CW00666117

FREUD

The life and work of Sigmund Freud continue to fascinate general and professional readers alike. Joel Whitebook here presents the first major biography of Freud since the last century, taking into account recent developments in psychoanalytic theory and practice, gender studies, philosophy, cultural theory, and more. Offering a radically new portrait of the creator of psychoanalysis, this book explores the man in all his complexity alongside an interpretation of his theories that cuts through the stereotypes that surround him. The development of Freud's thinking is addressed not only in the context of his personal life, but also in that of society and culture at large, while the impact of his thinking on subsequent issues of psychoanalysis, philosophy, and social theory is fully examined. Whitebook demonstrates that declarations of Freud's obsolescence are premature, and, with his clear and engaging style, brings this vivid figure to life in a compelling and readable fashion.

Joel Whitebook is a philosopher and psychoanalyst who maintained a private practice in New York City for twenty-five years. He is currently in the faculty of the Columbia University Center for Psychoanalytic Training and Research and Director of the University's Psychoanalytic Studies Program. He is the author of *Perversion and Utopia* (1995) and numerous articles.

Freud

An Intellectual Biography

Joel Whitebook
Columbia University, New York

CAMBRIDGE
UNIVERSITY PRESS

CAMBRIDGE
UNIVERSITY PRESS

University Printing House, Cambridge CB2 8BS, United Kingdom

One Liberty Plaza, 20th Floor, New York, NY 10006, USA

477 Williamstown Road, Port Melbourne, VIC 3207, Australia

4843/24, 2nd Floor, Ansari Road, Daryaganj, Delhi-110002, India

79 Anson Road, #06-04/06, Singapore 079906

Cambridge University Press is part of the University of Cambridge.

It furthers the University's mission by disseminating knowledge in the pursuit of education, learning, and research at the highest international levels of excellence.

www.cambridge.org
Information on this title: www.cambridge.org/9780521864183
DOI: 10.1017/9781139025119

© Joel Whitebook 2017

First published 2017
Paperback edition first published 2020

Printed in the United Kingdom by TJ International Ltd, Padstow, Cornwall

A catalogue record for this publication is available from the British Library.

ISBN 978-0-521-86418-3 Hardback
ISBN 978-1-108-82904-5 Paperback

For Charlie

I feel inclined to object to the emphasis you put on the element of petit bourgeois correctness in my person. The fellow is actually somewhat more complicated.

Freud to Stefan Zweig

The laborious compilations of the student of civilization provide convincing evidence that originally the genitals were the pride and hope of living beings; they were worshipped as gods and transmitted the divine nature of their functions to all newly learned human activities. As a result of the sublimation of their basic nature there arose innumerable divinities; and at the same time when the connection between official religions and sexual activity was already hidden from general consciousness, secret cults devoted themselves to keeping it alive among a number of initiates. In the course of cultural development so much of the divine and sacred was ultimately extracted that the exhausted remnant fell into contempt.

Sigmund Freud,
Leonardo

Stupidity is a scar. It can relate to one faculty among many or to them all, practical and mental. Every partial stupidity in a human being marks a spot where the awakening play of muscles has been inhibited instead of fostered. With the inhibition, the vain repetitions of unorganized, awkward attempts originally begin. The child's endless questions are already a sign of a secret pain, a serious question to which it has found no answer and which it cannot frame in its proper form . . . At the point where its impulse has been blocked a scar can easily be left behind, a slight callous where the surface is numb. Such scars lead to deformations. They can produce "characters," hard and capable; they can produce stupidity, in the form of deficiency symptoms, blindness, or impotence, if they merely stagnate, or in the form of malice, spite, and fanaticism, if they turn cancerous within . . . Like the genera within the series of fauna, the intellectual gradations within the human species, indeed, the blind spots within the same individual, mark the points where hope has come to a halt and in the ossification bear witness to what holds all living things in thrall.

Max Horkheimer and Theodor Adorno,
Dialectic of enlightenment

Contents

Acknowledgments   xi

Introduction   1

1   **Wandering Jews:
    From Galicia to Vienna**   17

2   **Freud's *Bildung***   57

3   **Science as Vocation**   85

4   **Starting Out in Vienna**   121

5   **A Theoretical Excursus**   159

6   **"Dear Magician"**   171

7   **Becoming the First Psychoanalyst** 198

8   **Jung and the Counter-Enlightenment** 234

9   **Exorcising the "*Odium Jungian*"** 267

10 **"What Is Painful May None the Less
    Be Real": Loss, Mourning, and *Ananke*** 313

11 **Making Sense of the Death Instinct** 343

12 **Leaving Heaven to the Angels and the
    Sparrows: Freud's Critique of Religion** 377

13 **Late Freud and the Early Mother** 407

Bibliography   455

Index   471

ix

Acknowledgments

While I have been working on this biography for the past ten years, I have been engaged with the questions addressed in it for the better part of three decades. I would therefore like to thank not only those friends and colleagues who have made a direct contribution to the current work, but also those – several of whom are no longer with us – who have contributed to my overall theoretical development during that period. They are Debbie Bookchin, Cornelius Castoriadis, Peter Dews, Stathis Gourgouris, Axel Honneth, Martin Jay, Joyce McDougall, Fred Pine, Christine Pries, Martin Saar, Inge Scholz-Strasser, Janine Chasseguet-Smirgel, Marcela Tovar, Marvin Wasserman, Albrecht Wellmer, Shoshana Yovel, and Yirmiyahu Yovel.

I owe a special debt of gratitude to those colleagues who took time from their demanding schedules to read different versions of my manuscript either in whole or in part: Richard Armstrong, Richard J. Bernstein, Werner Bohleber, Raymond Geuss, Marsha Hewitt, Kevin Kelly, and Robert Paul.

I have presented my work-in-progress in various venues over the past decade, and although the colleagues who provided me with valuable feedback are two numerous to cite, I would like to thank them for their contributions to the formulation of my position.

Then of course there have been my students – both at the New School for Social Research and at Columbia University. Out of a combination of an Oedipal desire to bring down their professor and genuine intellectual passion, they have regularly plied me with challenging questions that have pushed me to develop and articulate my thinking.

The members of two groups of colleagues must also be mentioned. The first are the analysts and academics who participated in the University Seminar on Psychoanalytic Studies that I chaired at Columbia for seven years. The stalwarts who hung in and struggled with *Moses and*

Monotheism for an entire academic year were especially helpful in helping me try to make sense of that baffling text. The second are the members of my CAPS (Center for Advanced Psychoanalytic Studies) group that meets at Princeton twice a year. As seasoned clinicians, they brought an essential extra-theoretical dimension to their discussions of the work I presented to them.

Susanna Margolis is an experienced editor who stepped in at a late stage of the project and, with her intelligence and skill, helped me bring it to completion. I was grateful to find her, for in a world of blogs and tweets Susanna is an exception: she still takes writing seriously. I would also like to thank Ariel Merkel for the steadfast editorial assistance she has provided me for many years.

Finally, it is difficult to express the debt of gratitude I owe to Hilary Gaskin, my editor at Cambridge University Press, for her patience and the confidence she displayed in my work over the past decade.

Introduction

Reappropriating Freud

Does the world need another biography of Sigmund Freud? The answer is an emphatic yes. Utilizing what we have learned from Freud Studies, advances in psychoanalytic theory, the feminist critique of the field, infant research, attachment theory, and extensive clinical experience working with the "unclassical patient" in the last half-century, a new biography will allow us to sort out important unanswered questions concerning Freud's life and address critical issues in contemporary psychoanalysis and philosophy.[1]

Before I began work on this volume, I tended to be skeptical about the hermeneutical principle that it was necessary for each generation to reappropriate the classics for itself.[2] What I saw as its relativist implications seemed unacceptable. Conducting the research for this biography, however, has changed my thinking on the subject. Although I had been studying, teaching, and writing about Freud as well as practicing psychoanalysis for over three decades, I had not undertaken a systematic reading of his oeuvre since I was a graduate student and a psychoanalytic candidate in the 1970s and 1980s. Furthermore, I had intermittently perused the more recent biographical literature and the burgeoning field of Freud Studies in the intervening years, but I had not kept abreast with them in a serious fashion. When I commenced my "second sailing" and returned to a systematic reading of Freud's texts for this project, something virtually

---

[1] See Sheldon Bach, "Classical technique and the unclassical patient," *Narcissistic states and the therapeutic process* (New York: Jason Aranson, 1993), 177–198.

[2] See Hans-Georg Gadamer, *Truth and method*, second revised edition, trans. Joel Weinsheimer and Donald G. Marshal (New York: Continuum, 1994), 284–290.

leapt off the page that I had failed to recognize earlier: *If the figure of the mother – especially the early pre-Oedipal mother – is not entirely absent, she plays a minimal and marginal role in Freud's thinking.* The mother is largely missing from Freud's self-analysis and from *The interpretation of dreams*, the work that grew out of it; from his *Case histories*, where she cries out for inclusion; from his theories of development and pathogenesis; and from his patriarchal theories of culture and religion. In what the philosophically trained psychoanalyst Hans Loewald calls his "official" doctrine, *Freud* focused almost exclusively on the figure of the father and maintained that the Oedipus complex was the "nuclear complex" not only of neurosis, but also of civilization. It can even be argued that Freud's austere construction of the psychoanalytic "set-up" and his theory of technique is Oedipal, insofar as it stresses neutrality, distance, abstinence, and cognition and eschews relatedness, gratification, and experience.

But if the mother is largely absent from Freud's work, her absence is itself a "presence." As the feminist theorist Madelon Sprengnether observes in her important work *The spectral mother*, she assumes "a ghost-like function," haunting the margins, shadows, lacunae, and interstices of Freud's oeuvre.[3] The early mother is in fact at the center of what Loewald refers to as Freud's "unofficial" position, and it will be our task to draw her out.

Once I recognized the fact of the missing mother, I had to ask myself why I had not recognized it three decades earlier, and I arrived at the following answer: When I began my research for this biography, I was situated within a different "hermeneutical horizon" – a different historical-interpretive context – from the one I had been located in when I read Freud as a graduate student and a psychoanalytic candidate. That earlier horizon can be sketched like this.[4] Though many of the tenets of the classical Freudian theory were still in place and the *ancien régime* had not yet crumbled, by the 1970s and 1980s the psychoanalytic establishment – especially the New York Ego Psychologists – was being challenged from multiple directions. The Second Wave Feminists' attack

---

[3] Madelon Sprengnether, *The spectral mother: Freud, feminism, and psychoanalysis* (Ithaca, NY: Cornell University Press, 1990), 5.

[4] This sketch most accurately describes the situation in the United States in general, and New York in particular.

on psychoanalysis for its misogynist bias was in full force – with *enragés* like Kate Millett, Shulamith Firestone, and Germaine Greer leading the charge – and they demonized Freud as the arch-ideologue of patriarchy; infant research was, as it were, in its infancy; the encounter between psychoanalysis and attachment theory had yet to occur; the question of how to treat "the unclassical patient" was at the top of the clinical agenda; and the theories of D.W. Winnicott, Margaret Mahler, and Heinz Kohut, which focused on the pre-Oedipal phase of development and the significance of the early mother-of-separation, were being hotly debated. The field, in short, was in a state of upheaval.

By the turn of the twenty-first century, the dust had largely settled and the discipline had substantially reconfigured itself. (This is not to say that contemporary psychoanalysis has resolved all its major theoretical and clinical questions – far from it.) Under the impact of the feminist criticisms and thanks in part to the contributions of feminists who had themselves become analysts – for example, Juliet Mitchell, Elisabeth Young-Bruehl, Jessica Benjamin, and Nancy Chodorow – psychoanalysts had entered a prolonged and intense period of reflection and self-criticism. (The criticisms arising from the gay and lesbian movements, which followed in the wake of the emergence of Second Wave Feminism, has also had a propitious effect on the field.) Consequently, mainstream psychoanalysis jettisoned many of its mistaken and embarrassing doctrines about female psychology and sexuality and radically transformed its views about femininity. Predictably, not only did the reconceptualization of femininity correct the absence of the mother in Freudian theory, but it also introduced the early mother into the center of its investigations. These developments in turn dovetailed with the expansion of infant research into a diverse and productive field and led to a rapprochement between psychoanalysis and the adjacent field of attachment theory. Through these developments, analysts acquired extensive knowledge regarding the earliest stages of development and the infant–mother relationship – topics with which they had previously been relatively unfamiliar.

The pre-Oedipal turn in psychoanalysis was also motivated by an urgent clinical concern – namely, the so-called "widening scope of psychoanalysis."[5] How, it was asked, should the supposedly new, non-neurotic

[5] See Leo Stone, "The widening scope of psychoanalysis," *Journal of the American Psychoanalytic Association* 2 (1954), 567–594.

patients who were appearing in analysts' consulting rooms with increasing frequency be approached? By the 1950s, analysts were regularly confronted with unclassical patients who did not conform to the "classical" picture of neurosis – that is, patients for whom the standard psychoanalytic technique had presumably been designed. Furthermore, it was often difficult to reach these patients, much less to help them, employing an unmodified version of classical technique.[6]

Spearheaded by Anna Freud, conservative analysts, who argued for the preservation and defense of classical theory and technique, occupied one pole of the debate surrounding "the widening scope."[7] They maintained that analysts should hold their ground and continue to do what they knew best – that is, only treat patients in the neurotic range of psychopathology and exclude non-classical patients from their caseloads. Located at the opposite pole of the debate were analysts who advocated widening the scope of psychoanalysis in two respects – regarding the range of patients the field treated and the scope of theory it fashioned to understand them.[8] And for analysts who managed to tolerate the uncertainty and who possessed the flexibility, curiosity, and perseverance to stick with these patients, the work often proved to be enormously productive and in fact led to a qualitative expansion of the scope and depth of psychoanalytic understanding.

[6] Whether the "classical patient" – "the good neurotic" – for whom it was claimed Freud devised "classical technique" ever existed is a debatable question. The relatively florid pathology of many of Freud's early supposedly hysterical patients seems to locate them beyond the neurotic range of the diagnostic spectrum. It may be the case that the early analysts did not understand enough about non-neurotic pathology to accurately diagnose the clinical syndromes they were observing. Many contemporary analysts argue, moreover, that primitive non-neurotic parts are constituents of every individual's personality, and it is only now, with our more finely tuned clinical perception, that we can accurately recognize them. Indeed, today it is often maintained that if the more primitive strata of the psyche are not reached and worked through, an analysis will remain radically incomplete.

[7] See Anna Freud, "Difficulties in the path of psychoanalysis," *Problems of psychoanalytic training, diagnosis, and the technique of therapy: the writings of Anna Freud*, vol. II (New York: International Universities Press, 1971), 124–156.

[8] For an attempt to rebut Anna Freud's conservatism see André Green, "The analyst, symbolization and absence in the analytic setting," *On private madness* (Madison, CT: International Universities Press, 1986), 30–59.

These unclassical patients, Loewald observes, often manifest bizarre "psychotic and psychotic-like states," appear intransigent in their rejection of the common-sense rationality that most of us take for granted, and can be extremely frustrating – even exasperating – to work with. But, he argues, they can also teach us something about "fundamental issues" concerning human nature. These individuals "are transfixed by" concerns possessing a "genetic depth and antiquity" that are not readily observable in higher-functioning patients. "There is," Loewald observes, something archaic about their mentality." It is not, however, only "archaic . . . in the sense of [being] antiquated . . . but also in the sense of belonging to the origins of human life and thereby to its essence and core."[9] Nonclassical patients

often give one the feeling that they are struggling with basic, primary dilemmas of human life in forms and contents that seem less diluted and tempered, less qualified and overshadowed by the ordinary, familiar vicissitudes of life, than is generally true of neurotic patients.[10]

When these people are able to articulate their experience, they provide us, Loewald maintains, with insight into the "psychotic core" of the personality, which is rarely accessible in higher-functioning individuals, though it is present in all of us.

In other words, the unclassical patients can offer us insight into the most archaic strata of the psyche, before significant differentiation between subject and object has occurred, and where the separation-individuation process is incipient at best. Unlike most of us, they do not take individuated life and separate existence "for granted." For them, "the objectivity of the object and the subjectivity of the self" that are presupposed in consensually validated public reality remain problematic.[11] As a result of the encounter with the "post-classical patient," the nature of the subject and the nature of the object have, in other words, become a problematic topic for psychoanalytic theory, a fact that in turn has important

[9] Hans Loewald, "The waning of the Oedipus complex," *The essential Loewald: collected papers and monographs* (Hagerstown, MD: University Publishing Group, 2000), 399–400.

[10] *Ibid.*, 400.

[11] *Ibid.*, 399–400.

ramifications for philosophy, especially modern subject-centered philosophy. Perhaps most importantly, "owing in part to analytic research" into the archaic dimension of the psyche, "there is a growing awareness of the force and validity of another striving, that for unity, symbiosis, fusion, merging, identification – whatever name we wish to give to this sense of and longing for nonseparateness and undifferentiation."[12] Freud, for reasons we will explore in detail, showed little interest in this striving; on the contrary, he manifested a powerful aversion to it.

As the developments I have enumerated indicate, the hermeneutical horizon that provided the backdrop for my "return to Freud" was shaped by two things: the assimilation and working-through of the feminist critique of psychoanalysis and the "pre-Oedipal turn" in the field. And this fact points to the answer to another question, namely, how it had been possible for earlier generations of analysts to "scotomize" (block the perception of) "the missing mother" in Freud's thought and work when today her absence is so apparent that it cries out for commentary. That our predecessors had been situated within a different hermeneutical context from ours – one which had not only been created by Freud, but which, for reasons that will become clear, had also systematically excluded the significance of the of pre-Oedipal mother – helps to account for the scotomization.

This explanation of how earlier analysts could scotomize what today appears to be an obvious fact also helped to convince me that the hermeneutical principle was correct.[13] As my research progressed and it became increasingly clear that the concepts of finitude and omnipotence occupy a central position in Freud's scientific worldview, I recognized that the hermeneutical principle was not only consistent with *but also demanded by* Freud's own position. As I hope to demonstrate, the acceptance of finitude – "resignation to *Ananke*" – is a fundamental desideratum of Freud's project. And to deny the contextuality of human knowledge, that it is always situated in a *particular* horizon, is to deny the finitude of human existence. Only an infinite disembodied mind could attain Absolute Knowledge that is *independent* of all particular contexts. And, as I will argue, contrary to the

---

[12] *Ibid.*, 401–402.

[13] This is not to say that I am no longer concerned with the problem of what might be called framework-relativism. It is only to say that whatever solution one arrives at must do justice to the full force of the hermeneutical claim.

popular caricature of Freud as a dogmatic positivist, for him, science in the prescriptive sense, does not consist in the certainty of Absolute Knowledge but is in fact its methodical adversary.

Accounting for "the Missing Mother"

Once the fact of the missing mother has been recognized, two further questions arise. How are we to account for it? And what are its consequences for Freud's life and thought, and, by extension, for the development of psychoanalysis? These are two questions that a contemporary biographer of Freud must confront, and providing answers for them will constitute a central task of my investigation.

Another relatively recent development will help us address the first question. At the same time that psychoanalysis was undergoing the transformations sketched above, Freud Studies was emerging as an independent academic discipline. In the past, research into Freud's life and the history of psychoanalysis had been conducted for the most part by analysts – that is, largely by physicians who lacked solid scholarly training. Furthermore, because they were members of a guild that is infamous for its contentiousness, their work was often distorted by the profession's internecine quarrels.

The members of the new field of Freud Studies, by contrast, are academically trained scholars who are better equipped to conduct rigorous research. While the emergence of this new discipline and the body of work it has produced undoubtedly represent a clear advance that should be applauded, it is nevertheless necessary to register a caveat. For the academic field of Freud Studies also creates its own distinct dangers – now from the opposite direction. Though the members of the new *Fach* are rigorously trained academics, they tend to lack the first-hand clinical experience that is sometimes believed to be a prerequisite for gaining a full understanding of psychoanalytic phenomena and ideas.[14] Their

---

[14] The work of Paul Ricoeur perhaps constitutes the most compelling counter-example to this belief. The French philosopher had no clinical experience, on the couch or behind it. Nevertheless, *Freud and philosophy*, his unsurpassed *chef d'œuvre*, exhibits a profound grasp of the deepest strata and innermost workings of Freud's thinking. See Paul Ricoeur, *Freud and philosophy: a study in interpretation*, trans. Denis Savage (New Haven, CT: Yale University Press, 1970).

scholarship runs the risk of becoming too professional, too tidy – that is, too intellectualized. When this occurs, their work fails to capture the sheer messiness of unconscious-instinctual life and thereby misses the affective-corporeal guts of true analytic experience. Ironically, despite their celebration of *jouissance*, indeterminacy, playfulness, desire, otherness, and so on, the tendency toward intellectualization is most pronounced in the dazzling theoretical acrobatics on display in the developments in French psychoanalysis inspired by Jacques Lacan – which are close relatives of poststructuralism. Their theoretical fireworks provide a way of circumventing the confrontation with what Freud called "the exigencies of life."[15]

Be that as it may, one important contribution of Freud Studies is especially pertinent to our first question. Over roughly the last three decades, historians of psychoanalysis have devoted considerable attention to the first three years of Freud's life, the years spent in Freiberg, a Moravian town, roughly 150 miles north of Vienna, now located in the Czech Republic. Prior to their work, knowledge concerning that era of Freud's development was relatively scant. Furthermore, the more recent socio-historical studies of the Freiberg period have dovetailed with another new area of research that was stimulated by the pre-Oedipal turn in psychoanalysis and interest in the early mother: namely, Sigmund's relationship to his own mother, Amalie Freud, during his first three years. As a result of this combined research, the received account of Freud's early development and relation to his mother has been seriously challenged. The conventional version presented a highly idealized picture of Freud's early years, depicting him as the beloved son of a young, beautiful, and adoring mother – what may be called the myth of "mein goldener Sigi" ("my golden Sigi"). The new research, however, suggests that the Freud's early years were marked by significant trauma involving marital discord, the death of his infant brother Julius, financial problems, maternal depression and absence, the sudden disappearance of his beloved *Kinderfrau* (nursemaid), as well as the loss of his childhood home and extended family – and that the idealized picture of that period, to a significant degree, served

---

[15] French Freud inherited this paradox from its progenitor, Surrealism. Though the Surrealists were the self-designated champions of the unconscious and the irrational, the highly intellectualized quality of the Surrealists' work is often striking.

a defensive function, namely, to deny their traumatic nature.[16] These idealizations, moreover, were initially promulgated by Freud himself and then taken over by his followers.

Two of Freud's biographers, Max Schur and Peter Gay, mention that there may have been serious difficulties in Freud's early relationship to his mother that might have had "unfathomable biographical implications," but they mention this only *en passant* and do not assign the difficulties or their implications a central position in their studies.[17] Schur, for example, wrote to Ernest Jones, Freud's first official biographer, "Altogether, there are many evidences of complicated pre-genital relationships with his mother which were perhaps never fully analyzed." But he not only cosigned his vastly understated observation to a letter and did not publish it, he also failed to analyse those difficulties himself.[18] And while Gay raises the subject, it does not play an essential role in his narrative of Freud's life. Indeed, it is buried deep in his massive work, not appearing until page 505.[19]

In retrospect, Freud's excessive idealization should have raised a red flag indicating that something was amiss. These new additions to our knowledge regarding Freud's early development make it possible to formulate a thesis to account for the fact of "the missing mother." The psychological strategy that Freud adopted for coming to grips with his traumatic early experience involved the repression, dissociation, or splitting–off not only of the representation of the early mother but also, more generally, of the entire maternal dimension and realm of early experience. This does not mean that the memories, images, and feelings dating from the Freiberg era were simply extinguished. Psychic life does not operate that way.

---

[16] Louis Breger's biography *Freud: darkness in the midst of vision* (New York: Wiley, 2000) first drew my attention to the new scholarship that challenged the received idealized account of Freud's early development. And Breger has rendered us an important service by bringing this recent research together and presenting a relatively comprehensive and lucid account of it. Breger, however, is a self-psychologist who obviously does not find Freud very appealing and has an axe to grind with him. Consequently, his study lacks hermeneutical charity toward his subject and has a "gotcha" quality to it. While his biography is factually informative and useful, his tendentiousness often distorts the analysis of the facts he has presented.

[17] Peter Gay, *Freud: a life for our time* (New York: W.W. Norton & Co., 1988), 503.

[18] Quoted in *ibid.*, 505.

[19] See *ibid.*, 503–507. For a critique of Gay in these matters see Breger, *Freud*, 381.

It means, rather, that they were sidelined – that is, banished to the more marginal or remote regions of Freud's psyche, where they maintained an "extraterritorial" existence that continued to have a powerful impact on Freud, although he was largely unaware of it. As Breger describes it,

> The traumatic experiences of Freud's first four years vanished from his aware-ness. In contemporary terms, the events and images were stored as physical and emotional sensations, but the memories were not available to consciousness; they were dissociated, not integrated into a coherent sense of self. They existed in a separate compartment [or compartments – JW] of his personality.[20]

In general, a psychoanalyst's theory can only advance as far as his own analysis has progressed. What Freud split off in his psychic life became split off in his thinking, thus determining the limitations in his "offi-cial" position, centering on "the father complex." But while the material from these disavowed and dissociated regions of his mind were excluded from Freud's "official" doctrine, as we will see, they appear in his "unof-ficial position," and, following Loewald, it will be our job to ferret them out, analyse them, and assess their ramifications for psychoanalytic theory.

My Second Theme

In addition to "the missing mother," the second theme that I will pursue in this study is "the break with tradition" – a theme that was also central to the major theorists of modernity. Freud's interest in the topic arose directly from the circumstances of his life; his family lived through the massive social and cultural dislocations that accompanied the process of modernization in Europe. In the course of only three gener-ations, the Freuds were transformed from traditional *Ostjuden* (Eastern European Jews), inhabiting one of the Austrian Empire's easternmost provinces, Galicia, into relatively modern secular Jews living in its capital, Vienna. As a result of the way he experienced that transformation and integrated his particular, dual Jewish-German inheritance, Freud came to identify himself as a partisan of the Enlightenment. However, while he clearly saw himself as such – that is, as a representative of the *Aufklärung* – his position with regard to it is far from straightforward and requires

---

[20] Breger, *Freud*, 17.

careful delineation. What is more, the complexity of his position, which is connected to the nature of his psychoanalytic discoveries, makes it possible for both sides in the debate, the pro-Enlightenment and the anti-Enlightenment camps, to claim him as their own. Because of this complex situation, the interpretation of Freud has served as a central point of contention in many of the controversies concerning modernity and the Enlightenment.

How the defenders of the Enlightenment can claim Freud for their camp is easy to see: They simply take his self-designation at face value and fail to probe it further. For example, Peter Gay's attempt to portray Freud as a representative of the Enlightenment *simpliciter* – as "the last *philosophe*" – is one-sided and fails to capture the nuances of his position.[21] From its inception, the Enlightenment began spawning opposing movements – which can be subsumed under the rubric of the Counter-Enlightenment – that continually have dogged its development.[22] The standard Counter-Enlightenment critique – which is largely directed at what is taken to be the eighteenth-century Kantian version of the *Aufklärung* and charges it with excessive rationalism, abstract Universalism, Eurocentrism, and Whiggish progressivism – must be taken seriously. And insofar as Freud's "official" doctrine corresponds to this "Kantian" position, *which it does in many ways*, it is subject to the same charges.

But Freud was no representative of the standard picture of the eighteenth-century *Aufklärer*. He joined the Enlightenment at a later stage of its development. He can be more accurately described – especially as he matured – as a representative of what the philosopher and Spinoza scholar Yirmiyahu Yovel calls "the dark enlightenment," which was a deeper, conflicted, disconsolate, and even tragic yet still emancipatory tradition within the broader movement of the Enlightenment:

From Machiavelli and Hobbes, to Darwin and Marx, and up to Nietzsche, Freud and Heidegger – and passing through Spinoza . . . – this process of

---

[21] Peter Gay, *A godless Jew: Freud, atheism and the making of psychoanalysis* (New Haven, CT: Yale University Press, 1987), chapter 1. In addition to having written an authoritative biography of Freud, Gay is also the author of a magisterial history of the Enlightenment.

[22] See Isaiah Berlin, *The magus of the north* (London: John Murray, 1993).

dark enlightenment proved a sharp awakening from religious and metaphysical illusions, incurring pain and conflict in its wake. For it challenged accepted self-images and enshrined cultural identities, and thereby endangered a whole range of vested psychological interests. But for those very reasons, it was also a movement of emancipation, serving to inspire a richer and more lucid self-knowledge in man, even at the price of unflattering consequences which often shock and dismay. This was the true "Oedipal drive" – not of Freud's Oedipus but of the original protagonist of Sophocles' tragedy, of whom Freud himself is an avid follower.[23]

As a representative of the dark enlightenment, Freud seriously engaged the truth claims of the Counter-Enlightenment and attempted to integrate them into a chastened but radicalized defense of the Enlightenment. As opposed to "post-modernism's" hypomanic celebration of "the end of reason" and "the end of the subject," this approach attempts to enlist the critique of reason and of the subject to formulate an "expanded" conception of rationality and subjectivity that is broader, richer, and more supple than its predecessor. This is the strategy that Hegel followed when he tried to do justice to the truth content of Romanticism in order to overcome the one-sided rationalism of the Kantian *Aufklärung*. And it is also the strategy that philosopher Theodor Adorno advocated for Critical Theory, arguing that psychoanalysis exemplified the attempt to confront "the irrational" and integrate it into a more comprehensive and less reified conception of rationality.[24]

What, one might wonder, is the connection between my two seemingly disparate themes – "the missing mother" and "the break with tradition"? I have argued that in response to his experience of the break with tradition, Freud became a dark enlightener, and that his theoretical task consisted in confronting the irrational in order to integrate it into a fuller conception of reason. Psychoanalytically, in addition to the unconscious, the irrational is also instantiated in the realm of archaic pre-Oedipal and pre-verbal experience, centering on the infant–mother relationship. Therefore, to the extent that the "official" Freud, owing to his early history, was unable

[23] Yirmiyahu Yovel, *Spinoza and other heretics*, vol. II: *Adventures in immanence* (Princeton, NJ: Princeton University Press, 1992), 136. See also, Marsha Aileen Hewitt, *Freud on religion* (Bristol, CT: Acumen, 2014), 76.
[24] See for example Theodor W. Adorno, *Lectures on negative dialectics: fragments of a lecture course 1965/1966*, ed. Rolf Tiedemann, trans. Rodney Livingstone (Malden, MA: Polity Press, 2008), 69–70.

to engage the maternal dimension in psychic life, he was also unable to explore the irrational and fulfill his theoretical program.

Biographical Truth

Freud's statement that "biographical truth is not to be had" is treated as holy writ by most of his biographers, who dutifully cite it as they commence their biographies of the man who asserted that truthful biographies are impossible.[25] (Talk about a problem of self-reference.) But the claim is not as self-evident as it is generally assumed and should be examined. The biographer's inability to overcome his need to idealize his subject is, according to Freud, a central reason why their efforts are doomed to failure:

Biographers are fixated on their heroes in a quite special way. In many cases they have chosen their hero as the subject of their special studies because – for reasons of their personal emotional life – they have felt a special affection for him from the first. They then devote their energies to a task of idealization, aimed at enrolling the great man among the class of their infantile models . . . To gratify this wish they obliterate the individual features of their subject's physiognomy, they smooth over all traces of his life's struggles with internal and external resistances, and they tolerate in him no vestige of human weakness or imperfection.[26]

Freud's skepticism about biography rests, in other words, on the assumption that biographers cannot achieve sufficient mastery of their need for idealization to gain a more or less mature perspective on their subjects and present relatively apposite portraits of them. But this assumption can be questioned. The founder of Self-Psychology, Heinz Kohut, among others asserts that, because of his discomfort with early narcissistic experience, Freud – who was prone to massive idealizations into his fifties – had a very limited understanding of idealization and how it might be addressed

---

[25] Freud made this statement in 1936, when he declined the novelist Arnold Zweig's proposal to write his biography. Sigmund Freud, *The letters of Sigmund Freud*, ed. Ernst L. Freud, trans. Tania and James Stern (New York: Basic Books, 1960), 430. The poet, psychotherapist, and general editor of the new Penguin edition of Freud's writings, Adam Phillips, is the latest biographer to declaim this principle in his biography of Freud. See Adam Phillips, *Becoming Freud: the making of a psychoanalyst* (New Haven,CT: Yale University Press, 2014), 25–28.

[26] Sigmund Freud, *Leonardo da Vinci and a memory of his childhood* (1910), *SE* 11: 130.

analytically. This is the source of his skepticism concerning the possibility of working through our idealizing tendencies in a "good enough way" so that we can perceive the affectively charged parental figures in our lives in a less distorted fashion. This skepticism amounts to a de facto expression of despair on Freud's part concerning the prospects for achieving maturity. To become mature, a child must relinquish his infantile, idealized images of his or her parental figures and come to terms with them as flawed, complex, and ambivalent human beings. If it goes well, this de-idealization process, which begins with the small circle of the family, should lead to a less distorted perception of psychosocial reality in general. Ideally, we would have less need for idealized grandiose figures – Caesars, *Führers*, party chairmen, Supreme Leaders, celebrities, as well as omniscient psychoanalysts – and might become mature democratic citizens in the broadest sense of the term. It has been observed that psychoanalysis is in a post-apostolic age. With the passing of the generations, no contemporary psychoanalyst can claim a direct line of lineage from Freud and the original founders of the field. In a sense, we are all orphans – and that is a good thing. It is my hope that, given this fact and the passage of time – and given our better understanding of idealization – we can form a more mature picture of Freud, so that we can love the creator of our field without idealizing him and vigorously criticize him without bashing him. The attitude I am making a plea for is exhibited in the following passage from the German psychoanalyst and Freud scholar Ilse Grubrich-Simitis. In it, where she is commenting on Freud's letters to his fiancée, she writes:

In reading the bundle of letters from the time of his engagement, as expected we encounter him as a breathtakingly energetic young man, a genius bursting with ideas, willing and able to conquer, as loving as he was affectionate. At the same time, however, we meet someone worn down and overburdened by misfortune, torn asunder and plagued by violent mood swings – a hot-tempered and thoroughly brusque individual, in the highest degree sensitive and vulnerable. In other words, our reading offers a realistic picture of a many-sided Freud far removed from shallow hagiographic idealizations and even more so from the grotesque distortions of the "Freud bashers."[27]

---

[27] Ilse Grubrich-Simitis, "Seeds of core psychoanalytic concepts: on the courtship letters of Sigmund Freud and Martha Bernays," paper delivered at the 47th Congress of the International Psychoanalytic Association in Mexico City, trans. Philip Slotkin, 2011, 15.

But it may be the case I am "chasing an illusion."[28]

Freud makes another comment concerning the difficulties with writing biography:

If a biographical study is really intended to arrive at an understanding of the hero's mental life it must not – as happens in the majority of biographies as a result of discretion or prudishness – silently pass over its subject's sexual activity or sexual individuality.[29]

The hermeneutical horizon that shaped my return to Freud was, as mentioned, formed by the rise not only of Second Wave Feminism, but also of the gay and lesbian movements that emerged from it. This fact also has important consequences for studying Freud today. It helps to remove some of the stigma surrounding the topic of homosexuality so that the subject can be discussed more openly and directly. And it served to bring the strength of Freud's "androphilic current," as he euphemistically referred to it, and the intensity of the homosexual dynamics in his relationships with Wilhelm Fliess and C.G. Jung, into relief. With the notable exception of Peter Gay, this topic had also been largely scotomized by Freud's earlier biographers. Let me be clear: what I am calling for is not an attempt to "out" Freud, but to understand his "sexual identity" more fully.

One thing should be made clear: my aim in this study is not to provide a comprehensive biography of Sigmund Freud. Because several excellent ones are already available, such an effort would be redundant. My aim rather is to provide a narrative of the relation between Freud's life and his work from a specific perspective, namely, that of the two themes I have described: "the missing mother" and "the break with tradition." While readers will find familiarity with basic facts of Freud's life useful, such familiarity is not absolutely necessary in order to follow my argument. If the reader wants to become better acquainted with those facts, they should consult the classic Freud biographies by Ernest Jones, Peter Gay, and Ronald W. Clark.[30] And for a succinct and lucid account of

---

[28] Sigmund Freud, *The future of an illusion* (1927), *SE* 21: 48.

[29] Freud, *Leonardo*, 69.

[30] Ernest. Jones, *The life and work of Sigmund Freud,* 3 vols. (New York: Basic Books, 1953); Ronald William Clark, *Freud: the man and the cause* (New York: Random House, 1980); and Gay, *Freud: a life for our time.*

the development of Freud's theory, Richard Wollheim's *Sigmund Freud* is an excellent resource.[31]

I would like to conclude this Introduction with one final remark. It is my hope that I have succeeded in presenting a compelling account of Freud's intellectual biography – that is, of the relation between the unfolding of his thinking and crucial developments in his life history; a relatively lucid elucidation of some of his important theories; and landing some solid blows against my theoretical opponents. (I have not attempted to hide my partisanship.) In addition to these goals, it is also my hope that I have succeeded in bringing Freud to life "in all his contradictions."[32] The creator of psychoanalysis was not simply the bourgeois paterfamilias or the hyper-rational man of science as he is often depicted – though his personality contained elements of both. Beyond that, he was a passionate, vital, and thoroughly human man, who possessed a unique combination of an uninhibited imagination with a capacity for steel-trap "Euclidean" ratiocination, and who was one of the most creative and fascinating figures of modernity.

[31] Richard Wollheim, *Sigmund Freud* (Cambridge: Cambridge University Press, 1981).

[32] "Man in all his contradictions" was the title of one of Freud's favorite books. See Gay, *Freud: a life for our time*, 86.

1

Wandering Jews: From Galicia to Vienna

The Break with Tradition

The break with tradition, the theme that preoccupied the great theorists of modernity – Hegel, Nietzsche, Marx, Durkheim, and Weber – was also at the center of Freud's life and work. In his case, in fact, the topic held a particularly visceral meaning, for his family had experienced all the dislocating effects of that historical rupture directly. In the course of three generations, the Freuds went from being parochial *Ostjuden*, Eastern European Jews living in the constricted world of Galician Jewry on the eastern periphery of the Austrian Empire, to secularized Jews inhabiting one of the most cosmopolitan capitals of Western Europe.

For observant Jews, tradition was a chain consisting of the uninterrupted transmission of the Torah from one generation to the next, and there is no doubt that Freud's father, Jacob (1815–1896), had been raised in that tradition. Jacob's father, Schlomo, was a rabbi, although whether orthodox or Hassid is unclear. What is certain, however, is that Schlomo saw to it that his son received a thorough education in the sacred texts and that Jacob perused them all his life; we have his granddaughter's observation that Schlomo was studying Talmud in Aramaic as an old man in Vienna.[1]

There is also no doubt that Jacob wanted to pass the tradition on to his son, Sigmund. But the unorthodox – or post-traditional – way in which he chose to do it attests to the fact that the hitherto seamless continuity of tradition had been broken. Jacob's actions provide an invaluable artifact for deciphering the inner tensions he experienced as a man with one

---

[1] Judith Bernays Heller, "Freud's mother and father," *Freud as we knew him*, ed. Hendrik M. Ruitenbeek (Detroit, MI: Wayne State University Press, 1973), 355.

foot in the world of traditional Jewry and the other in secular modernity. He did not require Sigmund to spend long hours hunched over the Gemarah, the Talmud and its commentaries, as he had done. Instead, when Sigmund was seven, Jacob began reading the family Bible to him – something the precocious young boy would soon be able to do on his own. Significantly, the book in question was the *Israelitische Bibel*, published by Ludwig Philippson, a prominent scholar of both religious and secular subjects, and his brother Phoebus. The choice of the Philippson Bible represents an altered relation to the chain of tradition and tells us much about Jacob's own relation to the customs and teachings of his forefathers.

As was customary, the Freud family Bible contained a *Gedenkblatt*, the commemorative page on which the significant events in the family's history were recorded. Jacob inscribed only four entries on the *Gedenkblatt*; the first was the date he purchased the Philippson Bible – 1 November 1848. That was a seminal year for Europe in general, when the storms of revolution – and headwinds of reaction – blew across the continent and disturbed the lives of many Jewish communities. At the time, Jacob was living in the town in which he was born, Tysmenitz in Galicia, which had been part of Poland until 1772, when it was annexed by the Austrian Empire, of which it remained a part until the end of the First World War. In Galicia in general and in Tysmenitz in particular, many of the conflicting currents destabilizing Jewish life in the mid-nineteenth century converged, and "the old traditions, and hence the organization of the Jewish community, were being fundamentally challenged."[2] The three major strands of Judaism – orthodox rabbinism, Hassidism, and the Haskalah, the Jewish Enlightenment – were at loggerheads with one another, and their clash constituted a challenge to traditional authority that was unsettling in the extreme.

Galician Judaism was a thoroughly communal affair, and the Halakha, the traditionally sanctioned body of law, encompassed all aspects of that way of life. The extreme poverty of the *shtetls* and the precariousness of life in general meant that mutual support and solidarity were absolutely essential for physical survival. In fact, as noted by psychoanalyst

[2] Marianne Krüll, *Freud and his father*, trans. Arnold J. Pomerans (New York: W.W. Norton & Co., 1986), 78.

Ana-Maria Rizzuto, physical survival was not a certainty; "many Jews" in the region "died of starvation . . . in spite of community efforts."[3] Collective cohesiveness was essential in this context, and the individual was under enormous pressure to conform to the regulations governing almost every moment of the day. A challenge to the cohesion of this closed community, with its "long-established theological and ritualistic system of thought and activity," constituted a threat not only to the collective identity of the group but also to the very existence of its members.[4]

The first threat came from Hassidism, a movement that challenged the authority of the orthodox rabbis by criticizing their formalism, scholasticism, and legalism, presenting instead a simple and comforting teaching that stressed emotion, spiritualism, and everyday experience. Freud believed that his father might originally have been a Hassid, but whatever Jacob's early exposure to Hassidism, another movement came to play a decisive role in his life: the Haskalah – the Jewish Enlightenment that modeled itself on the German *Aufklärung* – which sought to advance the process of the physical and spiritual de-ghettoization of the Jews begun with the Napoleonic reforms (1806–1808). Partisans of the Haskalah, known as *maskilim*, wanted to *transform* the Jewish tradition so that its member would achieve full participation in the wider world of modernity. Though secular and progressive, the *maskilim* were neither anti-religious nor anti-clerical per se. They were not, in other words, Yiddish-speaking *philosophes*; rather, they opposed only what they considered the atavistic elements in traditional Judaism and favored adopting the civic values of the host culture as well as its manners and mode of dress.

The Hassidim were utterly hostile to these radical and secular tendencies, while the *maskilim* were no less suspicious of Hassidic superstitions and magical practices. Ironically, however, by daring to criticize the rabbis, the Hassidim had demonstrated that the absoluteness of traditional authority could be challenged; they thereby unwittingly opened the door for the critique of orthodoxy in general and for the Haskalah's rationalist critique in particular.

[3] Ana-Maria Rizzuto, *Why did Freud reject God? A psychodynamic interpretation* (New Haven, CT: Yale University Press, 1998), 28.

[4] Emanuel Rice, *Freud and Moses: the long journey home* (New York: State University of New York Press, 1990), 87.

The *maskilim* passed through that door and set out to integrate their faith in God, Judaism, and the Torah with the advances of the Enlightenment – that is, "to transilluminate the substance of the Scriptures and the Talmud with the vision and the wisdom of the *Aufklärung*."[5] This led them to oppose the rabbinical prohibition on secular learning and to advocate the teaching of European science, philosophy, language, and literature as part of a Jewish education. But while they rejected the narrow Talmudism of orthodox studies, the supporters of the Haskalah retained the Bible as a centerpiece of the educational process. Extolled as a humanist text belonging to world literature – a work on a par with the *Odyssey* or *The Divine Comedy* – the study of the Bible was seen as a way to promote perhaps the most cherished value of the German Enlightenment, namely, *Bildung* (properly cultured character formation). That was precisely what the Philippson Bible represented; it is, and as the noted French psychoanalyst Didier Anzieu observes, a product of the Haskalah *par excellence*.[6]

In addition to the emphasis on secular learning, the *maskilim*, rejecting the traditional stress on ritual and ceremonialism, focused on Judaism's ethical teaching – especially its emphasis on truth and justice. Their interpretation of that ethical teaching largely converged with the progressive values of the Enlightenment. Echoing Kant and the leading figure of the Haskalah Moses Mendelssohn, the English translator of the Philippson Bible wrote that the "intellectual cultivation" of the Jewish population "could not fail" to bring about the recognition of "the right of private judgment [that is, the right of critical thinking] . . . and the claims of individual freedom."[7]

Tysmenitz, while remaining, like Galicia in general, a stronghold of rabbinical orthodoxy, was also a place where the Haskalah flourished.[8] Indeed, "some of the most active *maskilim* . . . came from Tysmenitz"[9] – many from Jacob Freud's own generation. This was no doubt due partly to the fact that Tysmenitz was a bustling commercial town. As the experience of

---

[5] Rizzuto, *Why did Freud reject God?*, 62.

[6] Didier Anzieu, *Freud's self-analysis*, trans. Peter Graham (Madison, CT: International Universities Press, 1987), 300.

[7] Quoted in *ibid.*, 40.

[8] See Mordecai Mayer Halevy et al., "Discussion regarding Sigmund Freud's ancestry," *Yivo: annual of Jewish social science*, vol. XII (New York: Yivo, 1958), 298.

[9] Krüll, *Freud and his father*, 88.

the Greek seafarer demonstrates, the trader who comes into contact with foreign ways of life often contributes to the erosion of the parochialism of his own local culture and promotes the spread of enlightenment. This happened in Tysmenitz, where Jewish merchants who "regularly attended the great markets of Breslau, Leipzig, and other German cities" brought back the news of what European modernity had to offer and thereby helped Tysmenitz develop into a center of the Haskalah.[10]

Jacob Freud, according to the historian Marianne Krüll, was among the first group of Galician Jews to "abandon the traditional ways and to build for himself a new life, both intellectually and materially."[11] Although he may not have been a full-blown partisan of the Enlightenment, he did become a new type of Jew, one "deeply anchored in both the Jewish religious and scholastic traditions" but enthusiastic about the modernizing tendencies in European culture.[12] Although, as Rizzuto observes, "there is no documented information to help us understand" the process that brought about this "drastic change" in Freud's father, there is one meaningful and suggestive piece of evidence concerning the outcome of that transformation, namely, the 1848 purchase of the bilingual Philippson Bible.[13]

One possibility is that Jacob purchased the Philippson in order to participate in a "Reading and Cultural Circle," established in Tysmenitz that year, that was dedicated to spreading the principles of the Haskalah.[14] The year itself, as noted, was significant for the tide of revolutions that swept through Europe and the radical reforms that followed them; among other changes, these reforms "heralded a new epoch for the Jews."[15] *De jure* if not *de facto*, the feudal system was abolished, and Austrian Jews were granted their full political and civil rights as a result of these upheavals. In fact, the events of 1848 confronted Galician Jews with the choice, as Rizzuto observes, of either "integrating into an emancipated and educated bourgeoisie or retreating into a secluded, homogeneously observant

[10] *Ibid.*, 84.

[11] *Ibid.*, 71.

[12] See Yosef Hayim Yerushalmi, *Freud's Moses: Judaism terminable and interminable* (New Haven, CT: Yale University Press, 1991), 62, and Rice, *Freud and Moses*, 94.

[13] Rizzuto, *Why did Freud reject God?*, 41.

[14] See Krüll, *Freud and his father*, 88.

[15] *Ibid.*, 95.

Jewish community." Jacob's acquisition of that particular Bible in that particular year suggests that the wave of progressive developments led him to choose the first option.

The Philippson family behind the *Israelitische Bibel* played a prominent role in the Haskalah as well as in Reform Judaism. The Philippson Bible, which took sixteen years to complete, was "a work of serious scholarship in the spirit of the *Wissenschaft des Judentums* (Science of Judaism) movement," the nineteenth-century movement that sought to apply the most sophisticated methods of contemporary scholarship to the study of Judaism.[16] A typical page of the new Bible showed the Hebrew text of the Old Testament on one side, its German translation on the other, and extensive notes at the bottom. The notes presented not just important works of Jewish and Christian exegesis and commentary, but also scholarly entries from such diverse fields as anthropology, ancient history, comparative mythology, religion, medicine, and even the botany of the Near East – all of which were meant to expand the reader's appreciation of the Old Testament. More striking still, the Philippson Bible contained 685 illustrations meant to evoke the historical, cultural, and physical context of the biblical narrative. These illustrations depicted biblical landscapes, towns, plants, animals, marketplaces, coins, utilitarian objects from everyday life, and even Egyptian gods, that is, images of foreign deities.[17] As Jacob Freud surely knew, these elements of the text he chose to purchase would have been condemned as sacrilegious – specifically, idolatrous – in the orthodox world of Judaism in which he had been raised.

The Philippson Bible that Jacob read to Sigmund was in effect the medium in which he introduced the Jewish tradition to his son. The impact was likely twofold: Exposure to the rich content and Enlightenment orientation of this very singular edition of the Bible had "an enduring effect upon the direction of [Freud's] interest," while we can also assume that the pleasure and intimacy the young Sigmund experienced while

---

[16] Moshe Gresser, *Dual allegiance: Freud as a modern Jew* (Albany, NY: State University of New York Press, 1994), 25.

[17] Rizzuto masterfully demonstrates the important role these images came to play in Freud's fantasy life. See Rizzuto, *Why did Freud reject God?*, especially chapters 6 and 7.

reading the Bible with Jacob had no less of an impact on his development
than the content he absorbed from the text.[18]

Wissenschaftlich the Philippson Bible certainly was, but its intent was
not to debunk. Rather, the purpose was to enhance religious experience
and deepen one's understanding of the tradition by drawing on everything human knowledge had to offer. Yet whatever their intentions, by
treating the biblical text as an object of science rather than of exegesis,
the Philippsons contributed to the *undermining of tradition*. It was not
simply an absence of secular education that had prevented Jews from
reflecting on their fundamental beliefs before the nineteenth century.
Such reflection simply could not arise within their closed worldview;
it was literally unthinkable. Among the orthodox, the belief that the Torah
was "of Divine origin and therefore immune to such critical scrutiny" was
"thoroughly ingrained."[19] A tradition is only a tradition in the strict sense
when it is structurally impossible to reflect on its basic tenets – on the
fundamental "idols of the tribe"– especially from an external standpoint.
The basic tenets are taken for granted and, to paraphrase Winnicott, the
idea of questioning them simply does not arise.[20] To treat a people's tradition reflectively, as one social formation and belief system among many
that emerged out of contingent historical forces – for example, to scientifically objectify the Jewish tradition and its beliefs as the Philippsons
did – is to deprive it of its strictly traditionalist character.

As the vehicle Jacob employed to transmit his twofold legacy to
Sigmund, the Philippson Bible unwittingly subverted his attempt. In
line with the ideals of the Haskalah, Jacob had wanted Sigmund to be
both religious and modern. Using the enlightened *Israelitische Bibel* as
the orthodox used the Torah and other sacred texts, he sought to instill a
feeling for his people's beliefs, stories, customs, values, and laws, *as well as
a sense of piety* in his son. And Freud had no doubt about the impact that
the "deep engrossment in the Bible story" had on him.[21] Jacob, however,

---

[18] Sigmund Freud, "An autobiographical study" (1925), *SE* 20: 8, and Rizzuto, *Why
did Freud reject God?*, 63.

[19] Rice, *Freud and Moses*, 89.

[20] Thus, even if one chooses to retain the beliefs of a tradition after critically reflecting
on them, the manner in which one holds the same beliefs has been radically altered. In
other words, one cannot choose to be a traditionalist.

[21] Freud, "An autobiographical study," 8.

not only passed the contents of the Bible on to his son via the Philippson version of the text; at the same time, he implicitly introduced Sigmund to the Philippsons' *reflective* approach to the holy text. *And the latter ultimately eclipsed the former.* For the precocious boy that Freud surely was, the scholarly footnotes too may have been influential, even at a relatively early age. Furthermore, the illustrations, which offered "a broad view of many other nations, other peoples and landscapes," as Rizzuto observes, must have produced a de-centering, Herodotian, anthropological attitude in Freud. They transported him beyond the parochial confines of Leopoldstadt, the crowded Jewish district in Vienna where he grew up. "The child exposed to this pictorial universe," as Rizzuto puts it, "became the man with boundless curiosity."[22] While Freud thoroughly absorbed the content of the Old Testament, he came to treat it as data – historical, anthropological, and social-scientific. In other words, it became objectified – that is, it became the subject matter for scientific exploration and interpretation that could reveal essential facts about human nature rather than the source of religious inspiration.

As followers of the Haskalah, Jacob and the Philippson brothers believed that religious faith and science were not incompatible. Critical reflection, so they believed, would not necessarily lead to the subversion of faith. In Freud's case, however, as in that of many others, a scientific examination of religion led to its rejection. After all, it was not a particularly large step from the *Wissenschaft des Judentum*, as Freud was introduced to it in the footnotes of the Philippson Bible, to Feuerbach, the young Hegelian who provided the template for both the Marxian and the psychoanalytic critiques of religion and who became Freud's favorite philosopher during his university years. Sigmund Freud moved beyond his father's tension-filled position, suspended between the world of Jewish traditionalism and the world of European modernity, and became a thoroughly secular Jew – "a godless Jew" – and, as such, a major figure in the project of autonomy.

Jacob's "Second First-Born" Son

The parochialism of the Eastern European *shtetl* is only one side of the Jewish experience. Another is the ability to leave the safety and familiarity of one's home, either by choice or under duress, venture into the

---

[22] Rizzuto, *Why did Freud reject God?*, 118.

unknown, and attempt to create a better life. It is striking that Jacob Freud, like many of his coreligionists, was registered as a *Wanderjude* (wandering Jew), the near-mythical term Galician officials used to register the merchants who traveled outside the province in order to make a living. It is not known what motivated Jacob's choice – he may have already experienced difficulty making a living on his own – but by 1844, at the age of twenty-nine, he entered into partnership with his maternal grandfather Siskind Hoffman, a merchant who had been plying his trade for forty years between Galicia and the westward province of Moravia. From then on, the two men "traveled perpetually between Galicia" and the Moravian town of "Freiberg, trading wool, woolen fabrics, suet, honey, anise, hides, salt and similar raw products."[23] Even if it was not the allure of modernity that initially drew Jacob out of Tysmenitz, he would have been exposed to its attractions once he began his travels. Moravia was located about 150 miles northeast of Vienna and lay closer to the center of the Empire. The Austrians therefore had more reason to integrate it into the Empire's legal system and administrative codes – which meant aggressively pushing for Jewish assimilation there – than in the distant eastern provinces. Nevertheless, anti-Jewish regulations were more stringently enforced in Moravia. Consequently, as Krüll observes, "the new forms of life had most probably been further disseminated . . . in Moravian Jewish communities . . . than in [Jacob's] own backward Galicia."[24] Freiberg, moreover, was a market town, that is, a place where Jacob would have encountered and observed modern Gentile merchants from other cities in the Empire. We can imagine the influence that these experiences had on this provincial Jew, who, prior to partnering up with his grandfather, had never ventured out of his native town.

During his sojourns in Moravia, Jacob left behind in Tysmenitz his wife, Sally Kanner, whom he had married in 1832, and their two sons Emanuel (b. 1833) and Philipp (b. 1834). We know much about Jacob's sons because, as Sigmund's older half-brothers, they played an important role in his life. Little is known, however, about Sally's background and fate. Did she die? Did Jacob divorce her? No one in the Freud family

[23] René Glickhorn, "The Freiberg period of the Freud family," *Journal of the History of Medicine and Allied Sciences* 24 (1969), 138. The town reverted to its old Czech name of Pribor after the First World War.

[24] Krüll, *Freud and his father*, 91.

seems to mention her in later years. Some scholars believe that she was
Jacob's second wife. This mystery, moreover, is one aspect of a larger
problem: Not much is known in general about the years between the time
Jacob began his travels and when he settled in Freiberg (1844–1852),
especially concerning the transformations in his inner life.

However, there is one piece of evidence that, in addition to the acquisition of the Philippson Bible, documents Jacob's separation from the world
in which he was raised. Prior to the reforms of 1848, Jews in the Austrian
Empire did not possess the right of free domicile but had to receive permission from the authorities to take up residence in a particular town.
Beginning in 1844, the Freiberg registries indicate that the partners Siskind
Hoffman and Jacob Freud continually applied and reapplied for permits to
temporarily reside there in order to conduct their affairs. The process went
on until 19 October 1847, when Jacob submitted an application only for
himself. The reasons for the break from his grandfather are also not known
but, for whatever reason, Jacob struck out on his own. On 10 July 1848, the
authorities grudgingly issued Jacob a harshly worded letter of "toleration,"
granting him residence for only three of the six months he had requested.
But the records show that by 1852 Jacob had asserted his right "as a citizen"
and "used his newly acquired freedom of residence to leave" the world of
the *shtetl* and move to "the predominately Catholic town of Freiberg."[25]
There he would be counted among the approximately one hundred Jews in
a population of about four thousand. Indeed, the devotion to the Virgin was
so intense in Moravia that the province was known as "Marian Garden" – a
fact that seems to have had some effect on Freud's attitude to the figure of
the Mother in Catholicism.[26]

Jacob married Amalie Nathanson (b. 1835) on 29 July 1855. Like Jacob,
Amalie was an *Ostjuden*. She was born in a northeastern Galician town near
the Russian border called Brody, spent two years with her older brothers
in Odessa, and moved to Vienna with her parents as a child. Jacob Freud
met Amalie in the Austrian capital, where he was probably doing business
with her father – also named Jacob – who was ten years his senior. The
marriage was most likely an arrangement between Freud and Nathanson,

[25] Rizzuto, *Why did Freud reject God?*, 34.

[26] Paul C. Vitz, *Sigmund Freud's Christian unconscious* (New York: The Gilford Press,
1988), 3.

and one can speculate about the factors surrounding the deal. To make up for the liability of being twenty years older than Amalie, Krüll conjectures that Jacob may have deceived Nathanson about his financial situation, presenting himself as more successful than he actually was. If this is indeed what happened, Krüll speculates, the deception would most likely have caused considerable disappointment and resentment in the young bride – feelings that would have been compounded as she discovered over time that her husband was in fact an inadequate provider.[27] While Nathanson had the asset of a beautiful young virgin to barter, Amalie's "exchange value" was most likely diminished by the fact that she suffered from a chronic but unspecified tubercular ailment – tuberculosis being known as the "Viennese disease."[28]

On 6 May 1856, ten months after their wedding, Jacob's bride gave birth to Sigmund – or Schlomo Sigismund, as he was officially named. The boy was born in Jacob's and Amalie's new home in Freiberg, where Jacob, at age forty-one, had finally settled after years of itinerant wandering. As his father's "second first-born," the infant must have embodied many of the feelings that are attached to a new beginning.[29] But Jacob's situation at the time was complicated. His father Schlomo had died only ten weeks before the grandson was born. At the same time that Jacob was creating a new life with a new family, therefore, he was also mourning the passing of his father.

Until this point, the only inscription in the Freud family Bible recorded the date Jacob purchased it. Now, however, he made two new entries on the *Gedenkblatt* of the Philippson Bible – commemorating the death of Schlomo his father and the birth of Schlomo his son. These two were clearly related in his mind. "The three generations [of Freuds]," Rizzuto observes, "are linked by their joint appearance on the commemorative page, connecting birth and death from generation to generation."[30] The two inscriptions, moreover, are placed so close together that they almost appear as one.[31] The closely related emotions of piety and mourning are

---

[27] See Krüll, *Freud and his father*, 97–98.

[28] See Rizzuto, *Why did Freud reject God?*, 37.

[29] See Krüll, *Freud and his father*, 108.

[30] *Ibid.*, 26.

[31] See *Ibid.*, 24–25.

connected in the *content* of both inscriptions. When Jacob records the date that Freud "entered into the covenant" via circumcision, the meaning is clear: He hopes that his son will walk "the straight path" as an observant Jew like his grandfather.[32] The fact, however, that Jacob chose to record these pious wishes in the reformed Philippson Bible also indicates discontinuity with the past and expresses optimism for his son's future as an emancipated Jew. By doing so, he was expressing the hope that Schlomo Sigismund would become a member of the emerging "new Jew[s] of the *Aufklärung*."[33] It is striking, Rizzuto observes, that Jacob "did not find it incongruous to write a reverent account of his orthodox father's death and burial in the bible that defied God's law."[34] Indeed, we can go further and say that Jacob's failure to recognize that incongruity borders on dissociation. And there is something even more incongruous if not dissociative about the final inscription that he entered on the *Gedenkblatt* when he presented the rebound Bible to Freud on his thirty-fifth birthday. While his son had by that point become a confirmed atheist and man of science, Jacob nevertheless evokes the hope he had expressed in the third inscription that Freud would follow in the righteous footsteps of his grandfather, and he exhorts him to return to the "Book of Books" that had so fascinated him as a young boy. This exhortation is often referred to as Jacob's "paternal mandate," and we will consider it when we examine *Moses and monotheism* in the final chapter.

By most accounts, Jacob was a "most enticing father for a young child."[35] Although one might have expected the father of the man who discovered the Oedipus complex to be stern and tyrannical, Jacob was reportedly gentle, devoted, jocular, and very sympathetic. The Jewish historian Yoseph Hayim Yerushalmi notes that the elder Freud "seems a poor candidate for a Jewish Laius"; indeed, "one almost wishes that Freud's father had been Hermann Kafka."[36] This raises the critical question of what motivated Freud to create a powerful and frightening image

---

[32] Quoted from Rabbi Jules Harlow's translation in Rice, *Freud and Moses*, 33.

[33] Rizzuto, *Why did Freud reject God?*, 64.

[34] *Ibid.*, 41.

[35] *Ibid.*, 63.

[36] Yerushalmi, *Freud's Moses*, 11.

of the father. Whatever the case, Jacob was a devotee of Jewish humor and loved to deflate pretensions with a joke. Though he was deeply intelligent and had educated himself extensively, he retained childlike qualities that made him especially attuned to children and able to delight them with his humor and stories.[37] Lest Jacob's innocent side mislead us, however, we should note that, at its best, it was an expression of what Nietzsche called a "second innocence," which involved a "peculiar mixture of deep wisdom and fantastic light-heartedness."[38] His grandson Martin interpreted the twinkle in Jacob's eye to mean: "'Isn't everything we are doing and saying here a great joke?'"[39] The loss of Jacob's own father shortly before his son was born, Rizzuto argues, would have caused him to form an especially intense tie to Sigmund:

> At the deeper layers of his psychic makeup, Jacob must also have transferred onto his son the longing awakened by his own "most poignant" paternal loss. His attachment to his son had a depth of feeling and need that went beyond an ordinary attachment. Sigmund became an idealized and overcathected image of a son . . . This child was to be, like the biblical Joseph, his great pride and consolation.

As a result, "Freud became the beneficiary of Jacob's warmth and geniality: Jacob attended to him tenderly, sharing his humor, his exciting stories, his personal wisdom."[40] Freud himself wrote that "a little boy is bound to love and admire his father, who seems to him the most powerful, the kindest and the wisest creature in the world."[41] And this attitude toward Jacob must have been true during Freud's early years. It seems that just as Jacob idealized him, Freud idealized his father. This must have made his disappointment with Jacob in later years that much more difficult to bear – or even to acknowledge.

---

[37] See Martin Freud, *Glory reflected: Sigmund Freud – man and father* (London: Angus and Robertson, 1957), 10.

[38] Friedrich Nietzsche, *The gay science: with a prelude in German rhymes and an appendix of songs*, ed. Bernard Williams, trans. Josefine Nauckhoff (Cambridge: Cambridge University Press, 2001); Jeffrey Moussaief Masson (ed.), *The complete letters of Sigmund Freud to Wilhelm Fliess: 1887–1904* (Cambridge, MA: The Belknap Press of Harvard University Press, 1986), 202.

[39] Martin Freud, *Glory reflected*, 10.

[40] Rizzuto, *Why did Freud reject God?*, 65.

[41] Sigmund Freud, *Some reflections on schoolboy psychology* (1914), *SE* 13: 242.

Jacob's idealization of Freud, however, went along with an abdication of his paternal function. The downside of Jacob's childlike charm and lightheartedness was his ineffectualness in dealing with the realities of life – especially the financial realities. Though he suffered a number of financial failures, Jacob always remained "hopefully expecting something to turn up." He could be likened to a *mitteleuropäische* Willy Loman.[42] There is in fact no record of Jacob ever making an independent living, and it may be that he could only succeed in partnership with others, such as with Siskind Hoffman or his two sons.[43] Jacob expected Freud not only to compensate him emotionally for the personal disappointments in his life, but to provide him with a considerable degree of financial support as well. Freud's marriage to Martha was in fact delayed for a number of years partly because he had to provide for Jacob during his engagement. This surely would have caused considerable resentment in the struggling and lonely young physician who was eager to marry his fiancée.

There are many reasons why a boy needs a firmly defined paternal figure, but two are perhaps primary. The first is to act as a psychological barrier between him and his mother – especially a frightening and difficult one – so that he can dis-identify with and separate from her. Second, a "good enough" Oedipal adversary – that is, one who is strong without being omnipotent – is necessary to help a boy contain and shape his aggression and to tame his omnipotence. Jacob's failure to fulfill the first of these paternal functions is one reason why Amalie remained such a frightening figure that Freud was never able to face, come to terms with, and integrate into his psychic life. This fact is of the utmost consequence for his life, his thinking, and the development of psychoanalysis. And as a result of Jacob's failure to fulfill the second of these paternal functions, Freud continually struggled with his own omnipotence and developed an excessive tendency for idealization, which launched him onto repeated quests to find an ideal father.

At the age of seventy-five, Freud wrote: "But of one thing I can feel sure: deeply buried within me there still lives the happy child of Freiberg, the first-born son of a youthful mother, who received his first indelible impressions from this air, from this soil."[44] This statement can be

[42] See Breger, *Freud*, 26–28.
[43] Rizzuto, *Why did Freud reject God?*, 61.
[44] Sigmund Freud, "Letter to the *burgomeister* of Pribor" (1931), *SE* 21: 259.

interpreted as a retrospective idealization of Freiberg and Amalie. But like most idealizations, it is not constructed from thin air. There was much about Freud's life in Freiberg that made it a felicitous place for a young boy to grow up. The town was nestled in the foothills of the Carpathian Mountains and surrounded by the woods, farmlands, and meadows "where Freud used to toddle with his beloved father" and romp with his nephew John and his niece Pauline as well as children from the Fluss household.[45] (We should note that this picture of Freiberg is associated with Jacob rather than Amalie.) Peter Gay observes that "nothing appears more desperately urban than psychoanalysis." Likewise, its founder strikes us as "the quintessential city dweller, laboring in his consulting room all day and his study all evening, taking his daily walks through the modern Vienna being built while he was a student and young physician."[46] But this picture of Freud overlooks another deep-seated side of Freud's character that he acquired during his years in Freiberg: the role that nature played in his emotional life. His affinity for the natural world was so strong that he seemed to require regular retreats from Vienna into the countryside, where he took long walks in the mountains and delighted in gathering mushrooms with his children. To whatever degree Freud's idealization of Freiberg was a retrospective fantasy – as all images of Eden are – its bucolic surroundings nevertheless provided him with an image of life before the Fall.

The Freuds' living conditions in Freiberg were as humble as the family constellation was complex. Sigismund was born at No. 117 Schlossergasse, a building owned by a Catholic blacksmith named Zajic whose family had inhabited it for four generations. The home was only 30 feet by 30 feet and contained two rooms on each floor.[47] Zajic retained the entire ground floor for his workshop, and his family resided in one of the rooms on the upper floor. Jacob Freud's family – which comprised Jacob, Amalie, Sigmund, and, by the time they left for Vienna when Sigmund was three-and-a-half, his sister Anna – was thus left with one small room on the upper floor for their quarters. Freud therefore spent his earliest life in cramped living conditions with virtually no privacy. We can assume that he was exposed

[45] Ernest Jones, *The life and work of Sigmund Freud*, vol. I: *1856–1900, the formative years and the great discoveries* (New York: Basic Books, 1953), 11.

[46] Gay, *Freud: a life for our time*, 10.

[47] Glickhorn, "The Freiberg period of the Freud family," 42.

to many of the elemental facts of life (e.g., bodily functions, sexuality, marital discord, pregnancy, birth, illness, and death) before he had the capacity to assimilate the excitement, anxiety, and confusion that such experiences engender in a small child.

All young children are genealogists. One of the earliest and most urgent questions that sets their curiosity in motion is, "Where do I fit in the kinship structure of my family?" or "Where do I fit into the chain of generations and division between the sexes that structures my world?" Given the complexity of the family constellation, which involved the anomalous entanglement of three generations, the task of mapping out Freud's genealogy would have given the Structuralist anthropologist Lévi-Strauss a run for his money. If we begin with the assumption that approximately twenty years separates the generations – which was even more accurate in the mid-nineteenth century than it is today – then Jacob, who was entering his fifth decade when Sigmund was born, was the proper age to have been his grandfather. Freud's half-brothers Emanuel and Philipp, who accompanied Jacob to Freiberg, were twenty-three and twenty-one years old respectively at Freud's birth. Thus, they were the appropriate age to have been Sigmund's father. Furthermore, Amalie, who was also twenty-one at the time of Freud's birth in 1856, was of the same generation as Emanuel and Philipp. In other words, she was young enough to have been Jacob's daughter rather than his wife, and of a suitable age to be married to either of his older sons – or to be either's lover.

In addition to the complexity of the family structure, its members were thoroughly enmeshed in their daily lives and lived in close physical proximity to one another: Philipp, a bachelor of whom Sigmund was not particularly fond, resided in a room directly across the street from Jacob's home, while Emanuel, his wife Maria, and their three children lived several blocks away at 42, Marktplatz. Moreover, all the members of the clan, including the women, worked together on a regular basis in the warehouse that housed the family's wool business. In short, they spent very little time apart from one another.

Of the three menfolk in the family, Freud's "strict eldest brother" Emanuel was the most solid, responsible, and financially successful in life.[48] He was also the one Freud liked the most and remained closest to

---

[48] Sigmund Freud, *The psychopathology of everyday life* (1901), *SE* 6: 227.

throughout his life. When Freud visited Emanuel, who had moved to Manchester, England, at age nineteen, and beheld the prosperous life that his brother had created for himself and his family, he allowed himself this impious thought: "How different things would have been if I had been born the son not of my father but of my brother."[49] Furthermore, Emanuel was the only one of the three men who had a relatively conventional marriage. Maria was the appropriate age to be his wife and she "came of 'good' Jewish stock: a long line of rabbis and Talmudic scholars."[50] Freud seemed to have valued this bit of middle-class order in his otherwise confusing familial world. Indeed, Krüll believes that he may even have modeled his choice of his own wife on his brother's selection of Maria, for Martha Bernays – whose grandfather was the chief rabbi of Hamburg – also possessed a solid *bürgerlich* characteristic and came from a good Jewish family.[51]

Emanuel and Maria had a son and two daughters: John was nine months older than Freud, Pauline was seven and a half months younger than Freud, and Bertha was two years his junior. While both John and Pauline were his playmates, the brother was the more important.[52] Freud remembered that he and his nephew were inseparable for his first three years. He reports that they not only "loved each other" but, like rivalrous brothers, incessantly "fought with each other" as well.[53] In fact, Freud believed that his relationship with John was so important that it "determined all [his] later feelings in [his] intercourse with persons [his] own age." The relationship was "ineradicably fixed in" his "unconscious memory" and provided the transference template for the many intensely conflicted relationships that Freud had in later life – for example, with Josef Breuer, Wilhelm Fliess, and Carl Jung.[54] He tells us:

My emotional life has always insisted that I should have an intimate friend and a hated enemy. I have always been able to provide myself afresh with both, and it

---

[49] *Ibid.*, 219–220.

[50] Krüll, *Freud and his father*, 123.

[51] *Ibid.*, 123.

[52] John and Pauline are the two children in the paper we will examine entitled "Screen memories."

[53] Sigmund Freud, *The interpretation of dreams* (1900), *SE* 4 and 5: xi, 630 and 483.

[54] Masson (ed.), *Letters to Fliess*, 268.

has not infrequently happened that the ideal situation of childhood has been so completely reproduced that friend and enemy have come together in a single individual – though not, of course, both at once or with constant oscillations, as may have been the case in my early childhood.[55]

Freud realized that this transference template was also constructed out of images of his relationship to his younger brother Julius, who died at the age of nine months.

A Lacanian analysis of kinship nomenclature can help us to clarify the confusing nature of this family structure. Sigmund was his boyhood comrades' uncle. One wonders what it must have been like for Freud to know that John – the larger, stronger, and older of the two – was his nephew. One boy, moreover, referred to Jacob as "father," while the other as "grandfather." Add to this that Amalie belonged to the same cohort as her stepsons, Philipp and Emanuel. Upon analysing this complex family tree, moreover, it immediately appears logical that the attractive and lively Amalie would have been appropriately matched with Philipp, a fun-loving bachelor her own age. It is not surprising that Freud made this connection and suspected that they were having an affair, a suspicion that may not have been unfounded. There is some speculation that Amalie and Philipp were in fact lovers, and this is one of the reasons why the families separated, with Jacob's moving to Vienna while Emanuel's and Philipp's emigrated to England.[56]

The Myth of "Mein goldener Sigi"

The picture of Amalie as a young, beautiful, and animated mother who unambivalently adored her 'goldener Sigi' is to a large degree a myth – a defensive idealization, first promulgated by Freud, and then uncritically continued by many of his followers. By almost all accounts Amalie was a difficult woman: infantile, dependent, demanding, and self-centered. Although she was beautiful, lively, sociable, and an efficient housekeeper, she was anything but a loving wife and mother. Borrowing from the "vulture imagery" that appears at several key places in Freud's work, the historian of psychoanalysis Paul Roazen observes that she was "a tough

---

[55] Freud, *The interpretation of dreams*, 483.

[56] See Krüll, *Freud and his father*, 125.

old bird."[57] And Judith Heller Bernays, Freud's niece from New York, who visited Vienna regularly, confirms this assessment. She emphasizes the selfish and tyrannical personality that lay behind the "charming and smiling" performance that her grandmother put on for strangers.[58] For Heller, her grandmother's insensitivity was exemplified by the way she deployed deafness to avoid dealing with anything "that might require her to bestow an extra measure of sympathy or consolation upon some member of the family." For example, when one of her granddaughters died at the age of twenty-three, Amalie ignored what must have been the distressed atmosphere in the household and simply acted as if nothing had happened. Despite the fact that "this granddaughter had visited her frequently in the past," Amalie never mentioned the tragic death, even when the girl's mother came to the house.[59] As Rizzuto summarizes the situation, Amalie "was especially incapable of attending to their emotional pain. She offered no consolation or protection. Instead, she demanded to be protected from any knowledge that might cause *her* any pain or remove her from center stage."[60]

Freud's son Martin, who also describes Amalie as a selfish and aggravating woman, adds a socio-cultural dimension to his assessment of her. The "Galician Jews," Martin notes, "were a peculiar race, not only different from any other races inhabiting Europe, but absolutely different from Jews who had lived in the West for some generations." These *Ostjuden*, he continues, "had little grace and no manners; and their women were certainly not what we should call 'ladies'. They were highly emotional and easily carried away by their feelings." As a "true representative of her race," Amalie – who it seems never learned German but continued to speak Yiddish her entire life – was "not easy to live with." When she was "unsettled and disturbed," she would not hide her feelings to protect "the peace of those around them." On the contrary, Amalie had no difficulty directly discharging her volatile emotions when they seized her. It would be mistaken, however, to think that Martin's portrait of his grandmother simply reflects the prejudices of an assimilated

[57] Paul Roazen, *Freud and his followers* (New York: New American Library, 1974), 45.

[58] Heller, "Freud's mother and father," 338.

[59] *Ibid.*, 339.

[60] Rizzuto, *Why did Freud reject God?*, 201.

German-speaking Jew – a "Yekke," as *Ostjuden* derisively refer to them – residing in England. Martin also expresses deep admiration for the vitality and tenacity of his Eastern European brethren: "Although in many respects" Galician Jews "would seem to be untamed barbarians to more civilized people, they, alone of all minorities, stood up against the Nazis. It was men of Amalie's race who fought the German army on the ruins of Warsaw."[61] It is safe to assume that Freud's pugnacity – as well as his superstitiousness and gullibility, which is so unexpected in a champion of reason like Freud – was partly inherited from has head-strong, spirited, and irrational Galician mother.

In a remark that is not meant to be altogether positive, Freud's daughter Anna Freud observes that her grandmother was "devoted to and proud of her [son], as Jewish mothers are."[62] The implicit criticism is that, behind its self-sacrificing façade, proverbial Jewish mother-love typically contains a sizeable dose of narcissism. Although Amalie kept her daughter Dolfi imprisoned at home to take care of her, she did not attempt the same strategy with Sigmund. As "a highly narcissistic and socially ambitious person who placed all her hopes on her first born son," Rizzuto observes, she needed him out in the world to slay dragons so that she could revel "in his glory." Indeed, Amalie continued to express "her sense of owner-ship over" her son "privately and publicly, even when he was an elderly man."[63] Commenting on Anna's description of the relationship, Rizzuto notes, "The fact that Amalie enjoyed 'petting and making a fuss over' [Freud] did not make him less 'terrified' of this overbearing, emotionally exhausting, willful mother, a mother who could see herself in her children but could not see them in their own right."[64] Freud's reported feeling that he was unlovable, which helped to create the more vulnerable parts of his self, must have stemmed in part from the sense that his mother loved him not for his own sake but as a "narcissistic object." As a dutiful son who, in Anna's view, "suffered his mother" rather than being "dependent on her," Freud visited Amalie's house every Sunday afternoon for lunch.

[61] M. Freud, *Glory reflected*, 11–12.

[62] Cited in Paul Roazen, *Meeting Freud's family* (Amherst: University of Massachusetts Press, 1993), 191. This quote is from a letter from Anna Freud to Kurt Eissler.

[63] Rizzuto, *Why did Freud reject God?*, 197–198.

[64] *Ibid.*, 201.

Because of his ambivalence, however, he invariably arrived late. Prior to the Sunday visits, the anxiety he experienced often caused him gastrointestinal distress, and he would procrastinate at Berggasse 19 while Amalie nervously paced the floor in anticipation of his arrival.

A volatile and self-centered mother, however, does not of itself make for a traumatic childhood. There was something more – namely, maternal depression that was caused by the many losses that Amalie experienced in rapid succession. Even before Sigmund's birth, the family had suffered several painful deaths. Jacob had lost at least one – perhaps two – wives, and his father Schlomo died shortly before the child was born. Furthermore, these deaths were "followed during the next years by a series of losses that would have a powerful traumatic effect on the young boy."[65] Amalie's brother Julius died a month before the birth of her second son who would bear his name. But the most catastrophic loss was surely the death of that boy himself, the younger Julius, who was born when Sigmund was eleven months old and died six to eight months later. There is good reason to assume that Amalie became depressed, withdrawn, and psychologically unavailable to Freud as a result and may have even spent some time away from him in Roznau, a spa to which she regularly retreated.

The point at which an event occurs in a person's life often determines whether that event will become traumatic. And because all of this took place when Freud was roughly between eighteen and twenty-four months of age, a critical point in a child's development when his or her self is in the process of consolidating, the young Sigmund would have been especially vulnerable. Moreover, given the fact that the family lived in a one-room apartment, it is likely that the young Freud was exposed to his brother's illness and perhaps even to his death at first hand. And although a mother's depression can develop for a number of reasons (e.g., post partum, death of a parent, marital difficulties), all "authors have understood," as André Green observes in a classic article, that the most disastrous depression is that which follows "the death of a child at an early age."[66] With the death of Julius, in the context of numerous earlier losses, Amalie became what Green calls "a dead mother."

[65] Breger, *Freud*, 11.

[66] André Green, "The dead mother," *On private madness* (Madison, CT: International Universities Press, 1986), 149 (emphasis in the original).

It must be made clear that Green's concept of "the dead mother" does not refer to "the psychical consequences of the death of a real mother," which, although devastating, are well known.[67] Rather, it pertains to the *psychological* death of a mother *"following maternal depression."* The catastrophic character of "the dead mother syndrome," moreover, results from the fact that her psychological death brings to "a sudden halt" a relation between the mother and child that, according to Green, had previously been especially "good" – that is, "rich and happy" and marked by "authentic vitality."[68]

It is reasonable to assume that there was a significant quantum of "goodness" in Amalie's relation to Freud – at least before her psychological death, and there is a considerable degree of correspondence between Amalie's and Sigmund's mother–son relationship and the situation that Green describes.[69] Green argues that the mother's psychological death – which, as a rule, occurs suddenly and unexpectedly – "brutally" transforms the child's image of her from "a living object" and "a source of vitality . . . into a distant toneless [and] practically inanimate . . . figure." In short, she becomes *"a mother who remains alive and physically present but who is, so to speak, psychically dead in the eyes of the young child in her care."*[70] The "frozen" character of the maternal object prevents internalizations that are necessary for healthy development, Green argues, and this creates significant lacunae in the individual's psychic structure. In an attempt to compensate for those "gaps in the fabric of the self" and to grapple with the massive "loss of meaning" that the catastrophe precipitates, individuals suffering from the dead mother syndrome often resort to extensive intellectualization and become involved in a compulsive search for meaning.[71] Who fits this description better than Freud?

In light of Freud's troubled relationship with Amalie, her difficult and narcissistic behavior, and her depression following Julius's death, Freud's apparent idealization of the mother–son relationship is clearly

---

[67] *Ibid.*, 142.

[68] *Ibid.*, 149.

[69] Green in fact presents an analysis of Freud's early years in terms of the dead mother complex. See Green, "The dead mother," 169–173.

[70] *Ibid.*, 142 (emphasis added).

[71] *Ibid.*, 151.

more complicated than the received interpretation would have us believe. In a well-known line, Freud states that the mother–son relationship "is altogether the most perfect, the most free from ambivalence of all human relationships."[72] (Late in life, and with good reason, Freud corrected himself and asserted that the relationship to one's dog constitutes the most unambivalent one that can be achieved in civilization.) Readers have generally taken this to mean that it constitutes a self-contained, reciprocal, and incomparably gratifying relationship – the only relationship in civilization that is free from mutual hostility. And to the extent that he needed to idealize his relationship with Amalie, Freud would have preferred that interpretation as well. The sentence preceding that famous description, however, indicates another side to the story: "A mother is only brought unlimited satisfaction by her relation with her son." Rather than referring to a reciprocal mother–son relationship, Freud appears *to be referring only to the mother's love for the son and what she gains from it.*[73] There are many types of love, and viewed in this light, the son is indeed loved by his mother, but loved as *a narcissistic object.* "Freud's oft-quoted remarks on the mother–son relationship," Krüll argues, are not "happy reflections on maternal love," as they are usually taken to be, "but rather . . . wry comments on maternal exactions." She maintains that "when he called the mother–son relationship 'free from ambivalence,' Freud clearly meant that it was so for the mother rather than for the son." Amalie did not love Freud "'maternally' in the full sense of the word," which is to say "unconditionally" in his own right, but only insofar as she could bask in the narcissistic glow of his talent and achievements.[74]

In his attempt to decipher the meaning of Mona Lisa's enigmatic smile, Freud argues that Leonardo refound his mother's imago in his model's face and reproduced it in his painting of *La Giaconda*. The same can be said about Freud's relation to Leonardo's painting – namely, in it he refound Amalie's face. His thesis is that the enigmatic nature of Mona Lisa's smile results from its "double meaning." It contains both "the promise of unbounded tenderness and at the same time sinister

---

[72] Sigmund Freud, *New introductory lectures on psycho-analysis* (1933), *SE* 22: 133.

[73] See Krüll, *Freud and his father*, 118; Madelon Sprengnether, *The spectral mother: Freud, feminism, and psychoanalysis* (Ithaca, NY: Cornell University Press, 1990), 79–80.

[74] Krüll, *Freud and his father*, 117–118.

menace."[75] The early mother can provide unfettered gratification as well as excruciating deprivation. Likewise, Freud's description of the artist's "unsatisfied" mother might also be applied to Amalie's dissatisfying relation with Jacob: "So, like all unsatisfied mothers, she took her little son in place of her husband."[76] And again he comments on the incomparable pleasure that mother experiences with her infant (son):

A mother's love for the infant she suckles and cares for is something far more profound for her later affection for the growing child. It is in the nature of a completely satisfying love-relation; which not only fulfills every mental wish but also every physical need.[77]

Note again that Freud's description of the profound pleasure that can be attained in the infant–mother relationship is one-sided; it only pertains to the mother. Furthermore, assuming that he was drawing on memories of his own childhood, his analysis of Leonardo's relation to his mother also support's Green's claim that the "dead mother" theory applies to Freud – a theory which assumes that there was relatively abundant goodness between Amalie and her son before she succumbed to depression following Julius' death. Freud believed Leonardo's mother had bestowed "unbounded tenderness" upon him. But her affection contained a "menace" in that it made "the privations that were in store for him" that much harder to bear.[78] A mother's seductive smile is "sinister," in other words, because whatever pleasure it promises and even provides cannot last, making the "privations" that follow that much more painful.

One incident that borders on the comical demonstrates the extent of Jacob's and Amalie's ambition: When, like all Jews in the Empire, these two *Ostjuden* were compelled to choose birthdates for themselves from the Gregorian rather than the Jewish calendar, they chose Bismarck's and Emperor Franz Josef's respectively.[79] And in another incident, Amalie took the fact that her infant was born in a caul as an indication that happiness and fame lay in his future. Indeed, she seemed to have been scanning

---

[75] Freud, *Leonardo*, 115.

[76] *Ibid.*, 117.

[77] *Ibid.*, 117.

[78] *Ibid.*, 115.

[79] Freud, *The interpretation of dreams*, 192.

the environment for signs that would validate her ambitions for her son. When an old lady in a pastry shop prophesied that her baby would grow up to become a great man, the superstitious *Galitzianer* treated this pronouncement as an unassailable prediction. Freud, however, greeted the old lady's prediction with more skepticism: "Such prophecies must be made very often; there are so many happy and expectant mothers, and so many old peasant women and other old women who, since their mundane powers have deserted them, turn their eyes towards the future."[80]

Amalie's considerable grandiosity – as well as Jacob's – undoubtedly manifested itself in her ambitiousness regarding Freud. Pondering his mother's influence, Freud wondered, "Could this be [a] source of my thirst for grandeur?" He observes that this sort of early maternal idealization can in fact result in success in later life, and tells us that he has

found that people who know that they are preferred or favoured by their mother give evidence in their lives of a peculiar self-reliance and an unshakeable optimism which often seem like heroic attributes and bring actual success to their possessors.[81]

Even if it were clear that Freud is referring to himself in this and other, similar passages – and it is not – Amalie's idealization of her *goldener Sigi* is more complicated and less benign than the description appears to suggest. It is in fact shot through with contradictions that correspond to numerous contradictions in Freud's thoroughly polytropic personality. On the one hand, there can be little doubt that internalizing the early idealizing love that Freud received from Amalie, as well as from his father and his nursemaid, played an essential role in forming the solid parts of Freud's personality – his strengths – without which his ability to endure extreme adversity and to realize his monumental achievements would be unthinkable. On the other hand, in addition to its positive effects, Amalie's intense (over-)investment in her son also contained an extremely narcissistic side that had more malignant consequences for his development.

For coexisting alongside his exceptional strengths within the structure of Freud's self are many of the rifts and vulnerabilities that typically stem from disturbances in the early pre-Oedipal stages of development.

---

[80] *Ibid.*, 192.

[81] *Ibid.*, 398.

A conviction that he was unlovable despite the tremendous recognition he received, extreme separation anxiety and demandingness regarding his love objects, a craving for idealization, oral addictiveness, and a tendency to somatization were among them. Let us examine for example the remarks he made concerning the effects of his parents' ambition for him. He does not refer to the self-confidence or optimism that it engendered in him but to his "thirst for grandeur," which, like his penchant for heroism, can represent a (sometimes desperate) striving to repair serious defects in one's self. Uncertainty about being loved often fuels the narcissistic thirst for glory. In his letters to Martha, Fliess, and Jung, Freud repeatedly confesses his nagging self-doubts and the feeling that he is unlovable. And as Rizzuto points out, "In spite of the fact that his mother obviously favored him and regardless of his assertion that favored sons are optimists, Freud was prone to pessimism."[82]

The picture seems to be this: To the extent that Freud could identify with and internalize his mother's idealizing love – as well as his father's and his nursemaid's – he was able to maintain his self-confidence in the face of deep doubts and extreme adversity. But insofar as he sensed that Amalie's love was narcissistic and that her *kvelling* (gushing) over him was hollow, these identifications and internalizations were precarious, and his sense of self tended to be vulnerable and brittle. His prodigious *but costly* capacity for self-mastery, however, often allowed him to mask these vulnerabilities. It may be the case, moreover, that in Freud, as in many other remarkable people, these radical contrasts in his personality helped to engender a creative character structure.

"The Original Catastrophe"

Freud's representation of the maternal imago was further complicated by the fact that he had a "second mother": a Czech Catholic nanny, the *Kinderfrau* who cared for him for the first two and a half years of his life.[83] We cannot be certain to what extent Amalie relied on the *Kinderfrau* prior

---

[82] Rizzuto, *Why did Freud reject God?*, 201.

[83] See Jim Swan, "Mater and nannie: Freud's two mothers and the discovery of the Oedipus complex," *American Imago* 31 (1974), 1–64.

to Julius' death, although it is safe to assume, given the stress she must have been undergoing and her lack of experience in caring for an infant, that it was relatively extensive. Once Julius died, however, it is clear, as Harry Hardin, an expert in early maternal loss, maintains, that the Czech nursemaid became Sigmund's "sole caretaker" – a position she retained until she abruptly disappeared six months later.[84]

Hardin argues that Freud's *Kinderfrau* not only tended to his physical needs, but, after the psychological death of his mother, also became his primary source of emotional support. She became, in other words, what analysts call "a substitute object," who replaced the mother he had precipitately lost.[85] It is important to note that the forgotten memories of the *Kinderfrau* emerged during the early, critical phase of Freud's self-analysis, which he had officially undertaken in response to Jacob's death. He had been driven into a period of intense mourning, in which many of the significant losses of his earliest years were reactivated as a result of the loss of his father. The timing of the discovery of these repressed memories indicates the important position that the *Kinderfrau* occupied in Freud's psychic development. And although scant, what Freud says about her is so laden with meaning that it gives us an idea of the significance she had for him.

Freud displaced many of the negative feelings that he kept split off from his representation of Amalie onto the extremely ambivalent representation he formed of his *Kinderfrau*. The picture that emerges from his remarks is of a woman who combines the features of both the "good mother" and the "bad mother" *in extremis*: nurturing and frightening, gratifying and reprimanding, praising and devaluing. Like his heroes Oedipus, Leonardo, and Moses, Freud had "two mothers," and the representation of each was itself deeply divided, although he tended to isolate his negative feelings toward Amalie. Freud's description of the *Kinderfrau* uses terminology that accurately applies to the apotheosis of the bad mother – namely, a witch. In addition to her being "an ugly, elderly, but

---

[84] Harry T. Hardin, "On the vicissitudes of Freud's early mothering – I: Early environment and loss," *Psychoanalytic Quarterly* 56 (1988), 639.

[85] In addition to *Ibid.*, see Harry Hardin, "On the vicissitudes of Freud's early mothering – II: Alienation from his biological mother," *Psychoanalytic Quarterly* 56 (1988), 72–86, and "On the vicissitudes of Freud's early mothering – III: Freiberg, screen memories, and loss," *Psychoanalytic Quarterly* 57 (1988), 209–223.

clever woman," he writes that "the prehistoric old nurse" was also a "strict disciplinarian" who treated him harshly if he "failed to reach the required standard of cleanliness."[86] Furthermore, like the archaic mother with her frightening phallic features, she both excited the pre-pubescent boy's sexuality and belittled the fact that he was immature and helpless.

A psychoanalytically informed biographer wishes that Freud had pro-vided more details when he writes that she was his "teacher in sexual matters," and that she "complained because [he] was clumsy and unable to do anything."[87] He reports an incident which must have been espe-cially confusing and terrifying to a small boy, especially since it involved a woman who was a stickler for hygiene: "She washed me in reddish water" – presumably reddish from her menstrual blood – "in which she had previously washed herself."[88] Freud makes an anomalous statement, which for some peculiar reason has received virtually no commentary in the literature and which throws the *idée reçu* that he abandoned the seduc-tion theory in 1897 into question. *The man who just one month earlier had supposedly renounced the seduction theory, which had portrayed the father as the villain and seducer, now states that his nursemaid was his seductress.* He writes, "I only indicate that the old man plays no active part in my case, but . . . that in my case the 'prime originator' was an ugly, but clever woman" who revealed the secrets of sexuality to him while simultaneously enlightening him about heaven and hell.[89] Because of his inability to face the frightening aspects of the early mother – what Professor of English Literature Coppélia Kahn has referred to as his "matrophobia" – which we will examine in detail – Freud could not register the significance of this stunning remark and left it hanging.[90]

Much to our astonishment, Freud's enlightenment about the after-life took place during regular excursions, in which his Czech nanny would escort young Schlomo Sigismund from one of Freiberg's numerous

---

[86] Masson (ed.), *Letters to Fliess*, 248.

[87] *Ibid.*, 269.

[88] *Ibid.*, 269.

[89] *Letters to Fliess*, 268.

[90] Quoted in Sprengnether, *The spectral mother*, 2 n. 2.

Catholic churches to another. (The town did not contain a synagogue.) On these pilgrimages, she would preach to him about "God Almighty and hell," and her sermons made such an impression on the young boy that he would re-enact them for his parents when he returned home.[91] That the Freud family allowed this Catholic woman to *schlep* their son around the churches of Freiberg, while attempting to instill a sense of religion in him, shows how secular – indeed, how blasé – they were concerning religious matters.

These expeditions with his *Kinderfrau* surely would have had a powerful impact on Freud's later views on Christianity and on religion in general. We must therefore ask what Freud's experience during these early encounters with Catholicism would have been like. As Vitz observes, Freud would have been exposed to the sensuality (*Sinnlichkeit*) of the churches, liturgy, and ceremonies: the paintings and statues of the Madonna and child and of the various saints, the distribution of the communion, the Latin of the Mass, the smell of the incense, the richly colored robes of the priests, the candles and the "bells, organ, and instrumental music, as well as choirs and chants and the various forms of music."[92] The last point is especially noteworthy, given Freud's strong aversion to music, which we will examine in due course. And as we have noted, not only was Moravian Catholicism "especially devout," but its "devotion to the Virgin Mary was so pervasive that" the region "became known as a 'Marian Garden'."[93] Thus, Vitz argues, while Freud would undoubtedly have observed the authority of the priests and picked up on "references to the Pope," the "strong masculine characteristics of Catholic Christianity would not have been" central to his experience. Rather, the Catholic world he was exposed to centered on the figure of the Madonna and was overwhelmingly feminine and maternal.[94]

The atmosphere in these churches, as Vitz emphasizes, was thus both profoundly sensuous (*sinnlich*) and permeated with a maternal presence. The combination of these two qualities must have made a lasting impression on Freud, for eighty-odd years later he not only connected them in

[91] Masson (ed.), *Letters to Fliess*, 268.

[92] Vitz, *Sigmund Freud's Christian unconscious*, 9.

[93] *Ibid.*, 3.

[94] *Ibid.*, 11.

Moses and monotheism but also adduced them as evidence of Catholicism's regressive character vis-à-vis Judaism.[95]

But whatever the impact of these excursions and whatever the *Kinderfrau's* shortcomings, Freud acknowledged his gratitude and his deep love for her without equivocation. He recognized that, along with fear and feelings of inadequacy, she had also instilled in him "a high opinion" of his own "capacities" and, like Jacob and Amalie, contributed to the self-assurance that allowed him to pursue his life's ambitions.[96] In the most important statement of all, Freud writes in the depths of his self-analysis that if he has the fortitude to complete the project, he "shall be grateful to the memory of the old woman *who provided [him] at such an early age with the means for living, and going on living.*" This assertion that his *Kinderfrau* had supplied him with the means of life helps to confirm the hypothesis that she stepped in to replace his "dead mother" who had succumbed to a debilitating depression. In other words, by serving as a "substitute object," this nanny enabled Freud to psychologically survive a profoundly traumatic period in his life. In a letter to Wilhelm Fliess – the charismatic ear, nose, and throat specialist with extravagant speculative proclivities, with whom Freud would form an intense relationship in the 1890s – he expresses his gratitude to his nanny, and his tender feelings break through: "As you can see, the old liking is breaking through again today."[97]

The traumas, however, did not end with Amalie's depression. At the age of two and a half, Freud also lost his *Kinderfrau* – the very person who had rescued him when his mother became psychologically unavailable. To make matters worse, with the birth of his younger sister Anna, he was at the same time struggling with the introduction of a new rival into his world. And on top of that, the loss of the nanny was abrupt and apparently unexplained. Later, during his self-analysis, when Freud asked his mother about the old woman, he was told that she had been caught stealing during Amalie's convalescence following the birth of Anna. Once the crime was uncovered, so Amalie informed Freud, his older half-brother Philipp called the police, and the *Kinderfrau* was promptly taken off to

---

[95] *Moses and monotheism* (1939), *SE* 23: 113.

[96] Masson (ed.), *Letters to Fliess*, 269.

[97] *Ibid.*, 269 (emphasis added).

jail, tried, and imprisoned. At the age of two and a half, Freud must have been confused not only by his mother's pregnancy and the appearance of a new infant, but also by the sudden – and apparently unaccounted for – disappearance of the nanny standing in for the absent Amalie. It has been argued that the disappointment and rage provoked by having been "abandoned" by his *Kinderfrau* – which is how a child of that age would have experienced it – contributed to Freud's hostility toward Catholicism as well as his longing for Rome. The argument is not without merit.[98]

In addition to the death of Julius, Amalie's depression, and the *Kinderfrau's* disappearance, Freud was subjected to yet another major loss early in his life. At approximately three and a half years old, "the happy child of Freiberg," as he referred to himself as a grown man, was uprooted from his first idyllic home, and after a year in Leipzig was transplanted to Leopoldstadt, the overcrowded and wretched Jewish quarter of Vienna.[99] The reason for this move is not entirely clear. It may have been due to the fact that Sigmund's older half-brothers Emanuel and Philipp were involved in illegal activities, or perhaps to the suspicion that Philipp was having an affair with Amalie. The official explanation was that Jacob's business failed because of developments in the local economy – circumstances that were beyond his control. This explanation has since been contested by later scholarship and by the fact that Ignaz Fluss and his family, who were friends of the Freuds, remained in the area and prospered.[100] Regardless of which "of these various reasons was responsible for the Freuds' departure," one thing is clear, as Krüll observes: "The adults in whose company little Sigmund left Freiberg were in a state of anxiety or even panic, and no explanation for this was given to Sigmund."[101] Therefore, at the same time as the grown-ups were transmitting their agitation to the young boy, they were also unavailable to help him contain his own fear, sorrow, and anger. No one was.

Another aspect of the exodus from Freiberg would have increased its traumatic impact even further – namely, that Freud lost "the close-knit, extended family that had provided [him] with what security he enjoyed

---

[98] See, for example, Vitz, *Freud's Christian unconscious*, 214–217.

[99] See Freud, "Letter to the *burgomeister* of Pribor," 259.

[100] Krüll, *Freud and his father*, 143.

[101] *Ibid.*, 146.

during his first three years." Not only did Freud's older half-brothers
Emanuel and Philipp "[vanish] from his life," but his "playmate and best
friend John and John's sister Pauline" disappeared with them, just as
his *Kinderfrau* had disappeared the previous year.[102] As evidence of the
strength of the family bonds that had been established in Freiberg, Freud's
biographer Ronald William Clark observes that Freud "maintained an
affection" for his relatives after their departure to England "that went
far beyond the family feelings of a typically tight-knit Jewish family."[103]
Clinical experience indicates, moreover, that "children without reliable
maternal attachments typically gain security from other relationships" –
often including their caregivers – "and their familiar surroundings."
Moreover, while the loss of his extended family further aggravated
Freud's early trauma, the growth of his nuclear family did not mitigate his
loneliness.[104] Freud did not view Anna and the four other sisters and one
brother who followed in rapid succession as allies. On the contrary, he saw
them as rivals for Amalie's affection and further evidence of her "betrayal."

As the editors of *Freud: the fusion of science and humanism* point out,
the central theme in idealizing transferences is "perfection."[105] They
maintain that children who experience a "premature disturbance of
[their] illusion of omnipotence" and suffer a traumatic de-idealization
of their parents – as Freud did – often create merger fantasies "with
idealized parental imagoes" in order to combat the disillusionment.
Because of the premature disappointment, the internalization of the
parents that is necessary for healthy development does not take place. As
a result, the psychic structures that should have been created through
that process of internalization are not formed. The consequence, as
articulated by Heinz Kohut, an analyst who has been at the forefront of
exploring the archaic and narcissistic strata of the psyche, is that "such
persons are forever . . . yearning to find a substitute [and] seeking with
addiction like intensity . . . to establish a relationship to people who
serve as stand-ins for the omnipotent idealized self-object – i.e. to the

---

[102] Breger, *Freud*, 16.

[103] Clark, *Freud: the man and the cause*, 13.

[104] See Breger, *Freud*, 16.

[105] John Gedo and George H. Pollock (eds.), *Freud: the fusion of science and humanism*, Psychoanalytic Issues monograph 34/35 (New York: International Universities
Press, 1975).

archaic precursor of the missing inner structure."[106] Kohut's description accurately described the idealization-hunger that Freud manifested for many years.

The Consequences of Freud's Early Traumas

It is in the appropriately entitled article "Screen memories" that Freud broaches the fact that his first three and a half years involved significant trauma. In that autobiographical paper, when Freud speaks of "the original catastrophe" that "involved [his] whole existence," in a thoroughly timid and circumspect way, he refers only to the departure from Freiberg. Regarding life in Vienna, he goes on to say: "Long and difficult years followed, of which, so it seems to me, nothing is worth remembering."[107]

The years in Vienna, however, are not the only thing Freud does not care to remember. While being uprooted from bucolic Freiberg and set down in the slums of Leopoldstadt would surely have been traumatic, "the original catastrophe" was significantly larger in scope than Freud could admit. The loss of his Moravian home was in fact a cipher – a "screen" to use the term he introduces in the article – for all the traumatic losses that had preceded it: Julius' death, Amalie's depression, the disappearance of his nanny, and the dispersion of his extended family. By restricting himself to the move and its aftermath, Freud could avoid remembering the catastrophes and traumas that had preceded it.[108]

It is a fundamental tenet of psychoanalysis that all important psychic phenomena are "over-determined": They are the result of a concatenation of multiple factors that generally include adaptive and defensive elements, which must be sorted out on a case-by-case basis.[109] Freud's response to the traumatic experiences of his early years is no exception.

---

[106] Heinz Kohut, "Creativeness, charisma, group psychology: reflections on the self-analysis of Freud," *Self-psychology and the humanities* (New York: W.W. Norton & Co., 1985), 189.

[107] Sigmund Freud, "Screen memories" (1899), *SE* 3: 314 and 312.

[108] See Breger, *Freud*, 16.

[109] See Robert Waelder, "The principle of multiple function: observations on overdetermination," *Psychoanalysis: observation, theory, application: selected papers of Robert Waelder*, ed. Samuel A. Guttman (New York: International Universities Press, 1977), 75–92.

Because he could not rely on the adults in his world to protect and care for him adequately, he was compelled to take over their tasks and was forced to develop his ego "prematurely" – that is, before he should have. As Freud himself recognized as an adult, he had not been allowed to fully indulge the "immature" experiences of "the magical years" that are a necessary condition for developing a truly mature self – which is to say, a self that is strong, flexible, and richly integrated.[110] Freud's "precocious" ego–development had undeniable advantages; it provided him with exceptional psychological strengths that enabled him not only to accomplish the monumental achievements associated with his name but also to endure a relentless onslaught of hardships that would have defeated most mortals.[111] At the same time, however, he paid a high price to attain those strengths.

The strategy Freud employed not merely to adapt, but to survive, resulted in significant restrictions in his character structure, and, as a result of them, in the range and flexibility of his thinking, remarkable as those qualities nonetheless were. The restrictions, in turn, had serious consequences for the development of psychoanalysis.

As we have seen, Breger argues that "The traumatic experiences of Freud's first four years" and the panoply of emotions attached to them, "were dissociated, not integrated into a coherent sense of self. They existed in a separate compartment of his personality, protecting him from their disruptive effects."[112] Although this defensive dissociation protected Freud and allowed him to function at an exceptionally high level, it also largely cut him off from the realm of early pre–Oedipal experience. And because the world of archaic experience was too dangerous for Freud to explore – to do so might bring back the overwhelming anxiety and sense

---

[110] See Breger, *Freud*, 25 and 31.

[111] Werner Bohleber has called my attention to a group of patients who, though they were subject to severe trauma in their early development, do not suffer from the serious and debilitating pathology that one might expect. Instead, because of particular psychological strengths they were able, as Winnicott puts it, to "hitch on to" developmental and adaptive forces within them and "yet make good." Indeed, their traumatic material may even be transformed into remarkable creative achievements. Freud can be counted as a member of this group. D.W. Winnicott, *Home is where we start from: essays by a psychoanalyst* (New York: W.W. Norton & Co., 1986), 31–32.

[112] Breger, *Freud*, 17.

of helplessness he had experienced as a child – it could not be integrated into his theory. The pre-Oedipal world that Freud had difficulty entering is primarily pre-verbal, affective, sensorial, and motoric in nature, and it *centers on the infant's relation to the early mother*. Because the child's primary developmental task during this phase is to separate satisfactorily from the symbiotic mother and to establish adequately differentiated representations of itself and of the object, its central theme is obviously "separation."[113] Other closely related themes – including "helplessness" and "loss" as well as "omnipotence" and "magic" – emerge in the infant's struggle to deny the profound psychic pain that separation entails.

As a result of the way he responded to his early traumatic experiences, Freud developed a phallologocentric – that is, masculinist and hyper-rational – character. The overwhelming anxiety we can assume he experienced during his first three and a half years and his inability to do anything about it instilled in him a deep hatred of passivity, helplessness, and dependence that lasted throughout his life. (It will therefore come as no surprise that helplessness became a central topic in his theory of human nature.) Freud's loathing of passivity and helplessness, moreover, produced an understandable counter-reaction: a valorization of self-sufficiency and independence that entailed an investment in activity, self-control, rationality, objectivity, moral rectitude, courage, and a disciplined work ethic. Indeed, according to Ernest Jones, Freud's associate, supporter, and first definitive biographer, Freud's "great dislike of helplessness and his love of independence" were two of his best-known "character traits."[114] In studying Freud's biography, however, a question often arises that is difficult to answer: When does his laudable and adaptive valorization of autonomy tip over into an idealization – if not a fetishization – of narcissistic self-sufficiency and create a counter-phobic contempt for passivity and dependency? There are important times when allowing oneself to be passive and dependent is not only "permissible" but is in fact necessary for achieving a fulfilled life – for example, when one is in love or in psychoanalysis. Unfortunately, however, Freud's fearful and contemptuous attitude toward passivity prevented him from

---

[113] See Margaret Mahler, Annie Bergman, and Fred Pine, *The psychological birth of the infant: symbiosis and individuation* (New York, Basic Books, 1975).

[114] Jones, *Freud* I, 129.

analysing it in himself, and this meant he could not adequately explore the significance of the topic for psychoanalytic theory in general, an inability that was responsible for a consequential limitation in his thinking.

We can describe Freud's character as phallocentric, the first half, so to say, of being phallologocentric, not because autonomy and independence – and the other attributes Freud associated with them – are in fact "masculine," but because *he thought they were*. He lionized these attributes at the expense of other personality traits that he devalued as "feminine" – for example, helplessness, passivity, dependence, emotionality, irrationality, lack of discipline, and an irresolute sense of morality. In addition to the misogynist prejudices of fin-de-siècle culture, personal factors served to engender Freud's "repudiation of femininity," which began as early as his fourth year and infused his personal relations and thinking up through one of his final publications. To cite an obvious example, the fact that his tempestuous mother was the personification of emotionality, irrationality, dependence, and lack of self-control led him to assume that those traits were "feminine" and to negatively invest them. There is, moreover, another deeper connection between Freud's "repudiation of femininity" and his relation to Amalie. In a mechanism, reversal, that lies behind much male misogyny, Freud took the passivity and helplessness that he experienced in the face of his powerful, uncontrollable, and frightening mother and projected them onto women in general. It was not he, the frightened little boy, who was passive and helpless, but the female members of the species. Indeed, because these are two of the defining attributes of being female as he saw it, girls and women deserve to be denigrated.

Although he registered caveats to the effect that the concepts of "masculinity" and "femininity" were largely conventional, the equation of femininity with passivity became almost axiomatic in Freud's thinking, and, except on a few rare occasions, he did not reflect on it. Furthermore, he made two other relatively dogmatic assumptions in conjunction with that presupposition. In addition to identifying femininity with passivity, he also equated male homosexuality with the "passive-female" position. Moreover, he took it as virtually self-evident that all men find the "passive-female" position intrinsically frightening and degrading. This is in fact a primary source of whatever misogyny existed in him: As a result of repudiating "femininity" in themselves, men also repudiate it in women. With several significant exceptions, Freud also believed that because men find the "passive-feminine" position so threatening, the topic of homosexuality is one of the most dangerous and difficult issues that a man can confront.[115] Perhaps until recently, this may have empirically been the case for many if not most men. And although Freud's "andro-philic side" is a complicated topic, it may have been true for Freud as well. Nevertheless, even if this is true, he dogmatically arrested his thinking on the subject. Rather than elevating this empirical state of affairs into a universal fact – as self-evidently given – he should have subjected it to analytic scrutiny. Freud's failure to do so delineates one of the major limitations in his thinking.

Freud's logocentrism is a correlate of his phallocentrism and completes his phallologocentrism. In addition to the other character traits that he extolled – namely, rationality, and the capacity for linguistic articulation – objectivity, which presupposes the relatively clear separation of subject and object, ranked among his most cherished values. And again Freud considered that these attributes, which were so essential to the formation of his "scientific" worldview, were distinctively masculine. It is safe to assume, as Breger points out, that Freud's logocentrism was partly a response to "all those female babies," the sisters who quickly arrived on the scene one after another and "lacked his verbal skills." In contrast to their rational and "civilized older brother," those baby girls "were the ones who could not control themselves; they were infantile creatures who gave way to their impulses, females incapable of the renunciation of pleasure."[116] Again, Freud's logocentrism entailed the devaluation of femininity. It is almost trivial to point out that without his prodigious capacity for reason, as well as his quasi-obsessive power of self-control, Freud could not have produced his monumental body of work. But it must also be pointed out that in cutting himself off from a major portion of the pre-verbal realm of archaic experience, he purchased these strengths at a considerable price.

Freud's Tin Ear

One place where Freud's almost phobic attitude toward archaic experience clearly manifested itself was in his strong aversion to music – with its "contentless forms and intensities and unaccountable emotions" – a dislike that was almost unheard of in the Vienna of Haydn, Mozart, Beethoven, and

---

[115] Masson (ed.), *Letters to Fliess*, 246.

[116] Breger, *Freud*, 31.

Schubert.[117] Recent research in neuropsychology has discovered that the incomparable power of music can partly be explained by the fact that it simultaneously excites all the strata of the mind-brain – from the most "primitive" to the most "advanced." For example, in addition to Bach's exquisite mathematical rigor, his music also reaches down into the earliest pre-verbal layers of early experience and has the power to "evoke powerful feelings" – ranging from grief to ecstasy – that are difficult to control.[118] In the beginning, the infant is enveloped in an undifferentiated sea of sound – a "primordial density" – out of which more determinate aural units later emerge.[119] The musicality of the mother's voice, with its variations in intensity, rhythmic impulses, and affective resonance, precedes the differentiation of the articulated phonemes of the *logos*. As distinguished from "inter-subjectivity," understood as the communication of linguistic meaning, music is one of the most effective media for achieving "inter-affectivity" – the communication of affective experiences and emotional states.

Amalie was very musical and, like other Viennese Jewish mothers with elevated cultural aspirations, she wanted her daughters to play the piano. Thus, when Freud's sister Anna was eight she began studying the instrument and would practice, as she reports, "by the hour." However, "though Sigmund's room was not near" the piano, "the sound disturbed him" when he was engaged in his studies. "His majesty the scholar" therefore laid down an ultimatum: Either the piano goes or he goes.[120] Not wanting to loose her *goldener Sigi*, Amalie deferred and had the instrument removed, making it impossible for his sisters to become musicians – and rendering the Freud household one of the only bourgeois homes in Vienna without a piano. Freud's son Martin observes that his tyrannical demand concerning this "one strange point" was out of character. Although the young Sigmund tended to be neither selfish nor spoiled – rather, he was

[117] Heinz Kohut, *The restoration of the self* (New York: International Universities Press, 1977), 294.

[118] Breger, *Freud*, 33.

[119] Hans Loewald, "Primary process, secondary process, and language," *The essential Loewald: collected papers and monographs* (Hagerstown, MD: University Publishing Group, 2000), 186.

[120] Anna Freud Bernays, "My Brother, Sigmund Freud," *Freud as we knew him*, ed. Henrik M. Ruitenbeek (Detroit, MI: Wayne State University Press), 142.

regarded as a self-controlled, considerate, well-mannered gentleman – the intensity of his aversion to music caused him to behave in this anomalous manner. Martin reports that Freud's "attitude towards musical instruments of any kind never changed throughout his life." There was never a piano in Berggasse 19, the building where he spent most of his adult life, and none of his children ever studied a musical instrument. But, his son adds, "I do not think the world has missed much through the total inability of any member of the Freud family to play 'The Blue Danube'."[121]

Freud's "extreme" and "atypical" aversion to music can be interpreted as an angry rejection of Amalie in two ways:[122] concretely, as his particular mother who had injured and infuriated him, and abstractly, as a representative of the maternal principle. By banishing the piano from the house, the young tyrant may have been punishing his mother directly for the "crimes" for which he held her responsible – her desertion to depression, volatility, self-centered demandingness, accession to the firing of the *Kinderfrau*, numerous pregnancies, and, as Freud suspected, her infidelity with Philipp. If this were indeed a punishment, it would serve not only to deprive her of something she cherished but also to thwart her aspirations for her daughters. Furthermore, as Breger suggests, because Freud viewed his volatile Galician mother as the exemplification of emotionality, his attempt to put "a lid on her musical interest" represented "part of his wider need to control emotion" in general. After all, as Breger observes, "music has the power to evoke a range of feelings in the listener, to carry one away on a tide of romantic passion or bring on sadness and grief." And, for reasons we are familiar with, "these were reactions that [Freud] had to suppress at all costs."[123]

To the limited degree that Freud could enjoy musical performances later in life, they were primarily operas – his favorites included *Don Giovanni, The Marriage of Figaro, Carmen,* and *Die Meistersinger* – that is, works *that contained librettos.* These two facts, that Freud associated music with Amalie and that he could only appreciate music if it was accompanied by words, tells us something more about the types of experiences and feelings that were dangerous and intolerable for him. Kohut suggests that music without words, what he calls "pure music," often transports us into psychic localities and feeling states connected with the pre-verbal

---

[121] M. Freud, *Glory reflected,* 19–20.

[122] Breger, *Freud,* 33.

[123] *Ibid.,* 33.

realm of the early mother–infant relationship. Unlike the domain that is mediated by language, which is made of "clearly defined and definable" experiences, this is a realm "of contentless forms and intensities and [of] emotions." Because Freud had been traumatized precisely at this level of psychic development, one marked by relative lack of determinacy, structure, and cohesion, it was too dangerous for him to "give himself over" to music because it threatened to transport him to those regions again.[124] Freud in fact explains his inability to enjoy music without words in terms of its indeterminacy, which makes it impossible for it to be grasped discursively:

Wherever I cannot do this [that is, understand something discursively], as for instance with music, I am almost incapable of obtaining any pleasure. Some rationalistic, or perhaps analytic, turn of mind in me rebels against being moved by a thing without knowing why I am thus affected and what it is that affects me.[125]

It is reasonable to assume that the mother's lullaby is one of the psychoanthropological sorts of music. The lullaby, however, is a siren's song that cuts two ways. It holds out the promise of merger, ecstasy, and bliss – of what Lacan called pure *jouissance* – but it simultaneously entails the terror and threat of dedifferentiation and loss of the self. As Max Horkheimer and Theodor W. Adorno, two major figures of the Frankfurt School, observe while commenting on Odysseus' encounter with the sirens on his return to Ithaca:

The fear of losing the self, and suspending with it the boundary between oneself and other life, the aversion of death and destruction, is twinned with a promise of joy which has threatened civilization at every moment.[126]

Ultimately, for Freud, this fear outweighed the *promesse du bonheur* contained in the realm of archaic experience – as well as his curiosity – and prevented Freud from exploring that region and the figure of the early mother in any detail.

[124] Kohut, *The restoration of the self*, 294.
[125] Freud, "The Moses of Michelangelo" (1914), *SE* 14: 211.
[126] Max Horkheimer and Theodor W. Adorno, *Dialectic of enlightenment: philosophical fragments*, ed. Gunzelin Noerr, trans. Edmund Jephcott (Stanford, CA: Stanford University Press, 2002), 26.

2

Freud's *Bildung*

Truth and Illusion in the City of Dreams

The mid-nineteenth century saw the modernizing forces of change roil through virtually every aspect of European life, and those forces were all converging in Vienna, the heterogeneous, fractious, and polyglot capital of the Habsburg Empire, at the time the Freud family relocated there in 1860. Freud's father (and mother) had already broken with the isolated, narrowly religious *Ostjuden* past into which they had been born, and the move from Freiberg to the capital represented the next step of their *passage*. Here their "goldener Sigi" would begin his education, come of age, wrestle with his passionate nature, and choose science as his profession. Here too, he would become the famously "godless Jew," the implacable liberal, the dedicated rationalist and champion of the Enlightenment who towered over the intellectual history of the twentieth century, and who will undoubtedly continue to influence our cultural life for some time to come – the monotonous litany proclaiming his obsolescence notwithstanding.

The Viennese context was all-important to Freud's formation. Owing to a stroke of fortune, his critical formative years began during Austria's "brief interlude of liberalism" following the country's defeat in the Austro-Prussian War;[1] the era saw the collapse of the aristocracy's (overt) domination of the government and the ascendance of the *Bürgerministerium*, the formation of a new Cabinet made up largely of middle-class professional men, many of them Jewish, who set out to modernize the baroque world of Austrian politics. The society and culture that resulted – and the milieu that Freud absorbed as a boy – was intellectually energetic and committed to social progress through science, education, and liberal politics.

---

[1] Horkheimer and Adorno, *Dialectic of enlightenment*, 69.

The decline of the aristocracy and of the church, moreover, allowed Austria
to enter its *Gründerzeit*, its period of capitalist takeoff, in the 1860s.

With the victory of the *Bürgerministerium*, the new species of secular Jew referred to by Rizzuto could enter arenas that had until recently
been the preserve of the Gentiles, and enter they did – into the universities, the professions, and the burgeoning capitalist economy.
Furthermore, with the decline of aristocratic patronage, these newly secularized Jews, who had a passionate, almost religious devotion to the arts,
became the primary supporters of Viennese culture.[2] "The glorious days
when the Esterhazys harbored a Haydn, the Lobkowitzes and the Kinskys
and Waldsteins competed to have a première of Beethoven in their
palaces . . . were gone," as the Viennese author Stefan Zweig observes,
and artistic production was moving into the marketplace where composers
like "Wagner, Brahms, Johann Strauss, and Hugo Wolf [did not receive]
the slightest support" from the aristocracy. This presented the wealthy
aspiring Jewish *Bürger* with an opportunity for social advancement. In
fact, middle-class Jews became so prominent in the cultural life of Vienna
that Zweig could wrote, "Nine-tenths of what the world celebrated as
Viennese culture in the nineteenth century was promoted, nourished, or
even created by Viennese Jewry."[3]

Little wonder that Jacob Freud decorated his home with portraits of
many of the new Jewish Cabinet Ministers. The message was clear: It was
now possible for Jews to have successful political careers – to seek and
hold power. "Henceforth," Freud notes, "every industrious Jewish boy
carried a Cabinet Minister's portfolio in his satchel."[4]

At the same time, mid-nineteenth-century Vienna, while struggling
to become modernized, was also a society focused on pageantry, pomp,
and spectacle, which were vigorously promoted by Austria's antediluvian
emperor Franz Josef to mask the vacuity, ineptitude, and fragility of the
Habsburg dynasty. Viennese society, as Freud's urbane and savvy colleague

---

[2] See Carl Schorske, *Fin-de-siècle Vienna: politics and culture* (New York: Alfred A.
Knopf, 1980), 8.

[3] Stefan Zweig, *The world of yesterday: an autobiography of Stefan Zweig* (Lincoln:
University of Nebraska Press, 1964), 22. It has been said that in Vienna and Berlin
during the second half of the nineteenth century, the Jews migrated from the
synagogue to the concert hall and the theater.

[4] Freud, *The interpretation of dreams*, 193.

Hans Sachs observes, was permeated by "play-acting" offstage as well as onstage – by "the policeman who warned a driver, the housewife who bargained for her cabbages, the tram-car conductor and the woman with a bundle, the prosecutor and the defendant."[5] Sachs makes an interesting observation that helps to capture the specific flavor of Viennese culture – namely, that this behavior should not be viewed as hypocritical because the dissemblance was institutionalized. "Artificiality and pretense," as Janik and Toulmin observe, "were the rule rather than the exception, and in every aspect of life the proper appearances and adornments were all that mattered."[6] In other words, everybody was aware of the game. And play-acting that is acknowledged as such, if only by a wink, is not, Sachs is arguing, hypocrisy in the strict sense.

Freud's politics and his secularism were forged in this milieu. What Carl Schorske, perhaps the foremost historian of fin-de-siècle Vienna, calls the era's "clear and confident mid-century liberalism" shaped Freud's entire political outlook, engendering in him the "political values he retained all his life" – his contempt for courtiers, aristocracy, and royalty, commitment to science and reason, and his respect for "British" integrity and industriousness – even after he became skeptical about politics.[7] And the rationalism prized by the culture bolstered the secularism that, as we shall see, both Freud's home life and his schooling also helped to engender.

It was during this period that one of the iconic events in the annals of Freudian lore took place, an incident that played an enormous role in shaping Freud's liberal sensibility. In their early days in Vienna, Jacob

[5] Hans Sachs, *Freud: master and friend* (Cambridge, MA: Harvard University Press, 1944), 32–33.

[6] Alan Janik and Stephen Toulmin, *Wittgenstein's Vienna* (New York: Simon and Schuster, 1973), 62.

[7] Schorske, "Politics and patricide," *Fin-de-siècle Vienna*, 189. Schorske's influential thesis, elaborated by his student William McGrath, was that, had the political situation gone better, Freud may very well have ended up a lawyer or even a politician. But there was no more of a chance that he would have become a lawyer than he would have remained a neurologist, as many of today's up-to-date analysts maintain. He was simply too ambitious. He wanted to fry really big fish – answer fundamental questions about the human condition – and those fish are not to be found in law or neurology. To be sure, he would have incorporated the most recent discoveries of neuropsychology into his theory of human nature – as he would have done with the relevant findings of all disciplines – but he would have not been a neurologist.

would take his son on walks around the city and share his views about the world with him. On one such *Spaziergang*, he recounted the story of an incident that had occurred when he still lived in Freiberg:

"When I was a young man," he said, "I went for a walk one Saturday in the streets of your birthplace. I was well dressed, and had a new fur cap on my head. A Christian came up to me and with a single blow knocked off my cap into the mud and shouted: 'Jew! get off the pavement!'"

The boy naturally wanted to know how his father had responded. And the answer he received was disappointing: "'I went into the roadway and picked up my cap,' was his quiet reply."

Jacob had offered the story as an illustration of how much things had improved politically since the Freiberg days, the implication being that such an incident could not occur in the liberal Vienna of the late 1860s. Sigmund, however, reacted to it differently. His father's response "struck" him "as unheroic on the part of the big strong man who was holding the little boy by the hand." In reaction to the disappointment, the boy's mind turned to another father–son scenario where the father, unlike Jacob, had maintained his ideal stature: "the scene in which Hannibal's father, Hamilcar Barca, made his boy swear before the household altar to take vengeance on the Romans." Freud believed that, "ever since that time," he had "identified with Hannibal, the leader who fought against the Romans."[8] Moreover, the fact that Hannibal was a Semite allowed Freud to construe this story as the struggle of Jews against the Catholic Church – the very embodiment of the forces of reaction that eventually helped to doom the liberal interlude of the *Bürgerministerium*.

Freud was deeply disillusioned with his father, but his revolt against him assumed a different form from that assumed by most members of the next generation. He was disappointed with Jacob *for not defending his liberalism strongly enough* – as symbolized by his submission to the anti-Semitic Christian. In contrast, after the failure of the *Bürgerministerium*, much of the Oedipal revolt of the following generation, exemplified in *Jung Wien* (The Young Vienna Movement), consisted of a rejection of their fathers' liberalism and a retreat into aestheticism, irrationalism, and decadence. Unlike *Jung Wien*, Freud did not reject Jacob's liberal values;

[8] Freud, *The interpretation of dreams*, 197.

on the contrary, he believed they ought to be defended more aggressively, with the vigor of a Hannibal. In so doing, as Schorske observes, "he shared more with . . . the confident rationalism of the orthodox liberal fathers" – "the men with qualities" – than with "the ambiguity ridden culture makers" of *Jung Wien*.[9] A paradox, however, emerged from this situation: by not revolting against mid-century rationalism of the fathers and by remaining committed to science, Freud unearthed what he believed to be the universality of Oedipal revolt.[10]

It is not hard to imagine how a world of ubiquitous dissemblance and role-playing – where life is conducted according to unwritten codes and everyone presents a cleverly crafted persona – could provide the impetus for an exceptionally curious and perceptive young man like Freud to crack those codes and unmask those personas in order to reveal the truer if less pleasant reality lying beneath the frothy surface, just as he had struggled to decipher the structure underlying his complicated family constellation in Freiberg. Nor is it difficult to see how the Viennese culture of beautiful illusion produced five of modernity's fiercest and most puritanical intellects – Karl Kraus, Adolf Loos, Arnold Schönberg, Ludwig Wittgenstein, and Freud – as a reaction against it.

This chapter explores the tensions and paradoxes of Freud's formative years as he made his way toward becoming, as he saw it, an *Aufklärer* and a man of science.

Leopoldstadt

The setting for "the long and difficult years" that Freud mentioned in "Screen memories" was Leopoldstadt in Vienna's largely Jewish Second District, where Jacob Freud eventually relocated his family after their departure from Freiberg. The contrast between the "peaceful pastoral countryside" that surrounded Catholic Freiberg and the urban squalor of Leopoldstadt could not have been starker.[11] The "slums" of the quarter,

---

[9] Carl Schorske, "Generational tension," *Thinking with history: explorations in the passage to modernism* (Princeton, NJ: Princeton University Press 1998), 154.

[10] *Ibid.*, 154.

[11] Siegfried and Suzanne Cassirer Bernfeld, "Freud's early childhood," *Freud as we knew him*, ed. Hendrik M. Ruitenbeek (Detroit, MI: Wayne State University Press, 1973), 188–189.

where most of the poor Jews like the Freuds lived, were "as bad as the worst in any Western city."[12] The appalling and unsanitary conditions that created predictable health problems were largely the result of waves of Jewish emigration into Vienna from the outlying areas of the Empire. What came to be called the "Jewish invasion" was a direct result of the 1848 revolution and the lifting of the problematic travel and residential prohibitions. The exponential growth of Vienna's Jewish community was accelerated under the *Bürgerministerium* in the 1860s. By the turn of the century, Vienna "had the largest Jewish community of any city in Western Europe," and "in all Europe . . . only Warsaw and Budapest had more Jewish residents."[13] Gay tells us that "when Burkhardt returned to the city in 1884, he found it thoroughly 'Judaized'– totally *verjudet*. It is a repulsive term," Gay observes, "that was to enjoy an ominous career in Freud's lifetime."[14]

The misery of the slums was intensified by the launch of capitalism in Austria, which occurred later than it had in Germany and France, and which saw ambitious, recently emancipated Jews ascend the rungs of the economic ladder until they came to dominate the Austrian economy (a prime example being Karl Wittgenstein, father of Ludwig) – while conditions in the slums simultaneously worsened.

Economic success, however, was not on the cards for Jacob Freud. Though he described himself as a "wool merchant" all his life, Jacob was "a man incapable of functioning on his own in the commercial and business world."[15] Without someone to back him up, as Süsskind Hoffman had done during the *Wanderjude* years and as Emanuel and Philipp had done in Freiberg, it was apparent that Jacob could not sustain a viable business. Yet despite his repeated failures, he remained an impractical dreamer always inventing new schemes who finally descended into a "state of fatalistic helplessness and even childishness" in his old age.[16] Because there is no record of Jacob paying any income tax in Vienna, we must ask how he

---

[12] Hannah S. Decker, *Freud, Dora, and Vienna 1900* (New York: The Free Press, 1991), 24.

[13] George E. Berkley, *Vienna and its Jews: the tragedy of success 1880s–1980s* (Cambridge, MA: Abt Books, 1988), 35.

[14] Gay "Freud: a life for our time," 20.

[15] Rizzuto, *Why did Freud reject God?*, 61.

[16] M. Freud, *Glory reflected*, 20.

supported his family, especially considering that Amalie gave birth to four daughters – Rosa, Marie, Adolfine, and Pauline – and a son, Alexander, during their first six years in Leopoldstadt.[17] It is likely that Jacob received financial assistance not only from Emanuel and Philipp, who had become prosperous businessmen in Manchester, but also from Amalie's father, Jacob Nathanson. The struggling young physician Sigmund also contributed to his father's support, causing him considerable hardship.

Jacob and Amalie began educating their son at an early age, and it must not have taken long to recognize that the idea of their "golden Sigi" was not just the wishful fantasy of "his majesty the baby" which every parent entertains, but that they were blessed with a truly exceptional child.[18] Sigmund was elevated to the position of family favorite, and "no sacrifice was too great" to advance his education.[19] We can assume that the four apartments that Jacob's family occupied between 1860 and 1875 comprised the small cramped quarters that typified Vienna's Jewish slum, with little room for privacy. Yet Freud's sister, Anna Bernays, reports that "no matter how crowded [the] quarters," a room was always set aside where Freud could pursue his studies. In their fourth flat in Vienna on Kaiser-Joseph-Strasse, Sigi occupied a "cabinet," described as a "long narrow" room at the top of the stairs with "a window looking on the street." He lived, worked, and entertained his friends in this monk's cell until his internship at medical school. Freud often took his dinner in the cabinet and proceeded to read late into the night so as not to interrupt his studies. Anna Freud Bernays explains that "the only thing that changed in this room" over the years "was the increasing number of crowded bookcases added to the writing desk, bed, chair and shelf which furnished it."[20]

Though he may not have been a *yeshiva bocher*, a yeshiva-attending Talmudic scholar in the traditional mold, one would be hard pressed to find someone who devoted himself to his studies more than Freud. "Reading and studying," Jones observes, "seemed to have filled the greater part of his life."[21] His almost obsessive devotion to his studies,

---

[17] Krüll, *Freud and his father*, 149.

[18] Sigmund Freud, "On narcissism: an introduction" (1914), *SE* 14: 91.

[19] M. Freud, *Glory reflected*, 19.

[20] Bernays, "My brother, Sigmund Freud," 141.

[21] Jones, *Freud* I, 21.

Breger argues, was central to the way in which his rigid character structure and need for self-control manifested themselves. In addition to being "'moral' – prudish, unexpressive, censorious – to an extreme degree," Freud, Breger maintains, "took up the mantle of the special achieving child, burying himself in his books and schoolwork and avoiding emotional entanglements – especially with girls."[22] Breger's hostility toward Freud prevents him from appreciating the other "adaptive" side of Freud's over-investment in his studies. Not only did his studiousness constitute a defensive means of controlling his emotional life, which he employed up through his years at Brücke's laboratory, it also constituted an example of successful "sublimation."[23] Whatever other factors may have been driving his studies, Freud tells us that he was also moved "by a certain greed for knowledge."[24] Surely the depth and intensity of Freud's pursuit of knowledge must also have sprung from a passionate love of learning for its own sake.

"Jewgreek is Greekjew": *Volksschule* and *Gymnasium*

It does not follow from the fact that Freud was ambivalent about Judaism that he did not love it – or, worse yet, that he was a "self-hating Jew," as the more chauvinistic defenders of the tribe sometimes assert. In fact, making the charge demonstrates an ignorance of Freud's own theory of ambivalence, which holds that we are most conflicted and ambivalent precisely about the things we love the most. The charge that Freud's ambivalence about Judaism proves that he was a "self-hating Jew" is therefore not only false; it is also banal.

It is true that, much as he tried to deny the traumatic nature of his first three years, Freud also felt it necessary to minimize the role of Judaism in his upbringing. As religious studies professor Reuben Rainey observes, "Freud's self-portrait presents us with a kind of infant *philosophe* sprung from the head of Zeus, who could well serve as a paradigm for a psychoanalytic vision of child development devoid of religious needs." This picture,

---

[22] Breger, *Freud*, 30.

[23] See Anzieu, *Freud's self-analysis*, 16.

[24] Freud, "An autobiographical study," 8 (translation altered). Gay's translation of *Wissbegierde* has been used rather than Strachey's because Strachey's is too tepid and does not capture the appetitive dimension of Freud's investment in learning.

however, "hardly fits what we know," especially what we have learned over the last thirty years, "about Freud's family background."[25] We will have ample opportunity to see that Freud, like Odysseus, was *polytropos*.[26] And one of the innumerable contradictions in this thoroughly *polytropic* individual is that while he felt compelled to deny the Jewishness of his upbringing, he never tired of reminding the world of the fact that he was a Jew.

It is equally true that many Jews of Freud's time and place and from similarly emancipated assimilationist families experienced conflict between their commitments to *Judentum*, Judaism, and to the German values of *Kultur*, *Humanität*, and *Bildung*. That is a story that has been recounted many times. In some cases – those of Karl Kraus, Gustav Mahler, and Arnold Schönberg, to name three examples – the tension led to conversion to Christianity, an act Heine considered the admission ticket to European society. And although the manner in which Freud navigated the intricacies of his "dual allegiance" was conflicted and complex, he never saw the two traditions *as irreconcilably opposed*.[27] In fact, Freud managed to integrate the two traditions within himself – a process, full of complexity, that can be illustrated in the way he incorporated what he learned from the age of six to eight at a Jewish *Volksschule* with what he learned from age nine to seventeen at the *Gymnasium*.

The prelude for this integration lies in the situation in Jacob and Amalie's household, for all education – in the fundamental sense of socialization or character-formation – begins at home. Considering Jacob's relation to Judaism, it is not surprising that the Freud household was relatively non-observant but nonetheless thoroughly Jewish at the same time – a combination that contributed to Freud's eventual conception of himself as "a godless Jew."[28] While Jacob spent a good deal of his time studying the holy texts, there is no record of his attending synagogue. Nor did the family observe the Sabbath. And although this

[25] Reuben M. Rainey, *Freud as a student of religion: perspectives on the background and development of his thought* (Missoula, MT: Scholars' Press, 1975), 24.

[26] "A man of twists and turns" (*The Odyssey*, trans. Fagles).

[27] See Gresser, *Dual allegiance*; and see also Marthe Robert, *From Oedipus to Moses: Freud's Jewish identity*, trans. Robert Manheim (New York: Anchor Books, 1976), 19.

[28] And this is exactly the way Freud's son Martin described their home at Berggasse 19, regardless of the fact that they celebrated Easter and Christmas. See Gresser, *Dual allegiance*, 86.

question is somewhat controversial, there is no direct evidence to support the claim that Freud was *bar mitzvahed*.[29] While the family did not follow kosher laws, we know from Freud himself that they observed the major Jewish holidays (for example, Rosh Hashanah, Yom Kippur, Purim, and Pesach) as late as 1874 – as well as Easter and Christmas. And despite the fact he had become an agnostic by the end of his *Gymnasium* years, Freud continued to attend these holiday celebrations even when he was in medical school, "grudgingly submitt[ing] to them in an attitude of ironic detachment."[30]

Regardless of the level of observance in the Freud household, it is important to consider another less tangible but perhaps more important factor, namely, the affective ambience of the home. This is created mainly by the innumerable conscious, preconscious, and unconscious exchanges that take place in everyday life. The affective flavor of the Freud home was thoroughly Jewish – dripping with *Yiddishkeit*. As a result, for Freud, what was *heimisch* – familiar or familial – was that which was Jewish.[31] As Gresser observes, "being Jewish" for Freud did not involve the observance of rituals and ceremonies but was rather identified with "a familial kinship, an intermingling of selfhood."[32]

There is evidence, moreover, that Yiddish was spoken in the household. Indeed, Freud's colleague Theodor Reik reports that Amalie never learned to speak proper German. Yiddish, maybe even more than other languages, has a very specific *Weltanschauung* sedimented within it – a *Weltanschauung* Freud absorbed from his surroundings. Even if he could not speak the language, as he claimed, he could certainly understand it. Yiddish, Gresser argues, was linked "to his Jewish home, literally *mame-loschen* [mother tongue], the affectionate term among Jews for the language."[33] Furthermore, when Freud expressed himself in a more intimate or unbuttoned mood in his letters, or when his "existence was threatened in any way," he often turned to Yiddish. On the other hand,

[29] See Yerushalmi, *Freud's Moses*, 123 n. 33, and Gresser, *Dual allegiance*, 50–51.

[30] Walther Boehlich (ed.), *The letters of Sigmund Freud to Eduard Silberstein, 1871–1881*, trans. Arnold J. Pomerans (Cambridge, MA: The Belknap Press of Harvard University Press, 1990), 167.

[31] *Heimish* in Yiddish.

[32] Gresser, *Dual allegiance*, 91.

[33] *Ibid.*, 113.

when he spoke in his official public or scientific mode, he generally cited Sophocles, Shakespeare, or Goethe just like every good *Gymnasiast* – that is, like a student at an elite *Gymnasium*.[34]

As we noted in Chapter 1, Jacob Freud had the capacity to remain light-hearted and jocular – even to a fault – whatever the adversity and disappointments that confronted him. He may have been feckless, but Jacob was a connoisseur of the Jewish joke, a lingua franca that even non-believers can use to communicate, as the Jewish philosopher Ernst Simon suggests, "the intimate familiarity of a shared psychic structure" to other Jews.[35] Freud's celebrated love of Jewish humor, which shows "a man at home with his Jewish attitude for life," was tied up with his love for his father.[36] This is attested to by the fact that he began his collection of Jewish jokes (and joined the B'nai B'rith) shortly after Jacob's death.

The affective flavor of the Freud home, therefore – the worldview captured in Yiddish as the mother tongue and epitomized in humor – was second nature to Freud throughout his life. This did not, however, prevent him from exhibiting the same prejudices against the *Ostjuden* common among assimilated Viennese Jews. In fact, his description of a family of Eastern Jews with whom he shared a train compartment is, according to Gay, as anti-Semitic as any "professional [Jew-baiter's]."[37] But when writing to his fiancée to share his vision of their future home, he pictures it in essentially Jewish terms: "Even if the form wherein the old Jews were happy no longer offers us any shelter" – that is, even if the traditional way of life is no longer available to us – "something of the core, of the essence of this meaningful and life-affirming Judaism will not be absent from our home."[38] It is this "'core' of his Jewishness" that Freud

[34] See Yerushalmi, *Freud's Moses*, 69, and Robert, *From Oedipus to Moses*, 59.

[35] Quoted in Gresser, *Dual allegiance*, 15.

[36] Martin S. Bergmann, "Moses and the evolution of Freud's Jewish identity," *Judaism and psychoanalysis*, ed. Mortimer Ostow (London: Karnac Books, 1977), 117.

[37] Gay, *Freud: a life for our time*, 19. For the passage Gay has in mind see Sigmund Freud, "Some early unpublished letters of Freud," *International Journal of Psychoanalysis* 50 (1969), 420.

[38] Ernst L. Freud (ed.), *The letters of Sigmund Freud*, ed. 22. Freud's basically affirmative attitude toward a Jewish upbringing can also be observed in the advice he gave Max Graf, the father of Little Hans, on how to raise his son: "If you do not let your

"sought to preserve . . . while simultaneously casting off the outer form that he believed consisted of theology, religious ceremony, obsessional legalism, and ritual observances."[39] And it was derived from the home life that Jacob and Amalie constructed in Leopoldstadt, the base from which he sallied forth at the age of six to begin his education.

Though we cannot be certain which of two Jewish *Volksschulen* he was enrolled in, it is clear that Freud attended a private Jewish elementary school from 1862 until 1864. In addition to the study of Hebrew and five hours of religious instruction a week, the school's curriculum would have reflected the brand of Reform Judaism found in the Philippson Bible, one that sought to interpret the principles of Judaism in terms of the values of modern European culture.

Adolf Jellinek, the head "*Prediger* [preacher] of the Viennese Jewish Community," articulated this outlook when he called for the building of a third temple "on the wreckage of religion" that would hallow and sanctify "the aspirations of modern society."[40] As opposed to the traditional *heder* and *yeshiva*, Judaism's old-fashioned pedagogical institutions, the *Volksschule* largely ignored the Talmud and the commentaries and focused its attention almost exclusively on the Pentateuch – the Five Books of Moses constituting the heart of the Jewish Bible. Freud's engagement with the Bible, which began at home with his father, in fact continued through the *Volksschule* and, as we will see, during his *Gymnasium* years as well. Thus, for the better part of a decade, he was exposed to "a curriculum . . . structured around a thorough study" of that text.[41] While he was thoroughly conversant with the biblical stories and "lived on terms of natural intimacy" with its heroes, identifying himself at various points in his life with Jacob, Joseph, or Moses, Freud's identification was with what he considered the text's ethical rather than its religious

---

son grow up as a Jew, you will deprive him of those sources of energy which cannot be replaced by anything else. He will have to struggle as a Jew, and you ought to develop in him all the energy he will need for that struggle. Do not deprive him of that advantage." Max Graf, "Reminiscences of Professor Sigmund Freud," *Psychoanalytic Quarterly* 11 (1942), 473.

[39] Rainey, *Freud as a student of religion*, 65.

[40] Quoted in *ibid.*, 15.

[41] For a detailed account of the role of religion in the curricula of Vienna's primary and secondary schools see *ibid.*, 36–52.

message.[42] Indeed, it can be argued that the Bible was in fact "his deepest patrimony."[43]

Freud's *Volksschule*, despite its adherence to Reform Judaism and to a relatively modern pedagogical approach, did not present its students with "a dispassionate analysis" of Judaism "in the spirit of *Religionswissenschaft*" – the science of religion. Instead the aim was to engage the children by kindling their imagination and affect. The "curriculum was designed to bring about a 'personal encounter' with the 'spirit of Judaism' through a careful analysis of major portions of the Pentateuch and synagogue prayers" – an encounter that emphasized "feeling" and "spiritual depth."[44] The fact that Freud was exposed to this affective encounter helps to explain the unique nature of his rationalism and how it contributed to his exceptional creativity. Marthe Robert, the French author who first broke the taboo on discussing Freud's Jewish roots, lest psychoanalysis be condemned as "a Jewish science," and undertook a detailed study of it, observes that Freud's adherence to his "'god Logos' never barred him from a profound experience of the inspired primordial images."[45]

Added to this was the impressive figure of Samuel Hammerschlag, a warm and passionate man who was an eminent pedagogue and an important and inspirational influence on Freud's *Bildung*. A prominent member of the *Kultusgemeinde*, the leadership organization of Vienna's orthodox Jews, Hammerschlag was the boy's teacher at the *Volksschule* and most likely also instructed him in Hebrew and religion at the *Gymnasium*, where both were required subjects. In addition to encouraging his studies, the instructor was known to lend his student money. The two became so close that Freud wrote to Martha, "There is such a secret sympathy between us that we can talk intimately together."[46] Freud reveals how down-to-earth and unpretentious Hammerschlag's sensibility was when he tells his fiancée that he "felt more at home" in the modest household of his "dear old Jewish teacher" where he had become a regular guest than

[42] Robert, *From Oedipus to Moses*, 38.

[43] Gresser, *Dual allegiance*, 88.

[44] *Ibid.*, 51, 34 and 38.

[45] Robert, *From Oedipus to Moses*, 38. One is reminded of the similarity between the copious illustrations of the Philippson Bible and the antiquities that surrounded Freud in his office pointed out by Rizzuto.

[46] The unpublished letter is cited by Jones, *Freud* I, 163.

he did "with the wealthy Schwabs."[47] Freud held Hammerschlag and his
family in such high regard that he named two of his daughters, Anna and
Sophie, after his mentor's daughter and niece.

Years later, on Hammerschlag's death in 1904, Freud wrote a deeply
affectionate and laudatory obituary, praising his teacher for his "sympathetic kindness" and gift for "leaving ineradicable impressions on the
development of his students." Furthermore, he pays Hammerschlag
the highest compliment when he likens him to the Hebrew prophets:
"A spark from the same fire which animated the spirit of the great Jewish
seers and prophets burned in him."[48]

But Freud also used the obituary to stake out his own position.
Hammerschlag's advocacy of Jewish particularity is too much for him –
Hammerschlag had contended that Jews should defend their particularity
not only in order to avoid the dangers of assimilation, but also because
following this course would increase their chances of making significant
contributions to universal culture. Freud in the obituary beats a retreat in
the direction of Apollonian restraint, advocating – at least implicitly – the
same sort of one-sided Universalism Hammerschlag criticized: "the ideal
of humanism of our German classical period . . . based on the foundation of philological and classical studies."[49] Such studies were the core
curriculum of the *Leopoldstädter Communal-Realgymnasium*, known as the
Sperlgymnasium, which was the local elite "high school" in Leopoldstadt
that Freud entered in 1865. There, he proceeded to carve out a stellar academic career. In his "Autobiographical study," Freud at age sixty-nine still
lets us know that he was the head of class for seven years and was granted

[47] *The letters of Sigmund Freud*, ed. Ernst L. Freud, 84.

[48] Writing to his fiancée from Paris, Freud boasted that Josef Breuer had attributed the
same "fire" to him that he had ascribed to Hammerschlag, when he told the young
physician that he "had inherited all the obstinate defiance and all the passions with
which our forefathers defended their Temple."

[49] Sigmund Freud, "Obituary for Professor S. Hammerschlag," (1904), *SE* 9: 256.
Something similar occured in a letter Freud wrote to Herzl when he sent him a copy of
The interpretation of dreams where he appears to be commending his efforts on behalf
of Zionism: "But at all events, may I ask you to keep the book as a token of the high
esteem in which I – like so many others – have held you since many years for the poet
and the fighter for the human rights of our people." Freud praises Zionism not as a
specifically Jewish movement but in terms of its attempt to provide Jews with their
(universal) "human rights." See Rainey, *Freud as a student of religion*, 70–71.

special privileges for his exceptional performance. Unsurprisingly, Freud graduated *summa cum laude* from the *Gymnasium*.

The Cult of *Bildung*

Classical studies were the pathway to and the requisite basis of *Bildung* – roughly translated as "education," "development," or "cultivation" – and Richard Armstrong, an impressive and original psychoanalytically oriented classicist, argues that the institution of the *Gymnasium*, where, Rainey tells us, two-fifths of the studies were devoted to the classics, played a critical role in the acculturation of many upwardly mobile young Jewish men.[50] At the time, Jews, as we saw, were replacing the aristocracy as the largest supporters of culture in Vienna, and they embraced the *Bildungsideal* of the *Gymnasium* with a fervor that reached a nearly religious pitch.[51] One novelist wrote of the period: Whereas "formerly the religious spirit proceeded from revelation, the present starts with *Bildung*."[52] The idealization – or fetishization – of *Bildung* was pervasive throughout the various modernist movements that arose in the Jewish community. The psychoanalysts, Socialists, and Zionists each believed their project represented the "true unfolding of *Bildung* and the Enlightenment."[53]

The Europeanizing Viennese Jews had good reason to invest so heavily in the ideal. As an alternative to religion, *Bildung* seemed to provide an entrée into European society that did not require the ignominy of

[50] Richard Armstrong, "Marooned mandarins: Freud, classical education, and the Jews of Vienna," *Classics and National Culture*, ed. Susan A. Stephens and Phiroze Vasunia (Oxford: Oxford University Press, 2010), 34–58. (Many of these quotes come from an earlier unpublished version of this article.) Rainey, *Freud as a student of religion*, 109.

[51] See Harry Zohn, "Fin-de-siècle Vienna: the Jewish contribution," *The Jewish response to German culture: from the enlightenment to the second world war*, ed. Jehuda Reinharz and Walter Schatzberg (Hanover, NH: University of New England Press, 1985), 144–145.

[52] Quoted in George L. Mosse, "Jewish emancipation: between *bildung* and respectability: from the enlightenment to the second world war," *The Jewish response to German culture: from the enlightenment to the second world war*, ed. Jehuda Reinharz and Walter Schatzberg (Hanover, NH: University of New England Press, 1985), 3.

[53] *Ibid.*, 15.

conversion.[54] In Humboldt's original conception, the idea of *Bildung* was democratic; its acquisition required no ethnic or national credentials. The works of classical literature, which constituted the core of the *Bildungsprozess*, were "considered a universal heritage." They were available to anyone, regardless of background, who was willing to put in the effort to acquire them. It was widely believed that one *gebildeter Mensch* – one cultured individual – met another *gebildeter Mensch* on equal grounds, not as a German or a Jew, but as a cultivated European.[55]

In addition to whatever extrinsic sociological motive of upward mobility was involved with the Jews' zeal for *Bildung*, another intrinsic factor was at work as well – namely, their own tradition, which placed such a high premium on learning. As Jaffe observes, "although Freud's intellectual tools came from his classical *Gymnasium* education, the impulses and motivations that put those tools in motion came from Freud's Jewish tradition and its inheritance."[56] The Jewish passion for learning that had been bottled up before emancipation in the narrow channels of Talmudic studies was now released "into the urban cauldron," where it could be redirected toward the broader cultural inheritance of the Western tradition.[57]

It was a fortunate and "decisive" fact, as the Jewish historian Gershom Scholem observes, not only that the Jews first encountered "German culture . . . on their road to the West," but also that German *Kultur* "had reached one of its most fruitful turning points" and was at its "zenith."[58] The intersection of the recently emancipated Jewish tradition and the

[54] See Gresser, *Dual allegiance*, 40.

[55] Richard Sterba describes the importance of the ideal of *Bildung* to Freud and the members of his early circle. Indeed, for his followers, Freud's charisma derived in no small degree from his superior *Bildung*: "Sigmund Freud was above all of us; his *Bildung* was of the highest level, as one can easily recognize in his publications and letters." Richard Sterba, *Reminiscences of a Viennese psychoanalyst* (Detroit, MI: Wayne State University Press, 1982), 81.

[56] Quoted in Gresser, *Freud's dual inheritance*, 80.

[57] William M. Johnston, *The Austrian mind: an intellectual and social history 1848-1938* (Berkeley: University of California Press, 1972), 29.

[58] Gershom Scholem, "Jews and Germans," *On Jews and Judaism in crisis: selected essays*, ed. Werner J. Dannhauser (New York: Schocken Books, 1976), 78. However, In contrast to the Germans, the Viennese, as Zohn points out, did not have a "Gershom Scholem to point out forcefully that the German-Jewish symbiosis there had no future." Zohn, "Fin-de-siècle Vienna," 145.

German *Aufklärung* produced a cultural efflorescence in literature, music, philosophy, politics, journalism, and science that lasted for approximately a century – roughly from the Revolution of 1848 through the Holocaust. Indeed, one can argue that the achievements during those hundred years rivaled the riches created by the "golden era" of Jewish culture on the Iberian Peninsula and have not been equaled since.[59]

It must also be noted, however, that the embrace of *Bildung* was not universal. Stefan Zweig, for one, found his school

a place where we had to assimilate the "science of the not-worth-knowing" in exactly measured portions – scholastic or scholastically manufactured material which we felt could have no relation to reality or to our personal interests. It was dull, pointless learning that the old pedagogy forced upon us, not for the sake of life, but for the sake of learning. And the only truly joyful moment of happiness for which I have to thank my school was the day that I was able to shut the door behind me forever.[60]

That an emphasis on classical studies can breed a sterile scholasticism is not a revelation. All too often, a classical education has been associated with cultural conservatism and externally prescribed norms of respectability, as it was with certain self-satisfied members of the *Bildungsbürgertum*, who could wax eloquent over Beethoven's kitschy Ninth Symphony but often found the exuberant freedom of his other late works too disturbing to tolerate.

By the same token, as Robert argues, because of classical education's fixation on the past – "nothing was true or beautiful or worthy of interest that had not been certified in the remote or recent past by authorities thought to be infallible" – it "left its adepts almost totally blind to modern cultural developments."[61] This is painfully obvious in Freud's conservative taste in art and literature and his complete inability to appreciate the European avant-garde, which was rooted in part in his inability to appreciate the more archaic realms of psychic experience. Non-representational painting and non-narrative novels were beyond his grasp. Freud's

[59] See Amos Elon, *The pity of it all: a portrait of the German-Jewish epoch, 1743–1933* (New York: Picador, 2003).

[60] Zweig, *The world of yesterday*, 29.

[61] Robert, *From Oedipus to Moses*, 53.

orientation in Vienna was, as Gay observes, toward the medical school, and he showed little interest in the experiments that were taking place all around him in the music, literature, architecture, design, painting, and philosophy of Vienna *moderne*.[62] Classicism's apolitical "overestimation of culture," moreover, which became "the mainstay of an ideology," left many of the students of the *Gymnasium* tragically ill-prepared for the real social, historical, and political events that were about to intrude violently into their lives.[63] Yet, despite these obvious defects, Freud, who had "turned the world upside down by revealing the impure source of all the creations of the spirit," remained enthralled by the classicist perspective. He never found "fault," Robert observes, "with his old teachers for the wrongness of their teaching methods or for their blind faith in a supposedly eternal, and for that very reason false, ideal."[64]

One reason why Freud did not turn his critical gaze on classicist culture, Robert argues, was his disinclination to tamper with the status of the *gebildeter Mensch*, which seemed to offer "the Jew an honorable way out of his spiritual ghetto." Furthermore, as she also suggests, because he had to "acquire" classical culture through "discipline and work," it would always remain foreign – "a second culture" for him, "despite the importance . . . it would assume" in his life. No matter how thoroughly he had mastered it, she maintains, Freud did not feel entitled to criticize humanist *Kultur*. Paradoxically, he was able to criticize Jewish culture because it was more *heimlich* – more familiar. When it came to Judaism, "his judgment was surer, more deeply motivated, and paradoxically, freer to express itself." Criticism can imply love, or at least a deep emotional engagement with the subject one is criticizing, and Freud's critique of Judaism certainly indicates its profound significance for him. For Freud, Robert argues, his acquired classical culture "remained on the reassuring surface of things as they should be, without any real relationship to the internal drama from which Freud derived his passionate thinking." Judaism, on the other hand, partook "of the ambivalence of all true life,

[62] Peter Gay, *Freud, Jews, and other Germans* (Oxford: Oxford University Press, 1984), 34.

[63] Robert, *From Oedipus to Moses*, 53.

[64] *Ibid.*, 56.

caught up in the endless circle of remorse and guilt, [and] was the driving force behind his strange destiny."[65]

Freud's appropriation of Hammerschlag's teaching – his embrace of the universalistic side of the Jewish tradition and minimization of its particularistic dimension – determined the way he navigated his dual allegiance and the tension between *Judentum* and *Bildung* throughout his career. Freud's reading of the Jewish tradition, as we will see in Chapter 12, was selective. He identified exclusively with Judaism's Mosaic strand and ignored a multitude of other trends. Furthermore, he construed the great prophet and lawgiver – who was himself the heir to Akhenaten's Egyptian Enlightenment – as an Enlightener *avant la lettre* who promoted monotheism, opposed "myth, magic and sorcery," was committed to "truth, order and justice," and, most importantly, valorized *Geistigkeit*, spirituality or intellectuality, over *Sinnlichkeit*, sensuality.[66] Freud, in short, assimilated Moses the prophet to Moses Mendelsohn, the nineteenth-century Jewish philosopher and champion of the *Aufklärung*. Moreover, like Moses, the modern-day *Aufklärer* (e.g., Kant, Marx, and Freud himself) were engaged in the critique of idolatry.[67] Just as Moses attacked the false gods in the name of the one true God, Freud and the *Aufklärer* criticized cultural illusions – especially the illusions of religion – in the name of science.

Love and Science: Gisela and Choosing a Profession

According to a psychoanalytic legend that Freud himself initiated, he discovered his calling to be a scientist in a sudden conversion-like experience when he was sixteen. During his *Gymnasium* years, under the influence of his fellow student Heinrich Braun – who became a famous Social Democratic politician and editor – Freud seemed to be moving toward a career in law and politics. But at the time he was about to complete his *Matura*, the final exam at *Gymnasium*, he claims to have had an epiphany: "It was hearing Goethe's beautiful essay [probably written by one of Goethe's students – JW], 'On Nature,' read aloud at a popular lecture by

[65] *Ibid.*, 59.

[66] *Ibid.*, 21.

[67] See Yerushalmi, *Freud's Moses*, 22.

Professor Carl Brühl just before I left school that decided me to become a medical student" in order "to take up the study of natural science."[68]

The Viennese-born psychoanalyst Kurt Eissler, however, challenges Freud's mythologizing account of his decision to study medicine, citing two letters Freud wrote to his childhood friend Emil Fluss, whom Sigmund had known since the days when both their families lived in Freiberg.[69] In these two letters, written several months before the recitation of the Goethe essay at the time of his *Matura*, Freud informs his friend of his decision to pursue a career in science. Eissler stresses the hesitating manner in which Freud slowly reveals the decision. And the coquettishness is not inappropriate, considering that the decision is closely bound up with the vicissitudes of his love life.[70]

In the context of discussing Fluss's relationship with his girlfriend, Freud writes in the first letter (17 March 1873) that he "can report what is perhaps the most important bit of news in [his] miserable life." This leads Fluss to believe that his pal is about to announce that he has fallen in love. But Emil's expectations are frustrated when Freud goes on to write that since "the matter is as yet undecided," he will not say "more about it at this stage," but will provide "more detailed news some other time." Then, in the second letter (1 May 1873), Freud corrects Fluss's misapprehension, explaining that the decision does not refer to a "relationship" but to a "plan" that "is as certain and as fixed as any human plan can be." Lifting "the veil of secrecy," he announces he has decided to be a natural scientist who will "gain insight into the age-old dossiers of Nature, perhaps even eavesdrop on her eternal processes."[71] Freud's "romance", it turns out, had "involved mother nature."[72]

---

[68] Freud, "An autobiographical study," 8. See also Sigmund Freud, *The question of lay analysis* (1926), *SE*, 20, 8; and Freud, *The interpretation of dreams*, 8. Because Vienna's famed medical school contained some of Europe's finest scientists, the idea of studying serious science there was not unusual.

[69] K.R. Eissler, "Creativity and adolescence: the effect of trauma in Freud's adolescence," *The Psychoanalytic Study of the Child* 33 (1978), 466–467.

[70] See William J. McGrath, *Freud's discovery of psychoanalysis: the politics of hysteria* (Ithaca, NY: Cornell University Press, 1986), 91.

[71] See Freud, "Some early unpublished letters of Freud," 423–424.

[72] McGrath, *Freud's discovery of psychoanalysis*, 89.

The romantic notion of nature expressed in the essay reflects the *Naturphilosophie* (Philosophy of Nature) that had been prevalent in Germany in the early part of the nineteenth century. It thus *derives from the very tradition that the positivist sciences – which Freud was about to embrace – were trying to quash.* Nature, as depicted in the essay, is not the disenchanted, reified extended quantifiable substance of the positivists but is rather, as Jones notes, "a beautiful and bountiful mother who allows her favorite children the privilege of exploring her secrets."[73] Gay observes that "the fragment that changed Freud's mind was an emotional and exclamatory hymn celebrating an eroticized Nature as an embracing, almost smothering, ever-renewed mother."[74] There is therefore a striking disconnect between the emotional longings expressed in the essay and the type of science in which Freud was about to immerse himself. While he was drawn to nature as a generous maternal object whose mysteries and riches he wanted to explore, the objectifying methods he chose to be trained in only fit nature insofar as it was conceived by Positivism – as a lifeless mechanism.

In order to understand the dynamics that animated Freud's choice of a career, it is necessary to examine another event that occurred roughly six months before these letters to Fluss, an event that in fact involved Emile's family. The Flusses had remained in Freiberg and maintained their friendship with the Freuds after their move to Vienna. When Freud was sixteen, he returned to Freiberg for the first time to spend his summer holidays with the Flusses. Freiberg was not only the scene of his original infantile loves, losses, and injuries. With its "really beautiful woods" that Freud had explored almost before he "had learnt to walk," the town also represented life before "the original catastrophe" – a pre-traumatic Eden to which he longed to return.[75] Such a visit could be expected to stir up turbulent emotions, and indeed it did.

While Freud defensively protected his ineffectual father by attributing Jacob's business failure in Freiberg to an economic crisis that had affected the entire region, Ignaz Fluss, who was in the same field as Jacob, flourished. He even opened several new factories in the region. One can assume that the difference between the Flusses' financial success and flourishing

---

[73] Jones, *Freud* I, 29.

[74] Gay, *Freud: a life for our time*, 24.

[75] Freud, "Screen memories," 312–313.

household and the Freuds' impoverished situation in Vienna did not escape the young man. This surely served to intensify his disappointment and resentment toward Jacob and led him to fantasize about what his fate might have been if he had been born to Ignaz instead – fantasies that were likely accompanied by considerable guilt.

During his stay in Freiberg, Freud experienced his first adolescent infatuation – what he referred to as "calf love," to downplay its seriousness – when he fell in love with the Flusses' thirteen-year-old daughter Gisela.[76] The shy young Sigmund kept his feelings to himself, writing to his other boyhood chum Eduard Silberstein that while "the affection appeared like a beautiful spring day," the "nonsensical Hamlet in me, my diffidence, stood in the way" of approaching the object of his desires.[77] Indeed, Freud kept his feelings so well hidden that when Gisela left Freiberg to return to school several days later, she had no idea of the passions stirring in her guest. The day before her departure, Freud notified Silberstein that he hoped Gisela's "absence" would give him back his "sense of security."[78]

But just the opposite proved to be the case. The "separation," which psychoanalysis suggests would have rekindled the losses of Amalie and the *Kinderfrau*, in fact brought Freud's "longings" for maternal love and succor "to a really high pitch." To console himself after Gisela's departure, he "passed many hours in solitary walks through the lovely woods" from his childhood "that [he] had found once more" – thus returning home to nature and the mother's body.[79] Freud, who stated that "every finding is a refinding," explained in a letter to his wife Martha thirteen years after the event that the object of his adolescent passion had not been Gisela per se. His love for the girl, as Jones describes it, was based "on some internal image of his own plainly derived from far deeper sources associated with his early home."[80] The fact that Freud's famous screen memory *"relating to"* his early childhood in Freiberg emerged at the time of the Gisela episode supports this interpretation.[81]

[76] *Ibid.*, 313.

[77] Freud, *Letters to Silberstein*, 16.

[78] *Ibid.*, 12.

[79] Freud, "Screen memories," 313.

[80] Jones, *Freud* I, 33.

[81] Freud, "Screen memories," 322.

The lush, idyllic quality of the alpine setting of Freud's screen memory is striking: "I see a rectangular, rather steeply sloping piece of meadow-land, green and thickly grown; in the green there are a great number of yellow flowers – evidently dandelions." This is an uncontaminated state of pristine nature prior to the Fall. Then, almost as if from a fairytale, "at the top of the meadow there is a cottage and in front of the cottage door two women are standing chatting busily, a peasant-woman with a handkerchief on her head and a children's nurse."[82] These two women in front of such a mythic domicile are reminiscent of Freud's two mothers, Amalie and the *Kinderfrau*. As usual, however, Freud "interprets upwards" and focuses on the phallic-sexual aspects of the memory, construing his own and his nephew John's mischievous behavior and the dandelions as their wish to deflower their female playmate. But the oral-maternal element of the memory is so redolent that we can almost taste the delicious black bread that the peasant woman feeds the children.

The emergence of these caring maternal images and feelings – this generous orality – was probably stimulated not only by the general atmosphere of material well-being that permeated the Fluss household, but more specifically by Freud's experience of Frau Fluss, whom he describes as the exact antithesis of his Amalie. Indeed, Freud suspects that his infatuation for Gisela may, in part, be tied up with the figure of her mother: "It would seem that I have transferred my esteem for the mother to friendship for the daughter . . . I am full of admiration for this woman whom none of her children can fully match."[83]

Freud explains his attraction to Eleonore Fluss by enumerating a catalogue of this woman's remarkable virtues, which in turn reveals much about his own system of values. Despite the limited circumstances of her upbringing, Frau Fluss, unlike Freud's own Galician mother, had "acquired an education of which a nineteen-year-old salon-bred young thing need not be ashamed." Freud was impressed that she had read the classics and "what she has not read she is conversant with." In addition to her impressive range of knowledge, Freud considered her an enlightened woman who possessed "sound judgment" in "guiding the household into the modern mainstream." Lest Silberstein get the wrong impression,

---

[82] *Ibid.*, 311.

[83] Freud, *Letters to Silberstein*, 17.

Freud informs him that Eleonore Fluss is no "frustrated bluestocking" without practical capabilities. In addition to overseeing an efficient household and raising seven children, "she plays a large part in running the [family] business."[84] In fact, Freud was "convinced that all the factory workers obey her as well as they do" her husband.

But along with these urbane observations, the extraordinarily precocious and highly inhibited young Freud also offers a glimpse into the deeper and more affect-laden sources of his infatuation with Gisela's mother. She provided him with maternal succor and tenderness at a time when he was experiencing acute physical and emotional distress. Here's what happened.

After Gisela's departure, Freud developed a terrible toothache. Having raved the whole day and exhausted every possible remedy, he resorted to "some pure alcohol to deaden the pain" and predictably "vomited violently but lost the toothache."[85] The illness had an unintended salutary effect. Frau Fluss cared for Freud "as for her own child." Freud gave Silberstein the following report:

The doctor was called, I slept upstairs that night, and got up the next morning well and without toothache. [Frau Fluss] asked me how I had slept. Badly I replied, I didn't sleep a wink. Or so it had seemed to me. Smiling, she said, I came to see you twice during the night, and you never noticed.[86]

Furthermore, this flawless woman knew how to draw the boy out: "She fully appreciates that I need encouragement before I speak or bestir myself, and she never fails to give it . . . As she directs so I speak and come out of my shell." Given his experience with his own mother, Freud cannot believe his good fortune and exclaims that he "cannot possibly deserve all the kindness and goodness she has been showing."[87] Frau Fluss, in short, was "certainly a contrast to Amalie." In her, Freud had "found the ideal mother, one who was not volatile and given to anger, one who could share his deepest intellectual and literary interests." And it was probably no

---

[84] *Ibid.*, 17.

[85] *Ibid.*, 18.

[86] *Ibid.*, 18.

[87] *Ibid.*, 18.

accident that this occurred "in Freiberg, the very place where he suffered his original losses."[88]

As a result of his encounter with Gisela and Eleonore Fluss, Freud found himself in an emotional "whirlwind" when he returned to Vienna. He felt overwhelmed and helpless in the face of the passions unleashed by his return to his childhood home.[89] One can assume that these emotions were double-edged. The experience of sexual excitement and maternal care most likely awakened memories of the "good" Amalie and the "good" *Kinderfrau* prior to Julius' death, the arrest of the nursemaid, and Freud's departure from his childhood home. A psychoanalyst would assume, however, that along with Gisela's departure, this reawakening would have also reminded Freud of the loss and anger of his early years. He was once again confronted with his belief that women were powerful and frightening creatures. Not only are they the source of the greatest excitement and a most exquisite gratification, but they can also leave one abandoned, frustrated, and desperate.

At this point in his life, however, Freud was not prepared to confront this belief and avoided it through an almost total "repudiation of femininity." For the next ten years, he withdrew into the life of a monastic scientist, and for the most part avoided close female contact, until he was hit by another whirlwind when he spotted Martha Bernays chatting with his sisters in the family's living room.

"The Gisela experience," as Eissler observes, "evidently precipitated intensive and extensive defenses."[90] One of the defenses that Freud resorted to is fairly crude and typical of adolescent boys, namely, denial and reversal of affect through derision. When Freud reports to Emile about the episode, he writes "there was more irony, yes mockery, than seriousness in the whole flirtation."[91] The nickname that Freud and his two schoolboy buddies assigned to Gisela in their correspondence, "Ichthyosaura," was not as innocent as it appears. Its ostensible derivation came from understanding that as "a female member of the Fluss family," Gisela, like the Ichthyosaura, was a "weibliches Flusswesen" (female river

[88] Breger, *Freud*, 37.

[89] Freud, "Some early unpublished letters," 419.

[90] Eissler, "Creativity and adolescence," 474.

[91] Freud, "Some unpublished early letters," 421.

creature).[92] As Eissler points out, Ichthyosaura is the ancestor of the 400 eels Freud would later dissect in Trieste in a painstaking attempt to locate their elusive testes and is "an aquatic reptile of dinosaurian proportions." It would seem therefore that the name had a less benign meaning in the unconsciousness of these adolescent boys. Eissler interprets the nickname to imply that "women are dangerous monsters, a fear-arousing species whose phallic nature seems obvious."[93] Eissler also notes that the letters Freud wrote to Silberstein while he was in Trieste suggest that, during his late adolescence and early adulthood, he experienced women as alien creatures with which he was afraid to interact. Freud writes to his friend that on his first day in the Adriatic port he was "filled with apprehension" when the city appeared to be "inhabited by none but Italian goddesses."[94] The young anatomist, however, was "not allowed to dissect human beings," as he was permitted to do with the other species he was getting to know, that is, the eels, and therefore had no way to get on more intimate terms with these Mediterranean beauties: "Physiologically, all that I know about them," he tells Silberstein, "is that they like to go for walks."[95]

Freud's mockery of Gisela reached its heights in his reaction to her wedding. The fact that it occurred three years after the visit to Freiberg shows how little Freud had been able to rid himself of her influence. The wounded lover expressed his scorn by "turning the object of his love . . . into an object of contempt"[96] in a pseudo-Homeric epithalamium to the bride and groom that he attached to a letter to Silberstein. When he had first met her, Freud had praised Gisela as a "Thracian" beauty, with an "aquiline nose," "long back hair," and "firm lips."[97] But now he derides Ichthyosaura, "who irresistibly conquered men's hearts and left them homesick," for her plumpness: "Spherical she appeared and gloriously rounded." Freud levels another charge at Gisela, which in his book was even more devastating: In addition to becoming a conventional bourgeois

---

[92] McGrath, *Freud's discovery of psychoanalysis*, 89.

[93] Eissler, "Creativity and adolescence," 471.

[94] Freud, *Letters to Silberstein*, p. 153. For some inexplicable reason, these goddesses all seem to have disappeared by the following day.

[95] *Ibid.*, 144.

[96] Boehlich, "Introduction," in *ibid.*, xx.

[97] *Ibid.*, 18.

Hausfrau knitting stockings and preparing herring, Gisela, Freud was appalled to learn, was going to keep a kosher home. He believed this decision was to please her Jewish husband "who in Germany studies the art of acquiring money." And he draws on the rich tradition of Yiddish insults delivered in the form of blessings to deliver his final punch to the two philistines:

> May blessings abound in their house; the roast never rest on the stove.
> May their ironclad safe be filled to the brim at all times,
> As so may they both live out their allotted span . . .
> Blessed with splendid livers and lungs,
> Never plagued by *spirit*.[98]

An earlier draft of the epithalamium, however, reveals the "wretched, abominable despair" that lay behind this clever literary production: "Woe is me, woe; I rage, pain sears my breast." Indeed, the desperation reached suicidal proportions when Freud asked to be sent "forthwith" potassium cyanide, hemlock, a sharp razor, and a revolver because he cannot bear to think of "the faithful bride in another man's arms."[99]

At this point, Freud's adolescent defenses of devaluation and reversal of affect have broken down, and what he attempts to replace them with illuminates the emotional underpinnings of his choice to become a physician/scientist. His declared solution, as recorded in a postscript to the epithalamium, is to close an era in his life – the era to which the Gisela affair belonged. Using the geological language that befits the discussion of a prehistoric creature like the Ichthyosaura, he declares: "Herewith the Formation comes to end." This closure will be achieved by renouncing magic, fantasy, and unconscious forces deriving from the archaic past and becoming vigilantly and resolutely oriented to reality. In an apparent reference to Prospero in Shakespeare's *Tempest*, Freud announces that he will bury his "magic wand" in order to institute a "new age" devoid of "secrets" – that is, the unconscious – an age "which has no need of poetry and fantasy." Furthermore, Freud's choice of women in the future shall not be based on influences emanating from the archaic psyche of "the gruesome primeval past," a time "when wild Creatures" like

---

[98] *Ibid.*, 137–138 (emphasis in the original).
[99] *Ibid.*, 188.

Ichthyosaura "could consume the oxygen of the atmosphere unpunished by man." Instead, Freud declares, his choices will be entirely grounded in the "present," consisting solely in "the children of man" instead of the descendants of dangerous creatures from the prehistoric world of unconscious memory.[100] Freud, Eissler argues, wanted to turn his back on the archaic "world of the id," with its power to "throw the self into perplexity and helplessness." From that point on, he continues, "only the *hic et nunc* of the external world were acceptable matters for attention."[101] And what is more concerned with "the *hic et nunc* of the external world" – with hard material reality – than the empirical sciences, with their reality-oriented methodology that seeks to bracket out subjective experience? Freud would, in short, use Reason-Science to contain his explosive passions.

[100] *Ibid.*, 138.

[101] Eissler, "Creativity and adolescence," 476. See also Matthew Von Unwerth, *Freud's requiem: mourning, memory, and the invisible history of a summer walk* (New York: Riverhead Books, 2005), 72–73.

3

Science as Vocation

WHEN FREUD, AGED SEVENTEEN, entered university in 1873, he did not hurry single-mindedly to pursue his declared course of study in science and medicine. Instead, he was drawn to philosophy and allowed himself a relatively free rein to explore the field. Yet within two years, upon returning from a trip to England in 1875, he abruptly declared a change of heart and mind. He vehemently denounced philosophy and presented himself as a hard-nosed man of science. Insofar as we consider the psychological aspects of Freud's about-face, it was part of his effort to contain the cauldron of emotions and desires broiling within him by submitting to the rigor of scientific thinking and the disciplined structure of scientific research.

And this strategy worked well. Under the aegis of a Positivist apprenticeship, it allowed him to maintain a relatively even-keeled if constricted existence during his university years. This accommodation, however, unraveled when he was forced to leave the university, fell in love, and travelled to Paris to study with the world-famed Jean-Martin Charcot, causing his repressed unconscious-instinctual life to rise the surface. The emotional and intellectual upheavals that Freud experienced in Paris were not entirely negative. On the contrary, they were essential to Freud's passage to his own métier: from a research scientist to a clinician pursuing philosophical questions via the study of psychopathology – in short, to becoming a philosophical physician. This chapter explores how Freud found his way to this new identity, which became the base on which psychoanalysis would be built.

Freud as Anti-philosopher

In addition to his idealization of the relationship with his mother and his denial of the extent of his Jewish education, Freud helped promulgate a third myth about himself – namely, that he was an anti-philosopher.[1] (How these myths are connected is unclear, but one suspects they are.) This became the "official position" within the world of psychoanalysis, although it is a distortion at best, as an examination of his intellectual career starting in his university years makes clear.

As noted, Freud on arrival at the University of Vienna was in no great rush to commence his presumed course of studies. The Medical School had no prescribed curriculum, and this freed the medical students to pursue their interests as they wished. The intellectually omnivorous Freud took full advantage of this liberty, following his interests into a number of different byways before he settled down to pursue his medical degree. In light of the supposed allegiance to science that he had declared at the time of his *Matura*, he made a curious announcement in a letter to Silberstein at the beginning of his university career: "Of the next, my first university year, I can give you the news that I shall devote all of it to purely humanistic studies, which have nothing to do with my later field." Considering his subsequent belief in the inseparability of clinical and "applied" psychoanalysis, his additional observation that those humanistic studies "will not be unprofitable for all that" is worth noting. Freud is clear that he does not want to be pinned to a particular curriculum but rather wishes to give his curiosity the maximum freedom to roam: "If anyone asks me, or you on my behalf, what I intend to be, refrain from giving a definite answer, and simply say: a scientist, a professor, or something like that."[2]

---

[1] Fritz Wittels, Freud's first and, as he puts it, "unsolicited biographer," introduced the term "anti-philosopher" (Freud, *The interpretation of dreams*, 14 n. 1). See Fritz Wittels, *Sigmund Freud: his personality, his teaching and his school* (London: George Allen & Unwin, 1924), chapter 2. For attempts to disprove the claim that he was an "anti-philosopher" see: Patricia Herzog, "The myth of Freud as anti-philosopher," *Freud: appraisals and reappraisals: contributions to Freud Studies*, vol. II, ed. Paul E. Stepansky (Hillsdale, NJ: Analytic Press, 1988), 163–189; Richard Asky and Joseph Farquhar, *Apprehending the inaccessible: Freudian psychoanalysis and existential phenomenology* (Evanston, IL: Northwestern University Press, 2006); and Alfred I. Tauber, *Freud, the reluctant philosopher* (Princeton, NJ: Princeton University Press, 2010).

[2] Freud, *Letters to Silberstein*, 24.

One place where Freud's intellectual perigrinations led him was to the classroom of the philosopher Franz Brentano, whom he described as a "remarkable man . . . and a damned clever fellow, a genius in fact, who is, in many respects, an ideal human being."[3] In line with the Freudian establishment's policy initiated by its founder himself, Jones too minimizes Freud's attraction to the airy field of philosophy in order to safeguard his *bona fides* as a tough-minded scientist. But this clearly distorts the facts. Where Jones casually states that Freud "took a glance at philosophy in Brentano's reading seminar" merely "once a week," in reality the student attended five of Brentano's courses from 1874 to 1876 – courses he was under no obligation to take.[4] Furthermore, accompanied by his friend Joseph Paneth, a devoted young Nietzschean, Freud visited the philosopher at his home on several occasions to challenge the professor's views. This certainly constitutes more than a "glance." It is worth adding that Brentano had written his *Habilitationsschrift*, the second thesis that a German academic must write to qualify for a professorship, on Aristotle's psychology.

Freud found Brentano's relation to religion vexing and struggled to come to terms with it. The philosopher was not only a believer but an ordained priest who had resigned from the priesthood because he could not accept the doctrine of papal infallibility. This is clearly something Freud would have admired. However, that such a brilliant and honest thinker who "abhors all glib phrases, all emotionality, and all intolerance of other views" – something Freud would also have admired – could be a believer confounded the young student. Freud, who had come to think of himself as a "godless medical man and an empiricist," was especially troubled by the fact that he found it so difficult to refute Brentano's

---

[3] *Ibid.*, 95.

[4] Jones, *Freud* I, 37. Jones was following Bernfeld, who wrote, "it is impossible that Freud at that time [his university years] or at any time for that matter was a follower of Brentano. One even wonders whether he would have cared to understand the finer points of his arguments" in this matter. See Siegfried Bernfeld, "Freud's scientific beginnings," *American Imago* 6 (1949), 190. James Barclay and James McGrath have done much to correct this misconception. See James R. Barclay, "Franz Brentano and Sigmund Freud," *Journal of Existentialism* 5 (1964), 1–36. See also McGrath, *The discovery of psychoanalysis*, 111–127. Peter Gay too is much more even-handed than Jones in his treatment of Freud's relation to philosophy. See Gay, *Freud: a life for our time*, 28.

arguments for the existence of God despite his concerted efforts to dismantle them.[5] This difficulty led Freud to recognize that he had found a worthy adversary in Brentano – a "sharp dialectician" against whom one can "hone one's wits."[6]

Making the man even more attractive in Freud's eyes was that he had stood up to the Church over the question of papal infallibility. Because of this opposition, he was such a controversial figure when he arrived in Vienna in 1874 that the emperor and cardinal both opposed his appointment to the university. "Freud's Hannibal phantasy," as McGrath observes, "would certainly have predisposed him to admire a man who had first defied the pope in resigning from the priesthood and had then defied both emperor and cardinal in accepting the Vienna position."[7]

Although Brentano was a German who resided in the German cultural sphere, his thinking was more akin to the British Empiricists than to the German Idealists. According to Freud, Kant "comes off very badly" in Brentano's eyes. While Brentano thought Kant's skepticism should be respected, he found him "an intolerable pedant" who does "not at all deserve the great reputation he enjoys." And, as Freud reports to Silberstein, Brentano held Kant's "successors Schelling, Fichte and Hegel" in even lower regard and viewed them all as "swindlers." On the other hand, Brentano's high opinion of Hume, whom he considered "the most precise thinker and most perfect writer of all philosophers," undoubtedly contributed to Freud's later Anglophilia.[8]

One thing Freud found congenial in Brentano's philosophy was that it managed *to be simultaneously scientific and dualistic*. This philosophical stance, McGrath argues, provided a significant part of the theoretical framework "within which Freud was later to make his own revolutionary discoveries."[9] The former priest emphatically rejected all forms of *a priorism*, "declared himself unreservedly a follower of the empiricist school," and insisted that philosophy and psychology – which, for him, were integrally

---

[5] Freud, *Letters to Silberstein*, 104.

[6] *Ibid.*, 107.

[7] McGrath, *Freud's discovery of psychoanalysis*, 11.

[8] Freud, *Letters to Silberstein*, 103-104.

[9] McGrath, *Freud's discovery of psychoanalysis*, 114.

connected – should be placed on firmly empirical scientific foundations.[10] It is important to note that a scientific and empirical approach did not entail a "one-sided" materialism for Brentano. In other words, *it was possible to be scientific and empirical without being baldly physicalistic and reductionist.*

Freud inherited Brentano's dualistic approach, which held that the scientific study of the psyche required the combination of two perspectives: On the one hand, the third-person external perspective of the natural scientist that approaches the psyche as an object, such as one finds in the study of the physiological basis of neurophysiology, animal and human behavior, child development, mental illness, and so-called primitive "mentalities." On the other hand, Brentano used a first-person perspective that examines internal representations from within the psyche, for example, through what Brentano called inner perception.[11] Brentano considered both approaches essential and privileged neither over the other. That the two dimensions are of equal status "methodologically" is, for the philosopher, the result of an important empirical fact: namely, that soma and psyche are in constant interaction with one another. In a recommendation that assumed obvious significance for Freud, Brentano suggests that it is especially fruitful to study borderline phenomena – hysteria is a prime example – in order to grasp both sides of their interaction. For the interaction between psyche and soma is particularly perspicuous in such cases.

Contra Jones, therefore, Brentano in fact had such a powerful impact on Freud that the sought to take a double doctorate in philosophy and zoology. He pursued this plan with the department of philosophy, but it never came to fruition.[12]

But Brentano was not the only measure of Freud's infatuation with philosophy. During his first year at the university, he also discovered the work of the young Hegelian philosopher Ludwig Feuerbach, whom he praises just as lavishly as he had Brentano. He wrote to Silberstein, "I revere and admire [Feuerbach] above all other philosophers."[13] Arguably, Feuerbach

---

[10] Freud, *Letters to Silberstein*, p. 102. Throughout his career Freud always held that fundamental theoretical concepts – "first principles" – ultimately rested on empirical evidence and could be altered in light of new experience. See especially Sigmund Freud, "Instincts and their vicissitudes," (1915), *SE* 14: 17.

[11] See *ibid.*, 13–14.

[12] See Freud, *Letters to Silberstein*, 95.

[13] *Ibid.*, 70.

had an even more profound effect on Freud than had Brentano, especially where his cultural writings are concerned.

Feuerbach, whose primary interest was the critique of religion, is historically remembered more for his influence on others rather than for his own contribution – especially for his influence on that other "master of suspicion," Karl Marx, as well as on Freud.[14] However substantially they may have differed on other issues, Marx and Freud both agreed on one point famously made by the latter: "The critique of religion is the premise of all critique."[15] In other words, they both believed that religion comprised the paradigmatic case of the illusory belief systems humanity has been forced to employ because of its immaturity – what Marx refers to as its "prehistory." Marx and Freud both argued that with the advent of modernity and the creation of modern science, it was both possible and desirable for humanity to overcome these illusions and achieve its maturity. The critique of religion was thus the premise of all critique in that it unmasked the paradigmatic form of false belief that had characterized the existence of the human species up until the present. It thereby promoted humankind's ascent to maturity – the central goal of the Enlightenment.

Feuerbach's theory of the genesis of religion centers on the concept of *projection*[16]. He argues that the privation and suffering of *Unlust* (unpleasure) – to use a Freudian term – experienced by embodied, sentient human beings, leads them to *project* their wishes for a fulfillment into the heavens. As Marx observed, the sensuous earthly family explains the Holy Family and not the other way around. In a statement that must have loomed large for the man who would write *The future of an illusion*, Feuerbach explains that he does not treat theology "as a mystical pragmatology as in Christian mythology, nor as ontology, as in speculative philosophy of religion, but rather as psychic pathology."[17] Religion, in other

[14] Ricoeur, *Freud and philosophy*, 32.

[15] Karl Marx, "Contribution to the critique of Hegel's philosophy of right," *Marx and Engels on Religion* (New York: Schocken Books, 1967), 41 (translation altered). The German term *Kritik*, which the text renders as "criticism," is more accurately translated as "critique." The alternative translation has the advantage of situating Marx's position in the German philosophical tradition that it grew out of.

[16] See Van Austin Harvey, *Feuerbach and the interpretation of religion* (Cambridge: Cambridge University Press, 1995), chapters 6 and 7.

[17] Quoted in McGrath, *Freud's discovery of psychoanalysis*, 106.

words, is the symptom that results from the projection into the heavens of wishes that arise in response to concrete human privation and suffering. And the prescribed treatment of the symptom follows from its etiology: One must try to remediate the suffering that causes the pathological projection in the first place. The logic of Marx's and Freud's positions is strictly parallel; only the content differs. For Marx, concrete suffering was to be ameliorated on the socio–economic plane of existence; for Freud, it was to be remediated in the psychosexual dimension of human life.[18]

As McGrath points out, Freud's encounter with the Philippson Bible, which approached religion through anthropology and the human sciences rather than through theology, would have made him especially receptive to Feuerbach's thinking.[19] But as he did with most of the philosophers who influenced him, the mature Freud fails to acknowledge how important Feuerbach was for the development of his thinking. Yet the young Hegelian's ideas are simply too integral to the main thrust of Freud's theory to be ignored. Freud may not acknowledge it, but his most important book on religion, *The future of an illusion*, is Feuerbachian to its core. Its major thesis – namely, that religion is the projected wish to be protected from the consequences of human helplessness – comes straight out of Feuerbach's *The essence of Christianity*.

In addition to these facts from his student years, statements Freud made in his later life also provide evidence of how deeply he was drawn to philosophy. In 1896, he informed Fliess that "as a young man [he] knew no longing other than for philosophical knowledge." And in the "Postscript" to his "Autobiographical study," published in1930, he tells us that

After making a lifelong *détour* through natural sciences, medicine and psychotherapy, [I] returned to the cultural problems which had fascinated me long before when I was a youth scarcely old enough for thinking.[20]

---

[18] Jürgen Habermas sought to unite these two masters of suspicion by subsuming both Marx's idea of ideology and Freud's concept of neurosis under a theory of false consciousness that could be understood in terms of "systematically distorted communication." Jürgen Habermas, *Knowledge and human interests*, trans. Jeremy J. Shapiro (Boston, MA: Beacon Press, 1969).

[19] McGrath, *Freud's discovery of psychoanalysis*, 105.

[20] Freud, "Postscript," "An autobiographical study," 72.

Similarly, in the "Postscript" to *The question of lay analysis*, written during the same period, he states:

After forty-one years of medical activity, my self-knowledge tells me that I have never really been a doctor in the proper sense. I became a doctor through being compelled to deviate from my original purpose; and the triumph of my life lies in having, after a long and roundabout journey, found my way back to my earliest path. I have no knowledge of having had any craving in my early childhood to help suffering humanity . . . In my youth, I felt an overpowering need to understand something of the riddles of the world in which we live and perhaps even to contribute something to their solution.[21]

If one takes logic, epistemology, and metaphysics as the essential subject matter of philosophy, then Freud, who displayed little interest in these topics, was not a philosopher in this strict academic sense. But the topics he refers to in these passages, which can most accurately be classified as philosophical anthropology, clearly belong to a more generous conception of the discipline.[22] Freud, it can be argued, came home not only to Judaism, but also to philosophy.

Furthermore, the magnitude of Freud's speculative *daemon* revealed itself, as we will see in Chapter 10, when he unshackled the restraints he had placed on it in the name of science and began to philosophize with reckless abandon after the First World War. At that point, he not only threw off the strictures of empirical science but also ignored the basic canons of modern philosophical discourse. That is, he blithely disregarded the supposedly inviolable beachhead that had been established by the reflective epistemological turn in modern philosophy – which excluded the sort of direct apprehension of the object claimed by the pre-modern ontological tradition – and began to make grandiose pronouncements

---

[21] Freud, "Postscript," *The question of lay analysis*, 253.

[22] Castoriadis parses this point somewhat differently: "This means that psychoanalysis is philosophical; but, despite what one might be tempted to say, it is not philosophy." Rather, he goes on, through its discovery of psychic reality and creation of a *techné* and a *praxis* for pursuing the goals that had traditionally been articulated by ethical theory, psychoanalysis contributes "to a renewal of the philosophical problematic." Cornelius Castoriadis, *Crossroads in the labyrinth*, trans. Kate Soper and Martin H. Ryle (Cambridge MA: The MIT Press, 1984), 34.

about the first causes or fundamental constituents of nature, *eros, strife, and thanatos*, with the naïveté of a pre-Socratic philosopher.

Thus the notion that Freud himself promoted – namely, that he was an "anti-philosopher" – is too simplistic to be taken at face value. Admittedly, his critique of philosophy is apt and penetrating, and his skepticism concerning the field is well taken. Certainly too, his introduction of psychic reality created a chasm in the history of rationality that calls into question the traditional definition of man as an *animal rationale* and sets the post-Freudian theoretical universe apart from everything that preceded it. But this chasm should be viewed as a provocation challenging philosophy to interrogate its idealist and rationalist prejudices, not as a wholesale condemnation of the field. (Unfortunately, few academic philosophers have taken up the challenge.) Freud's attempt to portray a total split between psychoanalysis and the Queen of the Sciences is, in short, inaccurate and leads to serious distortions.

A more accurate description of the situation is this: While Freud was fascinated by philosophy in his youth and through his first years at the university, at a certain point he abruptly turned against it in a relatively violent way, suppressed the fact that he had been deeply attracted to the field, and doggedly insisted that he was an empirical scientist. Like his idealization of his relationship with Amalie and the minimization of his Jewish schooling, his vehement rejection of philosophy and his assumption of the mantle of an empirical scientist also need to be accounted for. The passion that Freud invested in opposing philosophy suggests that he remained deeply drawn to it at some level and continued to struggle against the temptations it represented for him. As Freud himself taught us, the opposite of love is not hate but indifference. And Freud was anything but indifferent toward philosophy.

After his volte-face and subsequent denunciation of philosophy, discussed later in this chapter, Freud had few good things to say about philosophers – with the two notable exceptions of Spinoza and his beloved Plato. He tended to view the discipline as a domain of illusion, second in perniciousness only to religion. Philosophy, he argued, represents the pathological hypertrophy of the mind's "synthetic function" – its inherent drive to assimilate everything it encounters to itself. Philosophical thinking by its very nature, Freud argued, omnipotently presses for systematization and totalization. In this respect, the philosopher resembles the obsessional or paranoid subject. Because he cannot tolerate any gaps in experience, he tries to impose – that is, project – more order on experience than in fact exists. Freud delighted in Heine's mischievous observation that the philosopher tries to patch up "the gaps in the structure of the universe . . . with his nightcaps and the tatters of his dressing gown."[23] And for Freud, the attempt to forcibly impose the order and connection of our thoughts onto experience is the very definition of magical thinking.

What Freud failed to realize, however, was that his quarrel with philosophy for being in some sense "pathological" and his opposition to its aspirations to be totalizing and systematic were protestations he shared with several of the greatest philosophers of modernity – Nietzsche, Adorno, and the late Wittgenstein, for example – who were thoroughly rigorous but anti-systematic in their philosophical endeavors. One of the sources of Freud's multiply-determined suspicion of excessive systematization – of too much unification – was his discomfort with undifferentiated experience deriving from the earliest symbiotic stages of development – from the *unio maternalis*.[24] And while this suspicion was productive and led to his incisive critique of philosophy's pathological tendencies, his inability to handle the concept of unity also had serious negative consequences for his own theory.

Freud also objected to the fact that, unlike scientists, philosophers are not compelled to formulate their theories through the painstakingly piece-meal work of empirical research. Less encumbered by the constraints of empirical reality, they are free to formulate their theories through speculation – to frictionlessly spin their conceptual wheels without the resistance of the extra-conceptual world.

In addition to these theoretical objections, Freud's rejection of philosophy was also strategic. Considering that his scandalous and disquieting theories grew out of hypnotism – which was always threatened by a hovering specter of fraud, quackery, and charlatanism – he believed that his theories had a better chance of acceptance if they were wrapped in the cloak of tough-minded science.

---

[23] Freud, *New introductory lectures on psycho-analysis*, 161 n. 1. See also Freud, *The interpretation of dreams*, 490.

[24] Freud criticized Jung's theorizing for aiming at too much synthesis. See Ernst Pfeiffer (ed.), *Sigmund Freud and Lou Andreas Salomé letters*, trans. William and Elaine Robson-Scott (New York: W.W. Norton & Co., 1985), 60.

Freud's sudden and relatively violent turn against philosophy and the suppression of his own "daemon of creative speculation," to use Jones's phrase, requires psychoanalytic reflection.[25] Jones's position on this question is in fact relatively ambivalent. On the one hand, when he is operating as a psychoanalytic *apparatchik* trying to market the dubious new field to a skeptical world, he brushes aside the philosophical dimension of Freud's personality and the extent to which Freud had been actively engaged with the field – as we saw in his discussion of Brentano. Jones then works hard to sell Freud as a thoroughly kosher scientist.[26] But on the other hand, when he is not promoting the discipline, Jones presents a more complex and differentiated picture of Freud's relation to his philosophical *daemon* – his "fantastic self," as he refers to it.[27] For example, although he does not go into detail about the nature of the threat, Jones affirms psychoanalyst Fritz Wittels's "shrewd suggestion" that Freud may have turned away from his "bent towards speculative abstractions" because it felt too dangerous and he was "afraid of being mastered by it."

In other words, as Jones correctly suggests, Freud may have been threatened by the very intensity of his *Wissenstrieb*, his drive for knowledge, because it raised the specter of omnipotence, and Freud was afraid of becoming overwhelmed by it. Like drives in general, if *Wissenstrieb* becomes too powerful, it can pose a danger to the ego – by threatening to overwhelm it. The will-to-knowledge can also be a will-to-power. Furthermore, the pursuit of knowledge beyond a permitted limit can also be experienced as prohibitively dangerous for a variety of pre-Oedipal and Oedipal reasons. In fact, Jones reports that Freud confirmed Wittels's hypothesis. He told Jones that, "as a young man" he had read "very little" philosophy – which is not entirely accurate – because he "felt a strong

---

[25] Jones, *Freud* I, 431.

[26] These considerations are in fact responsible for the appearance of the *Standard Edition*. To promote their air of respectability, Jones saw to it that they were published in accordance with the format that was standard for British medical textbooks.

[27] Jones, *Freud* II, 431. For Freud's speculative drive see also Ilse Grubrich-Simitis, "Metapsychology and metabiology, on Sigmund Freud's first draft of 'Overview of the transference neurosis,'" *Freud, A phylogenetic fantasy: Overview of the transference neurosis*, ed. Ilse Grubrich-Simitis, trans. Alex Hoffer and Peter T. Hoffer (Cambridge, MA: Harvard University Press, 1987), 75–108.

attraction towards speculation and ruthlessly checked it."[28] His rejection of his attraction to philosophy was an effort to contain his speculative *daemon. The interplay between Freud's prodigious speculative drive and the various stratagems he employed to manage it throughout his life is one of the central leitmotifs of his biography.*

Regardless of its artificiality and possible theoretical price, Freud's choice to cloak himself in the mantle of a strict scientist proved to be felicitous. "His scientific mirage was a vital and even fertile illusion,"[29] observes Cornelius Castoriadis, the Greek-French philosopher, social theorist, and psychoanalyst. The scientific model provided him with scaffolding on which he could hang his theories and think them through – even to the point where they burst through the confines of that model. Furthermore, his "long detour" through science and medicine also helped him contain and discipline the excesses of his speculative drive, which was a necessary precondition for the discovery of psychoanalysis. For many years, the monastic and highly structured life of a scientific researcher, which was only disrupted by "the tumultuous urge of his love experience," provided him with a means of containing his erotic *daemon*, which was closely tied with his speculative one.[30]

Moreover, Freud could not have created the new discipline without his years of apprenticeship as an empirical researcher, where he internalized not only a scientific *ethos* but a scientific *hexis* (habit) as well: the habit of patiently and meticulously observing and working over data for extended periods of time and constructing theory in a methodical fashion. Without it, he would not have been able to discern the structure underlying the hyper-complex and hyper-ambiguous phenomena of clinical experience. Freud seems to have intuited on some level that, if he did not sufficiently rein in his speculative drive, he would end up as a quack like his wildly speculative friend and colleague Wilhelm Fliess. The fact that he chose to leave "A phylogenetic fantasy" – the twelfth of the "metapsychological papers" he composed during the lull in his practice brought about by the First World War – in the drawer rather than publish it is a testament

---

[28] Jones, Freud I, 29.

[29] Castoriadis, *Crossroads in the labyrinth*, 3.

[30] Ernest Jones, *The life and work of Sigmund Freud*, vol. II: *1901–1919, the years of maturity* (New York: Basic Books, 1955), 431.

to the fact that Freud was aware of the limits of acceptable speculation. He realized what should or should not be submitted to the public for its adjudication.[31]

Jones, however, could have gone further in exploring the dangers that philosophical speculation posed for Freud. While philosophy has historically been a male enterprise, if not an almost exclusively male fraternity, there is also a maternal stratum to the philosophical enterprise that has been largely obscured by its overwhelmingly phallocentric character.[32] When that maternal stratum is recognized – the stratum belonging to Ichthyosaura that Freud had renounced when he swore off poetry and fantasy and embraced science as his *Beruf*, his vocation or calling – it raises a question: Were Freud's difficulties with his undeniably strong attraction to philosophy somehow connected with his almost phobic discomfort with early experiences and the figure of the archaic mother? In an unusually creative and highly speculative paper, the American psychoanalyst Harry Slochower answers this question in the affirmative.[33] His thesis is that because perennial philosophy has been pursued as *Ursprungsphilosophie*, the philosophy of origins, that seeks to discover the foundation of all things (for example, philosophy, theology, ontology, or metaphysics), its genetic roots are in part located in the infant's symbiotic-like relation to its mother.

To support this claim, Slochower cites an analysis by Otto Fenichel in which the German psychoanalytic theorist argues that the metaphysical quest for the Absolute – the "All" characterized by limitlessness, timelessness, plenitude, fullness, and presence – derives from memories originating in the earliest undifferentiated stage of development. To use Freud's vocabulary, the "All" derives from the experience of what he called primary narcissism. "The development of the mind," Fenichel argues, "began with the All," and "metaphysical intuition wants to return to its starting point." The "All" that metaphysics seeks to recapture, however, only existed endopsychically and not in external reality. And the

---

[31] See Freud, *A phylogenetic fantasy: Overview of the transference neurosis*.

[32] It is striking that Plato gives the most important arguments in *The Symposium*, a homoerotic drinking party, in an exchange with Diotima – a woman.

[33] Harry Slochower, "Philosophical principles in Freudian theory: ontology and the quest for *matrem*," *American Imago* 32 (1975), 1–39.

fundamental error of metaphysics, Fenichel contends, is to mistake an endopsychic reality for an external reality.[34]

When considered from a psychological point of view, it is evident that beneath its highly elaborate systems of discursive articulation, metaphysics is also animated by a striving for "nonseparateness and undifferentiation," or "for unity, symbiosis, fusion, merging or identification," in the words of Loewald.[35] A consideration of Aristotle supports this hypothesis: In the *Metaphysics* (see especially Book ∧), one of the founding texts of the onto-theological tradition, the attributes he ascribes to god – *nous theos* – are almost identical to those Freud uses to describe the plenum-like state of "the primal psychical situation."[36] Aristotle's god is not only completely self-sufficient – *autarchic* – but, because he is pure actuality, does not experience deprivation, otherness, lack, or want. As a result, the Aristotelian god does not desire anything outside of himself. All other beings in the cosmos, however, are composed of some mixture of potentiality and actuality, and therefore experience privation and want to one degree or another. Thus, in a language reminiscent of Freud's explanation of our "fascination" with the narcissistic self-sufficiency of beautiful, self-contented, and self-contained women, "cats and large beasts of prey," and "great criminals," Aristotle contends that all beings in the cosmos desire the self-sufficient perfection of god.[37] As the "unmoved mover," Aristotle's *nous theos* functions as a unique beloved or object of desire: While he is self-contained, pure actuality, and devoid of all movement, the erotic attraction his autarchic perfection exerts on the rest of the cosmos is what sets it in motion. To be clear, this is not an attempt to reduce Aristotle's god to primary narcissism. It is only meant to suggest that Aristotle drew on mental images somewhere in his mind that derived from the experience of primary narcissism when he articulated his conception of god.

In light of these considerations, a comment that Freud made to psychologist Werner Achelis in 1927 is of particular significance. He informs Achelis that he found metaphysics, which he argues is a "survival from the

---

[34] Otto Fenichel, "Psychoanalysis and metaphysics," *Collected papers of Otto Fenichel: first series* (New York: W.W. Norton & Co., 1953), 25.

[35] Loewald, "The waning of the Oedipus complex," 402.

[36] Freud, "Instincts and their vicissitudes," 134.

[37] Freud, "On narcissism," 88–89.

period of religious *Weltanschauung*," not merely alien but also contemptuous. "Other defects in my nature," Freud observed, "have certainly distressed me and made me feel humble; with metaphysics it is different – I not only have no talent for it but no respect for it, either." And, although "one cannot say such things aloud," he also tells Achelis that he is well aware, as a secular Jew, of the "extent this way of thinking estranges [him] from German cultural life."[38]

The point is that Freud identified philosophy as such with metaphysics, and *qua* metaphysics he rejected it in its entirety. Despite his experience with Brentano, he showed no interest in exploring the possibility of non-metaphysical modes of philosophy – something Wittgenstein and the Vienna Circle were doing at that time in his own hometown. He had at his disposal the entire tradition of the human sciences, the aim of which was precisely to pursue philosophical questions with non-metaphysical means. Yet he chose not to explicitly align himself with these pursuits, although that was in fact exactly what he was doing. He preferred to polemicize against philosophy instead.

Returning to our admittedly speculative question, we know that Freud was uncomfortable with early undifferentiated experience connected with the imago of the archaic mother and avoided it almost phobically – something he would explicitly admit in the 1930s. Could he have perhaps intuited at some level of consciousness that beneath its extensive differentiation and discursive elaboration, philosophy, understood as a quest for the Absolute, represented the pursuit of a merger, of dedifferentiation and unification, and that the source of his suspicion of philosophy was that intuition? If this were the case, then Freud's complicated and complex hostility to the Queen of the Sciences is connected in a significant way to his difficulties with early undifferentiated experience related to the figure of the archaic mother.

Freud the "Philosophical Physician"

But as we have just noted, it is not necessary to equate philosophy with metaphysics. Approached in a more materialist and empiricist vein, philosophy can in fact work in conjunction with science. Empirical science

---

[38] *The Letters of Sigmund Freud*, ed. Ernst L. Freud, 374–375. I thank Werner Bohleber for calling my attention to this letter.

broadly conceived – that is, conceived as more than bald physicalism – can provide the material for philosophical reflection even as it helps discipline the field's speculative excesses through its empirical restraints and "relentlessly realistic criticism." *This conception in fact fits Freud's theoretical practice.* Furthermore, if, as we have argued, Freud was pursuing philosophical anthropology, he pursued it in a specific mode – namely, as what the French called a *médicin-philosoph*, a philosophical physician. This was a new persona that emerged in conjunction with the Enlightenment's critique of metaphysics and the creation of the human sciences, and it was a persona that fit Freud like a glove.[39]

Throughout Europe, representatives of the Enlightenment had grown impatient with the perennially *aporetic* nature of philosophy, which they believed continually spun its wheels, never answering its own fundamental questions, and failed to achieve progress. They concluded that the rigorist demand for apodictic foundations and totalized systems that had characterized "perennial" philosophy for a millennium and a half was, with a few exceptions, misconceived and should be abandoned.

In conjunction with these criticisms, Enlightenment philosophers in Germany, France, England, and Scotland also argued that the findings of the new sciences, especially the human sciences, could not be ignored in the name of philosophical purism. Their program therefore advocated addressing the traditional problems of philosophy empirically, by replacing the study of the metaphysical topics with the study of "Man." For example, Locke, who was himself a physician, argued that, instead of investigating formal logic, one ought to examine the workings of the empirical mind – that is, investigate empirical psychology. And in general, *an important strand of Enlightenment thinking viewed the human sciences as an alternative medium for pursuing philosophical questions.* In this view, these sciences were simultaneously scientific and philosophical, occupying a theoretical terrain somewhere between "philosophy and

---

[39] See John H. Zammito, "*Médicin-philosoph*: persona for radical enlightenment," *Intellectual History Review* 18 (2008), 427–440, and John H. Zammito, *Kant, Herder, the birth of anthropology* (Chicago: University of Chicago Press, 2002), especially chapter 6. I thank Fred Neuhouser for calling my attention to Zammito's illuminating work. Though Nietzsche had something somewhat different in mind, he also called for a "philosophical physician." See Nietzsche, *The gay science*, 6.

science."[40] They were philosophical in that they rejected scientism – that is, the claim that empirical science exhausts the domain of legitimate knowledge, instead insisting on the necessity of second-level reflection that went beyond the givens of first-level scientific discourse. And they were scientific in that they rejected philosophy's pretensions at self-sufficiency, its over-reliance on reflection, and its relative disregard for empirical experience. They instead took the empirical sciences as the point of departure for legitimate theorizing. And the creators of the human sciences held the figure of the physician in particularly high regard. Diderot believed, for example, that because the physician was on *intimate terms with our creaturely existence*, he possessed a privileged mode of access into the realm of human nature. Many physicians in fact made important contributions to the new sciences. Freud did not explicitly use the term "philosophical physician" to refer to himself, yet he came to understand himself to be just that. He would tell Wilhelm Fliess that "as a young man [he] knew no longing other than for philosophical knowledge," although he did not know how to pursue it. But, via the route of medicine and psychology, he believed he had found the means for attaining his "original goal" of philosophy. He would achieve it, as he later wrote, by replacing "metaphysics" with "metapsychology."[41] Freud began the transformation from an empirical research scientist into a philosophical physician while in Paris, where he went in 1885 to study with Jean-Martin Charcot. As a result of his experience with Charcot, he realized that the realm of psychopathology, the realm of "the sick soul," constituted the empirical object domain in which he could most fruitfully pursue the basically philosophical questions concerning human nature that had absorbed him since his youth. He also concluded that clinical practice, and not laboratory research, provided the best medium for pursuing such questions. "Through abnormality," as Thomas Mann put it, Freud would "succeed in penetrating most deeply into the darkness of human nature," into the sickness caused by the strain of man's "position between nature and spirit, between angel and brute."[42]

[40] Jürgen Habermas, "Between philosophy and science – Marxism as critique," *Theory and Practice*, trans. John Viertel (Boston: Beacon Press, 1973), 195–252.

[41] Masson (ed.), *Letters to Fliess*, 159 and 180, and *The psychopathology of everyday life*, 259.

[42] Thomas Mann, *Freud, Goethe, Wagner* (New York: Alfred A. Knopf, 1937), 11.

What happened to turn the anti-philosopher into the philosophical physician? The likely answer begins in England.

Freud's About-face

In the summer of 1875, Freud traveled to England to visit his half-brothers in Manchester. Philipp and Emanuel had become successful merchants, thriving family men, and proper Englishmen, albeit of the Jewish persuasion. Like the earlier trip to Freiberg, and for similar reasons, the visit with his family had an enormous impact on Freud. As he had with Herr Fluss, Jones explains, Freud wondered whether "his path in life would have been much easier . . . had he been Emanuel's son."[43] When he returned to Vienna, his Anglophilia was soaring. He wrote to Silberstein:

As for England itself, I . . . can say straight out that I would sooner live there than here, rain, fog, drunkenness, and conservatism notwithstanding. Many peculiarities of the English character that other Continentals might find intolerable agree well with my own makeup.[44]

Freud found the civic-mindedness, practicality, industriousness, and sense of justice of the British quite congenial. According to Schorske, in contrast to Vienna's detested courtiers, aesthetes, priests, and *Schlamperei*, Freud saw the English as "builders, stern and rational, of the liberal ego which, for [him], made England the classic land of ethical rectitude, manly self-control, and the rule of law."[45] In other words, Freud saw in the British the values associated with *Bürgersministerium*.

---

[43] Jones, *Freud* I, 24.

[44] Freud, *Letters to Silberstein*, 127.

[45] Schorske, "Freud: the psychoarcheology of civilizations," The *Cambridge companion to Freud*, ed. Jerome Neu (Cambridge: Cambridge University Press, 1991), 10–13. Seven years later, in a letter to Martha, written at a time of extreme frustration concerning his career in Vienna, Freud declares, "I am aching for independence so as to follow my own wishes. The thought of England surges up before me, with its sober industriousness, its generous devotion to the public weal, the stubbornness and sensitive feeling for justice of its inhabitants, the running fire of general interest that can strike sparks in the newspapers; all the ineffaceable impressions of my journey seven

Freud's decisive rejection of philosophy in favor of natural science occurred when he returned from Manchester, and the decision was clearly linked with his Anglophilia.[46] Freud momentarily displaced the titans of German culture – Goethe, Schiller, and Heine – from his pantheon and substituted for them the English scientists "Tyndall, Huxley, Lyell, Darwin, Thomson, Lockyer, et al.," whom he described as his "real teachers."[47]

Once back in Vienna, Freud was ready to descend from the heights of late-adolescent philosophical rumination to the more concrete reality of the material world. In his fourth semester at the university, he "switched from the less demanding 'zoology for medical students' to fifteen hours of zoology proper."[48] His professor was Carl Claus, one of the most prominent advocates of Darwin's cause in Germany, who had been brought to the University of Vienna to "modernize the department of zoology and bring it up to the level of other divisions at the university."[49] Claus offered Freud a coveted summer placement at the marine biology station he had established in Trieste, where he was assigned the infamous task of dissecting eels. Challenging the long-standing scientific tradition that the species were hermaphrodites, a Polish zoologist had reported a year earlier that he had discovered gonads in these aquatic creatures. Although Freud sliced up more than 400 eels in search of gonads, his findings were inconclusive. While it is natural to chuckle at the idea of "the future discoverer of the castration complex" cutting up buckets of eels in the attempt to discover their elusive testes, there is one point that should not be overlooked:[50] The unfulfilling exercise gave Freud the experience of approaching sexuality not "through the lens of social convention, but through scientific analysis

---

years ago, one that had a decisive influence on my whole life, have been awakened in their full vividness." Quoted in Jones, *Freud* I, 178–179.

[46] In the letter just cited, he wrote to Silberstein that he was "more suspicious than ever of philosophy." Freud, *Letters to Silberstein*, 128.

[47] *Ibid.*, 128, and quoted in Jones, *Freud* I, 178–179.

[48] Lucille B. Ritvo, *Darwin's influence on Freud: a tale of two scientists* (New Haven, CT: Yale University Press, 1990), 114. For a detailed discussion of Claus see *ibid.*, chapter 10.

[49] Gay, *Freud: a life for our time*, 31.

[50] Jones, *Freud* I, 42.

and evolutionary doctrine" – an experience that was crucial in the formation of the first psychoanalyst.[51]

Furthermore, Freud's scientific work also had a philosophical dimension. Although Darwin's name rarely appears in Freud's work, his influence on him, as the historian of science Frank Sulloway observes, was
so massive and pervasive that it was simply a given.[52] Darwin's theory
of evolution resulted in the constitution of a revolutionary new worldview, a naturalistic worldview in which human beings were to be understood immanently as thoroughly embedded in the natural world. After
Darwin's great discovery, there was much work to be done in a variety
of fields in order to complete the details of this new worldview. Freud's
pre-analytic scientific work, such as his investigation of the spinal cord
of the Petromyzon in the laboratory of physician and physiologist Ernst
Brücke, as well as psychoanalysis itself, can be seen as efforts to elaborate
and complete Darwinism.

It was to Brücke's laboratory that Freud moved when he grew dissatis-
fied with Claus, and it was there, in Brücke's Physiological Institute, that
he "found rest and full satisfaction" and "spent the happiest hours of"
his "student years."[53] On the surface, Freud's dissatisfaction with Claus is
difficult to explain. On paper, given the professor's credentials, he should
have been an ideal mentor for Freud; indeed, his work was not that different from Brücke's. The decisive factor seems to have been personal, and
Eissler suggests that it had to do with Freud's father hunger. Claus lacked
most of the qualities that Freud, given his experience with Jacob, required
in a mentor, while Brücke possessed them in abundance. First, whereas
Claus was only twenty years older than Freud, approximately the age of
his older half-brothers, Brücke was forty years his senior and roughly the
same age as Jacob. Furthermore, also like Jacob, Claus seems to have been
something of an ineffectual sad sack, with thwarted professional ambitions and unhappy personal relations that were filled with multiple losses.

Someone with Freud's filial history was likely to take Brücke, who led a
relatively blessed life, as an ego–ideal. The Prussian settled on his vocation

[51] George Makari, *Revolution in mind: the creation of psychoanalysis* (New York:
HarperCollins, 2008), 111.

[52] See Frank Sulloway, *Freud, biologist of the mind: beyond the psychoanalytic legend*
(New York: Basic Book, 1979), 238–239.

[53] Freud, "An autobiographical study," 9, and *The interpretation of dreams*, 206.

early, and successfully pursued it in a straightforward and uncomplicated way. He seems to have been fortunate in love as well; he sustained a long and successful marriage to an early sweetheart. One should note, however, that Brücke was not narrow and rigid in his interests. The son of an artist, he was a man of wide culture who possessed some artistic talent himself. He had attended a humanist *Gymnasium*, and he was fluent in French, English, and Italian. Even after he began medical school, he continued to pursue humanistic studies by attending classes in philosophy, logic, German Classics, and Greek at the university – much like Freud. Needless to say, Freud most likely found Brücke's *Bildung* impressive.

Not all attributes of Brücke's personality, however, were appealing to his students. In contrast to the more liberal and easy-going Claus, the Prussian Brücke was stern. He demanded that everything was to be *pünktlich* – precisely on time. Freud, who lived some distance from the Physiological Institute and often arrived late, recalls an incident when its Director confronted him with his lack of punctuality. Freud does not remember his mentor's words as much as his eyes. It was the gaze of the angry patriarch staring down at the disobedient son, much as Freud would later describe Moses staring down at the insubordinate Israelites when he descended from Sinai:

What overwhelmed me were the terrible blue eyes with which he looked at me and by which I was reduced to nothing . . . No one who can remember the great man's eyes, which retained their striking beauty even in his old age, and who has ever seen him in anger, will find it difficult to picture the young sinner's emotions.[54]

But rather than finding Brücke's strictness odious, Freud – who later wrote about the dangers of overly lenient fathers – seems to have welcomed it.[55] Indeed, one must wonder how Freud could have stated that he found "rest and satisfaction" as well as "happiness" pursuing his "neurohistological work . . . with an almost martinetlike superego figure such as Brücke" in the inhospitable environment of the Physiological Institute, which had "no gas and no water" and was "miserably housed

---

[54] See Freud, *The interpretation of dreams*, 422. Freud's colleagues often thought that he tried to emulate Brücke's gaze.

[55] See Sigmund Freud, *Civilization and its discontents* (1930), *SE* 21: 130 n. 2.

in the second story and basement of a dark and smelly old gun factory."[56] As we have seen, Freud had resolved to renounce all the violent feelings that were unleashed by his experience with Gisela and Frau Fluss – to renounce poetry and fantasy in favor of the realism of science. And for seven years, Brücke's highly disciplined laboratory provided him with an excellent external structure for containing those threatening emotions.

To carry out his repressive program, Freud literally narrowed his field of vision, spending hours staring into the small aperture of a microscope. It seems that nothing could be further "removed from" the approach to "nature which Goethe had presented in his essay, and which allegedly cast a spell of fascination upon Freud."[57] This severely circumscribed activity, however, was not only repressive; it also had an adaptive side. While this activity is "strictly bound to a frozen, unmoving picture" and may strike one as "static" and "boring," it also served the purpose, as Eissler observes, of imposing "maximal constraint on fantasy and the power of imagination" while also sharpening Freud's powers of objective observation. Furthermore, Brücke taught his student that microscopy did not have to be limited to mere description. Just as Freud would later develop an active form of listening as a result of his experience with Charcot, Brücke advocated an active mode of seeing: an attempt to perceive the genetic history frozen in the preparation under observation. "The dead image" could be "converted into something dynamic."[58] For example, from the observation of scattered cells under a microscope, Freud was able to reconstruct the evolutionary history of the spinal ganglion of the Petromyzon. As Eissler observes,

The strong repressive forces at work in this period of Freud's career did not constrain fantasy and imagination entirely. Certain limited freedoms were granted, but these did not include the freedom of the artistic mind when it converts daydreams into artistic products that abide by loose rules of aesthetics, but rather that of the scientist to interpret visual structures in conformity with the cold rules of reason and rationality that provided sufficient protection against derivatives of repressed drives.[59]

[56] Bernfeld, "Freud's scientific beginnings," 170, and Eissler, "Creativity and adolescence," 485.

[57] Eissler, "Creativity and adolescence," 486.

[58] *Ibid.*, 485.

[59] *Ibid.*, 20 n. 49.

Although experimentalism had become the dominant tendency in late nineteenth-century European science, Freud did not slavishly adopt the scientific methods of his day and, with his choice of the microscope, decided to remain an observationalist. Jones suggests that this decision may have partly resulted from the fact that Freud was temperamentally ill disposed toward experimental research. In his work in Brücke's Institute and later in the laboratories of neuropathologist Theodor Meynert, Freud had ample opportunity to undertake experimental projects in physiology, but in both situations chose histology – the microscopic investigation of anatomy – over experimentation. "Freud," as Jones puts it, "preferred the eye over the hand . . . passively seeing over actively doing," and had "an attraction to one, an aversion to the other."[60] Jones traced this aversion to an aspect of Freud's character: In whatever field he was engaged, Freud found intrusion into the material violent and distasteful. One of the reasons that he rejected hypnosis and replaced it with psychoanalysis was, as we will see in the next chapter, because he concluded that the earlier discipline, with its use of suggestion, was too "coarse" and violated the subject's autonomy. The philosopher Paul Ricoeur argues that Freud rejected the notion that knowledge is power in the strict Baconian sense. To be sure, he employed technique, but, as Ricoeur maintains, it was not a "technique of domination" but a "technique of emancipation."[61]

At the same time that Freud was relying on structure and discipline to contain the cauldron of emotions within him, a major paradigm shift was taking place in German philosophy and science: *Naturphilosophie*, the Philosophy of Nature, and its scientific offshoot, Vitalism, were giving way in the second half of the nineteenth century to Positivism. And Brücke, along with his contemporaries Emil du Bois-Reymond and Hermann Helmholtz, all of whom had studied with physiologist Johannes Müller, were major contributors to this transition. The *Naturphilosophen* maintained that nature was not a lifeless, mechanistic manifold but was animated by a life force – an *élan vital*. The Vitalists set out to demonstrate

[60] Jones, *Freud* I, 53. It is not entirely accurate to describe Freud's mode of seeing as "passive," for it involved a good deal of activity, but of a particular sort. It might better be described as "active receptivity."

[61] See Paul Ricoeur, "Technique and non-technique in interpreting", *The conflict of interpretations: essays and hermeneutics*, trans. Willis Domingo (Evanston, IL: Northwestern University Press, 1974), 177–195.

how that force worked in the world. Müller was a Vitalist, and a major thrust of his research sought to demonstrate how these life forces operated in the human body, especially in the brain. Ironically, as it turned out, it was only a relatively short step, as the historian of science and medicine George Makari observes, from Müller's Vitalistic position to the Positivists' mechanistic worldview. Helmholtz took that step when his scrutiny of his teacher's notion "of an irreducible life force" led to "questions about the nature of energy" in general. After the notion of vital force was stripped of its metaphysical trappings and transfigured into disenchanted physical energy, it became possible, so it was thought, to explain all natural phenomena by tracking "different transformations" of that energy.[62]

More specifically, there appeared to be nothing unique that characterized life – nothing in particular that set it apart from the rest of inanimate nature. Living organisms, it was argued, functioned according to the same laws as inorganic phenomena and could be exhaustively accounted for in terms of "dynamics, mechanics, and Newtonian laws."[63] With this principle as their point of departure, Müller's students, Young Turks like Helmholtz, Brücke, and du Bois-Reymond, having overthrown their mentor, advanced their own program. The Biophysicists, as they were known, set out to examine various biological phenomena in order to demonstrate that they could be exhaustively accounted for in mechanistic terms without recourse to any metaphysical or Vitalist principles. This, in principle, included psychological phenomena. In a letter to a friend, du Bois-Reymond enunciated what became known as the Positivist credo: that all living phenomena must be accounted for in terms of "the common physical–chemical forces" that are "active in the organism." Furthermore, if any new phenomena were discovered, they must be explained in terms of the same physio–chemical forces, or forces "possessing equal dignity."[64]

As a student of Brücke, Freud subscribed to this credo. Indeed, his various models of the "psychic apparatus" represent different attempts to

[62] Makari, *Revolution in mind*, 59.

[63] *Ibid.*, 59.

[64] Quoted in Siegfried Bernfeld, "Freud's earliest theories and the school of Helmholtz," *Psychoanalytic Quarterly* 13 (1944), 348.

explain the clinical phenomena that confronted him in accordance with
these principles. Whether or not he succeeded in living up to this credo,
depends, as we shall see, on how one interprets the phrase "possessing
equal dignity."[65]

Another important and related debate in nineteenth-century German
philosophy and science pitted the *Naturwissenschaften*, the natural sciences, against the *Geisteswissenschaften*, the human sciences. The proponents of *Geisteswissenschaften* argued that the human realm was
characterized by its own unique phenomena – for example, subjectivity,
meaning, and language – and that this uniqueness justified the existence
of an independent domain of human sciences (for example, sociology,
psychology, anthropology) of a status and with a methodology that differed
in essential ways from that of the natural sciences.[66] The Biophysicists
disagreed: *Wissenschaft* was *Naturwissenschaft – Punkt!* According to
them, subjectivity, meaning, and language were every bit as much occult
qualities as vital forces, entelechies, and final causes. Because they were
epiphenomena that could be explained away, the human sciences could –
and should – be reduced to the natural sciences.[67]

Positivism has recently come under attack as a reactionary movement –
a narrow and dogmatic form of scientism that cannot do justice to the
complexities of the human realm and is complicit in the technological
domination of nature. In conjunction with that broadside attack, it has

[65] See Sulloway, *Freud, biologist of the mind*, 65–66. Sulloway claims that the idea of a
"Helmholtz School" as presented by Jones and Bernfeld is not only inaccurate, but in
fact a myth. Nevertheless, even if the influence of the biophysicist and the Positivists
had waned by the time Freud entered Brücke's institutes, as Sulloway argues, the two
decades he spent as a research scientist were essential for his formation as a scientist.

[66] The proponents of the *Geisteswissenschaften* must be distinguished from the
Enlightenment thinkers who advanced the idea of a philosophical physician. Where
the latter believed that the human sciences should integrate empirical research with
philosophical reflection, the former held that the human sciences ought to remain
distinct *in toto* from the methodology of the natural sciences.

[67] See Makari, *Revolution in mind*, 59. This program was later taken up by the Logical
Positivists in their call for a "unified science," in which all putatively secondary
sciences like biology, sociology, and psychology would be reduced to the fundamental
sciences of chemistry and physics. See Rudolph Carnap, Otto Neurath, and Charles F.
W. Morris (eds.), *Foundations of the unity of science: toward an international encyclopedia of unified science*, vol. II (Chicago: University of Chicago Press, 1971).

become common to dismiss Freud as a Positivist. But it is important to
note that the Positivism of Freud's time was a progressive movement. It
was militantly anti-clerical and sought to consign "to the rubbish heap of
superstition all pantheism, all nature mysticism, all talk of occult divine
forces manifesting themselves in nature."[68] No wonder a progressively
oriented young man like Freud was attracted to it. In the long run, he was
not able to force all of his thinking into the Positivists' mechanistic world
picture. But as Ricoeur points out, Freud never disavowed the Positivists'
"fundamental convictions," and "like all his Vienna and Berlin teachers,
he continued to see in science the sole discipline of knowledge, the single
rule of intellectual honesty, a world view that excludes all others, especially that of the old religion."[69] While he insisted that he was a scientist, what *Wissenschaft* meant for Freud is difficult to determine – in part,
because he says so little about it. But it is clear that, for him, it did not
primarily represent a particular methodology or physicalist ontology. It is
also clear that it encompassed a demanding *ethos*. Beyond that, however,
it requires a considerable exertion of hermeneutical effort to construct
the full meaning that this normative idea had for Freud. We will return to
this question in Chapter 12.

The Great Charcot

Freud received a modest travel grant from his medical faculty to spend
four months, from October 1885 to February 1886, studying with Jean-
Martin Charcot in Paris. "When the twenty-nine-year-old doctor stepped
off the train" in the French capital, Makari observes, he was "ambitious
but poor." Though he had "tried his hand at" many things, he "still
had nothing to secure his future."[70] Freud's experience in Paris, however, proved to be a critical passage in his development that substantially
altered its trajectory.

---

[68] Gay, *Freud: a life for our time*, 34. See also Makari, *Revolution in mind*, 136.
[69] Ricoeur, *Freud and philosophy*, 72.
[70] Makari, *Revolution in mind*, 1.

Freud's tenure was at the Salpêtrière, the historic hospital complex that constituted a vast "museum of living" pathology.[71] An important motive for traveling abroad was to acquire further training in the treatment of "nervous disorders" – something that was hard to obtain in the world of Viennese psychiatry, which, unlike the French Clinical School, was strictly physiological in its orientation. But Freud on his arrival in Paris remained very much the research scientist: a neuroanatomist planning to dissect the brains of dead children, something Salpêtrière could supply in great abundance.

The impact of the charismatic Charcot, however, changed all that. Freud quickly lost interest in his "own silly things" and became fascinated by the Master's field of interest – hysteria – and thereby neurosis in general.[72] Charcot taught Freud that instead of dismissing neuroses as the mere dross of existence, one should treat them with the utmost respect because they could unlock important secrets of human nature. "Enter" the lowly realm of psychopathology, Charcot seemed to beckon, "for here too are gods."[73] By the time Freud returned to Vienna, he had made the transition from neurophysiology to psychopathology. He was no longer primarily a research scientist but had become, despite his antipathy toward medicine, a clinician. In neuroses – in "the sick soul" – Freud found the domain that would allow him to make the great discoveries concerning human nature he had been vainly pursuing elsewhere. In short, he had become a philosophical physician.

In addition to his transference to *le Maître*, Freud also developed a transference to the city of Paris itself, and it played a crucial role in the emotional and intellectual transformation he underwent there.[74] In contrast to the level-headed practicality that he admired in London, Paris was famous for its *fleurs du mal*, which included the hysterics of Salpêtrière. It was here that Freud opened himself to the world of the morbid and the pathological in a way he had formerly been reluctant

---

[71] Cited by Jan Goldstein "The hysteria diagnosis and the politics of anticlericalism in late nineteenth-century France," *Journal of Modern History* 54 (1982), 216.

[72] *The letters of Sigmund Freud*, ed. Ernst L. Freud, 86.

[73] This saying, which Charcot was fond of, is to be found in Aristotle who attributes it to Heraclitus. See Aristotle, *De partibus animalium*, trans. D.M. Balme (Oxford: The Clarendon Press, 1975), vol. I, 5. See also Anzieu, *Freud's self-analysis*, 176.

[74] See Schorske, "Freud: the psychoarcheology of civilizations," 8–24.

to do. In the vividly detailed letters he wrote to Martha, Freud often employs the language of dreams, magic, and fascination to describe his experience in the City of Light. Not only did the Assyrian and Egyptian rooms in the Louvre create "a dreamlike world," but he experienced Paris – "that magically attractive and repulsive city" – as "one long confused dream."[75] The young Viennese Jew compares Paris "to a vast overdressed Sphinx who gobbles up every foreigner unable to solve her riddles," and he informs his fiancée that the city "and all its inhabitants strike [him] as uncanny." Indeed, Parisians seem to be "of a different species from ourselves," a species "possessed of a thousand demons." They are "people given to psychical epidemics, historical mass convulsions, and they haven't changed since Victor Hugo wrote Notre Dame."[76] It was as if all the labile emotionality that Freud had tried to repress since the Gisela affair now confronted him in the boulevards of Paris.

While Vienna is primarily known as an aural town with a renowned musical tradition, Paris is the city of the gaze. Freud was drawn to as well as overly excited by the voyeuristic opportunities the city offered its visitors. He was especially attracted to the spectacle of the theater, but he often had to pay for the pleasure and stimulation of those excursions with migraines. Furthermore, just as the unworldly young scientist had been intimidated by the Italian goddesses in Trieste, he was now scandalized by the brazen exhibitionism of Parisian women and the shameless voyeurism with which the city's citizens crowded "round nudities as much as they do round corpses in the Morgue."[77] Freud tended to see the city itself as a "wanton, female temptress."[78] His remarkable assertion that the Parisian women are not particularly attractive cannot but strike one as defensive. The complexity of Freud's reaction to Paris is evidenced by the fact that the "favorite resort" of this secular, anti-medieval Jew was "the platform of Notre Dame." On his free afternoons, Freud would "clamber

---

[75] Freud himself spent considerable time in the morgue observing autopsies. Ernst L. Freud (ed.), *The letters of Sigmund Freud*, 174, 185, and 188.

[76] *Ibid.*, 187–188. Freud had the opportunity to witness a raucous political contest between the Monarchists and the Republicans, which influenced his view of crowds.

[77] *Ibid.*, 188. See Jeffrey Moussaieff Masson, *The assault on truth: Freud's suppression of the seduction theory* (New York: Farrar, Straus and Giroux, 1984), chapter 2. See also Janet Malcolm, *In the Freud archives* (New York: New York Review of Books Classics, 2002).

[78] Schorske, "The psychoarcheology of civilizations," 13.

about there on the towers of the church between the monsters and the devils" in the bestiary of the unconscious that he had struggled to repress for so long.[79]

With his penchant for military heroes, Freud was bewitched by "the Napoleon of neurosis," as Charcot was popularly known. Yet the content of *le Maître*'s teaching alone, however brilliant it may have been, cannot explain the impact he had on Freud. Charcot's charisma, "the magic that emanated from his looks and from his voice," also played a critical role.[80] Freud's intense transference to Charcot led him to tell Martha, in words that echo his hyperbolic description of Brücke, that "no other human being [had] ever affected [him] in the same way."[81]

By 1870 the Frenchman, who had already had a brilliant career as a neurologist, concluded, as Freud put it, "that the theory of organic nervous illnesses was for the time being complete."[82] Charcot then turned to the study of the neuroses in their own clinical terms. The transition from neurologist to psychopathologist was marked by the fact that the chair created for Charcot was specifically mandated to focus on the *névrose*. This was a shift from the chair of his predecessor, which had been in "mental pathology and diseases of the brain, the *encéphale*."[83] A serendipitous development at Salpêtrière helped to launch his study of hysteria: An organizational reshuffling at the hospital resulted in the creation of a unit that housed both epileptic and hysterical women. Charcot used his clout as the senior physician at Salpêtrière to get himself placed in charge of the unit. This move must have been difficult for many of his colleagues to comprehend, because they would have considered this a particularly unattractive appointment. Charcot's intention was to differentiate between epileptic and hysterical seizures – between those with an organic basis and those that were functional.

Charcot was a representative of the *psychologie nouvelle*, which officially began with Théodule-Armand Ribot in the 1870s but that could trace its lineage back a hundred years to the period before the French

[79] Freud, *The interpretation of dreams*, 469.
[80] Sigmund Freud, "Charcot" (1893), *SE* 3: 18.
[81] Ernst L. Freud (ed.), *The letters of Sigmund Freud*, 185.
[82] Freud, "Charcot," 19.
[83] See Goldstein, "The hysteria diagnosis," 234.

Revolution and the work of Franz Anton Mesmer.[84] As an early explorer in the realm of dynamic psychology, Mesmer understandably but inadequately conceptualized his discovery of magnetism as an actual physical substance. Yet if we overlook this misplaced concreteness, Mesmer's identification of the "healer's" charismatic power, which is similar to the *mana* of the shaman, and his insight into the essential role it plays in the therapeutic process constituted a major contribution to the history of psychodynamic psychotherapy. Mesmer realized, moreover, that it was necessary to enlist this magnetic power in order to establish the correct "rapport" between healer and patient – what Freud would later call the "transference" – and that such rapport provided an essential medium for effective treatment.

In the second half of the nineteenth century, the predominantly physicalist scientists in Vienna and Berlin avoided questions concerning the psyche or the soul, dismissing them as theological or metaphysical. But for whatever cultural reasons, the situation was different in France. With the creation of the *psychologie nouvelle*, as Makari observes, "the marvelous and miraculous made their way from isolated villages and abbeys and carnival halls, from exorcists and charlatans and old mesmerists, into the great halls of French academic science."[85] They transformed France into a hotbed of study for somnambulism, human automatisms, multiple personality, double consciousness, and second selves, as well as demonic possessions, fugue states, faith cures, and waking dreams.

In the 1870s, Ribot, at that time still at the École Normale Supérieure, later professor of experimental psychology at the College de France, adopted a two-pronged strategy to establish psychology as a rigorous natural science. In line with the rise of the human sciences, and against the philosophers, he argued that psychology must renounce metaphysics and forgo the right to pass judgment on transcendental questions. Furthermore, it had to give up its "armchair methods" and "employ the methods of natural science." On the other hand, against August Comte and the Positivists, who argued that an objective science of the psyche was impossible, Ribot contended that such a science could be and should

---

[84] See Makari, *Revolution in mind*, 10ff and Henri F. Ellenberger, *The discovery of the unconscious: the history and evolution of dynamic psychiatry* (New York: Basic Books, 1970).

[85] Makari, *Revolution in mind*, 11.

be obtained. Comte maintained that because psychologists relied on introspection to gain access to the inner world, and because this sort of self-observation is by definition subjective, an objective science of psychology was impossible.[86] Generally speaking, Comte's point, as Makari makes clear, constitutes an objection that every conscientious investigator of the mind must address: If psychology is objective, it is not objective in the same way that physics is objective, because the subject that is conducting the investigation inhabits the same mind that is being investigated. He or she cannot therefore be a neutral observer in the strict sense but must be necessarily implicated in the research.[87] In psychoanalysis, this question arises *a fortiori* in the problem of countertransference.

Ribot countered Comte by challenging his basic assumption that psychology was forced to rely exclusively on introspection. Much like Brentano, he argued that a valid science of the mind must combine introspection with the objective observation of behavior and physiological processes – referred to today as the first-person and the third-person perspectives. Introspective methods were necessary, he argued, to "get at mental phenomena," but introspective accounts could not be accepted at face value. Instead, "those subjective impressions needed to be stabilized and corroborated by a myriad of methods."[88] Furthermore, again like Brentano, Ribot argued that psychopathology had a special role in psychology. As a substitute for laboratory research, which is too difficult to conduct in psychology, he asserted that "the anomalies, the monsters of psychological order," can serve as "experiments prepared by Nature" for us.[89] The *psychologie nouvelle* had brought into its domain all the morbid, uncanny, dream-like, and quasi-occult phenomena – what Auden calls "the fauna of the night" – that theretofore had seemed beyond the reach of legitimate science.[90] Charcot, France's next famous psychologist, plunged in.

---

[86] *Ibid.*, 10–11.

[87] After the twentieth-century revolution in physics, the claim that physics fulfills this criterion of objectivity has itself become problematic.

[88] *Ibid.*, 12.

[89] Quoted in *ibid.*, 3.

[90] W.H. Auden, "In memory of Sigmund Freud," *Freud as we knew him*, ed. Hendrik M. Ruitenbeek (Detroit, MI: Wayne State University Press, 1973), 119.

"As a teacher," Freud tells Martha, "Charcot was positively fascinating." After his lectures, which were little works "of art in construction and composition . . . one could not get the sound of what he had said out of one's ears or the thought of what he had demonstrated out of one's mind."[91] But it was not just the artfulness of his lectures or the theatricality of his case presentations that impressed Freud. Charcot also created for his students a relaxed and egalitarian atmosphere in which they were free to question their teacher. This appealed to Freud's sensibility.[92]

Furthermore, the young German provincial, as Freud viewed himself while in Paris, was also taken with the neurologist's worldliness. Freud compares Charcot to "a worldly priest from whom one expects a ready wit and appreciation of good living."[93] The neurologist's marriage to a wealthy widow helped him pursue his epicurean life. He was famous for the *soirées* that he threw in his mansion on the Boulevard Saint-Germain. "*Le Tout Paris*" – the social, intellectual, and political elites of the city – attended these evenings in his home, which was "a kind of private museum with Renaissance furniture, stained-glass windows, tapestries, paintings, antiques, and rare books."[94] When Charcot invited the young, socially unsophisticated Jew to one such evening, he boasted that "Il y aura du monde" – the whole world will be there.[95] Freud wrote to Martha that he found these *soirées* so intimidating that he had to fortify himself before attending them with a dose of cocaine, which he began using while in Brücke's laboratory, in order to lessen the anxiety and "untie [his] tongue."[96] Indeed, the cocaine itself embodied Freud's conflicted experience in Paris: The white powder contained both the magic that tempted and excited him and the antidote to the anxiety that the magic aroused.

The visuality of Parisian culture was also manifested in Charcot himself. His Tuesday morning case conferences were theatrical spectacles in

---

[91] Freud "Charcot," 17.

[92] This estimation of Charcot's qualities as a teacher was not universally shared by all his students. See, for example, Ellenberger, *The discovery of the unconscious*, 92.

[93] Ernst L. Freud (ed.), *The letters of Sigmund Freud*, 175.

[94] Ellenberger, *The discovery of the unconscious*, 94.

[95] Ernst L. Freud (ed.), *The letters of Sigmund Freud*, 193.

[96] *Ibid.*, 193.

which young, hysterical women displayed all the florid and often eroticized symptomatology of the disease: convulsions, anesthesias, paralyses,
and trance-like states. Freud describes Charcot as a *visuel*. "Day after day,"
he would mull over material that confounded him. Then at one point, "in
his mind's eye, the apparent chaos presented by the continual repetition
of the same symptoms . . . gave way to order," and the "nosological pictures emerged." Like an Aristotelian *phronimos*, a man of practical reason,
Charcot would perceive the universal – the "type" as he called it – in the
particular. Freud was so impressed with Charcot's nosological capacities
that he compared him to Adam in the Garden of Eden, distinguishing
and giving names to all God's creatures.[97] This fundamentally empirical
approach, which bracketed theory in favor of direct observation, contrasted sharply with the highly theoretical Helmoltzian School. Voicing
his opposition to aprioristic theoretical approaches, Charcot remarked
that "theory is good, but it doesn't prevent things from existing." Given
his own suspicion about the excesses of theory, Freud found Charcot's
"way of seeing people and things without preconceived ideas" to his liking.[98]
Indeed, one of the things he took from the Frenchman was his method –
the patient and meticulous immersion in the clinical phenomena that
allowed theoretical generalizations to emerge.[99]

Charcot's greatest contribution, in Freud's opinion, was to establish
the legitimacy of hysteria as a diagnostic category. Hysteria, "the most
enigmatic of all nervous diseases," had been a protean entity that defied
clear conceptualization since its identification by the Greeks.[100] In the
mid-nineteenth century, it was viewed as a diagnostic pseudo-category,
"the wastepaper basket of medicine where one throws otherwise unem-
ployed symptoms," as one contemporary psychiatrist described it.[101]
Furthermore, if hysterics were no longer treated as witches possessed
by the devil, they were still seen as dissemblers and malingerers who
were not worthy of proper medical attention. The contempt in which

[97] Pierre Janet, one of France's other eminent psychologists, was more critical, arguing that Charcot simplified the phenomena in order to force them into neat categories.

[98] Ellenberger, *The discovery of the unconscious*, 753.

[99] For this entire paragraph see Freud, "Charcot," 12–13.

[100] *Ibid.*, 19. See Ilza Veith, *Hysteria: the history of a disease* (Chicago: University of
Chicago Press, 1965).

[101] Cited in Goldstein, "The hysteria diagnosis," 211.

they were held extended to the physicians who were supposedly duped by them. The fact that Charcot was not frightened of being made a fool of and threw "the whole weight of his authority on the side of the genuineness and objectivity of hysterical phenomena" served to establish the legitimacy of hysteria as a diagnostic category.[102] Hysterics were no longer dismissed as malingerers but perceived as legitimate patients entitled to serious medical treatment. Furthermore, Freud believed that Charcot had succeeded in introducing coherence into the whole "motley picture" of hysterical symptomatology.[103] He even claimed to identify the distinct stages which a full-blown hysterical attack passes though – a schema that did not, however, stand the test of time.

Charcot's demonstration that the origins of hysterical symptoms were psychological rather than physiological had a profound impact on Freud's development. The neurologist argued that, while hysterical symptoms mimic disorders that have a purely physiological origin, there are no underlying organic lesions. And by showing that somatic symptoms such as paralysis can be produced and removed in a patient through hypnotic suggestion, Charcot also demonstrated that hysterical symptoms are caused by ideas or representations.[104] Most important, this fact *points to the existence of an unconscious mental life. If hysterical symptoms are caused by representations, and if the person is not aware of those representations, then they must reside in a part of the mind that is outside of consciousness.* It is worth noting that by 1893 Freud argued that this out-of-awareness state is akin to sleep, while consciousness is akin to waking life. And although Charcot himself "did not follow this path" in pursuit of the clinical implications of his discoveries, by showing that hysterical symptoms are psychological and are caused by ideas, he nevertheless opened the door to the exploration of what Freud later called "psychic reality" and to therapeutic intervention into that realm.[105]

[102] Freud, "Charcot," 19.

[103] Sigmund Freud, "Preface and footnotes to the translation of Charcot's *Leçons du mardi de la Salpêtrière*" (1886), *SE* 1: 35.

[104] Freud helped to substantiate this thesis by demonstrating that the physical symptoms of hysteria do not conform to the anatomy of the actual body, but to the body as it is represented in the imagination of the hysteric.

[105] Freud, "Charcot," 20.

Freud was attracted to Charcot for political as well as scientific reasons. More accurately, the convergence of politics and science in his work appealed to the student. Like Freud, Charcot was an "enlightened secularizer," who wanted to use scientific critique as a weapon in the struggle for emancipation from what he understood as the religiously sanctioned superstition of the past.[106] Charcot's generation of psychiatrists, who came into their own in the Third Republic, tended to be Positivist and self-consciously anti-clerical; they distrusted and even detested the "Catholic church as a retrograde force militating against both scientific and social progress."[107] They considered the preceding generation, the psychiatrists of the Second Empire, to be backward-looking Romantics relying on the Church to protect their political position in the state-run system of psychiatric institutions. In this context, the fight to explain hysteria scientifically, rather than to subsume it under witchcraft, became a highly charged political issue. As the eminent historian of science and medicine Jan Goldstein observes, "The hysteria concept was a kind of capsule of the eighteenth-century Voltairean mentality, of the assault upon the clerical world view by the scientific world view."[108] Charcot himself had a keen interest in demonology and owned an extensive library that contained rare books on witchcraft and possession, some of which he republished in the *Bibliothèque diabolique*. And to strengthen his secularizing claims, he undertook a retrospective reexamination of medieval art, which attempted to demonstrate that the contorted and convulsed figures it often depicted were in fact hysterics rather than witches.

Charcot was an emancipator for Freud. By demythologizing hysteria and establishing its scientific legitimacy, he "had repeated on a small scale" the "act of liberation" in which "citizen" Philippe Pinel had "the chains taken off the poor madmen in the Salpêtrière"– an act that was depicted in a painting that hung on the wall of Charcot's lecture room.[109] By displaying André Brouillet's famous painting of Charcot examining a fainting hysteric, first exhibited in 1877, in his consulting room,

---

[106] McGrath, *Freud's discovery of psychoanalysis*, 58.

[107] Goldstein, "The hysteria diagnosis," 222.

[108] *Ibid.*, 237–238.

[109] Freud, "Charcot," 18.

Freud was declaring that he also belonged to this emancipatory tradition. Although Charcot's scientific reputation declined markedly after his death, his legitimization of hysteria as a diagnostic category and his demonstration of its psychological nature constitute an enduring legacy of influence on Freud.[110]

---

[110] It was precisely this emancipatory tradition that Michel Foucault set out to debunk in *The history of madness*, trans. Jonathan Murphy (New York: Routledge, 2007). For a critique of Foucault from a psychoanalytic perspective see Joel Whitebook, "Against interiority: Foucault's struggle with psychoanalysis," *The Cambridge companion to Foucault*, second edition, ed. Gary Gutting (Cambridge: Cambridge University Press, 2005), 312–347.

4

Starting Out in Vienna

Freud's return to Vienna from Paris in 1886 marked the end of his "moratorium," his prolonged delay in choosing a career that "characterizes the beginnings of many a creative worker."[1] The young physician, who did not completely leave the shelter of his parents' home until he was twenty-seven, had finished his university studies and earned his medical degree; dissected buckets of eels in Trieste; worked as a hard-nosed research scientist in Brücke's Physiological Institute for seven years; experimented with cocaine; served time training in general medicine under Meynert, psychiatry under Nothnagel (during which time he also dissected an impressive number of brains), and pediatric neurology under Kassowitz; and made the pilgrimage to Paris to study with the great Charcot. After all that, he found himself back in Vienna with two looming issues confronted him: establishing a practice and marriage. From Jacob, Amalie, and his *Kinderfrau*, Freud had internalized the belief that he was fated to accomplish great things. Yet he had failed to produce the great discovery he believed he was destined to make. In the meantime, the mundane realities of establishing a practice, getting married, setting up a household, and beginning a family – which required him to make a living – were rushing in on him.

The End of "the Lyric Phase"

On an evening four years before his return to Vienna, Freud, aged twenty-six, came home from his day at Vienna's General Hospital and caught sight of Martha Bernays seated in the family living room

---

[1] Erik Erikson, "Freud's 'The origins of psycho-analysis'," *International Journal of Psycho-Analysis* 38 (1955), 3.

surrounded by his sisters. The sight triggered something unprecedented, namely, Freud deviated from his habitual routine. Instead of immediately climbing the stairs to begin his evening's studies, he joined the convivial gathering of young women. That his future bride was "peeling an apple" was perhaps an intimation of Eve in the garden.[2] And Martha did indeed offer many temptations – or invitations – but one is especially pertinent to the themes we are tracing in Freud's life. Her attraction led him to open up, that is, to relax the rigid controls he had imposed on himself for many years, "experiment with new, less orderly and controlled ways of being," and allow "the submerged side of himself [to come to] life." The "deep inner needs [that] had been held in abeyance until this point," Breger observes, now "began to assert themselves."[3] *Eros* was unbound for the fist time since Freud's experience with Gisela and Eleonore Fluss in Freiberg ten years earlier. "It was," as Jones describes it, "a veritable *grande passion*" – anticipating the one he would experience, as we will see, with Wilhelm Fliess from 1887 to 1901. As Jones notes, Freud "was to experience in his own person the full force of the terrible power of love with all its raptures, fears, and torments" – all the passions of which his intense nature was capable."[4]

It is admittedly difficult to evaluate the state of being in love. Long before Freud created psychoanalysis and observed that love is a normal form of psychosis, he had written to his fiancée, "One is crazy when one is in love."[5] Much of Freud's behavior during his engagement with Martha, was moreover, as Grubrich-Simitis notes, "typical of late adolescence: the intemperance, the aspect of 'to heaven rejoicing, cast down unto death,' the sometimes strident contradictions, the restless questing, and the rapid pace of life." Additionally, there were external factors that undoubtedly increased the intensity and volatility of his feelings and behavior. For one thing, from the beginning of his extended engagement to Martha, Freud was continuously under extreme financial pressure. His income as a medical student and as an intern and resident at Vienna's General Hospital was meagre, and, as a Jew, his prospects for advancing his career were limited.

[2] Jones, *Freud* I, 103.

[3] Breger, *Freud*, 55–56.

[4] Jones, *Freud* I, 109.

[5] *Ibid.*, 132.

Consequently, he was constantly forced to borrow from his friends and colleagues – something he loathed, given the way he coveted his independence. To make matters worse, Freud had to expend a portion of his limited income supporting his family, leaving even less with which to marry and begin a family. On top of these financial pressures, Martha's strong-willed, widowed mother moved her family from Vienna to Wandsbek, a suburb of her hometown, Hamburg, so that for three of the four and a quarter years the lovers were engaged, they were largely separated from each other.

But while it is difficult to say when the normal craziness of being in love crosses a line and becomes "abnormal," there were aspects of Freud's behavior – even in light of the pressures on him at the time – that place it beyond the normal craziness that one finds in romantic infatuation. And the nature of these behaviors suggests that they originated in Freud's pre-Oedipal history. It is true that most passionate lovers are demanding, prone to jealousy, and find separation from their partners painful. But Freud's attempt to control Martha omnipotently, his jealousy, the fits of rage, and the extreme difficulty he experienced enduring their separation – as well as his conviction that he was unlovable and its concomitant need for constant reassurance – were of a different order of magnitude. Jones sums the situation up with a pithy formulation: "it seemed as if his goal was fusion rather than union."[6] Freud's inability to tolerate Martha's separateness and his attempt to control her without limit manifested themselves in his demand for total compliance, which is to say, for her "complete identification with himself, his feelings, his opinions."[7] Freud's behavior reminds one of a tyrannical child who attempts to deny his mother's independent existence by constantly and exclusively demanding her attention. Freud, who was not unaware of these tendencies, wrote to Martha that he was "so exclusive where [he] loved" and that he had "a tendency toward tyranny."[8]

A primary arena in which the battle for complete control was waged concerned Martha's mother Emmeline (neé Phillip). Martha's paternal grandfather, Isaac Bernays, had been the highly respected orthodox chief

---

[6] Jones, *Freud* I, 110.

[7] *Ibid.*, 122.

[8] *The letters of Sigmund Freud*, ed. Ernst L. Freud, 22.

rabbi of Hamburg, who had naturally raised his son, Berman Bernays, in an orthodox fashion. And like her husband, Emmeline had also been brought up in an orthodox home, which meant that Freud's fiancée was also raised in a strictly observant household. Martha was indeed close to her mother – in fact, incapable of criticizing her – and was also not ill disposed toward the family's observant environment, but Freud, as we might imagine, would have none of this. He became determined to transform Martha into a "heathen," demanding that she break completely with Emmeline's religious practices, which he considered nothing but superstition. The combination of Emmeline's strict orthodoxy and the fact that she had shanghaied Martha to Hamburg – which may have been partly motivated by the wish to separate her daughter from her impecunious and atheist fiancé – made her Freud's nemesis: "the enemy of our love," as he told Martha.[9] Freud seems to have missed the irony involved in his insistence that Martha renounce her family's orthodox brand of Judaism. For, as Breger observes, "it was precisely this Orthodoxy that prescribed the subservient position of women that Freud demanded of Martha."[10]

After considerable strife, Freud modulated his feelings and achieved a rapprochement with Frau Bernays; indeed, they developed a relatively warm relationship. At the same time, however, he succeeded in his program of transforming Martha, at least outwardly. When the couple finally married, Martha went along with establishing a completely secular household. No Sabbath candles were lit, nor did they even observe Passover – a holiday that is celebrated by many secular Jews, including Jacob. Freud's son Martin tells us: "Our festivals were Christmas, with presents under a candle-lit tree, and Easter, with gaily painted Easter eggs. I had never been in a synagogue, nor to my knowledge had my brothers or sisters."[11]

Although Martha complied with Freud's wishes for the sake of marital harmony, it came at a great inward cost. A cousin reported that Martha told her "how not being allowed to light the Sabbath lights on the first Friday night after her marriage was one of the most upsetting experiences

[9] *Ibid.*, 123.

[10] Breger, *Freud*, 62.

[11] Martin Freud, "Who was Freud?," *The Jews of Austria*, ed. Josef Fraenkel (Portland, OR: Vallentine Mitchell, 1970), 203.

of her life."[12] And when Freud died and she no longer had to sacrifice her wishes to please him, Martha immediately resumed the weekly ritual of lighting the Sabbath candles.

As always, however, the situation with Freud was not straightforward, and there was another side to his attitude toward Judaism – independent of its laws, ceremonies, and rituals – and how it ought to inform one's life. In a letter to Martha, Freud described an encounter he had with an "old Jew" who ran a print shop in Hamburg where he had gone to purchase stationery for her.[13] In the course of their conversation, it came out that the old man had been a student of Martha's grandfather. Freud's curiosity was naturally piqued, and he asked the man to describe his teacher to him. In contrast to his mother-in-law's brand of observant Judaism as he perceived it, Freud was pleased to hear that Martha's grandfather had been a man he could admire. Indeed, the portrait that emerged of Isaac Bernays reminded Freud of Lessing's Nathan the Wise. While orthodox, Bernays was far from being dogmatic but was rather an "extraordinary person" who "taught religion with great imagination and humaneness." His attitude was reflective. If someone "demanded a reason" for an apparent absurdity in the Scriptures, Bernays did not simply fall back on authority but was prepared "to step outside of the law and justify it for the unbeliever from there."[14] While Bernays's intentions remained religious, "religion was no longer treated as a rigid dogma" but had become "an object for reflection for the satisfaction of cultivated artistic taste and of intensified logical efforts." The rabbi promoted religion not dogmatically "because it happened to exist and had been declared holy," but reflectively "because he was pleased by the deeper meaning which he found in it or which he projected into it."[15]

[12] Quoted in Clark, *Freud: the man and the cause*, 89.

[13] Freud's second visit to the old man was on *Tisha B'av*, the holiday commemorating the destruction of Jerusalem by the Romans. Given the fact that psychoanalysis would be exiled from Europe in the thirties and form a Diaspora of its own, what Freud has to say in this context is interesting: "And the historians say that if Jerusalem had not been destroyed, we Jews would have perished like so many races before and after us. According to them, the invisible edifice of Judaism became possible only after the collapse of the visible Temple." Ernst L. Freud (ed.), *The letters of Sigmund Freud*, 19.

[14] *Ibid.*, 20.

[15] *Ibid.*, 21.

Perhaps the most significant fact that the old Jew conveyed to Freud was that Bernays "had been no ascetic." The rabbi believed that Jews were "made for enjoyment" and "despised anyone who lacked the ability to enjoy." Bernays stressed, moreover, that "the Law commands the Jew to appreciate every pleasure, however small, to say grace over every fruit which makes him aware of the beautiful world in which it is grown."[16] For all his erudition, Freud possessed an enormous capacity to enjoy the ordinary pleasures of life and strongly believed that their importance should not be underestimated. Freud concluded the letter by extracting some lessons from Bernays's "life-affirming" teaching for the way he and Martha ought to lead their life:

And as for us, this is what I believe: even if the form wherein the old Jews were happy no longer offers us any shelter, something of the core, of the essence of this meaningful and life-affirming Judaism will not be absent from our home.[17]

As we will see, Freud's assertion of his *bona fides* as a Jew rested on the claim that although he rejected its institutionalized form, he remained loyal to something essential to Judaism.

At several points during the engagement, Freud succumbed to fits of jealous rage. In the early episodes that concerned two men, Max Mayers and Fritz Wahle – who in fact had designs on Martha – Freud's jealousy, though extreme, was not entirely unfounded. However, in a later episode involving Martha's older brother Eli, Freud's suspicions were largely a figment of his imagination. One aspect of the earlier episodes provides some insight into the way Freud thought about himself. Far from being "my golden Sigi" – the son of a beautiful young mother who, having internalized her adoring gaze, became a supremely self-confidence man – Freud was plagued by "perpetual uncertainty" concerning his attractiveness and lovability. "Nature," he told Martha, had not endowed him with the "kind of talent that compels recognition."[18] Both of Freud's early rivals were artists, and Max was a musician to boot. As such, Freud told Martha, they possessed the magic to attract women, which he, as a drab rationalist and plodding man of science, did not:

---

[16] *Ibid.*, 21.

[17] *Ibid.*, 22.

[18] Jones, *Freud* I, 122 and 118.

I think there is a general enmity between artists and those engaged in the details of scientific work. We know that they possess in their art the master key to open with ease all female hearts, whereas we stand helpless at the strange design of the lock and have first to torment ourselves to discover a suitable key.[19]

As we will see, Freud later became convinced that he lacked the physicianly *mana* to elicit his patients' transferences, which are a necessary condition for clinical success. Freud also believed, not without reason, that the difficulties he encountered in his relationship with Martha – for example, his insecurity and lack of savoir-faire with regard to women – were partly the result of his not having begun his experience with the opposite sex at an early, more "appropriate" age. It was his belief, Jones tells us, "that he had never paid attention to girls" and that he paid "heavily for his neglect" in his relationship with Martha. Indeed, Freud wrote to her that his anguish during the courtship was "a punishment for not having fallen in love when I was nineteen instead of twenty-nine."[20]

The severe separation anxiety and fear of losing Martha throughout most of their engagement – "his desperate need for her love and reassurance" – reminds one of toddlers who have not achieved "object constancy," that is, the capacity to maintain a positive image of their mother when she is absent, which image enables them to tolerate the separation.[21] In a pattern that Freud would latter repeat in his relationship with Fliess, Martha's letters became a focal point for his separation anxiety. Not receiving a letter according to the demands of his internal clock could throw Freud into state of utter despair, especially when he was in a particularly vulnerable condition. But when one did arrive at the required time, it could magically elevate his mood and restore his psychic equilibrium. As he told Martha, "Only a letter from [her] made life worth living."[22] It is apt to compare Martha's letters (as well as Fliess's) to narcotic substances – for example, the cocaine or cigars that Freud was dependent on – for they could repair the gaps in the fabric of his self, referred to by Green. Indeed, Freud said as much, when he wrote to

[19] Quoted in *ibid.*, 111.
[20] Quoted in *ibid.*, 99 and 135.
[21] Breger, *Freud*, 59.
[22] Quoted in Jones, *Freud* I, 133.

Martha: "Smoking 25 [cigars] a day, I'm afraid, but when one's darling isn't there, one needs an anaesthetic."[23]

One year before they married, Freud remarked that Martha's absence from Vienna might have been for the best. If they had been in the same town, he suggests, not only would he have found their inability to marry more difficult to tolerate, but he would also have been constantly distracted from his work and would have become more demanding as a result. There was another consequence of the prolonged separation that Freud does not cite. He was an epistolary lover. Anticipating his later friendship with Fliess, the "lyric" phase of Freud's relationship to Martha was largely conducted through the medium of letters. Being in love always involves a large degree of fantasy – of the projection of one's inner world onto the beloved. But owing to his intrapsychic dynamics and the lovers' circumstances, in Freud's case the element of fantasy was significantly larger than the statistical norm. Martha's absence created a voluminous space that Freud could fill with his fantasies, which he did in the more than nine hundred letters, often filling up more than twelve pages, that he wrote to his fiancée. "With the protective distance between them, and with his literary skill at play," Freud, as Breger puts it, "could give free reign to his powerful yearnings for love," as well as his equally powerful imagination.[24]

This is not to say that the correspondence consisted entirely in fantasy. On the contrary, it also contained discussions of the important happenings in the couple's lives and those of their relatives and friends, of serious works of literature – including those of Cervantes, Balzac, and Dickens – and of the developments in Freud's work and career. Because Martha later wanted nothing to do with psychoanalysis, it has often been assumed that she had never been a partner in Freud's thinking. But as the couples' entire *Brautbriefe – Betrothal Letters* – have appeared and readers have had their opportunity to examine Martha's half of the correspondence, it has become clear that this was by no means the case. Indeed, as Grubrich-Simitis has demonstrated, Freud's bride was intensely involved in the discussion of some of Freud's most basic concepts – for example, sexuality, drives, and the unconscious – as they were emerging in their

---

[23] Quoted in Grubrich-Simitis, "Seeds of core psychoanalytic concepts."

[24] Breger, *Freud*, 95.

incipient form.[25] Furthermore, the picture that emerges of Martha in the *Brautbriefe* helps to correct the impression of her that Freud's letters might create, namely, that she was a stereotypically demure and submissive daughter of a respectable bourgeois family. On the contrary, she appears an intelligent, substantial, and independent woman, who in many ways was more than a match for Freud. Similarly, the flowery and overwrote prose that Freud often flourishes in his letters to his beloved – which are typical not only of the nineteenth century, but also of a man who is belatedly experiencing adolescent love – can be a source of embarrassment to the contemporary reader. At the same time, however, Freud's writing also contains vivid descriptions of the kaleidoscopic emotions that an infatuated lover can be subject to, as well as keen insights into the nature of love itself. Jones is not exaggerating when he observes that Freud's letters rank among "the great love literature of the world."[26] It is reasonable to assume, moreover, that Freud drew on memories of his own experience during these turbulent years when he formulated his mature psychoanalytic theories of love.

When Freud returned to Vienna and established his private practice, Breuer, Fleischl, Meynert, and Nothnagel referred patients to him; he also supplemented his income by working at Meynert's laboratory and Kassowitz's Pediatric Institute. Finally, after more than four years of deprivation and longing, Freud's "steadily dwindling savings," along with "his fiancée's modest legacies and dowry, wedding presents in cash from her family, and, above all, generous loans and gifts from wealthy

---

[25] Grubrich-Simitis, "Seeds of core psychoanalytic concepts," 7–12. S. Fischer Verlag is in the process of publishing the entire multi-volume *Brautbriefe*, as a result of the monumental editorial effort of the late Gerhard Fichtner, Ilse Grubrich-Simitis, and Albrecht Hirschmüller. Thus far three of the five volumes have appeared. As we will see in the next chapter, earlier, Anna Freud suppressed the publication of the full Freud/Fliess correspondence, believing it would show her father in an unfavorable light and damage his reputation. It was only after her death that a complete and uncensored edition of the letters was published. And Miss Freud would not permit the *Brautbriefe* to see the light of day for the same reason. It was not until 2011, that is, until twenty-nine years after her death, that the first volume made its appearance. Rather than detracting from our picture of Freud, both the Freud/Fliess letters and the *Brautbriefe* in fact enhance it by showing him in his full humanity.

[26] Jones, *Freud* I, 110.

friends," allowed the couple to scrape together barely enough money to marry.[27]

The wedding, however, presented a new and unexpected difficulty. Not only did Freud dislike formal ceremonies in general, he was especially opposed to Jewish weddings. After attending one when his friend Paneth married Sophie Schwab and gazing "at the scene with a fascinated horror," according to Jones, the young apostate "wrote a letter of sixteen pages describing all the odious detail in a spirit of malign mockery."[28] He was therefore relieved that the couple planned to marry in Wandsbek rather than Vienna. From Freud's point of view, this location was ideal because German law only required a civil service. Thus, he would be spared "the painful dilemma of either changing his 'Confession,' which Freud could never have seriously intended, or going through the elaborate ceremonies of a Jewish wedding, which he abhorred."[29] But there was a hitch. Much to Freud's dismay, Martha discovered that Austria did not recognize civil marriages, which meant that their German marriage would not be valid when they returned to Vienna. Therefore, two services – one civil and the other religious – were required and Freud grudgingly submitted to both. The civil service was conducted on 13 September 1886 in Wandsbek's Town Hall, and the religious service was held the following day. To make it "as easy as possible for" Freud to endure, Martha arranged for the latter to be held "in her mother's home . . . on a week day, when very few friends could attend." Having to cram for the occasion, Freud spent the two nights prior to the wedding "at the house of Uncle Elias Philipp, who was charged with the task of coaching him in the Hebrew *Broche* [prayers] he would have to recite" at the wedding.[30] One can only imagine what was going through the mind of the militant atheist when he stood under the *chuppe* (the traditional marriage canopy) and recited the Hebrew prayers.

To succeed over the long haul, Freud observed, a couple must successfully negotiate the difficult transition from the "lyric" to the "epic" phase

---

[27] Gay, *Freud: a life for our time*, 54.

[28] Jones, *Freud* I, 140. Freud would not have fared well in Great Neck, a Jewish suburb on Long Island where lavish weddings are a regular occurrence. The significance of Freud's intense antipathy toward rituals and ceremonies and its ramifications for his un-Durkheimian understanding of religion will be discussed in Chapter 11.

[29] *Ibid.*, 149.

[30] *Ibid.*, 150.

of their relationship.[31] Sigmund's and Martha's transition to their epic phase began when, after returning from a brief honeymoon, they took up residence in a four-room flat at Maria Theresienstrasse 8. Martha bore the couple's first three children of what would become a rapidly expanding brood in those small quarters: a daughter Mathilde in 1887, a son Martin in 1889, and a second boy, Oliver, known as "Oli," in 1891. It was not long before the couple required more space, and in the same year as Oli's birth the family moved into what would become their legendary residence at Berggasse 19 – where the Freuds would live for forty-five years, and where their paterfamilias would produce most of his work. Over the next several years, Martha gave birth to three more children in quick succession: Ernst in 1892, Sophie in 1893, and Anna in 1895.

It is clear from his letters to Fliess that Freud was a proud father and derived enormous gratification from his children. The pleasure, however, was not unalloyed. Even before their marriage, Freud predicted the corrosive effects that the epic stage would have on the couple's former happiness:

It is a happy time for our love now. I always think that once one is married one no longer – in most cases – lives for each other as one used to. One lives rather with each other for some third thing, and for the husband dangerous rivals soon appear: household and nursery. Then, despite all love and unity, the help each person had found in the other ceases. The husband looks again for friends, frequents an inn, finds general outside interests.[32]

The words proved to be prescient. As the couple began their "epic phase" at Berggasse, the passion that had characterized Martha's and Sigmund's engagement began to diminish. Almost immediately, they established a marital arrangement that the historians of psychoanalysis Lisa Appignanesi and John Forrester describe as "almost a caricature of the by then traditional division of labour."[33] Freud became increasingly absorbed in his work and was under enormous financial pressure. Not only did he have to feed, clothe, and shelter his growing family, but he also contributed support to his parents and his four unmarried sisters.

---

[31] Quoted in Jones, *Freud* I, 139.

[32] Quoted in *ibid.*, 140.

[33] Lisa Appignanesi and John Forrester, *Freud's women* (New York: Basic Books, 1992).

Moreover, while Freud was not the type to frequent pubs, he became "increasingly engrossed" in his work as it developed and began to communicate "primarily with his male colleagues." Although there are a few notable exceptions to this androcentrism, Freud's orientation toward men continued for the remainder of his career. As his project developed, psychoanalysis increasingly became "the recipient of his passion, time and energy," as Breger observes.[34] Work left Freud with little time or energy for anything else, other than regular card games and mandatory Sunday dinners at Amalie's.

To compound matters, whatever interest Martha may have had in Freud's work during their engagement quickly faded as his thinking developed in the direction of psychoanalysis. Indeed, she was indifferent toward Freud's creation for most of his career and even referred to it as "a form of pornography."[35] Appignanesi and Forrester observe that, "in later years, Freud's disciples were shocked and surprised to learn how little Martha knew or cared about psychoanalysis."[36] The couple's earlier rapport no longer existed, and she was unable to take an interest in the things that mattered the most to Freud. Appignanesi and Forrester suggest, however, that a lack of curiosity may not have been the only reason for Martha's indifference toward Freud's psychoanalytic work. It may have in fact been "part of their agreed-upon division of labour," and, so they argue, Freud may even have preferred it this way: it meant that he would not have to hear "doubts of the wisdom of his unorthodox methods of treatment from his wife." Appignanesi and Forrester also suggest that Martha may not have needed to know the details of Freud's work because her trust in it "was unshakable" in that "it rested on trust in his person." Finally, Martha may have tolerated her husband's absorption in his career because she was, as Freud himself observed in a letter to Marie Bonaparte, "fundamentally quite ambitious." Like his mother, Freud's wife was "quite satisfied" with the fame psychoanalysis brought to him.[37]

---

[34] *Ibid.*, 92–93, and Masson (ed.), *Letters to Flies*s, 129.

[35] René Laforgue, "Personal memories of Freud," *Freud as we knew him*, ed. Hendrik M. Ruitenbeek (Detroit, MI: Wayne State University Press, 1973), 342.

[36] Appignanesi and Forrester, *Freud's women*, 45.

[37] Quoted in Appignanesi and Forrester, *Freud's women*, 45.

While Freud was increasingly absorbed in his work, Martha had her own formidable assignment: managing the household and caring for her children. By all reports, she never adopted the more relaxed habits of the Viennese, but did an excellent job at putting her "Northern German virtue" to good use. Like a good *Hausfrau*, she valued discipline, cleanliness, and punctuality – sometimes to an obsessional extreme, according to her daughter Anna. Breger suggests that she substituted "duty and work for the intimacy that was missing in her marriage." According to him, "she was so committed to maintaining a spotless house that she would come to the dinner table with a pitcher of hot water and special napkin so that she could immediately remove any stains that were made on the tablecloth."[38] This may have been a source of contention with Freud, who was much more easygoing; in later years, he even argued that he should be allowed to feed his beloved dogs from the table.

At the same time, it would be simplistic to simply dismiss Martha as a stereotypical *Hausfrau*; she must have been more than that. Though her mode of domestic engineering may have been Prussian, visitors to Berggasse consistently reported that the atmosphere there was warm and congenial. While Freud's personality must have contributed to the *sympatische* environment, that could not entirely account for the ambiance. As Oskar Pfister, the Swiss Lutheran minister who trained as a psychoanalyst and became a lifelong friend of Freud's, observed:

I, who grew up fatherless and suffered for a life-time under a soft, one-sided bringing up, was dazzled by the beauty of that family life, which in spite of the almost superhuman greatness of the father of the house and his deep seriousness, breathed freedom and cheerfulness."[39]

It appears that Martha's and Freud's sexual life ended rather early.[40] According to Gay, by 1893, at the relatively young age of thirty-seven, Freud was living in abstinence.[41] In fact, Freud was surprisingly open

---

[38] Breger, *Freud*, 93.

[39] Heinrich Meng and Ernst L. Freud (eds.), *Psychoanalysis and faith: the letters of Sigmund Freud and Oskar Pfister*, trans. Erich Mosbacher (New York: Basic Books, 1963), 13.

[40] See especially Breger, *Freud*, 91–96.

[41] Gay, *Freud: a life for our time*, 162.

about this fact; indeed, at times he almost seems proud of his ability to tolerate the forbearance.[42] In 1897, he wrote to Fliess that "sexual excitement is of no use to someone like me."[43] (However, as we will see in the next chapter, Freud's involvement with Fliess generated considerable sexual excitement.) And in a letter to Fliess in 1900, he lamented the fact that his pleasures were so limited: "I am not allowed to smoke anything decent; alcohol does nothing for me [and] I am done begetting children."[44] This is not to say that Freud's views about sexuality were puritanical. As he wrote to the American analyst James Putnam:

Sexual morality as defined by society, in its most extreme form that of America, strikes me as very contemptible. I stand for an infinitely freer sexual life, although I myself have made very little use of that freedom.[45]

In this regard, Anzieu makes an interesting observation about Freud's libidinal economy. The French analyst contrasts Freud's attitude toward sexuality to that of "many of his male contemporaries," including his colleagues, a number of whom were engaged in quite active sexual lives. While these men were "libertine in their acts," Anzieu observes, "they were inhibited in thought and speech." Freud, on the other hand, "was reserved when it came to doing" – he did not take advantage of the "infinitely freer sexual life" he stood for – but was "transgressive when it came to knowing."[46] Where Kant exhorted us "to think for ourselves," Freud urged us "to think everything." Anzieu introduces a distinction between "expressive" and "reflexive" forms of sublimation that helps to illuminate the distinctive nature of Freud's creative processes. "Expressive" sublimation is the more common form of the process, in which "the sexual instincts" find expression and partial satisfaction in cultural objects of various sorts. In "reflexive" sublimation, the type of sublimation in which Freud was engaged, "the instincts," Anzieu writes, not only find satisfaction in the sublimatory process but also become its object. That is to say, Freud's

[42] See *ibid.*, 164.

[43] Masson (ed.), *Letters to Fliess*, 276.

[44] *Ibid.*, 404.

[45] *The letters of Sigmund Freud*, ed. Ernst L. Freud, 308.

[46] Anzieu, *Freud's self-analysis*, 51.

sublimatory and creative activity consisted in reflecting on the workings of the sexual instincts themselves.[47]

It is likely that all couples experience a degree of disillusionment when they enter their epic phase. Predictably, the usual factors – pregnancies, the arrival of children, managing a household, and an increased workload – lead to diminished passion and sexual interest. But there was something more going on with Freud. Although all lyrical phases rest on illusion to one degree or another, in his case the fantasy element, as we have seen, tended toward the extreme. We can compare the couple's separation to a petri dish, which, because it was relatively immunized against external reality, allowed Freud's fantasies – which found expression in his lyrical love letters – to grow with relatively few restrictions, while providing a container for them at the same time. It can be assumed, therefore, that the disillusionment he experienced as the epic phase progressed was that much more intense. If we agree with Breger that Freud's article "'Civilized' sexual morality and modern nervous illness" is in part autobiographical, then the following observation is pertinent. "The spiritual disillusionment and bodily deprivation to which most marriages are doomed," Freud observes, "puts both partners back in the state they were in before their marriage." But this is not a simple return to the *status quo ante*, for "they are poorer by the loss of illusion." And this statement applies *a fortiori* to Freud, given the magnitude of the illusion[s] that he lost.[48]

Emmeline Bernays, Freud's "sworn enemy," had unwittingly done him an enormous favour when she moved her daughter to Wandsbek. He was not forced to confront his fantasies with the realities of a flesh-and-blood person while Martha was away, but was able to maintain a fantasized love object that he could idealize in the extreme. So when they were finally able to live together, the relationship, to the extent it had been based on fantasy, could not withstand the test of everyday reality. As Breger observes:

They had weathered these tempestuous times, but then, once married, living – and sleeping – together, [Freud's] passion quickly faded. He was able to express a range of emotions during the engagement when their primary contract was by letter . . . He would give free reign to his powerful yearnings for love. But the

---

[47] *Ibid.*, 52.

[48] Sigmund Freud, "'Civilized' sexual morality and modern nervous illness" (1908), *SE* 9: 194–195.

courtship and engagement, conducted in literary form, had been filled with his fantasies, and the romance of them could not stand the reality of life.[49]

Furthermore, the restlessness and discontent he experienced when he was separated from Martha did not subside when they were finally united. He suffered from anxiety and depression as well as a variety of somatic symptoms, and he eventually sought to have his yearnings fulfilled elsewhere. Within a year after marrying Martha, Freud met Wilhelm Fliess, who lived in Berlin. He not only became the new object of Freud's desires, but letters again provided the primary medium in which the relationship unfolded. Gay argues, in fact, that Martha's failure to satisfy Freud's inchoate yet intense yearnings "virtually made Fliess necessary."[50]

Breuer

Another person from whom Freud demanded complete agreement was Josef Breuer, and that demand became one of the major reasons for their falling out. The two *Gymnasium*-educated Jewish physicians first met in Brücke's Physiological Institute in the late 1870s, where their common cultural background as well as their mutual commitment to biophysics and other shared scientific interests drew them to each other. They maintained their friendship via mail while Freud was in Paris, and they grew even closer when Freud returned to Vienna, where the younger physician spent considerable time as a guest in Breuer's home.

Breuer, who was known for his kindness and generosity, did not appear to be a man with any axes to grind. Not only was he free from excessive ambition but, unlike Brücke, Charcot, and Meynert, he was also unimpressed by "great men," not aspiring to become one himself. This fact, coupled with Freud's ambivalence about Breuer's generous support, caused some difficulty for the idealization-hungry younger man. Breuer earned considerable recognition as a successful researcher and "produced several works of permanent value" in physiology.[51] But his "caretaking nature," combined with his failure to advance his university career, led

---

[49] Breger, *Freud*, 95.

[50] Gay, *Freud: a life for our time*, 61.

[51] Freud, "An autobiographical study," 19.

him to move away from research toward the realm of clinical practice.[52] It is a testimony to Breuer's "supreme skill as a doctor" that "many distinguished members of the Medical School faculty," Brücke among them, selected him "as their personal physician."[53]

In 1882, before Freud left for Paris, Breuer reported the dramatic case of a vital, imaginative, strong-willed, and keenly intelligent young hysterical woman whom he had been treating, and his junior colleague became fascinated by what he heard. The woman's florid symptomology included hallucinations of snakes, paralyses, convulsions, anesthesia, deafness, and the inability to speak her native tongue, German, coupled with the simultaneous capacity to communicate in perfect English. While known to history as the Fräulein Anna O. of *Studies on hysteria*, the work Breuer and Freud coauthored in 1895, her name was actually Bertha Pappenheim. She came from the same wealthy Jewish milieu that produced Breuer and so many of the protagonists of the early history of analysis.[54]

Breuer's recognition of a split in the patient's consciousness – though not his explanation of it – and his discovery of the cathartic technique represent psychoanalysis in an embryonic form. In their sessions, Breuer observed "absences" in Anna's presentations, during which she would withdraw her attention, descend into an altered and confused state, and articulate "profoundly melancholic phantasies – 'daydreams,' she would call them – sometimes characterized by poetic beauty."[55] Anna later elaborated these absences into a second personality, which the French refer to as a *condition seconde*, and would enter into this personality either through hypnosis or on her own via auto-hypnosis.[56]

Raised in an orthodox and puritanical Jewish home that allowed no room for a girl's self-expression, Anna had been a bored and frustrated adolescent who retreated into daydreams to escape the tedium of her life. Breuer accurately considered those daydreams as precursors to the absences and *condition seconde* she later developed.

[52] Breger, *Freud*, 101.

[53] *Ibid.*, 101.

[54] See Josef Breuer and Sigmund Freud, *Studies in hysteria* (1893–1895), *SE* 2: 21–47.

[55] Sigmund Freud, *Five lectures on psychoanalysis* (1910), *SE* 11: 12.

[56] In a pregnant observation, Breuer recognized that the condition of the second personality resembled a dream state.

Anna O. is perhaps best known for virtually leading Breuer to the cathartic method, the forerunner of free association. Although many of her symptoms assumed a physiological form, Breuer came to realize that they were in fact symbolic – in other words, that they were meaningful, and could therefore be interpreted. Breuer agreed with Charcot that hysteria was caused by traumas, but, as opposed to the French neurologist, he understood those traumas as psychological rather than physical in nature. Hysteria, in short, was caused by ideas. Breuer argued, moreover, that the ideational content of a hysteric's symptoms consists in disguised memories – "monuments" or "memorials" – of the patient's "psychical traumas" from childhood.[57] Hence the famous dictum: *"Hysterics suffer mainly from reminiscences."*[58] The "fixation of mental life to pathogenic traumas," Freud observed, "is one of the most significant and practically important characteristics of neurosis."[59]

With Anna leading the way, Breuer also discovered that when her symptoms were traced back to those traumatic memories, they would dissolve. The method that he therefore adopted was this: to have Anna enter a state of auto- or doctor-induced hypnosis and follow each symptom, in order, to the traumatic memory that lay behind it; this would result in what he called a catharsis. In this manner, the symptom was "talked away." Breuer describes the process:

Each individual symptom in this complicated case was taken separately in hand; all the occasions on which it had appeared were described in reverse order, starting before the time when the patient became bedridden and was going back to the event which had led to its first appearance. When this had been described the symptom was permanently removed.[60]

It is important to stress that symptoms were not effectively "talked away" unless the "strangulated affect" that became attached to them when they were originally formed was discharged. It must be stressed that the "talking cure" – a term that Anna famously coined – is also an affective, that is to say, an energic cure, a fact that is missed in purely linguistic

---

[57] Freud, *Five lectures on psychoanalysis*, 18.

[58] Breuer and Freud, *Studies in hysteria*, 7 (emphasis in the original).

[59] Freud, *Five lectures on psychoanalysis*, 17.

[60] *Ibid.*, 35.

interpretations of psychoanalysis. If it is not accompanied by the appropriate affect, the mere recollection of the traumatic event – the mere act
of putting it into words – does not remove the symptom. Without the
energic component, one does not have a dynamic psychology.

Freud kept Breuer's account of the Anna O. case tucked away in his
memory for the better part of a decade. Before he made use of it for
his own clinical purposes, he had tried to drum up Charcot's interest
in Anna's specific case and in the cathartic method in general, but the
French neurologist was only interested in hysteria and hypnosis as topics
for research and uninterested in their clinical significance. It was only in
1889, after Freud's return to Vienna, when his use of hypnotic suggestion
with his patients reached an impasse, that he returned to the cathartic
method.

According to the received account, sexuality played the central role
in Breuer's abrupt termination of his treatment of Anna O. – as well as, in
the end, of the Freud–Breuer friendship. Indeed, Jones's dramatized narrative of the termination of Anna's treatment has become part of psychoanalytic lore. According to the Welshman, Breuer panicked in the face
of the sexualized transference that Anna had developed to him (which
included a case of hysterical pregnancy), grabbed his jealous wife, and
hopped on the Orient Express for a second honeymoon in perhaps the
most romantic of all cities, Venice – where, moreover, his daughter was
conceived.[61] It makes a great story, but unfortunately recent scholarship
has demonstrated that it is not true: there was no trip to Venice, and his
daughter was conceived a year earlier.[62] At that point, Freud stepped in
and assumed responsibility for Anna's treatment.

Nevertheless, even if the details of Jones's colorful narrative are inaccurate, Freud was convinced that an "untoward event" of some sort had
occurred at the end of Anna's treatment with Breuer, and that it concerned "the sexual motivation of [the] transference." Freud also believed
that this transference phenomenon provided a glimpse into the explosive

---

[61] See Jones, *Freud* I, 224–225.
[62] See Ellenberger, *The discovery of the unconscious*, 481–484; Albrecht Hirschmüller,
The life and work of Josef Breuer: physiology and psychoanalysis (New York: New York
University Press, 1989), 112–116 and 136–141; Breger, *Freud*, 122-123; and Makari,
Revolution in mind, 91–92.

potential of sexuality, which lay at the heart of "hypnotic rapport."[63] This is a critical point in the development of psychoanalysis.

Shortly after hearing Breuer's own account of the termination, Freud remarked in a letter to Martha, at that time still his fiancée, that this event was an important way-station on his path to discovering the full significance of transference. After recounting Breuer's version of the termination in the letter, Freud sought to reassure Martha with a self-deprecating statement: "For that to happen one has to be a Breuer."[64] In effect, he was telling Martha, "Don't worry; for a female patient to develop a sexualized transference to her physician, he must be as attractive as Breuer." The implication was that because Freud did not fit the bill, Martha had no need to be concerned that an eroticized transference situation could possibility arise with him. But when a patient later made an erotic advance towards him – the presumably unattractive physician was rescued by the lucky appearance of his housekeeper – Freud was forced to recognize that transference is to a large extent independent of the personal attributes of the doctor, that is, of the "real" situation.

There was one more item on Freud's agenda before he could put an end to his extended moratorium and truly "start out" on a career, marriage, and fatherhood – that is, he had to relinquish his hunger for father-mentors. When Freud met Fliess, he was in the process of separating from Breuer, who was the last in a series of father figures that included Hammerschlag, Brücke, and Charcot. As Fliess was being elevated into the role of the "beloved friend," Breuer was being cast off as the "hated enemy." Freud had reached the point, Breger suggests, where he no longer needed to be a "deferential apprentice" to an older "master" but was ready to strike out on his own and become the heroic and defiant revolutionary.[65]

The standard explanation suggests that Freud rejected Breuer because the latter, as an established bourgeois doctor, could not accept the scandalous proposition that sexuality was the exclusive cause of hysteria. This account is at best partial. As he had with Martha, Freud demanded unequivocal acceptance and affirmation from his colleague. It was necessary

[63] Freud, *History of the psychoanalytic movement*, 12.

[64] Quoted in Jones, *Freud* I, 225. See also Léon Chertok, "The discovery of the transference: towards an epistemological interpretation," *International Journal of Psychoanalysis* 49 (1968), 563.

[65] Breger, *Freud*, 125.

that Breuer accept his theory that sexuality was the cause of hysteria *in toto*; no light could exist between their positions. And Breuer did not deny the importance of sexuality; in fact, he stressed it even more strongly than Freud in *Studies on hysteria*. What he did deny was that it was the *explicans* for *all* cases of hysteria.

Freud's demand for utter loyalty erupted in an event that occurred in 1895 at the Vienna College of Medicine. Somewhat full of himself upon returning from Paris where he had studied with the Great Charcot, Freud delivered three lectures to that organization. In them, he defended his claim that sexuality played the decisive role in the etiology of hysteria and neurasthenia. The members of that august institution included a number of the city's most eminent physicians – among them, Krafft-Ebing. When the predictable objections arose during the discussion, as Makari informs us, it was Breuer who in fact "rose to defend his young colleague," and to testify that while he had originally been skeptical about Freud's thesis, careful clinical observation had convinced him of its validity. The theory, he assured his colleagues, was not a result of suggestion but had emerged from the material itself. Indeed, the supposedly bourgeois and conventional Breuer even chided "those men of science," as Makari refers to them, "who could not bring themselves to imagine sexual abuse, going so far as to say that they themselves were behaving like hysterics." But this was not enough for Freud. Although Breuer praised his "theory as a great advance," he also maintained that Freud at times "overstated" his case. While sexuality accounted for the origins of many cases of hysteria, for Breuer it was not the universal etiological factor in all of them. This was a reasonable and differentiated position. But Freud – who would later sing the praises of scientific skepticism and insist on the fallibility of all scientific theories – could not tolerate even this limited disagreement with his theory, and he broke with Breuer, a man who had treated him so generously, in a thoroughly unpalatable way.[66] It has even been suggested that Breuer's generous support contributed to Freud's brutal treatment of him. That is to say, it was Freud's way of reacting against having been dependent on Breuer.

In a remarkably balanced letter to the Swiss psychologist Auguste Forel in 1907, Breuer both provides an account of his position and sheds light

[66] Makari, *Revolution in mind*, 91–92.

on aspects of Freud's personality at the time.[67] Breuer explains that his
reasons for transferring Anna O. to Freud, as well as his decision to stop
treating hysterics, was not, as Freud would have it, because of the sexual
material that the case involved. Rather, it was owing to the fact that the
case was too demanding for a general practitioner like Breuer. Today, we
see a florid hysteric like Anna O., as well as many of Freud's other supposedly hysterical patients, as suffering not from neurotic disorders but
rather from a pathology closer to the borderline range of the diagnostic
spectrum. Extensive clinical experience has taught us how demanding
and exhausting work with these patients can be. Breuer simply concluded
that he could not accommodate Anna in his practice. "It was impossible,"
he wrote, "for a 'general practitioner' to treat a case of that kind without
bringing his activities and mode of life completely to an end." Therefore,
he "vowed" that he "would not go through such an ordeal again," and he
later referred other hysterical patients who came his way to Freud.[68]

Yet Breuer insists that, "together with Freud," he recognized "the
prominent place assumed by sexuality (*das Vordrängen des Sexualen*)" in
psychopathology. And he offers his Swiss colleague the same assurance
he offered the audience at the College of Medicine – namely, that Freud's
conclusions were based on sound clinical observation. At the same time,
he also observes that Freud sometimes tended to universalize the role of
sexuality in a way that was not supported by the evidence. In Breuer's
opinion, this over-reaching resulted partly from the absolutizing speculative tendency in Freud's scientific personality, and partly from his need
to view himself as an iconoclastic rebel. "Freud," Breuer writes, "is a
man given to absolute and exclusive formulations: this is a psychical need
which, in my opinion, leads to excessive generalization." And he suggests
that these excessive tendencies may result from "a desire *d'épâter le bourgeois* [sic]."[69]

But Breuer's view of Freud also remains positive, fair-minded, and tol-
erant. He continues to insist that his collaborator's insights are largely
"derived from experience," and that whatever exaggerations he introduces

---

[67] The letter is reproduced in Paul F. Cranefield, "Josef Breuer's evaluation of his
contribution to psycho-analysis," *International Journal of Psychoanalysis* 39 (1958),
319–322. See also Makari, *Revolution in mind*, 91.

[68] Cranefield, "Josef Breuer's evaluation of his contribution to psycho-analysis," 319.

[69] *Ibid.*, 320.

into the material can also be seen in objective terms. Breuer, moreover, views Freud's boldness as a necessary and healthy swing in the theoretical pendulum away from the purely physiological explanations of the psychiatric establishment of the time.

Hysteria and Hypnosis

Freud was capable of soaring flights of speculation, but he could also be a down-to-earth pragmatist. He had to be, given his responsibilities for supporting the residents at Berggasse 19 as well as contributing to the support of his parents and sisters. As he succinctly put it: "Anyone who wants to make a living from the treatment of nervous patients must clearly be able to do something for them." The problem was, however, that in 1887 he did not have much to offer the "neurotics" he was treating. Freud was not a natural physician: he doubted his abilities; and he possessed only a limited "therapeutic arsenal" to treat the wide array of disorders with which he was confronted.[70] The arsenal consisted of electrotherapy (that is, the application of an electronic stimulation to the affected part of the body), massage, hydrotherapy, rest cures, and hypnotic suggestion. With the exception of hypnosis, the other treatments were relatively ineffective in dealing with his patients' conditions. Consequently, he was under considerable pressure to refine his clinical skills post-haste.

In 1889, therefore, Freud traveled to Nancy to study with the famed hypnotist Hippolyte Bernheim. In contrast to Charcot, the very embodiment of Parisian urbanity and sophistication, Bernheim was a provincial doctor in Nancy and a representative of the French clinical tradition. He had been won over to hypnosis after witnessing Auguste Liébeault, "a slightly disreputable country doctor" and "old-time hypnotist," use it to cure one of his patients of sciatica.[71] What Freud observed when he traveled to France to observe Liébeault and Bernheim at work impressed him:

With the idea of perfecting my hypnotic technique, I made a journey to Nancy in the summer of 1889 and spent several weeks there. I witnessed the moving spectacle of old Liébeault working among the poor women and children of the

---

[70] Freud, "An autobiographical study," 16.

[71] Makari, *Revolution in mind*, 30.

laboring classes, [and] I was a spectator of Bernheim's astonishing experiments on his hospital patients.[72]

Freud had already become convinced of the reality of hypnosis when he observed Charcot's use of it at Salpêtrière, although the eminent neurologist only used it for research and did not pursue its possible clinical applications. Freud's experience in Nancy further convinced him of the reality of hypnosis, albeit within certain limits, and reinforced his belief in the existence of unconscious mental life. "I received the profoundest impression," he writes, "of the possibility that there could be powerful mental processes which nevertheless remained hidden from the consciousness of man."[73]

Bernheim's impact on Freud was not only clinical. The provincial small-time doctor had the audacity to launch a broadside attack against the great Charcot that resulted in a heated debate between the Nancy School and the Paris School, into which a sizeable portion of the international psychiatric community was drawn. And in sorting out where he stood vis-à-vis Bernheim and Charcot, Freud clarified his own position, which contributed to the creation of psychoanalysis.[74]

Bernheim's criticisms of Charcot were epistemological as well as substantive. He argued that Charcot's claim that an episode of Grand Hysteria invariably passes through a particular series of three delineable stages was empirically false. A growing body of evidence in the late 1880s had in fact supported Bernheim's position. What is more, Bernheim did not simply reject Charcot's stage-theory, but also tried to explain the origins of Charcot's error. In a skeptical trope that is familiar in the history of philosophy – and that is often deployed against Freud by his critics – Bernheim turned the content of the theory back onto the theorist. Because it involved contagion, the phenomenon of hysteria lent itself to this theoretical maneuver particularly well. The members of the Paris School, so Bernheim argued, were themselves suffering from the very hysteria they claimed to be describing. He maintained that a hysterical contagion had swept through the ranks of Charcot's followers, explaining why they championed his theory so enthusiastically. Bernheim also argued that the

---

[72] Quoted in Jones, *Freud* I, 238.

[73] *Ibid.*, 238.

[74] See Markari, *Revolution in mind*, 29–34.

members of the Paris School had actually *suggested* – "implanted," to use Foucault's term – the stages of a hysterical episode to their patients, who in turn proceeded to oblige their physicians by acting them out.

Bernheim did not stop there; he expanded this argument into a case for what philosophers call "the totalized critique of reason" – a self-liquidating critique that is so encompassing that it undercuts the position of the theorist making it. Charcot contended not only that hypnosis was a pathological process and that only hysterics could be hypnotized, but also that hypnotizability was a sure diagnostic indicator of hysteria. Against Charcot, Bernheim argued that hypnotizability was a normal phenomenon based on a universal feature of the human psyche – namely, *credulity* or *suggestibility*. While Freud believed that Bernheim's derivation of hypnotizability from an ordinary human phenomenon was his great contribution, he disagreed with Bernheim's use of this universal fact to advance an irrational view of human nature that would negate the very possibility of autonomous rational thought and judgment.[75] As Makari describes it:

Hypnosis, [Bernheim] believed, wasn't even necessary for suggestions to take hold of another person. Ideas passed from one unconscious mind to another all the time. The mind's windows were open, taking in commands, suggestions, and ideas from others and then mistaking foreign notions for their own. All human psychology was characterized by this gross "credulity." False impressions and ideas were readily accepted by the mind thanks to automatic, unconscious cerebration, the frailty of reason, and the all-too-human need to believe. Religion, education, tradition, morality, allegiance to the state, and social conventionality; the work of lawyers, politicians, professors, orators, charlatans, and seducers, all these were evidence of a world dominated by suggestion and credulity. Credulity was not odd or unusual, but rather was essential to normal psychological life.[76]

Indeed, Bernheim did not shy away from the implication of his position: that a scientific account of the human mind was impossible. *Bernheim's position rules out the possibility of a (relatively) independent and objective observer, (sufficiently) uncontaminated by suggestion, who could investigate*

---

[75] See Sigmund Freud, "Preface to the translation of Bernheim's *De la suggestion*" (1888), *SE* 1: 17–21.

[76] *Revolution in Mind*, 30. Makari rightly points out that Bernheim was in fact formulating "a rudimentary psychology of illusion." See his, "A history of Freud's first theory of transference," *International Review of Psychoanalysis* 9 (1992), 421.

the workings of the mind, including its suggestibility. In short, for him, a rational scientific subject is impossible. "There was no way for psychological scientists to stand outside this swim, for," as Makari observes, "they were being suggested to even as they were suggesting."[77] Suggestibility is what makes us vulnerable to the ruses of Descartes's diabolical evil genius.

Freud was confronted with a dilemma. On the one hand, the empirical evidence against many of Charcot's key theories was convincing, but he also accepted Bernheim's claim that suggestibility and credulity are ubiquitous psychological phenomena. On the other hand, like the members of the Paris School, he was determined to defend the possibility of a scientific theory of the human mind. *Freud's desideratum was therefore to acknowledge the full extent of human irrationality and nevertheless to retain a place for science and reason,* and, for the rest of his career, this was his pursuit. One might argue, in fact, that the desideratum became the defining problematic of his psychoanalytic project, and that the pursuit of this desideratum is what distinguishes Freud from both the irrationalism of the Romantics and the hyper-rationalism of the one-sided Enlighteners.

Freud's solution was to reject the idea that suggestibility is a brute fact that could not be further explained. Instead, he sought to make it an object of a scientific investigation. To do this, he turned to *intrapsychic reality*. Rather than focusing on "the hypnotic encounter as some interpersonal drama between a wide-eyed hypnotist and a swooning subject," as Makari observes, Freud turned his "attention to the intrapsychic conditions that made a man prone to another's suggestion."[78] Freud's goal was to provide a rational psychological account of the human tendency toward suggestibility – an account he developed in his attempt to explain our susceptibility to transference – and therefore toward irrationality. In other words, *Freud sought to formulate a rational theory of irrationality.*[79]

Freud's trip to Nancy did not produce the desired results. When he returned to Vienna, his success with hypnosis did not appreciably improve. In fact, he was never comfortable practicing hypnosis and perhaps for that reason was never particularly good at it. His discomfort with hypnosis

---

[77] Makari, *Revolution in mind*, 31.

[78] *Ibid.*, 33.

[79] See Otto Fenichel, *Problems of psychoanalytic technique* (New York: The Psychoanalytic Quarterly, 1941), 13.

illuminates an important aspect of his clinical *ethos*, which centered on the patient's autonomy, and of his personal Enlightenment *ethos* more generally. Hypnosis – through the hypnotic trance, the subject's exclusive focus on the hypnotist, the abdication of his or her critical faculties – is meant to induce a state of extreme thralldom, which is to say, extreme heteronomy in the hypnotic subject, who is effectively reduced to a state of "bondage" vis-à-vis the hypnotist.[80] Autonomous thinking presupposes the capacity spontaneously to initiate a train of thought independent of such external causes as one's bodily desires, the voice of authority, or the influence of a charismatic personality, to note just a few examples. And it is precisely this capacity that hypnotic suggestion puts out of commission.

In hypnotic suggestion, Freud argues, "a conscious idea . . . has been introduced into the brain of the hypnotized subject by an external influence and has been accepted by him as though it had arisen spontaneously" – as though it was the subject's own.[81] Suggestion is even more insidious in that it presents itself with a semblance of spontaneity: after subjects have been awakened, they experience the idea as though it had originated with them, which it had not. Suggestion, in other words, not only implants an idea in person's head but also masks the fact that it has been implanted, thus circumventing the subject's rational agency.

When he practiced hypnosis, Freud tells us, he experienced a feeling of magical power – of omnipotence. "There was something positively seductive," he writes, "in working with hypnotism. For the first time, there was a sense of having overcome one's helplessness; and it was highly flattering to enjoy the reputation of being a miracle-worker."[82] Yet he recognized that seductiveness was just that: merely seductive. The perks of playing the omnipotent doctor – the magical healer – were not attractive to him. Indeed, although Freud is often lambasted as an authoritarian patriarch, the psychoanalyst and social commentator Eric Erikson sees him differently. Erikson argues that, in a profoundly radical gesture, Freud rejected the role of the omnipotent patriarchal physician who prescribes treatment from on high and assumed the more "feminine" stance of a receptive

[80] Sigmund Freud, *Group psychology and the analysis of the ego* (1921), *SE* 18: 113.

[81] Freud, "Preface to the translation of Bernheim's *De la suggestion*," 77.

[82] Freud, "An autobiographical study," 17.

listener who enlists the patient as a co-worker in the enterprise.[83] In fact, Freud explicitly criticized hypnosis for being a "coarsely interfering method" and quickly gave it up for something he found more conducive.[84]

Freud's almost instinctive predilection for autonomy is evident in his reaction to Bernheim's treatment of a patient. When he heard Bernheim shout at a patient who was "unamenable" to hypnosis, "'What are you doing? *Vous vous contre-suggestionnez!*' [You are counter-suggesting] . . . a muffled hostility to [the] tyranny of suggestion" rose up in him. He considered this incident "an evident injustice and an act of violence. For the man certainly had a right to counter-suggestion if people were trying to subdue him with suggestion."[85] Freud believed, in other words, that the patient's autonomy entailed a right to counter-suggestion.

It will be argued in the next chapter that when Freud fell passionately in love with Wilhelm Fliess, he became completely enthralled with him and could not appropriate his own autonomy until he worked through that thralldom, that extreme heteronomy, and resolved it. It is therefore pertinent to say something about the intrinsic connection that Freud believed existed between hypnosis and being in love. He observes that from "being in love to hypnosis is evidently only a short step,"[86] so close is the connection between the two phenomena. Being in love both involves an "overvaluation," an idealization, of the object, which is spared all criticism, while every form of perfection is attributed to it. When we are in love, Freud maintains, "the object serves as a substitute for some unattained ego ideal of our own" – it represents what we would like to be. By loving the object, we seek to "procure in this roundabout way" the perfection we cannot achieve on our own. And to the degree that the object becomes "more and

---

[83] See Erik H. Erikson, "The first psychoanalyst," *Insight and responsibility* (New York: W.W. Norton & Co., 1994), 38. Castoriadis observes that the aim of psychoanalysis "cannot be reached, not even approached, without the self-activity of the patient . . . Psychoanalysis is . . . a practical/poetical activity where both participants are agents and where the patient is the main agent of the development of his own self activity." Cornelius Castoriadis, "Psychoanalysis and politics," *World in fragments: writings on politics, society, psychoanalysis, and the imaginary*, trans. and ed. David Ames Curtis (Stanford, CA: Stanford University Press, 1997), 129.

[84] Quoted in Jones, 53.

[85] Freud, *Group psychology and the analysis of the ego*, 89.

[86] *Ibid.*, 114.

more sublime and precious," our own ego becomes diminished and debased. Carried to its limits, the object can get "possession of the entire self-love of the ego" and consume it.[87] This, Freud argues, accounts for the "traits of humility, of the limitation of narcissism, and of self-injury" – the self-abasement that can occur when one is in love. It also accounts for the lover's "devotion" or "bondage" to the object.[88] The lover's credulity and distorted perception of the beloved results from the fact that when one's ego is surrendered to the object, one's faculty of reality-testing and one's capacity for judgment – that is, one's autonomy – are surrendered as well.

The hypnotic subject exhibits the same docility and credulity – that is, "the same humble subjection, the same compliance, the same absence of criticism, towards the hypnotist" that the lover manifests "towards the loved object." "Everything is even clearer and more intense in hypnosis" than it is in love, Freud agues, because while "the hypnotic relation is the unlimited devotion of someone in love," it excludes "sexual satisfaction."[89] In a provocative claim that is bound to offend the sentimentalist, he adds, "It would be more to the point to explain being in love by means of hypnosis than the other way round."[90] As we will see, what Freud has to say about the relation of hypnosis and love can be read almost as a gloss of the dynamics of his relationship with Fliess.

Resistance, Defense, and Transference

Before his trip to Nancy, Freud had experimented with an amalgam of Breuer's cathartic method and hypnotic suggestion, but he continued to experience unsatisfying results with this procedure. At a certain point, he decided to concentrate exclusively on the cathartic approach, but to augment it with hypnosis as a means for uncovering traumatic memories rather than as a medium for suggestion. He even contacted Breuer to get more information about Anna O., after which Freud reports that he eventually "worked at nothing else" but this approach.[91]

---

[87] *Ibid.*, 115.

[88] *Ibid.*, 113.

[89] This formulation might be taken as a description of analysis.

[90] *Ibid.*, 113–114.

[91] Freud, *Autobiographical study*, 21.

But he also ran into difficulties with this new procedure as well. He discovered that the "cures" he was able to achieve were often superficial and short-lived, and he found also that there were many patients he could not hypnotize – patients, moreover, who were clearly hysterics and therefore should *ex hypothesi* be hypnotizable. On the assumption that the cathartic method required that the patient be put into a hypnotic trance, he in effect had reached another impasse.

What Freud now required to treat his hysterical patients was this: a technique that could "bypass hypnosis and yet obtain the pathogenic recollections" in order to abreact them.[92] While he was searching for this technique, Freud remembered Bernheim had told him in Nancy, namely, that when subjects are awakened from a hypnotic trance, they seem to have forgotten what transpired while they were somnambulant, but in fact, Bernheim had found, they retained it. "Posthypnotic amnesia," in other words, was "not absolute, and . . . an individual can be brought, by certain procedures, to recall in his wakeful state what had happened during the hypnotic session."[93] To demonstrate this, Bernheim would inform patients in a post-hypnotic state that they in fact possessed the memories of what had transpired when they were somnambulant and, when he pressed them, they would produce those memories.

Freud therefore adopted a new approach: He would place his hands on the foreheads of patients who insisted they could not remember what they had experienced as children and *exhort* them to recall the forgotten material. "Hesitatingly at first," he reports, "but eventually in a flood and with complete clarity," the patients remembered.[94] Hypnosis, so it appeared, was not necessary to gain access to required traumatic material.

He therefore decided to drop the hypnotic approach and adopt the working assumption that "his patients knew everything that was of any pathogenic significance and that it was only a question of obliging them to communicate it."[95] (This new procedure is sometimes referred to as the "pressure technique.") In the first step, Freud would place his patients in

---

[92] Breuer and Freud, *Studies on hysteria*, 268.

[93] Ellenberger, *The discovery of the unconscious*, 114.

[94] Freud, "An autobiographical study," 28.

[95] Breuer and Freud, *Studies on hysteria*, 110. It is important to note the term "obliging" here.

a recumbent position on a couch and ask them to close their eyes. Then, sitting behind them, he would question them about the origins of their symptoms. His patients, he tells us, would invariably reach a point where they could not produce any more answers. When this break in the process occurred, Freud would "insist," or "oblige," them to concentrate even more intensely.[96] After as many tries as necessary, he claims that they regularly succeeded in recovering the memory.

One cannot over-emphasize the importance of the step that Freud was about to take – a step that would propel him beyond the proto-psychoanalytic psychotherapy of Breuer into the domain of *psychodynamics*, or psychoanalysis proper. He was on the verge of formulating the foundational concept of *resistance*, and of discovering its correlates, defense and repression. Freud had always been perplexed by the question of hypnotizability. Why, he asked, were some patients only partially hypnotizable, while others rejected hypnosis outright? He concluded that, although the mechanism might be more obvious in the second case – that of patients who rejected hypnosis outright – the phenomenon was essentially the same in both. "People who were not hypnotizable," he argued, "were people who had a psychical objection to hypnosis, whether their objection was expressed as overt unwillingness or not."[97] *The task therefore was to elucidate the nature of that "psychical objection."*

Reflecting on his experience with the cathartic method, Freud asked himself what occurred at the point where patients seemed to reach an impasse in their ability to produce further answers to his questions. Because this impasse could be overcome by an effort on his part, by "insistence," he concluded that there must exist "*a psychical force in the patients which was opposed to the pathogenic ideas becoming conscious (being remembered)*."[98] In short, he was encountering a force of "resistance" that he "had to overcome" with his own counter-force in order to gain access to the memories. It involved, Freud observed, "a question of *quantitative* comparison, of a struggle between motive forces of different degrees of strength or intensity."[99]

---

[96] In the beginning, he would press his hands on their forehead, but as time went by he dropped this procedure.

[97] Breuer and Freud, *Studies on hysteria*, 268.

[98] *Ibid.*, 260 (emphasis in the original).

[99] *Ibid.*, 270 (emphasis in the original).

Freud realized, moreover, that the resistance he encountered when pursuing the cathartic method *and* the "psychical objection" he ran into when trying to hypnotize patients were manifestations of one and the same force. With this insight, he introduced an economic–dynamic standpoint into his thinking – that is, the perspective that conceptualizes psychological phenomena in terms of the conflictual interplay of the intrapsychic forces that produce them. This standpoint ultimately became a foundation stone of the brand of psychoanalysis, associated with his name.

During the decade in which Breuer pulled back from the treatment of hysterics and opened the field for Freud, the young clinician labored to convince his reluctant senior colleague to publish their joint findings. While Freud was theoretically daring and eager to publish their findings, Breuer was a cautious, hesitant scientist who wanted more data to back up their claims. Indeed, Freud's irritation with Breuer's restraint contributed to their increasing estrangement throughout the 1890s. Yet once the work of the renowned French psychologist Pierre Janet appeared in France and threatened to scoop the field, Breuer agreed to the publication of a journal article, "On the psychical mechanism of hysterical phenomena: preliminary communication," in 1893.

And in 1895, Freud convinced a still-reticent Breuer to publish a complete book, *Studies on hysteria*. The distance that had developed between the two in the intervening years is evident in the immensely rich *Studies*, which is also a somewhat odd and heterogeneous work – as well as a crucial one. It contains the co-authored 1893 article, "Preliminary communication," Breuer's presentation of Anna O., Freud's presentation of four more case studies, a theoretical chapter by Breuer, and a chapter on therapy by Freud. The organization of the book is curious: whereas one might have expected the more speculatively inclined Freud to write the chapter on theory, Breuer actually authored it. Interestingly, it was Freud who contributed the chapter on technique. This is an example of how Freud's theorizing eschewed abstract speculation and generally worked from the ground up.

Freud believed that higher-level generalizations characteristically arise out of the attempt to address particular problems on the concrete level of clinical experience. "I was driven forward," he tells us, "by practical necessity."[100] The inner logic of that process, in which the solution of one

---

[100] Freud, *Five Lectures on psychoanalysis*, 22.

clinical problem leads to the formulation of the next, is so perspicuous
as to be stunning. Thus as soon as he identified the problem of resistance, Freud asks: "What kind of force could one suppose was operative
here, and what motive could have put it into operation?" The answer,
he tells us, "seemed to open before [his] eyes" when he recognized
that the force behind the resistance to remember the traumatic experience *and the force that caused the inaccessibility* were the same.[101] He called
this second force "defense" or "repression."[102] In short, *Freud's investigation of the psychodynamics of the clinical encounter led to the question of
pathogenesis – and would eventually lead to a theory of the psychic apparatus
to explain the pathogenic process.*

The next question followed just as clearly as the previous one: "What
is the motive for the defense?" Freud's answer is twofold. First, he argues
that, from a phenomenological perspective, a defense is set in motion
when a person is confronted with an idea of "a distressing nature." He
then explains that such an idea might arouse such negative consequences
as "the affects of shame . . . self-reproach and . . . psychical pain," as
well as "the feeling of being harmed." Because these affects are distressing, he maintains, a person would "prefer not to have experienced" them,
or "would rather forget" them.[103] The attempt to forget/reject a distressing idea is the defense.

Freud next offers what he would refer to as a "metapsychological"
account of defense, and in it he introduces the important notion of an
"incompatible idea." In one of his earliest discussions of the ego, Freud
uses one of Charcot's arguments and maintains that the psychical agency
of the ego consists in an organized, associative web of ideas – a synthetic
unity. From a metapsychological perspective, an idea is "accepted" when
the ego allows it to enter its web of associations. But when the ego encounters an "incompatible" idea – one which threatens the integrity of its
organization, thus causing pain – the ego defends itself and mobilizes "a
repelling force" to get rid of it.[104]

---

[101] Breuer and Freud, *Studies on hysteria*, 268–269.

[102] The two terms had not yet been distinguished.

[103] *Ibid.*, 269.

[104] *Ibid.*, 269.

Other concepts of the ego and defense eventually emerged in the development of Freud's thinking, in addition to it as a synthesizing web of ideas. But according to this account – which corresponds to Freud's "unofficial" inclusionary position – the goal of ego development is expansion, greater integration, and differentiation of its associative web. In other words, the strength of the ego is not to be measured in terms of its defensive or repressive capabilities. On the contrary, the subject attempts "to forget about" an incompatible idea, according to Freud, "because he [has] no confidence in his power to resolve the contradiction between [it] and his ego by means of thought activity." Subjects, in other words, institute defenses and reject "incompatible" ideas because they do not feel they posses the strength to tolerate and *integrate* such ideas into their egos. *The capacity for integration, which requires the ability to sufficiently tolerate the discomfort of incompatible ideas, is a crucial indicator of the capacity for psychic growth and analysability.*[105] In *Studies*, Freud is clear that the goal of treatment "does not consist in extirpating something . . . but in causing the resistance to melt and in this way enabling the circulation to make its way into a region that has hitherto been cut off."[106] Once the circulation is restored, the pathogenic idea can be integrated into the ego. *The goal of treatment, in other words, is the expansion of the ego's integrative web.*

But there is another problem. Even when the ego resorts to defense rather than integration, it cannot completely carry out the defensive task. "Both the memory-trace and the affect which is attached to the idea," Freud observes, "are here once and for all." In the best-case scenario, the excitation attached to the idea is substantially weakened when it is banished to what Freud calls a "second psychical group" and is cut off from communication with consciousness and the ego.[107] Because repression is never complete, however, there is always the potential for what was repressed to return – that is, always the potential for psychopathology. The form which the return assumes determines the nature of the pathology: When the energy that was attached to the incompatible idea is channeled into physical pathways, for example, the result is the

---

[105] As we will see in Chapter 9, this idea will reappear in Freud's theory of mourning.

[106] Breuer and Freud, *Studies on hysteria*, 291.

[107] Freud, *The Neuro-Psychoses of defense*, 49. The idea of "a second psychical group" is the precursor of the concept of the unconscious.

conversion to the organic symptoms of hysteria; when a "false connection" is established and the energy becomes attached to an unrelated idea, the result is the compulsive ruminations of obsessional neurosis.

At this point in his thinking, Freud conceptualizes defense in quasi-intentional terms; he even refers to a "counter-will."[108] This distinguishes him from his French competitor, Pierre Janet, as well as from Breuer, who both saw pathology as a product of "splitting." They considered splitting an original phenomenon that does not result from the quasi-intentional actions of the ego, but that takes place without intentionality, simply as a result of the inherent weakness of the ego's capacities for integration. Freud offers a quotidian analogy to illustrate the concept of this splitting process:

Janet's hysterical patient reminds one of a feeble woman who has gone out shopping and is now returning home laden with a multitude of parcels and boxes. She cannot contain the whole heap of them with her two arms and ten fingers. So first of all one object slips from her grasp; and when she stoops to pick it up, another one escapes her in its place, and so on.[109]

Freud, in contrast, argues that the splitting one observes in psychopathology is a secondary phenomenon, brought about by the ego's quasi-willful defensive maneuvers. "*The splitting of the content of consciousness,*" he asserts, "*is the result of an act of will on the part of the patient.*" In short, it is motivated. Freud is not maintaining, however, that the patient's primary motive is "to bring about a splitting of consciousness." It is rather to get rid of the distressing incompatible idea. When the unacceptable idea is banished to the second psychical group splitting occurs as an unintended consequence.[110]

The intentional nature of defense has important clinical implications. In fact, it makes psychoanalytic psychotherapy possible. Because the

[108] Sigmund Freud, "A case of successful treatment by hypnotism" (1892–1893), *SE* 1: 122.

[109] Freud, *Five lectures on psychoanalysis*, 21-22. Like so many of the simplified binomial oppositions in psychoanalytic theory, the one between splitting and defense broke down over time and today splitting can be seen as a mechanism of defense, albeit a primitive one. At the same time, contemporary analysts also recognize the existence of splitting that results from ego weakness rather than active defense.

[110] Freud, *The Neuro-Psychoses of defense*, 46.

defense, which determines the symptomology, is meaningful and motivated, it can be clinically addressed and reversed.[111] The rejected idea can
be integrated into the ego's organization. Indeed, the "cure" consists in
the reintegration of the incompatible into the ego.

The clinical question that then emerged was this: How does one coun-
teract the defenses? Since the defenses are instituted by willful acts, Freud
argues that one must find a way to suspend the will and help patients
"free themselves from intentional thinking." Just as Anna O. helped
Breuer create the talking cure, Freud's patient Frau Emmy von N.
helped him discover a procedure for suspending intentional thinking: free
association. In response to Freud's insistent questioning, the spunky Frau
Emmy told the doctor that he "was not to keep on asking her where this
and that came from," but "to step out of the way to let her tell [him]
what she had to say."[112] When Freud complied, he found out that Frau
Emmy's spontaneous speech was not "as aimless as it would appear."
Although "roundabout," it often led to "pathogenic reminiscences" of
which she would unburden herself "without being asked to." Amazed,
the Professor observed, "It was as though she had adopted my procedure and was making use of our conversation, apparently unconstrained
and guided by chance, as a supplement to her hypnosis."[113] Freud came
to believe that free association – the patient's willfully unwillful effort to
disregard all censorship and give voice to every thought that occurs to his
or her consciousness – provided a means of neutralizing the ego's intentionality and unearthing the repressed thoughts that underlay a patient's
symptoms.[114]

---

[111] In this period, Freud conceived of this intentionality in conscious terms. The
person made a conscious decision to repress the incompatible idea. But as his career
progressed and his conception of defense became more sophisticated, the idea of
defense, while it remained intentional, became more and more unconscious until,
in *The ego and the id*, he arrived at a full-blown idea of unconscious defense. As a
result, the uniquely psychoanalytic task, which Freud approached from a number of different angles, became to explicate this peculiar notion of unconscious
intentionality.

[112] Breuer and Freud, *Studies on hysteria*, 63.

[113] *Ibid.*, 56.

[114] Though it involves a suspension of the will, free association is an active process. To
be sure, it requires a peculiar indeed paradoxical sort of activity – the willful suspension of the will. And, as such, it is diametrically opposed to the passivity of hypnosis.

Because it played such an important role in later controversies, one point should be underscored here. In addition to whatever intellectual factors might motivate a patient to struggle against the resistances and to free-associate, "an affective factor, the personal influence of the physician," was also essential. In fact, Freud observes that it "alone is in a position to remove the resistance" in a number of cases.[115] Freud did not consider this problematic. He argues that the patient's positive feelings for the doctor – what he later refers to as "the unobjectionable part of the transference" – is a factor not only in psychoanalysis, but in every form of medical treatment. He never fully recognized the tension between his desire to eliminate the use of suggestion and promote the patient's autonomy and his willingness to exploit the patient's positive transference to the therapist.

Freud introduced a concept that is believed to be his (and Breuer's) most important discovery in the closing passages of his contribution on therapy, namely, transference. Although he had assured Martha it would never happen, Freud discovered transference when, as we noted, it was unwittingly thrust upon him. He reports that one day, as a female patient awoke from hypnosis, "she threw her arms around [his] neck." Luckily, he declaims, the awkward situation was interrupted with "the unexpected entrance of a servant." Trying to understand what had transpired, Freud clung to the assumption he had made in his letter to Martha: he was unattractive. Since he "was modest enough not to attribute the event to [his] own irresistible personal attraction," he believed he had "now grasped the nature of the mysterious element that was at work behind hypnotism" – the hypnotic rapport or transference.[116] Indeed, Freud concluded that hypnotism not only obscured but also exploited what was to be analysed, the specific character of the transference. This was a central reason why he abandoned hypnotism.

Freud introduced the notion of a "false connection" to account for the transference. He explains how it works by citing a similar situation in which another female patient wanted to kiss him. In the course of treatment, a wish to kiss somebody from her past had emerged in consciousness, "without any memories of the surrounding circumstance which would

[115] Breuer and Freud, *Studies on hysteria*, 283.
[116] Freud, "An autobiographical study," 27.

have assigned it to a past time." Because of the mind's compulsion to form connections, the wish had to be attached to a figure in the present. Since Freud was a prominent person in the patient's current experience, the wish became attached to him; a "false connection" – a "*mésalliance*" – was thus made between a figure from the past and someone in her present-day life. Realizing that her wish from the past was incorrectly associated with him, Freud learned his lesson. Whenever a comparable situation occurred, he claimed that he was able to adopt an objective stance and "presume that transference and a false connection have once more taken place."[117]

The question of what constitutes Freud's fundamental discovery has been debated often: Was it the meaning of dreams, the existence of psychic reality, free association, or even the psychoanalytic setup itself? Of course, the question is impossible to answer, and the whole exercise is a bit puerile. Nevertheless, his discovery of the ubiquity of transference and the way it is enacted inside and outside of the psychoanalytic setting is certainly a prime candidate for this distinction. Freud himself spent most of the 1890s entangled in a many-sided and tumultuous transference-drama with Wilhelm Fliess, a speculatively inclined ear, nose, and throat specialist from Berlin. If Freud had until then struggled against the crime of speculative excess, when he met Fliess he discovered a willing accomplice – indeed, an energetic facilitator.

[117] Breuer and Freud, *Studies on hysteria*, 303.

5

A Theoretical Excursus

BEFORE TURNING TO THE development of psychoanalysis per se and the thoroughly untheoretical, which is to say the tumultuous, erotic and affective dimension of Freud's relationship to Wilhelm Fliess in which it developed, some theoretical considerations might prove helpful.[1]

When Hans Loewald set out to determine the implications of the pre-Oedipal turn for classical Freudian theory, he steered clear of the schismatic debates – often motivated as much by psychoanalytic politics as by theoretical considerations – that were widespread in the field in the decades following the Second World War. Instead of debating the primacy of Oedipal versus pre-Oedipal development – of the paternal versus the maternal dimension of psychic life – he asked a different question: What is the relationship between the two phases of development, and how do they become hierarchically structured in the psyche? It was in pursuit of these questions that Loewald introduced the distinction between Freud's "official" and "unofficial" positions, and it is within that scheme that I will structure my narrative of Freud's life and work.[2]

Both positions can be elucidated across three dimensions: reality and the ego, the psychic apparatus and the pleasure principle, and mastery and maturity.

In Freud's "official" position, the "relationship between the organism and environment, between individual and reality," Loewald observes,

---

[1] While this theoretical discussion is intended to make the underlying orientation of this biography more perspicuous, it is not essential and may be skipped by the less technically inclined reader.

[2] See Joel Whitebook, "Hans Loewald: a radical conservative," *International Journal of Psycho-analysis* 85 (2004), 97–115.

centers on the father and is "understood as antagonistic."[3] The "primal psychical situation" that exists at the beginning of development is envisioned as one of separation and opposition. It pictures a self-enclosed infantile psychism, governed exclusively by one set of principles, opposed to an external "reality" that operates according to a different set of principles.[4] This picture of the initial stage of development gives rise to the impossible theoretical task of explaining how a primitive psyche thus conceived could break out of its monadic enclosure, turn to reality, and form a relationship with the "object." The notorious "pessimism" of Freud's late "cultural" writings – in which he argues that the "programme" of the pleasure principle that "dominates the operation of the mental apparatus from the start" is "at loggerheads with the world" – is in fact a logical consequence of this "official" conception of the relation of the psyche and reality.[5]

If the "official" position views reality as external and hostile to the psyche, then it follows that the ego's primary function is understood as defense. The ego's task is to protect the psyche from the dangers emanating from its (inner and outer) world. Its *synthetic function* – that is, its capacity to *integrate* reality rather than defend against it – is, if not entirely overlooked, largely minimalized.

Freud's "official" position contains two closely related theses: that the father comprises the primary representative of reality and that the child's entrance into reality is essentially violent. First, during the pre-Oedipal period, the father intrudes into and breaks up the infant's dyadic, symbiotic, and libidinous relationship with the early mother of the oral phase – the so-called breast-mother – thereby forcing the child to turn to the external world for gratification. Later, the violent induction into reality culminates with the "resolution" of the Oedipus complex, when the boy – "official" theory is almost exclusively concerned with the boy – under the threat of paternal castration, renounces the mother as an object of phallic desire, submits to the father, and is offered identification with him as compensation for his renunciation. Because this resolution results in a qualitative advance in internalization and in the structuralization of the psyche, it is seen as a major advance in the solidification of the ego and its relation to reality.

---

[3] Loewald, "Defense and reality," 28.

[4] Freud, "Instincts and their vicissitudes," 134.

[5] Sigmund Freud, *Civilization and its discontents*, 76.

Freud's "official" theory, which subscribes to a "discharge" or "tension-reduction" model of the mental apparatus, contains three inter-related postulates. The central task of the psychic apparatus, defined by the "constancy principle," is to reduce stimuli to a minimal point or to zero – that is, eliminate it completely. Because it accomplishes this task by "discharging" – "getting rid of" – instinctual stimuli, the tension-reduction model is an "exclusionary" model of the mental apparatus. The "constancy principle" is logically connected with the "pleasure/unpleasure" or simply the "pleasure principle," which defines pleasure as a decrease and "unpleasure" (pain) as an increase in tension. (The psycho-sexual roots of this *exclusionary* model are, it should be noted, located in the oral phase, where the baby *spits out* everything it experiences as unpleasant and retains everything it finds pleasurable.) Rather than growing through the integration of instinctual stimuli into itself, the exclusionary ego develops by ejecting such stimuli from its boundaries, which is to say, by narrowing rather than expanding its domain.

Freud first articulated his "official" model in 1895, when he wrote the *Project for a scientific psychology*. It was not until 1920, in *Beyond the pleasure principle*, that he was compelled to introduce a qualitatively new concept, *eros* – conceived as a countervailing synthetic force in mental life that strives to create greater unities by integrating and binding energy – into his thinking. Then in 1924, when his theory entered a profound crisis, with great reluctance Freud was forced to acknowledge the existence of "pleasurable tensions and the unpleasurable relaxation of tensions."[6] While these developments negated the fundamental postulates of his "official" doctrine, Freud did not pursue their implications with much vigor – something that would have resulted in a fuller articulation of his "unofficial" position.

Freud's "official" concept of maturity, Loewald argues, is a product of the nineteenth century's belief in "the dignity of science" – that is, the belief that, ontogenetically and phylogenetically, the scientific stage of development represents "a stage of human evolution not previously reached." According to Loewald, "scientific man is considered by [the official – JW] Freud as the most advanced form of human development"

---

[6] See Sigmund Freud, *Project for a scientific psychology* (1897), *SE* 1: 283–398, and "The economic problem of masochism" (1924), *SE* 19: 160.

and "has its counterpart in the individual's stage of maturity."[7] In his "official" mode, Freud in other words elevated the perspective of modern science into a prescription for both collective and individual development.

As many philosophers and social theorists have argued, the modern scientific world-picture contains the domination of nature as one of its innermost possibilities. *"Mastery" in this context thus means "domination."* When the scientific idea of maturity is postulated as the goal of individual development and psychoanalytic practice, the concept of *mastery qua domination* is implicitly posited at the same time.[8] When mastery thus conceived is directed outwards, it results in the domination of outer nature; the imperious ego attempts to unify the "multifariousness" of external nature under its principles. When it is directed inwards, the outcome is the domination of "inner nature," where the ego subjects the diffuseness of unconscious-instinctual life to its unifying principles.[9] It is important to note that both cases involve the forced integration of the heterogeneous – "bad synthesis."

Freud's "official" notion of maturity envisages what the philosopher, psychoanalyst, and social theorist Cornelius Castoriadis calls a "power grab," in which the more "advanced" strata of the psyche dominate the more "primitive": the ego dominates the id, consciousness dominates the unconscious, realistic thinking dominates fantasy thinking, cognition dominates affect, activity dominates passivity, and the civilized part of the personality dominates the instincts.[10] This official notion led to two of

---

[7] Hans Loewald, "On the therapeutic action of psychoanalysis," *The essential Loewald: collected papers and monographs* (Hagerstown, MD: University Publishing Group, 2000) 228.

[8] On psychoanalysis as "a technique of emancipation" as opposed to "a technique of domination" see Paul Ricoeur "Technique and nontechnique in interpretation," *The conflict of interpretations: essays and hermeneutics*, ed. Don Ihde, trans. Willis Domingo (Evanston, IL: Northwestern University Press, 2007), 177–195.

[9] A central thesis of the Frankfurt School, which provided the basis of their attempt to integrate psychoanalysis and critical theory, was that *the domination of external nature and the domination of internal nature mutually entail one another*. See especially Horkheimer and Adorno, *Dialectic of enlightenment*. See also Joel Whitebook, *Perversion and utopia: a study in psychoanalysis and critical theory* (Cambridge, MA: The MIT Press, 1996), chapter 3.

[10] Cornelius Castoriadis, *The imaginary institution of society*, trans. Kathleen Blamey (Cambridge, MA: The MIT Press, 1987), 104. See also Hans Loewald, "Ego and

Freud's more objectionable proclamations. In the first, he likened the work of analysis (and the work of civilization) to "the draining of the Zuider Zee." Maturity would thus consist in a state where all the "primitive" sludge of unconscious-instinctual life has been dredged out of mental life.[11] The second problematic remark is contained in "Why war," his exchange with Albert Einstein. Although Freud admits the proposition was utopian, he nevertheless declares that in principle "a dictatorship of reason" represents the "ideal" solution to the human predicament – as though he was totally unaware of the critique of reason to which he had made such a substantial contribution.[12]

Freud's "unofficial" position centers on the figure of the mother and holds that psychic life begins not with separation but with relatedness and unity. Likewise, from the "maternal" perspective, reality is viewed as neither external nor hostile to the psyche. "The primal psychical situation" is envisaged as what Mahler calls a "dual unity," in which mother and child are in some sense symbiotically "merged," but which also contains ego precursors that are the seeds of the infant's differentiation that constitute the precursors of the ego.[13] Equipped with innate developmental potentialities, children, when they experience otherness (canonically in the form of hunger), begin to *differentiate out* of – "detach" themselves from – the dual unity, and the ego precursors that are contained in the relatively undifferentiated state begin to develop into the mature ego.[14]

Where Freud's "official" paternal position begins with separation – that is, the self-enclosed psychic monad confronting an external object – and must explain how the infant can break out of its monad and establish a

---

reality," *The essential Loewald: collected papers and monographs* (Hagerstown, MD: University Publishing Group, 2000), 20.

[11] Sigmund Freud, *New introductory lessons on psycho-analysis* (1933), *SE* 22: 80.

[12] Sigmund Freud, "Why war" (1933), *SE* 22: 215. Jonathan Lear observes that in *The Republic* Plato advocates the same "oligarchic" model for integrating the *polis* and the psyche. In both cases, unity is achieved when "the rational element" expels the entity's disruptive and undesirable contents, that is, the poets and the drives, from its domain. Jonathan Lear, "Inside and outside *The Republic*," *Open minded* (Cambridge, MA: Harvard University Press, 1998), 219–246.

[13] Mahler, Bergmann, and Pine, *The psychological birth of the infant*, 55. Loewald uses a similar term: "undifferentiated psychical field."

[14] In this respect, the unofficial position also involves an element of pain. See Freud, *Civilization and its discontents*, 68.

relation with the object, the maternal perspective begins with unity, and separation emerges out of it. Once the process of separation has been set in motion, the nascent ego is faced with a new task: to reintegrate the equally nascent object – that is, to integrate what has become external reality – which has also emerged in the process of the differentiation. This alternation of differentiation from and reintegration of the object, Loewald argues, establishes the lifelong developmental process through which the psyche must continually negotiate and renegotiate its relation to reality – its separateness from and relatedness to the object. If this process comes to a halt, development becomes arrested, and one of the central tasks of clinical psychoanalysis is to set it back into motion. Indeed, while the arrest of this developmental process is one way to define psychopathology, its complete cessation would constitute psychic death.

If Freud's "official" position conceptualizes the primary function of the ego as *defense*, his "unofficial" position understands it as *synthesis*. "What distinguishes the ego," he writes, "is a tendency to synthesis in its contents, to a combination and unification in its mental processes."[15] As opposed to the "exclusionary" model where the unity of the ego is achieved through expelling or getting rid of psychic material, in this case the ego integrates itself by preserving the material of unconscious-instinctual life and holding it together, synthesizing it into larger and more differentiated unities.

For Freud, the plenum-like existence of the "primal psychical situation" – which is devoid of otherness, privation, and negativity and where each instinctual demand is "magically" eliminated by the mother's ministrations as soon as it arises – defines perfection.[16] Once that undifferentiated plenum has been dissolved, memory traces of it, as Castoriadis observes, exert a continuous "magnetic attraction" on the psyche, and this leads to our lifelong striving to recapture its perfection in one form or another. In addition to whatever neurological processes underpin the process, these memories constitute the developmental source of "the irresistible advance towards unity in mental life."[17] That Freud did not systematically address

---

[15] Freud, *New introductory lectures on psycho-analysis*, 76.

[16] The way Freud characterizes the perfect state of primary narcissism invites comparison with the way Aristotle describes the autarchic perfection of god as a *nous theos*.

[17] Freud, *Group psychology and the analysis of the ego*, 105.

this unifying conatus in psychic life until he introduced the concept of *eros* in the 1920s – and then did so only hesitatingly and inadequately – will be especially significant for our account of his intellectual biography.[18]

When the exclusionary/discharge model of the psychic apparatus was modified, it became necessary, Winnicott recognized, to reconceptualize the concept of pleasure that had been contained in it.[19] Winnicott attempted to do this by introducing a distinction between "climactic" and "nonclimactic" pleasure. The first is what Freud had in mind with the pleasure/unpleasure principle. It is tied to the demands of the body, equates pleasure with the reduction of tension, and corresponds to the discharge model of the psychic apparatus. The classic prototype is the satiated infant at the mother's breast after she has gratified his bodily needs.

The second type of pleasure, nonclimactic or "ego pleasure," as Winnicott describes it, lacks "instinctual backing" and has "no discharge."[20] The paradigm crisis that Freud's drive-reduction model of the psychic apparatus experienced in 1924 forced him to admit the existence not only of "nonclimactic" pleasures, but also of "pleasurable tensions."[21] To acknowledge an *increase of tension could itself be pleasurable*, however, was to implicitly negate the pleasure principle, one of the fundamental axioms of his entire theory. But Freud did not pursue the consequences of his new formulations in much detail, for to do so would have entailed a radical reformulation of his position that he was not prepared to undertake.

It should be pointed out that to deny tension can be pleasurable leads to an unacceptable conclusion, namely, that ego functioning and psychological development, which consist in the binding and synthesizing of the contents of unconscious-instinctual life and require an increase of tension, are only painful. It is impossible, in other words, to conceive of growth as in any sense a pleasurable process.

---

[18] See Jonathan Lear, "The introduction of eros: reflections on the work of Hans Loewald," *Journal of the American Psychoanalytic Association* 4 (1996), 673–698.

[19] See D.W. Winnicott, "The location of cultural experience," *International Journal of Psycho-analysis* 48 (1967), 369–370. See also Loewald, "Sublimation: inquiries into theoretical psychoanalysis," *The essential Loewald: collected papers and monographs* (Hagerstown, MD: University Publishing Group, 2000), 468; Ricoeur, *Freud and philosophy*, 322; and Castoriadis, *The imaginary institution of society*, 315.

[20] Winnicott, "The location of cultural experience," 369–370.

[21] See Freud, "The economic problem of masochism," 157–170.

By replacing the discharge/exclusionary model of the psyche with an inclusionary model, recognizing the ego's synthetic or integrative tasks alongside its purely defensive functions, and rejecting the equation of pleasure with tension-reduction, the "unofficial" theory also entails a reconceptualization of the "official" concepts of mastery and maturity, which, as we have noted, can be partly traced to the modern scientific worldview. "I believe it to be necessary and timely," Loewald writes, "to question the assumption, handed to us from the nineteenth century, that the scientific approach to the world and the self represents" the highest and most "mature evolutionary stage of man."[22] Loewald in fact goes further and suggests that "in its dominant current . . . psychoanalytic theory has unwittingly taken over much of the obsessive neurotic's" notion of the relation of the ego and reality – where maturity is defined as the ego's domination over the other dimensions of psychic life – and made it its own.[23] In other words, it has elevated a *pathological* conception of ego-formation into a *prescriptive* one. Moreover, the mature *qua* obsessional model of the ego – encapsulated in the Zuider Zee metaphor – is not only "an inaccessible objective" but also, as Castoriadis maintains, undesirable *in the extreme*.

How [he asks] can we conceive of a subject that would have entirely "absorbed" the imaginative function [tied to unconscious-instinctual life – JW], how could we dry up this spring in the depths of ourselves from which flow both alienating phantasies and free creation truer than truth, unreal deliria and surreal poems, the eternally new [and] how can we eliminate what is at the base of, or, in any case what is inextricably bound up with what makes us human beings – our symbolic function, which presupposes our capacity to see and to think in a thing something which is not?[24]

However, as opposed to romantics like Georg Groddeck (the man for whom the term "wild analyst" was coined) and the young Michel Foucault, the point is not to idealize unconscious-instinctual life – to celebrate the "demonic" and ignore its dark side. It is rather to recognize that it constitutes a repository of material that is essential for human flourishing.

---

[22] Loewald, "On the therapeutic action of psychoanalysis," 228.

[23] Loewald, "Defense and reality," 30.

[24] Castoriadis, *The imaginary institution of society*, 104.

That material, however, must be symbolized, sublimated, and integrated into "new synthetic organizations" of the psyche in which the "vital links" between "the lowest" and the "highest in human nature" are preserved.[25]

Mastery in this case, Loewald suggests, consists not in "domination" but in "coming to terms" with the material of unconscious-instinctual life by representing and articulating it.[26] Instincts are not dammed up or excluded, but channeled and organized in order to create richer and more differentiated structures of the psyche.

It must be emphasized that, in criticizing Freud's "official" doctrine, Loewald is not suggesting that we simply replace it with his "unofficial" position. The way to correct the one-sided hypostatization of Oedipal theory over pre-Oedipal is not, he observes, to substitute "a paternal concept of reality" with "a maternal one" – or, as André Green puts it somewhat more graphically, to replace "the Father of the horde with the Great Mother Goddess."[27] The psyche's central task is to achieve optimal integration with reality; contrariwise, the primary threat it faces is the loss of reality integration via the loss of the self or via the loss of the object. With regard to this task and its accompanying danger, the "paternal" and "maternal" perspectives each have their complementary advantages and disadvantages, and they themselves must be *integrated* into a more encompassing position.

Because the paternal castration threat contains its own dangers vis-à-vis reality integration, it is incorrect to consider it as "the prototype of reality" *as such*. But not to recognize it as "one factor in the constitution of reality" is also incorrect.[28] The father's intervention into the relatively undifferentiated infant–mother matrix, as we have seen, initiates the process through which the ego and reality differentiate out from each other.

The danger with the paternal perspective, however, is that the integration of psyche and reality will misfire because *too much distance* is created between ego and object. In that case, we are confronted with the classical Oedipal configuration, which envisages a detached imperious ego standing over against an objectified world that has been so roundly criticized by

---

[25] Loewald, *Sublimation*, 453.

[26] *Ibid.*, 461.

[27] Loewald, "Ego and reality," 14, and Green, *On private madness*, 253.

[28] Loewald, "Ego and reality," 14.

feminists, anti-positivists, and ecologists. The ego's apparent sovereignty is deceptive, for insofar as they have lost their relatedness to one another, both the ego and the object are relatively lost in the Oedipal constellation. Contrary to what might be assumed, ego and the object develop not in opposition to each other, but through their mutual integration.[29]

The paternal configuration, however, is not solely negative, nor is it entirely hostile. The danger that arises with the maternal perspective is the obverse of the one we have examined with the Oedipal structure: Reality integration can fail because of insufficient separation and distance. Since the maternal situation begins with a merger-like state, relatedness is not a problem; it is there *ab initio*. Difficulties arise when the ego fails to differentiate itself adequately or when, once it has achieved a degree of separation, the archaic mother's Siren song sucks it back and it merges into the maternal matrix. If the threat in the paternal case is *castration*, the danger in the maternal one is the loss of self and object through *reengulfment* by "the overpowering, annihilating mother." In short,

the original unity and identity, undifferentiated and unstructured, of psychic apparatus and environment is as much of a danger for the ego as the demand of the "paternal castration threat" to give it up altogether.[30]

It is at this point that the "positive non-hostile side of the father figure" comes into view: "Against the threatening possibility of remaining in or sinking back into the structureless unity from which the ego emerged stands the powerful paternal force."[31] To use Lacan's terminology, the "significance of the phallus" resides in its creation of a barrier between the incipient ego and the archaic "imaginary" mother.[32] Furthermore, in addition to his castration threat, the father also invites his son to identify with him as an "active, nonpassive" figure who can resist the mother's regressive pull.[33]

---

[29] For this reason the opposition of ego psychology to object relations theory is spurious.

[30] Loewald, "Ego and reality," 15.

[31] *Ibid.*, 15.

[32] Jacques Lacan, "The significance of the phallus," *Écrits*, trans. Bruce Fink et al. (New York: W.W. Norton and Co., 2006), 575–584.

[33] Loewald, "Ego and reality," 16.

Loewald pulls together the different strands of his analysis of "the profoundly ambivalent relation with parent figures at work in the constitution
of ego and reality."[34] On the one hand, "the unstructured nothingness"
that would result from the dedifferentiation of "ego" and "reality" – from
the dissolution of the *prinicipium individuationis* – in maternal reengulfment "represents a threat" that is "as deep and frightening as the paternal
castration threat." Both entail a loss of reality. "Reality is lost if the ego
is cut off from objects (castration threat)," and it "is lost as well if the
boundaries of the ego and object are lost (the threat of the womb)."[35]
As Loewald observes, "the ego pursues its course of integrating
reality" and displays its "remarkable striving toward unification and
synthesis" by navigating between these two dangers.[36] He also calls our
attention to one final paradox that points to the thorough ambivalence of
the concept of "unity." The same original experience of unity that occurs
in the "primary psychical situation" and, when it is projected ahead of the
ego, posits the *telos* of development as *differentiation*, *structuralization*, and
synthesis, also poses the greatest threat to development – that is, regression back into that *undifferentiated* and *unstructured* unity. The question is:
in what manner is that *telos* pursued?

Loewald's elucidation of Freud's "unofficial" position and his call for
the integration of the paternal and maternal, Oedipal and pre-Oedipal
perspectives on reality constitute a rejection of the "power grab" model
of maturity. Maturity can no longer be understood as the domination of
the supposedly more advanced strata of the psyche over the supposedly
more archaic; rather, it must be reconceptualized, as Castoriadis observes,
as involving "another relation between" them.[37] "The so-called fully
developed, mature ego," Loewald observes,

is not one that has become fixated at the presumably highest or latest stages of
development, having left the other behind it, but is an ego that integrates its
reality in such a way that the earlier and deeper levels of ego-reality integration
remain alive as dynamic sources of higher organization.[38]

---

[34] *Ibid.*, 17.

[35] *Ibid.*, 16.

[36] *Ibid.*, 17.

[37] Castoriadis, *The imaginary institution of society*, 104.

[38] Loewald, "Ego and reality," 20.

Freud makes a similar suggestive observation relatively *en passant* in *Inhibitions, symptoms and anxiety*, when he asserts that too much distance between the ego and the id is as pathological as too little. "The ego," he notes, "is an organization," and ideally it aims at maintaining "free intercourse" with all the other parts of the psyche so that they can "reciprocally influence" each other.[39] Unfortunately, he does not explore this ideal in sufficient detail.

Whatever the case, Freud's use of the term "intercourse" implies that the goal of development is not "an attained state" but, Castoriadis argues, an ongoing "active situation," in which the individual is "unceasingly involved in the movement of taking up again" the contents of his psychic life and reworking them into richer and more differentiated synthetic configurations. It does not, in other words, comprise a state of "'awareness' achieved once and for all," where the ego has established its dominance over the "lower" parts of the psyche. Rather, the aim is to institute "*another relation* between the conscious and the unconscious, between lucidity and the function of the imaginary ... *another attitude* of the subject with respect to himself or herself, in a profound modification of the activity–passivity mix, of the sign under which this takes place, of the respective place of the two elements that compose it."[40] Far from a "dictatorship of reason," what is being suggested is a less repressive organization of the psyche, a more propitious integration of its heterogeneous parts.

We remain loyal to Freud's intentions not by slavishly repeating and defending his ideas, but by subjecting them to an immanent critique and critically reappropriating them. One of the central aims of this intellectual biography is to do just that. It is too easy to find the mistakes in Freud's thinking; they are manifold and all-too-familiar. But this can also be said of Plato and Kant. The more fruitful enterprise is to elucidate the inner tensions in his project – in the problematic that he has bequeathed us – so that we can address its deficiencies and advance it beyond the point where Freud reached the unavoidable limits of his background and his personality.

With these theoretical considerations in mind, let us turn to the concrete history of Freud's creation of psychoanalysis.

---

[39] Sigmund Freud, *Inhibitions, symptoms and anxiety* (1926), *SE* 20: 98.

[40] Castoriadis, *The imaginary institution of society*, 104.

6

"Dear Magician"

Passion and Knowledge

When the feminist theorist Shirley Nelson Garner read the complete and uncensored edition of Freud's *Letters to Fliess* for the first time, she experienced a not uncommon reaction. "What was most apparent – and surprising – to me," she reports, "was that they are love letters." A "careful rereading" did not change her mind."[1]

Garner is right. Breger has observed that Wilhelm Fliess, an ear, nose, and throat specialist who lived in Berlin and had a penchant for extravagant speculations, was "the great love of Freud's adult life."[2] Indeed, it is not going too far to describe this love as an *amour fou*. With its nasal surgeries, cocaine use, numerological pseudo-science, homoerotic infatuation, ideas about male menstruation, quest for the perfect means of contraception, pitched battles over Freud's beloved cigars, egregious mistreatment of a female patient, grandiose flattery, and self-important scientific "congresses," their relationship at times assumed a level of "madness" that far exceeded the merely eccentric.

Yet, as this chapter will argue, that madness played an essential constitutive role as the medium through which Freud discovered psychoanalysis. That Freud, like the rest of us, was fashioned out of what Kant called "the crooked timber of humanity" out of which "no straight thing was ever made" is not an embarrassment that must be suppressed, although many "rationalists" – both detractors and defenders of Freud – seek to suppress it on the grounds that psychoanalysis must be immune to

---

[1] Shirley Nelson Garner, "Freud and Fliess: homophobia and seduction," *Seduction and theory*, ed. Dianne Hunter (Chicago, University of Illinois Press, 1989), 86.

[2] Breger, *Freud*, 152.

171

"irrational" passion.[3] In fact, only by rejecting the rationalist assumption that knowledge and passion are incompatible is it possible to develop a truly psychoanalytic stance, which is to say one that strives to be neutral, toward the founder of the field.

At the same time that we would become free to acknowledge the full extent of that crookedness, we would also be invited to explore "one of the most fascinating secrets of human nature" – namely, how Freud's wondrous achievements could have been hewn out of such "lowly" material. *The wondrousness of his accomplishments is in fact directly proportional to the crookedness of the timber.* In a supposedly radical stratagem that is old as the Greek Skeptics, Freud's adversaries often turn the methods of psychoanalysis back on the first psychoanalyst. And there is nothing wrong with this move per se. However, where his opponents seek to deploy the resources of psychoanalysis in a reductionist way in order "to blacken [Freud] . . . and drag [him] into the dust," those resources can also be deployed in the opposite way: to elucidate the genesis of his accomplishments.[4] That is what the relationship with Fliess illustrates. The really hard task for psychoanalysis is to produce a theory which is genetic (or genealogical) and non-reductionist at the same time.

Freud's relationship to Fliess was the heir to the passionate stage of his relationship with Martha. Gay suggests in fact that the emotional deficit in their marriage "virtually made Fliess necessary."[5] Freud met Fliess a year after he married Martha and put an end to the agonizing deprivation caused by his prolonged betrothal. Freud hoped that his marriage would free him from the agony and despair he had suffered during the seemingly interminable engagement. But, as Breger observes, a year after the wedding, not only did the "inner turmoil" that Freud had hoped the marriage would alleviate "remain," but "in fact, his anxiety, depression, and physical complaints got worse." When Freud met Fliess, he turned to him to fulfill "the inner yearnings" that had remained unsatisfied in his marriage.[6] The effect of the meeting was similar to that Freud experienced

[3] Immanuel Kant, "Idea of a universal history with a cosmopolitan intent," *Kant: political writings, second edition,* ed. Hans Reiss, trans. H.B. Nisbet (Cambridge: Cambridge University Press, 1991), 46 (translation altered).

[4] Freud, *Leonardo,* 63 n. 1.

[5] Gay, *Freud: a life for our time,* 61.

[6] Breger, *Freud,* 96.

when he first encountered Martha in his parents' living room at the age of twenty-six, an encounter that unleashed a torrent of emotions that had been under control for years through his submitting to the strict discipline of Brücke's laboratory. Meeting Fliess at thirty-one similarly released the repressed and split-off contents of his unconscious-instinctual life, which surged to the surface, increasingly focusing on Fliess as their primary object.

Once released, "the eruptive emotionality" he had struggled "most to master" fueled the fires of his relationship to Fliess and, concomitantly, of his self-analysis as well as of the creation of a radically new discipline.[7] One can argue that, without the sheer madness of Freud's relation to Fliess, psychoanalysis, as we know it, would not have been created. It provided the medium through which his great discoveries took place. It is possible that the process could have followed a different course. But Freud in fact achieved what autonomy was available to him, given his constitution, familial constellation, and socio-historical background, by first passing through a prolonged and extreme state of abject heteronomy in relation to Fliess.

In principle, the fact that Freud's monumental achievements grew out of his passionate entanglement with Fliess should not present a problem for psychoanalysts. Like the Plato of the *Phaedrus*, psychoanalysis does not hold that an intrinsic opposition exists between passion and knowledge. To be sure, when it is not contained, sublimated, and articulated, passion *can* fatally interfere with our attempt to know (or create). But the opposition between the two is a contingent possibility, not a necessity. Going further, the Platonic-psychoanalytic tradition does not only deny the existence of an inherent opposition between passion and knowledge, it also holds *that the right sort of passion* – "divine madness," *theia mania* as Socrates referred to it in that dialogue – is a necessary condition for creativity of any magnitude. And Freud's *amour fou* with Fliess, despite its unseemly side, should be viewed as the right kind of madness that was necessary for the creation of psychoanalysis.[8] Castoriadis provides us

---

[7] Gay, *Freud: a life for our time*, 61.

[8] See Plato, *The Phaedrus*, trans. Alexander Nehamas and Paul Woodruff (Indianapolis, IN: Hackett, 1995), 26–27.

with empirical examples refuting the claim that passion and knowledge are incompatible:

> Of course, one can easily contradict this line of reasoning [which holds that passion and knowledge are intrinsically opposed] with the obvious fact that all great works of knowledge have been motivated by a single-minded passion and tyrannical absorption in a single object – from Archimedes, whose death was a result of his unwillingness (in the face of enemy attack) to leave behind the latest experiment on which he was working, to the feverish mathematical writings of Evariste Galois, hastily penned on the night preceding his fatal duel.[9]

Freud's beloved Plato made another argument that accords with the views of psychoanalysis. He maintained that "divine madness" is closely related to *eros* (erotic desire), another Janus-faced phenomenon. We need only recall the story of Helen and the Trojan War to remind ourselves of the havoc that *eros* – with its potential for *hubris* (comparable to the psychoanalytic idea of omnipotence) – can wreak in human affairs. At the same time, in *The Symposium* Plato also sought to demonstrate that erotic strivings are an indispensable medium for attaining the highest forms of knowledge.

This Platonic-psychoanalytic position stands in stark contrast to the beliefs of most philosophers and scientists in what we may call the rationalist tradition as well as to the representatives of "common sense." The rationalists, as Castoriadis observes, are convinced that passion and knowledge "are mutually contradictory terms" and that the attempt to "unite" them is "absurd." Rationalists believe that "passion . . . can only disturb or corrupt the real work of knowledge, which demands detachment and cool-headedness"; as an inevitable source of interference and distortion in the pursuit of knowledge, passion exerts a distorting influence that must be methodologically neutralized.[10] The rationalist tradition therefore assumes that to demonstrate that a piece of knowledge or a cultural object has grown out of passion is ipso facto to invalidate it. According to this view, "the higher," as Nietzsche puts it, "is not *permitted* to grow out of the lower" – indeed, "is not permitted to grow at all."[11] Freud, in marked

[9] Cornelius Castoriadis, "Passion and knowledge," *Diogenes* 40 (1992), 76.

[10] *Ibid.*, 76.

[11] Friedrich Nietzsche, *Twilight of the idols: or how to philosophize with a hammer*, trans. Richard Polt (Indianapolis, IN: Hackett, 1997), 19.

contrast, views the process through which "higher things" emerge out of "lower things" – "second nature" out of "first nature" – as "one of the most fascinating secrets of human nature."[12]

Despite their heated and seemingly interminable debates, the Freud-bashers and the keepers of the faith in fact fit together hand-in-glove. Freud's most obstreperous opponents and his staunchest defenders share the rationalist assumption that by demonstrating that a cultural achievement arose out of the "slime of history," one nullifies its validity.[13] Both sides in the Freud Wars agree that if some of Freud's most important accomplishments could be traced to the "abnormal" or "pathological" parts of his personality and/or that his treatment of family members, colleagues, and patients, at times, could be shown as less than exemplary – even downright scandalous – then Freud's creation, psychoanalysis, would be discredited.

There is, needless to say, one difference between the two camps. Where Freud's adversaries are eager to carry out that demonstration in order to debunk him, his defenders are equally keen to block its execution in order to protect his professional and personal standing. For obvious reasons, Freud's relationship with Fliess – and, to a lesser degree, his relationship with Jung – constitutes an *experimentum crucis* for both parties. Because of its sheer madness – especially the egregious way the two respectable physicians treated their mutual patient Emma Eckstein – Gay calls it "the most dismaying episode" in Freud's life, and Freud's adversaries often adduce it as a clincher that, they believe, discredits Freud as a person and psychoanalysis full stop.[14]

The guardians of Freud's legacy did not heed the principle their leader enunciated at the beginning of *Leonardo* – which he at times honored only in the breach – in an attempt to preempt the charge that he was pathologizing the Renaissance genius. That principle states that "there is no one so great as to be disgraced by being subject to the laws which govern both normal and pathological activity with equal cogency."[15] In the

---

[12] Freud, *Leonardo*, 130.

[13] See Jean-Paul Sartre, *Being and Nothingness*, trans. Hazel Barnes (New York: Washington Square Press, 1956), 604–612.

[14] Gay, *Freud: a life for our time*, 82.

[15] Freud, *Leonardo*, 59.

decades following Freud's death, members of the inner circle of the Freud establishment were convinced that his enemies were numerous, determined, and a serious threat to his legacy and to institutionalized psychoanalysis. (Although the way the Freud establishment chose to deal with the threat is problematic, given the conservative climate of the 1950s, their worries were not entirely unfounded.) They therefore sought to deprive Freud's critics of potentially compromising material that might be used as ammunition against him. In their zeal to conceal the "lowly origins" out of which Freud's achievements had arisen, the keepers of the flame adopted a strategy of stringent censorship and repression. While the situation has improved, to this day, they continue to prevent countless documents and letters – many crucial for a scholarly understanding of psychoanalysis – from being examined.

Because publication of a complete and unexpurgated edition of Freud's letters to Fliess would have revealed how completely *meshuga* Freud was at times during the 1890s not to mention the scope and intensity of his homosexual infatuation with his colleague in Berlin, the full extent of his cocaine use – which, *contra* Jones, lasted until 1896 and only stopped at the time of his father's death – and the unforgiveable mistreatment of Emma Eckstein, the members of the Freud establishment blocked the publication of the letters for a full thirty-three years. The 284 letters that comprise Freud's half of the correspondence survived thanks to the efforts of Marie Bonaparte, a Greek and Danish princess and one of Freud's most devoted followers, who lived in Paris.

When Reinhold Stahl, a Berlin art dealer and bookseller who had purchased Freud's half of the correspondence from Fliess's widow in 1933, was in the French capital trying to evade the Nazis, he offered to sell them to the Princess. Immediately perceiving their signifcance, she purchased them and transported them to Vienna, where she deposited them in the Rothschild Bank. After the *Anschluss*, when the letters were no longer safe in a Jewish establishment, Bonaparte used the immunity with which her royalty endowed her to remove them from her safety deposit box, with the Gestapo looking on, and then to take them to Paris. There she deposited them in a vault at the Danish embassy, where they safely remained throughout the war. When Bonaparte informed Freud that she was in possession of his half of the correspondence, he asked that the letters be destroyed. Given their intimate subject matter and revealing nature, one can understand Freud's reticence about the letters ever seeing the light of day, but Bonaparte recognized that they also constituted a treasure trove for anyone interested not only in the creation of psychoanalysis, but also in the psychology of scientific creativity in general. She therefore contravened the wishes of the man she loved and to whom she was devoted, and she preserved the letters for posterity.

After Germany's surrender, the letters were transported across the English Channel – securely wrapped in a watertight package that would float to the surface in case the ship struck an errant mine – and transferred to a conflicted Anna Freud at her home at Marsefield Gardens. Like Bonaparte, Anna recognized that the interest of science constituted a compelling reason for disregarding her father's wishes, but she also wanted to protect his image. She therefore came up with a compromise. In 1950, long after Freud's death, in conjunction with Bonaparte and Ernst Kris, an eminent Viennese art historian and psychoanalyst who became one of the leaders of the New York Ego Psychologists, Freud's daughter published a limited and extensively edited collection of the correspondence in German that excluded what the three considered to be the compromising material. The English translation, published in 1954, is entitled *The origins of psychoanalysis.*[16]

After Anna's death, Jeffrey Masson retranslated the letters and published a complete edition, which appeared in 1985. And that publication in fact had the effect that the Freud Establishment predicted and feared. Freud's detractors quickly latched on to the controversial material contained in the letters and deployed it in an attempt to discredit Freud's achievements of the 1890s – that is, during the period he was laying the foundations of psychoanalysis – thereby, as the detractors believed, subverting the building blocks of psychoanalysis itself.

Freud's "Creative Illness"

Two steps are therefore required to gain a proper understanding of Freud's relationship with Fliess: the assumption that passion and knowledge are intrinsically opposed must be rejected, and Freud's *amour fou* with Fliess must be understood as a case of "divine madness." This makes it possible undefensively and unapologetically to acknowledge the full

[16] Marie Bonaparte, Anna Freud, and Ernst Kris (eds.), *The origins of psychoanalysis: letters to Wilhelm Fliess*, trans. Eric Mosbacher and James Strachey (New York: Basic Books, 1954).

extent of Freud's "madness" and to explore its essential role as a medium in which psychoanalysis was created. Even Ernest Jones, Freud's official biographer – or hagiographer, if one listens to his critics – who goes to great lengths to minimize Freud's attraction to philosophy, his use of cocaine, and his homoerotic infatuation with Fliess in order to present him as a strict scientist, is forced to acknowledge the intensity of the Professor's passion:

> In reading through the tremendous story I have outlined here one apprehends above all how mighty were the passions that animated Freud and how unlike he was in reality to the calm scientist he is often depicted. He was beyond doubt someone whose instincts were far more powerful than those of the average man, but whose repressions were even more potent. The combination brought about an inner intensity of a degree that is perhaps the essential feature of any great genius.[17]

Like Max Weber, Freud's passionate defense of reason represented, in no small part, his struggle to come to terms with his own passionate constitution.[18] As it did with Weber, the force field created by that struggle helped to generate his monumental oeuvre.

In the nineties, Freud the empiricist was "obligated to build [his] way out into the dark," which meant more or less stumbling from one discovery to the next, while getting diverted into unproductive byways and tributaries.[19] Retrospectively, however, we can discern an inner logic to the development of his thinking in the last decade of the nineteenth century. If the discovery of psychic reality – which, it can be argued, was Freud's great achievement during those "heroic years" – is taken as the *telos* of that development, then it becomes clear that he had to complete two interrelated steps before he could discover it. For one, it was necessary for Freud to complete the transition, set in motion during his fellowship with Charcot, from a neurophysiologist to a psychologist. That is, he had to give up a physicalist approach to the mind and make the psyche rather than the brain the object of his research. There was a personal clinical

---

[17] Jones, *Freud* I, 152.

[18] See Max Weber, "Science as a vocation," *The vocation lectures*, ed. David Owens and Tracy R. Strong, trans. Rodney Livingstone (New York: Hackett, 2004), 1–31, and Joachim Radkau, *Max Weber: a biography*, trans. Patrick Camiller (Madden, MA: Polity Press, 2009).

[19] Freud, *The interpretation of dreams*, 549.

concomitant to this theoretical advance: It also was necessary for Freud to move from diagnosing himself as a neurasthenic suffering from an actual neurosis that was caused by current factors in his life to accepting the fact that he was a "hysteric" – that is, a neurotic who, like his patients, suffered from a psychological "illness" rooted in the past. For Freud, these two thoroughly entangled transitions were a necessary condition for discovering psychic reality, and he accomplished them in and through his experience with Fliess. It was only when he resolved that relationship and separated from the Berliner that he could complete the process and appropriate his own capacities and accomplishments.

Freud argued that a patient must pass through an "artificial illness" tied up with the analyst, a transference neurosis, if the analysis were to succeed.[20] Although it was never fully recognized for what it was, Freud was in effect entangled in *a decade-long transference illness with Fliess*. Because it could not be analysed, it was erratic and volatile in the extreme and assumed multiple configurations. Freud's transference-infatuation with Fliess manifested many of the features that psychoanalysis inherited from hypnosis – for example, self-deprecation, gullibility, incredulity, fascination, submission, and exclusivity – and the first proto-analysis was of necessity a "wild" analysis. Furthermore, the resolution of that wild proto-analysis, though sorely incomplete, resulted in Freud's separation from Fliess, the creation of psychoanalysis, and the publication of *The interpretation of dreams*.

In a similar vein, the eminent historian of dynamic psychiatry Henri Ellenberger argues that, in addition to whatever organic factors may have been at work, the *daimons* that had been unleashed when Freud left the protective environment of Brücke's Institute were the primary source of his proliferating psychological and physiological symptoms in the 1890s. Ellenberger's thesis is that Freud was suffering from a "creative illness," understood as "a polymorphous creative condition that can take the shape of depression, neurosis, psychosomatic ailments, or even psychosis," and which can "occur in various settings and is to be found among shamans, among the mystics of various religions, in certain philosophers and creative writers." Typically, its onset "succeeds a period of intense preoccupation

---

[20] See Sigmund Freud, "Remembering, repeating and working-through (further recommendations on the technique of psycho-analysis)" (1914), *SE* 12: 154.

with an idea and a search for a certain truth." Although the symptoms are "painful, if not agonizing . . . the subject never loses the thread of his dominating preoccupation." Indeed, despite the fact that the sufferer "is almost exclusively absorbed with himself," a creative illness "is often compatible with normal, professional activity and family life." Even in cases where the subject "has a mentor who guides him through the ordeal (like the shaman apprentice with his master)," he undergoes experiences of "extreme isolation."[21]

As we will see, everything Ellenberger describes – the dedication to an ideal, the intense suffering, the outward normality of everyday life, and the presence of a shamanistic mentor – fits Freud's experience during the Fliess years to a tee. He also accurately describes the way Freud's creative illness ended at the close of the century – that is, with his break with Fliess and publication of *The interpretation of dreams*: "The termination is often rapid and marked by a phase of exhilaration. The subject emerges from his ordeal with a permanent transformation in his personality and the conviction that he has discovered great truths of the spiritual world."[22]

Freud's relationship to Fliess, as Ellenberger notes, has "puzzled . . . many analysts."[23] Gay, for one, asks how Freud, "the great rationalist," who was thoroughly bourgeois in his mores and habits, could have become so "credulous," to use Bernheim's term, as to become entangled in such an irrational situation.[24] Freud himself provides a partial answer to this question when he tells an incredulous Karl Abraham, his collaborator and "best pupil," that he "overlooked a great deal" regarding Fliess's cockamamie ideas and problematic behavior because he "once loved

---

[21] Ellenberger, *The discovery of the unconscious*, 447–448. Peter Homans has noted that another great theorist of the same era, Max Weber, also went through a "creative illness" that was strikingly similar to Freud's. When the sociologist emerged from a prolonged and paralyzing depression, he completely recast his life's project and published his *magnum opus*, *The Protestant ethic and the spirit of capitalism*. See Peter Homans, "Loss and mourning in the life and thought of Max Weber: toward a theory of symbolic loss," *Symbolic loss: the ambiguity of mourning and memory at century's end*, ed. Peter Homans (Charlottesville: University of Virginia Press, 2000), 225–238.

[22] Ellenberger, *The discovery of the unconscious*, 448.

[23] *Ibid.*, 449.

[24] Gay, *Freud: a life for our time*, 58.

him very much."[25] A person is willing "to accept something absurd," as he observed, "provided it satisfies profound emotional impulses."[26] Ellenberger's explanation, however, goes further. Because of their "rationalist" assumptions, many conventional analysts, he argues, cannot comprehend Freud's involvement in such an irrational relationship because they cannot countenance the shamanistic element in their Master's relationship to Fliess – and in the origins of psychoanalysis itself. Their need to inoculate psychoanalysis against the irrational and defend its *bona fides* as a kosher natural science, devoid of any taint of magic, leads them to deny its roots in "the history of the trance" – something that Freud affirmed on more than one occasion when he acknowledged his indebtedness to the hypnotists. Ellenberger contends, however, that "a perusal" of their correspondence "shows that during the crucial period of Freud's creative illness, Fliess had involuntarily and unconsciously stepped into a role resembling the shaman master's before the shaman apprentice, and of spiritual director to the mystic" – and, we might add, of the training analyst and the psychoanalytic candidate.[27] Given the deep affinity between hypnosis and being in love, elucidated by Freud himself, Ellenberger's thesis is perfectly coherent: Freud's *amour fou* and his "creative illness" were two aspects of the same phenomenon.

Like all transferences, Freud's transference to Fliess was not monolithic but protean, fluctuating, and composed of numerous intertwining strands. The often debated question of whether Fliess represented a powerful father, an early mother, a sibling, or some other persona for Freud is misconceived. At one time or another in Freud's transferences to his colleague from Berlin, he stood for all of these personas – and many others. Given our interest in Freud's relation to the early mother and his repudiation of femininity, one cluster of transference dynamics in the Fliess relationship is especially relevant. The adamance with which Freud adhered to the "active-masculine" position while denigrating "passivity" and "femininity" should raise the suspicion of an analytically oriented observer. It suggests that powerful counter-forces

[25] Ernst Falzeder (ed.), *The complete correspondence of Sigmund Freud and Karl Abraham: 1907–1925*, trans. Caroline Schwarzacher with the collaboration of Christine Trollope and Klar Majthényi King (New York: Karnak, 2002), 103.

[26] Sigmund Freud, *Delusions and dreams in Jensen's* Gradiva (1907), *SE* 9: 71.

[27] Ellenberger, *The discovery of the unconscious*, 449.

were at work pulling him in the opposite direction, and that he had to
constantly combat and ward them off. It has, in short, the flavor of a "reaction formation." As a result of the phallologocentric character that he
constructed in the wake of "the original catastrophe," Freud, as we have
seen, split off his "passive-feminine" strivings, which could therefore not
be integrated into "great organization of [his] ego."[28] Because these
strivings were out of awareness and could not therefore be modified, they
remained relatively unmodulated. They continued to live an "outlaw"
existence in dissociated regions of Freud's mind, where they retained the
potential to reassert themselves under the right circumstances. And this
is exactly what happened when Freud encountered Fliess: the intense
transference he formed to the Berliner – especially after he became his
patient – reactivated those passive-feminine strivings which surged to the
surface in various forms.

In the pre-Oedipal stratum of the transference, Freud undoubtedly
drew on memory traces of Amalie and his *Kinderfrau* and cast Fliess
in the role of an early mothering figure. Fliess became the omnipotent
breast-mother whom young children want to *surrender* to, believing she
possesses the magical power to eliminate privation and pain and restore
them to a state of blissful tranquility. On the Oedipal level, the Berliner
was cast into the transference role of the powerful father – especially in his
capacity as a doctor. In this case, Freud assumed a "passive-homosexual"
attitude toward his friend and colleague; he wished to *submit* to him and
be penetrated by this powerful phallic figure. Sprengnether makes the
important observation, however, that because the persona of the doctor is ambivalent, he does not fit neatly into this scheme.[29] Today the
culture of medicine has changed, partly as a result of the increased presence of women physicians, but in the past, especially in Freud's day, the
"father-doctor" could easily appear as the personification of patriarchal
power and authority to the small helpless child.[30] On the other hand,
however, insofar as children see the physician as a healer, he can bear a
strong resemblance to the breast-mother. Children believe that, like the

---

[28] Freud, *Inhibitions, symptoms and anxiety*, 153.

[29] Sprengnether, *The spectral mother*, 34.

[30] See Jacques Derrida, "'To do justice to Freud': the history of madness in the age
of psychoanalysis," trans. Pascale-Anne Brault and Michael Nass, *Critical Inquiry* 20
(1994), 244.

"good" mother, he possesses the magical elixir that can make their pain and suffering disappear. Just as the hypnotic subject submits to the hypnotist, Freud's transference to Fliess, in both its pre-Oedipal and Oedipal dimensions, gave rise to the wish to surrender/submit to him.

Ellenberger calls our attention to a particular figure in the history of medicine that can help us delineate Freud's relation to Fliess more precisely – namely, the religious healer, onto whom the patient projects "the 'archetype of the Savior.'"[31] Freud, the disillusioned man of science, who claimed to repudiate passivity, magic, and redemption, in fact yearned for magic from Fliess. Indeed, one letter to Fliess begins with the salutation "Dear Magician." And in another Freud declares, "I still look to you as the messiah."[32]

The Opening Phase

Breuer facilitated the first meeting between Freud and Fliess, who would replace him as Freud's primary collaborator. Fliess's interests ranged far beyond his otolaryngology, the field in which he specialized, and he came to Vienna in the fall of 1887 to pursue advanced studies in general biology and to visit his fiancée, Ida Bondy. That she happened to be Breuer's niece as well as his patient is a sign of the tight-knit, quasi-incestuous nature of Vienna's Jewish community. Following Breuer's suggestion, Fliess attended a series of lectures that Freud was delivering at the university, and a remarkable relationship developed. For seventeen years, the two young Jewish doctors – Fliess, like Freud's brother Julius, was two years Freud's junior – engaged in an extensive and passionate correspondence. Though we only have Freud's side, it is clear that they exchanged not only discussions of their practices, families, and the most intimate details of their private lives – including Freud's relatively acute psychopathology and sexual difficulties – but also numerous and sometimes lengthy manuscripts detailing, among other things, the latest developments in their theories, clinical points of interest emerging from their private practices, preliminary drafts of their scientific papers, constant updates about publication scheduling, and barbed

[31] Ellenberger, *The discovery of the unconscious*, 38.
[32] Masson (ed.), *Letters to Fliess*, 26 and 51.

gossip about colleagues.[33] Their correspondence was also punctuated by regular "congresses," where the two men met in various European cities and Alpine resorts for several days of intense "scientific" discussion – and who knows what else. The cultural climate and the psychoanalytic profession's homophobic prejudices may have prevented it from being acknowledged in the past, but today the intense homosexual dimension of the Freud–Fliess relationship is beyond dispute.[34] While psychoanalyst David Lotto observes that "sublimated eroticism was rampant" in the Freud/Fliess correspondence, the sexuality was not in fact always that sublimated.[35] Freud's letters are rife with barely disguised homoerotic allusions. Anticipating an upcoming congress, Freud wrote to Fliess, "I bring nothing but two open ears and one temporal lobe lubricated for reception."[36] One naturally wonders whether these congresses were more than scientific and whether Freud ever consummated his love for Fliess sexually. To date, we do not possess the evidence to investigate this question properly. It may be going too far to describe Freud the way he described Leonardo – namely, as "emotionally homosexual."[37] Nevertheless, in his last letters to Fliess, which will be discussed below, he is remarkably frank in acknowledging his "androphilic current."[38]

Contrary to what might be expected, the fact that Fliess lived in another city and that the two men rarely met did not present an obstacle to the relationship. On the contrary, the distance was a necessary condition for its success. Freud, as we have observed, was an epistolary lover, who conducted his two most intense love relations via the mail and largely played them out in his mind. As it had during his betrothal to Martha, the separation from the love object allowed Freud to create and maintain Fliess as a fantasy object onto whom he could project a panoply of thoughts and feelings. Fliess, moreover, had one distinct advantage over Martha.

---

[33] See Sulloway, *Freud, biologist of the mind*, 136.

[34] See Elizabeth Lunbeck, *The Americanization of narcissism* (Cambridge, MA: Harvard University Press, 2014), 83–103.

[35] David Lotto, "Freud's struggle with misogyny: homosexuality and guilt in the dream of Irma's injection," *Journal of the American Psychoanalytic Association* 49 (2001), 1294.

[36] Masson (ed.), *Letters to Fliess*, 193.

[37] Freud, *Leonardo*, 98.

[38] Masson (ed.), *Letters to Fliess*, 447.

Because Freud never shared a flat with his colleague, the experience of his beloved's quotidian creaturelieness never shattered his idealizations. They were shattered in a different way. "We must admire," as Kohut observes, "the cleverness of Freud's choice of Fliess, with whom he was not in direct contact most of the time." With that choice, he created a situation where "the distance between Vienna and Berlin" approximated "the behind-the-couch distance and invisibility of the ordinary analyst," thus keeping "disturbing reality input at a distance" as well.[39] Like the configuration of the analytic set-up, the 423 miles separating Vienna and Berlin created a fantasy space that allowed Freud the proto-analysand to construct a proto-transference object without which an analytic-like process cannot occur.

In addition to its more pathological and defensive side, Freud's attachment to Fliess also served positive and adaptive functions that help explain the attachment of this *Homo rationalis* to this brilliant charismatic charlatan. That the Berliner facilitated his work is high among them. Creative people, Didier Anzieu observes, often require someone to grant them permission to pursue their intuitions, and Fliess fulfilled this requirement for Freud in two ways.[40] First, he granted Freud permission to freely explore the realm of sexuality – to gaze at "the primal scene" in the broadest sense of the term. Though Breuer did not deny the importance of sexuality to the extent that Freud claimed he did, he was not enthusiastic about exploring the subject. Fliess was. Jones observes that, "far from balking at sexual problems," Fliess "had made them the center of his whole work." Although the theories of the two men ultimately proved to be incompatible, "it looked for some time as if they were exploring the forbidden territory hand in hand."[41] And more generally, the highly speculative Fliess also became the anti-Brücke, who gave his Viennese friend permission to pursue his own speculative impulses.

The second way in which Fliess granted Freud permission to pursue his thoughts was in compensating for missing psychic structures that could alleviate anxiety and boost Freud's sense of self and his mood. Because the internalizations that are necessary for healthy development did not

[39] Kohut, "Creativeness, charisma, group psychology," 181.
[40] See Anzieu, *Freud's self-analysis*, 108–114.
[41] Jones, *Freud* I, 296.

adequately take place in Freud's case, the psychic structures that they should have created were not formed, as we have seen, thus creating "gaps in the fabric of" his self. To compensate for "missing inner structure[s]" of this sort, individuals with a history of early parental disillusionment, as Kohut observes, tend to be "forever . . . yearning to find" idealized objects who can function as "a substitute" for the missing internalized objects. These stand-in objects are desperately needed to combat the threat of fragmentation, to regulate affect, and to maintain one's sense of worth and vitality, and are therefore typically pursued with "an addiction-like intensity."[42] (In light of Freud's addictive behavior regarding cocaine and cigars, we should note that an idealized object need not be a person.) Repeating his experience with Martha's letters, those from Fliess served as narcissistic supplies, Freud's "nectar and ambrosia," that could stabilize his psychic equilibrium and establish a sense of wellbeing.[43] When he received a letter from his *eromenos* (beloved), it had a euphoric affect that would elevate his mood, alleviate his anxiety and depression, and allow him to work with renewed vigor.[44] In May 1896, he wrote to Fliess that his "moral strength [was] exhausted" and that he needed an "infusion of vital strength" like the one Fliess had previously provided in Dresden.[45] And contrariwise, if Fliess's letters did not arrive in a timely fashion, Freud would become deflated and anxious.

Was Fliess crazy or a genius? At the time, it was not easy to determine.[46] By all accounts, he was an attractive, indeed magnetic man. Measured in conventional terms, Fliess was more successful than Freud, and there was reason to envy him. Not only did he live in Berlin, which Freud considered a more enlightened and progressive city than the Vienna he saw as encrusted with reactionary traditions, Fliess was also married to a wealthy woman, had a thriving practice, and was therefore free from the financial

[42] Kohut, "Creativeness, charisma, group psychology," 189.

[43] Masson (ed.), *Letters to Fliess*, 87.

[44] In an ironic nod to Freud's *Bildung*, Boyarin uses the Greek terms for homosexual lovers *erastes* and *eromenos* to describe his relationship with Fliess. See Daniel Boyarin, *Unheroic conduct: the rise of heterosexuality and the invention of the Jewish man* (Berkeley: University of California Press, 1997), 203.

[45] Masson (ed.), *Letters to Fliess*, 190.

[46] See Max Schur, *Freud: living and dying* (New York: International Universities Press, 1972).

anxieties that plagued his Viennese colleague. The two men moreover had much in common. They were both highly cultured young Jewish physicians, beginning their careers and expanding their families, with a shared predilection for uninhibited theoretical speculation and an intense interest in sexuality. Intellectually, Fliess seems to have been charismatic. Karl Abraham, a skeptical *Menschenkenner* – a judge of character – who later immediately saw through Jung, described him as a "fascinating" personality.[47] With his speculative flare and confidence in his own intellectual capacities, which bordered on grandiosity and dogmatism, Fliess could expound at length on innumerable subjects.

At the time the two men met, the Berliner's theoretical position, which posterity has come to view as "a remarkably well-developed form of pseudoscience," consisted in three components.[48]

First, his theory of the "nasal-reflex neurosis" postulated a connection between a heterogeneous group of symptoms – including migraines, dysmenorrhea, gastrointestinal difficulties, cardiac symptoms, and sinusitis – and pathogenic spots in the nose. He "treated" these symptoms either by cauterizing those spots or applying cocaine to them – something that must have perked the interest of Freud who was already using the substance when he met the Berliner. The assertion that there is a connection between the nose and the female genitalia was perhaps Fliess's most famous claim. To support it, he argued that the turbinal bone in the nose is structurally homologous with the female genitalia, that nasal mucosa and vaginal mucosa are similar in nature, and that the nose, like the vagina, can bleed. He construed the last point to mean that men can menstruate. The ENT specialist even claimed to have identified "certain 'genital spots' (*Genitalstellen*) inside the interior of the nose itself" which were directly connected with the genitals.[49] One implication of this theory is important for our narrative: If the nose is connected with the genitals and sexuality, then interventions into the nose have sexual consequences.

Second, Fliess's theory of biorhythms was more metabiological – if not numerological – but no less dubious than the theory of the nasal-reflex neurosis. He postulated the existence of measurable cycles that govern

[47] Quoted in Jones, *Freud* I, 289.
[48] See Sulloway, *Freud, biologist of the mind*, 141.
[49] *Ibid.*, 140.

many important biological functions in human beings and that could be used to predict important events in an individual's life – for example, gestation, birth, and death. In addition to a woman's familiar twenty-eight-day menstrual cycle, he made the even more eccentric claim that another twenty-three-day cycle could be observed in men and was an analogue of female periodicity. In a particularly baroque argument, he also maintained that although both cycles could occur in both sexes, the familiar twenty-eight-day cycle was a "female" one and connected with emotional functioning, while the newly discovered twenty-three-day cycle was "male" and tied to psychological processes. Even more grandiosely, the Berliner maintained that he had identified metabiological laws that not only were applicable "to the animal kingdom" but applied to "the whole organic world" – something Freud would repeat in *Beyond the Pleasure Principle*.[50]

Third, Fliess asserted that human beings are innately bisexual, a postulate that follows from the first two theories. To support this claim, he pointed to the supposed fact that the nose, an organ possessed by both sexes, is connected with sexuality, and he argued that if the twenty-eight-day and twenty-three-day cycles occur in men and women alike, then members of both sexes are made up of a mixture of masculine and feminine components – that is, are bisexual. Because of the powerful and unresolved homosexual dynamics in the Freud–Fliess relationship, the idea of bisexuality loomed large in the conflicts between them and was in fact at the center of their final break.

Insofar as Freud remained committed to a physicalist approach to "the psychic apparatus," he required the type of quantitative biological theory that Fliess – his "Kepler of biology" – seemed to be offering.[51] Furthermore, as long as Freud needed to maintain Fliess as an idealized object, he masked the incompatibility of his collaborator's physiological orientation and his increasingly psychological approach by maintaining that they were "amalgamated theories."[52] Fliess, Freud tried to convince himself, was providing the hard mathematical base, while he was contributing the soft psychological superstructure. But when Freud began to

[50] Quoted in *ibid.*, 141.

[51] Masson (ed.), *Letters to Fliess*, 320.

[52] *Ibid.*, 214.

discover psychic reality and eventually recognized, as his collaborator in fact told him in no uncertain terms, that Fliess's thoroughly deterministic physiological theory left no room for psychology – or psychotherapy – he could no longer maintain the self-deception, nor did he need to.

Although Freud's relationship with Fliess started slowly and only took off in earnest six years later with the so-called cardiac episode, his idealization-hunger is on full display in his first letter to his new colleague. As it had been with Martha, it was love at first sight. Who Fliess was mattered little, in fact could not have mattered much, given that Freud had little time to become acquainted with him. (But perhaps this is often true when anyone falls in love.) What mattered was that Fliess provided the right kind of screen onto which Freud could project his idealizations. Thus, in the stilted opening paragraph of his first epistle, Freud writes the following to a man he barely knows:

Esteemed friend and colleague:
My letter of today admittedly is occasioned by business, but I must introduce it by confessing that I entertain hopes of continuing the relationship with you and that you have left a deep impression on me which could easily lead me to tell you outright in what category of men I place you.[53]

As Freud taught us, the "overvaluation" of the object – idealization – seriously impairs a person's critical faculties, especially when one is in love. And his "overvaluation" of Fliess helps to explain how a person with Freud's keen intelligence could have acted so credulously regarding a person as dubious as Fliess.

Heart Ache

Throughout most of its history, the healing profession's practitioners have recognized a recurrent phenomenon: "patients" regularly develop transferences to their "doctors," and these transferences tend to become especially intense in serious life-threatening situations.[54] Freud's transference to Fliess took hold for real, as psychoanalyst John Gedo observes,

[53] Masson (ed.), *Letters to Fliess*, 15.
[54] See Freud's important pre-analytical paper "Psychical treatment" (1890), *SE* 7: 281–302.

190   Freud: An Intellectual Biography

when he became the Berliner's patient and submitted to his treatment.[55] We first hear about Freud's heart condition in the letter of 18 October 1893. It is clear that Fliess had not only discussed Freud's cardiac difficulties with him but had also been treating his colleague for various "neurasthenic" maladies – for example, migraines, nasal problems, gastrointestinal difficulties, and a chronic sinus condition. Not surprisingly, Fliess began by diagnosing his colleague's cardiac pathology as a case of the nasal reflex neurosis, and he treated him accordingly. There is reason to believe that Fliess operated on Freud's nose, or at least cauterized and applied cocaine to it, at some of their congresses in February 1895 – at the same time that he also operated on Freud's patient Emma Eckstein – and again in the late summer of that year.[56] In short, Fliess was *actively intervening into Freud's body*.

As the following letters indicate, the pump had been fully primed for Freud to view Fliess as an idealized man of medicine – or, better yet, as a medicine man, given the magical powers he attributed to him. In the letter dated 28 May 1888, Freud, who severely doubted his own capacities as a physician, tells the charismatic Fliess that he commands little authority with Mrs. A., a patient both men are treating, and laments the fact that Fliess's "power over spirits" – that is, his *mana* as a healer – "cannot be transferred to him."[57] Freud was aware of the mesmerizing power that Fliess's *mana* had on him and how it paralyzed his capacity for independent thinking. Confessing his credulity, he tells the Berliner, "I really believe you in everything."[58] Freud's transference to Fliess was indeed so powerful that he remained impervious to mounting evidence that would have punctured his idealizations had he had his wits about him. This helps to explain how Freud's idealization of Fliess and subjugation to him could have lasted for so long. Jones makes the point that Freud's fear of the

---

[55] John Gedo, "Freud's self-analysis and his scientific ideas," *Freud: the fusion of science and humanism*, ed. John Gedo and George H. Pollock, Psychoanalytic Issues monograph 34/35 (New York: International Universities Press, 1976), 305.

[56] See Jones, *Freud* I, 209, and Lotto, "Freud's struggle," 1289–1290.

[57] Masson (ed.), *Letters to Fliess*, 21. At the time, Freud, who was working to perfect his hypnotic technique and had just published a preface to Bernheim's book *De la suggestion*, was deeply involved in the topic of the doctor's "magical" effects on the patient. See Ellenberger, *The discovery of the unconscious*, 449.

[58] Masson (ed.), *Letters to Fliess*, 36.

intensity of his own intellectual power, of his own omnipotence, caused him to vastly exaggerate Fliess's while underestimating his own:

The self-deprecation of his capacities and his achievement he so often voiced in the correspondence with Fliess sprang not from an inner weakness, but from a terrifying strength, one he felt unable to cope with alone. So he had to endow Fliess with all sorts of imaginary qualities, keen judgment and restraint, over-powerful intellectual vigor, which were essential to a protective mentor.[59]

It was only after Freud had withdrawn the idealizations of Fliess, worked through the fear of his own omnipotence, and appropriated his true strength – which was formidable indeed – that he could create psychoanalysis and write the *Traumdeutung, The interpretation of dreams*.

It is inconceivable, however, that a man with Freud's exceptional intellect, who lionized independence and abhorred passivity, could have submitted to another man indefinitely without some sort of struggle. When the inevitable chinks began to appear in Fliess's armor, they provided a toehold that Freud's doubts fastened on to, and he entered into an internal struggle that saw him oscillating continually between credulity and skepticism, submission and assertiveness, and that lasted for at least another five years.

One of the first cracks to appear in Fliess's position pertained to an equivocation in his diagnosis of his patient's cardiac condition. At one point, Fliess changed his opinion and began to maintain that although nasal pathology continued to play a role, the main etiological factor in Freud's cardiac condition was nicotine poisoning – which meant Freud should give up his beloved cigars. Freud's critical faculties had not become so blunted that he did not recognize a contradiction – or at least an inner tension – when he was presented with one. On 11 December 1893, he wrote to Fliess, "The prohibition on smoking does not agree with the nasal diagnosis." And four months later he told Fliess outright that he was "especially suspicious of [him] because this heart affair of mine is the only one in which I have ever heard you make contradictory statements."[60]

Though his cigars have been the butt of endless jokes about Freud and psychoanalysis, his dependency on them was no laughing matter. When

[59] Jones, *Freud* I, 295.
[60] Masson (ed.), *Letters to Fliess*, 63 and 68.

Fliess retreated from the nasal diagnosis and argued that nicotine poisoning was responsible for the cardiac pathology, the struggle over Freud's
nicotine addiction and smoking became the primary stage on which the
drama of his submission to his colleague and physician was enacted. Max
Schur, the physician and friend who would become central to Freud's life
in his later years, tells us about the "endless series of attempts" on Freud's
part to "give up nicotine" and submit to Fliess that ensued from this
prohibition against nicotine.[61] Given that Freud smoked twenty cigars a
day, the strength of his addiction cannot be doubted.[62] Clinical experience
demonstrates that this sort of dependency – with its intense oral cravings
and yearning to reunite with the original object – is exceedingly difficult
to overcome. The dynamics of this struggle with Fliess can be observed
in the letter of 18 October 1893, which makes it clear that Freud's physician had "insisted quite firmly that" he stop smoking. Freud confesses,
however, that he has fallen off the wagon and is "smoking heavily" again;
he vows, "I shall scrupulously follow a prescription of yours."[63] Like most
pledges of this sort, however, this one rings hollow – and a bit sarcastic.

Then, in the letter of 19 April 1894, Freud informs Fliess that he has
submitted to his orders and abstained from smoking. And in a phrase containing barely disguised oral homosexual connotations, he also reports,
"I have in fact not had anything warm between my lips" for "three weeks."[64]
In the same letter, however, in which he tells Fliess that he has refrained
from smoking and endured the "misery of abstinence," – which was "far
greater than [he] ever imagined" – he also informs him that he had experienced "a severe cardiac misery, greater than [he] ever experienced while
smoking."[65] Furthermore, while the symptoms persisted despite his abstinence, they responded to digitalis. The conclusion was obvious: Nicotine
was not the cause of the cardiac pathology, and Fliess's diagnosis was mistaken. Yet Freud does not draw the conclusion. Furthermore, in the same
letter, Freud also reports that, in addition to the typical symptoms of a

---

[61] Schur, *Freud: living and dying*, 41.

[62] Against Jones's bizarre claim that Freud did not have an addictive personality,
see Anzieu's more plausible position. Jones, *Freud* II, 430 and Anzieu, *Freud's self-
analysis*, 43–45.

[63] Masson (ed.), *Letters to Fliess*, 60.

[64] *Ibid.*, 67.

[65] *Ibid.*, 67.

heart attack, he had been experiencing "a feeling of depression, which took the form of visions of death and departure in place of the usual frenzy of activity." And the disturbing depressive symptoms caused him to wonder whether the whole thing might be "hypochondriacal."[66]

The distraught patient needed some clarity and assurance in the midst of this confusion. Although he was in the process of disengaging from Breuer and replacing him with Fliess as his primary confidant, Freud turned to his older colleague, a renowned diagnostician, for a consultation. Freud suggested to Breuer that the correct diagnosis was not nicotine poisoning but "chronic myocarditis," an inflammation of the heart muscle, which could be aggravated by heavy smoking. Breuer did not immediately provide Freud with the unequivocal answer he had hoped for, but two months later – partly as a result of hearing about two similar cases – he consented to the myocarditis diagnosis. Both men agreed, moreover, that it might have been caused by a bout of rheumatic fever Freud had suffered several years earlier. Two additional facts, moreover, helped to confirm the diagnosis: The symptoms were not aggravated by nicotine, and they responded to digitalis.

Freud was not only conflicted about both Breuer and Fliess, he was also pulled in opposite directions by the implications, positive and negative, of each diagnosis.[67] On the positive side of nicotine poisoning proving to be the correct diagnosis, Fliess would be redeemed as a diagnostician and preserved as a magical healer. Moreover, the solution to the problem would be straightforward; however difficult to implement, the answer – namely, to stop smoking – would at least be clear. The prognosis would also be more optimistic insofar as the condition was not as life-threatening. On the negative side, however, if Freud's symptoms were caused by nicotine poisoning, he would have to break his nicotine addiction, something that was extraordinarily difficult and that would have a significant psychological consequence: He would become more heavily dependent on Fliess, substituting the Berliner's magic for the magic of his cigars. Freud would thus be required to forgo the relative emotional self-sufficiency that smoking provided him – its powers to stimulate, soothe, and relieve depression – and would instead be forced to rely on an actual

---

[66] *Ibid.*, 67.

[67] See Schur, *Freud: living and dying*, 48 n.19.

human being, who would be less available and reliable, that is, less under his control, to serve as the breast-penis that could provide him with the energy and comfort he needed.

The dilemma that would be caused by accepting a diagnosis of myocarditis is easy to see. While the prognosis would be worse in that it was significantly more life-threatening, Freud would not be required to give up nicotine – at least not completely. He could avoid the agony of withdrawal and abstinence and retain the powerful pleasure and anti-depressive effects his cigars provided him. And rather than submitting to Fliess, he could retain the emotional independence that his cigars provided him. Without the cigars, as the analyst Shelley Orgel observes, Freud would parent the child – that is, give birth to psychoanalysis, together with Fliess – perhaps fulfilling the fantasy of a bisexual pregnancy. With the cigars, on the other hand, Freud could retain his creative autarchy and, by being both mother and father to the offspring, perhaps fulfill a bisexual fantasy of another sort – namely, of omnipotent self-sufficiency.[68]

What is most striking is that, even after it became clear that nicotine poisoning was the wrong diagnosis, Freud struggled to abstain for some time. His emotional wish/need to submit to Fliess entailed a *sacrificium intellectus* that prevented him from drawing the obvious conclusion. The factor that finally led him to wholeheartedly resume smoking, however, involved something he was not prepared to sacrifice to Fliess, nor to anyone: his creativity and capacity to work. "Freud," Anzieu observes, "needed tobacco in order to concentrate his thoughts, attain a state of intellectual excitement and combat his tendency to depression."[69] Without his cigars, which allowed him to be "the master of [his] mood," Freud could not work to his fullest capacity.[70] Freud's work more or less coincided with his life, and to compromise his creativity would have perhaps been something worse than a physical death. It would have constituted the death of his identity, of who he was as an individual.

Of the three protagonists, Fliess, Breuer, and Freud, it was only the latter – *a man on the path to discovering psychic reality* – who raised the

---

[68] See Shelley Orgel, "Freud and the repudiation of the feminine," *Journal of the American Psychoanalytic Association* 44 (1996), 49–50. For the fantasy of a homosexual birth see Boyarin, *Unheroic conduct*, 203–205.

[69] Anzieu, *Freud's self-analysis*, 43.

[70] Masson (ed.), *Letters to Fliess*, 84.

possibility that his cardiac symptoms might be psychological in origin. On 11 December 1893, he wrote to Fliess that he not only had "the impression that the whole business is organic and cardiac," but that *something neurotic would be harder to take*" – a proposition that strikes one as counter-intuitive. What is going on? Freud is giving voice to an insight that must have been dawning on him as a result of his own struggles to understand his inner world and the inner worlds of his patients. For most people, it is more difficult to accept the existence and power of psychic reality than of external reality. Clinical experience repeatedly shows that patients often prefer an external threat – regardless of how dangerous – to one emanating from within. It is not uncommon for people who have struggled with a hypochondriacal fear of illness and death throughout their lives to suddenly become organized and face their destiny with realism and maturity when they receive a terminal diagnosis. Freud increasingly came to understand that the human mind is naturally oriented toward the external world and tends to vigorously resist the attempt to redirect its gaze inward – hence the ubiquitous tendency to "act out" in analysis. As he wrote to Albert Einstein:

All our attention is directed to the outside, whence dangers and satisfaction beckon. From the inside, we want only to be left in peace. So if someone tries to turn our awareness inward . . . then our whole organization resists – just as, for example, the oesophagus and urethra resist any attempt to reverse their normal direction of passage.[71]

This observation helps us understand the widespread hostility toward psychoanalysis. Freud not only dealt humanity a blow to its self-esteem when he demonstrated that the ego was not master in its own house. He also provoked its ire by violating human nature and inviting the human animal to turn its gaze to the inside.

Because Freud never systematically relinquished his model of the psychic apparatus as a self-enclosed unit, he was theoretically unable to fully articulate a point that is beyond dispute today: Analysis has an irreducibly two-person dimension and must pass, via the transference, through the mediation of another person, an interlocutor. In his practice, however, he demonstrates that, at some level of awareness, he recognized that another

---

[71] Quoted in Ilse Grubrich-Simitis, *Early Freud and late Freud: reading anew* Studies on hysteria *and* Moses and monotheism (New York: Routledge, 1997), 2.

person – namely, Fliess – was essential to the proto-analytic process he was engaged in. Freud explicitly tells his colleague: "I need you as my audience" and "you are the only other, the *alter*."[72] He in fact developed the same sort of exclusive focus, demandingness, and credulity vis-à-vis his Other that infants manifest toward their mothers, hypnotic subjects toward their hypnotists, and analysands toward their analysts. Furthermore, in addition to whatever projective functions Fliess may have served, he also provided a perhaps indispensable service: He was a "quality . . . critic and reader" of Freud's work.[73]

Finally, there was an elephant in the room when Freud and his consultants were discussing his cardiac pathology – namely, his cocaine use, of which Fliess, who has been likened to Freud's dealer as well as his physician, was certainly aware. Howard Markel, an expert in the field of addiction, notes that Freud also participated in the denial and "continued to . . . perversely . . . search for alternative explanations for his chest pain rather than seriously contemplate cocaine's potential role in the matter."[74] The popularity of cocaine, according to Markel, was "spreading like wild-fire" in Europe in the 1880s – thanks in no small part to the promotional efforts of its two manufacturers, Parke-Davis and Company of Detroit and Merck & Company of Darmstadt, Germany – and the substance became the topic of numerous articles in the scientific and medical journals.[75] When Freud, "ever the obsessive-compulsive scholar," came across these publications, he began collecting "stacks of papers and books" on the subject. What he discovered intrigued the young scientist in two ways. At the time, he was interested in the relation between the mind and the functioning of the brain and believed that cocaine might provide a propitious vehicle for studying it. He therefore began to perform a series of relatively legitimate experiments on himself, in which he attempted to measure the physiological and psychological effects that the substance produced in him. As he grew ever more captivated with the substance's potential to eliminate some of humanity's most serious afflictions – for

---

[72] Masson (ed.), *Letters to Fliess*, 313.

[73] *Ibid.*, 313.

[74] Howard Markel, *An anatomy of addiction: Sigmund Freud, William Halsted, and the miracle of cocaine* (New York: Pantheon Books, 2011), 173.

[75] *Ibid.*, 65.

example, anxiety, depression, and diminished libido – he began enthusi-astically to tout its wonders to his friends and colleagues based on limited scientific research. This had tragic and lethal consequences when he inju-diciously used it in an attempt to cure the morphine addiction of his friend Ernst von Fleischl. As he would later do with Fliess, the young scientist was seeking thaumaturgy; cocaine, so it seemed, was powdered magic. The magical powers that Freud attributed to the substance are abundantly apparent in a letter he wrote to Martha before an upcoming visit:

Woe to you, my Princess when I come, I will kiss your cheeks quite red and feed you till you are plump. And if you are forward you shall see who is the stronger, a gentle little girl who doesn't eat enough or a big wild man who has cocaine in his body. In my last severe depression, I took coca again, and a small dose lifted me to the heights in a wonderful fashion. I am just now busy collecting the literature for a song of praise to this magical substance.[76]

In the 1890s, when his psychic pain and physical symptoms continued to intensify, Freud not only took on an "inhuman workload," he also med-icated himself with sizeable quantities of cocaine in an attempt to grap-ple with his suffering.[77] Given the state of current scholarship, in which the history of Freud's cocaine use has been thoroughly and meticulously documented, it would be difficult to deny its contribution to his cardiac pathology. As Markel observes, "if forced to make a retrospective diagnosis, a physician today would be hard-pressed not to consider that Sigmund's car-diac symptoms were related to his cocaine use."[78] More significantly, it was only when his father died – that is, at the point where he was about to begin his systematic self-analysis – that Freud gave up the cocaine. "The cocaine brush has been put completely aside," he informed Fliess.[79] He would no longer seek an external "biochemical solution" to his suffering in the mag-ical power of cocaine. Rather, he would pursue the solution in a prolonged and systematic examination of his inner world through a self-analysis.[80]

---

[76] Quoted in Jones, *Freud* I, 81.

[77] Markel, *An anatomy of addiction*, 405.

[78] *Ibid.*, 173.

[79] Masson (ed.), *Letters to Fliess*, 201.

[80] Anzieu, *Freud's self-analysis*, 45.

7

Becoming the First Psychoanalyst

The Eckstein Affair

What became known as "The Dream of Irma's Injection," the first dream that Freud claimed to have completely analysed, is the centerpiece of the *Traumdeutung* and occupies a foundational position in the construction of psychoanalytic theory. It is meant to demonstrate Freud's central thesis: that a dream is the (disguised) fulfillment of a wish. Because of its importance, many eminent analysts have taken a crack at interpreting it. But Max Schur's 1966 treatment of that canonical text in "Some 'additional day residues' of the 'specimen dream of psychoanalysis'" perhaps had the greatest impact.[1] Indeed, Schur – who had been granted access to the complete Fliess Letters, sent shock waves through the analytic community when he revealed that Freud's and Fliess's scandalous mistreatment of Freud's patient Emma Eckstein provided background to the Irma Dream. But even Schur pulled his punches. It was only in 1984, when Jeffrey Masson published *The assault on truth: Freud's suppression of the seduction theory*, that the full extent of Freud's and Fliess's deplorable – and perhaps legally actionable – treatment of Eckstein became known.[2]

"The Eckstein affair" and the cardiac episode overlapped. On 24 July 1895, the day on which the "Dream of Irma's Injection" took place, the Freud family was vacationing in a wooded suburb of Vienna that was a popular retreat for the city's middle-class Jewish population, while

---

[1] Max Schur, "Some 'additional day residues' of the 'specimen dream of psychoanalysis,'" *Psychoanalysis – a general psychology: essays in honor of Heinz Hartmann*, ed. Rudolph M. Lowenstein, Lottie M. Newman, Max Schur, and Albert Solnit (New York: International Universities Press, 1966), 45–85.

[2] Masson, *The assault on truth*.

Freud was "slowly recovering from [the] cardiac episode."[3] Though its most acute phase had subsided, he was still anxiously preoccupied with a situation that he believed had brought him "very close to the end of [his] life."[4] Sprengnether makes the important observation that at the time of the Emma episode, Freud was occupying two positions, of "both doctor and patient":[5] He was simultaneously a doctor *actively* treating Eckstein and other patients, and a patient *passively* submitting to Fliess's treatment, including interventions into his body.

On the afternoon of the 23rd, the "peace and quiet" that Freud enjoyed was interrupted by a visit from Oscar Rie, who, in addition to being the family pediatrician, was one of Freud's "oldest friends" and belonged to the same circle of medical colleagues[6] (He is Otto in the dream.) Rie was a guest at the family summer house of one of Freud's patients, Emma Eckstein – Irma in the dream – and had ample opportunity to observe her condition. When Rie told Freud that Emma "was better but not quite well," Freud took his colleague's assessment as a "reproof" of his "professional conscientiousness," and this criticism provided the impetus for the dream.[7] That evening, Freud worked late into the night writing up Emma's case history, which he intended to present to Breuer (Dr. M. in the dream), a "leading figure" in their circle, as a brief to "justify" his handling of Eckstein's treatment.[8] Then, in his sleep, Freud continued to work on the self-justification, moving from person to person in an attempt to affix blame for his patient's woes. Indeed, the entire dream has the atmosphere of a courtroom drama, and the question of vindication – of who is a "good" doctor (or good patient) and who is not – is one of its central motifs.

Freud first focuses his critical gaze on Emma herself, whose treatment, he tells us, had ended in only "a partial success." Although he had succeeded in removing her "hysterical anxiety," he had not been successful in alleviating "all her organic symptoms." As the dream begins, Freud spies

---

[3] Schur, "Some 'additional day residues,'" 50.

[4] Masson (ed.), *Letters to Fliess*, 442.

[5] Sprengnether, *The spectral mother*, 34.

[6] See Anzieu, *Freud's self-analysis*, 131, and Freud, *The interpretation of dreams*, 106.

[7] Freud, *The interpretation of dreams*, 120.

[8] *Ibid.*, 106.

Irma as he enters a "large hall," where a gathering is taking place, and immediately whisks his patient to a window in order to examine her.[9] He realizes that he is "especially anxious not to be responsible for the pains she still had." One possibility occurs to him: to blame Irma herself for her symptoms. Emma had in fact been a recalcitrant patient, who had been "unwilling to accept" the "solution" Freud proposed to her in the form of an interpretation that explained her ailment in terms of sexuality. Consequently, doctor and patient were in a conflicted state – "at variance" with each other – when they broke for the summer holiday.[10] In the dream, Freud tells Irma that if she had accepted his solution, her pains would have been alleviated, but, because she had defied him, she was still suffering. It is, in short, her "*own fault.*"[11] Feigning naïveté, Freud asks, "Could it be that the purpose of the dream lay in this direction" – that is, of exculpating himself by blaming someone else?[12]

After attempting to lay blame for the treatment's failure at his patient's feet, Freud redirects his critical gaze onto himself. Indeed, in this segment of the dream, he seems intent on masochistically "collecting all the occasions which [he] could bring up against [himself] as evidence of lack of medical conscientiousness."[13] Irma had initially resisted Freud's attempt to examine her, but when she finally yields and opens "*her mouth properly,*" Freud observes her "*turbinal bones*" – that is, the bones, which, according to Fliess, are connected to sexuality – "*with scabs on them.*" This observation sparks a stream of anxious and self-incriminating associations. *Qua* patient, Fliess had recently cauterized Freud's own turbinal bones, and the sight of the scabs raises questions about his own "state of health."[14] *Qua* doctor, Freud, who tells us he "was making frequent use of cocaine to reduce some troublesome nasal swellings," becomes concerned over his capacities as a physician, especially with respect to one patient in particular: a woman "who had followed [his] example," that is, had consumed large amounts of cocaine, and had developed "an extensive

---

[9] *Ibid.*, 107.

[10] *Ibid.*, 106.

[11] *Ibid.*, 108 (emphasis in the original).

[12] *Ibid.*, 109.

[13] *Ibid.*, 112.

[14] Anzieu, *Freud's self-analysis*, 143.

necrosis of the nasal mucous membrane" as a result.[15] This association, in turn, leads him to the memory of what may have been the darkest hour in Freud's medical career – namely, his well-intentioned but reckless prescription of cocaine to von Fleischl, which led to the long and hellish death of this friend and colleague and brought down upon Freud the ire of Vienna's medical establishment.

After this exercise in self-laceration, Freud pivots once again and attempts to "shift blame away" from himself.[16] He now summons three of his closest medical colleagues and places each of them in the defendant's dock. His intention is to demonstrate that Irma's pains are organic in nature – which, for some peculiar reason, he believes would exonerate *him* given that he was treating her as a psychologist – and to turn the tables on and disparage the competence of the three medical colleagues. When he finishes his examination of Irma, Freud *"at once call[s] in Dr. M."* (Breuer), who offers the following opinion: *"It's an infection, but no matter. Dysentery will supervene and the toxin will be eliminated."* For technical reasons that need not concern us, Freud found Dr. M.'s opinion not simply problematic but "ridiculous."[17] Even at this relatively early stage in the development of psychoanalytic theory, Freud already understood that he, as the author of the dream, had cast Dr. M. in a disparaging position, and he asks the appropriate question: "What could be my motive for treating this friend of mine so badly?"[18] The answer: revenge against Dr. M., who, like Irma, had refused to accept his "solution," that is, his explanation of hysteria in terms of sexuality, "the factor to which [Freud] attributed the greatest importance in the origin of the nervous disorders."[19] In reality, the dream occurred after Freud had fallen out with Breuer over the role that sexuality plays in hysteria. Freud tells us that he "could no longer feel any doubt "that this part of the dream was expressing derision at physicians" who are "ignorant of hysteria" and who, like Irma, would not accept his general theory about the sexual etiology of neurosis.[20]

[15] Freud, *The interpretation of dreams*, 111.

[16] *Ibid.*, 114.

[17] *Ibid.*, 113 (emphasis in the original).

[18] *Ibid.*, 115.

[19] *Ibid.*, 116.

[20] *Ibid.*, 115.

The climax of the courtroom drama – in which Freud vindicates himself – occurs when he places in the dock Otto, whose report about Emma had instigated the trial. He unfavorably compares Otto to Leopold, another pediatrician in their circle. Both men had been Freud's assistants at the Kassowitz Institute for Children's Diseases, where he had observed their contrasting intellectual styles and the intense competition between them. Where Otto was quick but careless, Leopold was "slow but sure." In the dream it is "prudent" Leopold who comes up with the correct diagnosis: Irma was suffering from an infection that had migrated to her left shoulder.[21] Once the diagnosis had been articulated, the same thought simultaneously occurs to Freud and the other three physicians. As Freud's associations reveal, the thought constitutes the heart of the dream:

Not long before, when she was feeling unwell, my friend Otto had given her an injection of a preparation of propyl, propyls . . . propionic acid . . . trimethylamin (and I saw before me the formula for this printed in heavy type) . . . Injections of that sort ought not to be made so thoughtlessly . . . and probably the syringe had not been clean.[22]

The idea that "*injections of that sort ought not to be made so thoughtlessly*" takes Freud back to the preceding day, when he had the feeling that Otto's assessment of Emma was precipitous – "How thoughtlessly he jumps to conclusions!"[23] The idea that "*the syringe had not been clean*," moreover, contains "another accusation against Otto." In contrast to Otto's carelessness, Freud congratulates himself for his conscientious treatment of another female patient. Although he had administered twice-daily injections to her for several years, he "always took constant pains," he tells us, "to be sure the syringe was clean": he had not caused a single infiltration."[24]

At this point, Freud believes he has gathered the material he requires to interpret the "Irma Dream" and substantiate his central thesis. "*When the work of interpretation has been completed*," he writes, "*we perceive that*

[21] *Ibid.*, 112.
[22] *Ibid.*, 107 (emphasis in the original).
[23] *Ibid.*, 117 (emphasis in the original).
[24] *Ibid.*, 118.

a dream is the fulfillment of a wish," presented in a visual form.[25] And the wish that is represented as fulfilled in "the specimen dream of psychoanalysis," Freud maintains, is that he is not responsible for Irma's continued suffering – that he is *vindicated*. However, even if we grant Freud that he has established his central thesis, we are still left with the impression that there is something incomplete about his analysis. And he admits as much:

I will not pretend that I have completely uncovered the meaning of this dream or that its interpretation is without a gap. I could spend much more time over it, derive further information from it and discuss fresh problems raised by it.[26]

Freud, moreover, has no difficulty acknowledging that these gaps result from his attempt to protect his privacy: "Considerations which arise in the case of every dream of my own restrain me from pursuing my interpretative work." On the contrary, he combatively throws down a challenge to any critic who might contest this right to privacy: "If anyone should feel tempted to express a hasty condemnation of my reticence, I would advise him to make the experiment of being franker than I am."[27] One of the reasons that Freud wanted Marie Bonaparte to destroy the Fliess Letters is that they contained the "information" that he did not want to become public, namely, that the dream mirrors the unsavory "Eckstein affair." And when this becomes clear, something else becomes clear as well: the "Irma Dream" does indeed constitute the fulfillment of a wish, as Freud argues, but it is not the wish he claims it is.[28] The person Freud was struggling to exculpate – at least in the first instance – was not himself but Fliess.[29] The wish was to exonerate the great "healer" from the charge of professional incompetence, on a life-threatening scale, in his treatment of Freud's patient Emma Eckstein. Indeed, Schur observes that Fliess could "have been convicted of malpractice in any court for this nearly fatal error."[30]

[25] *Ibid.*, 121 (emphasis in the original).
[26] *Ibid.*, 120–121.
[27] *Ibid.*, 121.
[28] See Anzieu, *Freud's self-analysis*, 143.
[29] See *ibid.*, 144, and Schur, "Some 'additional day residues,'" 70.
[30] Quoted in Masson, *The assault on truth*, 68.

The Latent Meaning

Some time during the first two weeks of February 1895, Fliess visited
Vienna where, according to Masson, he operated on the noses of two
patients, Fräulein Emma Eckstein and her psychoanalyst, Sigmund
Freud.[31] "The exact nature of [Emma's] complaint," according to Masson,
"is unknown, but it appears that she suffered from stomach ailments and
menstrual problems."[32] Although Freud had believed that his patient's
symptoms were hysterical, to play it safe and rule out a diagnosis of orga-
nicity, he asked Fliess to examine her when he was in Vienna for the 1894
Christmas holidays. Fliess, needless to say, recommended doing what he
was predisposed to do: operate.

Though Fliess was an ENT specialist, he was not an old hand at nasal
surgery. He had extensive experience cauterizing and cocainizing the
nasal mucosa, but actual surgery was a new procedure for him. Masson
suggests that he was not highly experienced at performing this procedure;
in fact, Emma may have been the first patient he performed it on.[33] It
appears that Freud was aware of this fact and agreed to the intervention
only reluctantly. His reticence led him to suggest, in a letter dated 24
January 1895, that Fliess call in Robert Gersuny, a well-known plastic
surgeon who would play an important role in Eckstein's treatment, to
assist him in the surgery. We do not know how Fliess responded, but given
his later opposition to outside consultants, we can assume that he did not
greet the suggestion favorably. In the same letter, Freud tells his colleague:

Now only one more week separates us from the operation . . . The time has passed
quickly, and I gladly avoid putting myself through self-examination to ascertain
what right I have to expect so much from it.[34]

Freud is avoiding self-examination for fear that it might reveal his
"over-valuation" of Fliess. He adduces his "lack of medical knowledge"
to get himself off the hook as someone qualified to judge the proposed
procedure, and accedes to Fliess's treatment plan in a highly conflicted

---

[31] See *ibid.*, 81–82.

[32] *Ibid.*, 57.

[33] *Ibid.*, 60.

[34] Masson (ed.), *Letters to Fliess*, 107.

way. He writes that he "would not have dared to invent this plan of treatment on [his] own," but insofar as he has "some insight into the matter, the cure must be achievable by this route." He will therefore "confidently join" Fliess in it.[35] Thus, even before the surgery on Eckstein, Freud had serious doubts about Fliess's abilities and struggled to suppress those doubts.

The next critical letter is dated 4 March, which means it was written several weeks after Fleiss had operated on Emma, and, as Schur observes, it "already contains the whole conflict."[36] Freud begins by apologizing for having allowed an "unconscionably long" time to pass "without a reply" to Fliess's letter. This suggests that he had indeed been angry toward him. The tone, however, immediately turns affectionate. Freud informs his friend that he had ordered a photograph of the two of them – "beautiful we are not" – apparently taken immediately after Eckstein's surgery. In what is a remarkable statement given what we are about to hear, he tells Fliess that the photo reminded him of the "pleasure" he derived from having the Berliner "close by [his] side after the operation."[37] When Freud turns to the topic of Emma's recovery, however, the news is distressing, to say the least:

Eckstein's condition is still unsatisfactory: persistent swelling, going up and going down "like an avalanche"; pain, so that morphine cannot be dispensed with; bad nights. The purulent secretions have been decreasing since yesterday; the day before yesterday (Saturday) she had a massive hemorrhage, probably as a result of expelling a bone chip the size of a heller; there were two bowls full of pus . . .[38]

We could continue with Freud's recitation of these horrors, but this should suffice. The deteriorating situation led Freud to arrange for a consultation, and the particular syntax he uses when he breaks the news to Fliess indicates how concerned he was about the danger of alienating his "only Other."[39] "Since the pain and the visible edema had increased, I *let myself*

[35] *Ibid.*, 107.

[36] Schur, "Some 'additional day residues,'" 68.

[37] Masson (ed.), *Letters to Fliess*, 113. Jung would send a similar letter to Freud years later.

[38] *Ibid.*, 113.

[39] *Ibid.*, 72.

be persuaded" [*"lies sich mich bewegen"*], he writes, "to call in Gersuny."[40] Freud is saying in effect, "I'm not to blame, I still believe in you, but the forces of circumstance compelled me to seek an outside consultant." This device, however, does not alleviate Freud's fear of offending his colleague, and in an attempt to undo the damage and restore his friend's standing, Freud asks Fliess to "send his authoritative advice" concerning the situation.[41]

As if to remind Fliess that he is his other patient – and to make an implicit connection between Emma's condition and his own – Freud encloses with the 4 March letter a *"Case History"* – the case being his. The language he uses to describe his condition on the day Fliess left Vienna for Berlin – he speaks of "thick old pus clots," "purulent secretion," and "migraines" – is almost the same language he used to describe Emma's. But, rather than criticize Fliess for his unsuccessful treatment – not to mention the fact that his cardiac symptoms had also reappeared – Freud employs a torturous masochistic logic to disavow what was happening. He does adduce the evidence at his disposal not to criticize Fliess's treatment of him, but to show that Fliess's theory is correct. While the news that he is suffering from acute nasal and cardiac symptoms is "not designed to make one feel at ease," at least, Freud writes, "this information affords some pleasure because it emphasizes once again that the condition of the heart depends on the condition of the nose" – something he had stopped believing long before.[42] In other words, though it might be bad news for the patient that Freud is suffering in both organs, it was good news for the physician; it served to confirm Fliess's nasal reflex theory.

The letter at the epicenter of the whole affair is dated 8 March. And though it has been widely quoted, it is necessary to discuss it at length. Freud begins by giving Fliess a heads-up so he can prepare himself for the bombshell that is about to explode. He informs the Berliner that he is about to give him a "report which will probably upset [Fliess] as much as it did" him. He nevertheless expresses the hope that "you will get over it as quickly as I."[43] The fact of the matter is that, far from getting over it

[40] *Ibid.*, 113 (emphasis added).
[41] *Ibid.*, 114.
[42] *Ibid.*, 115–116.
[43] *Ibid.*, 116.

quickly, Freud wrestled with the aftershocks of the events he was about to describe for years. Freud informs Fliess that because Emma's condition continued to worsen, he turned to Gersuny for another intervention. The surgeon drained her nose, but "was otherwise rather reserved." Then, two days later, Freud was "awakened in the morning" to be informed that "profuse bleeding had started again, pain, and so on."[44] As Gersuny was unavailable, Freud contacted another surgeon, Rosanes, to attend to Emma, and he began by cleaning the area around Emma's nose and removing some blood clots. But "suddenly," he

> pulled at something like a thread, kept pulling. Before either of us had time to think at least half a meter of gauze had been removed from the cavity. The next moment came a flood of blood. The patient turned white, her eyes bulged, and she had no pulse. Immediately thereafter, however, he again packed the cavity with fresh iodoform gauze and the hemorrhage stopped. It lasted about half a minute, but this was enough to make the poor creature, whom by then we had lying flat, unrecognizable.[45]

Freud then says something that immediately sparks our curiosity: "At the moment the foreign body came out *everything became clear to me*." But, instead of telling Fliess – and us – what had become clear to him, Freud simply returns to his narrative, informing Fliess, that as soon as Emma's nose had been packed, he "fled to the next room," where he "drank a bottle of water, and felt miserable."[46]

The two things that happened next cast a disparaging light on Freud's masculinity. First, the "brave Frau Doktor" – though it is not clear who this figure is, her strength and equanimity stand in marked contrast to Freud's own weakness – "brought [him] a small glass of cognac and," after drinking it, he "became himself again."[47] Then, when he returned to the scene of the crime, "somewhat shaken," Emma greeted him with a castrating quip: "So this is the strong sex."[48] Instead of occupying the

---

[44] *Ibid.*, 116.

[45] *Ibid.*, 117.

[46] *Ibid.*, 117 (emphasis added).

[47] In a footnote, Masson reports that he was unable to track down who the Frau Doktor was. *Ibid.*, 118 n. 2.

[48] *Ibid.*, 117.

position of the powerful phallic Father-Doctor, Freud is cast in the position of a castrated female.

In the next paragraph of the letter, Freud begins a dance of disavowal and displacement – similar to the one we observed in the Irma Dream – which is designed to shield Fliess from criticism. It is at this point that Freud tells Fliess what it was that he had perceived with such clarity at the "moment" the hemorrhaging erupted. "I don't believe," he writes, "it was the blood that overwhelmed me." Rather, he thinks that his faintness resulted from "the strong emotions" that were "welling up in" him. What he says next leads us to expect that he not only understands the full significance of these events, but is prepared to acknowledge that Emma's difficulties were iatrogenic and to accept responsibility on his and Fliess's behalf: "So we had done her an injustice; she was not abnormal, rather, a piece of iodoform gauze had gotten torn off as you were removing it."[49] *Having articulated it so clearly, this is the conclusion Freud should have stuck with.* Instead, he immediately contradicts himself and lets Fliess off the hook again: "Of course, no one is blaming you, nor would I know why they should."[50] Freud then produces a series of rationalizations that amount to a case of defensive overkill. His first line of defense is to blame himself. He should not, he writes, have "tormented" Fliess by urging the Berliner "to operate in a foreign city where [he] could not follow through on the case." Second, he points out that the accident is not that uncommon but in fact happens to "the most fortunate and circumspect of surgeons." And, finally, Freud shifts the blame to Rosanes, who, he asserts, acted carelessly when he precipitously pulled the foreign body out of Emma's nose.[51]

In the aftermath of these events, Freud developed a severe depression – "I rarely have felt so low and down, almost melancholic; all my interests have lost their meaning."[52] In a letter dated approximately a month later, he tells Fliess that his state is "unbelievably gloomy" because "this Eckstein affair" was "rapidly moving toward a bad ending."[53] Yet another crisis had occurred that had spanned the previous three days.

---

[49] *Ibid.*, 117.

[50] *Ibid.*, 118.

[51] For this entire paragraph see *ibid.*, 117–118.

[52] *Ibid.*, 119.

[53] *Ibid.*, 124.

After Emma's nose had been packed and repacked several times, it was unpacked again, and "there was a new, life-threatening hemorrhage which [Freud] witnessed." The bleeding, he writes, "did not spurt, it surged." And, he continues, given "the pain, the morphine, the demoralization caused by the obvious medical helplessness, and the danger," Fliess could surely imagine the state Emma was in. This time, moreover, the attending physicians did not pull their punches; they identified Fliess's original intervention as the source of Eckstein's life-threatening situation. Indeed, the evidence is so overwhelming that even Freud is forced to concur – at least for a moment: "I am really very shaken," he writes, "to think that such a mishap could have arisen from an operation that" Fliess "purported to be so harmless."[54] Three weeks earlier he had written: "In my thoughts I have given up hope for the poor girl and am inconsolable that I involved you and created such a distressing affair for you."[55] Freud has it backwards. The person toward whom Freud should feel inconsolable is, as Masson points out, Emma, not Fliess.[56]

At this point, Freud possesses more than enough objective evidence to assemble an accurate picture of who Fliess is and what has happened – and to hold him accountable. But to do so would have meant giving up Fleiss as his idealized "Other," and that was a step that Freud was incapable of taking. Freud's tenacious refusal to register the evidence before his eyes is so extreme that, as Gay observes, if one did not know better, one would take it as an instance of "willed blindness."[57]

Doctor or Patient? Man or Woman?

Why does Freud's interpretation of the Irma Dream strike us as so unresolved? The complicated chemical formula that emerges in Freud's associations contains the answer. Freud notes that the formula's "*heavy type*" suggests that it is the "centerpiece" of the dream, but he does not pursue its meaning in the detail it deserves, and the interpretation therefore remains incomplete. Strachey calls our attention to a curious fact, that is,

---

[54] *Ibid.*, 124.

[55] *Ibid.*, 121.

[56] Masson, *The assault on truth*, 69.

[57] Gay, *Freud: a life for our time*, 57.

although Fliess is not mentioned by name, he "figures frequently" in Freud's analysis of the "Irma Dream," especially in relation to sexuality.[58] This observation itself leads to another odd feature of Freud's interpretation. At this point in his career, he was energetically promoting his thesis that sexuality comprises the primary determinant of psychopathology. But while there are a number of obvious allusions to the topic in the dream – for example, the intrusion into Irma's mouth, her injection with the dirty syringe, and her refusal to accept Freud's "solution" – the topic receives little direct attention. And there is yet another point that further compounds our perplexity. Despite "its quite special importance" in the dream, with the notable exception of the American psychoanalyst David Lotto, the significance of Trimethylamin (TMA) has rarely been discussed in the literature.[59] For reasons that will become apparent, "prudery" in the form of inhibitions regarding the connection between sexuality and the sense of smell – even among analysts – might help to account for this omission.

Freud himself raises the right question: "What was it, then, to which my attention was to be directed in this way by Trimethylamin?" In his attempt to answer it, he recalls "a conversation" he had with a "friend, who had . . . been familiar with [his] writings during the period of their gestation," where "the subject of the chemistry of the sexual process" was discussed. And in it his friend noted "that one of the products of sexual metabolism was Trimethylamin."[60] Freud now believes he recognizes why TMA occupied such a "prominent" position in the dream: because "so many important subjects converged upon" it. The formula for TMA refers to "the immensely powerful factor of sexuality," something Breuer and Emma refused to accept, and points "to a person whose agreement [Freud] recalled with satisfaction whenever [he] felt isolated in [his] opinions" – namely, Fliess, who not only accepted his "solution" to the problem of the neuroses, but also possessed the power to restore his sense of self. "Surely," Freud exclaims, "this friend . . . must appear again elsewhere in these trains of thoughts." And, sure enough, he does: in Freud's examination of Irma's oral cavity, where he observes her turbinal

---

[58] Freud, *The interpretation of dreams*, 116 n. 2 (emphasis added).

[59] Lotto, "Freud's struggle with misogyny."

[60] Freud, The *interpretation of dreams*, 116.

bones, which, according to the unnamed friend, have a "very remarkable" connection with "the female organs of sex."[61]

At this point, Freud correctly understands that the link between the nose and female sexuality holds the key to the meaning of these crucial passages in the all important "specimen dream of psychoanalysis," but he does not grasp the nature of that link correctly. *It pertains not to the structural similarities between the turbinal bones and the female genitalia, but to a more elemental bodily phenomenon: the connection between the sense of smell and sexual excitement.*

This is where Lotto makes his entrance. His thesis is that the "Emma Affair" served to solidify Freud's homosexual ties to Fliess. It is one instance, he maintains, of a "recurring triangle" in Freud's life, in which he forged a homosexual bond with a male companion by jointly treating a female victim in a misogynist and sadistic fashion.[62] "For Freud," Lotto contends, "shared sexual and aggressive" behavior "toward a woman was an integral part of the homosexual connection between himself and the other man."[63] There were earlier instances of the triangle, first involving Freud, his nephew John, and his niece Pauline, and then Freud, Eduard Silberstein, and Gisela Fluss. And there would be a later one, when Freud and Jung maltreated Jung's patient, student, and lover, Sabina Spielrein. But, Lotto argues, "the surgery on Emma's nose" constitutes the most extensive and consequential "repetition and reenactment of this paradigmatic misogynist and triangular relationship."[64]

Because we do not know what Fliess said to Freud about Trimethylamin's role in the "chemistry of the sexual processes," and because there are no references to the substance in the Berliner's three major works, "we are left to wonder," Lotto observes, "about the substance of these conversations about TMA and the chemistry of the sexual processes."[65] Given Freud's and Fliess's obsession with the nose, the discharges that emanate from it, and its connection with sexuality, it comes as no surprise when Lotto informs us that the sense of smell and sexuality converge

[61] *Ibid.*, 117.

[62] Lotto, "Freud's struggle with misogyny," 1300.

[63] *Ibid.*, 1304.

[64] *Ibid.*, 1301.

[65] *Ibid.*, 1291.

in the TMA. "The most prominent characteristic of TMA," which "the human nose can detect . . . at very low concentrations," is, he tells us, that it "smells strongly of rotting fish."[66] Moreover, its presence in vaginal secretions is responsible for the "fishy odor" that is often associated with a woman's sexual organs. At least as far back as Horace, "the world of misogynist humor" has mocked female sexuality by comparing the *odori di femmina* to the unpleasant smell of fish.[67] Because they were physicians, knowledgeable about the workings of sexuality, Freud and Fliess would surely have been aware of the connection between this particular smell and a woman's sexual chemistry.

How much raunchy misogynist humor did these two bourgeois gentlemen allow themselves in private when they were discussing the connection between TMA and female sexuality? This is a question that can never be answered. According to Lotto, however, the "Irma Dream" does suggest that the theme was present in Freud's unconscious associations. He claims that by signifying a shared disparagement of female sexuality, the reference to TMA constitutes a highly condensed piece of dream-work that allowed Freud to express his homosexual attachment to Fliess in a disguised form. Their bond was partly constituted through their shared sadism toward Eckstein and, in turn, reinforced by it.[68]

Lotto's argument is not as implausible as it might appear in light of the following consideration. It would be difficult to underestimate the importance that Freud attributed to the sense of smell in the psycho-sexual life of human beings throughout his career. In two famous footnotes that appear in *Civilization and its discontents*, published in 1930, he repeated almost verbatim an idea that he had already proposed to Fliess in the 1890s.[69] He argues that the assumption of an upright bipedal posture by our "ape-like" ancestors marked a critical advance in the civilizing process. Prior to that step, our predecessors were on all fours and therefore in constant proximity to the genital and anal regions of the other members of their cohort and to the smells associated with them. This meant that

[66] *Ibid.*, 1301.

[67] *Ibid.*, 1293.

[68] *Ibid.*, 1310.

[69] See Masson (ed.), *Letters to Fliess*, 279, and Freud, *Civilization and its discontents*, 99 n. 1. and 105–106 n. 2.

olfactory stimulation constituted a central excitatory factor in their sexual lives. The assumption of an erect gait, however, distanced our primate forebears from their relatively direct contact with those nether regions. Consequently, the sense of smell was superseded by the less immediate sense of sight – seeing the genitals rather than smelling them became primary – and olfaction was not only repressed but also devalued. As with every advance in the civilizing process, "the gods of a superseded period" were "turned into devils," and the entire realm of olfaction and anal eroticism became negatively invested with a sense of shame, filth, and disgust.[70]

Freud speculates that another transition occurred in conjunction with these developments: from the condition where females are sexually receptive only at episodic intervals – when they are in "heat" – to one where they are physiologically available for intercourse on a continuous basis. This transition was civilizing in two ways. By providing the male with an incentive to stick around, "the continuity of sexual excitement" promoted the formation of an ongoing nuclear family; by also uncoupling the sexual act from reproduction, it gave rise to new, distinctly human forms of non-procreative psychosexuality and emotional intimacy.[71] With this advance in civilization, the old deities were again "turned into devils." The scent that females emit in most non-human species during estrus is an "attractant," designed to excite the males in her group to be drawn to her. Indeed, the Greek and Latin terms (*oistros* and *oestrus*), from which our term "estrus" derives, carry the connotations of overpowering desire, insane passion, and frenzy. For example, in *The Republic*, Plato uses the term to describe "the tyrannized soul" that is "driven and drawn by the gadfly (*oistros*) of desire" and "will be full of confusion" (577e). According to Freud, however, with the assumption of an upright posture, the repression of the sense of smell, and the emergence of the menstrual cycle in the human species, "the taboo on menstruation" was instituted, and the hedonic valence of "olfactory stimuli" was "reversed."

As the "fateful process of civilization" with its "incitement to cleanliness" progressed, Freud believed that the *odore di femmina* ceased to function as an attractant and became repellent to most men.[72] To supplement

[70] Freud, *Civilization and its discontents*, 99 n. 1.

[71] *Ibid.*, 99–100 n. 1.

[72] *Ibid.*, 99–100 n. 1, 105 n. 3.

his "scientific" assertion that the advance of civilization entails the repression and degradation of sexual fragrances, he offers an example from the "commonplace prejudices" of civilized Europeans:

In spite of the undeniable depreciation of olfactory stimuli, there exist even in Europe peoples among whom the strong sense of genital odors which are so repellent to us are highly prized as sexual stimulants and who refuse to give them up.[73]

Prejudices indeed. According to the logic of Freud's theory, only neurotic men, that is, men who by definition have refused to submit to the demands of civilization, continue to find the scents of female sexuality – which provide a pathway to the powerful affects deposited in our primitive reptilian brains – pleasurable and exciting. It is hard to imagine, however, that Arthur Schnitzler, Gustav Klimt, and the other sensualists of the Vienna *Lusthaus* suffered from this aversion. Freud's observation says more about him than it does about the sexual proclivities of his contemporaries. Where Freud is incredulous that some European men continue to enjoy these olfactory pleasures, we should be taken aback by his incredulity. This is the repudiation of femininity at its most corporeal.

In one respect, Lotto's description of the Sigmund–Wilhelm–Emma triangle is obviously correct. It pictures Fliess and Freud, in their joint role as the active Father-Doctor, together on the same side of a triangle, and Emma, in her role as the passive woman and a patient, alone on the other. By arranging the surgery in spite of his serious doubts, and by stubbornly defending his friend – indeed, by even blaming the victim after the procedure was botched – Freud aligned himself with Fliess and participated in a sadistic attack on a female, as he had with his nephew John and his boyhood buddy Silberstein. This time, however, the attack masqueraded as a legitimate medical procedure. "Freud's misogynist and homosexual impulses," as Lotto puts it, "were stimulated by Fliess's . . . surgical error committed while operating on Freud's patient, Emma Eckstein."[74] By identifying with the aggressive, phallic, and sadistic Father-Doctor, Freud, as Sprengnether observes, repudiated the "passive position" of the castrated and bleeding female patient.[75]

---

[73] *Ibid.*, 106.

[74] Lotto, "Freud's struggle with misogyny," 1290.

[75] Sprengnether, *The spectral mother*, 34.

But the triangle can be configured in another way, with Freud and Eckstein grouped together and occupying one side of the figure, opposing Fliess who faces them on the other. In addition to his self-object transference to Fliess as a pre-Oedipal object, Freud, as we have seen, was also embroiled in a more advanced phallic-level transference to the wizard from Berlin. In this configuration, Fliess became the object of Freud's passive homosexual desire, and he wished to submit to and be penetrated by him. Because it located Freud in "the 'passive' position" – in the feminine/homosexual position as he defined it – Freud's identification with Emma was part and parcel of the second transference. The Berliner had treated Freud during his cardiac episode, cauterized and cocainized his nose shortly before the fateful operation on Eckstein, and planned to operate on him again at the end of the summer. Furthermore, like Emma, Freud suffered serious complications in the aftermath of Fliess's interventions. However much Freud wanted to repudiate it, there was one fact that could not be denied: Both he and Emma had occupied the passive/castrated position as Fliess's patients.[76] Given that both had "submitted to surgical intervention at the hands of Fliess . . . it is hard to imagine," as Sprengnether observes, "how Freud could have avoided a comparison between these two events and the possibility of a shared fate."[77] "*Madame Eckstein*," he must have thought, "*c'est moi*."[78] And "to be like Eckstein," Sprengnether observes, was "to be like a woman," offering herself "up as an object of Fliess' desire."[79] Sharing her fate was to share the fate of a castrated and bleeding female patient, that is, of "the suffering woman."[80] And this "mutilated creature," was a figure he wanted nothing to do with.[81]

From the other direction, Freud's formidable ambition and reverence for independence stood in opposition to this powerful multiply determined wish to submit to Fliess – and led to a struggle against it. A remarkably long and torturous process – in which Freud tried to

---

[76] *Ibid.*, 34.

[77] *Ibid.*, 30–31.

[78] Boyarin, *Unheroic conduct*, 213 (emphasis in the original).

[79] Sprengnether, *The spectral mother*, 31. See also Anzieu, *Freud's self-analysis*, 144.

[80] *Ibid.*, 30–31.

[81] *Ibid.*, 34.

exonerate Fliess by blaming Emma for her misfortunes – was required, however, before his striving for autonomy achieved the upper hand. That the essential incompatibility between Fliess's physio–numerological theory and Freud's psychological approach had to be camouflaged in Freud's defense of the Berliner's indefensible behavior helps to explain the bizarre quality of his efforts. The developments in Freud's life in the wake of Emma's surgery add support to the idea, originating with Melanie Klein, a central figure in the history of psychoanalysis, not only that creativity represents an attempt to repair the damaged object, but that the attempt at reparation often assumes a manic character.[82] The severe depression that Freud fell into following Fliess's botched intervention gave rise to a period of intense creativity. Aided by "a lot" of cocaine and nicotine, Freud took on an "inhuman workload," and, as Breuer reported at the time, his "intellect" was "soaring" like a "hawk."[83] With "psychology" having become Freud's "tyrant" and "consuming passion," he had made two important discoveries: that dreams constitute the fulfillment of wishes and that pathological and normal phenomena form a continuum.[84] Freud was in fact on the verge of uncovering "something from the very core of nature."[85]

More specifically, he was on the verge of recognizing that fantasies expressing sexual wishes (at this point he referred to them as "scenes"), which emanate from a person's inner world, are the cause of hysteria.[86] He was, in other words, about to make what we have argued was his most consequential discovery of the 1890s: the existence of psychic reality. But because the need to exonerate Fliess contaminated this critical insight into the nature of hysteria, he at first expressed this new insight in a thoroughly distorted way. A year after the surgery, Freud informs Fliess that he can now "prove" that Emma's "episodes of bleeding were

---

[82] Loewald notes that successful sublimation typically contains "a manic element." Loewald, "Sublimation: inquiries into theoretical psychoanalysis," 463.

[83] Masson (ed.), *Letters to Fliess*, 128, 134 n. 1.

[84] *Ibid.*, 140 and 129.

[85] *Ibid.*, 136.

[86] Schur notes that in the letters to Fliess during this period, the meaning of the term "scene" is undergoing a decisive change. Rather than denoting the memory of an actual event, as it had in *Studies in hysteria*, it is acquiring the meaning of an intrapsychic "fantasy." See Schur, "Some 'additional day residues,'" 83 n. 55.

hysterical" – that is, "occasioned by *longing*." This was a proposition made by the Berliner himself. Although this "proof" would succeed in getting Fliess off the hook, it conveniently overlooks an awkward fact. Originally, the ENT specialist diagnosed Emma's condition not as a case of hysteria but as a "nasal reflex neurosis," and he performed the surgery on the basis of that diagnosis. And Freud makes another assertion, namely, that Emma's longing was sexual in nature, which would accord with his psychogenic theory of hysteria. But rather than tracing this sexual longing to intrapsychic processes, he explains them in terms of Fliess's theory of periodicity. Emma's "episodes of bleeding," Freud tells his colleague, "occurred at sexually relevant times." Unfortunately, however, the incompliant "woman, out of resistance, [had] not yet supplied [him] with the dates" – something he promises to obtain for his colleague in the future.[87]

This mad-hatter reasoning, as the psychoanalyst Paul Schimmel notes, reveals "a desperate man, warding off a more realistic appraisal and probably the attendant depression."[88] It would only end when Freud resolved his transference to Fliess in a "good-enough" fashion, thus enabling him to perceive the Berliner in a more realistic light.[89] To accomplish this, it would be necessary for Freud to accept the existence and power of psychic reality in general, and this, in turn, required that he concede the existence and power of his own psychic reality. Only then could Freud gain conviction about the truth, uniqueness, and magnitude of his own ideas and see Fliess for who he was: a sophisticated and charismatic charlatan. It was the death of Freud's father that set this process of discovery in motion. Prior to Jacob's passing, however, in a last feverish attempt to provide a comprehensive "psychology for neurologists," Freud bade "farewell" to a physicalist approach to the mind.[90] In an unpublished manuscript,

---

[87] Masson (ed.), *Letters to Fliess*, 183 (emphasis in the original).

[88] Paul Schimmel, *Sigmund Freud's discovery of psychoanalysis: conquistador and thinker* (New York: Routledge, 2013), 94.

[89] Like all transferences, Freud's transference to Fliess was never fully resolved. Indeed, the idea of a fully resolved transference belongs to the register of omnipotence and is not on the cards for finite creatures like us. As we will see, he was still struggling with it a decade later during his relationship with Jung.

[90] Masson (ed.), *Letters to Fliess*, 127, and Anzieu, *Freud's self-analysis*, 159.

discovered with the Fliess Letters, that contained forty thousand words
and was entitled *Project for a scientific psychology*, he set out

> to furnish a psychology that shall be a natural science: that is, to represent psy-
> chical process as quantitatively determinate states of specifiable material particles,
> thus making those processes perspicuous and free from contradiction.[91]

Though a number of its ideas had a rich afterlife in the history of Freud's
thought, the *Project* constituted a *reductio ad extremum*, in which he pursued the logic of the quantitative-materialist approach so rigorously and
thoroughly that its fundamental untenability became apparent. No sooner
had the *Project* been completed than it was obsolete. On 8 November 1895,
Freud consigned it to the drawer, never to see the light of day. Regarding
the psychological significance of the *Project*, it was a defensive work by
means of which Freud attempted to keep psychic reality – in himself and
in others – at arm's length by "scientifically" objectifying it. With Jacob's
death, however, Freud could no longer maintain this sort of "hysteropho-
bic" strategy and he was forced to confront his inner world directly.[92]

The Most Poignant Event in a Man's Life?

Like many of the *idées reçues* having to do with Freud's biography, the
standard account of his reaction to his father's death does not add up. "By
the time he died," Freud told Fliess, Jacob's "life had long been over."[93]
Indeed, there is little evidence that the old man played much of a role
in his son's life during the 1890s. Prior to June 1896 – that is, up until
four months before his death – Jacob "had hardly been mentioned in the
correspondence with Fliess."[94] At the same time, there is no doubt that
"the old man's death affected [Freud] deeply," leaving him feeling "quite
uprooted" and throwing him into a profound psychological crisis.[95] The
experience was so powerful that it led Freud to assert, in the "Preface
to the second edition" of *The interpretation of dreams*, that the death of

---

[91] Sigmund Freud, *Project for a scientific psychology* (1895), *SE* I: 295.

[92] Anzieu, *Freud's self-analysis*, 160.

[93] Masson (ed.), *Letters to Fliess*, 202.

[94] Schur, *Freud: living and dying*, 105.

[95] Masson (ed.), *Letters to Fliess*, 202.

a father is "the most important event, the most poignant loss of a man's life" – an assertion that, as Gay notes, is by no means self-evident.[96]

To be sure, Freud harbored enormous unconscious anger toward his father that he was never able adequately to face. But it is clear from the letters he wrote at the time that Freud also had a deep affection for Jacob's "peculiar mixture of deep wisdom and fantastic light-heartedness," and he admired the way his father "bore himself bravely to the end, just like the altogether unusual man he had been."[97] Moreover, it must have been agonizing to watch the man who had led him through the woods surrounding Freiberg diminish, to see the man who had introduced him to the Philippson Bible as a small boy "waste away – shrink, as he had put it . . . long before his physiological death."[98] Nevertheless, given Freud's stage in life and relation to Jacob at the time, his reaction to his father's death, Gay argues, "was exceptional in its intensity."[99] And these considerations do not explain the magnitude and intensity of the crisis that was precipitated by his father's passing.

Freud himself came up with a convincing explanation but could not run with it. "In [my] inner self," he told Fliess, "the whole past has been reawakened by this event."[100] In the aftermath of Jacob's death, Freud was plunged into a state of acute mourning and began a systematic self-analysis – which he had previously pursued in a more or less ad hoc fashion – in an attempt to come to grips with the pain. This tells us that he had reconciled himself to the fact that what he was suffering from was a form of *psycho*-pathology, as opposed to neurasthenia or some primarily physical ailment. He wrote to Fliess that he had become his own "most important patient" and that his "self-analysis" had become the "essential thing" in his life.[101] Freud's creative illness had reached its peak; sickness, therapy and the pursuit of knowledge now converged in his self-analysis. "A psychologist," Nietzsche writes, "should he himself

[96] Freud, *The interpretation of dreams*," xxvi; Gay, *Freud: a life for our time*, 89. One wants to ask, "What about the death of a man's mother?"

[97] Masson (ed.), *Letters to Fliess*, 202 and 201.

[98] Schur, *Freud: living and dying*, 109.

[99] Gay, *Freud: a life for our time*, 88.

[100] Masson (ed.), *Letters to Fliess*, 202.

[101] *Ibid.*, 279 and 270.

become ill . . . will bring all of his scientific curiosity into the illness."[102]
Freud was no exception.

The problem, however, was this: Rather than confronting his "whole
past," Freud's conscious pursuit of his *Trauerarbeit*, his work-of-
mourning, and his self-analysis both remained narrowly focused on the
loss of his father. The restricted conception of the classical Oedipus
complex *as a "father complex"* that emerged from his self-analysis was a
consequence of the relatively limited analytical scope. The process that
was unleashed by Jacob's death, however, far exceeded the parameters of
that one loss, and this fact goes a long way toward explaining its severity.
His father's death, as he told Fliess, had "reawakened" his "whole past,"
and through "those dark pathways behind the official consciousness," it
had reactivated the split-off memories of the other losses in Freud's life,
especially those from his early years.[103] But Freud could only intuit and
not fully fathom the processes that had been set in motion in his inner
world.

In addition to the fact that, as we have seen, he refers to his *Kinderfrau*
as his "original seducer," there is something else problematic in the fact
that Freud "abandoned the seduction theory" and that this abandonment
constituted the founding act of psychoanalysis. The legendary event officially occurred on 21 September 1897 when Freud announced to Fliess,
"I no longer believe in my *neurotica* [theory of neurosis]." Before that
point, Freud maintained, as we have seen, that unconscious memories of
actual childhood traumas – primarily of a sexual nature – were the cause
of hysteria. The "continual disappointments" using a clinical approach
predicated on that assumption, however, led him to reevaluate the
theory.[104] And a straightforward quantitative calculation played a pivotal
role in his rejection of it: given the number of hysterics (neurotics) in
Vienna, the prevalence of sexual abuse would have to be so extensive as to
be implausible. More specifically, the number of "perverse fathers," who
were thought to be the primary culprits in child abuse, the theory would
have required strained one's credulity. Indeed, given the sheer implausi-
bility of the numbers, what is "astonishing," as Gay observes, is not "that

[102] Nietzsche, *The gay science*, 4.

[103] See Breger, *Freud*, 135–137.

[104] Masson (ed.), *Letters to Fliess*, 264.

Freud eventually abandoned the idea, but that he adopted it in the first place."[105]

In conjunction with his "abandonment of the seduction theory," Freud proposed a new theory of hysteria that can be summed up in a new formula: Hysterics, for the most part, suffer not from reminiscences of scenes of actual sexual experiences, but from unconscious fantasies of sexual scenes. The description by Jean Laplanche and J.-B. Pontalis in their masterly work *The language of psycho-analysis* unpacks the formula aptly: "Phantasies, even if they are not based on real events, now come to have the same pathogenic effect for the subject as that which Freud had at first attributed to 'reminiscences.'"[106]

This is where the situation becomes particularly thorny and must be carefully sorted out. Freud's adversaries often proffer a simplistic argument. When Freud abandoned the seduction hypothesis and replaced it with a theory of fantasy, they argue, he was ipso facto denying the existence and prevalence of actual child abuse. His critics often make the further claim that Freud's rejection of the seduction theory was a politically motivated cover-up of the reality of child abuse. The ambitious young physician, so the argument goes, did not want to offend Vienna's powerful patriarchs with the scandalous accusation that they were a gang of child molesters.[107] This itself, however, is a piece of politically motivated nonsense. Freud never claimed that the abuse of children was an uncommon phenomenon in contemporary society. He had spent too many hours working in Vienna's General Hospital and attending autopsies in Paris's legendary morgue, where he had ample opportunity to observe its consequences, to make such an assertion. Moreover, even if Freud had been, as many no doubt assumed, an assimilating Jewish go-getter, eager to stay on the good side of "The Man," he would never have promoted a scandalous theory contending that small children are sexual creatures who harbor murderous wishes toward their elders.

The point of contention is not *whether* actual traumas play a role in the formation of psychopathology. Freud never denied that they did. Rather,

---

[105] Gay, *Freud: a life for our time*, 91.

[106] J. Laplanche and J.-B. Pontalis, *The language of psycho-analysis*, trans. Donald Nicholson-Smith (New York: W.W. Norton & Co., 1973.), 363.

[107] The *locus classicus* of this position is Masson, *The assault on truth*.

the controversial questions (which are as hotly debated as they were at the beginning of the twentieth century) are these: What is the relative weight of fantasy versus actual experience – which is to say, the Real – in the genesis of psychopathology? And how do the fantasy and the Real interact in that process? It should be pointed out that Freud changed his position on these questions, as he did on many others, throughout his career; in fact, he returned to an emphasis on traumatic experience in his later writings.[108] But the radically new thesis that Freud was advancing with his 1897 change of paradigm was something different. In addition to whatever contribution the Real might make to pathogenesis, unconscious fantasies are a crucial factor. In their multiplicity of shapes and forms, psychological symptoms, much like dreams, comprise the disguised expression of unconscious fantasies, usually of a wishful and sexual nature. More broadly – and more consequentially for a general theory of the human mind – Freud's new account of neurosis also led him to postulate the existence of psychic reality as the interior realm in which those fantasies are produced.[109] Fantasies, he argued, "possess *psychical* as contrasted to *material* reality," and "*in the world of the neuroses it is psychical reality which is the decisive factor.*"[110]

In 1845, Marx asserted that German Idealism had stressed the "*active side*" in philosophy, that is, the side of the mind that actively organizes – constitutes, determines, arranges – our experience.[111] Approximately a half-century later, Freud – who in many important respects is the heir to "classical German philosophy," his renunciation of the Queen of the Sciences notwithstanding – substantially expanded the concept of the "*active side*."[112] He maintained that unconscious psychic reality

---

[108] See Grubrich-Simitis, *Early Freud and late Freud.*

[109] Freud's extensive discussion of the "dream-work" is meant to elucidate the process through which neurotic symptomatology is generated, which is closely analogous to the process through which the manifest content of a dream is generated. See Freud, *The interpretation of dreams*, chapter VI.

[110] Sigmund Freud, *Introductory lectures on psycho-analysis (part III)*, 1916–1917, SE 16: 368 (emphasis in the original).

[111] Karl Marx, "Theses on Feuerbach," *Karl Marx and Frederick Engels: selected works*, vol. I (Moscow: Progress Press, 1969), 13 (emphasis in the original).

[112] See Stanley Cavell, "Freud and philosophy: a fragment," *Critical Inquiry* 13 (1987), 391.

and the fantasies it produces determine our experience, especially our pathological experience, as much as Kant's categories and schemata – indeed, perhaps even more.[113] At this point in his career, Freud tended to essentialize unconscious psychic reality and maintained that it constituted "the core of our being."[114] The concept of psychic reality, according to Laplanche and Pontalis, designates "whatever in the subject's psyche presents a consistency and resistance comparable to those displayed by material reality" – that is to say, by the external world, including the external world of our own bodies.[115] With his introduction of psychic reality, Freud was postulating the existence of a heretofore undiscovered realm of mind – and of nature, insofar as the human mind is part of nature. For Freud, we are citizens of two worlds. "Material reality" impinges on and determines us from one direction, and "psychic reality" exerts itself on and determines us, with at least equal force, from another.[116]

It must be admitted that Freud's position in 1900, in contrast to the one he held in the 1930s, suffered from a degree of perhaps unavoidable one-sidedness. He had just made his great discovery of psychic reality. As a researcher does with an element in a scientific preparation, he set out to isolate this newly discovered region in order to explore and map it as vigorously as he could. Freud acknowledged the imbalance in his position, but justified it in terms of the historical context: He had uncovered the "active side" of unconscious psychic functioning, and his first priority was to highlight it in order to demonstrate its significance for pathological and normal functioning, even if a degree of distortion was the result. Regarding clinical theory, Freud believed he had made the crucial and novel discovery that the active unconscious mind plays a "decisive" role in determining psychopathology, and he attempted to fashion a distinctly psychoanalytic technique that corresponded to it. And with regard to the ethics of psychoanalysis, the postulation of psychic reality had important implications that, as Castoriadis has demonstrated, led to a

[113] The position that thinkers assume on this question is an important indicator of where to locate them on the rationalist–irrationalist spectrum.

[114] Freud, *The interpretation of dreams*, 603. This state of affairs changed when Freud introduced the more differentiated structural model in 1923 and did not essentialize any of the psychic agencies – neither the ego, the super, nor the id.

[115] Laplanche and Pontalis, *The language of psycho-analysis*, 363.

[116] See especially Castoriadis, *The imaginary institution of society*, chapter 6.

deepening of the Enlightenment's central ethical doctrine of autonomy.[117] Emphasizing the "active side," as Loewald argues, entails an ethics of "avowal." It posits a demand that I "own" and assume "responsibility" for my "interior foreign territory," that is, my unconscious-instinctual life.[118] I must acknowledge, "This is me, too."[119] Approaches to psychoanalysis and ethical theories that minimize or deny the power of psychic reality exempt themselves from this demand. One suspects that this is an important part of what motivates them.

Because Jacob's death initiated a process of prolonged and agonizing mourning in him, one is tempted to say that it forced the existence of psychic reality on Freud, and this, in turn, enabled him to emancipate himself from Fliess in a "good-enough" way. The extraordinary intellectual effort that Freud exerted in his *Trauerarbeit* and self-analysis was meant, as Anzieu argues, not only to counter "the depressive anxiety caused by the death of his father" but also to provide "a theoretical formulation" for the events "taking place in his unconscious." It was an effort, in other words, to extract a theory from what he was going through. Anzieu likens Freud's psychic experience – the tableaux of his inner world – to a "theater," in which he was witnessing a "profound upheaval" in his emotional life that was being "instigated" elsewhere, off stage, as it were.[120] Locating and explaining whatever was producing or causing that theatrical performance perhaps became Freud's primary theoretical task.

In that it is involuntary and virtually inescapable, mourning exhibits a hardness and durability that is characteristic of reality. Because one cannot get around it, one is more or less forced to confront it. (The extent to which the loss is confronted, moreover, determines the success of the mourning process.) As a laboratory for psychological research, mourning has a decided "advantage" over dreaming: it is more directly observable. Mourning, as Anzieu notes, "takes place during" the day as well as the

---

[117] See *ibid.*, 101–107.

[118] Freud, *New introductory lectures on psycho-analysis*, 57; and see Hans Loewald, "Psychoanalysis and the history of the individual," *The essential Loewald: collected papers and monographs* (Hagerstown, MD: University Publishing Group), 531–571.

[119] Castoriadis, *The imaginary institution of society*, 104.

[120] Anzieu, *Freud's self-analysis*, 182. See also Schimmel, *Sigmund Freud's discovery of psychoanalysis*, 115.

night and "can be monitored during the waking state instead of having to be reconstructed afterwards."[121] Observing and reflecting on his experience of mourning in the aftermath of his father's death produced an "insight" in Freud, the like of which "falls into one's lot but once in a lifetime."[122] It convinced him of the existence of psychic reality, understood as "an internal reality of the mind which cannot be reduced to the functioning of the brain or to conscious thought."[123] Because it is irreducible to brain functioning, on the one hand, psychic reality cannot be accounted for by neuropsychology; because on the other hand it cannot be reduced to conscious thought, it eludes the grasp of rational academic psychology. Psychic reality is enacted on a *"stage"* (*Schauplatz*) that *"is different from that of waking ideational life,"* and a radically new approach, a non-physicalist theory of the psychic apparatus, was required to apprehend it.[124]

To mourn successfully is to face the reality of the situation, which consists in loss of one sort or another, and results in giving up the lost object. The refusal to mourn, in contrast, can be understood as a refusal in fantasy to face reality, so that one is not compelled to relinquish the object but can retain it and avoid the pain of the resulting loss.[125] It was remarkable, as we have seen, how long Freud refused to face the reality of his relation to Fliess.

But the work of mourning can also engender a sense of conviction about the truth of one's psychic reality – and thereby about the truth of one's ideas. This is what happened with Freud, so that, as his confidence in his theories of dreams, of the unconscious, of the principles of mental functioning and so on increased, it progressively undermined his relationship with Fliess. He increasingly understood that his original mode of psychological theorizing was incompatible with the Berliner's quantitative-physicalist pseudo-science. This growing confidence in the truth and magnitude of his discoveries, moreover, led Freud not only to

[121] Anzieu, *Freud's self-analysis*, 182.

[122] Freud, *The interpretation of dreams*, xxxii.

[123] Anzieu, *Freud's self-analysis*, 182.

[124] Freud, *The interpretation of dreams*, 536 (translation altered; emphasis in the original).

[125] See Thomas H. Ogden, "A new reading of object relations theory," *International Journal of Psycho-analysis* 83 (2002), 772–773.

the disillusionment with Fliess and withdrawal of his idealizations from him, but also to an internalized recognition of the significance of his own achievements. He began to accept the fact that it was he, and not the hyper-speculative ENT specialist from Berlin, who was the great thinker. Needless to say, this process did not follow a straightforward trajectory. The work of de-idealization, separation, and internalization dragged on for another several years.

By 1900, however, as a result of his *Trauerarbeit*, self-analysis, separation from Fliess, and completion of *The interpretation of dreams* – a work that he described as a "reaction to his father's death" and "a portion of my own self-analysis" – Freud's creative illness terminated in a way that closely approximates Ellenberger's ideal-typical description of the phenomenon.[126] It was relatively "rapid," and, like the outcome of successful mourning, as Freud later described it, was "marked by a phase of exhilaration."[127] Moreover, we can agree with Sulloway that the heroizing depiction of Freud's trajectory during the critical decade of the 1890s, which pictures him as emerging from his self-analysis as a thoroughly sovereign and self-possessed man who had mastered all his conflicts, is an idealized exaggeration.[128] One need only look at his experience with Jung, in which Freud repeated many of the conflicts with Fliess, albeit at a significantly diminished volume, to see that this is not the case. We can reject the exaggerated idealizations, however, without denying that Freud emerged from "his ordeal with a" by no means negligible "transformation of his personality" and a "conviction that he had discovered truths of the spiritual world." Freud's "self analysis," Ellenberger observes, "transformed the unsure young practitioner into a self-assured founder of a new school, convinced that he had made a great discovery, which he saw as his

---

[126] Freud, *The interpretation of dreams*, xxvi.

[127] See S. Freud, "Mourning and melancholia" (1917), *SE* 14: 253–256. Schimmel argues that, although Freud did not make them public until 1917 after the First World War had impressed the theme of loss on him, some of the central insights that he gained during his self-analysis concerned melancholia. Indeed, as we will see in Chapter 9, Schimmel's claim that "Mourning and melancholia" may rival *The interpretation of dreams* in importance is not implausible. See Schimmel, *Sigmund Freud's discovery of psychoanalysis*, Chapter 7. For Freud's early discussion of melancholia see also Masson (ed.), *Letters to Fliess*, 98–105.

[128] See Sulloway, *Freud, biologist of the mind*, 3–5.

mission to give to the world."[129] Most importantly, Freud had taken hold of a private, excruciating, and crippling illness that had tormented him for years – and expressed itself in a variety of physical symptoms – and transformed it into a creative project of world-historical significance.

The public manifestations of Freud's self-analysis reflected the transformations that had taken place in his inner world. Undeniably, Freud's attempt at a self-cure was imperfect. How could it not be radically incomplete, given that it was the first analysis – and a self-analysis to boot? Though limited, the results were not, however, insignificant. On 2 March 1899, he wrote to Fliess:

> The result of this year's work appears to be the surmounting of fantasies; they have indeed lured me far away from what is real. Yet all this work has been very good for my emotional life. I am apparently much more normal that I was four or five years ago.[130]

The modesty is what is important here. The phrases "has been very good for my emotional life" and "much more normal" are written in the register of the "good enough." And this is as it should be for a man who, as we will see, went on to articulate a "scientific" worldview that centered on the renunciation of omnipotence and grandiosity and the acceptance of human finitude.

The interpretation of dreams provides the public evidence of what Freud had accomplished in the nineties. The work was completed in 1899, but as a way of indicating its Eurocentric optimism and progressive orientation it was given a publication date of 1900. This book, so the date was meant to announce, represents a major advance in science's march through the natural universe. The organization of the *Traumdeutung*, moreover, is heterogeneous. After a review of the literature in chapter 1, chapters 2 through 6 are *hermeneutical* and concerned with meaning: they instruct the reader on how to *interpret* dreams. But then the incomparable chapter 7, a canonical text in the history of Western science and philosophy, is *explanatory* – that is, it deals with causes, but not, however, in the usual material sense. In his culminating chapter, Freud sets out to introduce the new realm of psychic reality into scientific discourse and to elucidate a

---

[129] Ellenberger, *The discovery of the unconscious*. 448, 459.

[130] Masson (ed.), *Letters to Fliess*, 347.

particular mode of causal functioning. If psychic reality can be viewed as a stage on which inner experiences take place that are instigated elsewhere, as Anzieu maintains, then Freud introduces his theory of the psychic apparatus to explain how that instigation functions. Dreams, our paradigmatic specimen of psychic reality, are caused, in a sense to be clarified, by the psychic apparatus. Thus, Freud's question in chapter 7 is this: What must the psychic apparatus be like if dreams are as he described them in the previous six chapters?

Chapter 7 is the heir to the *Project* of 1895 – and, behind that, to Freud's scientific training in the Helmholtzian tradition, which he never entirely abandoned. The idiosyncratic way in which Freud transforms his earlier theory is crucial in determining the *sui generis* nature of psychoanalytic discourse.[131] On the one hand, Freud seeks, as he had in the *Project*, to *explain* psychological phenomena in terms of the movement and displacement of energy along determinable pathways. On the other hand, in chapter 7, he no longer attempts to locate those pathways in the physiology of the brain – to "localize" them. Instead, he informs us, he will "remain on psychological ground" and treat those pathways as "psychical" as opposed to "physical" localities, avoiding "the temptation to determine psychical locality in any anatomical fashion." Freud attempts to justify this procedure by way of analogy, comparing a psychical locality to the "ideal point" where an image occurs in a "microscope" or "telescope," which is not "situated" in any "tangible component of the apparatus." He defiantly declares, moreover, that he sees no "necessity to apologize for the imperfections of any similar imagery" as these imperfections are required for the formation of scientific models.[132] In the *Project*, Freud had proposed the paradoxical idea of a quantum of energy that cannot be measured. He is now proposing the equally paradoxical notion of pathways of psychic energy that cannot be localized in the brain. How one evaluates Freud's entire approach will be determined, in no small degree, by what one makes of these formulations. Are they meaningful paradoxes that are necessary in the attempt to comprehend the elusive phenomenon of the human psyche? Or are they simply incoherent?

[131] See especially Ricoeur, *Freud and philosophy*, 65.
[132] Freud, *The interpretation of dreams*, 536.

The way in which one answers another question will also play a significant role in determining one's evaluation of Freud's theoretical innovations. As we saw, when he was a student in Brücke's Institute, he endorsed the "Positivist Manifesto" and pledged to expunge any reference to occult qualities in the formulation of scientific theories. This required that all phenomena had to be explained using the principles of physics and chemistry – or of disciplines that possessed "equal dignity." Now, however, Freud has introduced the concept of psychic reality, which, as Laplanche and Pontalis define it, exhibits "a consistency and resistance" vis-à-vis our experience that is "comparable to those displayed by material reality." The question thus becomes whether or not the notion of psychic reality possesses the same "dignity" as the concept of "material reality" – that is, as the principles of physics and chemistry, as Laplanche and Pontalis seem to suggest? To put the question differently: Has Freud, with his introduction of psychic reality, discovered a new domain of the natural world and opened it for scientific exploration, as he claims? Or has the idea of psychic reality reintroduced the occult through the back door?

The Androphilic Current

Love can be viewed as a Goethean *Urphänomen*, that is, a particular phenomenon, which, if investigated properly, reveals universal truths about nature. Because love has its roots in the earliest phases of development, when a child's psychic structure is largely unformed and it is most dependent on the adults in its environment, it can teach us much about the nature of the ego and its relation to objects. Freud's life was as much a laboratory for his research as his consulting room, and his reflections on the way he and Fliess loved each other resulted in a conceptual scheme in which he thought out many of his most important ideas – on homosexuality, internalization, ego-formation, object relations, paranoia, and narcissism. Freud's thinking on homosexuality as expressed in the Fliess Letters constitutes a one-of-a-kind episode in his career. His reflections on the subject were never as open and searching – to the point of being contradictory – as they were when he was in the grips of his *amour fou* for Fliess.

On the one hand, as we have seen, Freud extolled the virtues of activity and independence at the same time as he disparaged passivity and dependence. He equated male homosexuality with the "passive-feminine" position and believed that it was, by its very nature, fundamentally "unacceptable" to the male ego. Thus he tells Fliess that "every instance [of] repression starts from the feminine aspect," and "what men essentially repress is the pederastic element."[133] Freud made an even stronger claim: Men often find their homosexual desires so intolerable that they project them – eject them from their psyches – so that they become the basis of paranoia. Furthermore, because most men view the homosexual parts of themselves as repugnant and shameful, they want to keep them concealed. (This was perhaps truer in Freud's day than it is in ours.) The prospect of having his mind read, even in the form of a "neutral" psychoanalytic interpretation, is therefore something that most men fear, as it could reveal their homosexual thoughts and desires – could "out" them. Moreover, unmasking another man's homoerotic thoughts and desires provides a "thought reader" with considerable advantage in the struggle for dominance and submission that structures much of the interaction between men. The "theoretical" debates about homosexuality, projection, and paranoia among the early analysts – who were naïve in the extreme in their understanding of the power of transference and reckless in analysing each other – often served as a screen for the power struggles, the transferences and countertransferences between them. For this reason they are often difficult to sort out. In light of the presumed connection between homosexuality and projection that was current at the time, to invalidate a colleague's idea as a "projection" – as an externalization of his unconscious thought processes – was, as Gay argues, to imply that he was a homosexual, "at least a latent one."[134]

On the other hand, in his final letters to Fliess, which are remarkable for their candor and their elegiac beauty, Freud's remarks on homosexuality are in a markedly different key. He no longer views the phenomenon negatively but commends the creative potential contained in "the androphilic current."[135] It seems clear, as Anzieu observes, that Freud had been exploring his erotic transference to Fliess in his self-analysis, and, in a misguided attempt at analytic candor, attempted to share

---

[133] Masson (ed.), *Letters to Fliess*, 273 and 246.

[134] Gay, *Freud: a life for our time*, 275.

[135] Masson (ed.), *Letters to Fliess*, 447.

what he had discovered with his interlocutor. But the Berliner had not been involved in anything resembling an analytic process and was therefore disturbed by the material Freud was reporting to him; he found it difficult to tolerate.[136] What is perhaps most remarkable is Freud's honesty about the female and homosexual parts of his personality, given the contempt for the "feminine-passive" position he had expressed on other occasions. Far from repudiating his femininity, he embraces it. "No one," he tells Fliess, "can replace for me the relationship with the friend which a special – possibly feminine – side demands."[137] In another letter, he makes it clear that by "friend" he means "male friend": "In my life, as you know, woman has never replaced the comrade, the friend."[138] Freud also tells Fliess that, because he does not reject his feminine side, he does "not share" the Berliner's "contempt for friendship between men." On the contrary, because of its sublimatory potential, he views homosexual libido in a positive light, observing, for example, "If Breuer's male inclination were not so odd, so timid, so contradictory . . . it would be a nice example of the accomplishments into which the androphilic current in men can be sublimated."[139]

Freud's attempt to initiate a discussion about homosexuality with Fliess seems to have produced a series of pointed exchanges concerning the question of "thought reading." Freud is no fool and recognizes that when the Berliner accuses him of being a "reader of thoughts," he is attempting to destroy the very foundations of his entire psychoanalytic project. To counter this strategy, Freud goes to the heart of the matter and rejects the assumption that "thought reading" is objectionable per se. In fact, in the following argument, he turns the tables on Fliess and criticizes him for his incompetence as a "thought reader." Fliess's wife had decided that the relationship between the two men – that is, their homosexual bond – was threatening the Fliess marriage, and Fliess had sided

---

[136] See Anzieu, *Freud's self-analysis*, 525–526.

[137] Masson (ed.), *Letters to Fliess*, 412.

[138] *Ibid.*, 447. It was only after he had parted ways with Jung, and his need for a powerful homosexual bond had perhaps been diluted that, beginning with his sister-in-law Minna Bernays and Lou Andreas Salomé, Freud formed intimate intellectual relationships with woman. However, they never assumed the same intensity as his earlier relationships with Fliess and Jung. See Anzieu, *Freud's self-analysis*, 543.

[139] Masson (ed.), *Letters to Fliess*, 447.

with her against Freud. The latter argues that Fliess had failed to recognize that the "threatening" idea had been "planted in her mind" by
Breuer; this failure on Fliess's part, Freud argues, demonstrates the limits
of the Berliner's "perspicacity." Freud quotes a statement that Fliess had
made in the context of justifying his behavior vis-à-vis his wife: "'The
reader of thoughts [that is, Freud – JW] merely reads his thoughts into
other people.'" And Freud rightly points out that, if this observation were
true, it would render all his psychoanalytic "efforts valueless."[140] In dismissing Freud's interpretations as mere projections every time they make
him "uncomfortable," Fliess had disqualified himself as Freud's "only
audience" and "must regard [Freud's] entire method of working as being
just as worthless as the others do."[141]

Freud introduces a distinction between "thought reading" and "magic"
without which a specifically psychoanalytic approach to the human mind
would be incoherent. He objects to a reference to "magic" that Fliess
had apparently made in an earlier letter, arguing that Fliess is using it
"as superfluous plaster to cover over [his] doubt about thought reading."
Freud's pithy rejoinder encapsulates the distinctive nature of the psychoanalytic project: "I remain loyal to thought reading and continue to doubt
'magic.'"[142] In other words, spurious forms of "thought reading" do exist,
and they should be rejected as "magic." But the psychoanalytic enterprise
only makes sense, Freud insists, if non-magical – "scientific" – modes of
thought reading are indeed possible.

Several years after the two men had broken off contact, a sad and
bizarre coda to the Freud–Fliess story played out, partly in the pages the
city's *feuilletons*, and involved two of Vienna's most notorious personalities, Otto Weininger and Karl Kraus. It centered on a priority dispute
over who had introduced the concept of bisexuality. While the topic of the
controversy is noteworthy, its details are difficult to determine and need
not concern us. For us, the important thing is the way Freud correctly
or incorrectly interpreted Fliess's behavior towards him. "My one-time
friend Fliess," he later explained to Jung, "developed a dreadful case of
paranoia after throwing off his affection for me, which was undoubtedly

---

[140] *Ibid.*, 447.

[141] *Ibid.*, 450.

[142] *Ibid.*, 440.

considerable."[143] Fliess, so Freud believed, could not accept his intense homosexual love for Freud. Consequently, when the relationship ended, he was unable to internalize his "object relation" to Freud and make it part of himself. Instead, he was forced to deny it and project it into the external world. And Fliess's display of "paranoia" during the priority scandal, Freud claimed, was the result of that projection.

Freud, on the other hand, presented a more "sanguine" interpretation of the way he had handled his own homosexuality, which echoed his comments on sublimation and "the androcentric current."[144] He maintained that he had overcome the trauma of the Fliess relationship by withdrawing "a piece of homosexual investment" and utilizing it – that is, sublimating it – "for the enlargement of [his] own ego."[145] And he made the further claim that by "overcoming [his] homosexuality" through this process of internalization, he had gained "greater independence."[146] Thus, he triumphantly declared, "I have succeeded where the paranoiac fails."[147]

Freud's victory lap, however, was hugely premature, for, as we will see, his conflicts over homosexuality reasserted themselves with considerable force in his relationship with Jung. What is more, there is much to be questioned in his diagnosis of Fliess's behavior and his generalizations about homosexuality and paranoia. Nevertheless, despite these qualifications, Freud's struggle to comprehend his love for Fliess produced a group of essential ideas concerning object-love, self-love, loss, internalization, ego development, and projection. And he later used these ideas in the formulation of his landmark theories on narcissism, loss, mourning, and ego-development.

---

[143] William McGuire (ed.), *The Freud/Jung letters: the correspondence between Sigmund Freud and C.G. Jung*, trans. R.F.C. Hull (Princeton, NJ: Princeton University Press, 1974), 121.

[144] Lotto, "Freud's struggle with misogyny," 1298.

[145] Ernst Falzeder and Eva Brabant (eds.), *The correspondence of Sigmund Freud and Sándor Ferenczi*, vol. I: *1908–1914*, trans. Peter T. Hoffer (Cambridge, MA: Harvard University Press, 1922), 221.

[146] *Ibid.*, 227.

[147] *Ibid.*, 221.

8

Jung and the Counter-Enlightenment

PETER HOMANS, A PSYCHOANALYTICALLY oriented sociologist of religion, rightly takes umbrage with an assertion by Jones that Freud's relationship with Fliess was "the only really extraordinary experience in [his] life."[1] The statement, as Homans notes, ignores the analyst's seven-year entanglement, from 1906 to 1913, with his younger colleague from Zurich, Carl Gustav Jung, which was anything but ordinary. Freud's relationship with Jung may not have reached the near-delirious extremes that characterized the Fliess affair, but it was in no way devoid of irrational passion. Likewise, maintaining the relationship with Jung did not require the same massive denial as did the Fliess affair, but the disavowal that Freud had to employ to preserve that mésalliance was considerable. In important respects, Jung can be viewed as Fliess *redux*. As Freud himself recognized, he relived many of the themes and conflicts that had animated his *amour fou* with Fliess with his younger colleague from Switzerland, only with less intensity.[2] Commenting to Ferenczi on Jung's increasingly problematic behavior, for example, Freud borrowed Leporello's phrase from *Don Giovanni:* "This music seems extraordinarily familiar to me," he wrote.[3]

Jung's Provocation

The disparagers of psychoanalysis like to point to the unsavory aspects of the competition between Freud and Jung to demonstrate that the entire enterprise is "nothing but" a guise for the will-to-power. While the

---

[1] Jones, *Freud* I, 287; and Peter Homans, *The ability to mourn: disillusionment and the social origins of psychoanalysis*, second edition (Chicago: University of Chicago Press, 1989), 18.

[2] See Gay, *Freud: a life for our time*, 277–283.

[3] Falzeder and Brabant (eds.), *Correspondence of Freud and Ferenczi*, vol. I, 457.

competition between the two men was cutthroat, its effect can be compared to that of the *agon* among the dramatists that produced the classics
of Greek tragedy – namely, it spurred Freud to produce a number of his
greatest works.[4] Official psychoanalytic historiography has often focused
on the "heroic" decade of the 1890s and the creation of psychoanalysis in order to promote the image of Freud as the isolated conquistador
who single-handedly discovered and mapped a new continent – and to
marginalize other figures in its history, especially Jung.[5] To be sure, Jung
did not serve as the midwife to the birth of psychoanalysis as Fliess had;
still, a number of Freud's most important and pivotal works are unimaginable without his provocation.[6] The list includes *Leonardo, Totem and
taboo*, "Psycho-analytic notes on an autobiographical account of a case
of paranoia" (*Schreber*), "Formulations concerning the two principles of
mental functioning," "The Moses of Michelangelo," "Mourning and
melancholia," and, most important, "On narcissism: an introduction."
*For our purposes, it should be stressed that by introducing the notion of primary
narcissism into psychoanalytic theory, Freud wittingly or unwittingly was also
introducing the early infant–mother relationship into his thinking, although he
did not pursue it in any detail.*

The standard account portrays Freud and Jung as the two great antipodal
representatives of the Enlightenment and the Counter-Enlightenment –
Aufklärung and *Gegenaufklärung* – within psychoanalysis. Although the
picture is not wrong, it is too general and requires elaboration. It is true, for
example, that Freud remained a partisan of the Enlightenment throughout
his career, but he did not champion the eighteenth-century's "Kantian"–
that is, the one-sided, rationalistic, and relatively innocent – version of it.

---

[4] Kohut points out that although ambition is a necessary condition for achieving
greatness, it is not a sufficient one. If it is not combined with ideals, Kohut argues,
ambition alone is unlikely to result in truly great work. See Heinz Kohut, "The forms
and transformations of narcissism," *Journal of the American Psychoanalytic Association*
14 (1966), 243–272.

[5] See Sulloway, *Freud, biologist of the mind*, 5–10; Homans, *The ability to mourn*, 6; and
Elisabeth Young-Bruehl, "A history of Freud biographies," *Subject of biography: psy-
choanalysis, feminism, and writing women's lives* (Cambridge, MA: Harvard University
Press, 1998), 104.

[6] See Cornelius Castoriadis, "Psychoanalysis: project and elucidation," *Crossroads
in the labyrinth*, trans. Kate Soper and Martin H. Ryle (Cambridge, MA: The MIT
Press, 1984), 62–63.

Freud, as we noted in the Introduction, was a representative of the so-called "Dark Enlightenment" and defended a later, more chastened, which is to say more mature, stage in the movement's development. Unlike the one-sided rationalist representatives – who can be found in psychoanalysis as well as philosophy – Freud's strategy for defending the Enlightenment did not "exclude" the claims of the Counter-Enlightenment out of hand.[7] Instead, he adopted a program closely resembling the one Adorno advocated, namely, to take up "all the reactionary arguments against Western culture" and place them "in the service of progressive enlightenment."[8] Though he did not always succeed, Freud, as a "dark" enlightener, sought to take the claims of the *Gegenaufklärung* seriously. And this meant doing justice to the truth content of the irrational. Freud, for example, seriously entertained the question of telepathy, something that troubled the more conventionally minded Jones.[9]

In psychoanalysis, one place where the irrational is located is the realm of archaic experience – that is, pre-individuated, pre-verbal, and pre-Oedipal experience. Jung, by asserting the importance of psychosis, myth, collective fantasy, the occult, and the early mother, forced Freud to venture out of his comfort zone and into the realm of archaic psychic life – albeit in a highly hesitant way. Despite the limitations of these forays into more

---

[7] The members of the Hartmann School are perhaps the prime representatives of psychoanalytic Kantianism. Habermas also offers an example of this exclusionary "Kantian" strategy. It can be observed in his interpretation of Freud, where he denies the radical otherness of the unconscious by his *ex cathedra* rejection of the distinction between "thing-representations" and "word-representations." And it is also evident in the way he hastily dismisses the contemporary proponents of the Counter-Enlightenment in *The philosophical discourse of modernity* rather than entering into a serious *Auseinandersetzung* with them. See Jürgen Habermas, *The philosophical discourse of modernity: twelve lectures*, trans. Frederick G. Lawrence (Cambridge, MA: The MIT Press, 1987), and Whitebook, *Perversion and utopia*, 179–196.

[8] Theodor Adorno, *Minima moralia: reflections from a damaged life*, trans. E.F.N. Jephcott (New York: Verso, 2006), 192. Loewald's "inclusionary" approach to rationality and the ego follows a similar strategy. Indeed, Loewald's admirable review of the Freud/Jung correspondence, in which he strives to do justice to the truth content of both men's positions, exemplifies this "inclusionary" approach. See Hans Loewald, "Book review essay on the *Freud/Jung letters*," *The essential Loewald: collected papers and monographs* (Hagerstown, MD: University Publishing Group, 2000), 405–418.

[9] See Marsha Hewitt's nuanced discussion of Freud's position vis-à-vis telepathy. Marsha Aileen Hewitt, *Freud on religion* (Bristol, CT: Acumen, 2014), chapter 4.

primitive layers of the psyche, Jung's provocation had one critical result: It pushed Freud to spell out his conception of science and to articulate his scientific worldview more comprehensively than he had before. That is, Jung's challenge spurred Freud to articulate his Enlightenment understanding of science *as the methodical adversary of magic and the omnipotence of thoughts*.

In his memoir, *Memories, dreams, reflections*, first published in 1961, Jung showed no hesitancy in declaring his allegiance to the anti-modernist Counter-Enlightenment and acknowledging his lifelong attraction to the mystical, the occult, the religious, the magical, and the irrational. He openly embraces the enchanted "world of the Knights of the Grail" as his *"own world . . . in the deepest sense,"* and makes it clear that his personal cosmos *"had scarcely anything to do with"* the world inhabited by Sigmund Freud the atheist, rationalist, and secular Jew.[10] Moreover, he attributes Freud's inability to appreciate the "entire complex of questions" surrounding the paranormal to his "materialist prejudice" and "shallow" positivism.[11] Jung, who grew up in two parochial Swiss towns, Laufen Castle and Klein-Hüningen, in which superstition, mysticism, and belief in the occult were commonplace, was, as Kerr observes, part of "a widespread reaction against modernity underway in German culture generally."[12] Insofar as Jung gave "a psychoanalytic cast to the general

---

[10] C.G. Jung, *Memories, dreams, reflections*, recorded and ed. Aniela Jaffé, trans. Richard and Clara Winston (New York: Vintage Books, 1989), 165 (emphasis added).

[11] *Ibid.*, 155.

[12] Because of the importance that the question assumed in the Freud–Jung relationship, we should note that the particular form of romantic anti-modernism that emerged in the German-speaking *Mitteleuropa* tended to be deeply anti-Semitic. Although "Jew hatred," Steven Beller argues, was intrinsic to Christianity, and "anti-Semitism," in one form or another, was ubiquitous throughout Western and Eastern European societies, the intense hostility toward modernity that took root "in German Central Europe" helps to explain why the Holocaust took place there and nowhere else. The particularity of German development, its *"Sonderweg,"* produced a hatred for modernity that was deeper, broader, and more lethal than in the rest of Europe. And because the Jews were demonized as the carriers of modernity in its multifarious and even contradictory manifestations – capitalism and socialism, cultural modernism, urbanism, cosmopolitanism, positivism, rationalism, and so on – it also produced a murderous strand of anti-Semitism that culminated in the Final Solution. Steven Beller, *Antisemitism: a very short introduction* (Oxford: Oxford University Press, 2007).

tendency to romanticize and idealize the rural and pastoral world which European civilization was irrevocably leaving behind," he did for psycho-analysis what Heidegger – who hailed from a similarly rural and religious background that harbored intense resentment toward the modern world – did for philosophy.[13]

Jung sought to dismantle modernity and somehow "re-enchant" the world in order to escape what he experienced as "the banality of [modern] life." To this end, he wanted psychoanalysis to become a new counter-religion. Freud, by contrast, sought to complete "the unfinished proj-ect of modernity" and the "disenchantment of the world," understood as the struggle to reach maturity by overcoming "magical thinking" and achieving "the omnipotence of thoughts."[14] But because he was a rep-resentative of the Dark Enlightenment, who had eschewed many of the utopian – which is to say, omnipotent – excesses of the movement, he did

---

[13] John Kerr, *A most dangerous method: the story of Jung, Freud, and Sabina Spielrein* (New York: Alfred A. Knopf, 1993), 339. On the comparison of Jung and Heidegger see Walter Kaufmann, *Discovering the mind*, vol. III: *Freud, Adler and Jung* (New Brunswick, NJ: Transaction, 2007), 290. At the end of the nineteenth century and the beginning of the twentieth, the European cultural landscape contained two avant-gardes. The first, aesthetic modernism, thrived in the continent's great metropolitan centers like London, Paris, Berlin, and Vienna and adhered to Rimbaud's credo "Il faut être absolument moderne." (Though it dealt with much of the same material, Freud's modernism was quite distinct from the aesthetic avant-garde's.) The second – which Lukács dubbed "romantic anti-capitalism" – moved in an opposite direction, maintaining that modernity constituted a fundamentally mistaken project that should be undone. The conservative avant-garde tended to abhor the manic excitement of the new metropolises – celebrated by Baudelaire, Walter Benjamin, and others – and to prefer the harmony that supposedly characterized rural life. Furthermore, it was "reactionary" in the strict sense in that it turned to an idealized image of the past in the hopes of discovering a way to break out of the modern world. See Jay Sherry, "Carl Gustav Jung, avant-garde conservative," doctoral dissertation, Freie Univeristät Berlin, 2008.

[14] See Jürgen Habermas, "Modernity: an unfinished project," *Habermas and the unfinished project of modernity*, ed. Maurizio Passerin d'Entrève and Seyla Benhabib (Cambridge, MA: The MIT Press, 1997), 38–58. Though there are important differences that should not be underestimated, Habermas's idea of "the project of modernity" bears a close affinity with Castoriadis's notion of "the project of autonomy." Both thinkers, moreover, drew extensively on Freud in formulating their positions. See Castoriadis, *The imaginary institution of society*, 101–114, and "Psychoanalysis and politics."

not, as Loewald observes, "proclaim" the modern worldview "as the end of all wisdom." He was moreover fully aware of the costs that modernity and "the civilizing process" in general exacted on the individual and on the species as a whole. Indeed, he did much to document those costs. Nevertheless, as Loewald maintains, he "saw" the completion of the modern project "as a necessary step, for the individual and for humanity as a whole, in the development toward greater maturity and sanity."[15]

The differing views held by the two men played out in various ways as their relationship developed. Jung, who was candid about his tendency to dissemble, would at times present himself as a respectable representative of modern science. His research with word-association tests did indeed constitute the first attempt to provide experimental verification for psychoanalysis and helped the fledgling discipline gain recognition in the world of academic psychiatry, beyond the marginal circle of Freud's Viennese followers. And although Freud's prescriptive conception of science differed in fundamental ways from the precepts of standard science, and while he was skeptical about the possibility of providing an experimental verification of psychoanalysis, he was nonetheless deeply grateful for Jung's contribution. Moreover, as the friction in the relationship increased, Jung, like Eugen Bleuler, his "chief" at the Burghölzli Hospital in Zurich, took Freud to task for what they considered his speculative indulgences and failure to conform to the canons of scientific rigor.

At the same time, and in line with his commitment to the Counter-Enlightenment, Jung could also assume the role of a staunch critic of "positivism" who condemned the scientific worldview as being soulless and superficial. In truth, however, it is impossible to determine exactly where Jung stood with regard to science.[16] Going well beyond the kind of inner *tension* evident between Freud's "official" and "unofficial" positions, Jung's pronouncements on science – first in his student years and later, and then after his break with Freud – frankly contradict one another. These contradictions, in turn, were tied to a central feature of Jung's personality: his strong tendency toward dissociation and splitting and his conscious decision to create a "false self."

---

[15] Loewald, "Book review essay on the *Freud/Jung letters*," 408.
[16] See especially Frank McLynn, *Carl Gustav Jung* (New York: St. Martin's Press, 1996), chapters 3 and 4. See also Makari, *Revolution in mind*, 189–192.

Whatever one ultimately makes of Jung's contribution, by representing the Counter-Enlightenment within psychoanalysis his intervention into the history of the field accomplished something crucial: It forced Freud to confront, however hesitatingly, the "truth claims" of archaic experience and of the irrational dimension of the psyche, and in so doing compelled him to alter – and deepen – his position in substantial ways.

The impact of Jung's provocation reached its culmination in Freud's publication "On narcissism: an introduction." Speculations about the *Zeitgeist* are always dicey and, as a rule, should be resisted. But one fact is difficult to ignore. *The interpretation of dreams*, which embodied all the Whiggish optimism of the nineteenth century, was published in 1900. "On narcissism," which was written under the pressure of Jung's irrationalism and which threatened to topple the entire theoretical construction that Freud's rationalist worldview was based on, was published in 1914, the same year that the progressivism and optimism of European bourgeois culture came crashing down in the trenches of the Great War. One has the nagging feeling that this coincidence, as the Trotskyists used to say, "cannot be accidental." And if we wanted to indulge *zeitgeistliche* speculations further, we would also note that Albert Einstein published his "General theory of relativity" the following year. In any case, an examination of the vastly different childhood experiences of Jung and Freud will help us understand their opposing worldviews.

The Childhood of an Apostate

The claim that Freud's childhood was more traumatic than had formerly been recognized is of recent vintage and remains relatively controversial. The same cannot be said of Jung. He is remarkably candid in acknowledging the numerous traumatic events that marked his early life, and he provides detailed descriptions of these events and of their consequences for his psychic development.[17] If Freud's relationship with his parents,

---

[17] We need not be distracted by the diagnostic debate regarding Winnicott's statement that "Jung, in describing himself, gives us a picture of childhood schizophrenia." The statement is meant to be strictly neutral, not condemnatory. It is intended to describe the "crooked timber" out of which Jung's personality was carved. Furthermore, Winnicott argues that Jung exhibited the strength to heal himself and put his experience to creative use. Winnicott's neutrality is manifest in his suggestion that the price

especially Amalie, was difficult, it never reached the catastrophic extremes that marked Jung's relations with his depressed and defeated father, Paul, and his floridly disturbed mother, Emilie Preiswerk Jung.

Unlike Jacob Freud, who, though infuriatingly irresponsible, was a deeply intelligent, lovable, and loving man, Jung's father was not an inviting figure to love or identify with. Paul Jung was the son of a vital, productive, and celebrated father who not only spent a year in prison for his radical political activities but also became a protégé of the German geographer, naturalist, explorer, and romantic philosopher Alexander Von Humboldt. Despite being a promising student at the university, Paul was never able to construct a successful life for himself;[18] he ended up a thwarted pastor in the Swiss Reformed Church, serving in several backwater parishes. Bitter, depressive, and irritable, Paul was no more successful in his married life than in his career. Emilie's penchant for the occult did not sit well with Paul's scholarly sensibility, and the two quarreled constantly, seem to have separated on several occasions, and, from what we can tell, had a sporadic sexual life at best.

Carl's image of the Christian community of which his father was a member was no more attractive than his picture of Paul as a parent. For Carl, who became fascinated with corpses after he rushed off as a boy to see one that had washed up on the shore of the nearby Rhine, Christianity was associated not with love and life but with darkness and death. There seemed to be no end of funerals to attend in a small Swiss town like Laufen Castle, and what most impressed Carl on these occasions was the ubiquitous blackness: the blackness of the hole in the ground that would receive

---

Jung paid for his "madness" was perhaps no greater than the price that Freud's "flight into sanity" exacted on him and the field he created. What we should be concerned with is the content of the British analyst's argument. In addition to whatever suffering it may have caused him, Jung's extensive experience with dissociative states and the split-self was, according to Winnicott, also productive. It provided him with special insight into the phenomena that derive from the first three years of life – into "the psychotic core" of the personality – before the self has coalesced. Freud's distance from the realm of pre-integrated experience, as we have observed, undoubtedly had something to do with his vaunted ego-strength. But that ego could also be too strong, too compulsively integrated, so that it prevented him from gaining access to the more diffuse forms of primitive experience. D.W. Winnicott, "Review of *Memories, dreams, reflections*," *International Journal of Psychoanalysis* 45 (1964), 450.

[18] See McLynn, *Jung*, 5–6.

the coffin, of the cloth that was draped over it, and of the mourners' black attire, which was similar to the "long frock coats with unusually tall hats and shiny black boots" that the sextons wore. The boy associated this blackness with his father's depression. Carl came to doubt Jesus's "love and kindness" because he associated "the people who talked most about 'dear Lord Jesus'" – that is, the clergy, including eight of Paul's relatives – with death. They were a gloomy lot indeed, outfitted like mourners, who seemed to spend most of their time presiding over funerals.[19]

Carl also grew skeptical about the seriousness and authenticity of Paul's commitment to Christianity, and he began to pity his father. In a poignant effort at connection, reparation, and idealization, the boy attempted to engage his father intellectually and ignite some sparks of theological passion in him. But when he queried Paul about the mystery of the Trinity, hardly an unsuitable topic for theological debate, the pastor answered that he knew "nothing about it."[20] While he respected his father's honest admission of ignorance, Carl took Paul's response as a confirmation of what he already suspected – namely, that the official theologians lacked answers to life's most urgent questions. Eventually, Jung came "to the conscious realization that his father clung to blind faith as a means of warding off the void of nihilism or atheism" – that is, of fending off meaninglessness.[21] Paul's tragedy, as his son saw it, was that he had neither the strength nor the courage to reject the conventional teachings of the Church and embrace a more uncompromising and heterodox form of religion, or to reject religion outright and become an atheist. Stuck in this paralysis, Paul steadily deteriorated emotionally and physically until he died in 1895 during Jung's first year of medical school at the University of Basel.

Jung reports that his sexual life began under his "father's aegis."[22] Although the details of his first sexual encounter are unclear, he tells us that at the age of eighteen, a man who was a friend of Paul's and a member of the clergy seduced him. This experience reinforced a connection between sexuality and religion that had already appeared in a decisive dream Jung had at approximately the age of five. The dream's setting is the field behind

[19] Jung, *Memories*, 9.

[20] *Ibid.*, 53.

[21] McLynn, *Jung*, 29.

[22] *Ibid.*, 35. See McGuire (ed.), *The Freud/Jung letters*, 95.

the Vicarage where the family lived, where Carl discovers "a rectangular, stone-lined hole in the ground," descends its "stone stairway," and comes upon "a doorway with a round arch closed off by a big heavy . . . sumptuous . . . green curtain." When the boy pulls back the "brocade" curtain, he observes a dimly lit "rectangular chamber about thirty feet long" with a red rug that runs "from the entrance to a low platform," upon which platform sits a magnificent "golden throne" – a "real king's throne from a fairy tale."[23] At this point we arrive at the center of the dream:

Something was standing on it which I thought at first was a tree trunk twelve to fifteen feet high and about one and a half to two feet thick. It was a huge thing, reaching almost to the ceiling. But it was of a curious composition: It was made of skin and naked flesh, and on top there was something like a rounded head with no face, no hair. On the very top of the head was a single eye, gazing motionlessly upward.[24]

While the dream "haunted" Jung for years, "it was only decades before [he] understood that" the massive trunk-like object represented "a ritual phallus" signifying "a subterranean God 'not to be named.'"[25]

After having the dream, Jung tells us, "Lord Jesus never [again] became quite real for me, never quite acceptable, never quite loveable." Throughout his youth, "whenever anyone spoke too emphatically about Lord Jesus," the thought of this secret phallic deity, Christ's "underground counterpart," intruded into his thoughts.[26] The experience of the phallic deity constitutes the intrapsychic beginnings of Jung's private, blasphemous counter-religion, which, he came to believe, was superior to his father's spiritually bankrupt brand of Christianity. Jesus had been transfigured into a dark underground sexualized god, and although Jung tried to construe this transfiguration as a new version of Christianity, it is difficult to see, as the eminent sociologist Philip Rieff observes, how it was "reconcilable with the old."[27] Profoundly disillusioned with his father, Jung

---

[23] Jung, *Memories*, 11–12.

[24] *Ibid.*, 12.

[25] *Ibid.*, 12.

[26] *Ibid.*, 13.

[27] Philip Rieff, *The triumph of the therapeutic: uses of faith after Freud* (New York: Harper and Row, 1966), 111.

created a fantasy of an idealized phallus to replace him. Similarly, after he
"repudiated the social and cultural idealization of the Christianity of his
childhood," Jung constructed a new deity, "a subterranean God 'not to be
named'" as a substitute for it.[28]

In addition to an idealization of the object, the dream also contains an
aggrandizement of the self. Jung does not present the dream as a private
mental happening, that is, as an occurrence within psychic reality. He construes it as a revelation from outside, in which a "superior intelligence" –
an "alien guest who came both from above and from below" – initiated
him "into the realm of darkness" so that he "could bring the greatest
possible amount of light into" it.[29] Jung struggles to defuse the disturbing
experience by idealizing it, and he shores up his fragile sense of self by
fantasizing that the esoteric knowledge of a secret God, immeasurably
more sublime than the conventional teachings of his father's Church, had
been revealed to him.

As John Gedo observes, Jung "eventually directed [his] desperate
need to idealize a male figure," embodied in the deified phallus, "onto
Sigmund Freud." But instead of the "godhead" he was seeking, he
encountered both "the archeological science of psychoanalysis" that
sought to unmask the illusory nature of all religion and a flawed man who
attempted to deflect Jung's attempts to idealize him. The disappointment
was "catastrophic."[30] It led him not only to his break with Freud but also
to a prolonged personal crisis of intense psychic disorganization that Jung
had to battle his way through in the decade following 1914. Gedo makes
the further point that not all the difficulties were on Jung's side. Freud's
inability to recognize Jung's need for idealization – something which he
in fact shared with the younger man, but in a less intense form – and his
failure to respond to this need in a sensitive way constituted one of the
factors that led to the failure of the relationship. In other words, Freud's
"failure in empathy" – his incomplete understanding of early narcissistic
phenomena and his inability to respond to Jung's demands for idealization – led to calamitous results.

---

[28] Peter Homans, *Jung in context: modernity and the making of psychology* (Chicago:
University of Chicago Press, 1995), 121.

[29] Jung, *Memories*, 13.

[30] John Gedo, *Portraits of the artist: psychoanalysis of creativity and its vicissitudes*
(New York: The Gilford Press, 1983), 255.

But if Jung's father was unloving and unlovable, his mother, Emilie Preiswerk Jung, suffered psychological difficulties that were florid, acute, and frightening – very different in nature from Amalie Nathanson Freud, who was narcissistic, depressive, and demanding. As one commentator observes, Emilie Jung "bore [her son] on July 26, 1875, and devoted herself thereafter to scaring the daylights out of him."[31]

Emilie had been raised in an environment that was rife with all sorts of paranormal happenings. Motivated by the belief that Hebrew was the language spoken in Heaven, her father, Samuel Preiswerk, became an eminent scholar of the Hebrew language and the Old Testament. His "greatest source of satisfaction was the knowledge that he would be able to read celestial newspapers."[32] An occultist and a spiritualist, Preiswerk set an empty chair at the nightly dinner table in order to communicate with his first wife's ghost. This evening ritual created a problem, however; it not only evoked the understandable jealousy of his second wife, but, as a clairvoyant herself, Emilie's mother had little patience for her husband's attempt to communicate with his first wife. "The battle of the psyches," McLynn observes, "was fought out in the Preiswerk household."[33]

Carl reports that he suffered a breakdown of sorts at the age of three when Emilie, after temporarily separating from her husband, was hospitalized for several months, during which time Carl was turned over to the care of a maiden aunt twenty years his mother's senior. One of his major symptoms at the time was general eczema. Often considered a disorder of the "skin ego" – that is, of the physical "envelope" that contains and defines the soma-psyche – the malady suggests that Carl was struggling with difficulties pertaining to the integration of the self.[34] Winnicott maintains that the boy's symptomatology indicates two things: that the developmental formation of his "unit-self" had been disrupted, and that Jung was beginning to deploy splitting and dissociation – which became

---

[31] Walter Kendrick, "Psychiatrist to the gods?, *The New York Times on line*, www.nytimes.com/books/97/09/21/reviews/970921.21kendrit.html, 1.

[32] McLynn, *Jung*, 7.

[33] *Ibid.*, 7.

[34] See Didier Anzieu, *The skin ego* (New Haven, CT: Yale University Press, 1989). See also Joyce McDougall, *Theaters of the body: a psychoanalytic approach to psychosomatic illness* (New York: W.W. Norton & Co., 1989).

two preferred defenses – to protect himself against the intolerable psychic pain caused by the separation and loss.[35]

The early separation from his mother took a tremendous toll, as Jung recognized, on his capacity for attachment and intimacy. "From then on," he tells us, "I always felt mistrustful when the word 'love' was spoken. The feeling I associated with 'woman' was for a long time that of innate unreliability."[36] He also recognized that this experience, having convinced him that all love objects were unreliable, gave rise to what he called his "polygamous nature." Indeed, Jung was indeed remarkably frank in describing his predicament in one of his last letters to his lover Sabina Spielrein. "Now," he admits, "I'm the one who is ill," and he candidly warns her: "When love for woman awakens with me, the first thing I feel is regret for the poor woman who dreams of eternal faithfulness and other impossibilities and is slated for a rude awakening."[37] Jung was famously critical of what he considered Freud's quasi-religious celebration of sexuality. The great irony, however, is that, while he accused Freud of vastly exaggerating the importance of *eros*, Jung had little mastery over his own sexuality, and it wreaked havoc in his personal life.

Emilie's strong dissociative tendencies undoubtedly contributed to Carl's own propensity for splitting. He reports that his parents' estrangement created an "atmosphere" in their old Vicarage that was so "unbreathable" he often felt like he was "suffocating."[38] Each evening, his mother and father would withdraw into their respective bedrooms, at which time Emilie would slip into dissociated states and become, as he puts it, "uncanny and mysterious." Jung describes a particularly disturbing incident:

At night Mother was strange and mysterious. One night I saw a faintly luminous indefinite figure stepping from her door, and its head came off at its neck and floated in front of it in the air like a little moon. A new head appeared immediately, but it came off too. This process was repeated six or seven times.[39]

---

[35] Winnicott, "Review of *Memories*," 451.

[36] Jung, *Memories*, 8.

[37] Quoted in Ronald Hayman, *A life of Jung* (New York: W.W. Norton & Co., 1999), 105.

[38] Jung, *Memories*, 19.

[39] *Ibid.*, 18.

The young boy did not know what to make of these experiences, and his attitude toward his mother was, shall we say, split. In his memoirs, he acknowledges that these apparitions were terrifying and precipitated a series of frightening anxiety dreams. At the same time, he also idealizes these bizarre experiences, claiming that they brought Emilie into contact with the transcendent reality of the spirit world. In contrast to her diurnal, bourgeois, conventional, and restrained self, when she inhabited these altered states, Jung saw her as a paragon of uncompromising and fearsome truthfulness – "a priestess in a bear's cave . . . archaic and ruthless . . . as truth and nature."[40] He expresses regret that these states were only transitory, so that he was never able to pin her down, for, he exclaims, she "would have had a wonderful interlocutor."[41]

As early as the age of twelve, having struggled to contain his inner turmoil through a series of dreams, fantasies, and bizarre rituals, Carl began to realize that, like his mother, he was subject to experiences of dissociation and splitting. He eventually concluded that his identity consisted in "two different persons."[42] Where his "No. 1 Self," as he dubbed it, comprised the "normal"– that is to say, the reality-oriented, adaptive, and consensually validated aspects of his personality – his "No. 2 Self," which emerged during dissociative episodes, represented the bizarre, split-off, private, archaic, and maladaptive parts of his self. Though the way of the world eventually forced Jung to embrace pragmatically his No. 1 Self – which was associated with his thwarted and depressed bourgeois father – Jung always harbored a degree of contempt toward this aspect of his personality, viewing it as mundane, compromised, and spiritless.

Similarly, he had the same conflicted attitude towards his No. 2 Self as he had to his mother's dissociated states: The No. 2 Self was simultaneously fascinating and terrifying, and he did not know how to comprehend it. Did No. 2 represent a sphere of "immeasurable darkness" and morbidity?[43] Or did its apparent darkness in fact constitute a superior form of illumination that disclosed a deeper form of truth, a "higher esoteric

[40] *Ibid.*, 50.

[41] *Ibid.*, 52.

[42] *Ibid.*, 18 and 45.

[43] *Ibid.*, 88.

wisdom" that transcended the more superficial truths shared by everyday life and the scientific standpoint?[44]

These questions involve a more general issue that underlies the Freud/Jung controversy: namely, how to interpret so-called anomalous, paranormal, or occult experiences. Do such experiences offer a privileged window into psychic life and human nature – *without validating the existence of any transcendent or extramundane phenomena*? In this case, they should be studied naturalistically, that is, through science. This was Freud's position, though it was not one of simple-minded materialism. Or do they constitute evidence for the existence of a realm of supernatural happenings that lie beyond the immanent perspective of the scientific worldview? This would eventually become Jung's position, but he followed a circuitous and vacillating path before he finally and fully arrived at it.

Although adopting the mantle of a tough-minded scientist was a centerpiece of Jung's No. 1 Self, there are reasons to question the firmness of his commitment to scientific rationality. For example, his first presentation at the Zofingia Debating Society at the University of Basel sounded a characteristic Counter-Enlightenment theme, "The limits of natural science," and mocked the followers of "Papa Du Bois-Reymond," the man who had articulated the "positivist credo."[45] At the end of his university years, Jung wrote a dissertation on the occult that did not make any claims for the existence of the supernatural and purportedly sought to demystify "the strange events of spiritism via natural science." What he failed to mention, however, was the personal experience that provided the background for his study.[46] For several years, Jung had credulously attended the séances of a fifteen-year-old psychic, Hélène Preiswerk, who was in fact his mother's cousin, before she came on to him sexually, and several of his buddies were able to convince him that her performances were

[44] *Ibid.*, 229.

[45] C.G. Jung, *The Zofingia lectures: the collected works of C.G. Jung supplementary volume*, ed. William McGuire (Princeton, NJ: Princeton University Press, 1983), 1–20. In the same lecture, Jung also identified scientific materialism with the spirit of Judaism. See Makari, *Revolution in mind*, 190–191.

[46] C.G. Jung, "On the psychology and pathology of so-called occult phenomena," *The psychology of the occult* (Jung extracts), trans. R.F.C. Hull (Princeton, NJ: Princeton University Press, 1978), 6–19.

based on "trickery."[47] McLynn maintains that, rather than his academic coursework, the experience of these séances – where Jung, the only man in the room, was surrounded by a coterie of his mother's daft spiritualist cousins – constituted his "true formation in his Basel University years."[48]

Ultimately, Jung decided in favor of the second alternative, his No. 2 Self. As a young man, however, utilitarian considerations and the fear of acquiring "the dubious reputation of a freak" – or, worse yet, going mad like Nietzsche – converged and propelled a "flight into health" and the creation of a socially acceptable "false self." Nevertheless, at the same time that Jung made a pragmatic decision to assume the posture of his No. 1 Self in his dealings with the world, he resolved that "under no circumstances" would he leave his No. 2 Self "behind" or "declare" it "invalid."[49] Throughout his youth and early adulthood, Jung in fact reinvented himself in a Zelig-like fashion in three very different situations: at a rough-and-tumble rural school, at an elite *Gymnasium*, and at the University of Basel, where he transformed himself into the Swiss equivalent of a back-slapping "good old boy," wholeheartedly threw himself into the shenanigans of Zofingia fraternity, and earned the nickname of the "Barrel" as a result of his "physical burliness and . . . beer-drinking capacity."[50]

And Jung's false self served him well. After he completed his university years, it enabled him to obtain a position at one of Europe's most prestigious psychiatric hospitals and to rise quickly through its ranks; to publish prodigiously and make a name for himself in the world of academic psychiatry; to establish a rich (if promiscuous) personal life, marry well, and establish a thriving private practice; and not only to become the historical collaborator of Sigmund Freud, but to achieve a degree of international recognition that at times rivaled that of his older colleague.

The problem, however, was that Jung's solution had been achieved through "willpower" and that the underlying unconscious conflicts were "suppressed" rather than sufficiently resolved.[51] The accommodation was

[47] Jung, *Memories*, 148.
[48] McLynn, *Jung*, 51.
[49] *Ibid.*, 87.
[50] See McLynn, *Jung*, 45; Jung, *Memories*, 24.
[51] McLynn, *Jung*, 28.

therefore vulnerable and could not be sustained in the long run. Finally, under the combined personal and theoretical pressure of his engagement with Freud, Jung's No. 2 Self and "old religiosity" broke through, causing him to make a decisive turn in the direction of the world of alchemy, mysticism, magic, archaic mystery rites, and so on. Occultism – "the black tide of mud" that Freud had urged Jung to combat – could no longer be contained.[52] The break between the two analysts, fated from the start but deferred far beyond any reasonable expiration date, could no longer be avoided.

Disenchantment, Disillusionment, and the Break with Tradition

As it had with Freud, living through "the break with tradition" became a defining experience in Jung's biography. The distinct way that each man negotiated that massive cultural mutation goes a long way toward explaining "many of the time-honored differences" between them.[53]

As history unfolded, Freud, the urban secular Jew, grew more and more skeptical about human nature and the prospects of reducing unhappiness – and about creating an alliance between Gentiles and Jews – but he never lost the basic commitment to rationality and science that he had internalized as a child of "mid-century liberalism," even though he had to revise his understanding of both.[54] Jung, on the other hand, had come of age in a rural and deeply religious milieu and was nineteen years Freud's junior. He therefore belonged to a later generation – the generation of *Jung Wien* – whose members had lost their faith in liberalism, rationality, and progress and instead embraced two prophets of the *Gegenaufklärung*, Wagner and Nietzsche, as their alternative.

Homans turns to Max Weber to elucidate the differences between Freud's Enlightenment and Jung's Counter-Enlightenment positions, asserting that although Weber defended science and the Enlightenment, albeit as part of a tragic vision, his theory of "disenchantment" provides

---

[52] McGuire (ed.), *The Freud/Jung letters*, 97, and Jung, *Memories*, 150.

[53] Homans, *The ability to mourn*, 144.

[54] After the break with Jung, he wrote to Ferenczi that Jews and *goyim* mix like "oil and water." Falzeder and Brabant (eds.), *The Freud/Ferenczi letters*, vol. I, 28 July 1912.

a sociological diagnosis for many of the ideas of the *Gegenaufklärung*.[55] Homans attempts to integrate the cluster of psychoanalytic concepts surrounding Freud's idea of disillusionment, for example, de-idealization, loss, and mourning, with Weber's sociological diagnosis – specifically, with his theories of the rationalization process, the loss of meaning, and the disenchantment of the world. That the thinking of these two theoretical giants converged is understandable, given that "the world which Weber described was the world in which Freud also lived, worked and thought – as did his patients and followers."[56] With the rapid modernization of Vienna, embodied in the construction of the city's *Ringstrasse*, the vertiginous processes that Weber was analysing were unfolding before their very eyes. From Weber's side, Homans deploys the psychoanalytic theory of mourning to give the sociologist's theory a Freudian twist:

With these concepts [of rationalization and disenchantment] Weber created a portrait of modern Western man living in a time of general mourning for the lost spontaneity and immediacy which the social formations and symbols of Western religious culture had built up and guaranteed. As these experiences and values eroded, they were replaced by rational, calculative operations, in every possible sphere of life.[57]

And from Freud's side, Homans makes the unconventional but not implausible claim that "object loss [is] the central intellectual theme of psychoanalysis as a whole," and he argues that "the de-idealization experience" described by Freud "fits lock-and-key with Max Weber's account of value change in modern Western culture, which he described with the ideas of disenchantment and rationalization."[58] In sum, Homans's central

[55] See Homans, *The ability to mourn*, 24–26. In light of the fact that Freud formulated his theories of "magical thinking" and "the omnipotence of thoughts" in his attempt to counter Jung's mystical and religious tendencies, we should note that the German term that is translated as "disenchantment" is *Entzauberung*, which literally means "de-magification."

[56] *Ibid.*, 26.

[57] *Ibid.*, 26.

[58] *Ibid.*, 26 and 4. Freud's impatience with grandiosity and penchant for de-idealization stand out in the fact that he was a virtuoso of Jewish humor. The Jewish joke is a diminutive form of critique that aims to "bring soaring ambitions down to humble earth – [Freud's] own as well as those of his friends [and] enemies." *Ibid.*, 63.

thesis holds that "de-idealization and its historical correlative, disenchantment" are "a master theme in Freud's life and thought."[59]

Freud and Weber also shared a profound skepticism regarding the idea
of progress that resonated with the mood of the Counter-Enlightenment.
Freud's *Civilization and its discontents* and Weber's *The Protestant ethic and
the spirit of capitalism* pose a seemingly insurmountable challenge to any
progressivist desire to substantially transform modern society and ame-
liorate humanity's situation in modernity. Both thinkers argue that the
modernization process contains an implacably self-vitiating dynamic – "a
dialectic of enlightenment" – that renders all prospects of progressively
transforming the socio–economic order impossible.[60] Whether it is understood in terms of a growing sense of "guilt" and "discontent" (*Unbehagen*)
or of an unbearable "iron cage," the *telos* of modernity is a dead-end.[61]

By drawing on his theory of mourning rather than *Civilization and its
discontents*, Homans presents a refreshing attempt to locate a "redemptive dialectic" in Freud's thinking that would undoubtedly be dismissed
as *démodé* by the anti-modernist *bien pensants* populating our cultural
landscape. He argues that psychoanalysis was not only the product of the
"long process" of collective disillusionment and loss that began "centuries ago, with its roots in the origins of physical science in the seventeenth
century and in the theology of the fourteenth," but the culmination and
fulfillment of it.[62] Most importantly, he does not view that culmination
as entirely negative. To be sure, Freud provided a comprehensive damage
report on modernity's – or civilization's – negative consequences. But his
project also constituted "a creative response to [that] disillusionment and
disenchantment." In contrast to Weber, who only saw a loss of meaning –
an "emptying out" – Freud, Homans argues, responded to modernity's
destruction of the traditional structures of meaning "critically and constructively" and sought "to replace what is lost with something new."[63]

---

[59] *Ibid.*, 82.

[60] Although they do not flag it as such, Horkheimer's and Adorno's *magnum opus*
represents, among many other things, an attempt at integrating Weber and Freud in
Dialectic of enlightenment.

[61] Freud, *Civilization and its discontents*, 134, and Max Weber, *The Protestant ethic
and the spirit of capitalism*, trans. Talcott Parsons (New York: Scribner's, 1958), 181.

[62] Homans, *The ability to mourn*, 4.

[63] *Ibid.*, 27 and 4.

Homans rejects the view, often expounded by the conservatives within its ranks, that psychoanalysis represents a species of *Kulturpessimismus*. He argues that, like "many other cultural achievements in the West," including "modern literature and modern art," psychoanalysis constitutes a call "to give up many of the illusions or 'enchantments' which traditional culture had praised" and to create new post-traditional "structures of signification" and "appreciation" to replace them.[64] De-idealizing inherited values and meanings can, in short, have a productive and creative outcome, and, as we will see, the theory of mourning explains how it can come about.

Homans rightfully turns to the work of the totally *sui generis* and important German thinker Hans Blumenberg to develop his idiosyncratic interpretation of Freud's response to modernity.[65] Blumenberg combatted the anti-modern polemics that were circulating among the conservative German cultural critics of his day (for example, Martin Heidegger, Carl Schmitt, and Karl Löwith), which have for some perverse reason been picked up by today's post-modern left. In an attempt to discredit the validity of the "modern age," these conservatives maintain that modernity lacks any intrinsic legitimacy, and that its central ideas and values – for example, progress and the dignity of the individual – are parasitical on Christian doctrines. They claim, in other words, that modernity constitutes a social formation that is legitimate not in its own right, but only derivatively, as a "secularization of Christianity." Against this line of argument, Blumenberg asserts that modernity instituted at least one radically distinctive principle that bestows inherent legitimacy on it; he calls this principle "the primeval right to [human] self-assertion."[66] This concept refers not only to humanity's technological domination of the

---

[64] *Ibid.*, 4 and 27. In a somewhat different sense, Marx also believed that the disillusionment caused by the process of capitalist modernization resulted in enlightenment. As he famously wrote, "All fixed, fast-frozen relations, with their train of ancient and venerable prejudices and opinions, are swept away, all newly formed ones become antiquated before they can ossify. All that is solid melts into air, all that is holy profaned, and *man is at last compelled to face with sober senses his real conditions of life, and his relations with his kind.*" Karl Marx, "Manifesto of the Communist Party," *Karl Marx: on revolution*, ed. and trans. Saul K. Padover (New York: McGraw Hill, 1971), 83.

[65] See Homans, *The ability to mourn*, 268–270, and 314–319.

[66] Hans Blumenberg, *The legitimacy of the modern age*, trans. Robert M. Wallace (Cambridge, MA: The MIT Press, 1988), 196.

natural world, made possible by the "mechanization of the worldpicture," but also to a more comprehensive and significant achievement of the scientific revolution of the sixteenth and seventeenth centuries – namely, the emancipation of "theoretical curiosity."[67]

In the middle ages, Blumenberg argues, the Church Fathers, most notably Augustine, condemned *curiositas* as a vice. The manifestation of curiosity was taken as evidence of a lack of humility and a prideful presumption of omnipotence.[68] Only God is omnipotent, and only He can possess knowledge of the entire world. If mortals assert an unlimited right to explore the world and acquire knowledge of it, they deny their fallen state and presume to put themselves in God's omnipotent position. Therefore, the battle to legitimate modern science consisted in the struggle not only to validate a mathematized conception of the universe, but also to defend the emancipation of "theoretical curiosity." Because it has a direct bearing on Freud's theories of science and religion, we should note that the fight to liberate "theoretical curiosity" went hand-in-hand with the critique of religion. If the prohibition of curiosity was intrinsically tied to an omnipotent God, who already knows the essence of all things, then the denial of His existence eliminates that ban and opens nature for exploration by the finite human mind. As we will see in Chapter 12, when one digs deep enough into Freud's theory of science and criticism of religion, one thing becomes apparent: His most fundamental value-commitment was to the *unrestricted exercise of the intellect*. Beyond all theological, ontological, and doctrinal questions, Freud's conviction that religious belief necessarily entails a profound *sacrificium intellectus* constitutes the core of his abiding hostility to religion. In short, the repudiation of omnipotence, secularism, and the defense of science hang together for Freud.

Blumenberg views the emancipation and vindication of "theoretical curiosity" – of the imagination – as the singular epochal accomplishment of modernity.[69] After Copernicus, Galileo, and Kepler deployed theoretical

[67] Eduard Jan Dijksterhuis, *The mechanization of the world picture: Pythagoras to Newton*, trans. C. Dikshoom (Princeton, NJ: Princeton University Press, 1966).

[68] See Homans, *The ability to mourn*, 318–328.

[69] On the liberation of the "imaginary," see Castoriadis, *The imaginary institution of society*, 168, and Castoriadis, "The discovery of the imagination," *World in fragments: writings on politics, society, psychoanalysis and the imagination*, ed. and trans. David Ames Curtis (Stanford: Stanford University Press, 1997), 213–245. In his massive

curiosity theoretically, "other ways of going beyond the boundaries" of the inherited worldview, what Paul Valéry called "curiosités de toute espèce" (every kind of curiosity) spread throughout modern culture, giving it its open, restless, and creative character – exactly what conservative anti-modernists excoriate as the source of modernity's nihilism and decadence.[70] Blumenberg singles Freud out as one of the central heroes in the emancipation of curiosity. After all, what is the "fundamental rule," by which the analyst instructs the patient to say whatever comes to mind, if not an invitation to think everything?

According to Blumenberg, Freud did for the human realm what the natural scientists had done for the physical world. Because he redirected the gaze of curiosity to explore the previously tabooed topic of the psychosexual roots of individual and collective identity, Freud could rightfully identify his accomplishment with those of Copernicus and Darwin. The identification "alone," Homans rightfully notes, "precedes all disputes about the existence of physicalistic laws of the mind (the metapsychology)."[71] Understanding modernity as the liberation of theoretical curiosity, and understanding Freud as a major contributor to that emancipatory project, is one way to delineate the fissure separating his project from Jung's romantic anti-modernism. By dismissing modern

---

history of "solitary sex" Thomas Laqueur argues that the nineteenth century stigmatized masturbation – as opposed to Onanism, for example – and instituted a coordinated struggle against it because autoerotic practices are connected with fantasy, which is to say, the imagination. To be sure, the Bible had condemned Onanism as sinful, but not because of its connection with mental processes. It was condemned, rather, because it wasted "seed." In the nineteenth century, however, the stigmatization of masturbation and the public struggle against it became based on the belief that it promoted the anti-social expansion of fantasy life. Interestingly, the criticism of masturbation was part and parcel of the opposition to the novel, which was viewed as dangerous for the same reason. Thomas Laqueur, *Solitary history: a cultural history of masturbation* (New York: Zone Books, 2003), chapter V. These typically nineteenth-century attitudes partly determined Freud's attitude toward masturbation. He was right, however, to recognize the narcissistic power of masturbation insofar as it can offer a safe and tempting retreat from the dangers of object relations. What he failed to adequately appreciate, however, is that masturbation fantasies, which were elaborated in private, could enrich and enliven a couple's erotic life when they overlap and the partners can share them.

[70] See Homans, *The ability to mourn*, 318.

[71] *Ibid.*, 320.

science as positivist, Jung ignores its epochal achievement: emancipating theoretical curiosity. His musings on alchemy, Native American folklore, and the *Bhagavad Gita* should not be mistaken for the exercise of theoretical curiosity; they are exotica.

Deus Defecatus

The substantial differences in the way Freud and Jung were disillusioned in no small degree accounts for their divergent views on modernity, science, and religion. For disillusionment to have a productive outcome, as it did with Freud, it must proceed in a felicitous way and unfold at a manageable pace. If it occurs too rapidly, de-idealization becomes traumatic and cannot be assimilated and constructively elaborated. As opposed to Jung's, Homans observes, "Freud's disenchantment with his religious heritage was a gradual and progressive one." Although the atmosphere in the home was dripping in *Yiddishkeit*, Jacob "had no interest in doctrinal truths or in ritual observances" and was more than willing to have his son "exposed to an urbanized, scientific, and humanistic culture."[72] Freud's relatively untraumatic disillusionment with the tradition of the past, in conjunction with the secularized Jewish environment in which he was raised, allowed him to become an uncompromising atheist who rejected religion *in toto*. He believed, moreover, that his experience as a Jew contributed to his ability to stand outside "the compact majority" and identify with the universal perspective of science. Personally, moreover, the support Freud found in Vienna's Jewish community, for example, with his "brothers" at the B'nai B'rith, made it possible for his "self-analysis to proceed bit by bit, so that Freud's ego was never completely overwhelmed by the unconscious forces, the emergence of which his social isolation had fatefully authorized."[73]

Jung was not as fortunate. "Such gradualness and support," according to Homans, were "denied to" him, causing a "precipitous and excessively rapid" disillusionment with the tradition in which he had been socialized.[74] In this respect, Jung can be compared to Nietzsche, whose proclamations that "God is dead" sometimes have a manic and counter-phobic ring to

---

[72] *Ibid.*, 149.

[73] *Ibid.*, 149.

[74] *Ibid.*, 149.

them. Because Jung's disillusionment "was precipitous, rage filled, and therefore, incomplete," the way he charted the inner world of the psyche and the outer world of culture and religion had to take a different form from Freud's.[75] That Jung's father, like Nietzsche's, was a member of the clergy is perhaps the most decisive difference between the two analysts' upbringings. Because religion had cast a large onerous shadow over Jung's childhood, it was necessary for him to create a response that was commensurate with its importance in his life. It may seem paradoxical that Jung's greater hostility toward religion led to a desire to create a blasphemous alternative to it rather than completely to reject it. But the paradox is only apparent, for, as Freud recognized shortly after his break with Jung, it is more difficult to give up an object that we have hated than one about which we are less ambivalent.

Jung's struggle with religion is encapsulated in "the cathedral fantasy," which, along with the phallus dream, constitutes one of the two nodal episodes in the development of his inner life. Jung himself tells us that his "entire youth can be understood in terms of [the] secret" in the fantasy "that occurred when he was a *Gymnasium* student in Basel."[76] One summer's day, when Jung was passing through the town's Cathedral Square, the beauty of the church glistening in the bright sunlight overwhelmed him. But in the midst of reflecting on the sublime beauty of the church and the world as a whole, and of fantasizing that God was perched on his throne above, surveying his miraculous creation, Jung was seized by a choking sensation that abruptly arrested his thinking. He realized that an awful thought was about to emerge and that he must exert every effort to suppress it lest he commit a terrible sin.

Jung obsessively struggled for two days to prevent the forbidden thought from becoming conscious but finally sensed that it was about to break through despite his struggle. He then entered into a convoluted, internal, "theological" debate that ultimately provided a rationale for surrendering to the temptation, while simultaneously aggrandizing his sense of self. God, Jung perversely reasoned, was not subjecting him to a run-of-the-mill ordeal meant to determine his ability to withstand temptation. This was not, in other words, on the same level as the struggle against

[75] *Ibid.*, 361 n. 1.
[76] Jung, *Memories*, 41.

masturbation. Instead, he was demanding a more stringent trial, requir-
ing Jung to risk "heaven and hell" in order to determine whether he had
the courage to violate his own "faith" and "reason" by thinking blasphemous thoughts. Thinking sacrilegious thoughts was precisely what God
wanted him to do! Through this tortured logic, Jung concluded that by
performing blasphemy, he would emphatically prove his faith.[77]

The young man therefore screwed up his courage and allowed the
thought to break through:

I saw before me the cathedral, the blue sky. God sits on His golden throne, high
above the world – and from under the throne an enormous turd falls on the spar-
kling new roof, shatters it, and breaks the walls of the cathedral asunder.[78]

At that moment Jung experienced "an unutterable bliss" – this can happen after a spectacular bowel movement – and construed this fantasy as
an act of grace rather than a massive anal assault on his father's religion.
Because he "had yielded to His inexorable demand" and allowed himself
to think "the forbidden thought," Jung tells us, "the wisdom and goodness of God had been revealed to" him. He was not only "chosen" by
God, but this experience, so he believed, represented an "illumination"
that revealed the superiority of his brand of religiosity over his father's.
Paul practiced religion in the prescribed, conventional way but, according
to his son, "did not know the immediate living God, who stands, omnipotent and free, above His Bible and His Church." Carl, on the other hand,
was convinced that he had formerly experienced this living deity directly
with his underground phallic deity and now with his *Deus defecatus*. By
transforming sin into virtue – into the will of God – Jung provided himself with a rationalization for his aggression toward his father and his
Church, treated it as a privileged gift from God, and elevated himself into
a superior spiritual position. This triumph allowed Jung to reject institutionalized religion in the name of a higher counter-religion.

As one might have predicted, however, Jung's manic victory over his
father and the religion of his childhood had its depressive underside. His
contact with the living God filled Jung with a sense of certainty, superiority, and elation that expunged the "almost unendurable loneliness" he

[77] *Ibid.*, 39.
[78] *Ibid.*, 39.

experienced in his mundane social life, but God's ability to "befoul His own Cathedral" also told him that God "could be something terrible."[79] The privileged knowledge of God's dual nature shackled Jung with a burden that would "overshadow his whole life" and turn him into a deeply "pensive" individual who could never decide whether he was "outlawed or elect, accursed or blessed."[80] Though Jung never disclosed the secret of the Cathedral fantasy – nor of the phallus dream – to anyone, he tells us that his "entire life can be understood" in terms of these two secrets.[81] Regardless of how onerous he found it and how he grew to hate it, Paul's Christianity had been at the center of Carl Jung's life. It had provided his world with structure, coherence, and meaning. We can be as attached to our "bad" objects as we are to our "good" ones – indeed, even more so – and when Jung rejected his father's religion, it created an enormous void in his life and engendered a devastating sense of loss. "My sense of union with the Church and with the human world so far as I knew it," he tells us, "was shattered. I had, so it seemed to me, suffered the greatest defeat of my life. The religious outlook I imagined constituted my sole meaning-ful relation to the universe had disintegrated.[82]

The *Mésalliance*

"The friendship" between Freud and Jung, Walter Kaufmann observes, is "harder to explain than the break," for while "the break was somehow inevitable . . . the friendship was not."[83] The causes of the relationship's demise are in fact so obvious that one has to explain why it did not occur earlier. How, one wonders, could such an obvious *mésalliance* have come about in the first place? A number of factors enter into the answer to this question, but Kaufmann calls our attention to a particularly important one, namely, "how lonely both" Freud and Jung "felt when they found each other."[84]

---

[79] *Ibid.*, 41 and 48.
[80] *Ibid.*, 40–41.
[81] *Ibid.*, 40–1.
[82] *Ibid.*, 56.
[83] Kaufmann, *Discovering the mind*, vol. III, 311.
[84] *Ibid.*, 314.

Viewed from the outside, things were steadily improving for both men during the first years of the twentieth century. Freud had published three important works (*Three essays on sexuality*, *The psychopathology of everyday life*, and *Dora*), had landed the assistant professorship that had eluded him for years, and had attracted a group of followers with whom he inaugurated the famous Wednesday Night Meetings that were to continue for decades. Furthermore, thanks in no small part to Jung, psychoanalysis was beginning to be recognized on the international stage. Yet, the loss of Fliess, his "only Other," left an enormous void in Freud's life that these developments could not fill. Intellectually, Freud never held his "gang" of marginal Viennese Jews in high esteem. Strictly speaking, they may not have been *Luftmenschen*, but none of them possessed the education or *Bildung* to serve as an adequate interlocutor for Freud, much less the kind of intellectual firepower Fliess had that had generated so much intellectual excitement in the 1890s. When Jung first wrote to him, Freud was not as desperate as he had been when he met Fliess, but the suddenness and intensity with which he became attached to Jung suggest that his emotional situation was relatively urgent. Freud confirms this suggestion in a letter he wrote to his Swiss colleague, telling him that he had been in a state of "honourable but painful solitude" and experiencing "terrifying moments" of doubt when he first heard from him as "a voice from the unknown multitude."[85]

Jung also made impressive strides at the beginning of the new century. In 1900, the year that Freud published *The interpretation of dreams*, Jung began a residency at one of Europe's most prestigious psychiatric hospitals, the Burghölzli on Lake Zurich, and rose through its ranks in an unprecedented five years to become its Assistant Director. Although Jung's mobilization of his No. 1 Self enabled him to achieve considerable professional success, he felt thwarted and disgruntled in his role as a staff psychiatrist and conventional scientist. He found life in the monastic world of Burghölzli "barren of meaning" and considered the institution's intellectual horizons too restricted – limited, as he describes those horizons, to "what was probable, average, commonplace," while excluding "everything strange and significant."[86]

[85] McGuire (ed.), *The Freud/Jung letters*, 82.
[86] Jung, *Memories*, 112.

Although Jung successfully practiced mainstream psychiatric treatment, pursued standard scientific research, and published extensively in prestigious journals, his mind was too restless and searching to find satisfaction within the limited possibilities of a conventional psychiatric career. He was in fact busy establishing himself in a métier that did not address the urgent personal questions that his No. 2 Self posed to him, which were often the same questions that animated his intellectual creativity. When it came to the things that mattered most – the serious questions that had preoccupied religion and philosophy for millennia – Freud and Jung both felt isolated at the time they found each other.

Kaufmann summarizes the situation this way. The feelings that brought Freud and Jung together were so urgent that they were unmanageable, making a workable modus vivendi between the two impossible. "In their different ways both men were exceedingly lonely." They therefore not only "came too close to each other too quickly" but "sought more in their friendship than was realistic."[87]

At the time he met Fliess, Freud saw himself as a powerless and unskilled neophyte and the Berliner as an omnipotent "magician," who would save him from his personal suffering, theoretical confusion, and professional stagnation. With Jung, despite defending a disconsolate scientific *Weltanschauung* against the Zuricher's religious position, Freud again looked to the younger colleague for salvation, which is to say, for magic. The redemption Freud hoped Jung could deliver, however, differed from the one he had sought from Fliess. This one was tied to his perception of his life-situation at the time and to the belief that Jung, as a Gentile, was in a position to deliver the goods. Freud was no longer a young novice embarking on an unconventional and uncertain career fraught with all sorts of danger. He was now a battle-scarred conquistador confronting the prospect of his physical and mental decline, as well as his eventual demise. At the time, "Freud felt old," as Kaufmann puts it, "and thought his work was done."[88] These feelings were not entirely unfounded. To be in one's fifties in 1907 meant something different from what it means today, especially given that Freud had already experienced a prolonged life-threatening cardiac illness, which gave him added reason to be concerned with his longevity.

---

[87] Kaufmann, *Discovering the mind*, vol. III, 316.

[88] *Ibid.*, 317.

The situation also gave him cause to worry about the future of psychoanalysis and to contemplate the question of his successor. Enter Jung.

An arrangement of reciprocal self-deception made it possible for this thoroughly improbable relationship to take hold and maintain itself for an improbable stretch of time. Each man was convinced he could convert the other to his point of view. The theory of sexuality, which Freud believed provided the litmus test for his entire position, constituted the major point of contention between them. From the outset, Jung informed his senior colleague that he had serious reservations about his "broadened conception of sexuality."[89] Nevertheless, Freud convinced himself that, over time and under his tutelage, the less experienced practitioner of psychoanalysis would come around. I "venture to hope," he wrote to Jung in one of their early letters, "that in the course of the years you will come much closer to me [on the question of sexuality] than you now think possible."[90]

From his side, Jung deceived himself about the strength and depth of Freud's commitment to atheism and naturalism and its corollary – namely, that the critique of religion was integral to his entire project, not to mention his identity. He could thus convince himself that he could convert "the apostate Jew" on the questions of religion, spiritism, and the occult.

Like his friendship with Fliess, Freud's relationship to Jung was shot out of the barrel of a gun. That the two men talked "virtually without a pause for thirteen hours" at their first meeting, which occurred at Berggasse 19 on a Sunday afternoon in March 1907, attests to the intensity of the encounter.[91] After Jung departed from Vienna for Budapest, Freud exhibited the same unrestrained enthusiasm and instantaneous idealization vis-à-vis his new Swiss partner that he had displayed toward Fliess following their first meeting twenty years earlier. What is most striking about Freud's initial reaction to Jung is how quickly – indeed, how eagerly – he was prepared to relinquish his throne to the younger man. Thus, a month after their first visit, Freud wrote:

Your visit was most delightful and gratifying; I should like to repeat in writing various things that I confided to word of mouth, in particular, that you have

[89] McGuire (ed.), *The Freud/Jung letters*, 25.
[90] *Ibid.*, 5.
[91] Jung, *Memories*, 149.

inspired me with confidence for the future, that I now realize that I am replaceable as everyone else and that I could hope for no one better than yourself, as I have come to know you, to continue and complete my work.[92]

While, as we have noted, there were good reasons for Freud to be concerned about the future of psychoanalysis, this unctuous proclamation far outstrips the demands of reality. Though he had recently discovered the Oedipus complex, Freud's behavior more closely resembled Lear's premature abdication than Laius's attempted infanticide. "Given his love of Shakespeare," Kaufmann observes, Freud should have realized that he would have been making "Lear's mistake of turning over his crown too early, before he was really ready to retire," thereby creating "an almost impossible situation."[93] But powerful intrapsychic forces prevented him from recognizing the applicability of Shakespeare's tragedy to his own case.

Freud was attracted to Jung by a complex amalgam of opportunistic and principled motives, some of which were based in emotionally charged fantasies, others in realistic calculations. From a "public relations" perspective, Jung undoubtedly "had his uses."[94] Freud's Viennese followers were a marginal and relatively depressive group lacking the requisite credentials and self-confidence to promote psychoanalysis in the larger world. On the other hand, when Jung presented as his No. 1 Self, he fitted the bill exactly. In contrast to the cerebral, bookish, and inhibited "gang" in Vienna, Jung appeared in Freud's eyes as a strapping, athletic, outgoing Gentile – "a *shaygetz* god," to paraphrase Philip Roth – who had all the attributes of a natural salesman and the credentials of a world-class scientist.

Furthermore, although Freud undoubtedly possessed enormous charisma, he doubted his own attractiveness and ability to promote his cause. Echoing feelings he had earlier expressed to Martha, he wrote to Jung, "I have always felt that there was something about my personality, my ideas and manner of speaking that people find strange and repellent." These feelings, it is reasonable to assume, are manifestations of the "gaps in the

[92] McGuire (ed.), *The Freud/Jung letters*, 27. See also Ludwig Binswanger, *Sigmund Freud: reminiscences of a friendship*, trans. Norbert Guterman (New York: Grune & Stratton, 1957), 10–11.

[93] Kaufmann, *Discovering the mind*, vol. III, 317.

[94] Gay, *Freud: a life for our time*, 201.

fabric" of Freud's self that resulted from his early failures of internalization. Freud perceived Jung, on the other hand, as "a healthy man" to
whom "all hearts open." He told the younger colleague that, as a "master
of the art of winning people," he was "better fitted for propaganda" and
therefore the one to be psychoanalysis's "emissary" to the wider world.[95]

In addition to his gregarious and convivial personality, Jung, as opposed
to the Viennese, also possessed the training, talent, and professional standing to effectively advance the psychoanalytic cause in the larger scientific
community.[96] As the psychologist John Kerr points out in his history of
the Freud–Jung relationship, in 1907 it was not clear "which man," Freud
or Jung, "was currently the more important of the two," and he suggests
that, "were a contemporary commentator asked to pick which of their
viewpoints would be most likely to endure, he surely would have picked
Jung's."[97] The fact that all the members of Freud's Viennese circle were
Jewish was also a decisive factor in Freud's choice of Jung as his successor.
Insofar as their Jewishness made it possible to dismiss psychoanalysis as a
parochial enterprise, it made the already daunting task of presenting the
blasphemous new discipline to the wider Christian world that much more
difficult.

Freud entreated Karl Abraham, his Jewish colleague who suspected
Jung of anti-Semitism, to exercise some forbearance, indeed, some masochism, toward his Swiss rival by pointing out that "it was only with
his emergence on the scene that psychoanalysis was removed from the
danger of becoming a Jewish national affair." The very fact that Jung is "a
Christian and a pastor's son," Freud told Abraham, made "his association
with us . . . all the more valuable."[98] Though Freud's judgments regarding
the significance of Jung's Christian upbringing were often distorted, his
concerns were based on more than a grain of practical truth. Let us recall
that the "politics in a new key" had already made their ugly appearance
in Vienna: Not only had populist gangs of anti-Semitic thugs marauded
through its streets, but Karl Lueger, the populist anti-Semite, had been
elected the city's mayor.

[95] McGuire (ed.), *The Freud/Jung letters*, 82 and 366.
[96] Kaufmann, *Discovering the mind*, vol. III, 313.
[97] Kerr, *A most dangerous method*, 134.
[98] Falzeder (ed.), *Correspondence of Freud and Abraham*, 38.

In addition to the strategic calculations underlying Freud's wish to recruit Jung for psychoanalysis, he was also motivated by an authentic desire to transcend the ghettoized consciousness of Jewish particularism and by a *principled* commitment to the *Universalität* of the Enlightenment that reached back to his student days with Hammerschlag. Because science was universal, psychoanalysis had to overcome the particularity of its origins and become more than "a Jewish science." Though Freud's cosmopolitan aspirations would later be dampened by his experience with Jung, at the time he met the young psychiatrist they were at their height.[99] Freud's attempt to form a close alliance with the son of a Swiss pastor represented a good-faith attempt to escape intellectual parochialism and fulfill the ideal of European cosmopolitanism. Because of Jung's exceptional talent and rigorous scientific training, Freud believed that it could be possible to achieve those universalist aspirations. To maintain this idealized picture of his Swiss colleague, however, it was necessary for Freud to overlook the regressive anti-modern strains that were so prominent in Jung's personality.

There is something deeply ironical, if not comical, about Freud's distorted estimation of Jung's personality, which unfortunately had tragic consequences. Although the traits that Freud responded to in the young psychiatrist could not have been entirely fabricated, they were largely manifestations of the false self that Jung had constructed to make his way in "the real world." Freud acknowledged that he became a psychologist in part to compensate for the fact that he was not a natural *Menschenkenner*. Jones suggests that Freud's character contained an unusual combination of naïveté and gullibility, which he may have inherited from his Galician mother, and a razor-sharp intellect. Credulity that allowed him to entertain seemingly far-fetched ideas that more conventional thinkers would simply dismiss along with a critical faculty that enabled him to realistically assess those ideas made for a combination that was a key to his creativity.[100] But when it came to navigating his way socially, the same naïveté could land him in trouble. One might say that Freud loved Jung "narcissistically" – that is, as someone he

---

[99] Kerr attempts subtly to disparage Freud's cosmopolitanism by reducing it to assimilationism. See Kerr, *A most dangerous method*, 235. See also Homans, *The ability to mourn*, 73.

[100] See Jones, *Freud* III, 401–2.

would like to be: a strapping, athletic, outgoing, and uninhibited *goyish* hero who would magically save him from the hostile Gentile world that surrounded him. Jung's No. 1 Self had to no small degree seduced the shaky *Menschenkenner*. Freud failed to realize in sufficient time that a fragile No. 2 Self lay behind No. 1, and this second self became increasingly evident as the psychological pressure of their developing collaboration intensified.

9

Exorcising the
"Odium Jungian"

T HOUGH THEY CONTINUED TO exchange letters concerning trivial business matters, the break between Freud and Jung occurred de facto at
a congress of the International Psychoanalytic Association held in Munich
in September 1913. After that meeting, the two men never saw each other
again. Given their ambitions, theoretical differences, radically different
personalities, and opposing worldviews, the break was fated from the outset. Only a concatenation of diverse factors, as noted, delayed the rupture
for a remarkably long time.

"A Religious Crush"

Freud had definite political and theoretical plans for his newly designated
successor. Politically, he wanted Jung to assume major organizational
responsibilities in the psychoanalytic profession. In terms of theory, he
hoped that his younger colleague would, as he put it, inject his "own personal leaven into the fermenting mass of my ideas," thereby promoting
the growth of psychoanalysis.[1] More specifically, Freud hoped that Jung
would incorporate two new fields, psychosis and mythology, into psychoanalysis and thereby expand its theoretical scope.

As a staff psychiatrist at Burghölzli, Jung had acquired extensive
experience working with psychotics, a patient population with which
Freud, as a private practitioner, had had little contact. Freud therefore
considered the Zuricher as superbly qualified, as he himself was not,
to construct a psychoanalytic theory of psychosis – delineated in the
specific way Freud saw it – and assigned him the task: Jung was to provide an explanation of psychosis in terms of Freud's theory of sexuality.

---

[1] McGuire (ed.), *The Freud/Jung letters*, 77.

"My selfish purpose," Freud confessed, "is to persuade you to continue and complete my work by applying to psychosis what I have begun with neurosis."[2] Likewise, growing up in a parsonage, the pastor's son had a more intimate and extensive knowledge of religious teachings and experience than did Freud, the non-religious Jew. Moreover, Jung's exposure to such teachings produced in him intense and conflicted feelings that led him to read extensively on the topics of religion, mythology, and folklore as a young man. This was a package of credentials that made Freud confident that Jung was the person to "conquer the whole field of mythology" and religion for psychoanalysis – by which he meant, to subsume these topics under his libido theory.[3]

The maladroit judge of character failed to recognize, however, that Jung was a rebellious son who harbored ambitions that rivaled his own. Given Jung's personality, there was not a chance in hell that he would become a subservient organization man – if for no other reason than that it demanded too much time, and Jung required all the time he could get to pursue his own sizeable ambitions. Those ambitions made it equally unlikely that Jung would have subordinated himself theoretically to Freud. Formulate a theory of psychosis and religion in terms of Freud's view of sexuality, as Freud had assigned him to do? Again, not a chance in hell.

Predictably, these became the two issues of theory over which Freud and Jung eventually parted ways. We have observed that Jung never fully accepted Freud's theory of sexuality, the touchstone of his entire project; instead, he attempted to account for both psychosis and religion in terms of his own theory of "General Libido," which is to say, de-sexualized libido. The debates over these issues between the two men occurred over two distinct periods: The first, over psychosis, occurred between 1907 and 1911, the year Freud and Jung, accompanied by Sándor Ferenczi, visited America and lectured at Clark University, and the second, the debate over religion, took place between 1911 and 1913, the year their relationship terminated. Conceptually, however, the two debates involve the same issues, sexuality being at their core; the debates are thus thoroughly intertwined and cannot be neatly disentangled.

[2] *Ibid.*, 168.
[3] *Ibid.*, 53.

The contentious issue of sexuality goes beyond its scientific and clinical significance to encompass larger questions of *Weltanschauung*. For Freud, as Loewald argues, sexual drives were "not just abstract constructs or concepts in a theory of motivation or personality." Despite what "scientists, doctors, ministers, judges" and "'the educated circles' . . . wanted to admit or know," these drives are "what made the human world go around."[4] Freud's theory of sexuality was part and parcel of his thoroughgoing and unsentimental naturalism – one might indeed say of his paganism. It was intended to serve as "an unshakeable bulwark" not only "against the black tide . . . of occultism," as he told Jung, but also against the "postures and gestures, self-denials, rationalizations, distortions and hideouts" – in short, against the hypocrisy and self-deception that "respectable society" uses to conceal "the true life and real power of the instincts."[5] To be sure, Freud's bearing and habits were those of an arch bourgeois, while Jung abounded with anti-bourgeois pretentions. Nevertheless, from Freud's perspective, Jung's flight from sexuality and into the occult amounted to the same thing: an attempt to evade "'the exigencies of life,' man's troubled existence."[6]

Of the debates between Freud and Jung that sprang from this core, the one over religion took place in print while the debate over psychosis was primarily confined to their private correspondence – with the important exception of Freud's case study of Daniel Paul Schreber, which appeared as "Psycho-analytic notes on an autobiographical account of a case of paranoia (Dementia paranoides)," in 1911.

The letters in which the psychosis debate was contained can be so obscure that it is often difficult to make sense of them. Indeed, at times, one can hardly glean what the two men thought they were up to. The obscurity is profound enough to raise the suspicion that the stakes in this debate were not just theoretical – or rather, that theory was used as the medium through which a more personal struggle was conducted. What is clear, however, is that *the question of the connection between sexuality and the relation to reality is at the center of the debate on psychosis*. It is at the

---

[4] Loewald, "On motivation and instinct theory," *The essential Loewald: collected papers and monographs* (Hagerstown, MD: University Publishing Group, 2000), 125.

[5] Jung, *Memories*, 150, and Loewald, "On motivation and instinct theory," 125.

[6] Loewald, "Book review essay on the *Freud/Jung letters*," 408.

center of Freud's defense of his scientific *Weltanschauung* against the challenge of Jung's Counter-Enlightenment stance. And it is at the center of the debate over religion; after all, what does it mean to assert that religion is an "illusion," as Freud did, but that it entails a fundamental distortion of reality?[7]

We see this from the very beginning of the correspondence between the two men. When they began their collaboration, Freud's hunger for an interlocutor and his desire to win Jung over was so consuming that he was insufficiently sensitive to Jung's psychological situation, and, sometime between 7 and 20 April 1907, he imprudently sent him a text entitled "A few theoretical remarks on paranoia."[8] The text, which prefigured "On narcissism: an introduction" by seven years, contained a sketch of the ideas he had formulated about homosexuality, withdrawal of libido, projection, and paranoia in the wake of the Fliess imbroglio. In sending it, Freud failed to appreciate how difficult it would be for the son of a Swiss pastor to absorb the material – which was as intellectually dense as it was emotionally distressing.[9] The stimulation of all this material pertaining to homosexuality seems to have been too much for Jung to absorb; he had to distance himself from Freud and take a "long pause" before responding to the text. Then, on 11 September 1907, "a real-life intrusion of homosexual libido," as the psychoanalyst Zvi Lothane puts it, emerged between "master and disciple."[10] Jung asked Freud to send him a photograph of himself:

Perhaps I may take this opportunity to express a long cherished and constantly repressed wish: I would dearly like to have a photograph of you, not as you used to look but as you did when I first got to know you. Would you have the kindness

---

[7] See Patrick Vandermeersch, *Unresolved questions in the Freud/Jung debate on psychosis, sexual identity and religion*, Louvain Philosophical Studies 4, trans. Anne-Marie Marivoet and Vincent Sansone (Leuven: Leuven University Press, 1991), 33.

[8] McGuire (ed.), *The Freud/Jung letters*, 38–40.

[9] See Leonard Shengold, "The Freud/Jung letters: the correspondence between Sigmund Freud and C.G. Jung, *Journal of the American Psychoanalytic Association* 24 (1976), 673.

[10] Zvi Lothane, "The schism between Freud and Jung over Schreber: its implications for method and doctrine," *International Forum of Psychoanalysis* 6 (1997), 107. See also Vandermeersch, *Unresolved questions in the Freud–Jung debate*, 135.

to grant this wish of mine sometime? I would be ever so grateful because again and again I feel the want of your picture.[11]

This request was an uncanny repetition of something that, as we have noted, had occurred twelve years earlier, when Freud, in a manifestation of his growing love for Fliess, had made the same request of the Berliner at the time of the Eckstein affair.

It is compounded in a letter dated 28 October 1907 in which Jung offers a remarkable revelation that flies in the face of his denial of the momentous role that sexuality plays in human affairs. After proclaiming his "boundless admiration" for Freud "as a man and a researcher," Jung reveals that he has a "religious crush" on his older colleague. (For some reason, this eye-catching incident has received scant attention in the literature.) While confessing that he is troubled by his feelings for Freud, Jung halfheartedly attempts to minimize their importance: "Though it does not really bother me, I still feel it is disgusting and ridiculous because of its undeniable erotic undertone." He also informs Freud that his homosexual feelings interfere with his interpersonal life, making "relationships with colleagues who have strong transferences to [him] downright disgusting." He seems to be saying that he has difficulty tolerating the sizeable transferences that often develop between analysts, given the nature of their work, because they might reveal his homosexual feelings. And he goes on to tell Freud, "I also fear the same reaction from you when I speak of my intimate affairs."[12] In a rare moment of critical self-awareness, Jung recognizes that, because of the necessity of concealing the deeper and more troubling aspects of his personality – that is, of his No. 2 Self – his relations with others remain superficial and unsatisfying. He then dismisses his insight by devaluing intimacy: "Consequently, I skirt around such things as much as possible, for, to my feeling at any rate, every intimate relationship turns out after a while to be sentimental and banal or exhibitionistic."[13] Jung seems to be oblivious to the fact that contempt for intimacy is incompatible with being a psychoanalyst.

The source of the religious crush, Jung informs Freud, is the sexual experience that he had with his father's colleague at the age of eighteen.

[11] McGuire (ed.), *The Freud/Jung letters*, 86.

[12] *Ibid.*, 95.

[13] *Ibid.*, 95.

"The abominable feeling comes from the fact that as a boy I was the victim of a sexual assault by a man I once worshipped," he explains.[14] Taken together, the dream of the deified phallus and having been assaulted by a man of the cloth help to explain the convergence of sexuality and religion in Jung's crush on Freud. And he says as much: "My old religiosity had secretly found in you a compensating factor which I had to come to terms with eventually, and I was able to do so only by telling you about it."[15]

Freud is only interested in 50 per cent of Jung's revelation. He is utterly indifferent to the sexual half of the confession but deeply concerned with the religious one. In a statement that turned out to be all too prophetic, Freud warns his younger colleague that the enactment of a religious transference would inevitably lead to rebellion: "A transference on a religious basis would strike me as most disastrous; it could end only in apostasy, thanks to the universal human tendency to keep making new prints of clichés within us."[16] That is to say, if Jung were to enact his religious transference, it would reactivate infantile prototypes ("clichés") in an intensified form and leave him caught between the two poles that emerge from the experience of infantile helplessness – "reverent submission and mutinous insubordination."[17] And this "could only result in" rebellion – that is, in "apostasy."

Freud attempts to reassure Jung by telling him, "I shall do my best to show you that I am unfit to be an object of worship," but there is something problematic about his effort.[18] He often asserted that "the rejection of suggestion" – the repudiation of the magical powers of the hypnotist – constituted the founding principle of psychoanalysis, and by refusing to play the role of the omnipotent analyst with Jung, he was simply conforming to that principle. But as the person who elucidated the nature and power of transference and resistance, there is something Freud should have understood – namely, unless Jung's need for idealization was addressed, presenting himself as a "real" object would likely

---

Ibid., 95.

[15] *Ibid.*, 97.

[16] *Ibid.*, 98.

[17] Sigmund Freud, "Psycho-analytic notes on an autobiographical account of a case of paranoia (Dementia paranoides)" (1911), *SE* 12: 52.

[18] McGuire (ed.), *The Freud/Jung letters*, 98.

be of little use. Thanks to Kohut, analysts now understand something about idealization that Freud did not, the first analyst having been notoriously uncomfortable with the topic. At times, idealizing transferences must be not only tolerated but allowed full expression if they are to be worked through. Otherwise, they go underground and become malignant. Rebuffing Jung's desire to idealize him, without providing an alternative fate for it, was not a viable solution. In fact, one can argue that it constituted a failure of empathy.

The 1909 trip to America was an inflection point in the relationship between the two men. They had been jointly invited to deliver a series of lectures at Clark University in Worcester, Massachusetts.[19] Accompanied by Sándor Ferenczi, they boarded the *George Washington*, a ship of the Norddeutscher Lloyd line, on 20 August 1909 and crossed the Atlantic from Bremen to New York. They spent several days taking in the sights of Manhattan, including the Lower East Side, Central Park, Chinatown, Columbia University, and the Metropolitan Museum, "where Freud was chiefly interested in the Greek antiquities."[20] Their lectures at Clark were attended by many of America's intellectual elite, including William James, and were received with considerable enthusiasm, leading Freud to proclaim emotionally, "This is the first official recognition of our endeavors."[21] Jung believed that the laurels of the Clark visit belonged to him as much as to Freud, and this served to further intensify his ambition as well as his grandiosity when he returned to Europe. A new degree of contentiousness and competition entered the interaction between the two men, finding its voice in various aspects of theory if not reflected in their correspondence.

The subject of Jung's religious crush was not mentioned again, as Jung apparently followed Freud's counsel that, with the help of some levity, he try to "sublimate" his eroticized religious yearning. This "solution," however, constituted an act of compliance rather than a viable resolution of any conflicts, which indeed went underground. Jung managed to keep his "old religiosity" under wraps for the better part of three years,

---

[19] See Gay, *Freud: a life for our time*, 106.

[20] Jones, *Freud* II, 56. Freud, who was experiencing prostatic and gastrointestinal difficulties while in New York, considered the city's scant supply of public toilets one measure of the low level of American civilization.

[21] Quoted in *ibid.*, 57.

but in February 1910, it resurfaced with a vengeance when Freud simply raised the possibility of forming a purely pragmatic alliance with the
well-intentioned but thoroughly bloodless International Order of Ethics
and Culture – the *Internationaler Orden für Ethik und Kultur*. Jung's florid
rant confirms Gedo's observation that he did not consider a disillusioned
science of the mind a desirable alternative to religion. What he was seeking,
rather, was the formation of a radical counter-religion, which he took to
be a "finer and more comprehensive task" that he envisioned for psychoanalysis. In response to the possibility, he told Freud that "2000 years of
Christianity can only be replaced by something equivalent."[22] Echoing
Nietzsche's *The birth of tragedy* – written at a time when the philosopher
was enamored of Wagner as the prophet of a radical transfiguration of
culture – Jung called for a movement that would

transform Christ back into the soothsaying god of the vine, which he was, and in
this way absorb those ecstatic instinctual forces of Christianity for the *one* purpose of making the cult and the sacred myth what they once were – a drunken
feast of joy where man regained the ethos and holiness of an animal. [Talk about
lionizing the instinctual! – JW] . . . What infinite rapture and wantonness lie
dormant in our religion, waiting to be led back to their destination! A genuine
and proper ethical development cannot abandon Christianity but must grow up
within it, must bring to fruition its hymn of love, the agony and the ecstasy over
the dying and resurgent god, the mystic power of the wine, the awful anthropoph-
agy of the Last Supper.[23]

One can only imagine how appalled a secular Jewish doctor with Freud's
sober sensibilities must have been when he received this rapturous hymn
to Dionysus and Christ.

Freud eschewed not only religious rapture but also the rapturous rebellion against it. This can be seen in a letter to Ferenczi, written somewhat
later than Jung's rant, in which, however, the opposition between Freud's
conception of psychoanalysis and Jung's could not be clearer. As part of
the Enlightenment project of autonomy, Freud tells his Hungarian colleague, "psychoanalysis signifies not only man's . . . emancipation from
religion," but also "from (unjustified) authority" – as well as "from" the
sort of "*exaggerated rebellion against it*" that Jung was often engaged in.

<hr>

[22] *Ibid.*, 178.
[23] *Ibid.*, 178.

Freud makes a remarkably self-reflective observation that, as we will see, has important implications for his views on science. His research, he writes, is motivated by "an urge towards de-occultization" – that is, toward disenchantment. But Freud admits that the urge itself might contain a defense against those magical strivings and, moreover, that his "wish to bring [scientific] clarity to these matters" might itself represent such a defense.[24] This admission requires something like a "critique of unpure reason" that asks the following question: How is a science of "de-occultation" that has not purged itself from all "magic-religious strivings" possible? We will return to this question in Chapter 12.

Although it is not evident in his measured response to Jung, the latter's paean to his idea of counter-religion must have enraged Freud. In his paper on "The Moses of Michelangelo," one of the two studies that he published of the Hebrew prophet, we get some insight into the way he struggled to manage this anger against Jung. Freud became immediately fascinated with Michelangelo's statue of Moses, which stands atop the tomb of Pope Julius II in the church of San Pietro in Vincoli in Rome, when he first viewed it 1901. In the paper, he reports that "no other piece of sculpture" had "ever made a deeper impression on him."[25] According to Gay, however, Freud "did not see the statue as an assignment for interpretation until 1912, when his association with Jung was going sour" and his rage had to be contained. Moreover, he drafted his study of it in late 1913, just before he fashioned "The history of the psychoanalytic movement" – perhaps the angriest piece Freud every published – "the 'bomb' he planned to throw at Jung and [Alfred] Adler," the first of the dissenters from Freud orthodoxy.[26] The obsessiveness with which Freud studied, measured, and drew the statue during "the three lonely . . . weeks" he spent in Rome in September 1913 surely constituted an attempt to manage his intense fury toward Jung, and his heterodox interpretation of the statue, which simply waves away the standard account, surely pertains to his dealings with his Swiss adversary. As opposed to the received narrative maintaining that Moses smashed the tablets on which the commandments

[24] Falzeder and Brabant (eds.), *Correspondence of Freud and Ferenczi*, 70–71 (emphasis added).

[25] Sigmund Freud, "The Moses of Michelangelo" (1914), *SE* 13: 213.

[26] Gay, *Freud: a life for our time*, 314.

were inscribed, Freud's interpretation employs a detailed analysis of the statue's structural features to argue that what the sculptor is depicting is exactly the opposite – namely, the decisive moment at which Moses *stopped himself* from hurling the tablets to the ground. Moses, in short, "kept his passion in check" in order to "preserve" the tablets.[27] In so doing, and this is Freud's general point, the prophet realized "the highest mental achievement that is possible in a man, that of struggling success-fully against an inward passion for the sake of a cause to which he has devoted himself."[28] As we will see in the final chapter, this interpretation anticipates Freud's study of the prophet in *Moses and monotheism*, where he praises what he sees as the renunciatory ethics of the Jews.

Freud, it is safe to assume, must have continually invoked this ideal to bolster himself in his struggles to control his anger toward Jung for the greater good of the psychoanalytic "cause." Thus, all things considered, his response to Jung's rapturous 1910 onslaught was remarkably mea-sured. For although it was not explicitly acknowledged as such, Jung's paean to Dionysus and Jesus marked the moment when things had gone too far: *de facto*, a boundary had been breached, and things could never be repaired. Nonetheless, hope against hope, Freud wanted to keep Jung in the fold. So he told Jung he was "glad to abandon" the Ethical Order idea, explaining that he had only entertained the alliance out of purely strategic considerations.

At the same time, however, Freud was also frank with Jung, though not in a strident way. He told his zealous younger colleague that he had not been looking to the organization as a "substitute for religion" – "I did not expect the Fraternity to become a religious organization any more than I would expect a volunteer fire department to do so!" He went on, however, to repeat to Jung something the latter certainly did not want to hear because it demarcated the unbridgeable chasm between them: "I am not thinking of a substitute for religion," Freud proclaimed; "this need must be sublimated." Even worse, Freud delivered what was in effect the ultimate blow – albeit again in an understated way: "But you mustn't regard me as the founder of a religion."[29] With "this self-revelation by

---

[27] Freud, "The Moses of Michelangelo," 229.

[28] *Ibid.*, 233.

[29] *Ibid.*, 295.

Jung and Freud's unequivocal rejection of his program," Gedo observes, "we . . . come face to face with the fundamental reason for their inevitable separation."[30] Traumatic de-idealization and apostasy it would be.

The Ghost of Fliess

The "religious-libidinal cloud" of his No. 2 Self notwithstanding, Jung was also a seasoned clinician and a savvy man.[31] It therefore did not require much effort for him to understand that Freud's reports on the Fliess affair contained thinly veiled messages for him. Thus, after Freud informed him that he had discovered the relationship between homosexuality and paranoia in his friendship with Fliess, Jung attempted to preempt a repeat performance between the two of them. Noting that "the reference to Fliess" was "surely not accidental," he asked Freud to allow him to "enjoy [his] friendship not as one between equals but as that of father and son."[32] The idea of a benign father–son relationship would, however, quickly become problematic, for shortly after Jung made his request, Freud elaborated the Oedipus complex, a "father complex" involving paternal domination, filial rebellion, castration, murder, and cannibalism. And all parties to the Freud–Jung conflict deployed the new theory to justify themselves in the struggles that ensued in their psychoanalytic hoard. Likewise, when Jung's tardy response to Freud's letters evoked memories of the latter's experience with Fliess, his younger colleague "assured" him that, "not only now but for the future . . . nothing Fliess-like is going to happen." But a number of "Fliess-like" things did happen between them.

It was in 1909 that Freud had assigned Jung the task of colonizing the field of mythology for psychoanalytic theory, and on 14 October of that year, several months after the return from America, Jung had written to Freud that he was prepared to execute his assignment. He informed Freud that he was in the "grip" of "archeology or rather mythology," and that he was "obsessed by the thought of one day writing a comprehensive account

---

[30] John Gedo, "Magna est vis veritatis tuae et praevalebit," *Annual of Psychoanalysis* (1979), 69.

[31] McGuire (ed.), *The Freud/Jung letters*, 298.

[32] *Ibid.*, 122.

of this whole field."[33] In the course of fulfilling his assignment, however, Jung countermanded Freud's instructions by producing an "account" of myth and religion that was distinctly anti-Freudian.

Over the next several years, the two men churned out a series of dueling theoretical positions that tore at the fabric of their relationship. The central point of contention concerned the nature of the libido, and the phenomenon of psychotic regression provided the point of contention that both men fought to account for. One of the key analyses that would articulate much of Freud's thinking on the topic was contained in his study of Daniel Schreber's *Memoirs of my nervous illness*; ironically, and perhaps fittingly, it was Jung who referred him to the work.

Freud was in the midst of working on his monograph on Leonardo da Vinci when Jung more or less handed him the memoirs, and, as Gay notes, the analysis Freud conducted in "Psycho-analytic notes on an autobiographical case of paranoia" was "a pendant to his 'Leonardo.'"[34] There is something peculiar about Jung taking credit for having introduced Freud to the Schreber memoirs, in which the distinguished, insightful, and articulate jurist candidly recounts his experience during years of entrapment in a world of psychotic delusions.[35] Although Jung was apparently not

---

[33] *Ibid.*, 157.

[34] Gay, *Freud: a life for our time*, 277. The *Leonardo* monograph, published in 1910, evidences Freud's ongoing preoccupation with Fliessian themes. Freud originally wanted Jung to conquer the realm of culture for psychoanalysis by subsuming it under his theory of sexuality, but in the aftermath of the trip to America he made his own foray into that domain for the first time with his study of the Renaissance master, presumably so that his rival would not trump him. Adhering to the program he had prescribed to Jung, Freud set out to account for Leonardo's artistic and scientific achievements in terms of his sublimated sexuality – more specifically, his homosexuality – a signal, Gay notes, that Freud was "not inclined to compromise on the inflammatory and divisive issue of the libido." McGuire (ed.), *The Freud/Jung letters*, 266, and Gay, *Freud: a life for our time*, 274.

Leonardo is an altogether anomalous text, the only other work in which Freud exhibits the same open and even sympathetic attitude toward homosexuality (and bisexuality) that we observed in his last letters to Fliess and the only "case study" that centers on the early mother – or mothers – for, like Freud and his heroes Moses and Oedipus, Leonardo had two mothers. The monograph also contains the first mentions of the polymorphic figure of the phallic woman and, more significantly, the concept of narcissism.

[35] See C.G. Jung, *The symbols of transformation: an analysis of a prelude to a case of schizophrenia*, second edition, *The collected works of C.G. Jung*, vol. V, Bollingen Series XX,

conscious of what he was doing, presenting the memoirs to Freud constituted a provocative and masochistic "Fliess-like" enactment. The work is
not only saturated with homosexual material, but it also provided Freud
with an abundance of evidence to prove his case against Jung concerning the connection between homosexuality and paranoia. To make matters even worse for Freud's religiously impassioned opponent, Schreber's
Memoirs also point not only to a substantial link between religion and paranoid psychosis but also to "voluptuous" sexual ecstasy as well. Why would
Jung have provided his adversary with this windfall, in effect handing
Freud the weapon he would use to defeat him? We need to delve somewhat
deeply into the Schreber memoirs to understand all that was at stake.

Daniel Paul Schreber was the son of a powerful father, "Daniel
Gottlob Moritz Schreber, an orthopedic physician, prolific author, and
well-known education reformer," who is remembered in Germany owing
to the "Schreber Gardens" that still dot its urban landscape.[36] He was
an up-and-coming civil servant in Saxony's judicial system who in 1884
ran unsuccessfully for the Reichstag; his first breakdown occurred in the
wake of that defeat, but after seven months in the Leipzig Psychiatric
Clinic he appeared to have recovered. The following year, Schreber was
appointed to the bench in Saxony, and in 1893 he was elevated to the

---

ed. Herbert Read et al. (Princeton, NJ: Princeton University Press, 1967), para. 458
n. 6 (this is a translation of the radically revised 1952 edition of *Symbole der Wandlung*).
Also Daniel Paul Schreber, *Memoirs of my nervous illness*, trans. Ida Macalpine and
Richard Hunter (New York: The New York Review of Books, 2000).

[36] Freud's study has been criticized from several directions, but perhaps most notably for concentrating almost exclusively on Schreber's hospitalizations and delusions,
while paying slight attention to the impact that his father had on his development.
Schreber *père* was a strict authoritarian, whose educational regimen included interventions to discipline the student's body that would have warmed the cockles of Michel
Foucault's heart. At times, it is difficult to distinguish the orthopedic apparatuses that
he used in his "therapeutic gymnastics" from the torture devices employed by the
Spanish Inquisition. Daniel had been subjected to these disciplinary exercises, and
many of his psychotic formations, Freud's critics point out, can be traced to them. For
example, Schreber's delusions included "a terrible *Kopfzusammenschnürungsmaschine*,
a machine tying his head together," that is, "a distorted version of a mechanical head
straightener that Moritz Schreber had used to improve" his son's posture." Gay,
Freud: a life for our time, 284. See also William G. Niederland, *The Schreber case:
a psychoanalytic profile of a paranoid personality*, second revised edition (New York:
Routledge, 1984).

post of *Senatspräsident*. Shortly thereafter, he experienced another mental collapse that was far more severe than the first. After a bout of insomnia and an attempted suicide, Daniel was again hospitalized in the Leipzig Clinic, where he remained for nine years. It was during this hospitalization that he wrote his *Memoirs of my nervous illness – Denkwürdigkeit eines Nervenkranken* – as a brief meant to support his petition to be discharged from the Clinic. Because of Schreber's intelligence, insightfulness, and impressive honesty, his memoirs provide an incomparable window into the delusionary world of a psychotic individual. They provided Freud, who as we have seen was only meagerly experienced with inpatients, the "clinical material" he needed to write a study of psychosis.[37]

Freud began studying the *Memoirs* in the spring of 1910 while he was examining the proofs of *Leonardo*; it was also the year he began work on the "Two principles of mental functioning," yet the Schreber memoir was the only reading material he brought along when he vacationed with Ferenczi in Sicily that summer. Freud took obvious delight in Schreber's "brilliant madness" and frank lucidity.[38] Never one to esteem the psychiatric profession, Freud wrote to Jung that the "wonderful" Schreber "ought to have been made a professor of psychiatry and director of a mental hospital."[39] Gay comments that Freud's joking about Schreber and his bandying "Schreberisms" around with colleagues can appear "a bit callous" in light of the wretched man's extreme suffering.[40] But like Shakespeare, Freud appreciated that the deep and unsettling truths that madmen and fools often express can be extremely funny. Moreover, black humor is ubiquitous in such clinical settings as those in which severely ill patients are treated; it is an understandable way of coping with the intense anxiety that these situations generate.

Freud's enthusiasm for his new "patient," however, was not unproblematic. His "rather manic preoccupation with Schreber," Gay observes, "hints at some hidden interest driving him on: Fliess" – "to study Schreber was to remember Fliess."[41] Freud said as much when he told

---

[37] Freud, "Psycho-analytic notes on an autobiographical account of a case of paranoia."
[38] Castoriadis, "Psychoanalysis: project and elucidation," 126.
[39] McGuire (ed.), *The Freud/Jung letters*, 311.
[40] Gay, *Freud: a life for our time*, 280.
[41] *Ibid.*, 279.

Ferenczi that while he was engrossed in Schreber's *Memoirs* on Sicily that summer, his "dreams were . . . entirely concerned with the Fliess matter."[42] One of the functions served by Freud's "highly tendentious reading of Fliess's mental history" was to promote his triumphalist claim that he had "succeeded" in "overcoming" his homosexuality where Fliess had failed and become paranoid. That is, he wanted to deny that there was more than a small "piece of unruly homosexual feeling" involved in his obsession with Schreber and his dealings with Jung.[43] His struggles with Adler in the winter of 1910, however, show that his defensive boasting exaggerated the extent of his mastery. As Freud reported to Jung, the Adler contretemps reopened "the wounds of the Fliess affair" and "disturbed the peace [he] otherwise enjoyed during [his] work on paranoia." He was therefore "not sure" that he could prevent his "own complexes" from infiltrating his work on Schreber.[44]

Tendentious though it may be, Freud's analysis of Schreber's psychosis confidently explains its genesis using the schema he had devised to account for the dynamics of the Fliess affair – namely, de-cathexis–repudiation–projection. Freud, we will recall, believed that when they separated and Fliess had withdrawn his love from him, the Berliner could not accept its homosexual nature and attempted to deny it by projecting it outwards. When we also recall that Freud's intense (homosexual) transference to Fliess took off when his colleague became his physician, one feature of Schreber's "nervous illness" is striking: His psychosis centered on the vicissitudes of his transference to Dr. Emil Paul Flechsig, the primary psychiatrist who treated him. At some level of consciousness, this fact must have resonated in Freud's psyche. Schreber's second and more florid psychotic episode began with *paranoia* – delusions that Flechsig was *persecuting* him. He was to "'be handed over to a certain person,'" namely Flechsig, and transformed into a woman, that is, emasculated, and "'surrendered to the person in question with a view to sexual abuse.'" His "'soul was to be murdered and [his] body used like a strumpet.'"[45]

---

[42] Falzeder and Brabant (eds.), *Correspondence of Freud and Ferenczi*, vol. I, 222.

[43] Andrew R. Paskauskas (ed.), *The complete correspondence of Sigmund Freud and Ernest Jones: 1908–1939* (Cambridge, MA: The Belknap Press of Harvard University Press, 1993), 182.

[44] McGuire (ed.), *The Freud/Jung letters*, 382.

[45] Freud, *Psycho-analytic notes*, 19.

The onset of these persecutory delusions raises the perplexing question that lies at the heart of Freud's interpretation of the case. After Flechsig had helped him recover during his first hospitalization, Schreber reports that he felt nothing "'but the liveliest gratitude' toward him and in fact "'paid him . . . an appropriate honorarium.'"[46] *What then caused this reversal of feelings, from warm gratitude to persecutory anxiety?*

To answer the question, Freud turns to the prodromal phenomena that preceded the newly elected *Senatspräsident's* collapse. Schreber himself identifies the most important of these early symptoms: "What especially determined my mental break-down was a particular night, during which I had a quite extraordinary number of emissions – quite half a dozen in one night." Freud argues that, "if we are prepared to admit that an emission cannot occur in an adult without some mental concomitant, we shall be able to supplement the patient's emissions that night by assuming that they were accompanied by homosexual phantasies which remained unconscious."[47] And a later experience of Schreber's lends support to this claim. Upon awakening from a dream referring back to the onset of his illness, "the idea occurred to him 'that after all it really must be very nice to be a woman submitting to the act of copulation.'"[48] To add further support to his case, Freud notes that during the time the night of the multiple emissions took place, Schreber's wife, who usually protected him "against the attractive power of the men about him," was away on "a short holiday."[49]

In the next step of his argument, Freud adduces the fact of Schreber's "friendly feeling for his doctor" after his first hospitalization, which he asserts constituted a positive transference that he had formed to Flechsig. Just as Freud had developed an eroticized transference to Fliess when the latter became his physician, so Schreber directed his unconscious homosexual desires – there is no evidence of any overt homosexual activities on his part – toward Flechsig. "The exciting cause of [Schreber's] illness," Freud argues, "was the appearance of a feminine (that is, passive

[46] *Ibid.*, 41.

[47] *Ibid.*, 45.

[48] *Ibid.*, 13.

[49] *Ibid.*, 45.

homosexual) wishful phantasy, which took as its object the figure of his doctor."[50]

It is here that we arrive at Freud's answer to the question concerning the genesis of Schreber's persecutory delusions. Schreber, like Fliess, who could not tolerate his sexual wishes for Freud, had to reject his attraction to Flechsig. The two steps Schreber took to defend against these unacceptable desires explain the genesis of his paranoia. In the first, Schreber employed the mechanism of reversal to deny his love: He transformed the proposition "'*I* (a man) *love him* (a man)'" into "'I do not *love* him – I *hate* him.'" The "internal perception" of hatred, however, was also, Freud argues, intolerable. Therefore, in the second step, he replaced it with an "external perception" – that is, he projected it outward thus creating a paranoid delusion. Furthermore, by transforming "'I hate him'" into "'*He* hates (persecutes) *me*,'" Schreber also justified his hatred.[51] "The person [Schreber] longed for," Freud concludes, "now became his persecutor, and the content of his wishful phantasy became the content of his persecution."[52]

Whether or not this analysis accurately describes the Schreber case, Freud, as was his wont, extracted a global generalization from it: In all cases of "dementia paranoides . . . a defense against a homosexual wish was clearly recognizable at the very centre of the conflict which underlay the disease."[53]

Freud went on to argue that the way in which Schreber's persecutory delusions subsided confirms the claim that passive homosexual wishes had been their cause. In a new phase of his illness, Schreber replaced Flechsig with the "superior figure of God" as the primary object of his preoccupations, and at that point his "alarming" paranoid delusions not only "ceased" but his "femaleness" became prominent.[54] Able now to express his passive-feminine wishes openly in a religiously sanctioned delusion – in which he was penetrated by light rays emanating from the sun, a symbol for God – he did not have to disguise those wishes in the form of

[50] *Ibid.*, 47.

[51] *Ibid.*, 63.

[52] *Ibid.*, 47.

[53] *Ibid.*, 59.

[54] *Ibid.*, 17.

his persecutory delusions. According to Freud, Schreber had previously "been a doubter in religious matters," but in the new phase of his psychosis, he constructed a theological system to justify his desires, and they displayed "as much ingenuity as every other theodicy."[55] For Schreber, the divine "Order of Things" not only "condoned" his homosexual submission to God's penetrations – which he found "voluptuous" – but also demanded them. It was not that Schreber wished to be transformed into a woman; it was that he had to be emasculated in order to fulfill a higher act of redemption.

The need for redemption arose from the nature of Schreber's psychotic regression, in which Schreber withdrew his "libidinal cathexis . . . from the people in his environment and from the external world generally," thereby creating a desolated internal landscape. This "internal catastrophe," Freud maintains, "was in turn projected outward in the form of an end-of-the-world fantasy in which the human race had been annihilated."[56] The *Senatspräsident*'s subsequent delusions, involving sexual intercourse with God, represent, according to Freud, Schreber's attempts "at recovery, a process of reconstruction" – that is, an attempt at redemption.[57] If he was transformed into a woman, God could impregnate him so that he could redeem mankind by giving birth to "'a new race of men'" who would repopulate the world after the catastrophe.[58] Schreber's grandiose theological solution accomplished two things at once: "His ego found compensation in his megalomania," a topic that will be examined in Chapter 12, "while his feminine phantasy made its way through and became acceptable."[59]

Even before Freud finished the analysis of Schreber, he was feeling pressure to become more specific about the notion of a universal Oedipus complex that he had introduced in *The interpretation of dreams* but had not fleshed out in much detail. The pressure came from Jung's initial forays into mythology and the advances that the Zurich School in general were

---

[55] *Ibid.*, 24 and 28. This observation is significant in light of Freud's later critique of religion, which he equates with theodicy, that we will examine in Chapter 11.

[56] *Ibid.*, 69–70.

[57] *Ibid.*, 71.

[58] *Ibid.*, 17 and 48.

[59] *Ibid.*, 48.

making in their studies of myth, folklore, fairytales, and religion. The Zurichers, John Kerr observes, believed "that analyses of mythological material" possessed "special authority" because of the "glimpses" it provided "into the soul," and that a scientific "prize" would go to the individual who produced a theoretical account of the "'mythopoetic' function."[60] To this end, they enlisted Jung's theory of psychological "complexes," formulated during his earlier work on association tests, and attempted to uncover the various complexes that were instantiated in myths, fairytales, and religious narratives. As their research progressed, however, the number of complexes seemed to be proliferating ad infinitum, raising the specter of "eclecticism" and, worse yet, "theoretical chaos."[61]

Seizing the opportunity, Freud made his move. He set out to capture the "prize" by identifying one "core" or "nuclear" complex (*Kerncomplex*) underlying not only all cultural production, but all neurotic formations as well. He did this by concretizing the Oedipus complex as a "father complex" – which holds, among other things, that the child (more specifically, the boy) both loves and hates the father.[62]

Though the idea of a *Kerncomplex* had only recently been minted, Freud had no difficulty declaring that "[i]n the Schreber case, we find ourselves once again on the familiar ground of the father-complex." Schreber's "struggle with Flechsig," he argues, "became revealed to him as a conflict with God, and we must therefore construe it as an infantile conflict with the father whom he loved."[63] Freud's inadequate knowledge of the details of Schreber's early life, he concedes, made it impossible for him to satisfactorily explain the genesis of his psychopathology. Consequently, he must "content" himself with a "shadowy sketch of the infantile material which was used by the paranoiac disorder in portraying the current material."[64] He speculates that it had something to do with the question of patrimonial lineage. (Let us recall that at the time he was reflecting on Schreber, he was also preoccupied with the question

---

[60] Kerr, *A most dangerous method*, 248–249.

[61] *Ibid.*, 249.

[62] See especially Sigmund Freud, "Notes upon a case of obsessional neurosis" (1909), *SE* 10: 200–220.

[63] Freud, *Psycho-analytic notes*, 55.

[64] *Ibid.*, 57.

of patrimony – of who would inherit his mantle after his death.) Schreber was childless, and Freud argues that his "frustration" at not bearing a son who could continue "the family line" was at the heart of his delusional construction.[65] This speculation is suggestive, but, had Freud been more willing to pursue the social as well as the intrapsychic dimension of Schreber's situation, he might have elaborated it more fruitfully. Freud does not place enough emphasis on a precipitating factor in Schreber's second psychotic decompensation: that he had been promoted to the rank of *Senatspräsident*. That is, he had been moved up the ladder of paternal authority. Did his conflicts over "becoming the father" in a more substantial way precipitate his crisis?[66] Finally, there is another question that must be asked: How could Jung have reacted when Freud – who had been the object of his "religious crush" – explained Schreber's religious system in terms of his "feminine" desire to be penetrated by God?

A scholarly issue regarding the Schreber text bears directly on one of our central concerns – namely, Freud's "repudiation of femininity." The literary theorist Jay Geller reports that in Freud's personal copy of Schreber's *Memoirs*, Freud underlined the term "Entmannung" and wrote in the margins "Kern de Sache" ("heart of the matter"). The German term that Freud found so important literally means "unmanning," and it is more or less descriptive and value-neutral. But as Geller notes, the translators of the *Standard Edition* translated *Entmannung* "as 'emasculation' and correlate[d] it explicitly with both physical and figurative castration," thus endowing it with a largely negative meaning. "The 'emasculated' Schreber," Geller observes, "is presented as a devirilized victim of phantasized sexual persecution." When femininity is equated with castration, "becoming a woman" is seen negatively, as something to be repudiated. By contrast, the translation of Schreber's *Memoirs* by Ida Macalpine, as Geller points out, opted for the unusual but literal English term "unmanning." This translation not only removes the stigma

---

[65] *Ibid.*, 57–58.

[66] Eric Santner has pursued this line of investigation and examined the connection between Schreber's case history and the structure of authority in the Germany of his day. Santner's analysis, however, errs in the opposite direction, for he pays inadequate attention to the psychodynamic dimension of the *Senatspräsident*'s crisis. See Eric L. Santner, *My own private Germany: Daniel Paul Schreber's secret history of modernity* (Princeton, NJ: Princeton University Press, 1997).

from the term, it also makes it possible to view Schreber's "feminiza-tion" in a positive light, as he did himself.[67] The *Senatspräsident* exalted the exquisite sexual pleasure, the "voluptuousness," he experienced when he was penetrated as a woman. Furthermore, equating it with castration obscures another positive aspect of femininity, the creativity of the moth-er's childbearing capacity, something that men often envy. Melanie Klein argues, for example, that "the capacity to give and preserve life is felt as the greatest gift and therefore creativeness becomes the deepest cause for envy."[68] Far from being diminished or degraded through his feminization, Schreber acquires the capacity not only to procreate but also to redeem humanity through his fecundity. *Schreber's fantasies are in fact a delusional panegyric to femininity*.

Freud's explanation of the mechanism of paranoia, which contains two claims, became the central issue in his dispute with Jung. The first claim maintains that, as evidenced in the end-of-the-world fantasy, the onset of psychosis begins with a regression, that is, the withdrawal of libidinal cathexis from the (object-)world. The second distinctively Freudian claim is that the process of libidinal de-cathexis entails a withdrawal of "general interest" in the world, and this in turn, *seriously impairs the individual's relation to reality*. "Disturbances in an individual's libidinal investment in the object world," Freud explains, can result in "abnormal changes in the ego," and these produce the loss of reality observable in psychosis.[69]

Freud had the following idea in mind when he formulated this expla-nation. When Fliess withdrew his libido from Freud – that is, lost him as a love object – it produced the disturbances in his ego that caused his paranoid distortion of reality; likewise, Schreber's attempt to de-cathect Flechsig resulted in alterations of his ego that gave rise to his psychotic delusions. Freud's thesis, in short, is this: *A person's investment in reality as such is dependent on, if not determined by, his or her libidinal* – by which he means sexual – *investment in the world*.

[67] Jay Geller, "Freud v. Freud: Freud's reading of Daniel Paul Schreber's *Denwürdigkeit eines nevernkranken, Reading Freud's reading*, ed. Sander Gilman et al. (New York: New York University Press, 1994), 181. See also Boyarin, *Unheroic conduct*, 216–219.

[68] Melanie Klein, "Envy and gratitude," *Envy and gratitude & other works, 1946–1963* (New York: Delacorte Press, 1975), 202.

[69] Freud, *Psycho-analytic notes*, 70 n. 2.

It is on this very point that Jung drew a line in the sand between Freud and himself. Citing the relevant passage from *Schreber*, Jung writes:

As for the libido problem, I must confess that your remark in the Schreber analysis [*SE* 7: 75, para. 3] has set up booming reverberations. This remark, or rather the doubt expressed therein, has resuscitated all the difficulties that have beset me throughout the years in my attempt to apply the libido theory to Dem. prae. [Dementia praecox – viz., psychosis]. The loss of the reality in D. pr. cannot be solved in this way. Not by me at any rate.[70]

Jung grants that Freud's concept of (sexual) libido is applicable to neuroses, but he maintains that it cannot account for the loss of reality occurring in psychosis. He agrees that a withdrawal of libido occurs in psychosis – he calls it "introversion" – but disagrees with Freud *about the nature of the libido involved in that regression*. Freud defined libido in a circumscribed way – namely, as *libido sexualis*. When Jung queried him about his conception, Freud replied:

Regarding your difficulty with "my" libido. In the first sentence of the *Theory of Sexuality* there is a clear definition in which I see nothing to change: The analagon of hunger, for which, in the sexual context, the German language has no word except the ambiguous "*Lust*."[71]

To be sure, Freud had broadened the concept of sexuality enormously, far beyond the way it is conventionally understood, but his notion of libido remained sexual in that it pertained to the erogenous zones of the body and the demands that the soma makes on the psyche for work.

The complex if not obfuscating strategy that Jung devised to get the better of Freud moved in opposing directions at the same time. Jung's theory cast itself as scientific – Darwinian – but it also prioritized the archaic world's unconscious fantasy. He thereby managed both to appear more progressive, but to be more regressive, than Freud. (The progressivist – "teleological" – trappings serve to mask the terrifying aspects of the regressive archaic world that Jung lionizes.) Jung attempts to outflank Freud, the ardent Darwinian, by using an evolutionary argument to introduce his opposing "genetic" theory of libido. At the beginning of human evolution,

---

[70] McGuire (ed.), *The Freud/Jung letters*, 287.

[71] *Ibid.*, 277.

he argues, there existed a "sexual primal libido." Its evolutionary function was elementary: To propagate the species by maximizing the contacts between ova and spermatozoa. At a later stage, Jung argues, "an increasing transformation of primal libido" occurred that produced "the secondary functions of allurement and protection of young."[72] Intentional strategies for attracting a mate and for protecting one's offspring were more efficient means of propagating the species than the shotgun approach of the earlier stage.

Because "allurement and protection of the young . . . presuppose a very different and very complicated relation to reality," according to Jung, the "function of reality" emerged from this "altered mode of procreation . . . as a correlate [of the] heightened adaptation to reality."[73] Furthermore, as a concomitant of this same process, a broadened, non-sexual form of libido was differentiated out of "the sexual primal libido," and this "desexualized primal libido . . . regularly and properly supported the function of reality."[74] Jung's concept of General Libido, which was the heir to his

---

[72] C.G. Jung, *Psychology of the unconscious*, trans. Beatrice M. Hinkle (Mineola, NY: Dover, 2002), 149. (This is a republication of the 1916 English translation of Jung's original edition of *Wandlungen und die Symbole der Libido*.)

[73] *Ibid.*, 149–150.

[74] *Ibid.*, 151. Jung, who surely knew better, grossly misrepresents Freud's theory of sexuality and obscures its radical innovations. The radicalism consists precisely in detaching human sexuality from the vital function of procreation and in distinguishing the sexual instincts from the self-preservative instincts. *Contra* Jung, for Freud, procreation – the heterosexual joining of genitalia for the purpose of reproduction – does not constitute the essence of the human sexual drive. On the contrary, an animal *Instinkt* ("instinct") has a natural object that is hard-wired in its genetic make-up to ensure the reproduction of the species, but the human *Trieb* – "drive" – does not. The object, Freud argues, "is what is most variable" about the human drive and is only loosely attached to it. Indeed, from a Darwinian perspective, the "defunctionalized" human *Trieb* raises a vexing problem. The variability of the object, so it would appear, runs counter to the theory of adaptation. Worse yet – as Jung obviously knew that Freud's theory contained a self-preservative drive. Indeed, he explained neurosis in terms of the conflict between the two drives, and insisted that his position was always dualistic because he was a conflict theorist and conflict requires two terms that can oppose one another. Jung's genetic or General Libido in fact hypostatizes the self-preservative instinct, while marginalizing the sexual instinct. Freud, "Instincts and their vicissitudes," 122. While Jung accused Freud's theory of sexual monism, it was he, with his theory of General Libido, who was the monist.

earlier notion of an undifferentiated "psychic energy," is, he tells us, roughly comparable to Schopenhauer's philosophical notion of the Will. Unlike a Freudian drive, which pressures us from behind, it is largely intentional and voluntary.

Jung also attempts to minimize Freud's position. Much as Newton's theory of mechanics was subsumed under Einsteinian physics, Jung argues that Freud's narrower doctrine of sexual libido should become a subset of his theory of General Libido.

The withdrawal of sexual libido can, according to Jung, explain the partial loss of reality that occurs in neurosis, but it cannot account for the massive break with reality occurring in psychosis. "The schizophrenic," he claims, "shuns reality more than merely the erotic afflux would account for."[75] That is to say, only the expanded theory of General Libido is commensurate with the massiveness of the psychotic's global break with reality.

But this is where things start to get peculiar. It is clear that Jung's theory of General Libido is meant to be teleological at the level of phylogeny – that is, it can explain the propagation of the species. But Jung makes two further arguments asserting that psychotic regression, *which is generally viewed as the apotheosis of failed adaptation*, is also "teleological." The first argument holds that psychotic regression is adaptive in that the individual retreats from an unbearable external world and constructs a more tolerable "intra-psychic reality."[76] This point is true but relatively banal, for all defenses, however catastrophic, serve an adaptive qua protective function in that they prevent an even greater catastrophe.

Jung's second claim is more audacious and more problematic. "Through a series of researches by the Zurich School," he argues, "it has become apparent . . . that the phantasmic substitution products which take the place of the disturbed function of reality [in psychosis] bear unmistakable traces of archaic thought." The relatively shallow regression occurring in neurosis, involving the withdrawal of sexual libido, does not unfold beyond the ontogenetic stratum – that is, beyond the psychic life of the individual; it thus produces fantasies constructed out of memory traces from one's individual history and parental imagos. In psychosis, on the

[75] Jung, *Psychology of the unconscious*, 152.
[76] *Ibid.*, 152.

other hand, the regression that results from the withdrawal of General Libido extends to a significantly deeper level. The fantasies it produces, Jung maintains, reach beyond the realm of individual psychic existence to collective archaic fantasies that have organized "the general human function of reality since antiquity."[77] Clinically, it is not clear why regression to the archaic strata of mental functioning should be therapeutically beneficial, but Jung maintained that they were. More generally, *Jung believed that this account of psychotic regression provided the bridge between his theory of psychosis and his interpretation of mythology. The archaic fantasies that emerge in psychotic delusions, he argued, are the same as those that underlie myths.*

Mythos and *logos*

When in October 1909 Jung first announced to Freud that he was turning his attention to the study of myth, Freud, outwardly at least, responded enthusiastically. "I was delighted to learn," he wrote on 11 November 1909, "that you are going into mythology" and "can't wait to hear of your discoveries."[78] As the competition and conflicts between the two men intensified, however, it became increasingly apparent to both parties that Jung's goal was to eclipse Freud and that the position he was staking out contradicted fundamental tenets of Freudian theory. Though he often tried to fudge their differences, in the book that eventually grew out of his research, *Transformations and symbols of libido* (the original German edition was translated as *The psychology of the unconscious*), Jung advanced a Counter-Enlightenment position that was diametrically opposed to Freud's Enlightenment principles. Sensing what was up, Freud plunged into the study of myth and religion; his fear, however, was that it was too late, that too much ground had already been ceded to his opponent. At one point, Freud became so frustrated by their exchanges that he declared, "Why in God's name did I allow myself to follow you into this field?"[79]

Because of the intrinsic difficulty of the work, not to mention the anxiety produced in Jung by challenging Freud the Father, the writing of

---

[77] *Ibid.*, 154.

[78] McGuire (ed.), *The Freud/Jung letters*, 260.

[79] *Ibid.*, 456.

Symbols proceeded in fits and starts. Freud was understandably keen to know what was up with the competition and continually urged his colleague to share his work-in-progress. But for the most part, Jung held his cards close to his vest. He did, however, allow Freud to see an early draft of a text that was published as "Concerning the two kinds of thinking"; this became the first chapter in *Symbols*.[80]

From Jung's rhetoric, it is clear that the paper was meant to be *prescriptive*, rather than a "value-free" analysis of two forms of mentation. When Freud read it, he must have plotzed (as his Yiddish-speaking mother might have said), for the irreconcilable differences between their worldviews are there for anyone to observe. Yet he was still not prepared to pull the trigger and break with his "crown prince." Instead, his response to Jung's article, "Formulations concerning the two principles of mental functioning," written in November 1910, presented Freud's own opposing position in an uncompromising but measured way that nevertheless does not declare, QED, the now unbridgeable split between them.[81] The reader is left to draw the conclusion.

In one of the founding acts of Western rationality, Heraclitus also distinguished between "two kinds of thinking" – one belonging to the private domain of the *cosmos idios*, the other to the public arena of the *cosmos koinos*. Where the first kind of thinking is exemplified by the self-enclosed dream, the second modality is "intersubjective," to use an anachronistic term from a much later date, and is mediated by the *logos*. In one fragment, the psychoanalyst Bertram Lewin observes, the pre-Socratic philosopher "stated that whosoever does not recognize the world in common is not of sound mind but insane, and he acts and speaks like a sleeper."[82]

---

[80] See McGuire (ed.), *The Freud/Jung letters*, 332, and John Forrester, *Language and the origins of psychoanalysis* (New York: Columbia University Press, 1980), 100.

[81] Sigmund Freud, "Formulations concerning the two principles of mental functioning" (1911), *SE* 12: 213–216. In 1911, the same year that *Schreber* was published, both papers appeared in the same issue of the *Jahrbuch für psychoanalytische und psychopathologische Forschungen*. See McGuire (ed.), *The Freud/Jung letters*, 563.

[82] Bertram D. Lewin, "Dreams and the uses of regression," *Selected writings of Bertram D. Lewin*, ed. Jacob A. Arlow (New York: The Psychoanalytic Quarterly, 1973), 329. As opposed to Descartes, who believed he had to exclude the world of the dream in order to ground the foundations of modern rationality, Freud followed a different course. His radical innovation consisted in the attempt to comprehend the private world of the dream with the intersubjective *logos* of science.

Heraclitus' oracular declarations contained an admonition: Wake up, as it were, from the nocturnal dream world of the *koinonia idia* and join the diurnal world of the public *logos*. This could be taken as a motto for the forward march of Western rationality and science.

Jung's fundamental move consisted in a transmutation of the Heraclitean scheme. He argued that when the *cosmos idios* – which includes dreams, psychosis, and unconscious fantasies – is plumbed in sufficient depth, one arrives not at the *cosmos koinos* of the *logos*, but at a realm where the collective myths of the species are articulated in images. Forrester points out one of Jung's primary motives for pursuing this strategy: He wanted to demonstrate that the "contents of psychosis," which are generally thought of as epitomizing a private world cut off from public reality, are "essentially non-individual in character." In psychosis, as Forrester puts it, "we are faced with" the material of "the raw unconscious, without any intervention of consciousness," and this is also the material of truth contained in trans-individual myths.[83] *Jung, in short, wanted to lionize psychosis as a domain of universal truth, thereby validating the standpoint of his No. 2 Self, and, beyond that, of his mother's dissociated states.*

Jung's first kind of thinking is "directive." It is narrow, intensive, logical, mediated by words, directed toward the outer world, and geared for adaptation to the environment. In other words, this first kind of thinking is roughly equivalent to what has been called "technical" or "instrumental" reason. It is, moreover, a kind of thinking that, Jung contends, produces mere "knowledge" rather than "wisdom."

To bring home the point, Jung rolls out a shopworn Counter-Enlightenment trope asserting that modern "positivist" science most fully exemplifies directed thinking. By enlisting this anti-positivist rhetoric, he can disregard an essential feature of Freud's project – namely, that it represents an attempt to fashion a more comprehensive, non-positivist

---

[83] Forrester, *Language and the origins of psychoanalysis*, 105. Early in his career, Freud subscribed to the romantic notion that the unconscious represents "the essence of our being" (*der Kern unseres Wesens*) and constitutes the locus of truth, and that the aim of analysis is to gain unmediated access to its contents. Later, however, he abandoned it as too simplistic. (Sigmund Freud, "An outline of psycho-analysis" (1940), *SE* 23: 197.) The criticism that the more mature Freud made of the Surrealists' program also applies to Jung – namely, it sought direct access to the unconscious, while disregarding the other agencies of the psyche, particularly.

form of science.[84] In conflating science and positivism, Jung unbur-
dens himself of Freud's arduous theoretical task of conceptualizing this
non-positivist model of science – and a non-positivist mode of scientific
rigor – and allows himself to glorify unconscious fantasy and myth as
embodying a more exalted brand of truth. When positivism and myth are
the only two alternatives left standing, myth may appear as the lesser evil.

But Jung's attempt to discredit the rigor of scientific rationality by
claiming that it is the direct descendant of scholasticism's obsessional
hair-splitting is disingenuous and false; in fact, he has it backwards.[85] As
Blumenberg noted, it was only when thinkers like Copernicus, Galileo,
and Kepler broke with scholasticism, stopped debating how many angels
can dance on a pin, and directed their theoretical curiosity to the natural
world that modern science was born.

The difficulties with Jung's position also become apparent in his discussion of the Greeks. "The antique spirit," he argues, did not "create . . .
science but mythology." This claim overlooks the widely accepted idea
that one of the defining achievements of Hellenic culture was to have
introduced the distinction between *mythos* and *logos*. The Greeks thereby
set in motion a process of enlightenment *qua* "demythologization" –
that is, the methodical critique of *mythos* in the name of *logos* – to which
Freud's critique of illusion is the rightful heir.[86] Jung's assertion that the
Greeks "lacked . . . training in directed thinking" stretches credulity; one
wants to ask: What about Parmenides, who virtually adumbrated the deep
structure that has governed philosophical thinking until our own day, or
Aristotle, who produced the first organon of rational thought?[87]

---

[84] See Ricoeur, "Technique and non-technique in interpretation."

[85] See Jung, *The psychology of the unconscious*, 22–23.

[86] See especially G.E.R. Lloyd, *Magic, reason and experience: studies in the origins of
and development of Greek science* (Cambridge, MA: Hackett, 1971), chapter 1. In an
observation that does not contradict the general argument of this book, but in fact
reinforces it, Lloyd points out that the Greeks counter-poised reason not only to
myth, but, perhaps even more vigorously, to magic.

[87] It is true that the Greeks did not apply the rigorous forms of thinking they had
invented to the technological conquest of nature, but it was not because they "lacked
the capacity," as Jung maintains (see Jung, *The psychology of the unconscious*, 20).
Rather, they made an ethical decision to suppress acquisitive economic practices (*chre-
matistica*) in order to preserve their traditions, values, and way of life – not to mention
that they had slaves who could do the work of machines. Consequently, the expansive

Jung refers to the second kind of thought as "non-directive," "phan-tasy," or "dream" thinking. Unlike the first, directive kind of thinking, this mode of mentation is not constrained to following "a definite path." Rather, it is "associative" and "necessarily leads to an automatic play of ideas," in which "thoughts" are free to "float, sink and mount according to their own gravity." Because it does not require the exertion demanded by directive thinking, non-directive thinking "does not tire us." Instead, Jung argues, once the directive constraints are removed, our non-directive thoughts turn – or regress – "away from reality" and find their "material" in "the past with its thousand memory pictures."[88] The content of this non-directive thinking, in short, derives from the past and is encoded in images rather than words. Unlike the first kind of thinking, which is most fully exemplified in positivist science, this second kind is represented by myths, dreams, and unconscious fantasies.

Like Freud, Jung subscribed to the belief, widely held at the time, in the contemporaneous theory that "ontogeny recapitulates phylogeny." It lent substance to his argument that "infantile thinking" and "dreams" are "nothing but a re-echo of the prehistoric and the ancient," and that if regression achieves a sufficient depth, as it does in psychotic regression, it reaches the archaic truths that are contained in "the oldest foundations of the human mind" and that find expression in humanity's mythic heritage. Compared to such truths, those of science pale in significance.[89]

But Jung dodges a fundamental question, as he must: Why are fanta-sies and myths created? In other words, what motivates their production? Jung begs off and informs the reader that "the interesting question of the 'why' of all of this we must here leave unanswered," and turns instead "to the historical problem," that is, the details of concrete myths.[90] Freud's answer to the question could not have been more unambiguous: *Fantasies and myths are motivated by pleasure*; they constitute hedonic attempts to fulfill wishes that are often but not necessarily sexual in nature. And when Jung notes *en passant* that "we imagine what we lack" – for example, "the

---

capitalist economy that made use of instrumental rationality later fueled the modern conquest of nature never emerged in ancient Greece. See Joel Whitebook, "Pre-market economics: the Aristotelian perspective," *Dialectical Anthropology* 1 (1978), 197–200.

[88] Jung, *The psychology of the unconscious*, 21.

[89] *Ibid.*, 28 and 36.

[90] *Ibid.*, 31.

poor man imagines himself to be a millionaire" – he in fact offers the same answer but does not acknowledge that he is doing so. What is more, in an assertion that bears on the contentious question of religion, Jung states that in a "dead, cold and indestructible" world, which is to say a disenchanted world, humans necessarily have a need for "phantasmic, indestructible optimism" – that is, for consolation – which is "far removed from all sense of reality." Rather amazingly, the example that Jung offers of a consoling myth confirms Freud's thesis that religion consists of wish-fulfilling illusions, namely, the mythical transfiguration of "the shameful death of Christ" into "the highest salvation and redemption."[91]

Freud was fully in accord with Jung's account taken as a *description* of myths as reality-denying wishful constructions. For him, however, that definition was grounds for subsuming mythical thinking, in which Freud included religion, under reality-oriented scientific thinking that explained the mechanism of wish-fulfillment truth. When the technical details of the debates over psychosis and mythology are stripped away, it becomes clear, as Patrick Vandermeersch observes, that the underlying philosophical issue separating Freud and Jung concerned the relation of *pleasure and reality*.[92] As we will see in Chapter 12, the conception of science that Freud finally arrived at can be described in the following way: It is a historical institution and a practice that methodically struggles against the distortions arising from the temptations of pleasure in order to gain a more "apposite" account of reality.[93]

Freud does not say so explicitly, but his "Two principles of mental functioning" – which seeks to investigate "the relation of . . . mankind in general to reality, and in this way [bring] the psychological significance of the real external world into the structure of our theories" – represents a rejoinder to Jung's "Two kinds of thinking."[94] Although Freud does not call it that, its argument constitutes a systematic refutation of the position Jung outlined in that paper, and it aims at overturning Jung's valorization of unconscious fantasy over reality-oriented thinking in order to

---

[91] *Ibid.*, 30.

[92] See Vandermeersch, *Unresolved questions*, 167 and 183–184 (emphasis added).

[93] Giovanni Vassalli, "The birth of psychoanalysis from the spirit of technique: What have we learned? What can we apply?, *International Journal of Psychoanalysis* 82 (2001), 11.

[94] Freud, "Formulations concerning the two principles of mental functioning," 218.

differentiate Freud's scientific-rational stance from his adversary's myth-ical *Weltanschauung*.

In the first instance Freud agrees with Jung. The "primary processes" that characterize the earliest form of infantile mentation – which are more or less equivalent to Jung's "phantasy thinking" – operate in the medium of images rather than in words, and continue to function in the uncon-scious of the adult. But Freud adds an additional point that is absent in Jung – namely, that the primary processes are governed by the pleasure principle, which means they seek to achieve immediate pleasure and avoid pain. The primitive psychism – Freud calls it "the purified plea-sure-ego" – will only represent what is pleasurable and will not represent what is painful.[95] Freud's paradigmatic example is the hungry infant, who, he speculates, hallucinates the breast – that is, represents gratification imagistically – when the real breast fails to appear. At some unspecified theoretical point, however, hallucinatory wish fulfillment stops function-ing, and "the psychical apparatus" is compelled, Freud argues, to "form a conception of the real circumstance in the external world." In this "momentous" developmental "step," the "*reality principle*," which func-tions through a "secondary process" – that is, through words rather than images – is introduced into the infant's psyche. The significance of this step cannot be overestimated. Thenceforth, "what was presented in the mind was no longer agreeable but was what was real, even if it happened to be disagreeable."[96]

This critical point requires clarification. After the First World War, as we will see, Freud tended to identify reality as "harsh reality." In 1911, however, he does not yet view reality as intrinsically painful, though it may or may not be. The critical point is located elsewhere: With the intro-duction of the reality principle, the psyche will represent reality *even though it may be unpleasurable*. In short, the axes of pleasure and reality have been separated. Because thinking is no longer determined by the pleasure principle, reality can be measured against the standard of truth.

Jung was frank; his goal was consolation – that is, the pleasurable recasting of unpleasurable reality. For Freud, the goal was truth: the disconsolate resigna-tion to reality even when – or especially when – it is painful.

[95] Freud, "Instincts and their vicissitudes," 136.
[96] Freud, "Formulations concerning the two principles of mental functioning," 219.

Most commentators agree that Freud did not achieve his *desideratum* in "Two principles," which was to explain how the reality principle could possibly be introduced into the primitive psychic apparatus.[97] Despite his failure to achieve it, Freud was nevertheless pursuing the proper goal, for instituting the reality principle – separating pleasure and reality – is a *condition sine qua non* for a rational-scientific stance toward the world. To be sure, one must posit a second-order pleasure – un-knowing. But in the first instance, rather than motivating thought, pleasure becomes an object of theoretical investigation. By contrast, from Jung's perspective, which saw the introduction of "realistic thinking" as a fall from mythical truth, the *desideratum* would appear uninteresting at best, if not downright misconceived.

Fantasy no longer occupies the privileged position in Freud's scheme that it did in Jung's. "With the introduction of the reality principle," he argues, only "one species of thought-activity" qualified as fantasy – the species that had been "split off . . . kept free from reality-testing and remained subordinated to the pleasure principle alone." Beginning in children's play and continuing "in *day-dreaming*," fantasy thought-activity "abandons dependence on real objects";[98] this independence from the reality principle defines this mode of thought as fantasy. Only in art, according to Freud, can the pleasure principle and the reality principle be reconciled, albeit "in a particular way," and this makes art a privileged activity, one in which artists "mold [their] fantasies into truths of a new kind." They use their "special gifts" and the aesthetic resources their culture offers them to articulate private fantasies in a way that achieves public significance.[99]

For Jung, psychosis and myth are tied together, and this is his explanation for that claim: When regression goes far enough, he contends, one discovers that the incestuous fantasies constitute the deepest layer

[97] There is also a consensus among commentators that, given Freud's theoretical presuppositions and model of the primitive psychic apparatus, he could not have achieved this *desideratum*. Laplanche argues, for example, that Freud's monadic starting point – which likens the infant to an unborn chick enclosed in an egg – makes explaining how the turn to reality could take place impossible. He argues, moreover, that the conundrum arising from Freud's model of the chick in the egg is precisely parallel to the *aporia* arising from a Cartesian starting-point in philosophy. "How can a self-enclosed idealism," Laplanche asks, "open out to the world?" The answer is that it cannot. Jean Laplanche, *New foundations for psychoanalysis*, trans. David Macey (New York: Basil Blackwell, 1989), 75.
[98] Freud, "Formulations concerning the two principles of mental functioning," 222.
[99] *Ibid.*, 224.

of mythological formations.[100] Given our interest in Freud's insufficient treatment of the maternal dimension, the fact that Jung's theory of incest *centers on the archaic mother and excludes the father is of the utmost importance.*[101] Incestuous desire, according to Jung, involves not the wish to possess the mother on the adult level of genital sexuality but to *reunite* with her on the pre-genital level or on the stratum of what Jung calls "presexuality." As Sprengnether observes, "womb fantasies" constitute the background for the incest taboo.[102] The function of the incest barrier is not to prevent the phallic penetration of the mother, but *to block reentry into her body, which is to say, to block dedifferentiation and reunification with the primal object.* In fact, phallic penetration can be understood as the mode of reentry. The mythical hero's quest, according to Jung, consists in the struggle to "escape the magical circle of the incestuous, and, therefore, pernicious object" – that is, to differentiate himself from the archaic mother and to achieve individuation.[103] The dangerous regressive threat of the archaic object finds representation in the various figures of "the terrible mother" that appear in mythology.[104] *Because Jung's theory of incest clearly articulates the powerful regressive attraction of the early mother – something that, as we have emphasized, Freud had great difficulty coming to terms with – it is a centerpiece of his "provocation."* Moreover, in light of our current knowledge, Jung's theory not only contains considerable validity but also has a particularly contemporary, if not French, ring to it.[105] And it pushed Freud to acknowledge the existence of the early mother and to deal with it as an issue, however inadequately.

---

[100] See Vandermeersch, *Unresolved questions*, 234.

[101] As an explanation of his "remissness as correspondent," Jung tells Freud, "I have allowed all of my libido to disappear into my work. This time," he tells his apprehensive colleague, "I have ventured to tackle the mother" in order to address the fundamental questions of religion. "So what is keeping me hidden is the [descent] to the realm of Mothers, where, as we know, Theseus and Peirithoos remained stuck, grown fast to the rocks." McGuire (ed.), *The Freud/Jung letters*, 487.

[102] Sprengnether, *The spectral mother*, 137.

[103] Jung, *The psychology of the unconscious*, 428.

[104] *Ibid.*, 196.

[105] See for example Janine Chasseguet-Smirgel, "The archaic matrix of the Oedipus complex," *Sexuality and mind: the role of the father and the mother in the psyche*, ed. Leo Goldberger (New York: New York University Press, 1986), 74–91.

Freud countered with *Totem and taboo*, published in 1913.[106] In its
famous or infamous fourth essay, entitled "Return of totemism in childhood," he set out, *contra* Jung, to explain the incest taboo in terms of the
father complex. Let us briefly recall its well-known argument. Originally,
a powerful primal father (*Urvater*) possessed unrestricted sexual access
to all the women in the primal horde. If any of the sons challenged him,
the *Urvater* would kill them, castrate them, or drive them out. The
father's omnipotence consisted in his unrestricted right to sexual gratification and to murder. However, at some point – perhaps as a result of
a technological advance – the sons realized that if they banded together
they could remove him; he could defeat any one of them individually, but
not as a group. The brothers therefore formed an alliance, rose up, and
murdered the *Urvater*. Once he had been removed, however, a state of
nature ensued – much as has happened in our own time after the removal
of an all-powerful leader: for example, Tito in the former Yugoslavia and
Gaddafi in Libya. Reasoning in a Hobbesian manner, the brothers recognized that the only way to escape a war of all against all was to relinquish their individual sovereignty (omnipotence) and enter into a social
contract.

There was an additional motivation for this social compact. The brothers had not only hated the Father, but also loved him, and Freud argues
that "after they had gotten rid" of him, "the affection which had all this
time been pushed under was bound to make itself felt." It reemerged "in
the form of remorse" – that is, "a sense of guilt . . . felt by the whole
group." Because of that remorse, "the dead father became stronger than
the living one had been." In an act of "deferred obedience," the sons
sought to undo their murder "by forbidding the killing of the totem [ani-
mal], the substitute for the father," and by renouncing "their claim to the
women who had now been set free." That is, the brothers renounced their
sovereignty, which in psychoanalytic terms means their omnipotence,
by forfeiting the right to unrestricted sexual pleasure and murder. The
renunciation of omnipotence through the creation of the social contract,
Freud argues, constituted the founding act of civilization. The "filial
sense of guilt" gave rise to "the two fundamental taboos of totemism" –
against incest and against murder – which not only correspond "to the

---

[106] Sigmund Freud, *Totem and taboo* (1913), *SE* 13: xi–164.

two repressed wishes of the Oedipus complex," but also comprise the two constitutive laws of civilization.[107]

After the publication of *Totem and taboo*, all parties to the Freud–Jung squabbles deployed the work's narrative to frame their own position. Jung himself, despite having rejected the "father complex" in favor of the primal mother, accused Freud of behaving like the *Urvater* who sought to reduce his pupils to "either slavish sons or impudent puppies."[108] For his part, Freud often perceived a "patricidal look" in Jung's eyes and believed that his designated heir was intent on dethroning him. To be sure, both men could make a plausible case for their opposing positions. But there was another side to the story as well, perceived only by Jung's wife, Emma. It was that Freud, at the same time that he wanted to dominate Jung also wished to submit to him, as he had wished to submit to Fliess. With remarkable insight and sensitivity, Emma queried Freud about his Lear-like eagerness to surrender the kingdom he had fought so hard to create to his "crown prince":

You can imagine how overjoyed and honoured I am by the confidence you have in Carl, but it almost seems to me as though you were sometimes giving too much . . . Why are you thinking of giving up already instead of enjoying your well-earned fame and success? . . . [Y]ou should rejoice and drink to the full happiness of victory after having struggled for so long.[109]

Empirical evidence for the proposition that Freud (unconsciously) wished to surrender to his younger colleague may be found in the two fainting episodes Freud experienced in Jung's presence, the second of which uncannily repeated an earlier incident involving Fliess.[110] Although both episodes testify to a struggle for dominance, the wish to dominate was not the only factor involved in these over-determined events. The first occurred in Bremen while Freud, Jung, and Ferenczi were waiting to board the *George Washington, en route* to New York. Freud had scored a minor victory by inveigling Jung into taking a drink; the beer-drinking

---

[107] *Ibid.*, 143.

[108] McGuire (ed.), *The Freud/Jung letters*, 543.

[109] *Ibid.*, 456–457.

[110] Let us not forget that Freud also passed out at the sight of Emma Eckstein's uncontrolled hemorrhaging.

"Barrel" of university days had become a teetotaler under the puritanical influence of his boss at the Burghölzli, Eugen Bleuler. But after Freud interpreted Jung's perorations on some recently discovered prehistoric corpses as an expression of death wishes directed toward him, he passed out forthwith.[111]

Freud fainted for the second time in a meeting that had been convened in a futile attempt to repair what was in fact an irreparable rift between Freud and Jung. It was held on 24 November 1912 at the Park Hotel in Munich, the same city in which the final break took place a year later. As in Bremen, events began with what appeared to be a victory on Freud's part. On the evening of the 23rd, he held a private discussion with Jung, who seemed to have come around and accepted his point of view. Freud's mood was therefore upbeat the following day when he met Jung, Jones, Abraham, and several other colleagues for lunch in the hotel's dining room. But when the discussion turned to Abraham's research on the Egyptian Pharaoh Amenhotep, that singular figure who under the name Akhenaten overthrew his father's polytheistic religion and replaced it with his own monotheistic creed, Freud became agitated.[112] Again, not only did Freud interpret the discussion of the Pharaoh's Oedipal attack on his father as an expression of death wishes toward him, but, having done so, he proceeded to slide "off his chair in a faint."[113] What happened next is especially pertinent to our analysis. Jung tells us:

Everyone clustered helplessly around him. I picked him up, carried him into the next room, and laid him on a sofa. As I was carrying him, he half came to, and I shall never forget the look he cast at me. In his weakness he looked at me as if I were his father.[114]

---

[111] Freud later traced this episode, as well as the following one, to his early experience of brother Julius's death and saw them as self-punitive acts arising out of survivor's guilt. There is no reason to doubt that this was one factor contributing to his fainting. See Falzeder and Brabant (eds.), *Correspondence of Freud and Ferenczi*, vol. I, 440.

[112] Not only had Freud suggested the topic of Akhenaten to Abraham, but the revolutionary pharaoh was to play a central role in *Moses and monotheism* (see Chapter 13). However, in that late work, Freud does not mention Abraham's important paper on the topic, which he had in fact praised when it was published, presumably because some of his colleague's arguments contradict his central patriarchal thesis.

[113] Jung, *Memories*, 157.

[114] *Ibid.*, 157.

According to Jones, the first words Freud spoke when he revived were these: "How sweet it must be to die."[115]

Jung thought he had perceived a longing for the father in Freud's gaze when he looked up. But two facts suggest an alternative interpretation for what was going on in Freud's mind during the period under consideration and therefore for the meaning of that gaze. One hint is found in the fact that Freud published his paper "The theme of the three caskets," to be examined in the following chapter, in the year that followed the events at the Park Hotel; he had clearly been thinking about its contents for some time. In it, he argued that, in one important respect, the figure of the mother coincides with the figure of death. The relation that a man has to "the woman who bears" and nurses him at the beginning of life, he argues, converges with his later relation with "the woman who destroys him" – that is, "Mother Earth" whose arms he returns to at the end of life. These two instantiations of the maternal dimension converge in that both are characterized by stasis: In death one returns to the tensionless peace one had experienced *in utero*.[116]

Another hint is that in the following year, as we are about to see, Freud postulated the existence of primary narcissism, which can be understood as continuous with experience and as an original state of undifferentiated fullness, devoid of privation and tension, which we strive continually to recapture once it has been broken up.[117]

Put these two considerations together and the following interpretation can be formulated: Freud's exclamation, "how sweet it must be to die," can be taken to mean "how sweet it must be to return to the early mother." In other words, while in a twilight state after he fainted, with Jung holding him, Freud could unwittingly express his otherwise disavowed wish for merger and reunion with the primary object.

Freud's own response to the episode, articulated in a letter to Jones, was to connect it with Fliess:

There must be some psychic element in this attack . . . for I cannot forget that 6 and 4 years ago I suffered from similar though not so intense symptoms in the *same* room of the Parkhotel [*sic*]; in every case I had to leave the table. I saw

---

[115] Jones, *Freud* I, 317.
[116] Sigmund Freud, "The theme of the three caskets" (1913), *SE* 12: 301.
[117] Freud, "On narcissism: an introduction," 75–76 and 94.

Munich first when I visited Fliess during his illness . . . and this town seems to have acquired a strong connection with my relation to that man.[118]

Freud, moreover, acknowledges to Jones that his androphilic libido was involved in the fainting episode: "There is some piece of unruly homosexual feeling at the root of this matter."[119] Something "Fliess-like" had indeed happened in Munich.

Freud knew that he had lost much of his authority vis-à-vis Jung as a result of having fainted. Yet despite the risk of being further diminished in his adversary's eyes, he nevertheless displayed remarkable psychoanalytic candor and offered his adversary his account of what had happened in Munich. "For a moment," Gay observes, "it seemed as though Freud was willing to reason with Jung."[120] He wrote to his Swiss colleague: "The dining-room of the Park Hotel seems to hold a fatality for me. Six years ago I had a first attack of the same kind there. A bit of neurosis that I ought really to look into."[121] Although Freud refers to "a bit of neurosis" rather than "some piece of unruly homosexual feeling," Jung likely assumed that a homosexual component was at work in his fainting. He did not, however, treat Freud's candor as a gesture of good will. On the contrary, evoking his own "Helvetic bluntness," Jung seized on the information as ammunition to attack Freud for having mistreated him.

My very best thanks for one passage in your letter, where you speak of a "bit of neurosis" you haven't gotten rid of. This "bit" should, in my opinion, be taken very seriously indeed . . . I have suffered from this bit in my dealing with you, though you haven't seen it and didn't understand me properly when I tried to make my position clear. If these [neurotic] blinkers were removed you would . . . [not] *underestimate* my work by a very wide margin.[122]

---

[118] Paskauskas (ed.), *Correspondence of Freud and Jones*, 182 (emphasis in the original). Schur reports that such a meeting with Fliess never took place, which in fact makes Freud's statement to Jones even more significant. It suggests that there was a connection between Fliess and Jung regarding passivity and surrender in Freud's mind and that he constructed a spurious memory of an early meeting at the Park Hotel to represent it. See Schur, *Freud: living and dying*, 269.

[119] Paskauskas (ed.), *Correspondence of Freud and Jones*, 182.

[120] Gay, *Freud: a life for our time*, 235.

[121] McGuire (ed.), *The Freud/Jung letters*, 524.

[122] *Ibid.*, 525–526.

In effect, Jung was telling Freud what senior analysts have often told junior colleagues, supervisees, and candidates when they present a problem: "You need to go back for more analysis."

While reaffirming his commitment to analytic candor and lamenting the fact that many analysts fire interpretations at one another as weapons in their rivalries – a practice that was not entirely alien to him – Freud suggests a modest "household remedy": that is, "let each of us pay more attention to his own than to his neighbor's illness."[123] But when Jung rejected this proposal and accused Freud of "sniffing out all the symptomatic actions in [his] vicinity, thus reducing everyone to the level of sons and daughters who blushingly admit the existence of their faults" so that he could "remain on top as father," it was too much. Freud dropped all efforts at collegial neutrality and informed Jung that his lack of insight into his pathology made it impossible for their collaboration to continue:

It is a convention among us analysts that none of us feel ashamed of his own bit of neurosis. But when one who while behaving abnormally keeps shouting that he is normal, it gives ground for suspicion that he lacks insight into his illness. Accordingly, I propose that we abandon our personal relations entirely.[124]

Jung's curt response was inscribed on a postcard dated three days later: "The rest is silence."[125]

The end of Freud's relation with Jung invites comparison with the way that his relation with Fliess had terminated. Both situations involved a dispute over the same general question: "Where does the problem reside, in your head or mine?" Regarding their relationship, Jung put it in a nutshell: "*Who's* got the neurosis?"[126] And Jung's question can be reformulated and applied to Freud and Fliess: "*Who's* got the homosexuality?"

In one form or another, this problem is endemic to psychoanalysis, a field holding that one's intrapsychic life has important consequences for one's theoretical position. Power and truth are therefore more thoroughly intertwined in psychoanalysis than in other fields. Once the ubiquity of

[123] *Ibid.*, 529.

[124] *Ibid.*, 539.

[125] *Ibid.*, 540.

[126] *Ibid.*, 535 (emphasis in the original).

transference and countertransference has been acknowledged, an opponent's truth claim can always be discredited as a projection. Whether
we like it or not, the specter of epistemological vertigo is intrinsic to
the field and helps to explain its history of unmodulated "scientific"
controversies.

But in another way, the endings of the two relationships, Freud–Fliess
and Freud–Jung, are markedly different. To be sure, Freud's last letters
to Fliess are not devoid of anger and regret. But they are also infused
with a sense of deep melancholy, arising from the loss of what had been a
profound love between the two men. The predominant tone in the final
exchanges between Freud and Jung, by contrast, is largely one of bitterness
and rancor. Furthermore, despite everything that had happened, Freud
stuck to his "sanguine" account of the way he had mastered his libidinal
investments and used the "Fliess model" to explain the mechanics of how
he was managing his increasing disappointments with Jung. For example,
after concluding that Jung's lethargy as a letter writer indicated a lack of
investment in the relationship, Freud, who admitted to being "a demanding correspondent," wrote:

I took myself in hand and quickly turned off my excess libido. I was sorry to do so,
yet glad to see how quickly I managed it. Since then I have become undemanding
and not to be feared.[127]

Were it only that easy.

Settling the Score

Something else has been typically overlooked in the discussions of the
Freud–Jung relationship. From our contemporary perspective, it can be
seen that the third essay of *Totem and taboo*, entitled "Animism, magic,
and the omnipotence of thoughts," also written in direct opposition to
Jung, is as important as the one that follows it containing the theory of the
primal horde. The substance of that third essay overlaps with the content
of "On narcissism: an introduction," a paper that represents Freud's not
fully successful effort to definitively rid himself of the "Odium Jungian."
Freud conveyed the difficulty of that effort when he told Abraham that

---

[127] McGuire (ed.), *The Freud/Jung letters*, 488.

the paper "bears all the marks . . . of a difficult birth."[128] He also told his colleague that after completing the article, he was not "having a good time" and had been suffering from "a great deal of headache" and "intestinal trouble."[129] The theoretical and personal stakes were high, and the struggle involved in writing "On narcissism" took a substantial toll on Freud emotionally as well as physically. As Gay observes, moreover, the extremes that Freud went to in his attempt to refute Jung subverted many "of his own long-held views," and those subversions led to the major theoretical revisions of his own position in the 1920s.[130]

In "On narcissism," Freud's strategy is to outflank Jung on what we have been arguing was the key point of contention between them – the nature of the libido in psychotic regression. Freud did so by providing an account of psychosis in terms of his "libido theory," which is to say, in terms of his *libido sexualis*. Freud's point of departure is a clinical phenomenon – namely, the megalomania that characterizes certain forms of psychosis, such as we observed, for example, with Schreber. That megalomania, Freud asserts, tells us "what happens to the libido which has been withdrawn from external objects in schizophrenia." Once that libido "that has been withdrawn from the world is directed to the ego," he maintains, it "gives rise to an attitude which may be called narcissism."

Let us put Freud's idea in rather crudely energic terms – and his argument is unapologetically energic: He is arguing that "the megalomania" manifested in psychosis results from the over-excitation of the ego occurring as a result of psychotic regression – that is, of the influx of a large quantity of libido into that ego. It is here that Freud makes his key move, asserting that this megalomania is not a "new creation" but is "a magnification of a condition which had existed previously," a condition that he refers to as *primary narcissism*. That is to say, "the narcissism which arises through the drawing in of object-cathexis [is] a secondary one, superimposed upon a primary narcissism" that is not always readily observable. And he describes that primary narcissism as "an original libidinal cathexis of the ego."[131]

---

[128] Falzeder (ed.), *Correspondence of Freud and Abraham*, 222.

[129] *Ibid.*, 225.

[130] Gay, *Freud: a life for our time*, 328.

[131] For this entire paragraph see Freud, "On narcissism: an introduction," 74–75.

The nature of his practice, Freud explains, had prevented him from recognizing the existence of primary narcissism earlier. Work with neurotic
patients is largely dominated by object–libido, that is, their transference
investments in their analysts, which make it difficult to observe the narcissistic aspects of their personalities.

The next step of the argument is particularly interesting, for it involves
"one of the most fascinating secrets of human nature" – namely, the process of sublimation. Freud draws on his own private preoccupation and
sublimates it into a general theoretical construction; that is, he takes the
schema of libidinal dynamics he had correctly or incorrectly devised to
explain his relationship with Fliess and transforms it into his "amoeba"
model of narcissistic investment. Freud proposes the following thesis: At
the same time as a portion of the "original libidinal cathexis of the ego" is
"later given off to objects," that initial ego–investment always "persists"
and remains "related to the object–cathexes" it externalizes. And he likens
this to the way "the body of an amoeba [remains] related to the pseudopodia which it puts out."[132] As we will see, Freud later generalizes this model
further to explain mourning and normal ego development.

Put in more down–to–earth and less "biological" terms, Freud's idea
is this: We all begin life with the largest portion of libido invested in
ourselves. After that, how well our development goes determines the fate
of our libidinal investments. To the extent that a "good enough" environment greets a child, he or she acquires the capacity to invest in "objects"
(people, the world, ideas, and projects), and to maintain that investment despite the inevitable disappointments they encounter – that is,
to love and to sustain love. On the other hand, to the degree that their
early experience is less than facilitating, or is, worse yet, traumatic, children become "narcissistic" in that they tend to cling to their original
storehouse of libido and find it difficult to invest in the world. What is
more, when they are capable of cathecting objects, those cathexes are
generally fragile and are quickly withdrawn in the face of disappointment, much as an amoeba withdraws its pseudopodia when it encounters
noxious stimuli in its environment. These children, in short, grow up to
be individuals who have difficulty loving – in the broadest sense – and
maintaining their love.

---

[132] *Ibid.*, 75.

Freud adduces another phenomenon to support the existence of primary narcissism – namely, "the omnipotence of thoughts" that he claims
can be observed in children and in so-called "primitive people." Like
"megalomania," it comprises "an over-estimation of the power of . . .
wishes and mental acts" and "a belief in the thaumaturgic force of words."
This omnipotence is also a feature of "magic," which Freud understands
as "a technique for dealing with the external world" and "a logical application of these grandiose premises."[133] If, as he argues, magic consists in
mistaking the order and connection of thoughts for the order and connection of things, it follows that if humans can control their thoughts, they
can control the external world. "It is easy," Freud writes, "to perceive
the motives which lead men to practice magic: they are human wishes" –
wishes, moreover, that deny the irreducible and uncontrollable independence of the external world.[134] What is more, magical thinking makes it
impossible for human beings to test their beliefs against reality and comprehend their "true position in the universe," which is to say: magical
thinking makes science impossible.

Our "primitive" ancestors, Freud argues, first began to surrender
their omnipotence and acknowledge *Ananke* – fate, destiny, the ineluc-
tability "which opposes our narcissism" – at their relatives' gravesides.
Our ancient forebears invented spirits as a way of grappling with the
unfathomable phenomenon of death as well as with their guilt at having
survived, thereby creating animism, "the first" proto-theoretical "picture
man formed of the world."[135] But animism constituted only a partial surrender of omnipotence. On the one hand, death – and *eo ipso Ananke* –
had to some extent been acknowledged; had it not been, there would be no
motive for creating spirits as a means of coping with it. But on the other
hand, the existence of spirits presupposes the existence of an afterlife and
thus denies the finality of death. With animism, therefore, the "same gesture" that acknowledged death simultaneously enabled primitive humans
to retain some of their omnipotence over it.

---

[133] *Ibid.*, 175. Freud provides a more extended anthropological analysis of the omnipotence of thoughts and magical thinking in the third essay of *Totem and taboo*, referred
to above.

[134] See Freud, *Totem and taboo*, 83.

[135] *Ibid.*, 93.

In Freud's progressivist scheme of historical development, animism corresponds to the first narcissistic stage of development. The locus of that omnipotence is the grandiose self: Like the narcissistic infant, the shaman shakes his rattle at the world to make it conform to his wishes. In the next step in Freud's Comtean schema, the religious stage of phylogenetic development corresponds to the ontogenetic stage of object love: omnipotence has been transferred from the "grandiose self" to the "omnipotent object."[136] Just as older children beseech their parents to fulfill their wishes, the religious congregation petitions its gods for the same reason. "At the religious stage," Freud concludes, humans "transfer [their omnipotence] to the gods but do not seriously abandon it in themselves, for they reserve the power of influencing the gods . . . according to their wishes."[137] Omnipotence, in short, has not been relinquished, but only reconfigured.

Freud himself, however, makes a grandiose claim when he asserts that it is only with the scientific stage of development – which corresponds to the stage of mature object love in the individual – that omnipotence is surmounted. "The scientific view of the universe," he argues, "no longer affords any room for omnipotence." Not only have humans "acknowledged their smallness and submitted resignedly to death and the other necessities of nature," but they have also "renounced the pleasure principle, adjusted [themselves] to reality and turned to the world for" the gratification of their desires.[138] We are inclined to recoil at Freud's Eurocentric Whiggishness and snicker at his naïve pronouncements, but there is nevertheless a valid kernel to what he is saying that should be defended and preserved. When we strip away the Eurocentrism and the teleological philosophy of history, this is what remains: For Freud, the

---

[136] Heinz Kohut, *The analysis of the self: a systematic approach to the treatment of narcissistic personality disorders* (Chicago: University of Chicago Press, 2009).

[137] Freud, *Totem and taboo*, 88. Weston La Barre observes: "Ultimately both magic and religion reflect individual narcissism that insists, inalternatively, that somewhere *there must* be an omnipotence to minister to one's whole conscious and clear, categorically sanctioned, sacred need. The environment *must be* what I, unself-questioningly, demand that it be. The absoluteness of the imperious id creates the Absolute." Weston La Barre, *The ghost dance: the origins of religion* (New York: Delta Books, 1972), 110 (emphasis in the original).

[138] Freud, *Totem and taboo*, 88 and 90.

goal – in science, life, and psychoanalytic treatment – is to master omnipotence and accept *Ananke* to the extent that is possible for finite creatures
like us.

Jung's Counter-Enlightenment provocation thus pushed Freud to articulate his conception of science more completely. And it also did something
more. Even if inadvertently, *his attempt to outmaneuver Jung on the question
of psychosis led him, as we have seen, to postulate the existence of primary
narcissism – and, moreover, to address the issue of the archaic or early mother.*

Though Freud's discussion of primary narcissism is not consistent,
one valid way of interpreting it is this: It consists in an original, undifferentiated state devoid of privation and externality, and, like the *inter utero*
condition, this plenum-like state provides the psyche with its primordial
experience of perfection. "The infantile ego," Freud argues, finds "itself
possessed of every perfection that is of value," but as the child "grows
up . . . the admonitions of others" and "the awakening of his own critical judgments" cause the breakdown of that state of primary narcissistic
perfection. However, because, "where the libido is involved," humans
are incapable of giving up a satisfaction [they] once enjoyed," they are
"not willing to forgo the narcissistic perfection" of the original stage of
development. Instead, they form an "ego ideal," which becomes "the
substitute of the lost narcissism of their childhood"; they project this ego
ideal into the future and pursue it in one way or another throughout their
lives.[139] Behind all the metapsychological terminology, Freud has in fact
posited a state of undifferentiated merger with the archaic mother, and
he has argued that, once it is dissolved, it exerts a magnetic force on us so
that we attempt to recapture it in a variety of ways over the course of life.

But the strategy Freud pursued to counter Jung's irrationalist challenge put his own rationalist position in jeopardy. By arguing that the
ego is the repository of the entire libido, Freud seems to have sexualized,
which is to say naturalized, the ego. This may seem like a minor point, but
it has major consequences that threaten Freud's scientific *Weltanschauung*.
For nature to be comprehended scientifically, there must logically be
something outside of nature – a knowing subject – that can do the com-
prehending. But if the ego is thoroughly sexualized, it becomes part of
nature, thereby subverting the necessary preconditions for science. It is

---

[139] Freud, "On narcissism: an introduction," 94.

not clear, as André Green observes, why Freud adopted such an extreme position in order to defeat Jung.[140] There were other theoretical options available to him. Perhaps his zealousness to vindicate his theory of sexuality caused him to go too far, but for whatever reasons he did. And the destabilizing effect that this had on his theory reverberated throughout the rest of his career and supplied considerable ammunition to his critics.

[140] See André Green, "One, other, neuter: narcissistic values of sameness," *Life narcissism death narcissism*, trans. Andrew Weller (New York: Free Associations Books, 2001), 4–7.

10

"What Is Painful May None the Less Be Real": Loss, Mourning, and *Ananke*

THE PAINFUL PERSONAL BREAK with Jung was followed by the catastrophic events of the First World War. As it would do at several points in his life, adversity, in this case the physical and psychological suffering caused by the war, ignited a burst of creativity in Freud. In addition to writing important series of articles on metapsychology and psychoanalytic technique, he also authored some of his most philosophical, literary, and seminal works in response to that world-historical cataclysm – works that provided the bridge to his late cultural writings.

Loss and Disillusionment

The topic of loss, which is more closely related to the pre-Oedipal theme of separation than to the *topoi* of "the father complex," moved to the center of Freud's thinking in the wake of his break with Jung.[1] It is true that "the controversy between Freud and Jung concerned theoretical matters," but as Matthew von Unwerth observes in his elegant *Freud's requiem*, "the exchange could not have been more personal."[2] We have seen that their relationship was complicated and involved enormous aggression on both their parts, but there is no doubt that Freud also loved Jung deeply, something a member of his circle attested to. And in addition to a loss on the personal plane, the break with Jung also entailed loss for

[1] Sprengnether perceptively observes that Freud attempted to obscure the changes that were taking place in his thinking through a bizarre theoretical stretch that equated separation with castration. See Sprengnether, *The spectral mother*, 138–140, 146, and 176.

[2] Matthew von Unwerth, *Freud's requiem: mourning, memory, and the invisible history of a summer walk* (New York: Riverhead Books, 2005), 39.

Freud in the dimension of culture. Freud, as we have noted, believed that Jung could help him realize the universalist and cosmopolitan aspirations for psychoanalysis. "When Jung failed to fulfill his symbolic function as a path of access into this surrounding and unfriendly cultural world," Homans observes, it was necessary for Freud not only to reexamine his relation to the broader culture and its values, but also "to face that world more directly, without a mediating figure."[3]

We have seen that the de facto break with Jung occurred in September 1913 at the IPA's Munich Congress. When the Congress adjourned, Freud, accompanied by his sister-in-law Minna – an intelligent woman, who was deeply interested in his work – decamped for Rome, where he called on "old Moses" and spent seventeen days in the Eternal City.[4] After the disappointment with Jung, his designated son and heir, Freud's androphilia appears to have subsided considerably, allowing him to establish his first intellectual friendships with two substantial women – in addition to Minna, Lou Andreas-Salomé. (Freud had a number of close relations with female colleagues in the years that followed, but none of them assumed the intensity of his attachment to Fliess and Jung.)

The Italian capital – which he had only been able to enter after having worked through his "Rome neurosis" in self-analysis – was a city Freud loved deeply. Homans suggests that although Freud was not fully conscious of it, Rome may have had a strong "maternal presence" for him because of its association with his Catholic nursemaid and the Madonna.[5] It was therefore an ideal place to recover from the wounds inflicted by Munich and the battles of the preceding several years. And the city did the trick. Echoing Goethe's and Max Weber's experience of Italy, Freud wrote to Abraham that "in the incomparable beauty of Rome, I quickly recovered my spirits and energy for work."[6] Rome was also a city that had a rich

---

[3] Homans, *The ability to mourn*, 73.

[4] The fact that Freud described them as "17 delicious days" has led many to conclude that the two were having an affair. Paskauskas (ed.), *Correspondence of Freud and Jones*, 227.

[5] Homans, *The ability to mourn*, 51.

[6] Falzeder (ed.), *Correspondence of Freud and Abraham*, 195. Rome also had a curative effect on one of Freud's illustrious contemporaries, Max Weber. It was only after a series of visits to the Eternal City that Weber was able to pull himself out of a severe depression that had more or less lasted for a number of years and had required a

and complex web of meanings in Freud's inner world. This made it an excellent "facilitating environment" for the burst of creativity that took place there, which involved the working-through of his relationship with Jung and the theoretical controversies that grew out of it. Freud's *italienische Reise* produced "The Moses of Michelangelo," "The history of the psychoanalytic movement," and "On narcissism."

After completing "On narcissism," Freud did not immediately take up the paradigm-challenging difficulties it had generated. It was clear to him that "the subversive direction he was taking," as Gay observes, required major theoretical revisions, and he was planning to use his 1914 summer holiday in Karlsbad as an opportunity to turn his attention to his own work after the distractions that psychoanalytic politics had caused him over the previous several years. But then, "with unexpected, ungracious suddenness," loss insinuated its way into his life in another way. "The world" – in the form of the First World War – "intruded," as Gay observes, "and for a time disrupted Freud's thoughts in a brutal and unimaginable way."[7] Consequently, he did not turn to the challenges posed by "On narcissism" directly. It was only after the war that Freud commenced the restructuring of his position in a fundamental way.

Much has been written about the Great War and its effects on Western consciousness. With the exception of the American Civil War, which had occurred on the other side of the Atlantic, the catastrophe of World War I was unprecedented. Because nothing involving destruction on this scale had ever happened before, it was perhaps even more traumatic than the other catastrophes that followed it in the twentieth century. When the Second World War broke out, trench warfare, in which hundreds of thousands of men died in a matter of days while the battle line barely moved, as well as the use of poison gas, tanks, and airplanes were already history. The parties to the Second World War knew therefore that it was possible for disasters like these to happen again. This is not a question of which World War, the First or Second, saw the greater slaughter. The point is rather that the Great War was perhaps experienced as a traumatic shock

---

hospitalization. See Peter Homans, "Loss and mourning in the life and thought of Max Weber: toward a theory of symbolic loss," *Symbolic loss: the ambiguity of mourning and memory at century's end*, ed. Peter Homans (Charlottesville: University of Virginia Press, 2000), 225–238.

[7] Gay, *Freud: a life for our time*, 142.

in a way that the Second World War was not. It constituted a massive historical rupture and created a chasm between the world that had had come before it and the one that would come after it. Commenting on the rupture to Frau Lou, Freud wrote: "I do not doubt that mankind will survive even this war, but I know for certain that for me and my contemporaries" – that is, for those Europeans who came of age prior to 1914 – "the world will never again be a happy place. It is too hideous."[8]

The unparalleled destructiveness of the Great War engendered an experience of collective and massive disillusionment in the West. Not only did it wreak havoc on Europe's material assets – her population, agricultural fields, and cities – it also did immeasurable and irreparable damage to her spiritual heritage, the heritage that Freud, as a *gebildeter Mensch*, most identified with. Viewed from the *longue durée*, it brought to an end a common European culture, which, in important respects, had enjoyed a continuous existence for more than a thousand years. Viewed from a more limited time span, the optimism and faith in rationality, progress, and science that had marked bourgeois culture prior to 1914 suffered their demise at Verdun and at the Somme, thus challenging the basic values of the bourgeois worldview, which in many important ways was also Freud's. Thus, in addition to the task of mourning actual death and material destruction on an unprecedented scale, Freud also faced the necessity of mourning the civilizational ideals that had shaped him. The war, moreover, raised troubling questions about human nature. How was it that human beings – and in this case the citizens of the world's presumably civilized nations – were capable of such barbarism? After the horrifying events of the war, it became difficult to maintain one's faith in the essential goodness, rationality, and sociability of the human animal. And if that faith was abandoned, one had to ask, what were the implications for individual and social existence?

The massive disillusionment engendered by the First World War amplified the strand of *Kulturpessimismus* that was already present in Freud's thinking. Nevertheless, as we noted, Homans attempts to identify a redemptive dialectic in Freud's views on disillusionment. His thesis is that disillusionment – specifically, the disenchantment and de-idealization

---

[8] Ernst Pfeiffer (ed.), *Sigmund Freud and Lou Andreas-Salomé letters*, trans. William and Elaine Robson-Scott (New York: Harcourt Brace Jovanovich, 1966), 21.

of the West's traditional and largely religious structures of meaning – is a necessary condition for the unique modes of enlightenment and emancipation that became possible in modernity. That is, while the break with tradition made the creation of new, post-traditional structures of meaning both necessary and possible, disillusionment with the inherited structure of beliefs – the displacement if not the destruction of false idols – was a *condition sine qua non* for gaining new post-traditional insights.

Homans argues, moreover, that *mourning* supplies the link between disillusionment and emancipatory enlightenment. Mourning, Freud notes, can be an "extraordinarily painful" process, but without its fruits, disillusionment is likely to result in despair, pessimism, and nihilism or, conversely, lead to the hypomanic denial of loss – all recognizable features of the modern constellation.[9] But with the mediation of mourning, disillusionment can lead to "an education to reality" and to the creation of new structures of meaning.[10]

Lamps Out all over Europe

A number of commentators have been bewildered by Freud's initial reaction to the war, which was one of nationalistic and militaristic enthusiasm. Despite his protracted *Kampf mit Wien* (struggle with Vienna), habitual grousing about the Habsburgs, and opposition to all forms of nationalism, when the war began Freud declared himself an Austrian patriot. He wrote to Abraham, "Perhaps for the first time in 30 years I feel myself an Austrian and would like to try it once again, with this not very hopeful Empire," and he declared that "my entire libido is given to Austro-Hungary."[11] Jones captures the perplexity those commentators experienced when he observes: "One would have supposed that a pacific *savant* of fifty-eight would have greeted [the war] with simple horror."[12]

---

[9] Freud, "Mourning and melancholia," 245.

[10] Freud, *The future of an illusion*, 49.

[11] Freud refers to his protracted "battle of Vienna" in a letter to his Martha in 1886. *The letters of Sigmund Freud*, ed. Ernst L. Freud, 206; Falzeder (ed.), *Correspondence of Freud and Abraham*, 265; quoted in Jones, *Freud* II, 171. Ellenberger observes, "Those Viennese who really disliked Vienna emigrated; those who loved it pretended to hate it, but stayed." Ellenberger, *The discovery of the unconscious*, 108.

[12] Jones *Freud* II, 171.

But instead of opposing the militaristic spirit of the day – or at least direct-ing some of his vaunted skepticism at it – for a while, Freud supported the Austrian cause with little reservation.

As a physician, he was assigned the task of evaluating conscripts who were petitioning to be exempted from duty because of psychological dis-orders, and one might think that he would have been sympathetic to the plight of these young men. Instead, we are rather stunned when we learn from Jones that Freud – who, early in his career, had fought against dis-missing hysterics as malingerers – "did not readily help neurotics to avoid conscription." This refusal would perhaps strike us as less offensive if he had justified it on purely nationalist grounds and simply maintained that these young men "should," as Jones puts it, "all try to help in the common interest" – in other words, if he had just maintained that Austria needed canon fodder for the front. But he did not. Moreover, Jones also informs us that Freud evinced no concern for the toll that the experience of war could take on a young conscript's psyche. Instead, like an unbend-ing patriarch extolling the virtues of a martial *ethos*, Freud asserted "it would do them good to do so," that is, to undergo the horrors of war.[13]

These disturbing facts aside, Freud's behavior was not as unusual as one might assume. By reacting in this way, he was not alone. As Gay observes, "Europeans of all stripes" – including "aristocrats, bourgeois, workers, and farmers; reactionaries, liberals, and radicals; cosmopolitans, chauvinists, and particularists; fierce soldiers, preoccupied scholars, and gentle theologians" – joined in greeting the advent of war with a fervor bordering on a religious experience.[14] It is difficult for us to comprehend this reaction given that we know what followed those heady days.[15] At the war's outset, however, two factors help to explain how this heterogeneous group of flag-wavers became swept away in the frenzy. Many of them believed that, like the wars in recent memory, this one would be fought on battlefields far removed from Europe's population centers and that

[13] *Ibid.*, 171.

[14] Gay, *Freud: a life for our time*, 347–348.

[15] One might argue on Freud's behalf that the extreme trauma that the new form of warfare would inflict on the combatants – what we now call PTSD – had as yet not been observed and diagnosed. In fact, the whole debate over "shell shock" did not emerge until the First World War and Freud as well as other analysts were participants in it.

it would be "noble, short and swift" – nothing like the prolonged war of attrition that ensued. Many also believed that the war would revive the chivalrous deeds and national glory of an earlier era, thus relieving them of the distinctly unheroic monotony of bourgeois existence.[16] With a few exceptions – Freud's brother Alexander being one of them – they did not foresee the nightmare that the new species of warfare was about to unloose on them.[17]

Freud in fact acted no differently from the many eminent European intellectuals who became ardent supporters of the war; notable exceptions include Albert Einstein, Bertrand Russell, Jean Jaurès, Rosa Luxemburg, and Romain Rolland. But there is also another point to be considered in his case: his penchant for heroism and martial valor. It is of course not unusual for a boy to have been fascinated with military heroics, especially in Freud's day, but his was particularly intense and lasted well into his adulthood – apparently into his fifty-eighth year. Freud's enthrallment with military heroes like Hannibal, Cromwell, and Napoleon can be traced in part to his disappointment with Jacob's weakness. And it can also be understood as an aspect of his "repudiation of femininity" resulting from his early trauma – that is, his contempt for helplessness, dependency, and passivity, which he equated with femininity, and his reaction against his own "passive/feminine" strivings. After all, what is more indomitable and free from any contamination of femininity for a little boy than a heroic soldier? As Jones puts it, Freud's initial "youthful enthusiasm for the war" constituted a reawakening, a remobilization if you will, of "the military ardors of his boyhood."[18]

These considerations raise the question of how to understand two facts about Freud's personality. On the one hand, it cannot be doubted that he exhibited authentic and incomparable courage throughout his life. On the other hand, however, we tend to wince when we observe this Jewish doctor from Leopoldstadt, who never underestimated the pleasures of bourgeois life – for example, his *Tafelspitz* at the Café Landtmann, his daily strolls on the Ringstrasse where he purchased his Trabucco cigars

[16] Makari, *Revolution in mind*, 306.

[17] Jones, *Freud* II, 171.

[18] Jones, *Freud* II, 171. Beginning in 1915, James Joyce wrote *Ulysses*, among other things, to mock the grandiosity of military heroism by transforming the hero of Homer's epic into a cuckolded Jewish salesman.

at a local kiosk, his weekly game of Tarock while schmoozing with his brethren at the B'nai B'rith, and his favored bottle of Barolo – striking the heroic pose of a conquering general or describing himself as a conquistador. This discomfort, however, should not prevent us from recognizing an important point that may help to sort out this seeming incongruity. Regardless of the adolescent flavor of this posturing and the distortions it introduced into his thinking and judgment, Freud's heroic self-conception also had *a decidedly adaptive side.*

For one thing, his heroic imago contributed to the speculative freedom that allowed Freud to make his great discoveries. Where Kant admonished us to throw off dogmatic authority and "think for ourselves," Freud did the sage of Königsberg one better, imploring us to reject all parental prohibitions and "fantasize for ourselves." He told Ferenczi, albeit with unconvincing modesty, that "the only . . . quality of the first rank" he had discovered in himself was "a kind of courage, which is unshaken by convention." It allowed him, he told the Hungarian, freely to produce a "succession of daringly playful fantasies" that could later be subjected to "realistic criticism."[19] Freud's intellectual machismo, moreover, invites comparison with that of another theoretical giant of the same period, Max Weber. Both men, it seems, set out to demonstrate how much untarnished reality they could face without external metaphysical or theological props.

It is difficult to imagine, moreover, how, without this heroic ego ideal, Freud could have endured the innumerable blows, almost impossible for us to countenance, that Fate dealt him. This is especially true with regard to his sixteen-year battle with cancer, a battle that required no fewer than thirty surgical interventions. As Freud himself suggests, it was perhaps necessary for him to cast *Ananke* – "the inexorable, unavoidable necessity" – as his "immortal adversary" in order to mobilize the mettle that was required to combat the illness and the other adversities that befell him. Freud's own case is an example of the human mind's need for meaning. He told his physician, Felix Deutsch, that he could submit to "a remorseless law of nature" but not to mere chance. Without "sublime *Ananke*" as his opponent, he declared, he would "fall prey to the miserable cowardice of a human being and . . . become an unworthy spectacle for

[19] Falzeder and Brabant (eds.), *Correspondence of Freud and Ferenczi*, vol. II, 55. Although, as we have observed, Freud's capacity to fantasize, prodigious as it was, reached its limits when it came to the psychic territory of pre-Oedipal experience.

others."[20] That Freud demonstrated so little empathy for the understandable fear that a mere "human being" experiences in the face of sickness and death – indeed, considered it contemptible – is another indication of how loathsome the idea of helplessness was for him.

These observations, however, raise two thorny questions that will be addressed in the next chapter but that ought to be noted here. First, how does one distinguish between "the resignation to *Ananke*" when it represents the genuine mastery exemplified by the Stoic sage versus when it serves as a manic defense against reality dressed up as heroism? Second, what is the relation between Freud's *psychological* deployment of the idea of *Ananke* as "a fulcrum or a pillar" that anchored the courage he needed to face the challenges that confronted him and his elevation of the concept into one of his basic theoretical terms?

Whatever the source of Freud's initial elation over the war, it could not go on indefinitely. By approximately the end of 1914, the horrifying realities of this new species of warfare were becoming apparent, and too much reality was impinging on him. Ironically – or sadly – once he recovered from his jingoist delusions, Freud recognized that his own theory could have predicted the massive destruction. He wrote to Lou Andreas-Salomé: "It is too hideous. And the saddest thing about it is that it is exactly the way we should have expected people to behave from our knowledge of psycho-analysis."[21] This statement leads one to wonder what Freud, who died at the very moment German tanks had rolled into Poland, would have thought had he lived to witness the Second World War and the Holocaust.

As the events unfolded, an elemental emotional consideration played a decisive role in overriding Freud's initial bout of jingoism: the welfare of his children – his actual children as well as his creative child, psychoanalysis. As he told Ferenczi, "that the children will be provided for" – which, he added, "for a Jewish father is a matter of life and death" – was his primary concern.[22] Of all the anxieties besetting Freud during the war, the one concerning his children's safety, especially the safety of his sons who were of military age, undoubtedly did the most to moderate his martial impulses.

---

[20] See Schur, *Freud: living and dying*, 357.

[21] Pfeiffer (ed.), *Freud and Andreas-Salomé letters*, 21.

[22] *The letters of Sigmund Freud*, ed. Ernst L. Freud, 65.

The first real crisis that the war caused the family, however, concerned his youngest daughter Anna. That Anna had been allowed to visit England in July 1914 shows how little the reality of the impending tragedy had been grasped in its opening weeks. When overt hostilities broke out, there was concern that she would be stranded in London. But thanks to Jones's political adroitness and connections, she was able to return home, with no less a chaperone than the Austrian Ambassador to Britain. The two travelers followed a roundabout route, which led them through Gibraltar and Genoa, until they arrived in Vienna in mid-August.

Freud's relief when "the Austrian authorities had rejected two of [his sons], and exempted the third" from military duty also indicates that his concern for their safety trumped his patriotic dedication to the war effort.[23] But this relief was short-lived, for Freud's oldest son, Martin, enlisted in August, and his other sons, as well as his son-in-law Max Halberstadt, followed him into the military. "In the spring [1915], when the bloodletting comes," Freud wrote to Ferenczi, "I will have three or four sons in it. My trust in the future after the war is very slight."[24]

Martin marched off to battle with a great sense of duty mixed with romantic excitement and was assigned to an artillery unit where he was decorated several times and promoted to the rank of officer. Throughout the war he was moved back and forth between the Eastern Front and Italy, which was where he was taken prisoner when the Austrian army broke down as the war was approaching its end. The fact that the Freud family did not know Martin's condition or whereabouts when the hostilities ended caused them considerable anxiety. It was not relieved until 3 December 1918 when a postcard arrived informing them that he was recovering in an Italian hospital, and he did not return to Vienna until the following May.

Freud's second son Oliver, who was in the process of completing a degree in engineering in 1914, was exempted from military service on medical grounds. Having avoided conscription, he wanted to take a number of engineering jobs in part to help his father with his finances. But Freud – perhaps remembering that his own father had failed to provide him with sound practical advice – convinced his son to complete his

---

[23] Gay, *Freud: a life for our time*, 352.
[24] Falzeder and Brabant (eds.), *Correspondence of Freud and Ferenczi*, vol. II, 37.

studies, which he did in June 1915. After receiving his degree in civil engineering, Oli took a job that was not only enormously difficult but also of great military importance: helping to construct a tunnel that ran under the Jablonica Pass in the Carpathian Mountains.[25] That took fifteen months, after which Oli finally enlisted in the army in December 1916, joined a battalion of sappers, and spent the remainder of the war stationed at various postings around Europe. He was about to be promoted to the rank of officer when the armistice was declared.

Although he saw his share of action, including one battle where the rest of his battalion was wiped out, and although he received a commendation for bravery, of Freud's three sons, Ernst seems to have had the easiest time of it during the war. After serving twenty-four months at the front, he was sidelined with a duodenal ulcer and an infection of tuberculosis – which continued to plague him his entire life – and spent the remainder of the war moving from hospital to hospital. While Freud evinced fatherly pride in the way his sons had acquitted themselves militarily, he must also have counted himself among the lucky when all three of them, as well as his son-in-law Max, returned home safely when it was over.

His spiritual child, psychoanalysis, on the other hand, did not fare as well. The field's orientation had always been international, with extensive correspondence between members and regular international congresses serving as its "lifeblood."[26] But the barriers erected by the war made the usual modes of interaction and communication difficult if not impossible. The necessity of cancelling the congress in Dresden, scheduled for September 1914, was an early sign that the war was real and that the field's internationalism was in jeopardy. A prime example of the difficulties is that of Ernest Jones, one of Freud's closest and most dependable lieutenants. As a Welshman living in England, one of the Allied countries, Jones technically became an "enemy." Communication with him became difficult and contact impossible. (Jones nevertheless was able to get

---

[25] It is a testament to Freud's love for his son as well as to his adventurousness that he made the twelve-hour trip to visit Oli at the construction site, and, at the age of sixty, "accompanied [him] on an inspection of the unfinished tunnel, which was a gymnastic performance involving climbing over a number of ladders and so on." Jones, *Freud* II, 203.

[26] Gay, *Freud: a life for our time*, 351.

letters to Freud through Switzerland and the Netherlands.) Jones himself describes the toll that the war took on the profession:

[N]ot surprisingly, there was little time, and less money, available for psychoanalytic journals; the *Jarbuch* ceased publication, while *Imago* and the *Internationale Zeitschrift für Psychoanalyse* (founded in 1913) soldiered on, much reduced in size. The Vienna Psychoanalytic Society, which had for years faithfully assembled every Wednesday night, now convened once every two weeks and, from early 1916 on, once every three weeks or even more sporadically.

Furthermore, because many analysts were physicians, they were called up for duty, only further exacerbating the situation. Although their mobilization did not prevent them from working for the cause in their spare time, it placed serious limits on how much they could accomplish.

"Helplessness and penury," Freud wrote to Abraham in December of 1914, were the two things he had "always . . . hated most."[27] And by severely depleting his finances, the war threatened both. Freud began the war with only five and a half hours of patients, and his practice fluctuated erratically throughout its duration. When his income did pick up during the war's later years, the increase did not keep abreast of the wartime inflation. By the time of the armistice, Freud had lost his life savings, which had been invested in life insurance (100,000 crowns) and Austrian State Bonds (150,000 crowns).[28]

Civilian life in Vienna deteriorated dramatically as the war progressed. The situation worsened substantially in 1915 after the Allies imposed a blockade on the Central Powers. Rationing cards became necessary simply to obtain "the coarse, unappetizing 'war bread'"; the black market flourished; and "food riots struck in May and October."[29] Then, in 1916, severe food shortages, resulting from a poor harvest, combined with a shortage of fuel to create a particularly severe winter. In a response to the crisis, "city households were allowed to heat only one room."[30] Like all the residents of Vienna, the inhabitants of Berggasse 19 must have found "the forlornness of unheated rooms . . . particularly dispiriting." Because of

[27] Falzeder (ed.), *Correspondence of Freud and Abraham*, 294.
[28] See Breger, *Freud*, 250. See also Jones, *Freud* II, 199–200.
[29] Breger, *Freud*, 245.
[30] *Ibid.*, 248.

the lack of heat, Freud could only write letters "with freezing fingers, and all ideas of scientific writing had to be given up during winter months."[31] It was simply too cold. Likewise, when the irregular Wednesday meetings did convene in the Professor's waiting room, members had to remain bundled in their overcoats.

There were times when food supplies were so low that the situation threatened the family's health. Jones reports that "in his letters Freud had to complain many times of the bitter cold and the difficulty of procuring enough food to keep in health; there was very definite undernourishment in those years."[32] At the same time, it cannot be denied that, owing to the generosity of patients and colleagues who provided them with provisions – including such non-essential items as cigars – the Freud family was somewhat buffered from the extreme suffering that the average Viennese experienced during the war. Until Hungary split from Austria in October 1918 and travel between Budapest and Vienna became difficult, Ferenczi and Anton von Freund – an exceptionally wealthy Hungarian brewer with a doctorate in philosophy who had been successfully treated by Freud – were able to smuggle "flour, bread and occasionally a few luxuries of food" into Vienna by "hook or crook."[33] But to discount the suffering that the Freud family experienced because of their relatively privileged position, as Breger does, borders on the obscene.[34] Freud the realist was in fact unapologetic about the advantages his position afforded him and seems to have accepted the gifts without appreciable conflict. In his characteristically jocular manner, he referred to his beneficiaries as his "quartermasters" and compared his family's situation to that of "a doctor's family in the old days" where patients "paid" for their treatment through barter, by bringing "gifts to the physician."[35] If anything bothered him about the gifts, it was that they highlighted his helplessness and dependence on others.

[31] Jones, *Freud* II, 194 and 192.

[32] *Ibid.*, 192.

[33] *Ibid.*, 192 and 194.

[34] Gay rightfully takes Breger to task on this score. Peter Gay "Review of *Freud: darkness in the midst of vision*," *Journal of the American Psychoanalytic Association* 49 (2001), 1075–1076.

[35] See Breger, *Freud*, 249.

The war had one unintended consequence of which Freud took full advantage. As Homans observes, it "virtually re-created in a fresh and even more forceful way the earlier isolation of the self-analysis." Freud's practice was at times reduced to a virtual standstill; traveling and correspondence had become difficult if not impossible. And he was deprived of the regular contact with colleagues that not only kept him up-to-date with his psychoanalytic troops but also helped him develop his ideas. Freud used an image of war to describe his situation to Ferenczi: "I am living, as my brother says, in my private trench. I speculate and write."[36]

But instead of being immobilized by the situation, Freud took advantage of the time it afforded him. He struck a chord of melancholy resignation when he wrote to Jones saying that "the only thing we can do is keep a glow of fire going on a few hearths until a more favorable wind will allow it to blaze up again," but in fact he did considerably more than that.[37] This is not to deny the existence of fallow stretches when he could not write. But Freud, who was a "great mourner," reacted to these losses the way he responded to numerous losses throughout his life:[38] with an outburst of creativity that would have been exceptional under the best of circumstances. Perhaps most remarkably, in seven weeks between 15 March and 4 May 1915, Freud composed the so-called "Metapsychological papers" that elucidated such basic concepts of psychoanalysis as repression, the unconscious, and the drives. The "upsurge in productivity" during the war years, as Schur observes, "was unequaled since *The Interpretation of Dreams*."[39] Writing to Abraham, Freud acknowledged this fact: "I think I regard the situation as a repetition of the initial one, when I was productive and – isolated."[40]

There was, however, an important difference between the works produced in the 1890s and those produced during the war years. As Homans observes, while the isolation caused by the war had the effect of "driving Freud once again inward, into his inner world," this time "he also turned his thoughts outward, toward the surrounding culture."[41] The social

---

[36] Falzeder and Brabant (eds.), *Correspondence of Freud and Ferenczi*, vol. II, 36.

[37] Jones, *Freud* II, 179.

[38] Homans, *Jung in context*, xlvi.

[39] Schur, *Freud: living and dying*, 292.

[40] Falzeder (ed.), *Correspondence of Freud and Abraham*, 313.

[41] Homans, *The ability to mourn*, 195.

orientation of Freud's thinking, which had begun during his confrontation with Jung, undoubtedly received further impetus from the traumatic experience of the war. Whereas an almost exclusive concentration on psychic reality had been necessary to create psychoanalysis, social reality could no longer be bracketed. And the texts that grew out of the First World War – Freud's "proto-cultural texts," as Homans called them – prepared the way for the towering cultural works of the twenties and thirties.[42]

Furthermore, the fear, uncertainty, and privations caused by the war seem to have put Freud in a "philosophical" cast of mind. He now gave increasing freedom to "his demon of creative speculation, which he had so ruthlessly checked in the early years of scientific work when he tied himself all day to the microscope," and which he continued to check for the two decades that followed.[43] As we will see, "Thoughts for the time on war and death" and "On transience" represent the first stirrings of Freud's speculative demon that would find full unbridled expression in *Beyond the pleasure principle* and the great cultural works of the last twenty years of his life.

This burst of creativity cannot be fully explained by a relatively mundane factor like the number of free hours that suddenly became available to Freud. Another more profound psychological process was also at work. Though it was not as severe as the depression he suffered following his father's death, "Freud's realization of the realities of the war," Schimmel argues, "did, in fact, precipitate a depressive state of mind and a significant experience of mourning" during its opening phases.[44] On 11 December 1914, for example, Freud wrote to Abraham:

After some nice results, my own works plunged into deep darkness; I go on because one cannot remain without "something to do" (*que haceres*, as the Spanish say), but often without enthusiasm and with only a slight expectation of solving the very difficult problems.[45]

In the same letter, Freud reports suffering somatic symptoms – "I am tormented by my own particular intestine" – as he had during his depressive

[42] Homans, *The ability to mourn*, 196.
[43] Jones, *Freud* II, 431.
[44] Schimmel, *Sigmund Freud's discovery of psychoanalysis*, 132.
[45] Falzeder (ed.), *Correspondence of Freud and Abraham*, 228.

episodes in the nineties.[46] Just as Jacob's death threw Freud into a depression and initiated the process of mourning that led to the composition of *The interpretation of dreams*, so the war, by shattering many of Freud's illusions and defensive idealizations, precipitated a process of mourning, which, according to Schimmel, resulted in a major reworking of his inner world and theoretical perspective.[47] The decline in patient hours itself may have created the "space" in which Freud was forced to experience his depression without the external distraction that work often provides from one's psychic pain. Schimmel contends that "Mourning and melancholia" – which, it is important to point out, is a companion piece to "On narcissism" – was the most important work Freud produced during this period, and he even claims that it rivals *The interpretation of dreams* in importance. Whether or not that claim is true, it cannot be denied that analysts have increasingly come to appreciate the importance of that paper in recent years.

Freud's Wartime Triptych

"Mourning and melancholia" comprises one panel of Freud's "wartime triptych," as Ricoeur has called it, the other two panels being "On transience" and "Thoughts for the times on war and death." In these three interrelated texts, which involve a sustained reflection on loss, mourning, and the opposition between pleasure and reality, Freud's thinking deepened substantially, assumed a more tragic hue, and became more directly philosophical. As part of that process, the reality principle was transformed, Ricoeur observes, from "a principle of 'mental regulation'" into "the cypher of a possible wisdom . . . beyond illusion and consolation."[48] The transformation resulted, in large part, from death's move to the center of Freud's conception of human reality.

Prior to the triptych, Freud's conceptualization of reality had been more or less pragmatic and commonsensical; it corresponded to reality as both the man in the street and the psychiatrist understand it, which is more or less the same understanding. It referred to perceptual reality

[46] *Ibid.*, 228.

[47] See Schimmel, *Sigmund Freud's discovery of psychoanalysis*, 128–133.

[48] Ricoeur, *Freud and philosophy*, 262 and 325.

testing and was simply taken as the opposite of the hallucination (or the dream.) Reality, in other words, was what remains when perceptions are shorn of hallucinatory distortions.[49] As we saw, moreover, reality and pain were located on separate axes but could coincide. Reality, in other words, *could be* but *was not necessarily* painful.

With the wartime triptych, this changed. When Freud now argued that transience and loss were constitutive of human reality, it acquired the attribute of intrinsic "harshness," which is to say, it became "harsh reality." And the acceptance of the reality principle or wisdom now consisted in "resignation to the inexorable order of nature" – resignation to what Freud calls necessity or *Atropos* – the inexorable or ineluctable.[50] Ricoeur believes that Freud's adoption of these Greek terms is a sign that his thinking has moved away from psychiatry, taken a philosophical turn, and entered a tragic register.

But "resignation to the ineluctable" is no easy task, for it is opposed by our intractable narcissism and need for consolation, which seek systematically to deny the harshness of reality in order to protect our vulnerable self-esteem, thereby presenting formidable obstacles to the fulfillment of Freud's program of disillusionment. "Resignation," Ricoeur argues, "is an affective task, a work of correction applied to the very core of the libido, to the heart of narcissism." And in a statement that flies in the face of all claims that passion and knowledge, affect and reason, must be separated, Ricoeur also writes, "consequently, the scientific world view must be incorporated into a history of desire."[51]

"Mourning and melancholia" is the most clinical of the three texts of the triptych, but its implications extend far beyond the consulting room. In that paper, Freud sets out to determine the specific nature of a pathological phenomenon – namely, melancholia – by comparing it to the normal phenomenon of mourning in order to identify the *specifica differentia* that separates them. And he uses his "model of the amoeba" to elucidate both processes. Just as the amoeba withdraws its pseudopod when it encounters a painful stimulus in its environment, so in both cases a person withdraws his or her investment in an object when confronted

---

[49] See *ibid.*, 262–263.

[50] *Ibid.*, 328.

[51] *Ibid.*, 332.

with loss. Mourning and melancholia are, as Freud puts it, both reactions to loss – loss "of a loved person, or the loss of some abstraction which has taken the place of one, such as one's country, liberty, an ideal and so on."[52] Furthermore, with one decisive exception, mourning and melancholia exhibit

the same painful frame of mind, the same loss of interest in the outside world . . . the same loss of capacity to adopt any new object of love (which would mean replacing him) and the same turning away from any activity that is not connected with thoughts of him.[53]

"This inhibition and circumscription of the ego," Freud argues, "is the expression of an exclusive devotion to mourning which leaves nothing over for other purposes or other interests."[54]

This, however, is where the similarities between the two phenomena end and the differences begin to appear. In "normal grieving," which is a long and painful process, mourners repeatedly summon up images of the lost object and "bit by bit" withdraw their psychic investment from it until reality testing triumphs and they accept the reality of the loss. The process is *emancipatory*, for when the work of mourning has adequately run its natural course, the libido that had been withdrawn from the object is freed to be reinvested in new objects – that is, to be reinvested in the world. Though drawn out and "extraordinarily painful," successful mourning runs its course and comes to a natural end.[55]

By contrast, two features of melancholy, which represents a failure of mourning, distinguish it from the normal process: It does not come to an end, and it is characterized by violent "self-reproaches." In Freud's primary argument, the second feature explains the first. "The melancholic," he writes, "displays something . . . lacking in mourning – an extraordinary diminution of his self-regard, and impoverishment of his ego on

---

[52] Freud, "Mourning and melancholia," 243.

[53] *Ibid.*, 244.

[54] *Ibid.*, 244.

[55] For Freud, the mourning process constitutes "a great riddle": "Why it is that this detachment of libido from its objects should be such a painful process is a mystery to us and we have not hitherto been able to frame any hypothesis to account for it." Sigmund Freud, "On transience" (1916), *SE* 14: 306.

a grand scale."[56] There is, moreover, something puzzling about these self-reproaches, for "the most violent of them are hardly at all applicable to the patient himself." However, "if one listens patiently to a melancholic's self-accusations," according to Freud, it becomes apparent "that with insignificant modifications they do fit someone else"– namely, the lost object. The melancholic's "self-reproaches," therefore, "are reproaches against a [lost] love object which have been shifted away from it on to the patient's own ego." When melancholics withdraw their libido in the face of loss, according to Freud, they internalize "the abandoned object," and establish an "*identification*" with it in their ego.[57] The problem that causes the mourning process to go awry is this: Prior to the internalization, the melancholic's attitude toward the object had been *ambivalent*, which means that an ambivalent – hated – object is now lodged like a pathogen in the person's ego. This in turn results in a split in the psyche, in which "one part of the ego," which Freud calls "conscience," "sets itself over against the other" – namely, over against the portion of the ego comprising the internalized object – and "judges it critically."[58] The critical agency's attacks on the (internalized) hated object are manifested in the melancholic's lacerating self-reproaches. When melancholics are attacking themselves, they are in fact attacking "the forsaken object" that they have internalized. In sum, "object loss was transformed into an ego-loss and conflict between the ego and the loved person into a cleavage between the critical activity of the ego and the ego as alerted by identification." As Freud puts it in one of his most famous formulations, "The shadow of the object fell on the ego."[59]

Freud's main thesis is this: Unless melancholics are able to identify the true (unconscious) object of their anger, these intrapsychic conflicts tend to be interminable, thus explaining why, as opposed to mourning, melancholia does not naturally run its course. Indeed, one of the great paradoxical discoveries of psychoanalysis is that we can more easily work through the loss of someone we loved well than someone to whom we were ambivalently attached.

---

[56] Freud, "Mourning and melancholia," 246.

[57] *Ibid.*, 249.

[58] *Ibid.*, 247.

[59] *Ibid.*, 249.

As we noted in Chapter 6, there is another layer to Freud's argument in "Mourning and melancholia." Melancholy, he argues, is a narcissistic disorder, and the extent to which individuals retain their libido and keep it invested in themselves – the extent to which, so to speak, the amoeba's energy remains invested in its body – is often correlated with their predisposition to melancholia. At the same time that melancholics are strongly (but ambivalently) fixated on their "love objects," their object choices have been made, according to Freud, on a "narcissistic basis," which means that their ties to the object are precarious. Consequently, "when obstacles come into" the object investments, melancholics tend to withdraw their pseudopodia, retreat to a narcissistic stance, and internalize the object. "The narcissistic identification with the [lost] object," Freud asserts, "becomes the substitute for the [former] object cathexis." Despite "the conflict with the loved person" – which reappears in the hostile relation between the critical agency and the ego – and despite the "incredible pain" arising from the attacks of the critical agency, melancholia has one powerful advantage: "The love object need not be given up."[60] In their refusal to mourn, melancholics strike an "unconscious 'deal with the devil'":[61] They are prepared to accept the debilitating anguish of their affliction in exchange for avoiding what they consider the greater pain of relinquishing the object. *The refusal to mourn is the refusal to accept the reality of loss and has consequences for the person's acceptance of reality as such.*

In his elegiac "On transience," a non-technical paper and one of his most glorious pieces of writing, Freud extrapolates broader philosophical conclusions from the clinical analysis of "Mourning and melancholia." As his position deepened philosophically, Freud came to view transience and thereby loss as essential constituents of human reality. From a philosophical perspective, the views he developed on these topics – as well as on mourning – were responses to "the loss of meaning" that accompanied the disenchantment of the world. The question that had to be addressed was this: What are we to make of the fact that when disenchantment stripped purpose and meaning from the world as a whole, it divested human existence of meaning at the same time? It would seem that Freud, a virtuoso

---

[60] *Ibid.*, 249.

[61] Ogden, "A new reading of object relations theory," 773.

of sardonic humor, had Hamlet in mind when he formulated the situation in a letter to Marie Bonaparte:

The moment a man questions the meaning and value of life, he is sick, *since objectively neither has any existence*; by asking this question one is merely admitting to a store of unsatisfied libido to which something else must have happened, a kind of fermentation leading to sadness and depression. I have an advertisement floating about in my head which I consider the boldest and most successful piece of American publicity: "Why live, if you can be buried for ten dollars?"[62]

According to Freud, the meaning of life is no longer a philosophical problem, for philosophically it has been solved – or dissolved: The world is disenchanted, and life is meaningless. It is a practical problem concerning the creation of meaning through the investment of libido. That is, given that the world is "objectively" meaninglessness – given that the workings of the rest of the universe are not aligned with the wishes arising from human nature – how should individuals deploy their libido if they are not to succumb to depression, and despair? And this question is closely related to Homan's claim, namely, that disenchantment and disillusionment can lead to emancipation and human fulfillment rather than to nihilism. The most desirable response to disenchantment, as Freud sees it, is that we become disillusioned – that is, resigned to disenchantment – and learn to invest to the fullest in the world despite its lack of objective meaning and the ubiquity of loss.[63] (Another possible response is to attempt to "re-enchant" the world, as Jung did.) And a practical task follows from this conclusion: If a fulfilled life consists in maximizing one's investment in a meaningless world, and if human experience is permeated by loss, then "the ability to mourn" – that is, *the ability to work through loss in order to invest* – is a precondition for achieving fulfillment.

The occasion for which "On transience" was written, von Unwerth suggests, tells us much about the work.[64] In 1915, Freud was invited to contribute to a volume entitled *Das Land Goethes* (*Goethe's Land*) that was meant to raise money for German libraries and, by celebrating the

---

[62] *The letters of Sigmund Freud*, ed. Ernst L. Freud, 436–437 (emphasis added).

[63] In this respect, Freud is fully in accord with the subjectivist orientation that dominated modern philosophy from Descartes to Kant: Meaning is entirely on the side of the subject.

[64] See Von Unwerth, *Freud's requiem*, 8–9.

nation's greatest humanist, to combat the wartime charge that Germany
was a barbaric nation. The list of contributors – which included Albert
Einstein, Hugo von Hofmannsthal, Arthur Schnitzler, Max Reger,
Richard Strauss, and more than a hundred distinguished figures from the
worlds of literature, science, politics, and the fine arts – was stellar. And
the volume's "lavish production" – its expensive reproductions of art-
works, manuscripts, and autographs, not to mention the large sheets on
which it was printed and its yellow silk binding – befitted the eminence
of its contributors.[65]

In light of Freud's esteem for Goethe, it was an offer that would have
been difficult to refuse:

Freud admired not only Goethe's creativity and his prolific achievements, but
also his personality, which, like his own, was that of a bourgeois gentleman –
learned, generous, humble, honest, and perhaps above all, forbearing in the face
of adversity. Throughout his life, in youth as in maturity, Freud looked to Goethe
as a model.[66]

As a star *Gymnasiast*, Freud had the classics at his fingertips – the ancient
Greeks, the Bible, Shakespeare, Leonardo, and Schiller – and could cite
them with ease. But as von Unwerth informs us, "the work cited more
than any other, to which Freud returns again and again for advice and
insight, was Goethe's *Faust*."[67] Years later, in 1930, Freud was awarded
Frankfurt's Goethe Prize, and, along with becoming a member of the
Royal Society, he viewed this as one of his most treasured honors. It is
therefore fitting, as von Unwerth also notes, that for this 1915 essay celebrating Germany's greatest *Dichter*, Freud chose the title from Goethe
himself. That title, "On transience" is in fact taken from the final lines of
Faust, Part II:

All transience
Is only a likeness;
The inadequate
Becomes event;
The indescribable is here realized;

---

[65] See *ibid.*, 8.
[66] *Ibid.*, 93.
[67] *Ibid.*, 92.

The Eternal Womanly
draws us onward.[68]

"These lines," von Unwerth observes, "are ambiguous in German, and almost nonsensical in translation," but for our purposes, two things can nevertheless be said about them.[69]

First, for both Goethe and Freud, "transience," *Vergänglichkeit*, is the "name for the human condition" insofar as it is "marked by time-boundedness and impermanence." Its adjectival form, *vergänglich*, according to von Unwerth, "recalls the word for 'mortal,' *sterblich*, which means literally 'like death' or 'having death.'"[70] The timing is also surely significant, for in 1915, the year in which Freud chose *Vergänglichkeit* as the title for his paper, his three sons and one son-in-law were serving in the Austrian army and the slaughter of the war was becoming fully apparent, thus making the fleetingness and – perhaps – the meaningless-ness of life difficult to ignore.

The second point to be made about these lines from *Faust* is this: While the meaning of *Das Ewig-Weibliche, the Eternal Womanly*, has been endlessly debated, to an analytically attuned ear the statement that "The Eternal Womanly/ draws us onward" resonates with Freud's theory of the ego ideal (and with his analysis in "The theme of the three caskets," to be addressed in the next chapter). In "On narcissism," we will recall, Freud argues that the ego ideal is the heir to primary narcissism. When the perfection that we experience as infants in our merged state with the symbiotic mother breaks down, as inevitably it must, we project it ahead of us and pursue it in various forms – life-enhancing as well as destructive forms – throughout our lives. In this respect, one can say that

---

[68] *Ibid.*, 97 (translation altered). The original German:

Alles Vergängliche
Ist nur ein Gleichnis;
Das Unzulängliche,
Hier wird's Ereignis;
Das Unbeschreibliche,
Hier ist's getan;
Das Ewig-Weibliche
Zieht uns hinan.

[69] *Ibid.*, 97.

[70] *Ibid.*, 99.

"The Eternal Womanly," understood as the perfection of the symbiotic mother projected into the future, continually "draws us onward."

The literary conceit Freud uses in the essay is to present his ideas about transience by describing an idyllic "summer walk" he had supposedly taken "through a smiling countryside in the company of a taciturn friend and of a young but already famous poet." Whether this walk actually occurred is an open question, but in any case, the poet's supposed inability to enjoy "the beauty of the scene around him" provides the point of departure for Freud's reflections on the topic:[71]

[The poet] was disturbed by the thought that all this beauty was fated to extinction, that it would vanish when winter came, like all human beauty and all the beauty and splendor that men have created or may create. All that he would otherwise have loved and admired seemed to him to be shorn of its worth by transience which was its doom.[72]

For some peculiar reason, Freud does not recognize that the two responses to transience that he is about to distinguish amount to the same thing – namely, the attempt to deny loss. The first response is the poet's state of "aching despondency," and the second consists in "rebellion against the fact asserted" described in the following passage:

No! It is impossible that all this liveliness of Nature and Art, of the world of our sensations and of the world outside, will really fade away into nothing. It would be too senseless and too presumptuous to believe it. Somehow or other this loveliness must be able to persist and to escape all the powers of destruction.[73]

But, as we will see, Freud asserts that the poet's attitude comprises a refusal to mourn, and that refusal itself constitutes a rebellion against the reality of transience and loss.

Evoking his principle that pleasure and reality are located on independent axes, Freud argues that "the demand for immortality is a product of

---

[71] Freud, "On transience," 305. Though Freud might have embellished the story by transposing it to a bucolic summer setting, von Unwerth plausibly argues that the conversation recounted in the paper refers to a dialogue that had in fact taken place in Munich, where Rainer Maria Rilke and Lou Andreas-Salomé were his interlocutors. Von Unwerth, *Freud's requiem*, 1–2.

[72] Freud, "On transience," 305.

[73] *Ibid.*, 305.

our wishes" that is motivated by the pleasure principle and therefore has no purchase in reality. He restates his claim that "what is painful" in this case, the loss he is describing, "may nonetheless be true."

But Freud's own position on the subject has an inauthentic ring. He cannot, he tells us, deny "the transience of all things," but he disputes "the pessimistic poet's view that the transience of what is beautiful involves any loss in its worth." Instead, he heroically declares: "On the contrary, an increase! Transience value is scarcity in time. Limitation in the possibility of an enjoyment raises the value of enjoyment." The notion that limited access to the object enhances enjoyment may be a strategical maxim that a coquet can usefully subscribe to, but is it true? To be sure, the rareness of a love object – that it stands out from the rest of mundane existence – enhances its value. But to claim that the fact that its transience and potential loss increase its value is not self-evident. One senses that this is another instance in which Freud strikes a heroic counter-phobic posture to combat the reality of loss. Manically celebrating the value of transience rather than simply resigning oneself to it can be a way of denying the pain it entails.

Be that as it may, Freud's thesis regarding the poet's attitude is that it represents a "revolt . . . against mourning" – which means a "rebellion" against the inexorability of loss. "The idea that all this beauty was transient," he argues, "was giving [the poet] a foretaste of mourning over its decease." And "since the mind," like the amoeba, "instinctively recoils from anything that is painful," intimations of the pain of loss and mourning caused the poet to recoil from the beauty surrounding him and prevented him from enjoying it.[74] The poet lacked confidence in his ability to mourn – to tolerate the pain it involves. He therefore withdrew his libido from the beautiful landscape and could not invest in it when he experienced "a foretaste of mourning." Assessing his prospects on life's balance sheet of pleasure and pain, the poet concluded that he would achieve more pleasure in the long run if he followed a defensive strategy and withheld his libidinal assets instead of investing them in the world.

Freud contends, however, that this is a flawed calculation. Considered solely in terms of the calculus of the pleasure principle, he argues that a strategy of withholding one's "mental assets" in order to avoid pain in fact

[74] *Ibid.*, 306.

yields less gratification in the long run than a strategy of investing in life. The second strategy, however, presupposes the confidence in one's ability to mourn – to tolerate life's volatility, as it were.

As its title suggests, the third panel of the triptych, "Thoughts for the time on war and death," brings this line of reasoning to bear on the historical situation then current. This is a work in two essays, in each of which Freud sets out to disabuse the reader of an illusion in the name of the reality principle. *The brutality manifested in this work, however, far outstrips even the most stringent demands of the reality principle or of Freud's ethic of honesty.* One can agree to the proposition that "what is painful may none the less be true," but it does not follow that the truth must be delivered in brutal fashion.

One fact in particular helps to explain the brutality. Freud presented an early version of the second essay, the more brutal of the two, as a lecture to the B'nai B'rith on the day that his son Martin had gone off to the army. We can reasonably speculate that Freud's attempt "heroically" – which is to say brutally – to confront the truth represented his way of coping with the pain that Martin's departure was surely causing him.

In the first essay, Freud suggests that the disillusionment brought about by the First World War was greater than that of all previous wars – partly because of the heightened expectations for humanity that nineteenth-century Europe, with its faith in progress, had engendered in its citizens. Freud provides a comprehensive catalogue of the unanticipated features of that war that were causing massive disillusionment among good Europeans: The unprecedented slaughter resulting from mechanized warfare; the new phenomenon of total war that did not spare non-combatants; the fact that "the great world-dominating nations of the white race" were behaving as barbarically toward each other as they did toward their "uncivilized" colonies;[75] the failure to respect the humanitarian regulations protecting the injured and the doctors, nurses, and ambulance drivers who cared for them; the retreat from European cosmopolitanism to jingoistic nationalism; the systematic use of propaganda and imposition of censorship;[76] the unprincipled behavior of intellectuals,

---

[75] Sigmund Freud, "Thoughts for the time on war and death" (1915), *SE* 14: 276.

[76] Ironically, Freud's nephew Edward Bernays, whose family had moved from Vienna to New York, was recruited by Woodrow Wilson to help develop America's propaganda campaign. After the war, Bernays, who can be seen as the first "spin *Meister*,"

academics, and scientists; and the destruction of Europe's rich and variegated landscape, to name a few.

"Well may the citizen of the civilized world stand helpless," Freud writes, "in a world that has grown strange to him – his fatherland disintegrated, its common estates laid waste, his fellow citizens divided and debased." But, he continues, "there is something to be said . . . in criticism of his disappointment," for "strictly speaking," the disappointment "is not justified" in that it "consists in the destruction of" illusory expectations of civilized Europeans. "We welcome illusions," Freud continues, "because they spare us unpleasurable feelings, and enable us to enjoy satisfaction instead." So in conclusion, "we must not complain . . . if now and again they come into collision with some portion of reality and are shattered against."[77]

The phrases "now and again" and "some portion of reality" are downright peculiar and inappropriate given the magnitude of the disillusionment accompanying the Great War. Moreover, the equanimity Freud seeks to convey with these phrases is the flipside of the heroic stance he strikes in other passages. One admires Freud's effort to look reality directly in the face; nevertheless, as there was with his "sanguine" claims about having mastered his homosexuality, there is something unconvincing about the sense of mastery he seeks to communicate in these passages.

Freud makes his case with a straightforward psychoanalytic argument. The nineteenth century's belief in civilization and progress had given rise to the illusory notion that evil had been eradicated from human nature.[78] But, he argues,

in reality, there is no such thing as "evil." Psychological – or, more strictly speaking, psycho-analytic – investigation shows instead that the deepest essence of human nature consists of instinctual impulses, which are of an elementary nature,

---

achieved enormous success and power by hijacking his uncle's insights and creating the new field of public relations. Freud struggled against the power of suggestion throughout his entire career, and the idea of manipulating the public through the discoveries of psychoanalysis contradicted everything he stood for.

[77] *Ibid.*, 280.

[78] In conjunction with the American triumphalism that followed the collapse of the Soviet Union, the idea that evil had been overcome also began to circulate in the United States. But it was quickly shattered by the events in Bosnia and Rwanda and by the attack of September 11, 2001.

which are similar in all men and which aim at the satisfaction of certain primal needs.[79]

This claim should not be mistaken for an affirmation of the notion of original sin. For, Freud argues, "these impulses in themselves are neither good nor bad," and their consequences are determined by the particular social condition in which they happen to be embedded. According to Freud, "the extraordinary plasticity of mental development is not unrestricted as regards direction."[80] On the one hand, the mutability of human nature accounts for our "susceptibility to culture" and explains how the constructive sublimation of our instinctual inheritance is possible in the proper socio-historical circumstances.[81] But on the other hand, these primitive impulses are never eliminated and always remain latent regardless of the level of "progress." Consequently, regression is always a possibility, and those instinctual impulses can reassert themselves under particular social circumstances. (As Monty Python observed, the Inquisition can return at any moment.) This is what happened with the First World War. The tomfoolery of Europe's thoroughly interconnected ruling class and the imbecility of its generals produced a concatenation of forces that precipitated massive collective regression, unprecedented in its magnitude. The lesson of Freud's analysis is not that human beings are inherently either good or evil. It is rather that every effort should be made to create the social conditions that obviate the type of regression that occurred after an Austrian crown prince was assassinated in Sarajevo.

Freud is even more scandalous in the second essay of "Thoughts," where he seeks to shatter our illusions about death, than he was in the first. Indeed, he makes an assertion that, as Ricoeur observes, would have been "odious" in the Vienna of 1915 when a sizeable portion of its sons were engaged at the Front.[82] With the war, he asserts, "life has become interesting again; it has recovered its full content." Life has been reinvigorated, he argues, because "death will no longer be denied," as it generally is in our "normal" attitude. "Now we are forced to believe

[79] Freud, "Thoughts for the time on war and death," 281.

[80] *Ibid.*, 285.

[81] *Ibid.*, 283.

[82] Ricoeur, *Freud and philosophy*, 329.

in it. People really die, and no longer one by one, but many, often tens of thousands."[83] Freud explains this brutal assertion with the following argument:

But this [normal] attitude of ours towards death has a powerful effect on our lives. Life is impoverished, it loses its interest when the highest stake in the game of living, life itself, may not be asked. It becomes . . . shallow and empty.[84]

With a heroic flare that might cause the reader some embarrassment, the self-proclaimed conquistador cites a historical example to illustrate the claim that "the tendency to exclude death from our calculations in life brings in its train many other renunciations and exclusions" that impoverish life. Against this tendency to deny death, he asserts "the motto of the Hanseatic League: 'It is necessary to sail the seas, it is not necessary to live.'"[85]

But Freud also offers another example that is more down-to-earth and intimate, and that helps us better understand what he is getting at behind the brutality and heroic posturing. He contrasts the superficiality of "an American flirtation, in which it is understood from the first that nothing emotionally consequential is to happen," to "a Continental love affair in which both partners must constantly bear its serious consequences in mind."[86] Both partners enter a Continental affair with a minimum of illusions, that is, with their eyes wide open, fully cognizant of the risk of loss and of the psychological anguish it might entail. But they enter it nevertheless because of the promise of richness and depth it offers. In an American flirtation, by contrast, the partners maintain the relationship on a superficial plane to avoid the risk involved in a deep investment, but at the same time they preclude its potential rewards. Like the young poet, by hedging their bets, they diminish their prospects of fulfillment. In light of this example, we can interpret Freud's assertion that life is impoverished to the extent that we "exclude death from our calculations." Death is the primary instantiation of transience and loss – of *Ananke* – that an individual encounters in life. And as Freud argues throughout the triptych,

[83] Freud, "Thoughts for the time on war and death," 291.

[84] *Ibid.*, 290.

[85] *Ibid.*, 291.

[86] *Ibid.*, 290.

the attempt to escape the reality of loss by refusing to invest in the world results in the impoverishment of life. Freud criticizes illusion not primarily in the name of some abstract notion of truth but in practical terms. "To tolerate life," he asserts, "remains the first duty of all living beings," and "illusion becomes valueless if it makes this harder for us." He thus offers the following maxim, "If you want to endure life, prepare yourself for death," which can be reformulated as, "If you not only want to endure life but also to enhance it, prepare yourself for loss and mourning."[87]

[87] *Ibid.*, 299–300.

11

Making Sense of the Death Instinct

W ITH THE END OF the First World War, Freud entered the third and
final phase of his career. The hostilities had ceased, yet the experience of loss and the confrontation with death that began with Jung's
departure and continued with the devastation of the war did not abate;
it only intensified. Furthermore, after 1918, the ravages of Fate struck
closer to home.

The split with Jung, however intense Freud's relationship with him
might have been, had constituted the loss of a colleague. Likewise, while
the very scale and consequences of the war constituted a traumatic blow
to Freud's sense of himself and of the world, and while the material hardship in Vienna had been severe, no one in his immediate world died as a
result of combat. Then, however, as Gay observes, "Freud was forced to
confront more than once what he had been almost wholly spared during
the war – mortality."[1] As the last two decades of his life unfolded, not
only did the topic of death assume an increasingly central position in his
thinking, but death as a reality came to dominate his personal existence
with a mercilessness that is difficult to imagine.[2]

Earlier, as we have seen, the topic of death had played a critical role
in the analysis of magic and the omnipotence of thoughts in *Totem and
taboo*. And in the wartime triptych, Freud laid the groundwork for his
later more fully achieved formulations on the subject. In the 1920s, he
took up the elements that had been present in the earlier analyses and
systematically elaborated them into his "scientific" worldview, with its

---

[1] Gay, *Freud: a life for our time*, 390.

[2] See Schur, *Freud*, Part III, and Mark Edmundson, *The death of Sigmund Freud: the
legacy of his last days* (New York: Bloomsbury, 2007).

truth ethic and aspiration to achieve "a wisdom beyond illusion and con-solation."[3] In addition to the theory of anthropological helplessness, the interpretation of death as the primary instantiation of *Ananke* served as a foundation stone for his new theoretical construction.

At the same time that he was reflecting on the significance of *thanatos* as a metapsychological problem, death in all its elemental creatureliness also inserted itself into Freud's life in a thoroughly untheoretical way. In a misguided attempt to protect the scientific purity of his theories and fore-stall any reductionist explanation of them, the "Kantian" Freud and some of his followers denied that his extended combat with illness and death had anything to do with his theoretical formulations. But this is simply implausible. How could they not?[4] Indeed, as with Socrates, the way Freud handled his death is integral to his philosophy and personal *ethos*: where the Greek philosopher voluntarily drank the hemlock, Freud had Max Schur inject him with 21 milliliters of morphine when it had become "meaningless" to continue his life. Perhaps this fact helps us understand Freud's rather perplexing assertion that "the organism wishes to die only in its own fashion."[5]

---

[3] Ricoeur, *Freud and philosophy*, 310.

[4] See footnote 21 below.

[5] Sigmund Freud, *Beyond the pleasure principle* (1920), *SE* 18: 39. Along with von Unwerth's *Freud's requiem*, Mark Edmundson's *The death of Sigmund Freud* is one of the finest studies of the founder of psychoanalysis to appear in recent years. Using straightforward non-technical language, Edmundson presents a complex and even-handed portrait of the man that – with the exception of W.H. Auden – "gets" what Freud was all about perhaps more than any author who has written about him. But an element of ambivalence breaks through in Edmundson's interpretation of Freud's assisted suicide, causing him to misinterpret the meaning of the act: "By dying as he did, Freud increased the length and breadth of the authoritative shadow that he would cast forward into time. He died in a way that would enhance his reputation as a leader, that would engender people's loyalty over the years, that would move them in the way that kings' and potentates' passing can do, move them with the majestic sense that here was a man who was more than a man. This was someone worth believing in with fervor and worth following into the future. Freud wanted to create belief and adher-ence down through the time, and – though it is not entirely tasteful to say as much – he arranged his death in such a way as to help him do exactly that." Edmundson, *The death of Sigmund Freud*, 229. Granted, Freud did not always live up to his ideals, but at his best he was committed to an ethic of maturity and autonomy, which strove to overcome omnipotence and grandiosity while coming to terms with human finitude.

Ananke at its Cruelest

Fate's first victim was Freud's Hungarian friend, colleague, and benefactor Anton von Freund, who had done much to support him personally and psychoanalysis as a movement. When Toni, as he was called, finally succumbed in January 1920, after a long and agonizing illness, Freud wrote to his colleague Max Eitingon, "He bore his hopelessness with heroic clarity, did not disgrace analysis."[6] That is, "he died," as Gay observes, "as Freud's father had died" – let us recall the beautiful letter Freud wrote to Fliess on the occasion of Jacob's death – "and as he himself hoped to die."[7]

When Freud observes that von Freund "did not disgrace psychoanalysis," it tells us something about the way he viewed the field that he had created beyond the mere fact that it was a "medical" profession. Freud sometimes referred to psychoanalysis as a *Bewegung* (movement), a term that is fraught with difficulties. Approaching analysis as a political movement on a par with Marxism, for example, has led to many of the unappetizing pathologies that have plagued the International Psychoanalytic Association and its affiliates throughout their history: bureaucratization, authoritarianism, exclusionism, and sectarian infighting.[8] But it

---

He detested royalty, and wanted not only to eliminate the magical aura that surrounds kings and potentates, but also to reduce omnipotence in our personal lives. Let us recall, Freud praised Leonardo, with whom he obviously identified, for casting off the authority of tradition and thinking for himself. Freud may have wanted his death to influence his followers, but it is mistaken to compare it to the grandiose pomposity of a royal funeral. It was meant to encourage those who subscribed to the analytic *ethos* to pursue their maturity and autonomy. The way Freud took his life, in other words, can be viewed as an exemplary act in which he sought to demonstrate his acceptance of finitude and adherence to the psychoanalytic *ethos* in order to encourage his followers to pursue their own autonomy after he left them. However, there may a paradox involved in Freud's suicide that Edmundson is getting at. As we will see, Freud's program that exhorts us to eschew our omnipotence and occupy the place of the merely human – to accept our situation as "simple shareholders on earth" – may itself be "more than human." The resurgence of religion and retreat from secularism in recent decades may be evidence that this is true.

[6] Quoted in Gay, *Freud: a life for our time*, 391.

[7] *Ibid.*, 391.

[8] Granted, the world is not a nursery and "trained ruthlessness" is, as Weber observed, often necessary to accomplish something in it, but Freud's instrumentalism at times approached Leninist proportions.

is perhaps more useful to understand what Freud was aiming at, a vocation or calling, a *Berufung*. Although it has often only been honored in the breach, that calling involved a demanding *ethos*, which transcended any calculus of political power and devoted itself to the things for their own sake. And that *ethos* served to unite its early adherents in a shared esprit de corps. As his comment to Eitingon indicates, Freud saw the question of how a person comes to grips with his or her death as central to that *ethos*.

Because Von Freund's death was a drawn-out process, it did not come as a shock and allowed Freud time to assimilate the event – to the extent that such assimilation is possible. But what followed occurred with a rapidity that was staggering. The next death was sudden and unexpected. On 22 January 1920, in fact the very day von Freund was buried, Freud received a telegram from his son-in-law Max Halberstadt in Hamburg informing him that his favorite daughter Sophie – "dear blooming Sophie," as Freud called her in a letter to Amalie – had contracted the deadly Spanish influenza that was sweeping through Europe in the aftermath of the war.[9] Not only was Sophie beautiful, but in Freud's eyes his twenty-six-year-old daughter was an exemplary wife and mother of two boys, one six and the other thirteen months. On top of that, she had been pregnant with her third child at the time of her death, which occurred four days after Freud had received word of her illness. "The news," Jones observes, "was a thunderbolt from a clear sky."[10]

Freud was then granted a reprieve of three years. But when Fate struck again, it was with unmitigated cruelty and twice. In April 1923, the year he published *The ego and the id*, he was diagnosed with the cancer that would be his constant adversary for the next sixteen years. Then, in June, Freud lost his favorite grandchild, Sophie's youngest son Heinele, to miliary tuberculosis. This may have been the most consequential loss of all. Freud was surprised by the unexpected intensity of his attachment to the boy, whose "advanced" intelligence would obviously have been a delight to his grandfather. "He was indeed an enchanting fellow," Freud wrote to two close colleagues in Budapest, "and I myself know that I

[9] Quoted in *ibid.*, 391.
[10] Ernest Jones, *The life and work of Sigmund Freud*, vol. III, *1919–1939, the last phase* (New York: Basic Books, 1957), 57.

have hardly ever loved a human being, certainly never a child, so much as him."[11] This was "*Ananke* at its cruelest," as Schur observes, and the ordeal – which was the only time Freud was seen to cry – tested his stoical resolve to the utmost.[12]

Perhaps because it had occurred immediately after the war, in an environment in which one was each day forced to steel oneself against bad news and had therefore already become "resigned to what fate had in store," not even the death of Sophie had caused Freud the agony he experienced when Heinerle died.[13] After the boy's death, he entered a period of profound mourning and dejection the likes of which he had never experienced before, although it conformed to the classical description he had given of melancholia. Almost all his psychic energy was directed at the lost object: He described himself as "obsessed by impotent longing for the dear child" and with nothing to invest in the world.[14] "Fundamentally," he wrote, "everything has lost its meaning for me."[15] Freud also felt that something had been killed in him and that he would never be able to invest in life again. He told his old friend Oscar Rie that Heinerle had "meant the future to [him] and thus has taken the future away with him."[16] And it is undoubtedly true that one never entirely recovers from a loss of this magnitude and that the death of his grandson must have introduced a cleavage in Freud's life that altered his view of the world.

But these sentiments did not represent the final word on the subject. As Schur observes, they were in part the expression of Freud's "old depression, grief and mourning," which had been "revived by the loss of his grandson." It would be difficult, Schur goes on, for "anyone who knew Freud closely during the subsequent years" to take those feelings "at face value." Freud not only maintained his old attachments and continued to make a monumental investment in his work, but he formed new ones as well. The point is that "Freud would not have survived without them."

[11] Quoted in Gay, *Freud: a life for our time*, 421.

[12] Schur, *Freud: living and dying*, 359.

[13] Gerhard Fichtner (ed.), *The Sigmund Freud – Ludwig Binswanger Correspondence, 1908–1938*, trans. Arnold J. Pomerans (New York: Other Press, 2003), 184.

[14] Quoted in Gay, *Freud: a life for our time*, 422.

[15] Quoted in Schur, *Freud: living and dying*, 358.

[16] Quoted in Gay, *Freud: a life for our time*, 422.

His "unbelievable resilience," however, cannot only be accounted for in terms of his "ego strength," prodigious as it was. Of equal importance was the fact that, as Homans noted, he was a "good mourner," and "his strength was fed constantly by his ability to love and to give."[17]

Considering the enormity of these blows, Freud's ability to recover was remarkable. Indeed, it was even somewhat unsettling, as he partially acknowledges, when he compares his suffering to that of Martha and Anna, who were "severely shaken in a more human sense" than he was.[18] His personal solution for contending with the abuses that Fate metes out to all of us – which allowed him to persevere in the face of this sudden onslaught of adversity and to endure the years of suffering that were to follow – consisted in two parts. The first was the resignation to *Ananke* – to "blunt necessity," as he put it in a letter to Eitingon.[19] Freud reaffirmed his stoical stance in a letter he wrote to Ferenczi in February 1920. He tells his concerned protégé that, as painful as Sophie's death was, it did not "overturn any attitude toward life" – that is, his disconsolate atheism. He remained lucid about the consequences of his position and accepted the fact that he had no right to protest his fortune: "Since I am profoundly unbelieving, I have no one to blame, and I know there is no place where one can lodge a complaint."[20]

We noted in the previous chapter, in addressing the question of Freud's heroism, that he recognized that his investment in the resignation to *Ananke* served a crucial psychological function, enabling him to contend with the ordeals to which he was subjected. And in *Beyond the pleasure principle* he considers the possibility that his theory of the death instinct and *Ananke* may in fact be a consoling illusion that allows us to "bear the burden of existence."[21] In the face of death, our own and the deaths of those we love, he argues, it might be "easier to submit to a remorseless law of nature, the sublime [*Ananke*], than to a chance which might perhaps have been escaped." But a reductionist explanation of his theory of *Ananke* does not constitute the final word for understanding Freud.

---

[17] Schur, *Freud: living and dying*, 360.

[18] Falzeder and Brabant (eds.), *Correspondence of Freud and Ferenczi*, vol. III, 6.

[19] Quoted in Jones, *Freud* III, 19.

[20] Falzeder and Brabant (eds.), *Correspondence of Freud and Ferenczi*, vol. III, 7.

[21] Freud, *Beyond the pleasure principle*, 45. The line is from Schiller.

Even if it is admitted that the theory owes its genesis to his need to overcome his sense of helplessness and provide him with consolation, he
insists that we must also "turn to biology in order to test [its] validity."[22]

In addition to his resignation to *Ananke* – Freud's capacity for mourning – the second arrow he had in his quiver for combating adversity was
to invest in the world through work. For him, *the proper response to the
meaninglessness of these two deaths – indeed, to the meaninglessness of death in
general – was work.* "Work and the free play of the imagination," he told
Pfister, "are for me the same thing, I take no pleasure in anything else."[23]
Harking back to his university years when the structure and orderliness of
Brücke's laboratory allowed Freud to contain his inner turmoil, he reas-
sured Ferenczi that the "eternally uniformly set clock of duty" (Schiller)
and the "friendly habit of being and acting!" (Goethe) would bring him
back to the world and allow him to continue with his projects.[24] These
citations from the classics notwithstanding, we begin to grow uneasy over
Freud's preternatural capacity for work when we read other remarks he
made to Ferenczi when apprising him of the details Sophie's death. They
have an almost dissociated quality to them. "My wife is very shaken," he
writes to the Hungarian analyst. "I think: *La séance continue*," which can
roughly be translated the work continues. "But," he continues, "it was a
bit much for one week."[25] A bit much indeed!

Yet, in two respects, it was work in the form of writing that constituted
Freud's way of coming to terms with Sophie's death; along with the act of
writing itself, he also grappled with her death in the content of the book he
was working on at the time, *Beyond the pleasure principle*. He thus attempted
to come to grips with the loss through the creation of meaning – a twofold process that involves the binding and shaping of psychic energy and

---

[22] *Ibid.*, 45. As we will see, the findings of biology in fact do not support the theory
of the death instinct as Freud conceived of it; in fact they tend to contradict it. Two
questions that are as important as they are difficult must be asked. The first is: How
do we distinguish between Freud's heroic resignation to *Ananke* as a manic defense
against the dread of helplessness and as the real accomplishments of a stoic sage? And
second, what is the relation between Freud's theory of the death instinct and *Ananke*
and its genesis in the contingent conditions of his psychic life?

[23] Meng and Freud (eds.), *Psychoanalysis and faith*, 34.

[24] Falzeder and Brabant (eds.), *Correspondence of Freud and Ferenczi*, vol. III, 7.

[25] *Ibid.*, 6.

symbolization. Just as our "primitive" ancestors, according to Freud, had posited the theory of spirits in an attempt to grapple with the phenomenon of death, so he postulated his theory of the death instinct – representing his effort to decipher the significance of death – in the work he wrote in response to the loss of his daughter. As we will see, *Beyond the pleasure principle* contains one of the most famous and most important discussions in Freud's entire oeuvre – namely, his addressing of the question of loss in his analysis of his grandson's "fort-da game." Where most adults would have seen little more than meaningless and perhaps irritating child's play, Freud's guileless curiosity allowed him to explore one of the most pressing questions confronting the human condition: How is it that we finite beings can tolerate the experience of loss?

Notwithstanding a few caveats, Freud evinced little hesitation in generalizing his personal strategy for dealing with the cruelty of fate and recommending it as a psychoanalytically formulated practical philosophy to the citizens of a disenchanted secular world. When we turn to Freud's theory of religion, however, it will be necessary to examine the following questions: Is this generalization valid? Or is the strategy of disconsolate resignation that Freud advances attainable only by "the few," that is, by those individuals uniquely endowed with his exceptional capacities? If the latter is the case, we must then ask what strategy is available for "the multitude," to use Spinoza's term, under conditions of a disenchanted secularized world. We will return to this problem in the next chapter.

Disavowal: That Peculiar State of Knowing and Not Knowing

In February 1923, three months before Heinerle's death, Freud began his struggle with cancer. It started when he discovered a growth in his mouth that turned out to be malignant. The development of his attitude toward his cancer followed a course that is not uncommon when one is facing a life-threatening illness. Through a long and ragged trajectory, it moved from disavowal to acceptance of the reality of the situation. The conflict in Freud's case, however, was more intense and complicated than in most. By this point in his life, he had fully articulated his so-called truth ethic, which centered on the repudiation of disavowal and the resignation to *Ananke*, and the pressure of this commitment made his struggle particularly dramatic. During the period under consideration, Freud wrote a letter to Romain Rolland, the French intellectual, musicologist, and political activist, whom he greatly admired in spite of disagreeing with his pronounced idealism and pacifist commitments. In the letter, it is clear that the question of facing reality was on Freud's mind. He contrasts himself to the Frenchman, who was dedicated to the idea of universal love – an idea that Freud describes as "the most precious illusion of mankind." As opposed to Rolland, however, he insists that he is committed to the destruction of all illusions, regardless of how "beautiful" they may be:

I, of course, belong to a race which in the Middle Ages was held responsible for all epidemics and which today is blamed for the disintegration of the Austrian Empire and the German defeat. Such experiences have a sobering effect and are not conducive to make one believe in illusions. A great part of my life's work . . . has been spent [trying to] destroy my own illusions and those of mankind.[26]

Yet, despite his principled stand against illusion – and despite the fact that he was a physician who inhabited the same world as a number of Europe's most eminent men of medicine – Freud as well as the doctors who treated him encountered enormous difficulty confronting his cancer without considerable "disavowal." In technical psychoanalytic terms, "disavowal" is not equivalent to "denial." With the latter, one simply refuses to register an unacceptable truth in its entirety. "Disavowal," on the other hand, involves splitting – a concept Freud also developed in his exploration of the question of reality during 1920s – that is, the puzzling situation of knowing-and-not-knowing something at the same time.

The fear that a doctor might order him to give up his beloved cigars, as Fliess had during the cardiac episode, combined with the more straightforward fear that the growth might indeed be malignant – in Schur's opinion, the first possibility "was much more threatening and unacceptable to Freud than surgery" – led Freud to procrastinate for two months before having the growth evaluated.[27] He also kept the news to himself, not informing his family or colleagues. And when he finally acted in the beginning of April of that year, 1923, he chose Maxim Steiner as the consultant, a close friend who, however, was not the best-qualified specialist for the job. This was part of a larger pattern in which Freud displayed a

---

[26] *The letters of Sigmund Freud*, ed. Ernst L. Freud, 341.

[27] Schur, *Freud: living and dying*, 350.

remarkably lackadaisical if not cavalier attitude toward his illness in its early phases.

By selecting a friend rather than an independent and expert consultant, Freud was perhaps at least unconsciously choosing someone who was less likely to be candid with him. And Steiner in fact proved incapable of leveling with his patient. Before the consultation, Freud himself had diagnosed the growth as "epithelioma," which meant it was a malignancy. In June, he informed Ferenczi that he had known it was cancer all along.[28] But three months earlier, his own estimation of the lesion was "not accepted" by Steiner, who offered the alternative diagnosis of "leukoplakia," a benign condition caused by smoking, and the part of Freud that needed to disavow the situation acquiesced and accepted his physician's judgment – at least for the moment.[29] "Now," Schur observes, "began a tragic chain of events which was to have far-reaching consequences."[30]

Only later that week, when Felix Deutsch, another friend and colleague, who was also Freud's personal internist, happened to visit him concerning other matters, Freud invited him to examine his mouth – warning Deutsch, "Be prepared to see something you won't like." And Deutsch was indeed shocked when he immediately recognized that he was observing an advanced stage of cancer. Yet, like Steiner, he offered Freud the less threatening diagnosis of a "bad leukoplakia," recommending, nevertheless, that the lesion be excised immediately. Hans Pichler, the director of the Vienna Surgical Clinic's Department of Oral Surgery – who later assumed responsibility for Freud's treatment and performed heroically over the course of fifteen years – was the obvious choice to perform the procedure. But again, Freud's conflicts concerning his illness led him to choose an inappropriate man, Markus Hajek, someone he had in fact openly disparaged in discussions with Deutsch. While Hajek was respected for his research and publications, he was considered "a somewhat mediocre surgeon." Moreover, Freud was convinced that Hajek harbored ambivalent feelings toward him. Nonetheless, he went ahead with the choice, and it resulted in something resembling "a grotesque nightmare."[31]

[28] Falzeder and Brabant (eds.), *Correspondence of Freud and Ferenczi*, vol. III.
[29] Paskausas (ed.), *Correspondence of Freud and Jones*, 521.
[30] Schur, *Freud: living and dying*, 350.
[31] *Ibid.*, 351.

The surgery was performed not in a private hospital but in Hajek's out-patient clinic. The facilities, as Schur, who later emigrated to the States, reports, "had no private wards" and "were as deficient" as the infamous "outpatient wards of the older New York City Hospitals." This meant that if serious complications developed, Hajek and his staff were not equipped to deal with them. Freud's family was not informed about the procedure, and – in an attempt to demonstrate that the situation was not particularly worrisome – Deutsch accompanied his patient to the hospital but did not stick around for the results, assuming that Freud would return home that day. But things did not go smoothly, and Freud experienced considerable bleeding during and after the surgery. Rather than transferring him, how-ever, to "the quite luxurious Löw Sanitarium" – the private hospital one block away where Emma Eckstein had been taken – Freud was deposited in the only space available, a tiny room with a cot, to recover.[32]

In a somewhat bizarre twist, a "cretinous" but kindly dwarf who was Freud's roommate in the cubicle probably saved his life.[33] When Freud started to hemorrhage profusely, he was unable, due to the hemorrhage, to call out for assistance. Compounding the situation, the bell for sum-moning the nurses was out of order. Luckily, the dwarf was there to run for help, and the bleeding was finally contained after considerable effort. When Martha and Anna received a phone call from out of the blue asking them to bring food and clothing to the hospital, they rushed to Freud's side, where they found him sitting in a kitchen chair, drugged and covered with blood. His daughter Anna rather than wife Martha remained at the clinic until Freud was discharged, thereby establishing the role she would play throughout his prolonged and grueling illness: She would be his pri-mary nurse-caregiver, the only person Freud would allow himself to be dependent upon. Evoking shades of Fliess's (and Freud's) mistreatment of Emma Eckstein, "Hajek showed no sign of contrition at his botched, nearly fatal performance."[34] On the contrary, "the next morning," he had the gall to demonstrate Freud's "case to a crowd of students," and he discharged his patient later that day.[35]

[32] *Ibid.*, 351–352.

[33] Jones, *Freud* III, 95.

[34] Gay, *Freud: a life for our time*, 420.

[35] Jones, *Freud* III, 90ff.

Beyond the proximity of the Löw Sanitarium and Hajek's disgraceful behavior, there are, as Sprengnether points out, more significant associations between Freud's experience as a patient and the Emma episode. At the time of the early calamity, as we saw, Freud's identifications were split. On the one hand, he was predisposed to identify with Fliess, the active phallic doctor. But on the other hand, as Sprengnether has argued, Freud, though he in no way wanted to, could not have completely avoided an identification with Eckstein – the helpless, bloody, castrated female patient, who had been violated by the sadistic surgeon. After all, Fliess had operated on his nose only shortly before the botched intervention on Emma. As Sprengnether observes,

when Freud developed cancer of the mouth, he suddenly found himself [again] in a situation parallel to that of Emma Eckstein, subject to surgical intervention on his oral and nasal cavities which led to hemorrhage.[36]

We can reasonably speculate that under those circumstances it would have been difficult for Freud to ward off identification with the helpless, bloody, castrated female whom he despised. And in general, we can assume, as Sprengnether maintains, that the onset of the cancer reactivated Freud's terror of helplessness, castration, passivity – in short, of femininity as he conceived it – which had been awakened during the Emma episode. This, in turn, would have reanimated the yearning for an omnipotent caregiver who could defend him against them. Significantly, during the final phase of his career, as the concept of separation began to compete with the concept of castration for priority of place, Freud elaborated the concept of helplessness into a systematic technical doctrine that assumed a central position in his theory.[37]

Having been subjected to a post-surgical course of painful (and ineffective) radium and X-ray therapy, Freud surely knew that the lesion was malignant. Yet, regardless of everything that had happened, the charade continued. Hajek allowed his convalescing patient to take his traditional three-month summer holidays, and Freud retreated to Bad Gastein in Austria and later across the border to Lavarone in the Trentino-Alto Adige region of Italy. But when Freud's suffering did not abate, at Anna's

---

[36] Sprengnether, *The spectral mother*, 174.
[37] *Ibid.*, 176.

urging, he summoned Deutsch for a consultation. And, although Deutsch saw that another more radical operation would be necessary, he continued to hold the entire truth from Freud. One reason for Deutsch's lack of candor with his patient was his own need for disavowal. Like Freud's other disciples, he had difficulty countenancing the fact that his larger-than-life mentor and master was mortal. Furthermore, as a physician and psychoanalyst, there was another less subjective and defensible reason for sparing his patient: clinical tact. This was the period when Freud was thoroughly immersed in his mourning for Heinerle, and one could legitimately argue that it was not advisable to burden him with the full truth of his illness.

However, although Deutsch's primary rationale for withholding the truth from his patient rested in part on legitimate clinical considerations, it in fact represented a profound failure to understand Freud's character. More specifically, it was the result of a misinterpretation of something Freud had said when the two men had met on 7 April. Freud had asked Deutsch to help him "disappear from the world" if his situation became intolerable. Deutsch concluded that Freud was contemplating suicide owing to his depression and despair and was therefore "unprepared to deal with reality."[38] In other words, he used the presumed risk of suicide to justify his lack of candor. Freud, however, was requesting something different, which, in a particular way, was an affirmation of life. He was asking Deutsch to help him end his life if his condition deteriorated beyond the point where it could no longer be deemed a properly human life but amounted to little more than mere biological existence – to "mere life" as opposed to "living well," to use Aristotle's distinction. Freud had told Pfister earlier that his "secret prayer" was to be "spared any wasting away and crippling of my ability to work because of physical deterioration."[39] Schur – the man whom Freud eventually chose to replace Deutsch as his personal physician because he could be trusted precisely on this issue – assures us that Freud "never contemplated suicide" in response to the innumerable losses and agonizing pain he was subjected

[38] Quoted in Schur, *Freud: living and dying*, 353.
[39] Meng and Freud (eds.), *Psychoanalysis and faith*, 35. Had Freud lived today, there would be little doubt about the contents of his "living will."

to. On the contrary, he fought to "prolong life to the bitter end," and only asked that it not be extended beyond the point where it had lost its integrity.[40]

Freud believed that in a situation in which one's life has been degraded beyond an acceptable threshold, taking one's life does not constitute an act of despondency and abdication. On the contrary, it constitutes a philosophical assertion of what autonomy an individual possesses, however slight, in an indifferent universe – his "scrap of independence."[41] It is an expression, in other words, of the circumscribed sovereignty of a finite being.

Deutsch failed to appreciate Freud's long-standing conviction that the ability to face death honestly was an essential ingredient of human dignity and autonomy. As early as an 1899 letter to Fliess, in an uncharacteristic reversal of the usual position, Freud extolled the superiority of Christianity over modern science and medicine with regard to its attitude toward death. Not only is the "art of deceiving the patient" practiced by most modern physicians unnecessary, Freud contended, it also debases the person. "What has the individual come to," Freud asks, and "how negligible must be the influence of the religion of science, which is supposed to have taken the place of the old religion, if one no longer dares to disclose that it is this or that man's turn to die?" With Christianity, the individual "at least has the last sacrament administered a few hours beforehand." Freud expresses the "hope that when my time comes, I shall find someone who will treat me with greater respect and tell me when to be ready." (At a critical point, he concluded that Schur was that person.) Again, as Gay observed, Freud views as exemplary the way his unassuming father had faced his death "and retained his beautiful composure to the end."[42]

In August, the members of Freud's inner circle, who had finally been apprised of the situation, were also meeting in northern Italy, in a town called San Cristoforo, where Deutsch and Anna joined them at a dinner at which they frantically debated the question of how to handle the situation. A decision was finally reached: They would put off informing Freud

[40] Schur, *Freud: living and dying*, 353–354.
[41] Freud, *Group psychology and the analysis of the ego*, 129.
[42] Masson (ed.), *Letters to Fliess*, 343–345.

about the true nature of his illness and would permit him to proceed with a trip to Rome that he had been eagerly looking forward to since April, for it would enable him to introduce his daughter Anna to his beloved city. And with the exception of a frightening episode on the night train from Verona to Rome where blood began to spurt out of Freud's mouth, the trip proved to be a great success, fulfilling the expectations of both parties. In Schur's opinion, "'Allowing' Freud to see Rome once more and to show it to Anna was the most humane and constructive action of those months."[43] Sadly, however, after this trip, Freud the exuberant traveler was only able "to spend a holiday away from Vienna or the nearby Semmering . . . twice more in his life, in 1929 and 1930."[44]

While Freud was in Italy, Deutsch contacted Pichler who had consented to perform the next surgery, which was deemed essential. Pichler, Schur tells us, was "the best type of German-Austrian," a thoroughly professional "man of the highest integrity," with little awareness of Freud's celebrity, who devoted himself to his patient without reserve for the next fifteen years.[45] He was also a true *Homo surgicus*, the type of man who was not intimidated by the aggressive quasi-heroic measures that were required to treat Freud properly.[46] Indeed, Pichler was so meticulous and thorough that he tested out the radical methods he had devised for Freud's surgery on an human corpse before the actual intervention.

The explicit acknowledgment of the cancer and the prospect of major surgery integrated Freud's psychological state and prepared him to face reality more directly. The vacillation ceased, and, from that point on, Freud not only conscientiously participated in his medical treatment, submitting to it in a soldierly way – always with Anna at his side – but also displayed extraordinary courage in the face of extreme pain and chronic discomfort. The stoical resignation to reality had been solidified.

Pichler carried out the surgery in two steps. The first, which took place on 4 October, was more or less preparatory. But the second, occurring a week later, involved the excision of massive portions of Freud's oral cavity.

[43] Schur, *Freud: living and dying*, 361.
[44] Jones, *Freud* III, 98.
[45] *Ibid.*, 101.
[46] Schur, *Freud: living and dying*, 363. After the *Anschluss*, Pichler appealed to the authorities on Freud's behalf.

"After slitting the lip and cheek wide open," Jones tells us, Pichler "removed the whole upper jaw and palate on the affected side," a procedure which, moreover, "threw the nasal cavity and mouth into one."[47] Remarkably, both procedures were carried out only under local anesthesia. When he came out of the second operation, Freud's heart rate measured 64, and he ran a high temperature for several days. He had to be fed through a tube in his nose, making it impossible for him to speak for some time, and he was administered fluids through his rectum. He was finally discharged on 28 October.

On 12 November, however, Pichler detected a suspicious spot in Freud's mouth that was immediately biopsied and proven to be malignant. "Now," Schur observes, "both Pichler and Freud proved their mettle. Most surgeons would have given up at this point."[48] Pichler, however, was candid with his patient and recommended further surgery, which Freud agreed to. The operation was actually performed that afternoon – again only using local anesthesia. Still further portions of his oral cavity were removed, again causing considerable pain. Pichler was finally satisfied and rightfully so. The operation was a success in that another malignancy was not discovered until 1938. Innumerable non-cancerous growths, however, which were partly the result of Freud's continued inability to stop smoking – this was one area, Freud admitted, where he could not establish "the dominance of the ego" – had to be surgically removed in the interim.[49] All in all, Freud underwent thirty-four operations (as well as several rounds of radiation therapy) in sixteen years – a period that included not only the agony of his illness, but the loss of many colleagues and friends, an international economic crisis that threatened his finances, the rise of anti-Semitism and fascism in Europe, the *Anschluss*, and his grueling emigration to London while in a severely compromised medical state.[50]

Freud's life had been preserved, but at an enormous cost. As a result of the "yawning cavity" that the surgery had created in his mouth, he was forced to wear a cumbersome prosthetic device, that Schur referred to as "the monster."[51] Because it was difficult to design one that fit

---

[47] Jones, *Freud* III, 99.

[48] Schur, *Freud: living and dying*, 363.

[49] *Ibid.*, 410.

[50] See *Ibid.*, 365.

[51] Jones, *Freud* III, 100.

properly, the prosthesis was a constant source of discomfort and pain. The very act of inserting it and removing it – which was Anna's job – was an ordeal, and sometimes required that the surgeon be summonsed to Berggasse 19 to carry it out. As a result of the disfigurement and the prosthesis, Freud's speech – which had been known for its eloquence, became defective, assuming a "nasal and thick" quality, "rather like that of someone with a cleft palate." The difficulty in communicating in turn caused Freud to withdraw from most of the professional activities that had formerly been a mainstay of his existence. Likewise, eating developed into such a disorderly affair that Freud – who was fastidious when it came to his physical appearance – generally chose to forgo companionship at meals and take them alone. What is more, the surgery had damaged his Eustachian tube and caused almost complete deafness on his right side. As this was the side that faced his patients, it eventually became necessary to reverse the position of his chair and the couch so that he could attend to their associations.

Freud loathed helplessness and dependence, and the way infantilization caused by the surgery certainly represented a violation of one of his most highly coveted possessions, his independence. When years later, during Freud's last days in London, Jones finally told him that Anna and his colleagues had debated whether or not to inform him about the true nature of his condition, Freud became furious. He looked at Jones "with blazing eyes" and declared "*Mit welchem Recht?*" (With what right?).[52] What right did those closest to him have to assume this paternalistic posture and deprive him of his autonomy?

Deutsch saw nothing wrong in the way he had handled the situation and claimed that, if it were to repeat itself, he would act in the same way. He did, however, recognize what the experience meant to Freud and honorably tendered his resignation, telling his patient "what had happened precluded in the future the complete confidence so essential in a patient–doctor relationship."[53] While Freud let Deutsch go as his personal internist, the two civilized gentlemen were able to reestablish a cordial friendship in the future. Freud, however, did not seek a replacement for another five years. His hesitancy was the result not only of his

[52] *Ibid.*, 93.
[53] *Ibid.*, 96.

experience with Deutsch, but, Schur suggests, also of the recognition
that the ubiquitous ambivalence that affects all human relations was bound
to be especially powerful in the "delicate" relation "between a physician
and a towering father figure such as he was."[54]

Freud's friends and family, however, came to the conclusion that the
continued absence of a personal physician was ill advised and Freud therefore set out to engage a new one. He had articulated the criterion for the
type of doctor he was seeking in the letter to Fliess cited above: "someone who will treat me with greater respect" than the typical doctor treats
his patient "and tell me when to be ready." At the time, Freud's friend
and follower Marie Bonaparte became impressed with a young physician
Max Schur, then thirty-one, when he treated her during a hospitalization, and recommended him to Freud. That he was a psychoanalytically
oriented internist, something of a rarity at the time, who had attended
Freud's "Introductory lectures" and was already in a personal analysis,
spoke in Schur's favor. On the other side of the ledger, however, Freud
was concerned that, because the relatively young man had not completed
his analysis, the same difficulties that had emerged with Deutsch might
manifest themselves in his case. At their first meeting, Freud immediately
placed his primary requirements for a patient–doctor relationship on the
table: it must be based on "mutual respect and confidence" and Freud
must always be told the complete truth. Schur's response apparently convinced Freud, but, before concluding the deal, there was one more item
on Freud's agenda. He made the same request of the young physician he
had made of Deutsch: "Promise me one more thing: that when the time
comes, you won't let me suffer unnecessarily."[55] Schur agreed and the two
men shook hands.

For Freud, the idea of "the harshness of life," which played an increasingly important role in the last phase of his career, was not merely an
abstract concept belonging to the realm of theoretical reflection. It was
also something that, after a certain point, Freud experienced concretely
on a day-to-day, if not minute-to-minute basis.[56] Pichler's notes record
that, in the year 1926 alone, "there were 48 office visits, one biopsy, two

[54] Schur, *Freud: living and dying*, 407.

[55] *Ibid.*, 408.

[56] See Ricoeur, *Freud and philosophy*, 250 and 323.

cauterizations, and constant experiments with three different prostheses involving attempt to preserve the few remaining teeth."[57] To be sure, the danger of reductionism is real and must be addressed. But we cannot allow it to prevent us from taking Freud's medical condition, in all its extremity, and the way he dealt with it as the background for our examination of the last phase of his career. To do otherwise, as Freud observed, would result in a picture of the man and his work that is not only "false," but "lifeless" as well.

The Theoretical Revisions of the Twenties

In the twenties, the serious anomalies that had emerged in "On narcissism" also led Freud to undertake a comprehensive revision of his theoretical position. He articulated his revised position in two primary works, *Beyond the pleasure principle* (1920) and *The ego and the id* (1923); this chapter examines the former, which bears more directly on the topics we are pursuing.

To begin with, *Beyond the pleasure principle* is arguably the most scandalous book in Freud's oeuvre, which is not lacking in scandalous books. Perhaps even more than *Moses and monotheism*, that other baffling work, its argument contains gaps big enough to drive a proverbial truck through and deploys highly questionable empirical evidence in a cavalier manner to suit its purposes.[58] Nevertheless, one of Freud's aims is clear: Though he was not sure how to go about it, after what the Great War had revealed about human nature, he wanted to fully incorporate "the work of the negative" into his theory.[59] Beyond that, however, it is difficult to determine exactly what Freud thought he was up to in *Beyond the pleasure principle* and just what sort of theoretical discourse he believed he was engaged in.

Something else about the impact of the war must be considered when interpreting this work: Freud's experience of it, as we have noted, precipitated a fundamental change in his theoretical attitude. Jones reports that as early as 1910, that is, while he was experiencing the impact of Jung's

---

[57] See Schur, *Freud: living and dying*, 389.

[58] Freud claims to ground his speculations in *Beyond the pleasure principle* in the findings of solid biological science, but he in fact deploys speculative metabiological theory of the most dubious sort.

[59] See Green, *The work of the negative*, chapter 4.

provocation, Freud had expressed "the wish with a sigh that he could retire from medical practice and devote himself to the unraveling of cultural and historical problems – ultimately the great problem of how man came to be what he is."[60] We do not know the precise reasons, but, after the war, Freud removed the shackles that he had placed on his speculative demon and allowed it to soar. Before that point, we have seen that he had vehemently – even counter-phobically – eschewed philosophical speculation. After it, the self-proclaimed anti-philosopher did not just begin to speculate; rather, he entirely disregarded the requirements that Kant's Copernican turn had laid down for modern philosophy and produced sweeping ontological pronouncements about the fundamental *archai* (constituents) of reality – for example, "Love" and "Strife" – with the naïveté of a Pre-Socratic.

Interpreters of *Beyond the pleasure principle* are confronted with two choices. They can either dismiss the work as a piece of indefensible speculation, as many of Freud's critics as well as his own psychoanalytic followers are prepared to do. Or they can adopt the attitude that the Jewish historian Salo Baron suggested concerning *Moses and monotheism* and assume that, if somebody of Freud's "stature" wrote the work, there must be something worth listening to in it.[61] In the latter case, an interpreter will grant Freud considerable hermeneutical charity and attempt to discover the meaningful content embedded in his speculative flights. One way to do that is to attempt to reconstruct Freud's metabiological theorizing in *Beyond the pleasure principle* in a way that uncovers a valid kernel. But while it may be fascinating to follow the intricate tributaries of Freud's theorizing, the questions that are pursued in this necessarily scholastic enterprise cannot, in the final analysis, be answered – even though oceans of ink have been spilt trying.

Instead, let us explore a less trodden path that does not aspire to the theoretical heights of Freud's investigations but can nevertheless yield fruitful results. It is an approach that employs the experience-based language of fundamental human realities – especially of the infant–mother relationship – rather than the abstract terminology of metabiological

---

[60] Jones, *Freud* I, 27.

[61] Salo Baron, "Review of *Moses and monotheism*," *American Journal of Sociology* 45 (1939), 471.

theory. And it is an approach predicated on the assumption that, if Freud's understanding of early development had been more thorough, it might have enabled him to articulate what he was struggling to express in his closely related analyses of the death drive, the pleasure principle, and *eros* in *Beyond the pleasure principle* – without resorting to dubious metabiological speculations.

However, before this alternative approach per se is presented, something must be said about Freud's line of argument in *Beyond the pleasure principle*. His strategy is to introduce the work of the negative into his theory by examining three phenomena that appear to contradict his fundamental assumption that the pleasure principle governs psychic life: the "war neuroses," child's play, and the anti-therapeutic force that some patients exhibit in psychoanalysis. While following the pleasure principle exclusively can produce maladaptive consequences insofar as it results in a conflict with the reality principle and interferes with adjustment to the demands of society, the pleasure principle is not unequivocally negative or destructive. On the contrary, it is a eudemonistic principle of mental functioning that provides coherence to psychic life, and without it experience would become unstructured and chaotic. After examining his three counter-examples that appear to contravene the pleasure principle, in one of the shaky steps in his argument, Freud makes the following assertion: The three cases provide sufficient grounds for positing a "compulsion to repeat" – the phenomenon in which an individual appears to violate the pleasure principle by repeatedly returning to a traumatic, which is to say painful, event or seeking out circumstances in which such an event might recur. While this repetition compulsion may not contradict the pleasure principle per se, Freud maintains, it operates "independently of it and to some extent in disregard of it."[62] Moreover, he describes the repetition compulsion as "malignant" and "demonic" – that is to say, as a manifestation of the work of the negative.[63]

Next, in an even more problematic move, Freud attempts to derive the existence of a death instinct from the compulsion to repeat, arguing that the compulsion seems "more primitive, more elementary, more

[62] Freud, *Beyond the pleasure principle*, 35.
[63] *Ibid.*, 21.

instinctual than the pleasure principle it overrides."[64] Indeed, Freud's derivation of the death instinct from the repetition compulsion is based on nothing more than a "suspicion":

At this point we cannot escape a suspicion that we may have come upon the track of a universal attribute of the instincts and perhaps of organic life in general which has not hitherto been clearly recognized or at least not explicitly stressed. *It seems, then, that an instinct is an urge inherent in organic life to restore an earlier state of things* which the living entity has been obliged to abandon under the pressure of external disturbing forces; that is, it is a kind of organic elasticity, or to put it another, the expression of the inertia in organic life.[65]

Freud's next step is not simply problematic; it is wrong. "*The earlier state of things*" that an instinct seeks to restore, he claims, is the inanimate state that existed before life and vital tensions emerged. And from this assertion he "deduces" the death instinct. The "goal of all organic striving," he argues,

must be an *old* state of things, an initial state from which the living entity has at one time or another departed, and to which it is striving to return . . . If we are to take it as a truth that knows no exception that everything living dies for *internal* reasons – becomes inorganic again – then we shall be compelled to say that "'*the aim of all life is death.*'"[66]

Where the force of the "must" comes from is unclear. Whatever the case, the argument is this: All living things strive to restore an earlier condition; that condition consists in the inorganic and tensionless state that existed before life emerged; therefore, all living things seek death – hence the death instinct.

As Freud certainly knew, the argument does not hold up either in terms of biology, where instincts are taken as a feature of organic life in general, or in terms of psychology, where they are viewed as pertaining to the individual human psyche.[67] Indeed, Freud's argument, as Laplanche and Pontalis observe, "might well" seem "absurd from the standpoint of the

---

[64] *Ibid.*, 23.

[65] *Ibid.*, 36 (emphasis in the original).

[66] *Ibid.*, 37 (emphasis in the original).

[67] See Sulloway, *Freud, biologist of the mind*, ch.11.

biological sciences."[68] That organisms strive to preserve themselves is a defining feature of life. To that end, they create a boundary, a "membrane" between their inner world and their environment, and they seek to preserve their "identity" by regulating their metabolic exchanges with their surroundings in order to maintain their internal homeostatic equilibrium.[69] Maintaining that homeostatic balance may indeed often require an organism to reduce its internal excitation to a target level; it may require an increase of excitation as well. But the notion that an organism strives to reduce its excitation beyond that target to zero – that is, to the point where it would die – simply contradicts the basic principles of biological theory.

The same criticism applies *mutatis mutandis* to Freud's position considered from the standpoint of psychology. Throughout his career, there was an ambiguity in Freud's discussion of "the principle of constancy," which was held to govern the functioning of the mental apparatus. In certain formulations, "constancy" refers to a tendency in the psyche that seeks to maintain a "favorable level of energy" by decreasing (or increasing) excitation to achieve the proper homeostatic target.[70] But in other formulations, "the principle of constancy" is understood as "a principle of inertia," which means that the psyche seeks to rid itself of all excitation and return to a state of *complete quiescence*.[71] And this is the way Freud (ambiguously) characterizes it in *Beyond the pleasure principle* when he states that "the dominating principle of mental life, and perhaps of nervous life in general, is the effort to reduce, to keep constant or *remove internal tension due to stimuli*" – that is, to return to a zero state – and, he argues, this "fact is one of the strongest reasons for believing in the death instinct."[72]

The intuitions behind Freud's unacceptable metabiological arguments can be redeemed and articulated by turning to another one of his texts, "The theme of the three caskets."[73] The paper harkens back to Freud's discussion of "The three fates" in *The interpretation of dreams*, and in

---

[68] Laplanche and Pontalis, *The language of psycho-analysis*, 344.

[69] See Hans Jonas, "Is God a mathematician? The meaning of metabolism," *The phenomenon of life: toward a philosophical biology* (Evanston, IL: Northwestern University Press, 2001), 64–98.

[70] Laplanche and Pontalis, *The language of psychoanalysis*, 343.

[71] See *ibid.*, 347–348.

[72] Freud, *Beyond the pleasure principle*, 55–56 (emphasis added).

[73] Sigmund Freud, "The theme of the three caskets" (1913), *SE* 12: 290–301.

both cases he not only addresses the figure of the Mother directly, but also connects her to death, and thereby to *Atropos* (the inexorable or ineluctable), which can be taken as more or less equivalent to *Ananke*. Published in 1913, "The theme of the three caskets," as Sprengnether points out, was written at a time when the break with Jung was approaching and the two men were debating Bachofen's theory of matriarchy.[74] This was also the period when Freud had plunged into the study of mythology and folklore in an attempt to catch up with Jung who was forging ahead in these areas, and he constructs his argument in "The three caskets" through a bravura excursion through these fields – and through an analysis of *King Lear*.[75]

His point of departure, however, is another Shakespeare play – namely *The Merchant of Venice* and specifically the scene in which Portia's suitors are asked to choose among three caskets – of gold, silver, and lead respectively. Freud attempts to discover the scene's meaning by associating to it as though it were a dream, and he reaches the following conclusion: "The caskets are also women, symbols of what is essential in woman, and therefore of woman herself – like coffers, boxes, cases, baskets, and so on," and the theme depicted is "a human one, *a man's choice between three women*."[76] Freud then turns to other seemingly disparate examples from cultural history involving similar triadic constellations – for instance, Lear's daughters, Paris's choice of Aphrodite over the other two goddesses in Offenbach's *La belle Hélène*, and the prince's three attempts to find Cinderella – and claims to uncover a unifying theme connecting them. While the third option is the most desirable, he argues, the qualities characterizing it represent Death – for example, the casket's paleness, Cordelia's silence, *Hélène*'s dumbness, and Cinderella's hiddenness. Focusing on the mute Cordelia, Freud formulates his thesis: The third sister represents "Death itself, The Goddess of Death." Since that is so, he continues, "the sisters are known to us. They are the Fates, the

[74] See Freud, *The interpretation of dreams*, 206–208. See also Sprengnether, *The spectral mother*, 212–213.

[75] It must be admitted that Freud's analysis in "The theme of the three caskets" may be no less bravura than his argument in *Beyond the pleasure principle*. But at least it is not presented as a scientific demonstration.

[76] Freud, "The theme of the three caskets," 292.

Moerae, the Parcae of the Norns, the third of whom is called Atropos, the inexorable."[77]

Where the Horae, "the hours," represent natural law and preside "over the regular order of nature" – for example, the cycle of the seasons – the Moerae "watch over the ordering of human life," that is, "the ineluctable severity of Law and its relation to death and dissolution." Man, Freud argues, can only perceive "the full seriousness of natural law" when it affects him personally and directly. The Moerae accomplish this by teaching him "that he too is part of nature and therefore subject to the immutable law of death" – that he "owes nature a death," to cite one of Freud's favorite lines from Shakespeare.[78] For humans, in other words, one's own death is the primary instance in which natural necessity confronts him. And insofar as it is ineluctable, that is, insofar as death cannot be eluded, experiencing it chastens our omnipotence, a necessary step in achieving maturity.

At this point, however, a "contradiction" seems to emerge. On the one hand, Freud's analysis points to the conclusion that his examples stand for the necessity of submitting to the inexorability of death. On the other hand, the examples all involve a choice that is presumably free. In a statement that he will later modify, Freud asserts: "No one chooses death, it is only by fatality that one falls a victim to it."[79] Freud believes that psychoanalytic theory allows him to resolve this apparent contradiction. The idea that one can choose the inexorable constitutes *a denial through a reversal of meaning*. Instead of representing the terrifying figure of Death that must be submitted to, the third figure is transformed into "the fairest and most desirable of women," whom one freely chooses. "Choice," Freud asserts, "stands in the place of necessity, of destiny."[80] In other words, through an act of reversal, subjugation to necessity is denied and transformed into the freedom to choose.

Freud turns now to *King Lear* and concludes "The theme of the three caskets" with a passage that bears directly on our concerns. The old

---

[77] *Ibid.*, 296.

[78] *Ibid.*, 298–299.

[79] *Ibid.*, 298. His modification of this statement will bear directly on the way he confronted his own death.

[80] *Ibid.*, 299.

king's choice among his three daughters, he argues, illumines "the three inevitable relations that a man has with a woman." They are "the woman who bears him, the woman who is his mate and the woman who destroys him." These are in turn "the three forms taken by the figure of the mother in the course of a man's life – the biological mother herself, the beloved who is chosen on her model, and lastly the Mother Earth who receives him once more" – in other words, the womb-mother of symbiosis, the tomb-mother of death, and the woman a man chooses between the two. Because Lear is an old man, Freud argues, "it is in vain" for him to desire "the love of woman as he had it first from his mother." Therefore, "the third of the Fates alone, the silent Goddess of Death, will take him into her arms."[81]

Returning to our earlier observation, we should note that this idea of a death instinct emerges from Freud's attempt to grapple with anomalies generated by his theory of narcissism. There is in fact an inner logic at work and it is this: Because the death drive consists in "an aspiration towards the level zero," it is, as Green argues, the logical heir to the quietude of primary narcissism.[82] The theory of the ego ideal in "On narcissism," as discussed in Chapter 10, suggests a way in which "the woman who bears" us and "the woman who destroys" us, in one important respect, coincide; it is a coincidence that makes Freud's postulation of a wish to return to a tensionless state more plausible. The argument runs as follows:

In the stage of primary narcissism, infants, who are in an undifferentiated relation with the womb-mother, experience a state of perfection consisting in an absence of tension, privation and otherness – that is, in a perfect condition of *complete quiescence*. Once primary narcissism breaks down and separation emerges, according to Freud, we project that experience of perfection ahead of us and, as we have observed, seek to recapture it in one form or another throughout our lives. When the wish to reinstate the original perfection is sublimated and pursued in a differentiated and realistic way, it can promote development and produce some of life's most cherished accomplishments. But as post-classical psychoanalysis has taught us, in addition to our more "advanced" developmental strivings, at a deeper stratum of psychic life – at its psychotic

---

[81] *Ibid.*, 301.
[82] Green, *The work of the negative*, 86.

core – we retain an ineradicable wish to recapture primary narcissism, understood as an undifferentiated state, directly, without mediation. In this case, "the earlier state of things . . . that we seek to restore" is the state of *perfection qua quiescence* we experienced with the womb-mother. Because this would be tantamount to death, the wish for symbiosis and the wish to die – the figure of the womb-mother and of the tomb-mother – converge.

Although, as Laplanche and Pontalis observe, the implication "always remained problematic for Freud," the death instinct nevertheless "evokes a profound link between pleasure and annihilation" and therefore suggests that death may not be an entirely negative phenomenon – indeed, that it might even be "an object of desire that beckons us."[83] Death holds out the promise of tranquility, of liberating us from the strife and suffering – the vital tensions – that are the inevitable concomitants of life. It frees us from what Winnicott famously described as the constant "strain of relating inner reality and outer reality" that the *principium individuationis* imposes on us.[84] As Horkheimer and Adorno observe, "The effort to hold itself together attends the ego at all its stages, and the temptation to be rid of the ego has always gone hand-in-hand with the blind determination to preserve it."[85] Moreover, the wish to restore the original state of perfection cuts both ways. At the same time as it promises the bliss that would result from a merger with the object, it also contains the threat of the terror that would result from the dissolution of the ego.

Horkheimer and Adorno elucidate this two-sided situation through their interpretation of the Siren episode in the *Odyssey*. The Sirens stand for both the first and the third mothers of "The three caskets." Their song, like the mother's lullaby, extends the promise of "unfettered fulfillment" – unalloyed *jouissance* in Lacan's terms – that we assume the infant experiences *in utero* and during the early period of extra-uterine life. But if the voyager surrenders to that song and strays from the path of maturation, then his ego will be dashed and shattered on the rocky shores

---

[83] Laplanche and Pontalis, *The language of psycho-analysis*, 273. See also Ricoeur, *Freud and philosophy*, 319, and Herbert Marcuse, *Eros and civilization: a philosophical inquiry into Freud* (Boston: Beacon Press, 1966), 25. We will return to the problematic nature of this idea for Freud when we examine his discussion of the oceanic feeling.

[84] D.W. Winnicott, *Playing and reality* (London: Tavistock, 1971), 240.

[85] Horkheimer and Adorno, *The dialectic of enlightenment*, 26.

of the Sirens' island, like the bodies of the sailors who had gone before.[86]
We will return to this topic in the final chapter when we examine Freud's
discussion of the oceanic feeling.

Eros: "Builder of Cities"

Having followed his speculations about a tension-reducing tendency in living beings to the point where it appears to contradict the self-preserving
characteristics of the organism, Freud calls a halt to this "extreme line of
thought" and comments, "Let us pause and reflect . . . it cannot be so" – that
is, it cannot be the case that the death instinct is the only principle governing the existence of living things.[87] This leads him to postulate the existence of *eros*, a life instinct that moves in the opposite direction and binds
energy into greater unities. The scandalous aura surrounding the notion
of the death instinct, Jonathan Lear suggests, may have led many analysts
to believe that its introduction constituted the "true and unsettling innovation in psychoanalytic theory" in the twenties.[88] Furthermore, because
Greek is thought of as the language of philosophy, the Greek terms *eros* may
have caused them to view its introduction as "a minor emendation," a mere
"philosophical flourish," in Freud's thinking.[89] But just the opposite is the
case. The concept of the death instinct had in fact been present in Freud's
thinking almost from the beginning. It was there *in nuce* when Freud introduced his discharge model of the mental apparatus in the 1890s and its
two correlated axioms: namely, the constancy hypothesis that held that the
function of the mental apparatus was to reduce psychic tension if not to
zero then to a minimum; and the pleasure principle that equated pleasure
with the reduction of tension. The death instinct was in fact a logical derivative of these two axioms. The way its articulation "took psychoanalysts
by surprise" was therefore, as Loewald remarks, unjustified.[90] *Eros* was in

---

[86] See *Ibid.*, 44–49, and Whitebook, *Perversion and utopia*, 145–146.

[87] Freud, *Beyond the pleasure principle*, 39.

[88] Loewald, "Sublimation," 468–469.

[89] Jonathan Lear, "The introduction of eros: reflections on the work of Hans Loewald,"
Journal of the American Psychoanalytic Association 44 (1996), 674.

[90] Hans Loewald, "Discussion: Max Schur, 'The id and the regulatory principles of
mental functioning,'" *The essential Loewald*, 62, and "On internalization," *The essential
Loewald*, 79.

fact the radically new feature that Freud introduced into his theory in the 1920s. This point, as Loewald observes, cannot be emphasized enough. As a tension-increasing dynamic, he argues, *eros* is "a force . . . sui generis, not reducible to" – that is to say, it is "beyond" the pleasure principle.[91] To be sure, the concept of *eros* was anticipated by Freud's ideas of bound energy and the synthetic function of the mind. But it was not until relatively late in his career, and then only with great reluctance, that he confronted and fully articulated its meaning. "Why," Loewald correctly asks, did "he [feel] much less at home" with *eros* "than he did with the death instinct?"[92]

Freud describes *eros* or the life instinct as an anti-entropic force that counteracts the entropic tendencies of the death instinct in the organism by forming "ever greater unities" – a process, which, moreover, entails an increase in tension.[93] *Eros* and its life-preserving function, Freud argues, can be observed in the behavior of simple cellular organisms. For example, when some germ cells break away from the organism of which they are a part, they do not follow the internal path of the death instinct. Instead, they unite with other germ cells, and through this union create an increase in tension and initiate a new chain of vital development. In this way, the activity of the germ cells works "against the death of the living substance and succeed[s] in winning for it what we can only regard as potential immortality" – that is, immortality for the trans-individual protoplasm, not for the singular organism.[94] If the death instinct is conservative in that it wants to return to an earlier state of things, *eros* is conservative in an opposite sense: it strives to conserve life.

In what might be described as attachment theory on a cellular level, Freud argues that the organism on its own, isolated from other organisms, is vulnerable to the death instinct and cannot defend itself against it. The life preserving "of the germ cell," according to Freud, is "only made possible" by becoming joined with another organism and creating a greater unity.[95] Not only must a germ cell coalesce "with another cell similar to itself and yet differing from it," but this "union with the living substance

[91] Loewald, "Discussion: Max Schur," 62.

[92] Loewald, "Sublimation," 469.

[93] Sigmund Freud, "Two encyclopedia articles" (1923), *SE* 18: 258.

[94] Freud, *Beyond the pleasure principle*, 40.

[95] *Ibid.*, 40.

of a different individual also increases . . . tensions" and introduces "what may be described as 'vital differences.'" This "influx of fresh amounts of stimulus" into the two organisms through their union has a "strengthening and rejuvenating effect" on both parties.[96]

Put in simple economic terms, the increase in energy that results from the union counteracts the disintegrative forces of the death instinct. This suggests another intrinsic connection, between narcissism and death. When an organism operates alone *narcissistically* – it succumbs to death; when it invests in objects and unites with other organisms, its vitality is enhanced. "A strong egoism," that is, "a strong investment in the self," Freud argues, "is a protection against falling ill, but," he continues, "in the last resort we must love" – in other words, invest in others – "in order not to fall ill." What is more, "we are bound to fall ill if . . . we are unable to love."[97]

By introducing a tension-increasing dynamic into his theory, Freud in fact violated one of its basic postulates, but he did not face the consequences of this move until four years later in "The economic problem of masochism." And when he did take it up, he did not pursue the logic of his new position as far as he should have. For reasons that are not entirely clear, in the 1924 text, Freud could no longer ignore the ramifications of his doctrine of *eros*. Earlier, the fact that the pleasure principle and the death instinct – insofar as they were both defined in terms of tension reduction – ended up on the same side of the ledger did not seem to cause him discomfort. Now it did. In the 1924 text, he states that the implication that the pleasure principle "would be entirely in the service of the death instinct" is unacceptable; "this view," he exclaims, "cannot be correct."[98]

In order to block the identification of pleasure and death, Freud, in what amounts to a revision of his fundamental position, adopts a new conception of pleasure that no longer equates it with the reduction of tension. In other words, he now admits the existence of *pleasurable tensions*:

It seems that in the series of feelings of tension we have a direct sense of the increase and decrease of amounts of stimulus, and it cannot be doubted that there are pleasurable tensions and unpleasurable relaxations of tensions.[99]

[96] *Ibid.*, 55.

[97] Freud, "On narcissism," 85.

[98] Freud, "The economic problem of masochism," 159–160.

[99] *Ibid.*, 160.

He cites the most obvious example of pleasurable tension, sexual excitation, but notes it is not the only one.

Then, in a move that can only be described as stunning, Freud retracts his doctrine of the pleasure principle. "Pleasure and unpleasure," he argues, can no longer be "referred to as an increase or decrease of a quantity," although they retain some reference to it. Having made that move, it becomes incumbent on Freud to provide "a *revised* pleasure principle," and he does in fact make a feeble effort in that direction. "It appears," he continues, that pleasure and unpleasure "depend not on this *quantitative* factor, but on some characteristic of it which we can only describe as a *qualitative* one." With this introduction of a qualitative factor, Freud appears to retract – or at least decenter – the "economic" point of view that had been central to his thinking since the *Project*. In an observation that is suggestive at best, he raises the possibility that this qualitative factor may have something to with the rhythm that accompanies the rise and fall of stimulation. Pleasure would still be understood with reference to the build-up as well as the discharge of tension. The process, however, would no longer be understood in terms of discrete climactic episodes, but in terms of how it functions over time. With respect to how this would work, however, Freud is forced to admit, "We do not know."[100] This is as far as he was able to go in the reconceptualization of pleasure.

Freud's lack of understanding of early infant–mother experience was a major source of his inability to theorize *eros* fully and recognize its ramifications for his overall theoretical position. Freud admits that he has not been able to find a "scientific explanation" of "the origin of the sexual instinct," and its "relation to its object." In lieu of such an account, the best he could do was turn to the "fantastic" realm of myth. He examines the myth that explains the source of erotic attraction, recited by Aristophanes in *The Symposium* of Plato. The myth cannot but remind us of Freud's discussion of primary narcissism and the ego ideal. It posits an original state of unity – of merger or symbiosis – which is subsequently broken apart and which Aristophanes' mythical creatures thereafter strive to restore.[101] And it also reminds us of the connection between narcissism and omnipotence in Freud's thinking. In that original state, according to

[100] *Ibid.*, 160.

[101] Freud, *Beyond the pleasure principle*, 59.

the myth, human beings were blessed with a double endowment, thus making them self-sufficient: Each individual had four hands, four eyes, four feet, two genitals and so on. At a certain point, however, because of the threat that these powerful creatures posed to the gods – because of the threat of their *hybris*/omnipotence – Zeus split them in two, and, after that, each divided creature sought to reunite with its other half in order to reinstate the original unity. This drive to restore the original state of unity, Aristophanes explains, is the motive force behind the desire for erotic union in all its de-sublimated and sublimated forms.

Freud, however, did not have to turn to mythology to find an account of the drive toward unity in the psyche and the modes of pleasure associated with it. In principle at least there were avenues of empirical research that he might have used to explore this topic – avenues that have in fact been followed since his death through clinical and experimental investigations of the early infant–mother relationship. As in Aristophanes' myth, they posit an original experience of unity that imparts a drive to recapture it once it has been lost. In this demythified approach, the original experience of union pertains no longer to our mythical ancestors but to what Loewald calls the "undifferentiated infant–mother matrix" that under "good enough" conditions is established with the birth of every child. The early infant–mother relationship involves two interrelated processes of binding. At the same time as the child binds itself to its mother, developing a relationship with her, she binds – organizes and articulates – the infant's disorganized unarticulated inner experience by containing and mirroring it back to him/her. In addition to synthetic tendencies that arise from the hardwiring of the human mind, the erotic striving for unification – for reunification – derives from the memory of that undifferentiated matrix.

Symbolization and Loss

Freud's famous discussion of his eighteen-month-old grandson Ernst's *fort-da* game, as we mentioned, addresses a question at the heart of the human dilemma: How is the toleration of loss possible. The boy would repeatedly play the game at the point where he was forced to separate from his mother Sophie. When she would leave, Ernst would take small objects and throw them away so that they ended up in places where it was difficult to locate and retrieve them. Then, on finding the object, Ernst would let out with "a loud, long-drawn-out 'o-o-o-o,' accompanied by an expression of interest and satisfaction." Sophie, who joined Freud in his observations, agreed that this utterance was not a meaningless sound, but "represented the German word *'fort'* [gone]."[102]

Further observation led Freud to conclude that Ernst was playing a game, and its meaning became apparent to him when he witnessed a particular version of it that involved "a wooden reel with a piece of string tied round it." The boy would skillfully throw the reel "over the edge of his curtained cot, so that it disappeared, while uttering his "expressive 'o-o-o-o.'" This, however, was only the first half of the game. For his grandson would then pull "the reel out of the cot again by the string and [hail] its reappearance with a joyful *'da'* [there]." In general one only witnessed "the first act" of the game, but, Freud concluded, "there is no doubt that the greater pleasure was attached to the second act" and that what he and Sophie had observed "was the complete game – disappearance and reappearance."[103]

Reaching this conclusion allowed Freud to answer the question he had been pondering throughout the time he was observing his grandson at play: How could Ernst, who was strongly attached to his mother, allow her "to go away without protesting" – that is, how could he accomplish "the renunciation of instinctual gratification" that was necessary in order to separate from her? He answered that by symbolically restaging, that is, symbolizing, his mother's "disappearance and return," Ernst compensated himself for that renunciation and could therefore tolerate it. It would be difficult to overestimate the significance that Freud attached to his grandson's symbolic play. He applauds Ernst's renunciation-of-instinct-through-symbolization as his "great cultural achievement."[104] *Symbolization, in short – insofar as it binds the distress caused by separation and makes the mastery of loss possible – is essential to the ascendance to culture.*

In praising his grandson's "great cultural achievement," Freud is gesturing in the direction of a profounder point concerning the human predicament. In the "wartime triptych," he had argued that transience is

---

[102] Freud, *Beyond the pleasure principle*, 14–15. For a sensitive analysis of the interaction between Freud and Sophie in this context see Appignanesi and Forrester, *Freud's women*, 60.

[103] Freud, *Beyond the pleasure principle*, 15.

[104] *Ibid.*, 15.

constitutive of human reality; it defines our finitude. That finitude is permeated by absence and loss, which bring us incredible pain. This leaves human beings with a fundamental question – namely, how is it possible to tolerate these inevitable experiences of loss and pain? Freud famously insisted that he had no consolation to offer us in the face of a meaningless and indifferent universe, though "at bottom that is what [we] are all demanding."[105] What he does offer in the face of harsh reality, however, is one admittedly not very powerful solution: the creation of meaning through symbolization, which goes hand-in-hand with the creation of psychic structure. Both can only be achieved through the process of mourning. In short, for Freud, the solution to the human predicament – insofar as there is a solution – presupposes "the ability to mourn."

Writing *Beyond the pleasure principle* was one of the primary ways in which Freud mourned Sophie's death; working on it was part of his *Trauerarbeit*. In an observation that resonates with his discussion of the first mother of "The three caskets," Freud notes a connection between writing and absence and loss. "Writing," he tells us, "was in its origin the voice of the absent person; and . . . a substitute for the mother's womb," which was "the first lodging for which in all likelihood man still longs, and in which he was safe and felt at ease."[106] In writing *Beyond the pleasure principle*, Freud simultaneously enacted the theories as he formulated them. His analysis of the "*fort-da*" game, a centerpiece of the book, concludes that symbolization – the creation of meaning – is the most effective way to respond to loss. In short, Freud, "the good mourner," struggled to "come to terms with" Sophie's death by following his own prescription. To combat the pain, he mobilized the hypomania of extreme theoretical exertion and struggled to create meaning.

---

[105] Freud, *Civilization and its discontents* (1930), *SE* 21: 145.
[106] *Ibid.* 43.

12

Leaving Heaven to the Angels and the Sparrows: Freud's Critique of Religion

IN A LETTER TO Oskar Pfister, the founder of psychoanalysis raised the following question: "Incidentally, why was it that none of all the pious ever discovered psycho-analysis? Why did it have to wait for a completely godless Jew (*gottloser Jude*)?"[1]

Although this question to his Swiss colleague, which Freud never answered directly, assumes the form of a throwaway, it should be treated with the utmost seriousness. It can provide an entrée into Freud's theory of religion that will lead us into the center of his unique position on the subject, beyond the all-too-familiar epistemological, ontological, and theological debates that never go anywhere. Furthermore, Freud's views on religion are not extraneous "cultural" supplements to his fundamental theory, as many clinically oriented psychoanalysts claim. That is, they are not "applied psychoanalysis"; rather, these views belong to the core of Freudian theory. Examining them can therefore illuminate some of the deepest structures of his thinking. Indeed, it can be argued that to unpack what Freud meant by "a godless Jew" is to elucidate one of the most fundamental strata of his project.

"An Apostate Jew"

With his provocative question to Pfister, Freud was throwing down a gauntlet. The idea of a "godless Jew" may at first sight appear to be a meaningless contradiction in terms rather than a pregnant paradoxical formulation to be elucidated. This is the way many of his defenders as well as his opponents have construed it in order to dismiss it – albeit from different directions.

[1] Meng and Freud (eds.), *Psychoanalysis and faith*, 63.

From one direction, a secularist ally like Peter Gay rejects the second term of the couplet and accepts the first, maintaining that Freud was an unqualified atheistic and materialist. "The first part of that claim, the godlessness," Gay writes, "has I think, now been firmly established. But a Jew? That question still remains unanswered."[2] Gay in fact makes the remarkable claim that Vienna's heavily Jewish milieu was of no consequence for the formation of Freud's theory and that he "could have developed his ideas in any city endowed with a first-rate medical school and an educated public large and affluent enough to furnish him with patients."[3] Yerushalmi makes short shrift of Gay's claim: "This hyperbole might be apt for Freud's pre-analytic work on the nerve cells of crayfish or the gonads of eels, but surely not on the interpretation of dreams or on human sexuality."[4] Moreover, as the philosopher Richard J. Bernstein stresses, "the most important issues here are not only biographical, they are conceptual."[5]

Gay is correct in describing Freud as a champion of the Enlightenment, but, as we have seen, the first psychoanalyst defended a later, darker, and more conflicted version of the Enlightenment than the one Gay attributes to the *philosophes*. Gay, adhering to an abstract notion of Enlightenment universalism, attempts, as Yerushalmi maintains, to throw "a *cordon sanitaire*, if not around Freud, then around psychoanalysis, shielding it from any taint of historical or cultural conditioning."[6] Like the "official" Freud who, for example, attempted to deny that Sophie's death had anything to do with his postulation of the death drive, Gay believes that to defend the scientific legitimacy of psychoanalysis – to prevent it from being written off as "a Jewish science" or a product of Freud's personality – one must purge it of any hint of particularity, including and especially Jewish particularity. But Gay is subscribing to what Yerushalmi calls "that canard of the Enlightenment" (it would be more accurate to say "of the abstract Enlightenment") – that is, "the false and insidious dichotomy between the 'parochial' and the 'universal.'"[7]

[2] Gay, *A godless Jew*, 113.

[3] *Ibid.*, 10.

[4] Yerushalmi, *Freud's Moses*, 116 n. 24.

[5] Richard J. Bernstein, *Freud and the legacy of Moses* (Cambridge: Cambridge University Press, 1998), 86.

[6] Yerushalmi, *Freud's Moses*, 116 n. 24.

[7] *Ibid.*, 98.

To impose that binary opposition on the topic would prevent us from ascertaining what Freud meant by "a godless Jew" and thereby from understanding the genesis and nature of his project. It would also ignore Freud's firm conviction that his particularistic Jewish tradition in fact contained crucial resources on which he drew to ascend to the standpoint of a critical and objective scientist. Yerushalmi reminds us of a critical point that is often missed: "The past not only subjugates; it also nourishes."[8]

From the other direction, religious Jews often take offense at Freud's formulation and reject the first term of the couplet, insisting that the idea of a "godless Jew" is not simply an incoherent notion but a sacrilege. Freud's self-description is adduced as proof that he not only rejected Judaism but was hostile to it – "a self-hating Jew." An especially difficult problem arises when religious individuals, either Jewish or Gentile, also hold Freud in high esteem. For example, Freud never stopped insisting that he was "an infidel Jew" and that he had a "completely negative attitude to religion . . . in any form," but a colleague like Pfister consistently had to deny his godlessness.[9] They cannot tolerate the fact that a man who, in their eyes, possessed unsurpassed intellectual depth, creativity, and personal integrity was an atheist – indeed, that his atheism was constitutive of his achievement.

Pfister found Freud's atheism so intolerable that he not only denied Freud's adamant insistence that he was a non-believer, but also made an utterly *meshuga* claim, one that rivals the fetishist's equation of a shoe with a penis: Namely, that Freud was not a Jew but a de facto Christian of the highest order, although he was not aware of it. At the same time as it is extraordinary, comical, presumptuous, and offensive, the extremity of Pfister's daft assertion demonstrates how threatening the idea of atheism can be – a fact that is not always recognized and deserves serious psychoanalytic investigation. The passage therefore should be cited at length:

[I]n the first place you are no Jew, which to me, in view of my unbounded admiration for Amos, Isaiah, Jeremiah, and the author of Job and Ecclesiastes, is a matter of profound regret, and in the second place, you are not godless, for he who lives

[8] *Ibid.*, 78.
[9] Sigmund Freud, "A religious experience" (1928), *SE* 21: 170, and Meng and Freud (eds.), *Psychoanalysis and faith*, 110.

the truth lives in God, and he who strives for the freeing of love "dwelleth in God" (First Epistle of John, iv, 16). If you raised to your consciousness and fully felt your place in the great design, which is to be as necessary as the synthesis of the notes is to a Beethoven symphony, I should say of you: A better Christian there never was.[10]

When Freud's daughter Anna came across this bizarre letter after her father's death, she incredulously wrote to Jones asking, "What in the world does Pfister mean here, and why does he want to dispute the fact that my father is a Jew, rather than accepting it."[11]

If Pfister made the completely *meshuga* assertion that Freud was an exemplary Christian, Freud makes the utterly *chutzpahdik* (cheeky) claim that, despite his "godlessness" – as we will see, it is precisely because of it – he represents "the essence" of what it is to be a Jew. In the "Preface" to the Hebrew translation of *Totem and taboo*, Freud presents a précis of what he means when he says he is a "godless Jew":

No reader of [the Hebrew version of] this book will find it easy to put himself in the emotional position of an author who is ignorant of the language of holy writ, who is completely estranged from the religion of his fathers – as well as from every other religion – and who cannot take a share in nationalist ideals, but who has yet never repudiated his people, who feels that he is in his essential nature a Jew and has no desire to alter that nature.

He then poses a question to himself: "Since you have abandoned all the common characteristics of your countrymen, what is there left to you that is Jewish?" And it is in his answer to this question that Freud makes his impertinent claim: "A very great deal, and probably its very essence." Furthermore, although that essence cannot now be expressed "clear in words," Freud argues, "no doubt, it will become accessible to the scientific."[12] Freud does not explicitly tag it as such, but as we will see in Chapter 13, in his interpretation of the Mosaic tradition, which is one strand of Judaism among many, Freud provides his "scientific" account of what he takes to be the "essence" of Judaism.

---

[10] Meng and Freud (eds.), *Psychoanalysis and faith*, 63.

[11] Quoted in Gay, *A godless Jew*, 82 n. 27.

[12] Freud, *Totem and taboo*, xv.

Religion and "the Sacrifice of the Intellect"

The future of an illusion presents another example of why Freud's work cannot be separated from his life. Schur observes that the 1927 monograph, probably his best-known tract on religion, was inextricably bound up with his experience of the cancer that was slowly destroying him. Sprengnether argues, as we have seen, that Freud's surgeries would have reactivated not only memories of the "infantile helplessness" he had experienced as a young child but also his identification with Emma Eckstein.[13] In short, he found himself in the position of a helpless, castrated female, passively suffering surgical intrusions into his body, a position that he loathed. Where Emma had to submit to Fliess's knife, Freud had to submit to Pichler's. (As we know, he had also submitted to Fliess's.)

In his notes, Pichler observes that Freud continually reflected on what he was going through in his treatment and attempted to extract whatever insights he could from it.[14] That the questions of the cancer and of illusion were linked in Freud's mind is evident in his rebuff to Eitington who tried to reassure Freud by telling him that the latest version of the prosthesis Pichler had devised for him was "nearly" perfect. Freud, who was determined to face his situation with a minimum of illusion, excoriated his well-intentioned colleague in a letter:

That "nearly" has its source in a not-yet abandoned illusion that Pichler will succeed in removing the last trouble spot and that I shall be able to associate with people without thinking more about the spot on my jaw than about the person. But the last spot is always the next-to-last . . . And so this illusion takes the path all others take.[15]

For Freud, the question of illusion stands behind the question of religion, and behind the question of religion stands the question of death. This is as it should be, for is it not true that death constitutes one of the essential concerns of most religions? And where can one plumb the question of death more deeply and directly than in one's own life – in "my" existential death – as opposed to some theological or philosophical abstraction?[16]

---

[13] Sprengnether, *The spectral mother*, 176 and 174.

[14] See Schur, *Freud: living and dying*, 396.

[15] Quoted in *ibid.*, 396.

[16] See Ricoeur, *Freud and philosophy*, 329.

As the Pragmatists argue, philosophical questions do not arise out of thin air but emerge from the problems that experience poses to us. Freud had reflected on the question of death earlier in his life, but having his body assaulted by cancer raised those reflections to an entirely new level of intensity.

The future of an illusion, which returns to topics Freud addressed in *Totem and taboo* and "Thoughts for the time on war and death," is one of his most uncharacteristic and least successfully realized works. Its Whiggish optimism contrasts sharply with Freud's brand of jocular pessimism, and its manifesto-like, polemical style lacks the subtlety that we expect from the recipient of the Goethe Prize. The work has therefore been regularly dismissed as an inferior "progressivist fantasy."[17] As with *Totem and taboo*, the criticisms of the 1927 text's Eurocentrism, progressivism, and naïve faith in science are well founded and must be taken seriously. Nevertheless, as with Freud's earlier excursus into anthropology, an immanent critique can reconstruct a valid core of *The future of an illusion* that should be preserved and defended. And again, the way to pursue the critique is to read the work's "unofficial" pre-Oedipal content against its "official" Oedipal doctrine.

Where the standard reading of *Totem and taboo* concentrates on "the father complex" – that is, the primal horde and the patricidal crime – we saw that the work also contains a narcissistic layer, concerning animism, omnipotence, and magical thinking, that illuminates its meaning in a substantially different way. Similarly, the received interpretations of *The future of an illusion* also concentrate on its Oedipal dimension – specifically, Freud's thesis that the wish for the powerful father constitutes the source of religion. But the text also contains a pre-Oedipal layer, largely concerned with the problem of helplessness and the wish for omnipotence arising from it, which can correct some of its more glaring deficiencies and help us elucidate Freud's interrelated theories of science and religion.

Freud is not so naïve as to believe that theological disputations generally convince anyone. Indeed, it is his position that emotions rather than reason almost always decides fundamental life questions – although he in fact contradicts the position in *The future of an illusion*. He feels compelled nevertheless to rehearse several of the classical arguments against

---

[17] Jonathan Lear, *Freud* (New York: Routledge, 2005), 210.

religion, while acknowledging, with an element of feigned modesty, that
he is not offering anything new that had not already been articulated by
his illustrious predecessors – presumably Hume, Voltaire, and Diderot –
"in a much more complete, forcible and impressive manner."[18] But for
two reasons, the "'*quia absurdum*' ['I believe because it is absurd'] of the
early Father of the Church" assumes particular significance for him.[19]

First, Freud believes that the *Credo* provides him the knockout punch
he needs to silence his opponents. Freud sees it as an admission of defeat
in which the defenders of religion admit that they cannot rationally justify
their beliefs. For him, the *Credo*, like all declarations of faith, amounts
to nothing more than a "self-confession," that is, a description of one's
private experience. Because it lacks intersubjective standing, it cannot
command our assent.[20] "Ignorance is ignorance," he argues, and "no right
to believe anything can be derived from it."[21]

There is a difficulty with Freud's position, however, that he does
not recognize. His religious adversaries can agree with his *description*
of their position *but not take it as a criticism*. According to them, Freud
fails to acknowledge the existence and value of "a noetic element above
and beyond reason," and this constitutes the major point of contention
between them.[22] But Freud will have no truck with the idea of extra-
rational truth. He simply declares *ex cathedra* not only that "there is no
appeal to a court above that of reason," but also that "what science cannot
give us we [cannot] get elsewhere"; he evinces no interest in disputing the
question.[23] Indeed, how could one dispute it, he might ask, except within
reason?

Freud is not interested in the Nietzschean question of how reason
comes to be valorized in the first place. Like Nietzsche, the first psychoanalyst was a post-metaphysical thinker who viewed the attempt to

---

[18] Freud, *The future of an illusion*, 35. With his modesty, Freud ignores the fact that
the psychoanalytic dimension adds something fundamentally new to the traditional
critique of religion.

[19] *Ibid.*, 28.

[20] *Ibid.*, 55 and 28.

[21] *Ibid.*, 32.

[22] William B. Parsons, *The enigma of the oceanic feeling: revisioning the psychoanalytic
theory of mysticism* (Oxford: Oxford University Press, 1999), 5.

[23] Freud, *The future of an illusion*, 56.

provide legitimating foundations for rationality as a misguided and fruit-
less enterprise. But as a psychologist, he could have made an important
contribution if he had examined "the charisma of reason" – that is, the
question of how reason becomes cathected as one possible form of thought
among many. Freud ironically acknowledges that there is a difficulty lurking in his position when he refers to "our god *Logos*," but he stops there
and does not pursue the problem further.[24]

In addition to dismissing the *Credo* as irrational, Freud was interested
in it because it is connected with the question of theodicy. Those who
write about religion typically begin with the observation that the phenomenon is too multifarious to be subsumed under a single concept; they
then proceed, with varying efforts at justification, to offer the definition
they will adopt. For Freud, religion is essentially *theodicy* – that is, the
attempt to provide a rationale for the ultimate meaninglessness of human
existence as well as for the inexorability and ubiquity of human suffering.
(Freud admits that his conception of religion fits the case of Catholicism
most accurately.) Not only does Freud utterly reject this attempt to provide a rationale where, as he sees it, none possibly exists; he also believes
the attempt has negative consequences for the human intellect.

In his classic work *The sacred canopy*, the eminent sociologist of religion
Peter Berger argued that our individual and collective existence is continually threatened by "contingency."[25] Meaninglessness, suffering, and
terror are always lurking at the boundaries of our organized human existence. Or, as Castoriadis puts it, our structured human "cosmos" is always
threatened by the "chaos" – the "abyss of meaninglessness" underlying it.[26]
Contingency continually threatens to break through, Berger argues, in
"limit-experiences" – for example, epidemics, famines, migrations,
floods, wars, and especially death – that disrupt our habitual modes of
existence.[27] Therefore, he contends, the central task of every society is to
shield its members from the threat of "anomic terror" by providing them

---

[24] *Ibid.*, 54.

[25] See Peter Berger, *The sacred canopy: elements of a sociological theory of religion* (New
York: Anchor Books, 1967), chapters 1–3.

[26] Cornelius Castoriadis, "Institution of society and religion," *World in fragments:
writings on politics, society, psychoanalysis, and the imagination*, ed. and trans. David
Ames Curtis (Stanford, CA: Stanford University Press, 1997), 324.

[27] See Berger, *The sacred canopy*, chapters 1–3.

with world-maintaining systems of meaning (*nomoi*) that cover over the ultimate fact of contingency – or, short of that, rationalize to the extent that it can be rationalized.[28] These meaning-bestowing belief systems are theodicies.

Castoriadis argues that the overwhelming majority of societies have been "heteronomous" in that they have posited the existence of extra-human entities – mythical ancestors, the gods, God, and so on – to conceal the underlying meaninglessness and to ground their *nomoi*. Religion *qua* theodicy, Castoriadis argues, cannot accept the existence of the abyss, and the function of the sacred is to mask the fact that the "fundamental idols of the tribe" are groundless human creations.[29] Or as the important and largely forgotten psychoanalytic anthropologist Weston La Barre puts it in *The ghost dance*, "the function of sacred culture is to protect men from clear knowledge of their predicament at all times."[30]

The taboo against addressing that predicament and thereby questioning the collective's "sacred core" leads to the interdiction against the exercise of curiosity – against the uninhibited exercise of the intellect – characteristic of most "traditional" societies, including medieval Catholicism. It was only with the liberation of theoretical curiosity in modernity that the sacred core of society could be interrogated. Max Weber holds that because any attempt to demonstrate "that the course of the world [is] *meaningful*" will necessarily fail, all theodicies will be "compelled at *some* point to demand the credo *non quod sed quia absurdum*" – that is, will be compelled to demand a "sacrifice of the intellect."[31] Christianity had the bad luck to arrive on the historical scene after philosophy had been invented.[32] And according to Weber, the early Church Fathers' hostility toward philosophy was well advised. For when later Catholic theologians like Aquinas accepted the demands of philosophy and attempted to provide a philosophical justification of Christianity, they revealed its insurmountable

---

[28] *Ibid.*, 22.

[29] Castoriadis, "Institution of society and religion," 312.

[30] La Barre, *The ghost dance*, 207. See also Émile Durkheim, *The elementary forms of religious life*, trans. Karen E. Fields (New York: The Free Press, 1995), 215; see also Castoriadis, "Institution of society and religion," 324.

[31] See Max Weber, *From Max Weber: essays in sociology*, ed. and trans. H.H. Girth and C. Wright Mills (Oxford: Oxford University Press, 1958), 351–353.

[32] See Castoriadis, "Institution of society and religion," 314.

internal contradictions, thereby opening the door to skepticism and eventually to secularism.

Freud is in full agreement with Weber's claim that religion necessarily entails a sacrifice of intellectual curiosity; indeed, this is one of his central indictments of it. Freud's own "credo," as Gay observes, "recognizes no boundaries to his systematic curiosity, no exemption from his voyeur's privilege."[33]

Helplessness as an Anthropological Fact

Believing he has dispensed with several of the most important canonical arguments supporting religious beliefs, which, as he saw it, were shaky to begin with, Freud draws the following conclusion:

[Of] all the information provided by our cultural assets it is precisely the elements which might be of the greatest importance to us [namely, the "information" contained in religious doctrines] and which have the task of solving the riddles of the universe and of reconciling us to the sufferings of life – it is precisely those elements that are the least well authenticated of any.[34]

"In other matters," he observes, "no sensible person will behave so irresponsibly or rest content with such feeble grounds for his opinions and for the line he takes." Why is it then, Freud asks, that it is "only in the highest and most sacred things that he allows himself to do so"?[35]

His answer is this: The force of religious ideas derives from their being "illusions" – that is, beliefs motivated by wishes. "The secret of their strength," he argues, "lies in the strength of" the wishes they fulfill, which are in fact "the oldest, strongest and most urgent wishes of mankind." He maintains, moreover, that "the terrifying impression of helplessness in childhood aroused the need for protection . . . through love," and, in a problematic if not peculiar claim to be examined below, he claims that that protection "was provided by the father."[36] Freud's central thesis is that "the longing for the father is the root of the need for religion."[37]

[33] Gay, *A godless Jew*, 46.
[34] Freud, *The future of an illusion*, 27.
[35] *Ibid.*, 32.
[36] *Ibid.*, 30.
[37] *Ibid.*, 22.

He argues further that, in addition to reconciling people to the toll that civilized social life exacts from them, religion's primary theodicean task is to "exorcize the terrors of nature [and] reconcile men to the cruelty of fate, particularly *as it manifests itself in death.*"[38] However far civilization's scientific and technological conquest of the external world may advance, a substantial portion of our natural environment will still elude our control and defy us. "No one," Freud writes, "is under the illusion that nature . . . will ever be entirely subject to man."[39] In some of his most inspired and heroic prose, Freud enumerates several of "the elements" that "seem to mock all human control":

The earth, which quakes and is torn apart and buries all human life and its works; water, which deluges and drowns everything in a turmoil; storms, which bow everything before them; there are diseases, which we have only recently recognized as attacks by other organisms; and finally there is the painful riddle of death, against which no medicine has yet been found, nor probably will be. With these forces nature rises up against us, majestic, cruel and inexorable.[40]

Freud's explanation of the particularly painful injuries that fate deals us beyond brute physical suffering leads us to the core of his doctrine of human nature, his "philosophical anthropology," which provides the basis for his theory of religion. It rests on the concept of *Hilflosigkeit* – helplessness. Laplanche and Pontalis point out that it is not always recognized that "this common word . . . has a specific meaning in Freudian theory," and that it "constitutes a permanent reference-point for" him that "deserves to be singled out and translated consistently." They hold that "this state of helplessness is an essentially objective *datum* – the situation of impotence in which the newborn human infant finds itself," and that it has enormous consequences for an individual's later life.[41]

---

[38] *Ibid.*, 17 (emphasis in the original).

[39] *Ibid.*, 15.

[40] *Ibid.*, 15–16. Freud's soaring rhetoric again points to the double-edged nature of his heroism. Portraying *Ananke* as a noble adversary may have allowed him to summon up his heroic self-image and mobilize the courage necessary for the prolonged and arduous combat with the cancer. This does not mean, however, that whatever psychological factors were at work, "resignation to *Ananke*" is praiseworthy.

[41] Laplanche and Pontalis, *The language of psychoanalysis*, 189. While the newborn is far more pre-adapted to reality than the early analysts recognized, the effort on the

Freud argues that nature's assaults are especially devastating – indeed, traumatizing – because they bring "to our mind once more" the "weakness and helplessness" we experienced as small children, which "we thought to escape through the work of civilization."[42] The terror that adults experience when confronted with the destructiveness of nature is not simply an appropriate response to objective danger. Nature's assaults can become catastrophic, in no small part because they can reawaken the "weakness and helplessness" we experienced as infants, thereby evoking the "original situations of danger" and retraumatizing us.[43] Freud's doctrine of *Hilflosigkeit* thus constitutes a biologically grounded elaboration of the philosophical theme of human finitude, and it allows us to draw a direct line from Kant the *Aufklärer* to Freud the dark enlightener. Like Kant, Freud believed that the goal of enlightenment is to overcome "immaturity." But where Kant's explication of the concept of immaturity is largely philosophical, Freud explains it in concrete anthropological terms.[44]

Anthropology tells us that the emergence of a specifically human animal was the result of a problem that arose in the course of evolution. The ecology of hunter cultures, according to La Barre, created "an adaptive premium on larger forebrains." This distinctive feature of human anatomy makes possible three attributes of cooperation that are required for successful hunting: the invention of better tools, the use of linguistic symbols for communication and strategic coordination, and the regulation of "unedited raw hindbrain impulses of erotism and aggression." This "massive specialization in forebrain," La Barre observes, made

---

part of infant researchers to depict a "competent" baby is in part politically motivated. It represents an effort to radically attenuate Freud's doctrine of helplessness and thereby undercut his pessimistic anthropology that is predicated on it.

[42] Freud, *The future of an illusion*, 16.

[43] Freud, *Inhibitions, symptoms and anxiety*, 155.

[44] This is the way that the Frankfurt School and Castoriadis interpreted Freud's relation to Kant. See Martin Jay, *The dialectical imagination: a history of the Frankfurt School and the Institute for Social Research, 1923–1950* (New York: Little Brown, 1973), chapter 3; Theodor W. Adorno, *Negative dialectics*, trans. E.B. Ashton (New York: Routledge, 1990), 211–299; and Joel Whitebook, "Weighty objects: on Adorno's Kant–Freud interpretation," *The Cambridge companion to Adorno*, ed. Thomas Hahn (Cambridge: Cambridge University press, 2004), 51–78. See also Tauber, *Freud, the reluctant philosopher*, 132–133.

the transformation of "man into a culture-bearing, learning animal" possible.[45]

The dramatic enlargement of the brain, however, created a serious evolutionary conundrum. To accommodate the growth of the proto-human brain, the size of the primate's skull had to increase proportionally. Consequently, at some point, the head of the fetus became so large in comparison to the birth canal and the mother's pelvis – which is more constricted than the pelvises of our four-legged ancestors owing to the requirements of bipedalism – that birth became more difficult and potentially more dangerous. To this day, the late and much-admired biologist Stephen Jay Gould observes, the birth of the human infant remains "a tight squeeze," making it "difficult compared with that of other mammals."[46] *Thus a condition that was necessary for the further evolution of the species – namely, an enlarged brain – simultaneously endangered that very evolution.*

To solve the problem, nature made a decision, so to speak, that was of the utmost consequence for the human species – indeed, it was constitutive of the human species. To prevent the infant's head from growing so large inside the womb that it would endanger its birth, its gestation period was shortened and it was born "prematurely." As a result, the human infant emerges from the womb at an earlier stage relative to its total development than the young of other species. "Its intra-uterine existence," as Freud put it, "seems short in comparison with that of most animals."[47] Moreover, because of this evolutionary innovation, much of the development that takes place *in utero* in other species occurs after the human infant emerges from the womb.[48] Gould states the prematurity

---

[45] La Barre, *The ghost dance*, 85.

[46] Stephen Jay Gould, *Ever since Darwin: reflections in natural history* (New York: W.W. Norton & Co., 1977), 74.

[47] Freud, *Inhibitions, symptoms, and anxieties*, 154. Gould points out that, "if women gave birth when they 'should,' – that is, at the point where the human newborn had acquired the same features that their primate relatives possess at birth – then they would carry their child for 'about a year and a half.'" Gould, *Ever since Darwin*, 74.

[48] For example, Gould tells us that "the brains of many mammals are essentially fully formed at birth," but "since the brain never gets very large, this poses no problem for birth." On the other hand, because of its shortened gestation period, at birth the human brain "is only one-fourth its final size" and must achieve most of its growth outside of the womb. *Ibid.*, 75–76.

thesis – which is by no means uncontroversial – somewhat provocatively, claiming that "human babies are born embryos, and embryos they remain for about the first nine months of life."[49]

The helplessness resulting from the infant's "prematurity" has another decisive ramification for our species: its extended dependency. The human child must remain dependent on its parents for a period of time that is unmatched in the animal kingdom. Furthermore, contrary to Freud's designation of the father as the primary protector of the young child, these evolutionary developments give rise to *the unique position of the mother in the human species*. As La Barre argues, "the human female's specialization in maternity," in protecting and caring for the young, is "the response . . . to this strikingly unfinished bodily dependency."[50] Helplessness and dependency, however, are not the end of the story, for they coexist together with the infant's enlarged brain. *And this combination gives rise to a form of adaptation – namely, a characteristically human mode of flexible learning that is unique to our species.*

Other species are endowed with "fixed instincts" (*Instinkte*) that are efficiently but narrowly adapted to one ecological niche, making it difficult for them to adapt to another niche for which they were not preprogrammed. The same specific hardwiring that is highly functional within circumscribed parameters also places serious limits on their flexibility and ability to learn. If a frog is taken out of its lily pond, the niche to which it is specifically adapted, and placed in a foreign environment, chances are it will not survive. On the other hand, the "defunctionalization" of our biological equipment led anthropologist Terrence Deacon to ask: "Would it be too humbling to see ourselves as a somewhat genetically degenerate, neurologically dedifferentiated ape?"[51] Rather than possessing "adult-adaptive instincts" (*Instinktes*), we are equipped with non-specialized plastic brains and mutable polymorphic drives (*Triebe*) that make possible "labile learning from others" – that is, education in the broadest sense of the term (*Paideia* or *Bildung*). Two functions thus

[49] *Ibid.*, 72.

[50] La Barre, *The ghost dance*, 86. See also Laplanche and Pontalis, *The language of psycho-analysis*, 214–217.

[51] Deacon is quoted in Robert N. Bellah, *Religion in human evolution: from the Paleolithic to the Axial Age* (Cambridge, MA: The Belknap Press of Harvard University Press, 2011), 87.

dovetail in the child's extended period of dependency. *The helplessness that results from its unfinished bodily state and meager instinctual endowment make socialization* qua *education necessary. And the prolonged period of the human child's dependence on its parents in conjunction with an enlarged brain and mutable Triebe make it possible.* Helplessness and extended dependency have two other consequences for the human animal. Love plays a more important role in our lives than it does in the lives of other species; and because our maturation process lasts so long and can become derailed at numerous points along the way, vulnerability to neurosis is intrinsic to our constitution.

The immaturity and helplessness of the human child, La Barre maintains, provides an "experimental matrix" that contains an equipotentiality for the genesis of "magic and religion" on the one hand, or for "the scientific world-view" on the other.[52] As helpless children, we confronted the seemingly omnipotent Otherness of our physical and socio-familial environments, an Otherness that was beyond our control, and this drove us – and to one degree or another continues to drive us – to pursue omnipotent solutions that seek to deny that helplessness.[53] (This is especially true at times of crisis and stress.) La Barre asserts that because of this species-specific childhood experience, magic and religion are exclusively human phenomena:

An animal without *prolonged infancy* in a *nuclear family* has no *experiential basis* for regressive belief in magic or religion. Elephantine waving of branches at the Moon, whatever it is ethologically is not ethnologically religious behavior, and the conditioned irrationality of golden hamsters is not superstitious magic. Only once long-dependent infants can invent magic. Only oedipal [and pre-Oedipal – JW] apes can have religion.[54]

In addition to magic and religion, however, this constellation contains the possibility of a different outcome. Though Freud does not systematically spell it out, his anthropological assumptions entail a normative implication and practical (clinical) program that places it squarely in the

---

[52] La Barre, *The ghost dance*, 87.

[53] The Kleinian analysts refer to these as "manic defenses."

[54] Weston La Barre, *Shadow of childhood: neoteny and the biology of religion* (Norman: University of Oklahoma Press, 1991), 146. La Barre was writing before the pre-Oedipal turn in psychoanalysis.

Enlightenment tradition. If immaturity – "infantilism" – defines our original situation, then maturity constitutes the goal of his Enlightenment program as it did for Kant's.

There is, however, a difference between the two thinkers: Where Freud agrees with Kant's general definition of maturity as "the ability to think for oneself," he attempts to provide it with concrete psychoanalytic content. If the condition of immaturity engenders the quest for omnipotence and magic, then the ability to think for oneself – "epistemological maturity," in La Barre's terms – is only possible to the extent that the omnipotence of thoughts has been chastened and worked through.[55] If our imagination is dominated by omnipotent parental imagoes who supposedly posses the solution to life's unanswerable questions, the ability to compensate us for our suffering, and the power to heal our wounded narcissism, thus restoring our wholeness, then it is impossible for us to assume responsibility for our situation and think for ourselves. Moreover, to the extent that one's thinking is determined by omnipotent parental imagoes, that "thinking" is determined by fear and inhibits independent and critical thought. Lacan's perverse attempt to stand it on its head notwithstanding, Freud's dictum that "where id was, there shall ego become" is the motto for this Enlightenment program.

La Barre calls our attention to a seemingly paradoxical aspect of the concept of immaturity. The playfulness of childhood may seem to be the antithesis of tough-minded scientific thinking, but, he argues, the retention into adulthood of the immature "purposeful purposelessness" of play is essential for critical thinking, which is to say, for mature scientific thinking. Developmental researchers now recognize that without a sufficient playful activity, the young of many species will not develop into properly mature adults. And for our species, the significance of play is even greater: It teaches us "to learn and innovate" as well as to "improvise."[56] In other words, the retention of the capacity for playfulness into adulthood is a necessary condition for creative and adaptive thinking. (Freud often observed that he found it difficult to distinguish theorizing from fantasizing.) While it is important for cultures to hand down "the answers to old questions" – this is one way to define tradition – it may

---

[55] La Barre, *The ghost dance*, 113.
[56] La Barre, *Shadow of childhood*, 108.

be even more important for them "to ask new questions that may lead to new answers" that foster more successful adaptations. Playful modes of thinking retained into adulthood can operate outside what Castoriadis calls the "inherited modes of thought" and are a primary source of the ability "to think otherwise" – of the critical ability that is necessary to prevent "the hardening of the categories."[57] La Barre suggests that "the *retention* of this free play may even be necessary for *human thinking* as such . . . Indeed, a strong tendency to think independently is the hallmark of the properly mature person."[58]

Freud's Prescription

As we have seen, when Freud was a university student, he informed Silberstein that Feuerbach was the philosopher he admired most. Yet, although *The future of an illusion* is a thoroughly Feuerbachian text, the post-Hegelian thinker is never mentioned in it. This is one example of Freud's desire to conceal the philosophical roots of his project and present himself as an empirical scientist. But in *The future of an illusion*, Freud makes use of Feuerbach's central notion of *projection* to diagnose the problem of religion.[59] His argument, as we have seen, is a *reductio ad anthropon*. The anxiety engendered by our anthropological helplessness produces the wish for a powerful and beneficent father who will shield us from the cruelties of fate and compensate us for our suffering. The images associated with this strong and providential paternal figure, images derived from the child's experience with the actual father, are *projected* into the heavens where they are transfigured into the imagery of religion. Freud's "prescription" for the *Religionsproblem* follows from his Feuerbachian "diagnosis." If its genesis consists in the *projection* of the fears arising out of existential helplessness, then the solution is to come to terms with our basic anthropological condition, which is to say, with our finitude and helplessness. Remove the source of the projections, and the projections will also be removed.

[57] Castoriadis, *Imaginary institution of society*, 169, and Le Barre, *Shadow of childhood*, 109.
[58] Le Barre, *Shadow of childhood*, 109.
[59] See Harvey, *Feuerbach and the interpretation of religion*, chapter 5.

These considerations allow us to spell out Freud's normative concept of maturity. Immaturity, "infantilism," consists in being at the mercy of one's helplessness; maturity, on the other hand, is the result of working through that helplessness and reconciling ourselves to it without any false promise of "consolation." Mature men and women, Freud writes, will have "to do without the consolation of religious illusion" and to "bear the trouble of life . . . and the cruelties of reality" autonomously, on their own. As he tells the reader in the final passages of *Civilization and its discontents*:

> I have not the courage to rise up before my fellow-men as a prophet, and I bow to their reproach that I can offer them no consolation: for at bottom that is what they are all demanding – the wildest revolutionaries no less passionately than the most virtuous believers.[60]

To be sure, the achievement of maturity necessitates the radical decentering of our "incorrigible narcissism" and constitutes a painful blow to our self-esteem.[61] But in the long run, Freud maintains, the benefits of a mature existence outweigh these narcissistic injuries. Gaining those benefits will not be easy, and Freud describes the difficulties it entails:

> Men will, it is true, find themselves in a difficult situation. They will have to admit to themselves the full extent of their helplessness and their insignificance in the machinery of the universe; they can no longer be the centre of creation, no longer the object of tender care on the part of a beneficent Providence. They will be in the same position as a child who has left the parental house where he was warm and comfortable. But surely infantilism is to be surmounted. Men cannot remain children forever; they must in the end go out into "hostile life." We may call this *"education to reality*."[62]

Let us be explicit about the *desideratum* of Freud's disconsolate position: It is to resign ourselves to a disenchanted world – that is, to accept "the full extent of [our] helplessness and . . . insignificance in the machinery of the universe." The uncharacteristic Whiggishness of *The future of an illusion* is on full display in this passage. The confidence expressed in the passage's assured tone, however, results from rhetorical flourishes rather

---

[60] Freud, *Civilization and its discontents*, 145.

[61] Ricoeur, *Freud and philosophy*, 334.

[62] Freud, The future of an illusion, 49.

than sound arguments. One wants to know from what source the force of the terms "surely," "cannot," and "must" derives. In other words, what in Freud's belief authorizes him to present these developments as historically necessary?

No sooner has Freud completed his discussion of helplessness than he immediately registers a critical qualification to forestall a possible misinterpretation of his position. Religious opponents might argue that what Freud sees as the mature individual's acceptance of his helplessness and finitude is equivalent to what the Christian understands as humility and the acknowledgment of one's sinfulness. Freud admits that, initially, the two positions are in fact the same: The mature citizen and the believer both renounce their omnipotence and accept their finitude. But this is as far as the comparison goes. For mature individuals, the acceptance of their finitude – of their helplessness and mortality – is the end of the story: full stop. The Christian faithful, however, do not stop there; they add a second step, positing the existence of an afterlife and of an omnipotent and providential god who will eventually compensate them for all their suffering:

Death itself is not extinction, is not a return to inorganic lifelessness, but the beginning of a new kind of existence which lies on the path of development to something higher. In the end all good is rewarded and all evil punished, if not actually in this form of life then in the later existences that begin after death. In this way all the terrors, the sufferings and the hardships of life are destined to be obliterated.[63]

While the faithful renounce omnipotence *ab initio*, Freud argues, they resurrect it, so to speak, in this second step. They get something more out of the bargain as well, thanks to a masochistic but ingenious deal devised by St. Paul. In return for embracing their supposed sinfulness and accepting Christ, believers are relieved of the sense of guilt that plagues the legalistic Jews, and they are promised that all the pain and suffering of their earthly existence will be redeemed in the afterlife.

The attempt to assimilate the Freudian position to Christian doctrine rests on a tacit equation of finitude and sinfulness. Granted, both concepts are defined in terms of our creatureliness and material constitution.

---

[63] *Ibid.*, 19.

But Freud is not only a "godless Jew," he is also a pagan. Indeed, in this respect, the two tend to coincide. As opposed to the Christian viewpoint, for Freud our status as natural creatures is not a source of shame; indeed, the entire concept of sin – which must be distinguished from destructiveness – is utterly alien to him.[64] Instead, like Spinoza – and as opposed to Christianity which disparages our animal inheritance – Freud believes that reading humanity back into nature is emancipatory and will lead to a more fulfilled existence.

Because Freud eschewed philosophy in the strict sense, he did not attempt to provide a "transcendental" justification for his basic moral and ethical principles à la Kant. The arguments he uses to advocate his prescriptions have the status of *prudential recommendations* rather than *rigorous demonstrations*. Although they are not amenable to rigorous proof, there are compelling reasons to accept them. The economic-energic standpoint may be out of fashion in contemporary psychoanalysis, but Freud's position is, as André Green argues, fundamentally a theory of "meaningful investment" (*Besetzung*), and his arguments in this context – which return to the motifs of The "wartime triptych" – are unabashedly economic.[65] Not only does religion exact an unacceptable toll on our intellect, but, for Freud, it also *represents an ill-advised allocation of our psychic resources.* By investing our mental assets in the phantasmagorical rewards of a world beyond, we divert them from our this-worldly existence and diminish our possibilities for fulfillment. It is Freud's view that if we were to withdraw those cathexes from the heavens and reinvest them in our life on earth, we would enhance our capacity to flourish. As opposed to the omnipotent Faustian will-to-power that seeks to dominate our natural habitat and our fellow humans, the reallocation of our psychic investments would liberate our power – our *energia* (potentiality) – "as honest smallholders on this earth," that is to say, as finite beings. Despite the narcissistic blow that this reinvestment would entail, and despite the fact that it would not produce the phantasmagorical prizes that religion dangle in front of the faithful, it would result in greater

[64] The naturalistic idea of innate destructiveness is not the same as the theological notion of original sin.

[65] Green, *The work of the negative*, 85.

fulfillment – and self-respect – in the long run. This is how Freud presents his positive doctrine, his *utopia of finitude*:

Of what use to them is the mirage of wide acres in the moon, whose harvest no one has yet seen? As honest smallholders on this earth they will know how to cultivate their plot in such a way that it supports them. By withdrawing their expectations from the other world and concentrating all their liberated energies into their life on earth, they will probably succeed in achieving a state of things in which life will be more tolerable for everyone and civilization no longer oppressive to anyone.[66]

Freud's "truth ethic" is not only a cognitive doctrine; it is also practical. It holds that by pursuing the path of truth – that is, by eschewing comforting illusions and consoling theodicies – one's chances of achieving a fulfilled life are enhanced. To mark his membership in the tradition of heretical Jewish thinkers founded by Spinoza, Freud concludes this passage with an ironical quote from another member of that tradition, Heinrich Heine, whom he describes as "a fellow-unbeliever" (*Unglaubensgenosse*) – the term that Heine uses to describe Spinoza: "We leave Heaven to the angels and the sparrows."[67]

Because Freud did not feel the need to have his work philosophically vindicated, he did not explicitly discuss his relation to Spinoza at any length in his published work. But he did not hesitate to acknowledge his esteem for the philosopher both as a thinker and as a human being: "Throughout my long life I [timidly] sustained an extraordinarily high respect for the person as well as for the results of thought [*Denkleistung*] of the great philosopher Spinoza."[68] Moreover, although Freud never addressed the details of Spinoza's philosophy, his basic theoretical orientation was Spinozist:

I readily admit my dependence on Spinoza's doctrine. There was no reason why I should expressly mention his name, since I conceived my hypotheses from

---

[66] *Freud, The future of an illusion*, 50.

[67] *Ibid.*, 50. Heine's remark prefigures the feelings expressed by another heretical iconoclast, John Lennon, in his composition *Imagine*.

[68] Quoted in Yovel, *Spinoza and other heretics*, 139.

the *atmosphere* created by him, rather than from the study of his work. Moreover, I did not seek a philosophical legitimization."[69]

In Spinoza, as Yovel observes, "Freud could see a reflection of himself – a solitary young revolutionary, adhering to a truth excavated from under the surface of the ruling culture, and facing hostility and scorn as a result." The Jewish philosopher was, Yovel writes, "a kind of distant brother of Freud, his brother in the honesty of his thought and the difficulty of his path, in his solitude and his genius" – and a brother in unbelief.[70]

Science and the Standpoint of Finitude

Freud's doctrines of helplessness and finitude hold the key to understanding the conception of science on which his critique of religion is based. Science does not coincide with the tenets of nineteenth-century Positivism, as Freud's critics often maintain. It is not defined by any particular theory or methodology, whether Aristotelian biology or quantum physics. Independent of how it happens to be instantiated at any given historical moment, science is the mode of thought and practice that befits the finite human mind. It is an institutionalized praxis predicated on the recognition of the human animal's innate tendency omnipotently to deny reality – the human penchant for magical thinking – *and it constitutes the methodical struggle against it.*[71]

The charge that Freud was a Positivist has become monotonous. It is too facile. It must be granted, however, that two facts can be adduced to support it. First, Freud was trained by Brücke, a leading representative of the Helmholzian School, and he endorsed Emil du Bois-Reymond's "Positivist Manifesto." And second, his "official" rhetoric often seeks to

---

[69] Quoted in *ibid.*, 139.

[70] *Ibid.*, 130.

[71] Bernard Williams argues that the commitment to truthfulness, accuracy, and the methodical and systematic attempt "to get things right," rather than the prescription of a correct methodology, distinguishes science from other forms of discourse and practice. And, like Freud, he believes that this pursuit requires constant vigilance against the misleading temptations created by "fantasy and wish." Bernard Williams, *Truth and truthfulness: an essay in genealogy* (Princeton, NJ: Princeton University Press, 2002), 45.

promote psychoanalysis as a strict science.[72] Both Freud's pre-analytic practice – which eschewed experimentalism and quantification, two hallmarks of late nineteenth-century Positivism – and his comments about the nature of science beyond the "official" rhetoric belie the claim that he was a Positivist. Furthermore, as we noted, Freud was deeply influenced by Goethe, who attempted to develop an alternative to Newton's reigning mathematical model of science.

The most striking thing about Freud's prescriptive notion of science was how little he had to say on the subject. Freud's conception of science is anti-foundational: It is grounded not on basic theoretical concepts that are assumed to be certain, but – as the important opening paragraphs of "Instincts and their vicissitudes" make clear – on provisional observational terms that are always open to revision.[73] Freud opposed science to philosophy for he believed that science proceeds in a piecemeal and cumulative fashion, repudiating all attempts at totalization and finality. Similarly, although science, as he conceived it, is rigorous, it does not strive for complete systematization. Instead of subordinating itself to the demands of a comprehensive overarching system, it builds its theories from below – that is, from empirical experience and the nature of the evidence.[74] This feature distinguishes it from religion, philosophy, and the various forms of *Weltanschauungen* that seek to provide an all-encompassing guide to reality.[75]

Perhaps most importantly, science is fallibilistic. Indeed, for Freud, this may be the feature that most distinguishes it from religion. He tells his religious interlocutor in *The future of an illusion*:

[72] Freud not only learned the details of the methodology of his Positivist teachers, he also internalized their scientific *ethos*: "Freud," as Ricoeur observes, "will never disavow [his mentors'] fundamental convictions." The conception of science he developed came to differ from theirs in radical ways, but Freud, "like all his Vienna and Berlin teachers," continued to see "in science the sole discipline of knowledge, the single rule of intellectual honesty, a world view that excludes all others, especially that of the old religion." Ricoeur, *Freud and philosophy*, 72.

[73] Freud, "Instincts and their vicissitudes," 117–118.

[74] See Kaufmann, *Discovering the mind*, vol. III, 77.

[75] Its rejection of totalizing systematization also distinguishes science from paranoid and obsessional systems of thought as well. At times, as Castoriadis remarks, only a hair's breadth seems to separate the "brilliant madness" of Schreber from the "mad brilliance" of Leibniz. Castoriadis, *Crossroads in the labyrinth*, 129.

Observe the difference between your attitude to illusions and mine. You have to
defend the religious illusion with all your might. If it becomes discredited . . .
then your world collapses. There is nothing left for you but to despair of everything . . . From that bondage I am, we are, free. Since we are prepared to renounce
a good part of our infantile wishes, we can bear it if a few of our expectations turn
out to be illusions.[76]

Scientists claim only that their theories provide the best possible way
of accounting for the data at that particular moment; they acknowledge
that their positions may be – indeed, if they are principled, *should* be –
superseded by later developments.[77] When that happens, the scientists
whose theories have been supplanted are prepared to relinquish those
theories – although not, one hopes, without a productive fight that may
itself enhance the science. Freud had only to observe the developments
in the physics of his day to see that this was true. And although it would
obviously run up against his most deeply seated inclinations, Freud
would have to admit that the scientific worldview and institution that
emerged in two specific places at two specific points in history (that is,
in ancient Greece and modern Europe) might one day be falsified. In
principle, if this were to happen, he would be compelled to withdraw his
investment in it.

Freud's assertion in *Totem and taboo* that modern science has renounced
the pleasure principle and completely replaced it with the reality principle is an embarrassing howler.[78] The claim is in fact self-contradictory,
although Freud does not recognize it. *The assertion that science has overcome omnipotence in toto is an omnipotent assertion.* It is not made from the
standpoint of finitude – the standpoint that science claims to occupy –
but remains within the register of omnipotence. Freud's error, however,
does not negate the idea that the proper task for the mature human mind
is to struggle against the omnipotence of thoughts. *The opposition to
magical thinking stands, but it must be elucidated in a non-omnipotent*

---

[76] Freud, *The future of an illusion*, 54.

[77] Samuel Beckett makes a Popperesque declaration that could serve as a maxim for
scientific fallibilism: "Ever tried. Ever failed. No matter. Try again. Fail again. Fail
better." Samuel Beckett, *Worstward ho* (New York: Grove Press, 1983), 2. I thank my
son Charlie Whitebook for calling my attention to the connection between Beckett's
admonition and the scientific outlook.

[78] See Freud, *Totem and taboo*, 90.

fashion – that is, within the register of finitude.[79] One's "faith" in reason must be elucidated after the fall of the Absolute, in a post-metaphysical and post-theological modality. The methodical struggle against the omnipotence of thoughts is an "infinite task," which the finite human mind can only approach asymptotically, in a "good enough" fashion. Indeed, the idea of a completed science, like the idea of a fully analysed individual, is an omnipotent illusion.

Two Difficulties with Freud's Position

These comments on finitude and science point to a deeper problem that is latent in Freud's thinking – namely, how difficult it is for large-brained apes like us to overcome omnipotence and magical thinking. There is something paradoxical about Freud's position, for his decentered anti-utopian affirmation of the merely human may be seen as utopian – as a utopia of finitude. Freud ironically acknowledges that his position comprises a chastened vision, telling us that our "god *Logos*" who watches over it is "not a very almighty one."[80] Yet this chastened vision remains utopian insofar as it suffers from the problem that plagues all utopias – it may be unattainable. In contrast to our usual idea of utopia, Freud's goal is not to create a land overflowing with milk and honey and devoid of privation and suffering, but simply to make our lives "as honest smallholders on this earth . . . more tolerable." But here's the rub: *Its very modesty is what makes it so difficult for creatures like us – with our incorrigible propensity for omnipotence, grandiosity, and magic – to realize this goal.* Freud claims that his position is naturalist, that it dispenses with all sentimental idealizations, and that it confronts human beings as they really are. But the yearning for omnipotence and magic and the wish for consolation may be intrinsic pieces of nature – of human nature.

---

[79] The question of how to elucidate the standpoint of finitude without appealing to the infinite – or the standpoint of immanence without appealing to the transcendent – remains a vexing philosophical problem of the first order. (Kant's transcendental philosophy represented a heroic attempt that failed.) For a deep and sustained reflection on the problem see Aristides Baltas, *Peeling potatoes and grinding lenses: Spinoza and young Wittgenstein converse on immanence and its logic* (Pittsburgh, PA: University of Pittsburgh Press, 2012).

[80] Freud, *The future of an illusion*, 54.

The possibility that most members of the human species may have no interest in signing on to the program of maturity as Freud defines it must be taken seriously. Elitist though it may sound, the demand that individuals "admit to themselves the full extent of their helplessness and their insignificance in the machinery of the universe" is, after all, a tall order, one that may be unlikely to appeal to most ordinary citizens, only approachable by a minority of individuals. Peter Berger – who was once one of the foremost defenders of the secularization thesis but who later concluded that it had been misconceived – notes that the human need for a consoling theodicy may be ineradicable:

Secular ideologies do not in the long run satisfy the need of human beings to give meaning to personal experience, especially that of pain and loss. They do not supply a *theodicy* in the broad sense given by Max Weber to an originally theological term for God in the presence of suffering and evil.[81]

The problem is already present in a contradiction in Freud's position, though he does not thematize it. On the one hand, Freud states that religion addresses "the oldest, strongest and most urgent wishes of mankind," including, one assumes, the wish for consolation. On the other hand, he never systematically addresses what would become of those wishes in a post-religious society – what alternative fate might await them. Rather, Freud for the most part seems to assume that, with the spread of science and process of secularization, the wish for consolation will simply wither away. But given the anthropological facts of helplessness and extended childhood dependency as Freud himself has delineated them, this is hardly plausible. Furthermore, "the desecuarlization of the world" during the past half-century has done much to undermine progressivist confidence that religion is on its way out.[82]

Pfister posed a question to Freud regarding his clinical approach that is equally applicable to his disconsolate worldview and critique of religion. Why, the Swiss minister asks, if analysts have nothing to offer their patients but the unvarnished truth about a "despoiled universe," should

---

[81] Peter Berger, "Paradox or pluralism: review of Michael Walzer's *The paradox of liberation: secular revolutions and religious counterrevolutions*," *Jewish Review of Books* 6 (2015), 14.

[82] See Peter Berger, *The desecularization of the world* (New York: William B. Eerdmans, 1999).

"the poor devils" not prefer to remain "shut up in their illness" rather than "entering that dreadful icy desolation"?[83] Likewise, why should believers relinquish their faith if all that Freud's Enlightenment critique of religion can offer them is resignation to their helplessness and insignificance in a disenchanted world? Why indeed? The response that Freud offers to disillusionment on the individual level and disenchantment on the collective level is, as Homans asserts, the acceptance of loss and the creation of new meaning and psychic structures through mourning. But this is extremely tough medicine, and Freud himself suggests that "only a few are capable of overcoming" infantilism.[84] Indeed, from the inception of psychoanalytical practice, many analysts have believed that classical analytic technique in the strict sense is only for the "few" – that only a small part of the patient population is "analysable."

Religion may not constitute a cognitive system that can compete with the science's truth-claims about "reality," but, as Durkheim argued, the religious impulse, like sexuality and aggression, is a permanent feature of human reality that every conceivable human society must find a way to accommodate. It is therefore incumbent on a proponent of secularization like Freud to propose possible "functional equivalents" for religion, as Durkheim called them, in a post-religious society.[85]

But as we noted, Freud never pursued the question of what post-religious alternatives might be available to those who reject his program of disillusionment; he offered no alternative program for the disillusionment. Here he might have followed the example of his "fellow unbeliever" Spinoza, who was more politically realistic in this regard.[86] Where Freud observed that not everyone was capable of overcoming infantilism, Spinoza argued that only the few can attain "the first kind of knowledge" – that is, strict philosophical knowledge, which is based on reason alone and which, like classical analytic technique, eschews the imagination. But Spinoza did not stop there. He conceptualized a "second kind of

[83] Meng and Freud (eds.), *Psychoanalysis and faith*, 116.

[84] *Ibid.*, 118. Freud acknowledges this when he quotes Goethe: "He who possesses science and art also has religion; but he who possesses neither of the two, let him have religion!" *Civilization and its discontents*, 74 n. 1.

[85] Durkheim, *The elementary forms of religious life*, 432. This idea was suggested to me by the late Ruth Stein.

[86] Yirmiyahu Yovel pointed this out to me.

knowledge" appropriate to "the multitude." It is opposed to religion in that it is not based on fear, superstition, and illusion, but it does not aspire to the rational purity of strict philosophical truth. And in contrast to philosophy, it does not hesitate to employ the emotions, affects, and imagination to promote the right beliefs and dispositions in the multitude. A psychoanalytic interpretation of Spinoza's "second kind of knowledge" might be a fruitful way to begin envisioning a functional equivalent to religion from a psychoanalytic point of view. In fact, analysts, with their knowledge of unconscious mental life, fantasy formation, group processes, the sado-masochistic dynamics of authority, and so on are in a particularly advantageous position to envisage such equivalents. This is an area where psychoanalysis might make a unique contribution to today's controversies regarding religion.

The second problem with Freud's position is this. Though he does not use the terminology we have been employing, Freud himself raises the question of the relation between his official and unofficial positions – more specifically, between his theory of the father complex and his doctrine of helplessness – and he does so through one of his favorite literary devices: an imaginary interlocutor (who was modeled on Pfister). But although he raises the right question, Freud's response to his interlocutor's objection amounts to a brush-off rather than a full-throated engagement with it. Furthermore, the glaring blunder contained in that brush-off is symptomatic of his inability fully to engage the figure of the early mother.

After observing that Freud had previously discussed the origins of religion in *Totem and taboo*, his interlocutor continues:

But there it appeared in a different light. Everything was the son–father relationship. God was the exalted father, and the longing for the father was the root of the need for religion. Since then, it seems, you have discovered the factor of human weakness and helplessness [associated with the pre-Oedipal realm], to which indeed the chief role in the formation of religion is generally assigned, and now you transpose everything that was once the father complex into the terms of helplessness.[87]

The interlocutor is in effect inquiring into the relationship between the Oedipal and (underdeveloped) pre-Oedipal strata of Freud's theory.

---

[87] *The future of an illusion*, 22.

Freud begins his explanation of the relation "between the father complex and man's helplessness and need for protection" by stating what is in fact the correct position:[88]

[T]he mother, who satisfies the child's hunger, becomes its first love-object and certainly also its first protection against all the undefined dangers and threats in the external world – its first protection against anxiety, we may say.[89]

Because of that inability to engage with the early mother, however, Freud cannot stick with this critical insight. He quickly takes flight from it and, in the process, commits the embarrassing howler mentioned above – one that evades the often terrifying power of the archaic mother: "In this function [of protection] the mother is soon replaced by the stronger father, who retains that position for the rest of childhood."[90] In a related passage, Freud also denies the power of the seemingly omnipotent mother and argues that the experience of religious "grandeur" derives exclusively from the primal father.[91] Because of his commitment to the Oedipus complex as his fundamental explanatory device, Freud is compelled to assimilate the idea of helplessness to the figure of the father. These passages demonstrate that Freud's anxiety concerning pre-Oedipal experience placed serious limits on not only his theory of psychic life but also his account of religion. A more satisfactory psychoanalytic theory of religion would have to fully encompass the maternal dimension. We will return to this topic in our discussion of *Geistigkeit* in the next chapter.

Again, biographical considerations can help us understand Freud's adopted extreme position regarding consolation. We can reasonably surmise that Freud's traumatic disappointment in Amalie and his *Kinderfrau* – as well as in Jacob's inability to step in and compensate for their maternal failures – made it difficult for him to trust that this environment could be a source of support, comfort, and satisfaction. Consequently, part of the *phallologocentric* character that Freud fashioned in response to his early traumata consisted in a repudiation of dependency – a repudiation of "the passive-feminine" attitude – and a near-fetishization of self-sufficiency.

---

[88] *Ibid.*,. 23.

[89] *Ibid.*,. 24

[90] *Ibid.*, 24.

[91] Freud, *Moses and monotheism*, 128.

His extreme repudiation of consolation was a consequence of this hypomanic idealization of independence. In this regard, a letter Freud wrote to Fliess on his first trip to Rome is significant; in it, he comments on his reaction to the medieval – that is to say, Catholic – stratum of the Eternal City as follows:

> The atmosphere troubled me. I found it difficult to tolerate the lie concerning man's redemption, which raises its head to high heaven – for I could not cast off the thought of my own misery and all the other misery I know about.[92]

With his rejection of consolation, Freud in effect is saying this: "Don't try to lure me out of my hard-won independence and lucidity with your false promises of solace. I've suffered too much. I know too much. I will not be duped again."

For Freud to have attained true maturity as he defined it – that is, true acceptance of his finitude – he would have had to have relinquished his fetishization of independence and acknowledged that, like the rest of us, he was in need of comfort. But this would have required him to confront and work through the extreme fear of helplessness that had resulted from his early traumas, and this was not something he was prepared to do. As Sprengnether points out, the only place where he was able to acknowledge his helplessness, dependency, and need of support was with his daughter Anna – his Antigone – who heroically nursed him through his protracted struggle against cancer.[93] One must ask: Did he refind his *Kinderfrau* in his daughter?

---

[92] Masson (ed.), *Letters to Fliess*, 449.
[93] See Sprengnether, *The spectral mother*, 176–177.

13

Late Freud and the Early Mother

IT HAS BEEN THE persistent thesis of this work that a lacuna in Freud's own psychological development colored and limited his theoretical work. Simply put, his difficulties with the figure of the early mother proved to be the source of a range of wrong-footed theoretical formulations. Freud was not entirely unaware of his deficiencies. As we shall see in this chapter, particularly in his correspondence with his friend, the author Roman Rolland, his explanation of his shortcomings is relatively deep – deeper even than that of the very sharp, perceptive Rolland. Echoing comments he makes regarding his limitations vis-à-vis the exploration of the more archaic dimension of psychic life, Freud writes to Rolland that, "while I have dug to a certain depth for their roots . . . it isn't easy to pass beyond the limits of one's nature."[1]

Rolland accurately explains Freud's deficiencies in terms of the latter's commitment to "critical reason," but he does not examine the psychological aspects of that theoretical commitment. Freud, however, by referring to "the limits of one's nature," at least points in the direction of a psychological account. This tells us that Freud had more than an inkling of the problem. The lacuna in his development – his discomfort with the mother – continued to inform his work through all the later years of his life, which were also beset with nearly overwhelming external difficulties. That is what this chapter will explore.

Freud's "Hellenic" investment in "critical reason" – that is, his Parmenidean–Apollonian commitment to differentiation, determinacy, and clarity – is overdetermined. On the one hand, it represents an authentic sublimatory accomplishment, achieved in part through lengthy education and scientific training, which had gained a considerable degree of freedom from its genetic roots. But on the other hand, these Parmenidean–Apollonian

[1] Ernst L. Freud (ed.), *The letters of Sigmund Freud*, 232.

proclivities served a defensive function. They prevented Freud from entering the more irrational, diffuse, fluid, and indeterminate areas of experience,
represented in philosophy by Heraclitus, in mythology by the chthonic
deities, and in psychoanalysis by the archaic mother. Freud in fact acknowledged his resistance to these more shadowy nether regions, admitting that "it
is very difficult for [him] to work with these almost intangible quantities."[2]

There is no question that the Parmenidean moment is an absolutely
necessary moment in the defense of "critical reason." Without a commitment to the rigors of differentiation, determinacy, and clarity, we
would be left in a "night in which . . . all cows are black," as Hegel put
it.[3] Rationality and science would be impossible. But the rationalist tradition is also subject to its own "pathologies."[4] These include not only
rigid formalism, excessive systematization, dogmatic scientism, and the
idealization of mathematics, but also difficulty dealing with affects, the
irreducible equivocality of ordinary language, and the vicissitudes of
development. At their worst, these deformations make it impossible to
capture the multitude of phenomena that elude rationality's conceptual
grid – what Adorno called "the addenda."[5] Much of post-Hegelian philosophy has been concerned with addressing the pathologies of reason
and the concomitant pathologies of the subject.

Freud occupies an ambiguous position in this context, which might be
expected given that he was a transitional figure with one foot planted in
the nineteenth century and the other in the twentieth. With his discovery
of psychic reality, the essentially perverse nature of human sexuality, and
the instinctual roots of an ego that is "not master in its own house," he
contributed as much as any modern thinker to the critique of reason and
of the subject. But the historical and cultural limits of his time as well as
the psychological limits of his personality prevented him from pursuing
the critique further. That he had serious limitations, which are apparent to
us, is true but almost trivial, for it is true of the significant figures in every
field. Instead of perseverating over those limitations, we should marvel at

[2] Freud, *Civilization and its discontents*, 72–73.

[3] G.W.F. Hegel, *The phenomenology of the spirit*, trans. A.V. Miller (Oxford: Oxford
University Press, 1997), 13.

[4] See Axel Honneth, *Pathologies of reason (on the legacy of critical theory)*, trans. James
D. Ingram (New York: Columbia University Press, 2009).

[5] Adorno, *Negative dialectics*, 226.

how far Freud – like all truly great thinkers – transcended his limitations and pursued his subversive investigations *in spite of them*. Where he left off should be our point of departure, and we should use the abundant resources he gave us to pursue our investigations.

"To Me Mysticism Is Just as Closed a Book as Music"

Freud's difficulties with the figure of the early mother are particularly perspicuous in the important first chapter of *Civilization and its discontents*, written as a response to Roman Rolland. Like Oskar Pfister, Rolland was an interlocutor and correspondent whom Freud deeply respected, although they had substantial differences regarding religion. They also disagreed on such topics as intuition versus rationality, the significance of mystical experience, and the perfectibility of humankind. But despite these differences, Freud's admiration for Rolland's character, for his principled and courageous political stances, his cosmopolitanism, scholarly accomplishments, and artistic creativity even surpassed his respect for the integrity of the Swiss minister.[6] His praise for the Frenchmen – a pacifist, musicologist, scholar, and Nobel laureate – could not have been higher. In the opening paragraph of *Civilization and its discontents*, Freud describes Rolland as one of the "few men" who is not motivated by the false values of "power, success and wealth" but instead pursues "what is of true value in life."[7] And in a tantalizing confession that appears in his last letter to Rolland, Freud tells him, "I have rarely experienced that mysterious attraction of one human being for another as vividly as I have with you," adding, "it is somehow bound up, perhaps, with the awareness of our being so different."[8] If Freud had said more about the mystery of that attraction, we might have learned a great deal about his psychology.

Upon its publication in 1927, Freud forwarded a copy of *The future of an illusion* to Rolland, whose scholarship embraced, among so many subjects, Eastern religion, and the reply he received consisted in two parts. Rolland agreed with Freud's critique of all organized religion – that is, of

[6] Rolland was perhaps best known as the author of *Jean Christophe*, a famous novel based on the life of Beethoven. He was awarded the 1915 Nobel Prize for literature.

[7] Freud, *Civilization and its discontents*, 64.

[8] *The letters of Sigmund Freud*, ed. Ernst L. Freud, 406.

official churches of every sort as well as of their doctrines, credos, and systems of belief – but he also expressed regret that Freud had not examined
what Rolland called "the true source of religious sentiments." Entirely
distinct from doctrine, this phenomenon, in Rolland's description, provides "the religious energy which is seized upon by the various Churches
and religious systems, directed by them into particular channels, and
doubtless also exhausted by them." It is "a feeling," consisting in "a sensation of 'eternity,' a feeling as of something limitless, unbounded – as
it were 'oceanic.'" It is, moreover, "a purely subject fact, not an article
of faith," and it "brings with it no assurance of immortality" nor of any
other extra-psychic facts. Nevertheless, Rolland argues, "one may . . .
rightly call oneself religious on the ground of the oceanic feeling alone,
even if one rejects every belief and every illusion."[9]

Freud found Rolland's idea of an oceanic feeling unsettling. It left
him "no peace," he admitted, which is probably why it took him nineteen months to respond to Rolland's letter.[10] (Almost a decade later, he
would report that he was unable to find any peace regarding the Moses
legend, which "haunted [him] like an unlaid ghost."[11]) Freud begins his
published response to Rolland's claims in the first chapter of *Civilization
and its discontents* by stating that he "cannot discover this 'oceanic' feeling
in" himself; he then proceeds to present an unsatisfying treatment of the
topic that is symptomatic of the substantial deficiencies in his ability to
deal with pre-verbal, that is to say pre-Oedipal, phenomena.[12] In his letter
to Rolland, Freud adds the following admission: "To me mysticism is just
as closed a book as music," an acknowledgment that he is as tone-deaf
to the *unio mystica* as to music.[13] The unstated fact is that Freud's being
closed off to both phenomena springs from a single origin – his fear of the
unio maternalis, the union of the infant with its mother.

Meanwhile, in his attempt to address the oceanic feeling in his reply to
Rolland, Freud becomes evasive. The man who undertook the analysis of
the seemingly self-contradictory notion of unconscious affect begs off by

[9] Freud, *Civilization and its discontents*, 64.

[10] Ernst L. Freud (ed.), *The letters of Sigmund Freud*, 388.

[11] Freud, *Moses and monotheism*, 103.

[12] Freud, *Civilization and its discontents*, 65.

[13] Ernst L. Freud (ed.), *The letters of Sigmund Freud*, 388.

claiming that "it is not easy to deal scientifically with feelings." The best one can do, he maintains, is to "fall back on the ideational content which is most readily associated with feeling" – that is, translate affect into cognition, the pre-linguistic into the linguistic. Accordingly, he proposes that the notion of the oceanic feeling be translated into the idea of "a feeling of an indissoluble bond, of being one with the external world as a whole." This proposal is not in itself objectionable, but in a murky passage Freud goes on to make the following assertion: "This seems to be something rather in the nature of an intellectual perception, which is not, it is true, without an accompanying feeling-tone, but only such as would be present with any other act of thought of equal range."[14]

Freud now introduces an important distinction between the existence of the oceanic feeling as such on the one hand and its significance and function regarding the origins of religion on the other. Freud acknowledges that his inability to locate the feeling in himself does not grant him the "right to deny that it does in fact occur in other people." On the contrary, his failure to experience it might actually indicate something about his own individual psychic make-up that prevents him from recognizing something that exists in (many) others. He then offers a separate argument: If the oceanic feeling does in fact exist, it does not follow that Rolland is interpreting it correctly or that it constitutes "the *fons et origo* of the whole need for religion."[15] For the purposes of our investigation, the question of whether the oceanic feeling represents the primary source of religion is secondary. It is more important to grasp its full significance for the understanding of early development and the formation of psychic structure, regardless of its significance for religious experience. So while the unofficial Freud timidly broaches the topic, the official Freud quickly draws back from it.

Freud then makes an assertion that is problematic as well as revealing. He remarks that the notion of an "immediate feeling" of our connection with "the world around" us "sounds so strange and fits in so badly with the fabric of our psychology that one is justified in attempting to discover a psycho-analytic, that is, genetic, explanation for such a feeling."[16]

[14] Freud, *Civilization and its discontents*, 65.

[15] *Ibid.*, 65.

[16] *Ibid.*, 65.

But what may be self-evident to Freud is by no means obvious to every-one. The notion may sound strange only to someone with his particular psychological make-up. Similarly, one can counter by arguing that the idea only accords poorly with *his* psychology because of the Oedipal lim-itations of "official" psychoanalytic theory.

More striking yet, Freud provides the correct genetic account of the oceanic feeling but fails to draw the right conclusions from his spot-on analysis. His account points to the universal existence of an undifferen-tiated pre-Oedipal stratum of psychic life, but he is unable to register its full existence. He argues that the common conception of the ego as an autonomous, unified, and well-delineated entity – that is, "marked off distinctly from everything else" – is "deceptive." The domain of the ego actually continues "inwards, without sharp delimitation, into an uncon-scious mental entity which we designate as the id."[17] As he argues in another text, we should not think of the boundaries separating the agen-cies of the psyche as "sharp frontiers" that can best be delineated with the sort of precise lines that one finds on a map. Rather, it is more accurate to visualize them as "areas of colour melting into one another as they are presented by modern artists."[18]

Freud also contends that, with one exception, in its normal non-pathological functioning, the ego maintains a "clear and sharp line of demarcation" between intrapsychic and extrapsychic reality, subject and object. That one "unusual" yet non-pathological exception is "the state of being in love," in which "the boundary between ego and object threatens to melt away."[19] Freud's account of the ego's relation to the external world, however, is itself also "deceptive." Because of his latent Cartesianism, Freud does not recognize that, in addition to being in love, there are many other non-pathological states in which a differentiated subject–object relation becomes relatively fluid. In light of what we have learned from the pre-Oedipal turn in psychoanalysis and from experience working with the non-classical patient, "the objectivity of the object and the subjectivity of the subject," as Loewald noted, no longer appear as the clear-cut facts that they did for Freud.[20]

[17] *Ibid.*, 66.

[18] Freud, *New introductory lectures on psycho-analysis*, 79.

[19] Freud, *Civilization and its discontents*, 66.

[20] Loewald, "The waning of the Oedipus complex," 399.

Freud rightly observes, however, that, to the extent that it exists, the feeling of a relatively autonomous, integrated, and differentiated ego "cannot have been the same from the beginning" but "must have gone through a process of development." *He therefore postulates the existence of a primary undifferentiated stage of development – akin to what he earlier called primary narcissism – and offers a perspicuous account of the separation-individuation process and the introduction of the reality principle.* "An infant at the breast," Freud notes, "does not as yet distinguish his ego from the external world as the source of the sensations flowing in upon him" but only "gradually learns to do so, in response to various promptings," especially those having to do with the experience of unpleasure.[21] Through this process, the ego – which originally included everything – "separates off an external world from itself" and establishes itself as a relatively distinct and independent entity. "Our present ego-feeling," according to Freud, "is, therefore, only a shrunken residue of a much more inclusive – indeed, an all-embracing – feeling which corresponded to a more intimate bond between the ego and the world about it."[22]

Freud is now in a position to present his genetic account of the oceanic feeling:

If we may assume that there are many people in whose mental life this primary ego-feeling has persisted to a greater or less degree, it would exist in them side by side with the narrower and more sharply demarcated ego-feeling of maturity . . . In that case, the ideational contents appropriate to it would be precisely those of limitlessness and of a bond with the universe – the same ideas with which my friend elucidated the "oceanic" feeling.[23]

Freud's formulation, however, discloses a critical problem in his position. If this "primary ego-feeling" persists in "many people," then the idea of an oceanic feeling hardly "sound[s] so strange" as Freud believes it does. On the contrary, on the basis of our current knowledge of early development and the genesis of the ego, we are confident that memory

---

[21] Freud, *Civilization and its discontents*, 67–68.

[22] *Ibid.*, 68. It should be noted that Freud does not say that the self-enclosed archaic ego turns to a reality that is separate from it, as he had in "Formulations concerning the two principles of mental functioning." Rather, he says that it "separates off an external world from itself." This is a crucial distinction.

[23] *Ibid.*, 68.

traces of early merger-like experiences with the archaic breast-mother are encoded in all of our psyches. It is only that some people have more access to these traces than others who, like Freud, are defensively cut off from them. (This is a *psychological* claim that is entirely independent from the issue of whether those feelings constitute the *fons et origo* of religion.) Indeed, today we are more inclined to say, following Loewald, that lack of access to the early undifferentiated strata of the psyche is itself a form of pathology that limits the possibilities of achieving a richly integrated self and a fulfilled life. Likewise, as opposed to our psychoanalytic forebears, we no longer tend to view "the so-called fully developed mature ego" as "one that has become fixated at the presumably highest" and most differentiated "stage of development." We are more apt to consider a felicitous form of ego-organization as one "that integrates its reality in such a way that the earlier and deeper levels of ego-reality integration remain alive as dynamic sources of higher organization."[24]

Though we are not primarily concerned with the thesis that the oceanic feeling constitutes the *fons et origo* of religion, the way Freud rejects it is illuminating. After offering a comprehensive and convincing analysis of the origins of the oceanic feeling in the undifferentiated experience of the infant–mother matrix, he summarily dismisses the argument that it should "be regarded as the source of religious needs" and reverts to his theory of the strong father. In a telling argument, he asserts that "the claim does not seem compelling" because "a feeling can only be a source of energy if it is itself the expression of a strong need." And he goes on to assert that he "cannot think of any need in childhood as strong as the need for the father's protection," which means that "the part played by the oceanic feeling, which might seek something like the restoration of limitless narcissism, is ousted from its place in the foreground." Freud concludes his analysis by reiterating the position he had taken in *The future of an illusion*: "The derivation of religious needs from the infant's helplessness and the longing for the father aroused by it seems incontrovertible."[25] The fact of the matter is, however, that Freud's inability to engage with the figure of the early mother and his repudiation of the symbiotic wish in himself prevented him from acknowledging that the

[24] Loewald, "Ego and reality," 20.
[25] Freud, *Civilization and its discontents*. 72.

desire to restore "limitless narcissism" is one of the strongest sources of energy in psychic life.

There is an even more peculiar difficulty with Freud's claim that the "longing" for the strong protective father constitutes the source of religion. It is at odds with the very theory of helplessness and infantile danger situations that he was developing at exactly the same time that he was also composing his texts on religion.[26] As we observed, Freud stated the correct position in *The future of an illusion* – namely, that "the mother, who satisfies the child's hunger, becomes . . . its first protection against the undefined dangers which threaten it in the external world, its first protection against anxiety." But he then beat a hasty retreat from that position, asserting that the mother's "protective function is soon replaced by the stronger father, who retains that position for the rest of childhood."[27]

It comes down to this: While the dangers against which the father protects the child should not be minimized, from a developmental perspective they belong to a relatively late epoch of psychic life. They presuppose the existence of an ego that is sufficiently separated from the external world so that it can represent nature and the dangers emanating from it – so that one can be aware of them. But, as Freud noted, the existence of a relatively differentiated ego "cannot have been [there] from the beginning," and the most primordial form of helplessness that the infant experiences – and the attendant dangers to that helplessness – date from an era before the differentiated ego is formed. In this context, helplessness consists in the incipient ego's inability to process the powerful, somatically based excitations that impinge upon it and thereby to reduce the build-up of destabilizing tension. The threat is precisely the danger of being overwhelmed by excessive stimuli. Indeed, it can be argued that being flooded by unbound excitation represents the primordial form of trauma.

A central task of the mother or mothering figure during the early stages of development is to protect her infant from this flood of stimulation. Through her ministrations to her baby's physical needs, she must eliminate potentially traumatic excitation, against which the baby is helpless, in order to maintain its homeostasis and keep it stable within. In light of Freud's debate with the quintessentially musical Rolland, it is significant

---

[26] See Freud, *Inhibitions, symptoms and anxiety*, 137.

[27] Freud, *The future of an illusion*, 24.

that the musicality of the mother's voice is one of the most effective resources in the maternal repertoire for soothing an infant's distress and restoring its psycho–affective composure. The nursing situation is more than a means of delivering nutrition. The danger of losing the early breast-mother is not only the danger of losing a "need–satisfying object" – "the cupboard mother" – it is simultaneously the danger of losing the agent that, by reducing tension through the satisfaction of somatic needs, pro-tects the child from the danger of traumatic excitation.

Furthermore, the threat of ego–loss remains with us throughout life and is no less a danger than the later threats that emanate from the exter-nal world. Freud's own experience of something approximating this early form of trauma to one degree or another – when Amalie, Jacob, and his *Kinderfrau* were unable to protect him from overwhelming anxiety – eventually resulted in his flight into premature adulthood and his defen-sive construction of a relatively rigid phallologocentric character.

Rolland, anticipating the later analysis of Heinz Kohut, took Freud's resistance to music as a manifestation of a gap in his psychic structure that resulted in serious limitations in his intellectual persona, his theory, and in his clinical practice. In fact, he had become intrigued by the analyst's antipathy to music even before receiving Freud's gift of *The future of an illusion* in November, 1927. Vacationing in Vienna during the previous July, Rolland had met Princess Marie Bonaparte, who happened to be a guest at the same hotel. It was in conversations with Bonaparte and several of her colleagues, the analyst D.J. Fisher tells us, that Rolland learned that "Freud was closed off to music," that in fact he "had a 'total, irremissi-ble occlusion to it." Rolland, Fisher reports, was "troubled . . . by this piece of information." That Freud, who seemed to be the very person-ification of uninhibited curiosity, had neither "perceived the cathartic possibility" of music nor inquired into "the roots of his resistance to [musical experience]" in order to overcome it "baffled" the musicologist. The Frenchman also raised a pertinent question concerning the clinical implications of Freud's imperviousness to music: "How could he ever read into the subconscious of souls, if he does not possess the key to the language of the subconscious?"[28]

---

[28] D.J. Fisher, "Sigmund Freud and Romain Rolland: the terrestrial animal and his great oceanic friend," *American Imago* 33 (1976), 18. (The quotations within this pas-sage are from Rolland's correspondence.)

And as the debate over religion unfolded, Freud himself observed that his resistance to music and his antipathy toward religion, at least in its more mystical manifestations, were closely related. Because the question of the meaning of religion touches on the very nature of the human animal, it was again difficult for Rolland to reconcile Freud's imperviousness to mysticism with his prodigiously unrestricted curiosity. In fact, for Rolland, this fact constituted a serious anomaly for the psychoanalytic student of human nature, and he told the self-proclaimed intellectual conquistador, "because 'nothing human is unknown to you,'" he could "hardly believe that mysticism and music are unknown to you."[29]

Rolland's explanation of this anomaly is not incorrect, but it does not go far enough. "I think you distrust" music and mysticism, he tells Freud, "because you uphold the integrity of critical reason, with which you control the instrument" – an apparent allusion to both the musical instrument and the instrument of the mind.[30] And Freud tends to agree with his friend's assessment. After receiving Rolland's biographical study of two Indian mystics, Freud wrote the perhaps somewhat disingenuous reply: "I shall now try with your guidance to penetrate into the Indian Jungle from which until now a certain blending of Hellenic love of proportion, Jewish sobriety, and philistine timidity have kept me away." Freud's reference to "the Indian Jungle," it should be noted, calls to mind the image of "the dark continent" that he had used to describe female psychology three years earlier in *The question of lay analysis*.[31] His reply now to Rolland acknowledges that he should have "tackled [the topic of mysticism] earlier, for the plants of this soil shouldn't be alien to me."[32]

Rolland maintains that although Freud's suspicion of mysticism and music was connected to his desire to defend "critical rationality," his resistance to the more fluid, indeterminate, and intensive realm of "intuitive" experience that mysticism and music represent actually limited how far he could carry out that defense. Freud's "extreme rationalism," he

[29] Quoted in Parsons, *The enigma of the oceanic feeling*, 176.

[30] *Ibid.*, 176.

[31] Ernst L. Freud (ed.), *The letters of Sigmund Freud*, 392. See also Freud, *The question of lay analysis*, 212.

[32] Ernst L. Freud (ed.), *The letters of Sigmund Freud*, 232. He also speculated that female analysts might have more success exploring that earlier rejoin and he turned out to be right, Melanie Klein and Margaret Mahler being two prime examples.

argues, can result in an irrationality of its own. Reason and the ego do not develop most felicitously by narrowing themselves and excluding what is alien to them. Rather, they advance and enrich themselves by encountering and integrating their "Other" into their domain. "The work of Eros" consists in creating "greater unities" by integrating the heterogeneous. Rolland tells his tone-deaf interlocutor, "Since birth, I have taken part in both the intuitive and the critical," and "I do not suffer from a conflict between their opposing tendencies." And he turns to music to make his point: "The musician makes harmony with the enemy forces, and at the same time finds in it his greatest joy." Harmony – *felicitous synthesis* – that brings conflicting forces together is the goal in music as it should be in psychic life. As opposed to the false reconciliation of musical kitsch, serious harmony does not consist in the elimination of the conflicting forces. Rather, music achieves its dynamics and liveliness through the difficult synthesis of opposing forces. The "official" Freud, with his exclusionary model of the psychic apparatus, could not appreciate this point. The "unofficial" Freud, however, with his doctrine of *eros* and his inclusionary model of the psychic apparatus, gleaned that the right kind of synthesis is the *desideratum*, but he could not fully explore the implications.

In fact, Freud only implicitly – and perhaps out of some sort of unconscious design – addresses the topic of felicitous integration. It occurs in a lengthy excursus in the first chapter of *Civilization and its discontents*, in which Freud indulges his passion for history and travel, as well as his love of Rome, and presents a detailed analysis of the stratified temporal-physical structure of the Eternal City. The stated purpose of the discussion is narrowly delimited. In order to explain how the early undifferentiated ego-states that account for the oceanic feeling can coexist alongside the maturely developed ego, Freud offers an overall explanation of how things are preserved "in the sphere of the mind."[33] But the implications of his analysis go far beyond his stated intention. Loewald believes that this excursus in fact provides one of the primary resources available to us for constructing Freud's "unofficial" position.

Freud begins his discussion with a reminder that, according to psychoanalytic teaching, "forgetting" something does not consist in the "annihilation" of its "memory-trace." In fact, the opposite is true: "In mental life

[33] Freud, *Civilization and its discontents*, 69.

nothing which has once been formed can perish . . . everything is somehow preserved."[34] He turns to his description of Rome to demonstrate
how this preservation takes place. With obvious delight, he leads us on a
detailed tour of his beloved city, showing how survivals from different historical epochs – the ancient, the medieval, and the Renaissance – coexist
in the modern city and are perceptible to the observer with a well-trained
eye. He tells us that "all [the] remains of ancient Rome" he is describing
"are found dovetailed into the jumble of the great metropolis which has
grown up in the last few centuries." After guiding us on an extended tour
of the Eternal City, Freud decides to rein in the pleasures of indulgence
and tells us "there is clearly no point in spinning our phantasy any further." In fact, because it is based on spatiality, the continuation of the
urban analogy actually "leads to things that are unimaginable and even
absurd."[35] Because two things cannot simultaneously occupy the same
space, at some point the city must break down as a model for explaining
the simultaneous coexistence of survivals from different epochs.

Not so in the realm of the human mind. Because it is not constrained
by the conditions of spatiality, there are no limits on the coexistence of
material from different developmental strata in the psyche. "Thus,"
Freud concludes, "we are perfectly willing to acknowledge that the
'oceanic' feeling exists in many people, and we are inclined to trace it
back to an early ego-feeling."[36] The implications of his analysis, however,
go far beyond the topic of the oceanic feeling and bear on the questions
of development, maturity, and psychic flourishing. According to the official position, development is seen as a more or less unilinear process in
which each "more advanced" stage supersedes and eliminates the more
"primitive" one before it, culminating in the ascendance of the supposedly rational and autonomous ego. Likewise, maturity is understood as
the ascendance of the mature ego to the top of the psyche's hierarchical
organization and its domination over the putatively more primitive stages
of development.

But drawing on Freud's urban analogy, development can be envisaged in a different way. Just as the history of Rome did not consist in

[34] *Ibid.*, 69.

[35] *Ibid.*, 70.

[36] *Ibid.*, 72.

a unidirectional unfolding in which each successive epoch replaced and eliminated its predecessor, so psychic development should not be seen as a strictly progressive process in which the "advanced" supersedes and eradicates the "primitive." Likewise, on this conception, the goal of development should be viewed not as a "power grab by the ego," but *as a felicitous constellation in which "free intercourse" is established between the more advanced and the more primitive strata of the psyche.*[37] From the "unofficial" perspective, this becomes the question concerning the goal of development: What are the most desirable forms of differentiated psychic integration – of the unification of the psyche – and the most felicitous modes of communication between the various strata?[38]

A Minoan–Mycenean Civilization

Although the intensity of Freud's reaction to Jacob's death is hard to explain, it nevertheless threw him into a profound, turbulent, and protracted emotional crisis. The experience, as we noted, led him to make the by no means self-evident statement that the death of his father "is the most important event, the most poignant loss, of a man's life."[39] His reaction to his mother's death, which occurred in September 1930 when she was ninety-five, was altogether different. To be sure, Freud realized that he could not discern the possible effects of Amalie's death in the "deeper levels" of his psyche, but on "the surface" he remained curiously unmoved.[40] He reported to Ferenczi that "this great event . . . had a strange effect on me. No pain, no mourning."[41] (It is entirely plausible that the emotional effects were so powerful that Freud had to numb himself to them.) Furthermore, Amalie's golden Sigi did not attend her funeral, but sent his daughter Anna instead. The ostensible reason for his absence was his infirm condition, but it is difficult to believe that there was not more going on, that it was not also an act of avoidance. Just as he

[37] Castoriadis, *The imaginary institution of society*, 104. See also Freud, *Inhibitions, symptoms and anxiety*, 98.
[38] See Loewald, "Ego and reality," 20.
[39] Freud, *The interpretation of dreams*, xxvi.
[40] Paskauskas (ed.), *Correspondence of Freud and Jones*, 637.
[41] Falzeder and Brabant (eds.), *Correspondence of Freud and Ferenczi*, vol. III, 399.

had difficulty dealing with Amalie in life, so he had difficulty dealing with her in death.

What Freud experienced "on the surface" in reaction to his mother's death was a twofold sense of liberation, and the way he describes it contains a muted expression of his hostility toward her. In a letter to Jones, he begins by expressing a relatively familiar platitude that one often hears from mourners who lack Freud's characteristic candor. Given her advanced years and helplessness, he was relieved, so he tells the Welshman, that she had finally been delivered from her suffering. But given what Freud himself has taught us about our ubiquitous ambivalence toward the dead, and given what we know about his own biography, it is difficult to imagine that this seemingly benign sentiment did not mask death wishes Freud harbored toward his mother. Realistically, it would have been difficult for Freud, the dutiful Jewish son, to simply say that Amalie was a difficult, selfish, insensitive, and volatile woman, and that being "emancipated" from her incessant demands was a relief.

Amalie's death, Freud reports, granted him an increase "in personal freedom" in another more unusual way. "Since it was always a terrifying thought that she might come to hear of my death," he told Jones, "I was not allowed to die as long as she was alive, and now I may."[42] In short, now that Amalie had died, he was free to die as well. This comment echoes Freud's observation in *Beyond the pleasure principle* that the ability to follow their own distinctive path to death is one way mortal beings can realize what autonomy is available to them in a life circumscribed by *Ananke*. In other words, insofar as Amalie's death increased Freud's freedom to die in his own fashion, it also increased his autonomy.

There is yet another way that Amalie's death liberated Freud, and it had important consequences for the development of his theory. Her death freed him to explore the realm of female psychology and sexuality in a way that had previously not been possible for him. He had timidly broached the topic of "femininity" in a number of earlier papers, especially the 1925 paper on "Some psychical consequences of the anatomical differences between the sexes," but he was now able to confront it more directly, and he did so in two texts that were published in 1931 and 1933 – albeit still with self-acknowledged limitations.

[42] Paskauskas (ed.), *Correspondence of Freud and Jones*, 637.

In general, a text should be approached with a maximum of "hermeneutical charity," and one should attempt to make sense of it in its own
terms before turning to external considerations. One species of text, however, tends to contravene this general principle – that is, a text that is
"mutilated" in the extreme. Freud, for example, believed that the text
of a dream constitutes the paradigm of a mutilated text, and he devised
his theory of the dream-work to *explain* and undo those mutilations in
order to arrive at their latent meaning. Likewise, he believed that the Bible
represented a mutilated text, and he adduced the tendentiousness of the
rabbis to explain and correct its distortions so that he could decipher its
true meaning. Reading Freud's late papers on femininity, it is difficult to
escape the conclusion that they are also mutilated texts. (We will see that
the same thing can be said about *Moses and monotheism*.) The abundance
of peculiarities, blind spots, and outright howlers contained in them suggests that powerful extra-textual forces were impinging on their composition. And given the general argument of this study, it is reasonable to
assume that those forces were connected with Freud's discomfort with
women, his almost phobic attitude toward the early mother, and the
suppression of his early years. Karen Horney's observation that Freud's
"picture of feminine development differs in no case by a hair's breath
from the typical ideas that the [frightened – JW] boy has of the girl" is
indeed well taken.[43]

When Second Wave Feminism burst on the scene in the 1960s and
1970s, Freud was attacked as one of the foremost ideologues of patriarchy,
and he quickly became an arch-nemesis of the Movement. The texts we are
about to consider, as well as the debates that had surrounded them in the
1930s, became the center of heated controversies. At that time, the questions being hotly debated concerned the difference between clitoral and
vaginal orgasms, about whether such a difference in fact existed, whether
clitorises were truncated penises and women truncated men, penis envy,
the nature and function of castration anxiety, and women's supposedly
diminished moral capacity. Today, however, there is a broad consensus
that many of Freud's ideas on femininity were not simply wrong but at
times downright daft. We will therefore consider these earlier topics only

---

[43] Karen Horney, "Flight from womanhood: the masculinity-complex in women, as
viewed by men and by women," *International Journal of Psycho-analysis* 7 (1926), 327.

insofar as they bear on our concern – that is, the earliest, relatively undifferentiated stages of development and the archaic mother.

Freud's exploration of "the sexual history of women," as Strachey refers to it, contained implications that could have subverted his "official" Oedipal doctrine and led him to a full elaboration of his "unofficial" position, had he pursued them.[44] It is in those investigations, Strachey observes, that "the pre-Oedipal phase in women gains an importance which we have not attributed to it hitherto."[45] Indeed, in a statement that appears to recant one of his fundamental tenets, Freud declares that "it would seem as though we must retract the universality of the thesis that the Oedipus complex is the nucleus of the neurosis."[46] It is not clear, however, how seriously he took this declaration in practice, and, as we will see in *Moses and monotheism*, he never retracted the claim that the Oedipus complex constitutes the nuclear complex of civilization. Always the good *Gymnasiast*, Freud turns to an example from antiquity to dramatize the magnitude of this revision. "Our insight into this early, pre-Oedipus . . . phase," he writes, "comes to us as a surprise, like the discovery, in another field, of the Minoan–Mycenean civilization behind the civilization of Greece."[47] Furthermore, he acknowledges that his tin ear for archaic experience had made it difficult to recognize this archaic civilization earlier:

Everything in the sphere of this first attachment to the mother seemed so difficult to grasp in analysis – so gray with age and shadowy and almost impossible to revivify – that it was as if it had succumbed to an especially inexorable repression.[48]

Freud also acknowledges that his unreceptiveness to the maternal transference – which would cast him in a "feminine position" – also contributed to his inability to perceive those early developmental layers. For the maternal transference is perhaps the primary stage on which those layers of development can be revivified and explored in analysis.

[44] Sigmund Freud, "Some psychical consequences of the anatomical distinction between the sexes" (1925), *SE* 19: 245.

[45] Sigmund Freud, "Female sexuality" (1931), *SE* 21: 225.

[46] *Ibid.*, 226.

[47] *Ibid.*, 225.

[48] *Ibid.*, 226.

Prior to his late papers on femininity, Freud subscribed to a theory of sexual monism. It held that there is only one path of sexual development, exemplified by the male, that a girl is a boy *manqué*, and that her development should be understood by analogy to his. The new theory, by contrast, postulates an independent line of female development and maintains that the nature of the little girl's pre-Oedipal relation to the mother distinguishes her line of development from the little boy's. We will see, however, that the revision is not as radical as it appears, for Freud retains some of the most problematic and misogynistic elements of his older theory. More significantly, *Freud analyses the pre-Oedipal phase not in terms of the separation-individuation process, which would have constituted a major revision, but in terms of the development of the libido and the girl's entry into the Oedipus complex, thereby continuing his earlier approach.*

There is one respect moreover in which the theory of sexual monism remains true, but Freud fails to recognize it. The sexual development of both sexes begins "monisitically," that is to say, *in the same way*. Because *difference as such* – separation – must be established before *sexual difference* can emerge as a developmental theme, the little boy and the little girl, as Joyce McDougall argues, are confronted with the same task during the earliest stages of development.[49] But because Freud had to deny that the pre-Oedipal stage applied equally to the little boy and the little girl, he could not appreciate the full significance of this point.

Freud's new theory remains monistic insofar as he begins with the observation that the original love object is the same for infants of both sexes – namely, the mother. Given that fact, he argues that the boy's developmental task is more straightforward and less fraught with potential pitfalls than the girl's. If he follows a heterosexual trajectory, the boy's development begins with a person of the opposite sex as his first libidinal object, and it culminates with a person of the opposite sex as his adult love object. In other words, according to the "normal" scheme of male development, a boy begins his erotic life with a woman, his mother, as his object, and, if he successfully traverses the Oedipus complex, refinds her as an adult in the woman chosen on the basis of her imago.

---

[49] See Joyce McDougall, *Theaters of the mind: illusion and truth on the psychoanalytic stage* (New York: Routledge, 2013), 226.

But the girl's developmental path is, Freud argues, riskier insofar as she must negotiate two difficult changes in order to enter the Oedipus complex and achieve mature femininity. The first change concerns her love object. The girl begins with a person of the same sex as her first erotic attachment, but she must then accomplish a change of object and transfer her libidinal investment to a person of the opposite sex – namely, to her father. According to Freud, this necessity renders a girl's development path more vulnerable to derailment, and, as a rule, women find homosexuality less alien and threatening than do men.

According to the new theory, the little girl must make a second change, shifting the primary locus of sexual pleasure from her clitoris to her vagina, and this change is closely connected with the first. It is here that we observe how little Freud's thinking has actually changed. In one crucial and invidious way, the theory of sexual monism remains in place: He still views the clitoris as a truncated penis. When a little girl observes a penis and compares her clitoris to it, according to Freud, she concludes that her organ is inferior *in virtue of its smaller size*. And in one of his most infamous arguments, he asserts not only that the little girl interprets her lack of a penis to mean that she is castrated, but also that her "castrated" state constitutes the biological "bedrock" of femininity.[50] Moreover, the belief that she is "castrated" gives rise to the girl's "penis envy" and the virtually ineradicable wish to obtain the male organ. Two factors in turn converge to cause the girl to then denigrate her mother and repudiate her as a love object. Freud claims that when the girl observes that her mother does not possess the esteemed phallus – that she too is a defective creature – she blames her mother for her own "castrated" state, leading the girl to denigrate her mother and reject her as a love object. For Freud, the rejection of the mother in favor of the father, and the rejection of the clitoris in favor of the vagina – that is, in favor of the proper receptacle for a man's penis – thus go hand-in-hand and are the necessary prerequisites for achieving mature femininity.

Freud's texts discussing the clitoris and the girl's "castrated" state are themselves mutilated in the extreme. Because his arguments are so peculiar and wide of the mark – so completely upside-down – it is reasonable to assume that they are a symptom that something disruptive is

---

[50] Sigmund Freud, "Analysis terminable and interminable" (1937), *SE* 23: 252.

at work in the composition of them – namely, his discomfort and lack of familiarity with female sexuality, probably deriving from his limited sexual experience and his gynephobia.[51] If one examines the physiological characteristics of the clitoris, it becomes apparent that Freud's portrait of it as an inferior organ is inaccurate and counter-phobic – indeed, that his theory of phallic monism is defensive. In effect, Freud's theory of sexual monism and the fetishist's theory of the phallic woman, which Freud also addressed during the period we are considering, amount to the same thing: Both are defensive and are meant to "disavow" the reality and significance of the vagina.[52] Where Freud disavows the significance of the vagina by creating a theory of clitoral inferiority, the fetishist denies the existence of the female organ by creating a fetish.

With regard to Freud's claims about the clitoris, the actual state of affairs is exactly the opposite of the one he describes. It can even be argued that the clitoris is in fact a "superior" sexual organ. Freud concludes that the clitoris is inferior to the penis by virtue of its size. Size, however, is not only a trivial basis for comparison, it also masks important attributes of the clitoris that are frightening to many men and must be suppressed in a phallocentric *Weltanschauung*. The clitoris is in fact by no means a small anatomical structure: The greater portion of the organ is located in the interior of the body, and the pea-sized portion that can be observed only comprises its exterior "cap." More importantly, considered as a vehicle for delivering pleasure, the clitoris is actually "superior" to the penis. Although this claim is not entirely uncontroversial, it is generally agreed that, where the clitoris contains 8,000 nerve endings and is associated with 15,000 others throughout the pelvic region, the penis contains only 4,000.[53] Indeed, the claim is often made that the clitoris is the only organ in human anatomy that is exclusively designed to provide pleasure.

---

[51] Tragically, Freud's misguided ideas about female anatomy and sexuality led Marie Bonaparte to subject herself to a surgical procedure in which her clitoris was moved closer to her vagina in an attempt to correct her lack of sexual responsiveness. The procedure did not accomplish its aim.

[52] See Sigmund Freud, "Fetishism" (1927), *SE* 21: 149–158.

[53] Interestingly, like the clitoris, the foreskin is often thought to contain 8,000 nerve endings. This fact might give credence to a theory of sexual monism from a different angle. Some experts argue that the clitoris and foreskin branched off from the same evolutionary source.

It is unlikely that most men are aware of these anatomical details. It is not uncommon, however, for them to have experienced a woman's greater orgasmic capacity and their difficulty in keeping pace with their sexual partners. In other words, men are often frightened of the formidable orgasmic power of female sexuality, which is superimposed on top of their fear of the seeming omnipotence of the archaic mother. And this threatening fact is one of the primary sources of misogyny. To bolster their vulnerable self-esteem, many man resort to machismo in the broadest sense of the term. They combat the threat of female sexuality by engaging in various forms of phallic braggadocio – ranging from the athletic to the intellectual – and repudiate women as castrated, helpless, dependent, silly, which is to say "hysterical," creatures, lacking in sexual desire. In short, just as Freud denied the power of the archaic mother – who possesses the seemingly omnipotent capacity to provide the most exquisite pleasure and to inflict the most unbearable frustrations – by minimizing her importance and replacing her with the father, so also did he disavow the formidable sexual capacities of a mature woman by advancing his embarrassingly defensive theory of clitoral inferiority and the derivative nature of female development.

For our purposes, Freud's continuous equivocations concerning pre-Oedipal development represent one of the most important features of his papers on femininity. At the same time as he acknowledges "the complete identity of the pre-Oedipus phase in boys and girls," he repeatedly undoes that acknowledgment and attributes the characteristic phenomena of pre-Oedipal development only to the girl.[54] In his analysis of this developmental stage, he uses the terms "the girl" and "the child" interchangeably, never mentioning the little boy, without any apparent awareness that he is doing so. To have fully affirmed the existence and significance of the pre-Oedipal phase in male development, Sprengnether observes, would have severely undermined his official theory and "threaten[ed] his idealization of the Oedipal bond between mother and son."[55] Moreover, in what can only be described as acts of dissociation, Freud offers several examples of pre-Oedipal phenomena that are lifted almost verbatim from his own childhood, and then attributes them exclusively to

[54] Freud, "Female sexuality," 241.

[55] Sprengnether, *The spectral mother*, 162.

the little girl, as if to say, "They do not pertain to boys and therefore do not apply to me."[56]

Needless to say, anger at not having been outfitted with a penis would apply only to the girl. But the other reasons Freud cites for the girl's anger at her mother apply equally to both sexes – and apply a fortiori to Freud's own early history. Freud cannot simply state the fact that boys and girls harbor the same grievances regarding the breast-mother. He begins a passage by addressing the girl's accusations that "her mother . . . did not suckle her long enough" and thus deprived her of "enough milk." Freud, however, quickly takes flight into a general anthropological discussion of the experience of "children . . . in our monogamous civilization." He voices skepticism about the claim that in our modern cultures, where infants are "weaned from the breast after six or nine months," children seem to remain "forever unsated" – as opposed to children of primitive cultures in which the "mother devotes herself exclusively to her children for two or three years." Against this argument, he maintains that "if one analysed children who had been suckled as long as the children of primitive peoples, one would [probably] come upon the same complaint." According to Freud, a child's anger at the breast-mother for not having provided enough gratification is a trans-cultural phenomenon that derives from the nature of our instinctual make-up. It results not from actual external events such as maternal deprivation – and is therefore not remediable by external actions – but from the inherent "greed of a child's libido."[57]

With this claim, Freud has moved far from the idea that anger at the breast-mother is the exclusive provenance of the little girl. It not only pertains to both sexes, but does so in virtue of the insatiability of the species' instinctual endowment. This is Freud at his most biologistic, and if this claim were accurate, it would virtually exclude the possibility that a child's environment could have any impact on his or her experience and development. It is undoubtedly true that human instincts can never be fully satisfied, and that an underlying sense of lack is therefore intrinsic to the human condition. But Freud's argument rules out the possibility of "good enough mothering," a term coined by the English

[56] See Breger, *Freud*, 31.
[57] Freud, "Female sexuality," 234.

pediatrician and psychoanalyst D.W. Winnicott – a kind of salutary maternal experience that imparts to the child "basic trust" that the world is a "good enough" place where one can find adequate gratification.

Freud's flight into biology is also a flight from his own biography. We do not know the details of Freud's early feeding history. We do not know, for example, if Amalie breast-fed him, and, if so, for how long. But we do know that Amalie became pregnant with Julian when Sigmund was approximately ten months old, so that, had she been breast-feeding him, it would have come to an end at that point. And it is generally believed that Amalie became depressed and withdrawn after Julian's death, which means that she would not have been in a position to provide Freud much in the way of maternal gratification. We also know that he lost his *Kinderfrau*, who had served as his mother substitute, when she abruptly disappeared at the time Amalie was giving birth to his first sister, Anna. Yet rather than accept the anger at the suffering these actual mothering figures may have caused him, Freud deflects the anger onto the supposed insatiable "greed" of a child's libido, thereby masochistically turning it back onto his own "badness." Freud, the sworn opponent of the Catholic Church, seems to be saying that the hunger of the infant is an original sin.

Freud's answer to a pertinent question concerning "a general characteristic of infantile sexuality" could have been lifted from the pages of his own life history. But he again appears to be totally dissociated from the personal background to his claim. Acknowledging that a boy's ambivalence toward his mother "is certainly no less strong than that of the girl," Freud raises the obvious question: "How is it" that they "are able to keep intact their attachment to their mother?" They can accomplish this feat, he answers, "by directing all their hostility onto their fathers."[58] While Jacob's fecklessness must have been irritating in the extreme, it does not provide a satisfying explanation for the intensity of the anger that Freud claims he harbored toward him. Why Freud needed to transform this lovable but exasperating *Luftmensch* from Galicia into Mozart's *Commendatore* requires explanation. The proposition that Jacob provided a receptacle for the displaced anger toward Amalie is one element of an answer. That Freud needed to envision Jacob as a powerful father who could function as a barrier against his frightening mother is another.

---

[58] *Ibid.*, 325.

But it makes no sense to go as far as a tendentious anti-Oedipal theorist like Louis Breger and reduce Freud's formulation of the "Oedipal story" to a "comforting myth" that allowed him to flee from the intolerable terrors associated with the archaic mother.[59] Sprengnether offers a less simplistic and more differentiated view – namely, that Freud's "construction" of his Oedipal theory is "a complex compromise formation," which, like all psychic accomplishments, contained adaptive and defensive elements.[60] *Contra* Breger's one-sided approach, it would be more fruitful to follow Loewald and attempt to understand how the pre-Oedipal and Oedipal strata of development become structured in the psyche.[61]

More examples could be supplied concerning a child's envy when new hungry siblings arrive on the scene, and the mother's seductiveness, as well as her interdiction against masturbation that apply equally to both sexes, but the point should have been fully established by now. One last comment, however, is in order. Freud observes that "perhaps the real fact is that the attachment to the mother is bound to perish, precisely because it was the first and was so intense." Yet then, in a flight into maturity, he launches into a discussion of why second marriages for women are gener-ally more successful than their first which more appropriately belongs in a nineteenth-century novel of manners than in a work of psychoanalytic theory. He thereby evades the point that, for both sexes, the reason the attachment to the pre-Oedipal mother is not only "bound to perish" but will do so painfully and with lifelong consequences is that it is *the first experience of separation*. The break-up of "the primal psychical situation," of the undifferentiated relation to the archaic mother, is the first intru-sion of separateness, of harsh reality, into the child's universe.

Geistigkeit: A Problematic Concept

The date was 2 August 1938. The lamps were about to go out all over Europe for the second time in less than thirty years, and the International Psychoanalytic Association was holding its fifteenth Congress in Paris. It was the last meeting that the organization would convene before most of

---

[59] Breger, *Freud*, 19.

[60] Sprengnether, *The spectral mother*, 4.

[61] See Loewald's canonical paper, "The waning of the Oedipus complex."

its members from continental Europe were forced into exile (many had already fled, returning only for the Congress) and before the death of its founder the following year. It was therefore Freud's last opportunity to address his assembled followers before taking leave of them, but he was by then already dying of cancer in London and too weak to attend, and so – as he had in 1930 when he was awarded the Goethe Prize and again when his mother was buried – he dispatched Anna to represent him. The text that he chose for his daughter to read on that occasion was a section from his final major work, *Moses and monotheism*. The title of the section is "Der Fortschritt in der Geistigkeit," which Strachey translates as "The progress in intellectuality," but, as we will see, the question of translation requires further scrutiny.

Just as Moses sought to put his affairs in order and provide the Israelites with his last testament before ascending Mount Nebo to die at the age of one hundred and twenty, so also, it has often been suggested, Freud drafted his final testament in *Moses and monotheism* before, like "another important Jew who died in exile," he returned "to the earth in London" at eighty-three.[62] The text as a whole, however, is not a suitable candidate to serve that function. Freud himself repeatedly apologized for its severe deficiencies, likening it to "a bronze statue resting on clay feet."[63] *Moses and monotheism* is, as Edward Said suggests, a specimen of *Spätstil* – "late style" – and the sovereignty that "lateness" conferred on him permitted the dying founder of psychoanalysis to produce a work that is as defiantly strange and singular as Beethoven's late quartets.[64] Freud wrote to Arnold Zweig, "We will forgo all misery and criticism and indulge in our fantasies about Moses."[65] The resulting work is confused, repetitious, tortured, lacunary, and, at points, even bizarre – one might say "mutilated." To this day, many if not most analysts are exasperated and embarrassed by *Moses and monotheism* and wonder how what Ilse Grubrich-Simitis calls this "jagged quarry" could exist "in the midst of such a classical landscape

[62] Auden, "In memory of Sigmund Freud," 116.

[63] Freud, *Moses and monotheism*, 17.

[64] Edward Said, *Freud and the Non-European* (New York: Verso, 2003), 28–29. See also Theodor W. Adorno, *Beethoven: the philosophy of music*, trans. Edmund Jephcott (New York: Polity Press, 2002), 123–137.

[65] Ernst Freud (ed.), *The letters of Sigmund Freud and Arnold Zweig*, trans. W. and E. Robson-Scott (New York: New York University Press, 1972), 122.

of manuscripts."[66] The section of it that Anna was given to read to the Congress, however, is an appropriate text to serve as Freud's last testament. Its relatively lucid composition and straightforward if not one-sided exhortation make it well suited for rallying the troops. Whatever the more esoteric and obscure truths embedded in *Moses and monotheism*, the passage that Anna delivered in Paris contained the exoteric message that Freud wanted his followers to carry with them after his death.

Throughout his life, Freud had identified with Moses in various ways, and when it came to drafting his last testament he saw a specific parallel between his situation and the lawgiver's. Moses had devised an elitist, severe, and uncompromising monotheistic doctrine that he attempted to impose on the common people from above – Freud refers to them as the "mob" – but which they ultimately found intolerable. According to Freud's presentation of the legend, Moses's demands were indeed so intolerable that the Israelites rose up and murdered him.[67] Freud believed that he had also subjected a "gang" of Viennese quasi-*Schlampere* to his equally "harsh" doctrine, and that they too had difficulty rising to its rigorous demands. There had already been the defections of Adler, Rank, and Jung – not to mention the heterodoxy of Mrs. Klein and her group in London – and Freud suspected that his discontented followers,

---

[66] Grubrich-Simitis, *Early Freud and late Freud*, 53. The extraordinarily lucid and rigorous "An outline of psychoanalysis," written at the same time, presents a condensed and dogmatic exposition of Freud's fundamental ideas that eliminates any suspicion that his mental capacities had declined. See Freud, "An Outline of Psycho-Analysis," 141–209.

[67] Just as Freud ignores the fact that an attempted infanticide preceded patricide in his treatment of the Oedipus legend – that Laius tried to kill Oedipus as an infant before his grown son actually murdered him – he also fails to mention a similar fact in the biblical story: namely, in the course of one day, Moses executed – "purged" – thousands of his "counter-revolutionary" followers who had danced before the Golden Calf, before the survivors rose up against him. It is striking that Freud praises the Levites, the elite members of Moses's "vanguard party" who carried out the bloody purge and kept the memory of Moses's vision of monotheism alive during the long period of "latency" until it finally returned from repression and was rekindled in Kadesh. Freud's affirmative view of the Levites' "Leninism" invites comparison with the function he envisioned for the "Committee" – the trustworthy "central committee" of his own "vanguard party" – that was constituted after the arch-deviationist, Jung, had been "purged." See Michael Walzer, *Exodus and revolution* (New York: Basic Books, 1985), 55–66.

who remained "murmurers" as long as he was alive, would become overt "blasphemers" once he died.[68] And Freud's suspicions about the resistances within his ranks applied a fortiori to the public at large.

A number of Jewish commentators seek to deny that, throughout his life, Freud held "a completely negative attitude toward religion in any form"; they want to claim him as a prodigal son who, after years of wandering in the desert of atheism, returned to the fold and made peace with the tribe at the end.[69] They often argue that, by taking up the Bible in the 1930s, Freud was complying with "the paternal mandate" that Jacob had inscribed in the family's Philippson Bible on the occasion of his son's thirtieth birthday, and that he was fulfilling his father's entreaty to return to the "Book of Books." Although the claim is not false per se, stated in this general way it is, as Richard Armstrong argues, sorely inadequate:

Some see in Freud's late-life interest in Jewish history a clear pattern of departure and return, and while I agree with this characterization generally, I would like to qualify just how one is to understand "return." For it seems brutally clear that Freud's "return" to the Jewish tradition in *Moses and Monotheism* is no facile reconciliation, nor a death-bed lapse into some suitably modified form of piety.[70]

As was demonstrated in Chapter 2, Freud identified with Judaism not only at the end of his career but throughout it, although in the thirties he embraced his identification with Judaism more thoroughly and more publicly.[71] As the sociologist Philip Rieff points out in his important study *Freud: the mind of a moralist*, despite Freud's skepticism about every variety of national pride and his uncompromising atheism, in

---

[68] Bela Grunberger observes that almost all the so-called dissidents, in one way or another, attempted to assert the importance of the early mother against Freud's concentration on "the father complex." But where orthodox Freudians criticized their attempts as deviations from the correct position, they should be understood as efforts to correct the one-sidedness of Freud's official patricentric position. Cited in Léon Chertok and Isabelle Strenger, *A critique of psychoanalytic reason: hypnosis as a scientific problem from Lavoisier to Lacan*, trans. Martha Noel Evans (Stanford, CA: Stanford University Press, 1992), 102.

[69] See for example Rice, *Freud and Moses*.

[70] Richard H. Armstrong, *A compulsion to antiquity: Freud and the ancient world* (Ithaca, NY: Cornell University Press, 2005), 248.

[71] See Robert, *From Oedipus to Moses*, chapter 2.

Moses and monotheism he manifests enormous pride in his identification with Moses – while interpreting him as an ancient precursor of the *Aufklärung*.[72]

Armstrong's claim that Freud's "return" to Judaism was no simple act of filial piety is correct. Indeed, to say that his "homecoming" was "ambivalent" is far too tepid; it was *thoroughly conflicted*. Freud undoubtedly had a deep affection for the tradition his father had imparted to him and identified with it. But his "return" to Judaism also included an act of patricidal destruction directed at "the religion of the fathers." He took what was his father's and "made it his own" by devouring and cannibalizing that patrimony and spitting it out in a radically altered form. This conjunction of identification and parricide is unsurprising to an analyst, for, according to Freud's own theory, most creative acts of any magnitude necessarily include both elements.[73] As we will see, in an assertion of Oedipal triumph he declares that he represents the culmination of the religion of the fathers by rendering it obsolete.

One important factor that brought about the work on Moses, argues Grubrich-Simitis, was the onslaught of traumatic assaults Freud experienced in the 1930s. We have observed that he was a man who deplored helplessness and exhibited "an indomitable aspiration to

---

[72] See Philip Rieff, *Freud: The mind of a moralist* (Chicago: University of Chicago Press, 1979), 257–259.

[73] See Whitebook. "Hans Loewald: a radical conservative," 98. When Freud's anti-secular critics claim that he became more sympathetic to religion in *Moses and monotheism*, they obscure his position to their own advantage. As opposed to the more rationalist *Future of an illusion*, in the later work Freud displays a greater appreciation of the enormity of the *power* that religion exerts over human beings. "There is," he observes, "an element of grandeur about everything to do with the origin of religion," which, he admits, was "not matched by the explanations we have hitherto given." *But grandeur is not truth*. In fact, its source is *purely emotional*, namely, the awe invoked by the powerful father. Freud came to realize that the force of religion is far greater than he had formerly recognized, but he continued to believe that its content was *false*. *Moses and monotheism* consists in an Enlightenment-style critique of religion, which repeats the argument of *Totem and taboo* almost verbatim, and continues to liken it to psychopathology – in fact it becomes delusionary rather illusionary – and traces its origins to the murder of the primal father. He explicitly states that he remains as convinced of his theory of the primal hoard as he had been in 1912. Freud explains the "religion of the fathers," as well as all religions, in terms of the *Urvater* of the primal horde. Freud, *Moses and monotheism*, 128 and 58.

independence" – almost to a fault.[74] Yet, after his lifelong effort to maintain his self-sufficient autonomy, these late-life assaults, bombarding him from several directions, threatened his physical and psychological integrity, dramatically increased his actual helplessness, and severely diminished his independence. Grubrich-Simitis argues that it was in no small measure in response to the multiple traumas that confronted him in the 1930s that Freud began to struggle with the figure of Moses, which "tormented [him] like an unlaid ghost." These traumas form the psychological context within which *Moses and monotheism* and specifically "Der Fortschritt in der Geistigkeit," Freud's final testament, were written.[75]

The first trauma was the most immediate and most personal: the cancer. As the disease progressed, Freud was progressively reduced to a situation resembling the child-like helplessness he despised. "From the onset of this illness to the end of his life," Jones informs us, Freud, the proud patriarch, "refused to have any other nurse" – that is, to be dependent on any other human being, including his wife – except "his daughter Anna."[76] And she performed her task with unflinching stoicism and courage. "What Lear wishes for and briefly obtains," Sprengnether observes, "Freud enjoy[ed] to the end of his life: his daughter's 'kind nursery.'"[77] One might say that he refound his "good" *Kinderfrau* in his daughter.

The second traumatic threat was social and political in nature: the spread of European anti-Semitism and the rise of Hitler. Compared to many of those surrounding him, Freud's political judgment was not commensurate with the demands of the situation, and he denied the full extent of the danger for some time, despite the fact that the interventions into his life, beginning in 1933, were repeated and harsh. His books were burned, his training and research institutes disbanded, and his publishing houses closed. Remarkably, despite his hatred of the institution, he even entertained the quasi-delusional notion that Austria's Catholic Church would protect him and the field he had created from the Nazis; it did not happen.

Grubrich-Simitis offers the following explanation for Freud's difficulty in confronting the situation. In addition to the understandable reluctance

---

[74] Grubrich-Simitis, *Early Freud and late Freud*, 59.

[75] Freud, *Moses and monotheism*, 103.

[76] Jones, *Freud* III, 96.

[77] Sprengnether, *The spectral mother*, 115.

of a frail old man, consumed with cancer, to leave the town where he had lived and worked for eighty years, to undertake an arduous journey to a foreign country, and to confront the demands of immigration, "the sheer quantitative level of the traumatic flood of stimuli in the experience of being impotently at the mercy of political persecution, serious illness and old age may have triggered a regressive process that" interfered with Freud's reality-testing.[78] It was only when the full danger concretized itself in his immediate life that Freud came to his senses, formed an accurate assessment of the threat, and agreed to emigrate to London.

The *coup de grace* occurred on 22 March 1938, when Anna was summoned to the Gestapo Headquarters in Vienna, a destination from which few detainees returned, as most were shipped off to one concentration camp or another. Both Anna and her brother Martin, who feared, but never received, a similar summons, were aware of the possibility of torture and had called on Max Schur to supply them "with a sufficient amount of Veronal" to end their lives should it prove necessary. Schur also "promised to take care of Freud as long as possible."[79]

Jones, who knew Freud well, describes that day "as the blackest" in the analyst's "life."[80] He tells us that Freud "spent the whole day pacing up and down and smoking an endless series of cigars to deaden his emotions." When Anna returned to Berggasse 19 seven hours later, exhausted but unharmed, her usually restrained papa – whose diary entry for that day simply read "Anna bei Gestapo" – could not hide his emotions. Shortly thereafter, he informed his son Ernst that he had decided to move to London "to die in freedom."[81] As the family was preparing to depart from Vienna, two events occurred that capture Freud's indomitable personality. When several members of the SA visited Berggasse 19 to catalogue its contents, the women of the house sought to unsettle them by acting in a hyper-cooperative manner. While Martha placed the household money, which did not amount to much, on the dining room table, "Anna," Jones tells us, "escorted them to the safe in another room and opened it." While the men were debating whether to abscond with the meager loot, "a

[78] Grubrich-Simitis, *Early Freud and late Freud*, 78.
[79] Schur, *Freud: living and dying*, 498.
[80] Jones, *Freud* III, 223–224.
[81] Quoted in Gay, *Freud: a life for our time*, 626.

frail and gaunt figure," as Jones describes him, appeared in the doorway. "It was Freud," who had been "aroused by the disturbance." He directed his frown and "blazing eyes that any Old Testament prophet might have envied" at the thugs, "completing," as Jones puts it, "the visitors' discomfiture." Claiming they would return another day, "they hastily took their departure."[82]

Freud's behavior in the second incident epitomizes his sovereignty, pluck, and humor. Before the Nazi authorities would allow him to leave, he was required to sign an affidavit attesting to the fact that the Germans had not mistreated him. Jones reports that "when the Nazi Commissar brought it along Freud had of course no compunction in signing it." He did, however, request that he be allowed to add a sentence to the document, which read: "I can heartily recommend the Gestapo to anyone."[83]

Freud left Vienna on 4 June 1938 on the Orient Express and spent the following night as a guest in Marie Bonaparte's elegant Parisian home. The next day, he arrived in the city he had loved since his youth, where Londoners of every stripe – from its scientific and literary elite to its tabloid journalists and Cockney cabbies – welcomed him with remarkable exuberance, an experience to which the reticent Professor, who had led a largely private existence, was quite unaccustomed.

From these threats to his professional identity and physical safety, Freud's return to the "Book of Books" may have served as a kind of shelter, for while it did not represent a straightforward return to the fold – to the "faith" of his fathers – it can be understood as a homecoming of a different, more intimate sort. Ana-Maria Rizzuto points out how, in 1896, after his father's death, Freud began to collect his antiquities – which seemed to have leapt off the pages of the Philippson Bible that he had read with Jacob – in an attempt to recreate that early intimacy and comfort himself in the face of that loss. Then in 1935, in the midst of overwhelmingly traumatic circumstances, Freud announced, as Grubrich-Simitis points out, that "after a lifelong *détour* through the natural sciences, medicine, and psychotherapy," he had returned to, had come home to, "the cultural problems which had fascinated" him when he "was a youth scarcely old enough for thinking" – that is, to the questions that had first fired his

---

[82] Jones, *Freud* III, 219.

[83] *Ibid.*, 226.

imagination when he was reading the family Bible with Jacob.[84] This adds an important psycho-affective meaning to the theoretical significance of Freud's research into the Moses legend in the 1930s. By immersing himself in the Bible, Freud may have again been (unconsciously) attempting to recreate the atmosphere of warmth and intimacy he had shared with Jacob when they read the Philippson text together – a way of containing the psychic pain he was experiencing in the face of being subjected to almost unfathomable loss and trauma.

There was another primary motive for engaging with the figure of the biblical prophet, as Grubrich-Simitis suggests, and that was "to allay the grinding disquietude he felt about the future of his work."[85] His anxiety concerning his legacy was undoubtedly a central concern, and, as we have seen, Freud often mobilized his heroic self-image to negotiate nearly intolerable situations. Just as he had turned to Hannibal, Cromwell, and Napoleon in the past, he now turned to Moses and compared himself to him to confront the many-sided trauma that was facing him. Although psychoanalysis would continue to be "politically persecuted and suppressed" by the forces of barbarism that were enveloping Europe, and although it would undoubtedly be confronted with minions of backsliding dissidents in the future as in the past, Freud could reassure himself with his version of the Moses story that this need not mean it would be extinguished.[86]

Like Arnold Schönberg, who reverted to Judaism and began to compose his opera *Moses und Aron* when he was forced to flee Europe, Freud on a similarly conscious level turned to Moses in an attempt to understand the rise of Hitler. The more obvious and less troubling question to ask at the time would have been this: What was it about the German (and Austrian) character and culture that gave rise to Nazism? But because of his consistent commitment to self-reflection, Freud asked a different question – one that he knew would not go down well with his persecuted co-religionists: What was it about "the particular character of the Jew[s]" that had "earned [them] the hearty dislike of every other people" throughout much of history?[87]

---

[84] Grubrich-Simitis, *Early Freud and late Freud*, 85.

[85] *Ibid.*, 61.

[86] *Ibid.*

[87] Pfeiffer (ed.), *Freud and Andreas-Salomé letters*, 204 and Freud, *Moses and monotheism*, 105.

This question presupposes a specific psychological theorem. Contrary to a popular conception, paranoia does not consist in pure projection "into the blue" but attaches itself onto some anchor, however minimal, that exists in extra-psychic reality.[88] Nor is prejudice a purely projective phenomenon. As with paranoia, it also "leans on" some feature in the person who is persecuted. If they are honest with themselves, individuals who have been the object of hatred often recognize that something in them provided a hook for their persecutor's projections. But having made this psychological point, we must immediately register a warning to forestall a particularly pernicious and not uncommon interpretation of it. To say that there is something about the Jews that provokes anti-Semitism – or that there is something about any persecuted group that provokes their persecution – *in no way implies that they got what they deserved.*

Freud answers the question in the following way. What he considers the highest achievement of the Jewish people, namely, their comprehensive articulation of a monotheistic worldview that is fully "dematerialized" or transcendent, is at the same time the source of the remarkable hatred that has regularly been directed at them.[89] Freud takes one of "the precepts of the Moses religion" to be of central importance: "the prohibition against making an image of God," or, to put it differently, "the compulsion to worship a God whom one cannot see."[90] By analysing the prohibition against images – the *Bilderverbot*, as it is often referred to – he believes he can elucidate the civilizational significance of Jewish monotheism as well as the enmity toward the Jews. His thesis is that this prohibition introduced "an advance in *Geistigkeit*" into world history:

[It] meant that a sensory perception was given second place to what may be called an abstract idea – a triumph of *Geistigkeit* over sensuality or, strictly speaking, an instinctual renunciation, with all its necessary psychological consequences.[91]

---

[88] Sigmund Freud, "Some neurotic mechanisms in jealousy, paranoia and homosexuality" (1922), *SE* 18: 226.

[89] We should note that while the revolutionary Egyptian Pharaoh Akhenaten first enunciated the monotheistic vision, according to Freud it fell to Moses and the Israelites, whose "peculiar psychic aptitude" was well suited for the task, to complete his project. Freud, *Moses and monotheism*, 111.

[90] *Ibid.*, 112–113.

[91] *Ibid.*, 113.

The question of how to translate *Geistigkeit* into English is controversial and encompasses important substantive issues concerning Freud's theory. The German term *Geist* is richly polysemic in a way that the candidates for its English translation are not. It is therefore difficult to convey its multiple meanings and full resonance with any single one of them.[92] For example, although Katherine Jones's choice to translate *Geistigkeit* as "spirituality" in the first English translation of *Moses and monotheism* has the advantage of capturing the extra-cognitive and emotional reverberations contained in the German, it fails adequately to convey the term's reference to reason and the intellect. We can therefore understand James Strachey's decision to translate *Geistigkeit* as "intellectuality" in the *Standard Edition*. By not mentioning "spirituality," he not only avoids any hint of Jungian vaporousness, but also highlights the supreme value that Freud attached to the intellect. Predictably, however, Strachey's choice errs in the opposite direction: It can strike one as overly cognitivist and lacking in emotional resonance. Because of its polysemic nature, *Geistigkeit* can be interpreted as a "tertiary" concept, and, at its best, it prescribes us the task of sublating or sublimating the binomial opposition between intellectuality and spirituality at a higher level of integration.

According to the standard chronology, the invention of monotheism by Akhenaten and Moses occurred before the Axial Age, but as Egyptologist and cultural historian Jan Assmann suggests, it can be viewed as an axial phenomenon. The feature unifying the diverse achievements that are generally subsumed under the idea of the Axial Age – for example, the contributions of Confucius, Socrates, Buddha, and Jeremiah – is, Assmann argues, "a breakthrough to a kind of transcendence."[93] In one way or another, axial figures posited a sphere of second-order being and thinking – for example, a notion of a "dematerialized" God with the Jews and the idea of Reason with the Greeks – that made it possible to both understand and criticize first-order thinking and the world as it is given. To use Hegel's language, this breakthrough to transcendence raised the human species out of its immediate natural existence and elevated it to the level of self-reflective *Geist*. The point to be stressed is that positing

---

[92] See Bernstein, *Freud and the legacy of Moses*, 31.

[93] Jan Assmann, *Of God and gods: Egypt, Israel, and the rise of monotheism*, George I. Mosse Series in Modern European Cultural and Intellectual History (Madison: University of Wisconsin Press, 2008), 79.

the existence of a transcendent sphere creates a standpoint from which "actually existing thinking and reality" can be criticized. Moses's introduction of monotheism made a new form of critique possible, and, for Freud, this is perhaps its most significant accomplishment; it is the one that he appropriated. *The Mosaic critique of idolatry, in other words, was the precursor of Freud's own destruction of the idols through the psychoanalytic critique of illusion.*

That the assertion of the demands of *Geistigkeit* over those of *Sinnlichkeit* – sensuality – requires the "renunciation" of instinctual life and the devaluation of the body constitutes the linchpin for Freud's explanation of anti-Semitism. To accomplish "higher" *geistig* achievements, one must renounce and repress the distracting perceptions and seductive temptations offered by the material world, as well as the immediate demands of inner nature – that is, of the drives. Like most obsessional attempts to control the instincts, the *geistig* demand for renunciation among the Jews steadily proliferated over "the course of the centuries" until, according to Freud, legalist prohibitions assumed a central position in Judaism. "The religion" that began with the *Bilderverbot* developed "more and more . . . into a religion of instinctual renunciations." He observes that as the Prophets never tire of reminding us, "God requires nothing other from his people than a just and virtuous conduct of life – that is, abstention from every instinctual satisfaction."[94]

Freud's celebration of *Geistigkeit* is unabashedly androcentric and patriarchal. He offers a particularly concrete and somewhat strained explanation of why the "turning from the mother to the father points to a victory of *Geistigkeit* over sensuality – that is, an advance in civilization."

---

[94] Freud, *Moses and monotheism*, 118–119. Though it may partly represent the envy of an unathletic *yeshiva bocher*, the Hellenophilic Freud praises the Jews' decision to pursue "intellectual labours" at the expense of "physical activity," as opposed to the Greeks' attempt to integrate mind and body, as "the worthier alternative." His rationale – namely, that their almost exclusive concentration on the intellect has "helped to check the brutality and tendency to violence" in the Jewish people – rings especially hollow in today's world. But there is another way in which Freud remains a Greek. Insofar as he sharply extols *Geistigkeit* over *Sinnlichkeit* and lionizes the mind at the expense of the body, Freud is, Assmann points out, a Platonist, and his position suffers from many of the same difficulties as Plato's dualistic philosophy that constructs an opposition between "highest" and "lowest." Jan Assmann, *The price of monotheism*, trans. Robert Savage (Stanford, CA: Stanford University Press, 2010), 99–100.

He argues that because birth, the physical emergence of the infant from the mother's body, is an observable fact, "maternity is proved by the evidence of the senses." By contrast, insofar as no comparable empirical evidence existed in Freud's time for establishing the identity of the father, he could contend that "paternity" was a "conceptual" matter – that is, "a hypothesis, based on an inference and a premise."[95] We might note that, prior to the discovery of DNA, this was an argument that legions of deadbeat dads deployed in less *geistig* situations. The triumph of patriarchy over the chthonic deities – of the Father of the primal horde over the Great Mother – represents an advance in *Geistigkeit* because the determination of paternal lineage relies on "conceptual" considerations – inferences, rather than "sensual" evidence.

Freud's account of "the advance in *Geistigkeit*" is not only a celebration of the "triumph" of patriarchy; it is also an expression of Freud's devaluation of the pre-Oedipal realm, and represents and entails a debasement of the maternal dimension. The early breast-mother, with the warmth, comfort, smells, closeness, and pleasure that she offers her child is, after all, the apotheosis of *Sinnlichkeit*. From the heights of the *geistig* Mosaic perspective, that sensuality, as Grubrich-Simitis shows, is demonized as "the fleshpots of Egypt," which can be understood as a "metaphor" for the temptation to return to a state of symbiotic merger with the archaic mother.[96] An observation by the anthropologist and practicing psychoanalyst Robert Paul lends support to Grubrich-Simitis's thesis. He argues that insofar as Moses's adopted mother is the pharaoh's daughter, Egypt can be viewed as representing maternity as such.[97]

Freud had a particular template in mind for explaining anti-Semitism: It is the hatred of Akhenaten and Moses, resulting from the demand for renunciation they imposed on the multitude writ large. After Akhenaten's

---

[95] Freud, *Moses and monotheism*, 114. Despite recent feminist attempts to minimize the Patriarchal nature of the Jewish tradition, Robert Paul argues that "as it stands, the Torah bears the marks of works written by, for and about men, in which the feminine dimension of life is pushed into the background and in which women are rarely seen as protagonists." Paul does, however, seek to uncover a latent maternal dimension in the biblical text. See Robert A. Paul, *Moses and civilization: the meaning behind Freud's myth* (New Haven: Yale University Press, 1996), 97–102.

[96] Grubrich-Simitis, *Early Freud and late Freud*, 72.

[97] Paul, *Moses and civilization*, 98.

death, in reaction to his anti-sensual and aniconic revolution-from-above – which sought to eradicate the abundant visuality of Egyptian culture and religion – the priests he had purged allied with the common people and angrily rose up in a counter-revolution that eradicated every trace of the Pharaoh's monotheistic worldview. By the same token, when the Israelites in the desert found they could no longer tolerate the renunciations that Moses's ascetic and dematerialized monotheism was imposing on them, they not only danced naked around the Golden Calf and yearned to return to "the fleshpots of Egypt," but, if Freud is to be believed, they also revolted against their leader and murdered him.

The central conflict at the heart of the notion of "an advance in *Geistigkeit*" can be formulated in the following way. On the one hand, the introduction into history of a thoroughly "dematerialized" monotheistic religion constituted an undeniable epochal advance and represents one of the Jews' greatest contributions to civilization. On the other hand, the demand for renunciation that is integral to it has provoked formidable resentment among the other peoples of the world. It is here that we arrive at Freud's central thesis concerning anti-Semitism: *The anger that the Gentile world harbors toward the Jews for having imposed that demand for renunciation on them is the central cause of the Jew-hatred that has regularly flared up over thousands of years.* Writing during the Nazi period, Horkheimer and Adorno make the point aphoristically: "Because [the Jews] invented the concept of the kosher," which exemplifies their reununciatory ethic, they "are persecuted like swine."[98] We might add that, because persecutory structures of thought typically obey primary processes, the Jews are often simultaneously condemned as hypersexual and lascivious.

As we have seen, in his 1918 letter to Oskar Pfister, Freud had asserted that only "a completely godless Jew" could have discovered psychoanalysis.[99] In his 1930 "Preface to the Hebrew translation of *Totem and taboo*," as we also saw, he upped the ante and asserted that it was he, a non-believing psychoanalyst, who in fact embodied the "very essence" of Judaism – although "he could not [at that time] express that essence in words."[100] In response

---

[98] Horkheimer and Adorno, *Dialectic of enlightenment*, 153.

[99] Meng and Freud (eds.), *Psychoanalysis and faith*, 63.

[100] Freud, *Totem and taboo*, xv.

to Freud's description of himself as "a godless Jew," Pfister had made, as
we noted, the thoroughly screwy assertion that no "better Christian" than
Freud ever existed. Now, Freud is in effect making the equally impertinent
claim that no more essential Jew than he had ever walked the earth. Far
from having abandoned the tribe, he is impudently asserting that, precisely
as an "apostate Jew" – the Jew as iconoclast – he is the essential Jew. Though
Yerushalmi, author of *Freud's Moses*, clearly bristles at the idea, he is forced
to conclude that Freud's "secret" is not only that he is "a godless Jew," but
also that psychoanalysis "is godless Judaism."[101]

   How can Freud make the seemingly outrageous claim that he embodies
the essence of Judaism? The Jewish tradition is a vast, variegated, and heterogeneous phenomenon, and, as Gershom Scholem observes, "everyone
cuts the slice suiting him from the big cake."[102] The slice that Freud chose
to cut was the Mosaic strand in that tradition, which, as he understood
it, centered on the critique of idolatry. Identifying the Mosaic tradition
with Judaism in that way allows Freud not only to assert his *bona fides*
both as an atheist and as a Jew, but also to make the scandalous claim that,
as a godless psychoanalyst, he had realized the essence of Judaism. In
effect, he assimilates Moses the prophet to Moses Mendelssohn, the fig-
urehead of the Haskalah, and construes the Mosaic critique of idolatry –
the rejection of magic and superstition in the name of "Ma'at," truth
and justice – as the ancient prefiguration of the modern Enlightenment's
disenchanting critique of illusion. *Freud's claim is, in short, that psychoanalysis constitutes the culmination of the Mosaic tradition.* It has carried the
critique of the false gods to the point where it is no longer a matter of the
idolatrous nature of this or that particular religion. Instead, it has reached
a threshold where the critique demonstrates that *religion as such* is, as it
were, idolatrous – false, illusory. One might say that the *Standard Edition*
becomes the new Torah.

   Bernstein suggests that, although he does not explicitly index it as
such, Freud in fact articulates in *Moses and monotheism* the essence of
Judaism he had gestured at in the "Preface" to *Totem and taboo*; it is an
essence epitomized in the notion of "Der Fortschritt in der Geistigkeit"
that Freud introduced in his late work on Moses. There is no doubt that

[101] Yerushalmi, *Freud's Moses*, 99.
[102] Scholem, *On Jews and Judaism in crisis*, 265.

Bernstein is in some sense correct when he claims that "this is a legacy with which Freud proudly [identified]" and wanted to honor at the end of his life.[103] The claim, however, is also problematic, in no small part because the concept of *Geistigkeit* is itself problematic, and Bernstein does not sufficiently pursue its problematic aspects.

Whatever its positive content, there is one thing, as Freud saw it, that the essence of Judaism was not: flabby. The feature of the Judaic tradition – more precisely of the Mosaic tradition – that he cherished and identified with was its critical rigor, manifested in its hostility to icons and idols. He valorized linguistic articulation over imagistic mentation because it allowed for greater determinacy and rigor. Freud believed, moreover, that the internalization of that iconoclasm enabled him to stand outside the "compact majority" – including the compact Jewish majority – and adhere to a transcultural standard of scientific objectivity. The flattering self-images that a group creates to boost its collective narcissism – "the idols of the tribe" – should not, he believed, be exempted from that skeptical rigor. Indeed, he may have been bending over backwards to demonstrate his commitment to cosmopolitan and universalist values when he asserted that Moses was an Egyptian, telling his critics that he refused to "put the truth aside in favour of what are supposed to be [the] national interests" of his own people, regardless of the profound historical crisis that was threatening them.[104]

But Freud's hortatory celebration of *Geistigkeit* in *Moses* is itself flabby; it does not live up to the critical iconoclasm that he saw as an essential contribution of the monotheistic revolution. Granted, given the multiple traumas that confronted him at the time – his cancer, the uprooting of the professional infrastructure he had created, Hitler's massive attack on the Jews, and his emigration to London – we can understand why Freud may have relaxed his critical standards and painted an idealized and inspirational portrait of his people.[105] Nevertheless, in so doing, he retreated from the skeptical and thoroughgoing iconoclasm that was essential to his Jewish ego ideal. The concept of *Geistigkeit* is too uncritical and affirmative – indeed, too un-analytic – and contains more than a whiff

---

[103] Bernstein, *Freud and the legacy of Moses*, 84.

[104] Freud, *Moses and monotheism*, 7.

[105] See Grubrich-Simitis, *Early Freud and late Freud*, 61.

of sanctimony and self-satisfaction. One can imagine a Reform rabbi in pre-war Berlin presenting a variation of Freud's encomium to *Geistigkeit* as a sermon to the respectable members of the Jewish *Bildungsbürgertum* – the very people against whom Franz Kafka, Gershom Scholem, and Walter Benjamin revolted.

The "third ear" of every self-respecting analyst should perk up at the mention of *Fortschritt*, for, as Freud taught us, there is no unambiguous progress in psychic life or in cultural history. Every advance exacts its price. In this respect, enlightened psychoanalytic thinking is similar to mythical thought, which holds, as Horkheimer and Adorno put it, that "everything that happens must atone for the fact of having happened."[106] The cost of creating monotheism was the repression and debasement not only of sensuality and the body but also of the maternal dimension. One of the most problematic features of Freud's celebration of *Geistigkeit* is his uncritical affirmation of its thoroughly androcentric and patriarchal orientation.[107] The reader is indeed taken aback when Freud criticizes Christianity's reintroduction of the figure of the mother as "a cultural regression" from the transcendent heights of Jewish monotheism to a more primitive stage of religious development based on "the great mother goddess."[108] It could in fact be argued that the rehabilitation of the maternal dimension was a crucial factor in Christianity's triumph over Judaism in popularity. Let us not forget that Freud experienced the *Sinnlichkeit* of Catholicism when he visited the churches of Freiberg, a city deeply devoted to the cult of the Madonna.

There is also a more insidious side to Freud's affirmation of paternal *Geistigkeit* and denigration of maternal *Sinnlichkeit*: It can be seen as identification with the aggressor – namely, with Pauline Christianity. The adoration of the Madonna may be one aspect of Christianity, but

---

[106] Horkheimer and Adorno, *Dialectic of enlightenment*, 8.

[107] In an attempt to de-vilify Freud for the feminists, Juliet Mitchell argued in her path breaking *Psychoanalysis and feminism* that the founder of psychoanalysis was not advocating patriarchy, but describing and analysing it. As much as one would like to accept Mitchell's attractive thesis, it does not hold up to scrutiny – at least in *Moses and monotheism*. The work unequivocally commends the virtues of patriarchy. Juliet Mitchell, *Psychoanalysis and feminism: a radical reassessment of Freudian psychoanalysis*, second revised edition (New York: Basic Books, 2000).

[108] Freud, *Moses and monotheism*, 88.

Paul's teachings, which criticize *Israel carnalis* and Jewish legalism in the name of Christian spirituality, are more central to its history.[109] As Robert Paul observes, the opposition between "spirituality" and "carnality" is at the heart of Paul's denunciation of the Jews.[110] Indeed, Assmann notes that "it could be said that Christianity is primarily and fundamentally distinguished by a principle that could no better be characterized than with Freud's phrase, 'progress in [spirituality].'" Assmann is content to conclude that, although "it is not without a certain irony," Freud's "use of a Christian topos" to articulate what he believed to be the greatest accomplishment of the Jewish people "was quite unintentional."[111] Yet the whole thing is too peculiar to be left there and invites analytic scrutiny. It would seem that Freud's eagerness to valorize the Jews led him to a certain identification with the aggressor.

The monolithic androcentrism of *Moses and monotheism* has a psychological and a political source. Psychologically, Grubrich-Simitis argues that because Freud had never successfully confronted "the catastrophic events of [his] own early childhood," largely connected with his relation to his mother, when memories of his early traumatic experiences were stirred up by the traumas of the thirties, he could only address them through displacement – that is, from the maternal world onto world history.[112] Instead of excavating his own pre-history and his relation to the archaic mother, Freud turned to an excavation of the "primeval" history of civilization through what Schorske calls his second "Egyptian dig."[113]

Schorske goes on to argue that, in addition to whatever psychological factors were undoubtedly at work, the masculinist bias of *Moses and monotheism* also results from Freud's political attempt to create an idealized picture of Akhenaten's Enlightenment and Moses's continuation of it in order to enhance the Jews' conception of themselves and stiffen their mettle in the struggle against Nazi barbarism. Egypt, Schorske points

---

[109] See Daniel Boyarin, *Carnal Israel: reading sex in Talmudic culture* (Berkeley: University of California Press, 1993).

[110] Paul, *Moses and civilization*, 36.

[111] Assmann, *The price of monotheism*, 101.

[112] Grubrich-Simitis, *Early Freud and late Freud*, 68.

[113] Carl Schorske, "To the Egyptian dig: Freud's psycho-archeology of cultures," *Thinking with history: explorations in the passage to modernism* (Princeton, NJ: Princeton University Press, 1998), 191–215.

448 Freud: An Intellectual Biography

out, replaced Greece as the ancient culture that Freud idealized. Though the Jews had never achieved "an honored place in the gentile history" of Athens, Rome, or Vienna, "in Egypt," he argues, according to Freud's narrative, they "became the *Kulturvolk* that rescued the highest gentile civilization from the unholy alliance of priests and ignorant people." The implicit message in *Moses and monotheism* is thus that "in modern times, the Jews, and cultured gentiles were, through exodus and exile, [likewise] saving Europe's enlightened civilization from Hitler."[114]

Writing at the time of the Berlin Olympics, Freud may have believed that to accomplish his goal it was necessary to portray the Jews not simply as a *Kulturvolk*, but specifically as a "masculine *Kulturvolk*"; he therefore emphasized "Moses's imperial manliness."[115] As Schorske maintains, by demanding instinctual renunciation, the prophet "liberated the Jews not so much from Egyptian bondage as from their instinctual drives." Moses was "a father" who transformed childish people "into a father-people" – into a mature, manly, and tenacious *Kulturvolk*, whose commitment to *Geistigkeit* allowed them to survive even as they elicited the intense hatred of the Gentile world.[116] In short, it was the demands of this "monumental" history, in Nietzsche's sense, of the ancient Near East that gave rise to the androcentric and patriarchal biases of *Moses and monotheism* and caused Freud to extol the "masculine" virtues of *Geistigkeit* and to debase the "feminine" and "maternal" values of *Sinnlichkeit*.

It's worth remembering that Freud's earlier forays into the study of Egypt were first aroused when, sitting by Jacob's side, the young Sigmund had read the Philippson Bible, with its numerous woodcuts depicting various aspects of the ancient Near East. Schorske tell us that after 1900 – that is, after his "conquest of Rome" – Freud's curiosity about Egypt asserted itself and "nurtured interests [in him] that were in drastic contradiction to the faith of his fathers and even to the male orientation of psycho-analysis." Indeed, according to Schorske, Freud's "first Egyptian digs" raised "ultimate and even dangerous questions of the psyche" to which

---

[114] *Ibid.*, 209.

[115] *Ibid.*, 209. Richard Armstrong drew my attention to the fact that the Olympics, with its celebration of masculine physicality and athleticism, constituted part of the backdrop for *Moses*.

[116] *Ibid.*, 209.

Freud had previously "devoted scant attention."[117] Jewish law, psychoanalyst Janine Chasseguet-Smirgel observes, is suspicious of "mixture,"
and many "Biblical prohibitions are based on a principle of division and
separation" – of what one can touch and not touch, what should be kept
distinct and apart.[118] Exactly the opposite is the case with the Egyptian
world that Freud was exploring in the first years of the twentieth century.
It was characterized by mixture, ambiguity, and bi-polarity, especially
with regard to bisexuality, a topic Freud was keenly interested in, in the
aftermath of his relation with Fliess.

In *Leonardo*, for example, Freud turns to Egyptian mythology to interpret the artist's early memory of when what Freud believed was a vulture
struck the boy on the mouth with its tail while he was resting in his cradle.
The memory, Freud argues, comprises a homosexual fantasy, in which the
vulture represents the phallic mother inserting her penis into the boy's
mouth. With this interpretation, Schorske points out, "a new [bisexual]
figure" appears "on the psychoanalytic scene: the phallic mother."[119]
Because we are not primarily interested in Leonardo's psychic life but
in Freud's, the fact that the interpretation was infamously based on a
mistranslation (the Italian word Freud took for "vulture" actually meant
"kite") is beside the point. For us, what is important is that Freud arrived
at his interpretation of the memory through associations to the Egyptian
goddess Mut, an early hermaphroditic Egyptian mother deity, who had
the head of a vulture and is generally depicted as possessing a phallus.

Contrary to the heterosexual bias that tends to characterize Freud's
"official position," in this text he praises the bisexuality of the Egyptian
gods. In a remarkable statement, he notes "expressions of the idea that
only a combination of male and female elements can give a worthy representation of divine perfection."[120] Schorske argues that just as the Egyptian

---

[117] *Ibid.*, 205.

[118] Janine Chasseguet-Smirgel, "Perversion and the universal law," *Creativity and
Perversion* (New York: W.W. Norton & Co., 1984), 8.

[119] Schorske, "To the Egyptian dig," 206.

[120] Freud, *Leonardo*, 94. In this context, Freud raises the mind-boggling question of
why humans endow "a figure which is intended to embody the essence of the mother
with a mark of male potency which is the opposite of everything male." Had he been
able to face the frightening power of his own mother, he might have been able to
provide a better answer to this question than the dubious one he formulated with the
castration complex.

world, with its indeterminate sexuality, can be viewed as the archaic history of humanity, so the pre-Oedipal world, with its unintegrated drives, can be seen as the archaic history of the individual. Unfortunately, the excavation of bisexuality and pre-Oedipal development in *Leonardo* that Freud undertook on his "first Egyptian dig" remained a relatively isolated event that he did not systematically pursue in his later work. To do so might have resulted in destabilizing and fruitful insights that could have been productive and might have prevented many serious errors in the development of psychoanalysis.

To accomplish his androcentric construction, Freud had to ignore the findings of two authors he was familiar with. The first was J. H. Breasted, one of the major sources for the argument of *Moses and monotheism*. Breasted had roots, according to Schorske, "in the progressivist spirit of America's New History," and sought to chart "Egyptian culture as it struggled out of chthonic darkness to the achievements of rational enlightenment in the reign of his hero, Akhenaten." Indeed, Freud's "portrait of Akhenaten" as a rational enlightener, expounding a demanding, rational, androcentric, and puritanical doctrine, "is firmly grounded in Breasted's account."[121] At the same time, however, Breasted also presented another deeply sensual side to Akhenaten's personality and dynasty that Freud completely ignored. For example, in contrast to the rigid and geometric Egyptian art that had preceded it, the works of Akhenaten's reign display "a sensuous, naturalistic plasticity worthy of *art nouveau*." The "frescoes depicting Akhenaten and his beautiful queen Nefertiti in tender communion," according to Schorske, "radiate the joy of *Sinnlichkeit*." None of this sensuality, however, can be found in Freud. Instead, he "selected from Breasted" only what served his purposes in connecting "the Egyptian Enlightenment" with the *geistig* portrait he wished to create of the Jews. "In his copy of Breasted's history," Schorske tells us, "Freud marked only those passages" that helped him further his aims.[122]

There is something particularly striking about the second text Freud chose to ignore, namely, Karl Abraham's "Amenhotep IV."[123] Not only

---

[121] Schorske, "To the Egyptian dig," 109–110.

[122] *Ibid.*, 110.

[123] Karl Abraham, "Amenhotep IV: a psycho-analytical contribution towards the understanding of his personality and of the monotheistic cult of Aton," *Clinical papers and essays on psycho-analysis*, ed. Hilda C. Abraham, trans. Hilda C Abraham et al. (New York: Bruner Mazel, 1955), 262–290.

had he proposed the topic of Akhenaten to his colleague from Berlin, but he had also praised the article, which emphasized the feminine side of the Pharaoh's personality and cultural innovations, when it was published in 1912. It has often been observed that there is a double Abrahamic repression in *Moses and monotheism*: of Abraham the patriarch and founder of the Jewish people, and of Abraham the author of this important article. According to Karl Abraham's paper, Akhenaten's character is distinctly androgynous. Moreover, the young Pharaoh not only was deeply attached to two powerful women, his mother Queen Tiy and his beautiful wife Nefertiti, but was also deeply influenced by them. It may be the case in fact that Queen Tiy was the source and inspiration for her son's mono-theistic revolution, *which would mean that the origins of monotheism were matriarchal*. While there was undoubtedly a *geistig* side to Akhenaten, according to Abraham he was no ascetic: both his personality and the culture that surrounded him contained a deeply sensual dimension.

The idea that everything has its price, as noted, is not foreign to psychoanalysis. And the price that Freud paid for creating an image of the Jews that would strengthen them during perhaps the most profound crisis they had faced was the exclusion of the feminine and maternal dimension from his thinking. As Schorske puts it, "For the sake of the Jews in Hitler's *Götterdammerung*, Freud banished from his mind the promising insights into sexuality and culture he had found in Egypt, and abandoned them in *Moses and Monotheism*."[124] Given the Nazi's fetishization of masculinity, Freud's political decision is understandable, but the price he paid for it was "the repudiation of femininity." Those of us who arrived on the scene after the feminist critique of psychoanalysis, which, in many important respects, dovetailed with the field's pre-Oedipal turn, have a responsibility to recoup that dimension without idealizing it.

Biological Fact or Lack of Curiosity?

Like *Moses and monotheism*, "Analysis terminable and interminable" can be viewed as a last testament, but of a different sort. Written in 1937, it was Freud's last paper; in it, he sought to incorporate the results of the systematic examination of the ego he had begun in the 1920s into his theory of technique, and to sum up his views about the clinical prospects of

[124] Schorske, "To the Egyptian dig," 213.

psychoanalysis. Given the argument of this study, one fact about "Analysis terminable and interminable" could not be more striking: It ends with a discussion of "the repudiation of femininity." *That is to say, in the final passages of his final paper, Freud addresses a topic that, we have been arguing, is one of the central motifs in his intellectual biography.* It is important to note that "the repudiation of femininity" pertains to both sexes, but manifests itself differently in each. In women, it assumes the form of "a wish for a penis," and in men it appears as "the struggle against passivity."[125]

Freud wrote these closing passages in an attempt to counter the therapeutic optimism that Ferenczi had expressed in a 1927 paper on termination.[126] The Hungarian analyst had argued that, for both sexes, overcoming the "castration complex" – that is, overcoming "the repudiation of femininity" – constitutes the criterion of a "complete" analysis:

> Every male patient must attain a feeling of equality in relation to the physician as a sign that he has overcome his fear of castration; every female patient, if her neurosis is to be regarded as fully disposed of, most have got rid of her masculinity complex without a trace of resentment by implications of her female role.[127]

Freud, however, thought that Ferenczi was asking "a great deal":

> At no other point in one's analytic work does one suffer more from an oppressive feeling that all one's repeated efforts have been in vain, and from a suspicion that one has been "preaching in the winds" than when one is trying to persuade a woman to abandon her wish for a penis on the ground of its being unrealizable or when one is seeking to convince a man that a passive attitude to men does not always signify castration and that it is indispensable in many relations in life.[128]

Freud adduces a biological explanation to account for this intractable state of affairs: "The repudiation of femininity can be nothing else than a biological fact, a part of the great riddle of sex." The wish for a penis and the struggle against passivity constitute a stratum of biological "bedrock"

---

[125] Freud, "Analysis terminable and interminable," 231.

[126] Sándor Ferenczi, "The problem of termination in analysis," *Final contributions to the problems and methods of psycho-analysis*, ed. Michael Balint, trans. Eric Mosbacher et al. (New York: Bruner Mazel, 1955), 77–87.

[127] *Ibid.*, 84.

[128] Freud, "Analysis terminable and interminable," 252.

that sets an unsurpassable limit to the scope of psychoanalytic enlighten-ment.[129] One does not have to be an opponent of the biological dimension of Freud's thinking to recognize that he often postulates a biological fact to account for a phenomenon he cannot explain psychologically, thereby reining in his curiosity and putting a halt to further exploration – as he does when he postulates the existence of this biological "bedrock."

The nearly ubiquitous fear of passivity in men, Freud argues, con-stitutes the ultimate limit of their analysability; it prevents them from submitting to the requisite passivity that is necessary for the analytic process. According to Freud, "the rebellious overcompensation of the male produces one of the strongest transference-resistances." A man, he observes, "refuses to subject himself to" the analyst as "a father-substitute, or to feel indebted to him for anything, and consequently he refuses to accept his recovery from the doctor."[130] *But rather than passively submitting to the struggle against passivity as a biological fact, Freud should have become actively curious about this transference-resistance and actively analysed it.* That would have been the proper analytic stance. But because Freud's lifelong fear of the "passive-feminine" parts of his own person-ality prevented him from analysing it in himself, he could not sufficiently analyse it in his male patients.

Though these considerations are important for psychoanalytic tech-nique, they have implications that go beyond the clinical setting and bear on one of the most urgent topics on our cultural agenda, namely, the struggle against misogyny. We inhabit a psychoanalytic universe that has been transformed by the pre-Oedipal turn and a cultural uni-verse that has been reconfigured by feminism, fundamental alterations in family structures, and the sexual revolution. We are therefore in a position to confront "the repudiation of femininity," both clinically and culturally, in a way that Freud, the nineteenth-century patriarch, could not. Although it has not always understood itself in those terms, that confrontation has been taking place for some time, in the proliferation of post-conventional identities and "neosexualities" that has been under-way since the 1960s.[131] Despite their excesses, obvious difficulties, and

[129] *Ibid.*, 252.

[130] *Ibid.*, 252.

[131] See McDougall, *Theaters of the mind*, chapter 11.

occasional downright silliness, the significance of these developments should not be underestimated.

Confronting the repudiation of femininity is obviously beneficial to women. It should diminish misogyny and eliminate anachronistic restrictions on their personal, professional, and sexual development. But the repudiation of femininity also takes a serious toll on men. It results in the culture's distorted conception of masculinity, which often finds its *reductio ad absurdum* in various manifestations machismo. If men did not have to repudiate the feminine – that is, the tender, dependent, vulnerable, receptive, and nurturing – parts of themselves, their possibilities for a fulfilled life would also be greatly enhanced. For those of us who still identify with psychoanalysis as one of the great cultural movements of modernity, the task, as noted by Mark Edmundson, chronicler of Freud's last years, is to use the resources with which the reluctant Patriarch provided us to criticize the patriarchy that he often seemed to embody – and perhaps to forgive him his lapses. For as W.H. Auden observed in his memorial for Sigmund Freud, "If some traces of the autocratic pose, the paternal strictness he distrusted, still clung to his utterance and features, it was a protective coloration for one who'd lived among enemies so long."[132]

---

[132] Auden, "In memory of Sigmund Freud," 118.

Bibliography

Abraham, Karl. 1955. Amenhotep IV: a psycho-analytical contribution towards the understanding of his personality and of the monotheistic cult of Aton. *Clinical papers and essays on psycho-analysis*. Ed. Hilda C. Abraham. Trans. Hilda C. Abraham et al. New York: Bruner Mazel. 262–290.

Adorno, Theodor W. 1990. *Negative dialectics*. Trans. E.B. Ashton. New York: Routledge.

   2002. *Beethoven: the philosophy of music*. Trans. Edmund Jephcott. New York: Polity Press.

   2006. *Minima moralia: reflections from a damaged life*. Trans E.F.N. Jephcott. New York: Verso.

   2008. *Lectures on negative dialectics: fragments of a lecture course 1965/1966*. Ed. Rolf Tiedemann. Trans. Rodney Livingstone. Malden, MA: Polity Press.

Anzieu, Didier. 1987. *Freud's self-analysis*. Trans. Peter Graham. Madison, CT: International Universities Press.

Appignanesi, L. and Forrester, J. 1992. *Freud's women*. New York: Basic Books.

Aristotle. 1972. *De partibus animalium*. Trans. D.M. Balme. Oxford: The Clarendon Press.

Armstrong, Richard H. 2005. *A compulsion to antiquity: Freud and the ancient world*. Ithaca, NY: Cornell University Press.

   2010. Marooned mandarins: Freud, classical education and the Jews of Vienna. *Classics and national cultures*. Ed. Susan A. Stephens and Phiroze Vasunia. Oxford: Oxford University Press. 34–58.

Asky, Richard and Farquhar, Joseph. 2006. *Apprehending the inaccessible: Freudian psychoanalysis and existential phenomenology*. Evanston, IL: Northwestern University Press.

Assmann, Jan. 2008. *Of God and gods: Egypt, Israel, and the rise of monotheism*. George L. Mosse Series in Modern European Cultural and Intellectual History. Madison: University of Wisconsin Press.

   2010. *The price of monotheism*. Trans. Robert Savage. Stanford, CA: Stanford University Press.

Auden, W.H. 1973. In memory of Sigmund Freud. *Freud as we knew him*. Ed. Hendrik M. Ruitenbeek. Detroit, MI: Wayne State University Press. 116–119.

Bach, Sheldon. 1993. Classical technique and the unclassical patient. *Narcissistic states and the therapeutic process*. New York: Jason Aranson. 177–198.

Baltas, Aristides. 2012. *Peeling potatoes and grinding lenses: Spinoza and young Wittgenstein converse on immanence and its logic.* Pittsburgh, PA: University of Pittsburgh Press.

Barclay, James R. 1964. Franz Brentano and Sigmund Freud. *Journal of Existentialism* 5: 1–36.

Barker, Pat. 2014. *The regeneration trilogy.* London: Hamish Hamilton.

Baron, Salo. 1939. Review of *Moses and monotheism. American Journal of Sociology* 45: 471–477.

Beckett, Samuel. 1983. *Worstward ho.* New York: Grove Press.

Bellah, Robert N. 2011. *Religion in human evolution: from the paleolithic to the Axial Age.* Cambridge, MA: The Belknap Press of Harvard University Press.

Beller, Steven. 2007. *Antisemitism: a very short introduction.* Oxford: Oxford University Press, 2007.

Berger, Peter. 1967. *The sacred canopy: elements of a sociological theory of religion.* New York: Anchor Books.

1999. *The desecularization of the world.* New York: William B. Eerdmans.

2015. Paradox or pluralism: review of Michael Walzer's *The paradox of liberation: secular revolutions and religious counterrevolutions. Jewish Review of Books* 6: 13–15.

Bergmann, Martin S. 1977. Moses and the evolution of Freud's Jewish identity. *Judaism and psychoanalysis.* Ed. Mortimer Ostow. London: Karnac Books. 111–142.

Berkley, George E. 1988. *Vienna and its Jews: the tragedy of success 1880s–1980s.* Cambridge, MA: Abt Books.

Berlin, Isaiah. 1993. *The magus of the north.* London: John Murray.

Bernays, Anna Freud. 1973. My brother, Sigmund Freud. *Freud as we knew him.* Ed. Henrik M. Ruitenbeek. Detroit, MI: Wayne State University Press. 140–147.

Bernfeld, Siegfried. 1944. Freud's earliest theories and the school of Helmholtz. *Psychoanalytic Quarterly* 13: 341–362.

1949. Freud's scientific beginnings. *American Imago* 6: 163–196.

Bernfeld, Siegfried and Bernfeld, Suzanne Cassirer. 1973. Freud's early childhood. *Freud as we knew him.* Ed. Hendrik M. Ruitenbeek. Detroit, MI: Wayne State University Press. 118–196.

Bernstein, Richard J. 1988. *Freud and the legacy of Moses.* Cambridge: Cambridge University Press.

Binswanger, Ludwig. 1957. *Sigmund Freud: reminiscences of a friendship.* Trans. Norbert Guterman. New York: Grune & Stratton.

Blumenberg, Hans. 1988. *The legitimacy of the modern age.* Trans. Robert M. Wallace. Cambridge, MA: The MIT Press.

Boehlich, Walther (ed.). 1990. *The letters of Sigmund Freud to Eduard Silberstein, 1871–1881.* Ed. Walther Boehlich. Trans. Arnold J. Pomerans. Cambridge, MA: The Belknap Press of Harvard University Press.

Bonaparte, Marie, Freud, Anna and Kris, Ernst (eds.). 1954. *The origins of psychoanalysis: letters to Wilhelm Fliess.* Trans. Eric Mosbacher and James Strachey. New York: Basic Books.

Boyarin, Daniel. 1993. *Carnal Israel: reading sex in Talmudic culture*. Berkeley: University of California Press.

1997. *Unheroic conduct: the rise of heterosexuality and the invention of the Jewish man*. Berkeley: University of California Press.

Breger, Louis. 2000. *Freud: darkness in the midst of vision*. New York: Wiley.

Breuer, Josef and Freud, Sigmund. 1893–1895. *Studies in hysteria*. SE 2: xxix–320.

Carnap, Rudolph, Neurath, Otto, and Charles F.W. Morris (eds.). 1971. *Foundations of the unity of science: toward an international encyclopedia of unified science*, vol. II. Chicago: University of Chicago Press.

Castoriadis, Cornelius. 1984. *Crossroads in the labyrinth*. Trans. Kate Soper and Martin H. Ryle. Cambridge, MA: The MIT Press.

1984. Psychoanalysis: project and elucidation. *Crossroads in the labyrinth*. Trans. Kate Soper and Martin H. Ryle. Cambridge, MA: The MIT Press. 46–118.

1987. *The imaginary institution of society*. Trans. Kathleen Blamey. Cambridge, MA: The MIT Press.

1992. Passion and knowledge. *Diogenes* 40: 75–93.

1997. The discovery of the imagination. *World in fragments: writings on politics, society, psychoanalysis and the imagination*. Ed. and trans. David Ames Curtis. Stanford: Stanford University Press. 213–245.

1997. Institution of society and religion. *World in fragments: writings on politics, society, psychoanalysis and the imagination*. Ed. and trans. David Ames Curtis. Stanford: Stanford University Press. 311–330.

1997. Psychoanalysis and politics. *World in fragments: writings on politics, society, psychoanalysis and the imagination*. Ed. and trans. David Ames Curtis. Stanford: Stanford University Press. 125–136.

1997. *World in fragments: writings on politics, society, psychoanalysis and the imagination*. Ed. and trans. David Ames Curtis. Stanford, CA: Stanford University Press.

Cavell, Stanley. 1987. Freud and philosophy: a fragment. *Critical Inquiry* 13: 386–393.

Chasseguet-Smirgel, Janine. 1984. Perversion and the universal law. *Creativity and perversion*, New York: W.W. Norton & Co.

1986. The archaic matrix of the Oedipus complex. *Sexuality and mind: the role of the father and the mother in the psyche*. Ed. Leo Goldberger. New York: New York University Press. 74–91.

Chertok, Léon. 1968. The discovery of the transference: towards an epistemological interpretation. *International Journal of Psycho-analysis* 49: 563.

Chertok, Léon and Strengers, Isabelle. 1992. *A critique of psychoanalytic reason: hypnosis as a scientific problem from Lavoisier to Lacan*. Trans. Martha Noel Evans. Stanford, CA: Stanford University Press.

Clark, Ronald William.1980. *Freud: the man and the cause*. New York: Random House.

Cranefield, Paul F. 1958. Josef Breuer's evaluation of his contribution to psychoanalysis. *International Journal of Psychoanalysis* 39: 319–322.

Decker, Hannah S. 1991. *Freud, Dora, and Vienna 1900*. New York: The Free Press.

Derrida, Jacques. 1994. "To do justice to Freud": the history of madness in the age of psychoanalysis. Trans. Pascale-Anne Brault and Michael Nass. *Critical Inquiry* 20: 227–266.

Dijksterhuis, Eduard Jan. 1966. *The mechanization of the world picture: Pythagoras to Newton*. Trans. C. Dikshoom. Princeton, NJ: Princeton University Press.

Durkheim, Émile. 1995. *The elementary forms of religious life*. Trans. Karen E. Fields. New York: The Free Press.

Edmundson, Mark. 2007. *The death of Sigmund Freud: the legacy of his last days*. New York: Bloomsbury.

Eissler, K.R. 1978. Creativity and adolescence: the effect of trauma in Freud's adolescence. *The Psychoanalytic Study of the Child* 33: 466–467.

Ellenberger, Henri F. 1970. *The discovery of the unconscious: the history and evolution of dynamic psychiatry*. New York: Basic Books.

Elon, Amos. 2003. *The pity of it all: a portrait of the German-Jewish epoch, 1743–1933*. New York: Picador.

Erikson, Erik. 1955. Freud's "The origins of psycho-analysis". *International Journal of Psycho-analysis* 38: 1–15.

——— 1994. The first psychoanalyst. *Insight and responsibility*. New York: W.W. Norton & Co. 17–47.

Falzeder, Ernst (ed.). 2002. *The complete correspondence of Sigmund Freud and Karl Abraham: 1907–1925*. Trans. Caroline Schwarzacher with the collaboration of Christine Trollope and Klar Majthényi King. New York: Karnac.

Falzeder, Ernst and Brabant, Eva (eds.). 1992. *The correspondence of Sigmund Freud and Sándor Ferenczi*, vol. I: *1908–1914*. Trans. Peter T. Hoffer. Cambridge, MA: Harvard University Press.

——— 2000. *The correspondence of Sigmund Freud and Sándor Ferenczi*, vol. III: *1920–1933*. Trans. Peter Hoffer. Cambridge, MA: Harvard University Press.

Fenichel, Otto. 1941. *Problems of psychoanalytic technique*. New York: The Psychoanalytic Quarterly.

——— 1953. Psychoanalysis and metaphysics. *Collected papers of Otto Fenichel: first series*. New York: W.W. Norton & Co. vol. II, 8–26.

Ferenczi, Sándor. 1955. The problem of termination in analysis. *Final contributions to the problems and methods of psycho-analysis*. Ed. Michael Balint. Trans. Eric Mosbacher et al. New York: Bruner Mazel. 77–86.

Fichtner, Gerhard (ed.). 2003. *The Sigmund Freud – Ludwig Binswanger Correspondence, 1908–1938*. Trans. Arnold J. Pomerans. New York: Other Press.

Fisher, D.J. 1976. Sigmund Freud and Romain Rolland: the terrestrial animal and his great oceanic friend. *American Imago* 33: 1–59.

Forrester, John. 1980. *Language and the origins of psychoanalysis*. New York: Columbia University Press.

Foucault, Michel. 2007. *The history of madness*. Trans. Jonathan Murphy. New York: Routledge.

Freud, Anna. 1971. Difficulties in the path of psychoanalysis. *Problems of psychoanalytic training, diagnosis, and the technique of therapy: the writings of Anna Freud*, vol. II. New York: International Universities Press. 124–156.

Freud, Ernst (ed.). 1972. *The letters of Sigmund Freud and Arnold Zweig*. Trans. W. and E. Robson-Scott. New York: New York University Press.

Freud, Martin. 1957. *Glory reflected: Sigmund Freud – man and father*. London: Angus and Robertson.

——— 1970. Who was Freud? *The Jews of Austria*. Ed. Josef Fraenkel Portland OR: Vallentine Mitchell.

Freud, Sigmund. 1886. Preface and footnotes to the translation of Charcot's *Leçons du mardi de la Salpêtrièère*. *SE* 1: 21–22.

——— 1888. Preface to the translation of Bernheim's *De la suggestion*. *SE* 1: 75–85.

——— 1890. Psychical treatment. *SE* 7: 281–302.

——— 1892–1893. A case of successful treatment by hypnotism. *SE* 1: 115–128.

——— 1893. Charcot. *SE* 3: 27–24.

——— 1895. Project for a scientific psychology. *SE* 1: 283–398.

——— 1899. Screen memories. *SE* 3: 299–322.

——— 1900. The interpretation of dreams. *SE* 4 and 5: xi–630.

——— 1901. The psychopathology of everyday life. *SE* 6: 1–279.

——— 1904. Obituary for Professor S. Hammerschlag. *SE* 9: 255–256.

——— 1907. Delusions and dreams in Jensen's *Gradiva*. *SE* 9: 3–95.

——— 1908. "Civilized" sexual morality and modern nervous illness. *SE* 9: 177–204.

——— 1909. Notes upon a case of obsessional neurosis. *SE* 10: 153–320.

——— 1910. Five lectures on psychoanalysis. *SE* 11: 1–58.

——— 1910. Leonardo da Vinci and a memory of his childhood. *SE* 11: 59–138.

——— 1911. Psycho-analytic notes on an autobiographical account of a case of paranoia (Dementia paranoides). *SE* 12: 3–84.

——— 1911. Formulations concerning the two principles of mental functioning. *SE* 12: 213–216.

——— 1913. Totem and taboo. *SE* 13: xi–64.

——— 1913. The theme of the three caskets. *SE* 12: 290–301.

——— 1914. Some reflections on schoolboy psychology. *SE* 13: 239–244.

——— 1914. The Moses of Michelangelo. *SE* 13: 209–237.

——— 1914. On narcissism: an introduction. *SE* 14: 67–102.

——— 1914. Instincts and their vicissitudes. *SE* 14: 105–140.

——— 1914. Remembering, repeating and working-through (further recommendations on the technique of psycho-analysis). *SE* 12: 145–156.

——— 1915. Instincts and their vicissitudes. *SE* 14: 109–140.

——— 1915. Thoughts for the time on war and death. *SE* 14: 273–302.

——— 1916. On transience. *SE* 14: 303–308.

——— 1916–1917. Introductory lectures on psycho-analysis. *SE* 15 and 16: 13–463.

——— 1917. Mourning and melancholia. *SE* 14: 237–258.

——— 1920. Beyond the pleasure principle. *SE* 18: 3–66.

——— 1921. Group psychology and the analysis of the ego. *SE* 18: 67–143.

1922. Some neurotic mechanisms in jealousy, paranoia and homosexuality. *SE* 18: 221–232.

1923. Two encyclopedia articles. *SE* 18: 235–262.

1924. The economic problem of masochism. *SE* 19: 155–172.

1924. Resistances to psychoanalysis. *SE* 19: 213–222.

1925. Some psychical consequences of the anatomical distinction between the sexes. *SE* 19: 241–258.

1925. An autobiographical study. *SE* 20: 2–70.

1926. Inhibitions, symptoms and anxiety. *SE* 20: 77–178.

1926. The question of lay analysis. *SE* 20: 177–258.

1927. The future of an illusion. *SE* 21: 1–56.

1927. Fetishism. *SE* 21: 149–158.

1928. A religious experience. *SE* 21: 167–172.

1930. Civilization and its discontents. *SE* 21: 3–148.

1931. Female sexuality. *SE* 21: 221–244.

1931. Letter to the *burgomeister* of Pribor. *SE* 21: 259.

1933. New introductory lessons on psycho-analysis. *SE* 22: 1–182.

1933. Why war. *SE* 22: 195–203.

1937. Analysis terminable and interminable. *SE* 23: 209–254.

1939. Moses and monotheism. *SE* 23: 1–138.

1940. An outline of psycho-analysis. *SE* 23: 141–207.

1960. *The letters of Sigmund Freud*. Ed. Ernst L. Freud. Trans. Tania and James Stern. New York: Basic Books.

1969. Some early unpublished letters of Freud. *International Journal of Psychoanalysis* 50: 419–427.

1987. *A phylogenetic fantasy: overview of the transference neurosis*. Trans. Alex Hoffer and Peter Hoffer. Ed. Ilse Grubrich-Simitis. Cambridge, MA: Harvard University Press.

Gadamer, Hans-Georg. 1994. *Truth and method*. Second revised edition. Trans. Joel Weinsheimer and Donald G. Marshal. New York: Continuum.

Garner, Shirley Nelson. 1989. Freud and Fliess: homophobia and seduction. *Seduction and theory*. Ed. Dianne Hunter. Chicago: University of Illinois Press. 86–108.

Gay, Peter. 1984. *Freud, Jews, and other Germans*. Oxford: Oxford University Press.

1988. *Freud: a life for our time*. New York: W.W. Norton.

1988. *A godless Jew: Freud, atheism, and the making of psychoanalysis*. New Haven, CT: Yale University Press.

2001. Review of *Freud: darkness in the midst of vision*. *Journal of the American Psychoanalytic Association* 49: 1075–1076.

Gedo, John. 1976. Freud's self-analysis and his scientific ideas. *Freud: the fusion of science and humanism*. Psychoanalytic Issues monograph 34/35. Ed. John Gedo and George H. Pollock. New York: International Universities Press. 286–306.

1983. *Portraits of the artist: the psychoanalysis of creativity and its vicissitudes*. New York: The Guilford Press.

Geller, Jay. 1994. *Freud v. Freud: Freud's reading of Daniel Paul Schreber's* Denkwür-
digkeiten Nervenkranken. *Reading Freud's reading.* Ed. Sander Gilman et al.
New York: New York University Press. 180–210.

Glickhorn, René. 1969. The Freiberg period of the Freud family. *Journal of the History
of Medicine and Allied Sciences* 24: 37–43.

Goldstein, Jan. 1982. The hysteria diagnosis and the politics of anticlericalism in late
nineteenth-century France. *Journal of Modern History* 54: 209–239.

Gould, Stephen Jay. 1977. *Ever since Darwin: reflections in natural history.* New York:
W.W. Norton & Co.

Graf, Max. 1942. Reminiscences of Professor Sigmund Freud. *Psychoanalytic
Quarterly* 11: 455–467.

Green, André. 1986. *On private madness.* Madison, CT: International Universities
Press.

    1986. The analyst, symbolization and absence in the analytic setting. *On private
madness.* Madison, CT: International Universities Press. 30–59.

    1986. The dead mother, *On private madness.* Madison, CT: International
Universities Press. 142–173.

    1999. *The work of the negative.* Trans. Andrew Weller. New York: Free Associations
Books.

    2001. "One, other neuter: narcissistic values of sameness." *Life narcissism, death
narcissism.* Trans. Andrew Weller. New York: Free Associations Books. 3–47.

Gresser, Moshe. 1944. *Dual allegiance: Freud as a modern Jew.* Albany: State University
of New York Press.

Grubrich-Simitis, Ilse. 1987. Metapsychology and metabiology, on Sigmund Freud's
first draft of "Overview of the transference neurosis." *Freud, A phylogenetic
fantasy: overview of the transference neurosis.* Ed. Ilse Grubrich-Simitis. Trans.
Alex Hoffer and Peter T. Hoffer. Cambridge, MA: Harvard University Press.
75–108.

    1997. *Early Freud and late Freud: reading anew.* Studies on hysteria *and* Moses and
monotheism. New York: Routledge.

    2011. Seeds of core psychoanalytic concepts: on the courtship letters of Sigmund
Freud and Martha Bernays. Paper delivered at the 47th Congress of the
International Psychoanalytic Association in Mexico City. Trans. Philip Slotkin.

Habermas, Jürgen. 1969. *Knowledge and human interests.* Trans. Jeremy J. Shapiro.
Boston, MA: Beacon Press.

    1973. Between philosophy and science – Marxism as critique. *Theory and practice.*
Trans. John Viertel. Boston: Beacon Press. 195–252.

    1987. *The philosophical discourse of modernity: twelve lectures.* Trans. Frederick G.
Lawrence. Cambridge, MA: The MIT Press.

    1997. Modernity: an unfinished project. *Habermas and the unfinished project of
modernity.* Ed. Maurizio Passerin d'Entrève and Seyla Benhabib. Cambridge,
MA: The MIT Press. 38–58.

Halevy, Mordecai Mayer, et al. 1958. Discussion regarding Sigmund Freud's ancestry.
Yivo: annual of Jewish social science, vol. XII. New York: Yivo. 297–300.

Hardin, Harry T. 1988. On the vicissitudes of Freud's early mothering – I: Early environment and loss. *Psychoanalytic Quarterly* 56: 628–644.

1988. On the vicissitudes of Freud's early mothering – II: Alienation from his biological mother. *Psychoanalytic Quarterly* 56: 72–86.

1988. On the vicissitudes of Freud's early mothering – III: Freiberg, screen memories, and loss. *Psychoanalytic Quarterly* 57: 209–223.

Harvey, Van Austin. 1995. *Feuerbach and the interpretation of religion*. Cambridge: Cambridge University Press.

Hayman, Ronald. 1999. *A life of Jung*. New York: W.W. Norton & Co.

Hegel, G.W.F. 1997. *The phenomenology of the spirit*. Trans. A.V. Miller. Oxford: Oxford University Press.

Heller, Judith Bernays. 1973. Freud's mother and father. *Freud as we knew him*. Ed. Hendrik M. Ruitenbeck. Detroit, MI: Wayne State University Press. 334–340.

Herzog, Patricia. 1988. The myth of Freud as anti-philosopher. *Freud: appraisals and reappraisals: contributions to Freud Studies*, vol. II. Ed. Paul E. Stepansky. Hillsdale, NJ: Analytic Press.

Hewitt, Marsha Aileen. 2014. *Freud on religion*. Bristol, CT: Acumen.

Hirschmüller, Albrecht. 1989. *The life and work of Josef Breuer: physiology and psychoanalysis*. New York: New York University Press.

Homans, Peter. 1989. *The ability to mourn: disillusionment and the social origins of psychoanalysis*. Second edition. Chicago: University of Chicago Press.

1995. *Jung in context: modernity and the making of psychology*. Chicago: University of Chicago Press.

2000. Loss and mourning in the life and thought of Max Weber: toward a theory of symbolic loss. *Symbolic loss: the ambiguity of mourning and memory at century's end*. Ed. Peter Homans. Charlottesville: University of Virginia Press. 225–238.

Honneth, Axel. 2009. *Pathologies of reason (on the legacy of critical theory)*. Trans. James D. Ingram. New York: Columbia University Press.

Horkheimer, Max and Adorno, Theodor W. 2002. *Dialectic of enlightenment: philosophical fragments*. Ed. Gunzelin Noerr. Trans. Edmund Jephcott. Stanford, CA: Stanford University Press.

Horney, Karen. 1926. The flight from womanhood: the masculinity-complex in women, as viewed by men and by women. *International Journal of Psychoanalysis* 7: 324–339.

Janik, Alan and Toulmin, Stephen. 1973. *Wittgenstein's Vienna*. New York: Simon and Schuster.

Jay, Martin. 1973. *The dialectical imagination: a history of the Frankfurt School and the Institute for Social Research, 1923–1950*. New York: Little Brown.

Johnston, William M. 1972. *The Austrian mind: an intellectual and social history 1848–1938*. Berkeley: University of California Press.

Jonas, Hans. 2001. Is God a mathematician? The meaning of metabolism. *The Phenomenon of life: toward a philosophical biology*. Evanston, IL: Northwestern University Press. 64–98.

Jones, Ernest. 1953. *The life and work of Sigmund Freud*, vol. I: *1856–1900, the formative years and the great discoveries*. New York: Basic Books.

1955. *The life and work of Sigmund Freud*, vol. II: *1901–1919, the years of maturity*. New York: Basic Books.

1957. *The life and work of Sigmund Freud*, vol. III: *1919–1939, the last phase*. New York: Basic Books.

Jung, C.G. 1967. *The symbols of transformation: an analysis of a prelude to a case of schizophrenia*. Second edition. *The collected works of C. G. Jung*, vol. V. Bollingen Series XX. Ed. Herbert read et al. Princeton, NJ: Princeton University Press.

1978. On the psychology and pathology of so-called occult phenomena. *The psychology of the occult* (Jung extracts). Trans. R.F.C. Hull. Princeton, NJ: Princeton University Press. 6–19.

1983. *The Zofingia lectures: the collected works of C.G. Jung supplementary volume*. Ed. William McGuire. Princeton, NJ: Princeton University Press.

1989. *Memories, dreams, reflections*. Trans. Clara Winston. New York: Vintage.

2002. *The psychology of the unconscious*. Trans. Beatrice M. Hinkle. Mineola, NY: Dover.

Kant, Immanuel. 1991. "Idea of a universal history with a cosmopolitan intent." *Kant: political writings*. Second edition. Ed. Hans Reiss. Trans. H.B. Nisbet. Cambridge: Cambridge University Press. 41–53.

Kaufmann, Walter. 2007. *Discovering the mind*, vol. III: *Freud, Adler and Jung*. New Brunswick, NJ: Transaction.

Kendrick, Walter. 1997. "Psychiatrist to the gods? *The New York Times* online. www.nytimes.com/books/97/09/21/reviews/970921.21kendrit.html.

Kerr, John. 1993. *A most dangerous method: the story of Jung, Freud, and Sabina Spielrein*. New York: Alfred A. Knopf.

Klein, Melanie. 1975. Envy and gratitude. *Envy and gratitude & other works, 1946–1963*. New York: Delacorte Press. 176–235.

Kohut, Heinz. 1966. The forms and transformations of narcissism. *Journal of the American Psychoanalytic Association* 14: 243–272.

1977. *The restoration of the self*. New York: International Universities Press.

1985. Creativeness, charisma, group psychology: reflections on the self-analysis of Freud. *Self psychology and the humanities*. New York: W.W. Norton & Co. 171–214.

2009. *The analysis of the self: a systematic approach to the treatment of narcissistic personality disorders*. Chicago: University of Chicago Press.

Krüll, Marianne. 1968. *Freud and his father*. Trans. Arnold J. Pomerans. New York: W.W. Norton & Co.

La Barre, Weston. 1972. *The ghost dance: the origins of religion*. New York: Delta Books.

1991. *Shadow of childhood: neoteny and the biology of religion*. Norman: University of Oklahoma Press.

Lacan, Jacques. 2006. *Écrits*. Trans. Bruce Fink et al. New York: W.W. Norton & Co.

2006. The mirror stage as formative of the I function as revealed in psychoanalytic experience. *Écrits*. Trans. Bruce Fink et al. New York: W.W. Norton & Co.
75–81.

2006. The significance of the phallus. *Écrits*. Trans. Bruce Fink et al. New York:
W.W. Norton & Co. 575–584.

Laforgue, René. 1973. Personal memories of Freud. *Freud as we knew him*. Ed.
Hendrik M. Ruitenbeek. Detroit, MI: Wayne State University Press. 341–349.

Laplanche, Jean. 1989. *New foundations for psychoanalysis*. Trans. David Macey. New
York: Basil Blackwell.

Laplanche, J. and Pontalis, J.-B. 1973. *The language of psycho-analysis*. Trans. Donald
Nicholson-Smith. New York: W.W. Norton & Co.

Laqueur, Thomas. 2003. *Solitary sex: a cultural history of masturbation*. New York:
Zone Books.

Lear, Jonathan. 1996. The introduction of eros: reflections on the work of Hans
Loewald. *Journal of the American Psychoanalytic Association* 44: 673–698.

1988. Inside and outside the republic. *Open minded*. Cambridge, MA: Harvard
University Press. 219–246.

2005. *Freud*. New York: Routledge.

Lewin, Bertram D. 1973. Dreams and the uses of regression. *Selected writings of
Bertram D. Lewin*. Ed. Jacob A. Arlow. New York: The Psychoanalytic Quarterly.
329–352.

Leys, Ruth. 2000. *Trauma: a genealogy*. Chicago: University of Chicago Press.

Lloyd, G.E.R. 1971. *Magic, reason and experience: studies in the origins of and development of Greek science*. Cambridge, MA: Hackett.

Loewald, Hans. 2000. Book review essay on the Freud/Jung letters. *The essential Loewald: collected papers and monographs*. Hagerstown, MD: University
Publishing Group. 405–418.

2000. Defense and reality. *The essential Loewald: collected papers and monographs*.
Hagerstown, MD: University Publishing Group. 3–21.

2000. Discussion: Max Schur, "The id and the regulatory principles of mental
functioning." *The essential Loewald: collected papers and monographs*. Hagerstown,
MD: University Publishing Group. 53–68.

2000. *The essential Loewald: collected papers and monographs*. Hagerstown, MD:
University Publishing Group.

2000. On internalization. *The essential Loewald: collected papers and monographs*.
Hagerstown, MD: University Publishing Group. 69–86.

2000. Primary process, secondary process, and language. *The essential Loewald: collected papers and monographs*. Hagerstown, MD: University Publishing Group.
178–206.

2000. Psychoanalysis and the history of the individual. *The essential Loewald: collected papers and monographs*. Hagerstown, MD: University Publishing Group.
531–571.

2000. Sublimation: inquiries into theoretical psychoanalysis. *The essential Loewald:
collected papers and monographs*. Hagerstown, MD: University Publishing Group.
439–530.

2000. On the therapeutic action of psychoanalysis. *The essential Loewald: collected papers and monographs.* Hagerstown, MD: University Publishing Group. 221–256.

2000. The waning of the Oedipus complex. *The essential Loewald: collected papers and monographs.* Hagerstown, MD: University Publishing Group. 384–404.

Lothane, Zvi. 1997. The schism between Freud and Jung over Schreber: its implications for method and doctrine. *International Forum of Psychoanalysis* 6: 103–115.

Lotto, David. 2001. Freud's struggle with misogyny: homosexuality and guilt in the dream of Irma's injection. *Journal of the American Psychoanalytic Association* 49: 1289–1313.

Lunbeck, Elizabeth. 2014. *The Americanization of narcissism.* Cambridge, MA: Harvard University Press.

Mahler, Margaret S., Pine, Fred, and Bergman, Annie. 1975. *The psychological birth of the human infant: symbiosis and individuation.* New York: Basic Books.

Makari, George. 1992. A history of Freud's first theory of transference. *International Review of Psychoanalysis* 9: 415–432.

. 2008. *Revolution in mind: the creation of psychoanalysis.* New York: HarperCollins.

Malcolm, Janet. 2002. *In the Freud Archives.* New York: New York Review of Books Classics.

Mann, Thomas. 1937. *Freud, Goethe, Wagner.* New York: Alfred A. Knopf.

Marcuse, Herbert. 1966. *Eros and civilization: a philosophical inquiry into Freud.* Boston: Beacon Press.

Markel, Howard. 2011. *An anatomy of addiction: Sigmund Freud, William Halsted, and the miracle of cocaine.* New York: Pantheon Books.

Marx, Karl. 1967. Contribution to the critique of Hegel's philosophy of right. *Marx and Engels on religion.* New York: Schocken Books. 41–58.

1969. Theses on Feuerbach. *Karl Marx and Frederick Engels, selected works*, vol. I. Moscow: Progress Press. 11–12.

1971. Manifesto of the Communist Party. *Karl Marx: on revolution.* Ed. and trans. Saul K. Padover. New York: McGraw Hill.

Masson, Jeffrey Moussaieff. 1984. *The assault on truth: Freud's suppression of the seduction theory.* New York: Farrar, Straus and Giroux.

(ed.). 1986. *The complete letters of Sigmund Freud to Wilhelm Fliess: 1887–1904.* Cambridge, MA: The Belknap Press of Harvard University Press.

McDougall, Joyce. 1989. *Theaters of the body: a psychoanalytic approach to psychosomatic illness.* New York: W.W. Norton & Co.

2013. *Theaters of the mind: illusion and truth on the psychoanalytic stage.* New York: Routledge.

McGrath, William. 1986. *Freud's discovery of psychoanalysis: the politics of hysteria.* Ithaca, NY: Cornell University Press.

McGuire, William (ed.). 1974. *The Freud/Jung letters: the correspondence between Sigmund Freud and C.G. Jung.* Trans. R.F.C. Hull. Princeton, NJ: Princeton University Press.

McLynn, Frank. 1996. *Carl Gustav Jung.* New York: St. Martin's Press.

Meng, Heinrich and Freud, Ernst L. (eds.). 1963. *Psychoanalysis and faith: the letters of Sigmund Freud and Oskar Pfister.* Trans. Erich Mosbacher. New York: Basic Books.

Mitchell, Juliet. 2000. *Psychoanalysis and feminism: a radical reassessment of Freudian psychoanalysis.* Second revised edition. New York: Basic Books.

Mosse, George L. 1985. Jewish emancipation: between *Bildung* and respectability: from the Enlightenment to the Second World War. *The Jewish response to German culture: from the Enlightenment to the Second World War.* Ed. Jehuda Reinharz and Walter Schatzberg. Hanover, NH: University of New England Press. 1–16.

Niedland, William G. 1984. *The Schreber case: a psychoanalytic profile of a paranoid personality.* Second revised edition. New York: Routledge.

Nietzsche, Friedrich. 1997. *Twilight of the idols: or how to philosophize with a hammer.* Trans. Richard Polt. Indianapolis, IN: Hackett.

———. 2001. *The gay science: with a prelude in German rhymes and an appendix of songs.* Ed. Bernard Williams. Trans. Josefine Naukhoff. Cambridge: Cambridge University Press.

Ogden, Thomas H. 2002. A new reading of object relations theory. *International Journal of Psychoanalysis* 83: 767–782.

Orgel, Shelly. 1966. Freud and the repudiation of the feminine. *Journal of the American Psychoanalytic Association* 44: 45–67.

Parsons, William B. 1999. *The enigma of the oceanic feeling: revisioning the psychoanalytic theory of mysticism.* Oxford: Oxford University Press.

Paskauska, Andrew R. (ed.). 1993. *The complete correspondence of Sigmund Freud and Ernest Jones: 1908–1939.* Cambridge, MA: The Belknap Press of Harvard University Press.

Paul, Robert A. 1996. *Moses and civilization: the meaning behind Freud's myth.* New Haven: Yale University Press.

Pfeiffer, Ernst (ed.). 1966. *Sigmund Freud and Lou Andreas-Salomé letters.* Trans. William and Elaine Robson-Scott. New York: Harcourt Brace Jovanovich.

Phillips, Adam. 2014. *Becoming Freud: the making of a psychoanalyst.* New Haven, CT: Yale University Press.

Plato. 1995. *The Phaedrus.* Trans. Alexander Nehamas and Paul Woodruff. Indianapolis, IN: Hackett.

Radkau, Joachim. 2009. *Max Weber: a biography.* Trans. Patrick Camiller. Madden, MA: Polity Press.

Rainey, Reuben M. 1975. *Freud as a student of religion: perspectives on the background and development of his thought.* Missoula, MT: Scholars' Press.

Reinharz, Jehuda and Schatzberg, Walter (eds.). *The Jewish response to German culture: from the Enlightenment to the Second World War.* Hanover, NH: University of New England Press.

Rice, Emanuel. 1990. *Freud and Moses: the long journey home.* New York: State University of New York Press.

Ricoeur, Paul. 1970. *Freud and philosophy: a study in interpretation.* Trans. Denis Savage. New Haven, CT: Yale University Press.

———. 1974. Technique and nontechnique in interpretation. *The conflict of interpretations: essays and hermeneutics.* Trans. Willis Domingo. Evanston, IL: Northwestern University Press. 177–195.

Rieff, Philip. 1966. *The triumph of the therapeutic: uses of faith after Freud*. New York: Harper and Row.

1979. *Freud: the mind of a moralist*. Chicago: University of Chicago Press.

Ritvo, Lucille B. 1990. *Darwin's influence on Freud: a tale of two scientists*. New Haven, CT: Yale University Press.

Rizzuto, Ana-Maria. 1998. *Why did Freud reject God? A psychodynamic interpretation*. New Haven, CT: Yale University Press.

Roazen, Paul. 1974. *Freud and his followers*. New York: New American Library.

Robert, Marthe. 1976. *From Oedipus to Moses: Freud's Jewish identity*. Trans. Robert Manheim. New York: Anchor Books.

Sachs, Hans. 1944. *Freud: master and friend*. Cambridge, MA: Harvard University Press.

Said, Edward. 2003. *Freud and the non-European*. New York: Verso.

Santner, Eric L. 1997. *My own private Germany: Daniel Paul Schreber's secret history of modernity*. Princeton, NJ: Princeton University Press.

Sartre, Jean-Paul. 1956. *Being and nothingness*. Trans. Hazel Barnes. New York: Washington Square Press.

Schimmel, Paul. 2013. *Sigmund Freud's discovery of psychoanalysis: conquistador and thinker*. New York: Routledge.

Scholem, Gershom. 1976. *On Jews and Judaism in crisis: selected essays*. Ed. Werner J. Dannhauser. New York: Schocken Books.

Schorske, Carl. 1980. *Fin-de-siècle Vienna: politics and culture*. New York: Alfred A. Knopf.

1991. Freud: the psychoarcheology of civilizations. *The Cambridge companion to Freud*. Ed. Jerome Neu. Cambridge: Cambridge University Press. 8–24.

1998. To the Egyptian dig: Freud's psycho-archaeology of cultures. *Thinking with history: explorations in the passage to modernism*. Princeton, NJ: Princeton University Press. 191–218.

1998. Generational tension. *Thinking with history: explorations in the passage to modernism*. Princeton, NJ: Princeton University Press. 141–156.

1998. *Thinking with history: explorations in the passage to modernism*. Princeton, NJ: Princeton University Press.

Schreber, Daniel Paul. 2000. *Memoirs of my nervous illness*. Trans. Ida Macalpine and Richard Hunter. New York: The New York Review of Books.

Schur, Max. 1966. Some "additional day residues" of the "specimen dream of psychoanalysis". *Psychoanalysis – a general psychology: essays in honor of Heinz Hartmann*. Ed. Rudolph M. Lowenstein, Lottie M. Newman, Max Schur, and Albert Solnit. New York: International Universities Press. 45–85.

1972. *Freud: living and dying*. New York: International Universities Press.

Shengold, Leonard. 1976. The Freud/Jung letters: the correspondence between Sigmund Freud and C.G. Jung. *Journal of the American Psychoanalytic Association* 24: 669–683.

Sherry, Jay. 2008. Carl Gustav Jung, avant-garde conservative. Doctoral dissertation, Freie Univeristät Berlin.

Slochower, Harry. 1975. Philosophical principles in Freudian theory: ontology and the quest for matrem. *American Imago* 32: 1–39.

Sprengnether, Madelon. 1990. *The spectral mother: Freud, feminism, and psychoanalysis*. Ithaca, NY: Cornell University Press.

Sterba, Richard. 1982. *Reminiscences of a Viennese psychoanalyst*. Detroit, MI: Wayne State University Press.

Stone, Leo. 1954. The widening scope of psychoanalysis. *Journal of the American Psychoanalytic Association* 2: 567–594.

Sulloway, Frank. 1979. *Freud, biologist of the mind: beyond the psychoanalytic legend*. New York: Basic Books.

Swan, Jim. 1974. Mater and nannie: Freud's two mothers and the discovery of the Oedipus complex. *American Imago* 31: 1–64.

Tauber, Alfred I. 2010. *Freud, the reluctant philosopher*. Princeton, NJ: Princeton University Press.

Vandermeersch, Patrick. 1991. *Unresolved questions in the Freud/Jung debate on psychosis, sexual identity and religion*. Louvain Philosophical Studies 4. Trans. Anne-Marie Marivoet and Vincent Sansone. Leuven: Leuven University Press.

Vassali, Giovanni. 2001. The birth of psychoanalysis from the spirit of technique: What have we learned? What can we apply? *International Journal of Psychoanalysis* 82: 3–25.

Veith, Ilza. 1965. *Hysteria: the history of a disease*. Chicago: University of Chicago Press.

Vitz, Paul C. 1988. *Sigmund Freud's Christian unconscious*. New York: The Gilford Press.

von Unwerth, Matthew. 2005. *Freud's requiem: mourning, memory, and the invisible history of a summer walk*. New York: Riverhead Books.

Waelder, Robert. 1977. The principle of multiple function: observations on overdetermination. *Psychoanalysis: observation, theory, application: selected papers of Robert Waelder*. Ed. Samuel A. Guttman. New York: International Universities Press. 75–92.

Walzer, Michael. 1985. *Exodus and revolution*. New York: Basic Books.

Weber, Max. 1958. *From Max Weber: essays in sociology*. Trans. and ed. H.H. Girth and C. Wright Mills. Oxford: Oxford University Press.

———. 1958. *The Protestant ethic and the spirit of capitalism*. Trans. Talcott Parsons. New York: Scribner's.

———. 2004. Science as a vocation. *The vocation lectures*. Ed. David Owens and Tracy R. Strong. Trans. Rodney Livingstone. New York: Hackett. 1–31.

Whitebook, Joel. 1978. Pre-market economics: the Aristotelian perspective. *Dialectical Anthropology* 1: 197–200.

———. 1996. *Perversion and utopia: a study in psychoanalysis and critical theory*. Cambridge, MA: The MIT Press.

———. 2004. Hans Loewald: a radical conservative. *International Journal of Psychoanalysis* 85: 97–115.

———. 2004. Weighty objects: on Adorno's Kant–Freud interpretation. *The Cambridge companion to Adorno*. Ed. Thomas Hahn. Cambridge: Cambridge University Press. 51–78.

2005. Against interiority: Foucault's struggle with psychoanalysis. *The Cambridge companion to Foucault.* Second edition. Ed. Gary Gutting. Cambridge: Cambridge University Press. 312–347.

Williams, Bernard. 2002. *Truth and truthfulness: an essay in genealogy.* Princeton, NJ: Princeton University Press.

Winnicott, D.W. 1964. Review of *Memories, dreams, reflections. International Journal of Psychoanalysis* 45: 450–455.

1967. The location of cultural experience. *International Journal of Psychoanalysis* 48: 268–372.

1971. *Playing and reality.* London: Tavistock.

1986. *Home is where we start from: essays by a psychoanalyst.* New York: W.W. Norton & Co.

Wittels, Fritz. 1924. *Sigmund Freud: his personality, his teaching and his school.* London: George Allen & Unwin.

Wollheim, Richard. 1981. *Sigmund Freud.* Cambridge: Cambridge University Press.

Yerushalmi, Yosef Hayim. 1991. *Freud's Moses: Judaism terminable and interminable.* New Haven, CT: Yale University Press.

Young-Bruehl, Elisabeth. 1998. A history of Freud biographies. *Subject of biography: psychoanalysis, feminism, and writing women's lives.* Cambridge, MA: Harvard University Press.

Yovel, Yirmiyahu. 1992. *Spinoza and other heretics,* vol. II: *Adventures in immanence.* Princeton, NJ: Princeton University Press.

Zammito, John H. 2002. *Kant, Herder, the birth of anthropology.* Chicago: University of Chicago Press.

2008. *Médicin-philosoph*: persona for radical enlightenment. *Intellectual History Review* 18: 427–440.

Zohn, Harry. 1985. Fin-de-siècle Vienna: the Jewish contribution. *The Jewish response to German culture: from the Enlightenment to the Second World War.* Ed. Jehuda Reinharz and Walter Schatzberg. Hanover, NH: University of New England Press. 144–145.

Zweig, Stefan. 1964. *The world of yesterday: an autobiography of Stefan Zweig.* Lincoln: University of Nebraska Press.

Index

"A Few Theoretical Remarks on
Paranoia", 270
Abraham, Karl, 180, 302, 306
   "Amenhotep IV", 450–451
   Freud's letters to, 314, 317, 327
   on Jung, 187, 264
Achelis, Werner, 98–99
"active side" (philosophical concept), 222
Adler, Alfred, 281, 432
Adorno, Theodor W., 56, 94, 369, 443, 446
Akhenaten (Amenhotep), 75, 302, 440,
   442–443, 447, 450–451
America, Freud and Jung's trip to, 273
American flirtation vs. Continental love
   affair, 341
amnesia, post-hypnotic, 150
amoeba, Freud's model of, 329, 332
"Analysis Terminable and Interminable",
   451–452
Ananke, 309, 311, 341, 344, 347, 366, 421
   Freud's resignation to, 6, 320–321,
   348–349, 350
androcentrism, Freud's, 132, 447
androphilia, 15, 53, 184, 229–233, 304, 314
Anglophilia, Freud's, 102–103
animism, 309–310, 382
"Animism, Magic, and the Omnipotence of
   Thoughts", 306
Anna O. (Bertha Pappenheim), 137–140, 149,
   152, 156
anthropology, 388–389
anti-philosophy, Freud's, 86–99
anti-Semitism
   Freud's explanation for, 441, 442–443
   Jung's suspected, 264
   rise of, 237, 435–438, 445
anxiety, Freud's, 127–128, 136, 172, 416

in childhood, 42, 50–51
Fliess and the alleviation of, 185–186
prior to his Sunday afternoon visits to
   Amalie, 37
and use of cocaine, 116
Anzieu, Didier, 20, 185, 194, 224–225,
   228, 230
Appignanesi, Lisa, 131–132
Aquinas, 385
archaic mother. *See* early mother
Aristophanes, 374
Aristotle, 294, 355
   conception of god, 98
Armstrong, Richard, 71, 433
Assmann, Jan, 440
atheism, Freud's, 262, 348
   debate over, 377–380, 433–434, 443–444
Auden, W.H., 115, 454
Augustine, 254

Bach, Johann Sebastian, 54
Bachofen, Johann Jacob, 366
Barron, Salo, 362
Beethoven, Ludwig van, 53, 73
Benjamin, Jessica, 3
Benjamin, Walter, 446
Berger, Peter, 384, 402
Bernays, Anna Freud (Freud's sister), 31
   birth of, 429
   on Freud's quarters, 63
   piano playing, 54
Bernays, Berman, 124
Bernays, Eduard, 338n
Bernays, Eli, 126
Bernays, Emmeline (Freud's mother-in-law),
   123–124
Bernays, Isaac, 123, 125–126

Bernays, Martha. *See* Freud, Martha Bernays
    (Freud's wife)
Bernays, Mina, 314
Bernheim, Hyppolite, 143–146
    on posthypnotic anmesia, 150
Bernstein, Richard J., 378, 444–445
Beyond the pleasure principle, 161, 348,
    349–350, 361–365, 421
    and the mourning of Sophie's death, 376
Bible. *See* Philippson Bible
Bildung, 71–75
biographical truth, 13–16
birth, Freud's, 31
birth process, evolution of, 389–390
bisexuality, 188
    controversy over introduction of concept, 232
    in *Leonardo*, 449–450
black humor, 280
Bleuler, Eugen, 239, 302
Blumenberg, Hans, 251, 253–256, 294
Bohleber, Werner, 50n
Bonaparte, Marie, 132, 333
    and the Freud/Fliess letters, 176–177, 203
    hosts Freud in London, 437
    and Rolland, 416
    and Schur, 360
Braun, Heinrich, 75
"break with tradition", 10–13, 17–24
    Jung's experience, 250
Breasted, James H., 450
Breger, Louis, 10, 50, 124, 132, 430
    on the assertion of Freud's inner needs, 122
    Freud family during First World War, 325
    Freud's aversion to music, 55
    Freud's correspondence with Martha, 128
    Freud's devotion to study, 63–64
    Freud's logocentrism, 53
    Martha's obsessive household
        management, 133
    on Wilhelm Fliess, 171
Brentano, Franz, 86–90, 99
Breuer, Josef, 33, 129, 136–143, 149, 156, 210
    diagnosis of Freud's heart condition, 193
    as Dr. M. in the Irma dream, 199, 201
    importance of sexuality, 185
    introduction of Freud to Fliess, 183
    male inclination, 231
    pathology as a product of splitting, 155
    Studies on hysteria, 152

Bondy, Ida, 183
Brouillet, André, 119
Brücke, Ernst, 64, 104–109, 121, 136, 140
Brühl, Carl, 76
Buddha, 440
Burghölzli Hospital (Zurich), 239, 260

Case histories, 2
Castoriadis, Cornelius, 96, 162, 164, 166, 169,
    173, 223, 384–385
castration complex, 103, 286–287, 354,
    422, 452
castration threat, paternal, 160, 168, 167–169
cathartic technique, 137–139, 149–150, 152
Catholic Church, Austria's, 435
Catholicism. *See* Roman Catholicism
character, Freud's, 265. *See also* personality,
    Freud's
Charcot, Jean-Martin, 85, 101, 110–120, 136,
    138, 139, 140, 153, 178
    Bernheim's criticisms of, 144–146
    use of hypnosis, 144
Chasseguet-Smirgel, Janine, 449
child abuse, 220, 221
children, Freud's. *See also individual children*
    birth of, 131
    Freud's anxiety and their involvement in
        the First World War, 321–323, 338
Chodorow, Nancy, 3
Christianity, 385–386, 395–396, 446–447
    and death, 356
    Jews' conversion to, 65
    Jung's disillusionment with, 256–259
    Jung's views and experience of, 241–244
    secularization of, 253
Civilization and its discontents, 212, 217, 252,
    409–410
Clark, Ronald W., 15, 48
Claus, Carl, 103, 104
clitoris, 422, 425–426
cocaine
    Fliess's application to Freud's nose, 190
    Freud's prescription of to von Fleischl,
        200–201
    Freud's use of, 116, 176, 196–197, 200–201
Confucius, 440
consolation, 328, 329, 349, 401, 402
    Freud's repudiation of, 394, 405–406
    Jung on the need for, 296, 297

constancy principle, 161
Copernicus, 254, 255, 294
Counter-Enlightenment, 11, 12, 235–237,
        239–240, 248, 252, 270, 291, 293, 311
"creative illness", 179–183, 219
creativity, Freud's
    depression and, 216
    effect of First World War on, 313, 325–328
    in Rome, 315
    and his smoking habit, 191–194
critical reason, 407–408, 417
curiosity, theoretical, 254–256

da Vinci, Leonardo, 39
    Freud's monograph on, 278. See also
        Leonardo
    relationship to mother, 40
Dark Enlightenment, 12, 236, 238
Darwin, Charles, 103, 104, 255
Das Ewig-Weibliche, the Eternal Womanly, 335
Das Land Goethes (Goethe's Land), 333–334
daydreams, 137
Deacon, Terrence, 390
dead mother syndrome, 37–38, 40
deafness, Freud's, 359
death, 343–344
    of close friends and family, Freud's
        responses, 345–350
    life after, 395
death drive, 363
death instinct, 348–350, 363–365, 368–369,
        370–372
defense, 151, 153–157
de-idealization, 251, 253, 256
demonic possessions, 114
depression
    Freud's creativity and, 216
    Freud's episodes of, 136, 172
    Freud's following the Eckstein affair, 208, 216
    maternal, 37–38
Descartes, René, 146
Deutsch, Felix, 320, 352–353, 355–356,
        359–360
Diderot, Denis, 101, 383
digitalis, 192
disenchantment, 333
disillusionment, 256–257, 333
    caused by First World War, 316–317, 338–339
    Freud's idea of, 251–252

Freud's program of, 329, 403
    marital, 135
    parental, 186
    religious, 256–259
divine madness, 174
Dora, 260
double consciousness, 114
Dr. M. (Josef Breuer), 199, 201
Dream of Irma's Injection, 198–203, 209–212
dreams, 158, 293, 295
    interpretation of. See Dream of Irma's
        Injection
    Jung's phallus dream, 242–243, 257, 272
drives, 128
du Bois-Reymond, Emil, 107, 108, 248
Durkheim, Émile, 17, 403

early mother, 2–3, 8, 9, 40, 97, 168, 303, 311,
        404–405, 408, 442, 447
    Fliess as, 181–182
    Freud's difficulties with, 99, 407, 409,
        414, 422
    infant development and, 423, 429–430
    infant's relationship with, 51, 56, 160
    Jung's theory of incest and, 299
    Kinderfrau (Freud's nanny) as, 44
    omnipotence of, 427
Eckstein, Emma, 175, 176, 190, 210, 353
    Freud's identification with, 353–354, 381
    as Irma in Freud's dream, 198–203
    treatment of, 203–209
    triangular relationship with Freud and
        Fliess, 211, 214–217
"economic problem of masochism, The", 372
Edmundson, Mark, 344–345
education, Freud's, 63–64, 68–71
eels
    Freud's dissection and study of, 82,
        103–104, 121, 378
ego, 170, 412–414, 415, 418–420, 451
    and the id, 162
    defense of itself, 153–156, 164
    development of, 163, 166, 167–168
    infantile, 311
    inhibition and circumscriptions of, 330
    libidinal cathexis of, 307–308, 312
    melancholia and, 331
    preservation of, 369
    and reality, 168–169

Ego and the id, The, 346, 361
ego ideal, 311, 335, 368
ego-formation, 229
Egypt/Egyptian culture
  Freud's interest in, 447–451
Egyptian Enlightenment, 75
Einstein, Albert, 163, 195, 240, 319, 334
Eissler, Kurt, 76, 82, 84
  Freud's learning under Brücke, 106
Eitingon, Max, 345, 348, 381
electrotherapy, 143
Ellenberger, Henri, 179–181, 179–181, 226
Emmy von N., 156–157
Enlightenment, 235–236, 378
  Freud's involvement with, 10–12
  Jewish, 18, 19–22, 23, 24, 444
  and philosophy, 100–101
  project of autonomy, 274
  vs. Counter-Enlightenment, 250
Erikson, Eric, 147
eros, 122, 161, 165, 174, 246, 363, 370–374, 370–374, 418
erotic desire. *See eros*

faith cures, 114
fantasy and fantasies, 221–223, 298–299
  creation of, 295–296
  homosexual, 449
  Jung's cathedral fantasy, 257–259
  of a sexual nature, 216
  theory of, 221
  unconscious, 293, 294, 295, 296
father complex, 10, 220, 277, 313
  and helplessness, 393, 404–406, 414–415
  Jung's rejection of, 301
fathers, perverse, 220
Faust (Goethe), 334–335
femininity
  Freud's, 231
  Freud's papers on, 421–428
  Freud's repudiation of, 52–53, 81, 181, 214, 286–287, 319, 354, 451, 452–454
Fenichel, Otto, 98
Ferenczi, Sándor, 321, 420
  on the castration complex, 452
  Freud's letters to, 234, 274–275, 320, 322, 326, 348–349, 352
  help given to the Freud family during First World War, 325

vacation with Freud in Sicily, 280–281
visit to America with Freud and Jung, 268, 273, 301
Feuerbach, Ludwig, 24, 91, 393
Fichte, Johann Gottlieb, 88
financial pressures, Freud's, 122–123, 131, 324
finitude, 6, 376, 393, 395–397, 398, 400–401, 406
Firestone, Shulamith, 3
First World War, 313
  disillusionment engendered by, 315–317, 339
  effect on Freud's creativity, 325–328
  effect on Freud's finances, 324
  effect on psychoanalysis, 323–324
  Freud's family in, 321–323
  Freud's reaction to, 317–321
  impact on *Beyond the pleasure principle*, 361–362
Fisher, D.J., 416
Flechsig, Dr. Emil Paul, 281–283, 285, 287
Fleischl von Marxow, Ernst, 129
  Freud's prescription of cocaine to, 197, 200–201
Fliess, Wilhelm, 33, 101, 122, 127, 140, 351
  behaviour, Freud's interpretation of, 232–233
  Freud links his fainting attack with, 303–304
  in Freud's analysis of the Irma Dream, 210
  Freud's enthrallment with, 148
  Freud's letters to, 171, 176–177
    on Christianity, 356
    on his family life, 131
    on his *Kinderfrau* (nanny), 46
    on his unloveableness, 42
    on homosexuality, 229, 230–231
    on Rome, 406
    on self-analysis, 227
    regarding Emma Eckstein, 204–208
    regarding Jacob, 218
  Freud's relationship with, 136, 159, 171–173, 175, 225
    breakdown of, 225–226, 305–306
  Freud's loneliness following breakdown of, 260
  Freud's love, 229, 233
  homosexual element, 15, 184, 192, 211–212

Freud's transference to, 189–190, 214–217, 230, 281
    nasal-reflex neurosis, 187
    paranoia, 281
    theory of bisexuality, 188
    thoery of biorhythms, 187–188
    treatment of Emma Eckstein, 203–209
    tribunal bones and sexuality, 200
Fluss, Eleonore, 78–81, 106, 122
Fluss, Emile, 81
    Freud's letters to, 76
Fluss, Gisela, 78–84, 106, 122, 211
Fluss, Ignaz, 47, 77
Forel, Auguste, 141
"Formulations concerning the two principles of mental functioning", 292
Forrester, John, 131–132, 293
fort-da game, 350, 374–376
"Fortschritt in der Geistigkeit, Der", 431, 435, 444
Foucault, Michel, 120, 145, 166
Franz Josef, Emperor, 58
free association, 138, 156–157, 158
Freiberg, 25, 26, 61
    departure from, 48
    Freud's early years in, 8–10
    Freud's idealization of, 27–28
    Freud's return for a holiday, 77–81
French psychoanalysis, 8
Freud, Adolfine (Dolfi, Freud's sister), 36, 63
Freud, Alexander (Freud's brother), 63, 319
Freud, Amalie Nathanson (Freud's mother), 416
    age at Freud's birth, 32
    ambition, 40–41
    birth of Freud, 27
    character and personality, 34–36, 245
    comparison with Eleonore Fluss, 81
    depression, 37–38, 49
    dismissal of the *Kinderfrau*, 46
    early mothering, 429
    Freud's idealization of relationship with, 93
    Freud's impressions of, 31
    Freud's reaction to her death, 420–421
    Freud's rejection of, 55
    Freud's relationship with, 8–9, 36–42, 241
    Freud's traumatic disappointment in, 405
    language spoken, 66
    marriage to Jacob, 26–27

musicality, 54–55
    relationship with Philipp Freud, 34
Freud, Anna (Freud's daughter), 70, 356
    birth, 46, 131
    care of Freud during his illness, 353, 354, 359, 406, 435
    defense of classical theory and technique, 4
    Freud's letters to Fliess, 177
    on her grandmother, 36
    on her mother's obsessive household management, 133
    and the outbreak of First World War, 321–322
    on Pfister's letter, 380
    represents Freud at the IPA Paris Congress, 431–432
    summoned to Gestapo headquarters, 436–437
Freud, Anna (Freud's sister). *See* Bernays, Anna Freud
Freud, Bertha (Freud's neice), 33
Freud, Emanuel (Freud's half-brother), 25, 32–34, 62
    departure, 48
    Freud's visit to, 102
    and move to Leopoldstadt, 47
Freud, Ernst (Freud's son), 131, 436
    involvement in First World War, 323
Freud, Jacob (Freud's father), 58, 405, 416
    alleged business failure, 47
    ambition, 40
    character and personality, 241, 429
    death, 217–218, 345
        Freud's reaction to, 43, 218–220, 224–226, 328, 420, 437
    economic struggle in Leopoldstadt, 62–63
    family losses, 37
    as a father to Freud, 28–30
    Freud's disillusionment with, 59–61
    Jewish traditions transmitted to Freud, 17–24
    Judaism, 65–68, 256
    marriage to Amalie Nathanson, 26–27
    marriage to Sally Kanner, 25–26
    and the Philippson Bible, 17–24, 433
    recording of Freud's birth, 27–28
    settles in Freiberg, 26
    travels as a merchant, 24–25

Freud, John (Freud's nephew), 31, 33–34, 48,
    211, 214
Freud, Julius (Freud's brother), 8, 34, 37, 40,
    43, 49, 429
Freud, Maria (Emanuel Freud's wife), 32–33
Freud, Marie (Freud's sister), 63
Freud, Martha Bernays (Freud's wife), 33,
    69, 81, 113
  birth of children, 131
  Freud's correspondence with, 127–129, 186
    descriptive language, 112
    on Charcot, 116
    on cocaine, 196–197
    on his adolescent passion, 78
    on self-doubts and his
      unloveableness, 42
    on transference, 140
  Freud's illness, 353
  Freud's relationship with, 121–136,
    172–173
  household management, 132–133
  lack of interest in Freud's work, 132
  marriage, 30
  visit from Nazi SA, 436
Freud, Martin (Freud's son), 29, 124, 436
  birth, 131
  on Freud's aversion to music, 54–55
  involvement in First World War, 322, 338
  opinion of his grandmother, 35–36
Freud, Mathilde (Freud's daughter), 131
Freud, Oliver (Oli, Freud's son), 131
  involvement in First World War, 322–323
Freud, Pauline (Freud's niece), 31, 33, 48,
    211
Freud, Pauline (Freud's sister), 63
Freud, Philipp (Freud's half-brother), 25,
    32, 34, 62
  departure, 48
  dismissal of Freud's Kinderfrau, 46
  Freud's visit to, 102
  and move to Leopoldstadt, 47
Freud, Rosa (Freud's sister), 63
Freud, Schlomo (Freud's grandfather), 17,
    27, 37
Freud, Sophie (Freud's daughter). See
    Halberstadt, Sophie Freud
Freud family
  effect of the First World War on, 324–325
  Judaism, 65–68

living conditions, 31–32
  structure, 32–34
Freud Studies, 7–8
Freund, Anton von, 325
  death of, 345–346
fugue states, 114
future of an illusion, The, 90, 91, 381–384,
    393, 394, 399–400, 409, 414, 416

Galileo, 254, 294
Garner, Shirley Nelson, 171
Gay, Peter, 11, 15, 31, 62, 74, 133, 220,
    278, 386
  death of Anton von Freund, 345
  denial of the influence of religion on
    Freud's theories, 377–378
  effects of First World War, 315
  Europeans' reaction to First World
    War, 318
  Freud and Schreber, 280
  Freud's anti-Semitism, 67
  Freud's homosexuality, 230
  Freud's reaction to his father's death, 219
  Freud's relationship with Fliess, 172,
    175, 180
  Freud's relationship with his mother, 9
  Freud's relationship with Jung, 304, 307
  Freud's "willed-blindness", 209
  mortality, 343
  nature, 77
gay and lesbian movements, 15
Gedo, John, 189, 244, 274, 277
Geisteswissenschaften (human sciences), 109
Geistigkeit (spirituality/intellectuality), 75,
    431, 439–448
Geller, Jay, 286
German Idealism, 88, 222
Gersuny, Robert, 204, 206, 207
God
  Aristotle's concept of, 98
  Freud on, 395, 401, 404, 439, 441
  Jung's views of, 244, 257–259
  omnipotence of, 254
  Schreber's desire to be penetrated by,
    283–284, 286
Goethe, Johann Wolfgang von, 75, 103, 106,
    314, 333–335, 399
good enough mothering, 428
Gould, Stephen Jay, 389

grandiose self, 310
Great War. *See* First World War
Greeks, 294
Green, André, 37–38, 167, 312, 368, 396
Greer, Germaine, 3
Gresser, Moshe, 66
grieving, normal, 330
Groddeck, Georg, 166
Grubrich-Simitis, Ilse, 122, 128, 431,
    434–436, 437–438, 442, 447

Hajek, Marcus, 352–354
Halakha, 18
Halberstadt, Ernst (Freud's grandson),
    374–375
Halberstadt, Heinerle (Freud's grandson),
    346–347, 350
    Freud's mourning for, 355
Halberstadt, Max (Freud's son-in-law), 322
Halberstadt, Sophie Freud (Freud's
    daughter), 70
    birth, 131
    death, 346, 347, 376
      and the death drive, 378
      Freud's response, 348–350
    observations of her son Ernst, 348–350
Hamlet, 78, 333
Hammerschlag, Samuel, 69–71, 75, 140, 265
Hannibal, Freud's identification with, 60
Hardin, Harry, 43
Haskalah (Jewish Enlightenment), 18, 19–22,
    23, 24, 444
Hassidism, 19
Haydn, Joseph, 53
health, Freud's
    at the time of the Eckstein Affair, 198–199
    battle with cancer, 321, 346, 350–361,
      381–382, 431, 435, 445
    fainting episodes, 301–304
    heart condition, 190–197
    intestinal problems, 37, 327
Hegel, Georg Wilhelm Friedrich, 17, 88
Heidegger, Martin, 238, 253
Heine, Heinrich, 65, 94, 103, 397
Heller, Judith Bernays (Freud's neice), 35
Helmholtz, Hermann, 107–108
helplessness, 50–52, 91, 147, 319, 321, 324,
    344, 354, 359, 382, 398, 402–403
    anthropological, 393

and the father complex, 393, 404–406,
    414–415
    Freud's, 51, 325, 349, 381, 434–435
    infantile, 272, 381, 387–388, 390
Heraclitus, 292–293, 408
"history of the psychoanalytic movement,
    The", 315
Hitler, Adolf, 435, 445
Hoffman, Siskind, 25, 26, 30, 62
Hofmannsthal, Hugo von, 334
Homans, Peter, 234, 250–253, 255, 256, 314,
    326, 348, 403
    Freud's trip to Rome, 314
    Freud's views on disillusionment, 316–317
homosexuality, 15, 53, 229–233
    as element in Freud's fainting
      episodes, 304
    fantasy, 449
    Freud and Jung's exchanges on, 270–272
    Freud's, 339
    in Freud's relationship with Fliess, 15, 184,
      192, 211–212
    paranoia and, 277, 279, 281
    Schreber's unconscious desires, 282
Horkheimer, Max, 56, 369, 443, 446
Horney, Karen, 422
human automatisms, 114
Humboldt, Alexander Von, 72, 241
Hume, David, 88, 383
Huxley, Thomas, 103
hydrotherapy, 143
hypnosis, 94, 137
    and hysteria, 143–149
hypnotizability, 151
hysteria, 89, 111, 113, 117–120
    Anna O. case, 137–140
    Freud's new theory of, 221
    Freud's theory of, 216–217
    and hypnosis, 143–149
    stage theory, 144–146, 144–145

id, 162
idealization
    of Amalie and Freiberg, 8–9, 31
    and biography, 13–14
    of Fliess, 189, 190
    Freud's desire for, 49
    Jung's need for, 244, 272
illusion, 381–382

immaturity, 391–393
  as the goal of enlightenment, 388
incest, Jung's theory of, 299
incestuous fantasies, 298
infants
  pre-maturity thesis, 389–390
  relation to early mother, 51, 56, 160
Inhibitions, symptoms and anxiety, 170
internalization, 229
International Psychoanalytic Association,
  345, 430
interpretation of dreams, The, 2, 179, 180, 191,
  218, 227–228, 240, 260, 284, 328, 365
Irma's Injection Dream. *See* Dream of Irma's
  Injection
irrational, the, 236
irrationality, rational theory of, 146
Israelitische Bibel. See Philippson Bible

James, William, 273
Janet, Pierre, 152, 155
Janik, Alan, 59
Jaurès, Jean, 319
jealousy, Freud's episodes of, 126–127
Jellinek, Adolf, 68
Jeremiah, 440
Jewish traditionalism vs. secularism, 17–24
Jews
  dual allegiance, 65
  Galician, 35–36
  in Leopoldstadt, 61–62
  secular, 58
  and Viennese culture, 71–75
Jones, Ernest, 9, 15, 51, 63, 78, 87, 89, 102,
  359, 435
  Anna O.'s sexual transference, 139
  effects of the First World War, 323–324
  Freud and philosophy, 94–96, 97
  Freud in love, 122
  Freud's character, 265
  Freud's choice of histology, 107
  Freud's fainting attack, 303
  Freud's letter regarding Amalie's death, 421
  Freud's passion, 178
  Freud's reaction to First World War,
    317–318, 319
  Freud's relationship with Fliess, 190–191
  Freud's relationships with girls, 127
  helps Anna return home, 322

nature, 77
  visit by Nazis to the Freud family, 436–437
  on Wilhelm Fliess, 185
Jones, Katherine, 440
Judaism
  and control of the instincts, 441
  Freud on the essence of, 443–445
  Freud's attitude to, 124–126, 377–380
  Freud's identification with, 75
  Freud's introduction to, 17–24
  Freud's relation to, 64–71
  Freud's return to, 433–434
  traditional vs. secular, 17–24
Jung, Carl Gustav, 15, 187, 211, 226, 232,
  366, 432
  ambitions, 268
  appearance, 249, 263, 266
  disillusionment with religion, 256–259
  early life, 240–248
  Freud's letters to
    on Schreber, 280
    on self-doubts, 42
  Freud's plans for, 267–268
  Freud's unconscious desire to submit to,
    301–303
  impact on Freud of his provocation,
    234–240
  introduction of Schreber's *Memoirs* to
    Freud, 278–279
  Memories, dreams, reflections, 237
  personality, 263–264, 265–266
    his two selves, 247–250, 260–261, 266,
      271, 277
  relationship with Freud, 33, 175, 234,
    259–266
    break up of, 267, 305–306, 313–314
    the need to idealize Freud, 244
  religious crush, 271–272, 273, 286
  study of mythology, 284–285, 291–299
  theory of pyschological complexes, 285
  Transformations and symbols of libido,
    291–292
Jung, Emilie Preiswerk, 241, 245–248
Jung, Emma, 301
Jung, Paul, 241–242, 257, 258, 259

Kafka, Franz, 446
Kahn, Coppélia, 44
Kampf mit Wien (struggle with Vienna), 317

Kanner, Sally, 25
Kant, Immanuel, 20, 170, 171, 223, 320, 396
 Brentano's opinion of, 88
 concept of immaturity, 388
 definition of maturity, 392
Kassowitz, Max, 121, 129
Kassowtiz Institute for Children's Diseases,
 202
Kaufmann, Walter, 259, 261, 263
Kepler, Johannes, 254, 294
Kerr, John, 237, 285
Kinderfrau (Freud's nanny)
 dismissal/loss of, 8, 46–47, 49, 55, 78,
 81, 429
 Freud sees in Anna, 406, 435
 Freud's traumatic disappointment in,
 405, 416
 influence on Freud, 42–47, 121
 memory traces of, 182
 "as original seducer", 220
Klein, Melanie, 216, 287, 432
Klimt, Gustav, 214
Kohut, Heinz, 3, 13, 48, 186, 273, 416
 "pure music", 55
Krafft-Ebing, Richard von, 141
Kraus, Karl, 61, 65, 232
Kris, Ernst, 177
Krüll, Marianne, 21, 25, 33, 39, 47

La Barre, Weston, 385, 388–389, 390–393
Lacan, Jacques, 8, 56, 168, 392
Laplanche, Jean, 221, 223, 229, 364,
 369, 387
Lear, Jonathan, 163, 370
Leonardo, 235, 280, 449–450
Leopold (in Irma's dream), 202
Leopoldstadt, 24, 49, 61–64
 Freud family move to, 47
Letters to Fliess, 171, 198, 203, 218, 229
Lévi-Strauss, Claude, 32
libido, 278, 333
 Fliess's withdrawal from Freud, 287
 Freud's and Jung's differing opinions on,
 287–291
 Freud's, 306
 Freud's and fainting, 304
 Freud's theory, 307–308, 311
 Jung's theory, 268
Liébeault, Auguste, 143

life instinct. *See eros*
Lockyer, Norman, 103
Loewald, Hans, 98, 224, 412, 414
 eros, 371
 Jung's anti-modernity, 239
 Oedipal vs. pre-Oedipal development,
 Freud's "official" and "unofficial"
 positions, 2, 159–169, 418, 430
 sexual drives, 269
 unclassical patients, 4–5
 undifferentiated infant–mother
 matrix, 374
logocentrism, 53
logos, 292–294
Loman, Willy, 30
London, Freud's emigration to, 358,
 436–437, 445
Loos, Adolf, 61
loss, 313–317, 341–342
 of extended family, effect on Freud, 47–48
 symbolization and, 374–376
Lothane, Zvi, 270
Lotto, David, 184, 210, 211–212, 214
love, 229
 Freud's first, 78–84
 maternal, Freud's longing for, 78–81
 state of being in, 229
 and hypnosis, 148–149
Löwith, Karl, 253
Luger, Karl, 264
Luxemburg, Rosa, 319
Lyell, Charles, 103

Macalpine, Ida, 286
magic
 and omnipotence, 309–310
 and religion, 391–392
 and science, 275
 and thought reading, 232
magical power
 attributed to cocaine, 197
 attributed to Fliess, 190, 193, 261
 children's belief in, 182–183
 Freud's feeling of, 147
magical thinking, 94, 238, 309, 382, 398,
 400, 401
Mahler, Gustav, 65
Mahler, Margaret, 3, 163
Makari, George, 108, 110, 114, 141, 146

Manchester (England), Freud's visit to, 102–103
Mann, Thomas, 101
Markel, Howard, 196, 197
Marx, Karl, 17, 222, 253
  critique of religion, 90–91
masculinity, 52, 454
  challenges to Freud's, 207–208
maskilim, 19–21
massage, 143
Masson, Jeffrey, 177, 198, 204, 209
masturbation, 258, 430
material reality, 223
maturity, 161–163, 166, 169, 392
  developoment of, 419
  Freud's attainment of, 406
  Freud's concept of, 393–394
Mayers, Max, 126
McDougall, Joyce, 424
McGrath, William J., 88, 91
meaning of life, 333
megalomania, 307
melancholia, 329–332, 347
memories, traumatic
  Freud's method of inducing recovery of, 150–151
  and hysteria, 138
Mendelssohn, Moses, 20, 444
Mesmer, Franz Anton, 114
metaphysics, 98–99
Meynert, Theodor, 107, 129, 136
Millett, Kate, 3
misogyny, Freud's and Fliess's, 211–212
Mitchell, Juliet, 3
modernity, 10–11, 252–256
  Jung's attempts to dismantle, 237–239
Mona Lisa, 39–40
monotheism, 440, 446. *See also Moses and monotheism*
Moravia, 25
Moses, 75, 105, 431, 435, 442–443
  assimilation with Moses Mendelssohn, 444
  Freud's identification with, 432, 438
  invention of monotheism, 440–441
Moses and monotheism, 28, 276, 361, 362, 422, 423, 431–435, 444, 451
  Abrahamic repression in, 451
  androcentric and patriarchal biases of, 447–448

"Moses of Michelangelo, The", 235, 275–276, 315
mother, the missing, 2–3, 6
  accounting for, 7–10
mother–infant relationship, 40
mother's musicality, 54, 56, 416
mother–son relationship, 38–39
mourning, 316–317, 329–332
  creation of meaning and, 376
  Freud's, 219–220, 224–226, 347, 349
  psychoanalytic theory of, 251–252
"Mourning and Melancholia", 235, 328, 329–332, 329–332
Mozart, Wolfgang Amadeus, 53
Mrs. A., 190
Müller, Johannes, 107–108
multiple personality, 114
music, Freud's aversion to, 53–56, 410, 416–418
mysticism, 237, 410
  Freud's suspicion of, 416–417
myth/mythology, 284–285, 291–299

Nancy, Freud's visit to study hypnosis, 143–146
narcissism, 229, 307, 329, 392, 414. *See also* "On narcissism: an introduction"
  Amalie Nathanson Freud's, 36, 38, 41, 245
  collective, 445
  death and, 372
  maturity and, 394
  melancholia and, 331–332
  omnipotence and, 373
  primary, 97–98, 235, 303, 307–311, 335, 368–369, 373, 413
nasal reflex neurosis, 190, 206, 217
Nathanson, Jacob, 63
Nathanson, Julius, 37
nature, Freud's affinity with, 31
Naturphilosophie (Philosophy of Nature), 77, 107
Naturwissenschaften (natural sciences) vs. *Geisteswissenschaften* (human sciences), 109
Nazis, 36, 176, 435–438
Nefertiti, 451
neurasthenia, 141
Newton, Isaac, 399
nicotine poisoning, Fliess misdiagnoses, 191–194

Nietzsche, Friedrich, 17, 29, 94, 174, 219,
    249, 250, 383, 448
    religion, 256
    The birth of tragedy, 274
Nothnagel, Hermann, 121, 129

object relations, 229
occult/occultism, 245, 250, 269
    belief in, 237
    Jung's dissertation on, 248
    Jung's mother and, 241
oceanic feeling, 370, 410–412, 410–412,
    413–414, 418, 419
Odysseus, 56, 65
Odyssey, Siren episode, 369–370
Oedipal revolt, 59–61
Oedipal vs. pre-Oedipal development,
    Freud's "official" and "unofficial"
    positions, 1–2, 159–170, 382, 404–405,
    418, 423–430
Oedipus complex, 2, 28, 263, 277, 284–285,
    301, 382, 404–405, 423–425
omnipotence, 6, 30, 95, 174, 300, 308–311,
    382, 392, 400–401
    Freud's, 147, 190–191
    in infants, 48, 51
    of God, 254
    of the archaic mother, 427
    of thoughts, 237, 238
    renunciation of, 227, 254, 300–301, 395
"On narcissism: an introduction", 235, 240,
    270, 306–307, 315, 328, 335, 361, 368
"On transience", 327, 328, 332–338
Orgel, Shelley, 194
Otto (Oscar Rie), 199, 201–202

Paneth, Joseph, 87, 130
Pappenheim, Bertha. *See* Anna O
paranoia, 229, 439
    homosexuality and, 279
    mechanisms, 287
    Schreber's, 281, 283–284, 285
paranormal, 237
    Emilie Praiswerk Jung and, 245, 246–247
    Freud's interpretation of, 248
    Jung's interpretation of, 248–249
Paris, Freud's experiences in, 110–120
Parmenides, 294
passion and knowledge, 171–177

Paul, Robert, 442
penis envy, 422, 425–426, 428, 452–453
personality, Freud's, 41–42, 263–264,
    319–320
Pfister, Oskar, 133, 349, 355, 377, 402, 404,
    409
    on Freud's religious beliefs, 379–380,
    443–444
phallocentrism, 52, 53
phallogocentrism, 51 53, 405
phallus, significance of, 168
Philippson, Ludwig, 18
Philippson, Phoebus, 18
Philippson Bible, 18, 21–24, 27–28, 68, 91,
    219, 433, 437–438, 448
Phillips, Adam, 13
philosophical anthropology, Freud's study of,
    92, 99–102, 387
Physiological Institute, 105
Pichler, Hans, 352, 357–358, 360, 381
Pinel, Philippe, 119
Plato, 93, 163, 170, 174, 213
pleasurable tensions, 372–373
pleasure, climactic and nonclimactic, 165
pleasure principle, 161, 160–161, 165, 297,
    337, 361–365, 371
    revision of, 373
    vs. reality principle, 296–298, 336–337
Pontalis, J.B., 221, 223, 229, 364, 369, 387
Positivism, 77, 107, 109–110, 119, 239,
    398–399
Preiswerk, Samuel, 245
prejudice, 439
pressure technique, 150–151
primal horde theory, 306, 382
primitive psychism, 297
Project for a scientific psychology, 161, 217–
    218, 228
projection, 393
    and homosexuality, 230
psyche, 89, 114
psychic reality, 118, 158, 178–179, 189,
    194–195, 216, 217–218, 222–226,
    227–229, 244, 327, 408
    extra, 412, 439
    intra, 146, 290, 412
"Psychical Consequences of the
    Anatomical Differences between
    the Sexes", 421

Psycho-analytic notes on an autobiographical account of a case of paranoia (Dementia paranoides), 278

psychology, establishment as a natural science, 114–115

psychopathology, 101, 111, 115, 154, 164
  discussion of Freud's with Fliess, 183
  factors in the formation of, 221–224
  place of sexuality in, 142
  splitting in, 155

psychopathology of everyday life, The, 260

psychosis, Freud's and Jung's debates on, 269–270

question of lay analysis, The, 92, 417

Rainey, Reuben, 64, 71

Rank, Otto, 432

rationalist tradition, 174–175

reality principle, 328–329, 338
  vs. pleasure principle, 296–298, 336–337

Reger, Max, 334

Reik, Theodor, 66

religion
  and theoretical curiosity, 254
  Brenanto's approach to, 87–88
  disillusionment with, 256–259
  Feuerbach's theory on the genesis of, 89–91
  Freud's and Jung's debates on, 267–277
  Freud's theory of, 350, 382–386

religious beliefs, Freud's
  his father's influence on, 17–24
  his *Kinderfrau*'s (nanny) influence on, 45

repression, 151

resistance, 151–153

rest cures, 143

"Return of Totemism in Childhood", 300

Ribot, Théodule-Armand, 113, 114–115

Ricoeur, Paul, 107, 328–329, 340

Rie, Oscar, 199, 347
  as Otto in Irma's dream, 201–202

Rieff, Philip, 243, 433

Rizzuto, Ana-Maria, 19, 21, 27, 29, 35, 36, 42, 58, 437

Roazen, Paul, 34

Robert, Marthe, 69, 73–75

Rolland, Romain, 319, 350–351, 407, 409–411

Freud's resisitance to music, 415–418

Roman Catholicism, 45, 385–386

Rome
  Freud's description of, 418–419
  Freud's visit to, 314–315, 356–357

Rosanes (surgeon called on to attend Emma Eckstein), 207, 208

Roth, Philip, 263

Russell, Bertrand, 319

Sachs, Hans, 59

sadism, toward Emma Eckstein, 211–212

Said, Edward, 431

Salomé, Lou Andreas, 314, 316, 321

Schelling, Friedrich Wilhelm Joseph, 88

Schiller, Friedrich, 103

Schimmel, Paul, 217, 327, 328

Schmitt, Carl, 253

Schnitzler, Arthur, 214, 334

Scholem, Gershom, 72, 444, 446

Schönberg, Arnold, 61, 65, 438

Schorske, Carl, 59, 102, 447–451

Schreber, 235

Schreber, Daniel Gottlob Moritz, 279

Schreber, Daniel Paul, 278–288
  Memoirs of my nervous illness, 278–281

Schubert, Franz, 54

Schur, Max, 326, 347, 358
  assistance given during First World War, 436
  becomes Freud's physician, 360
  Freud's alleged contemplation of suicide, 355
  Freud's attempts to give up nicotine, 192
  Freud's cancer diagnosis and treatment, 351–353
  Freud's relationship with his mother, 9
  Freud's trip to Rome, 357
  on *The future of an illusion*, 381
  injection of Freud with morphine, 344
  on the mistreatment of Emma Eckstein, 198, 203, 205
  opinion of Pichler, 357

Schwab, Sophie, 130

science, influences on Freud's decision to study, 75–84

second selves, 114

Second Wave Feminism, 2, 15, 422

Second World War, 315

seduction theory, 44
  Freud's abandonment of, 220–221
self
  consolidation of, 37
  loss of, 56
self-analysis, Freud's, 46, 173, 197, 224–227, 256, 326
  erotic transference to Fliess, 230
  following Jacob's death, 43, 219–220
  Rome neurosis, 314
  the mother missing from, 2
separation, 313
separation anxiety, Freud's, 42, 127–128
sexual abuse, 220
  suffered by Jung, 272
sexual development, 423–425
sexual drives, 269
sexual monism, 423–426
sexuality, 128
  and the nose/sense of smell, 187–188, 210–214
  as cause of hysteria, 140–142, 201
  culture and, 451
  Freud's views on, 134–135
  importance of, 185
  infantile, 429
  in Irma's injection dram, 200
  Jung's, 246
  presexuality, 299
  and religion, 242, 246
sexuality, female, 421–427
  link with the nose, 211–212
sexuality, Freud's, 15, 339
  Kinderfrau (Freud's nanny) and, 44
  marital, 133–136
  in his relationship with Fliess, 184, 192, 211–212
sexuality, theory of, 288, 312
  Freud and Jung's differing opinions on, 262, 268–269
Shakespeare, William
  King Lear, 366, 367–368
  The Merchant of Venice, 366–367
Silberstein, Eduard, 211, 214
  Freud's letters to
    on Eleonore Fluss, 79–80
    on England, 102
    on Feuerbach, 89, 393
    on Gisella Fluss, 78, 82–83

on intended study at university, 86
on the opinions of Brentano, 88
on women, 82
Simon, Ernst, 67
Slochower, Harry, 97
smoking habit, Freud's, 191–194
Socrates, 173, 344, 440
soma, 89
somnambulism, 114
soul, 114
Spielrein, Sabina, 211, 246
Spinoza, Baruch, 93, 350, 397–398
spiritualism, 245
  Jung's experience of, 248–249
splitting (of the ego), 155–156
Sprengnether, Madelon, 182, 199, 215, 299, 366, 381, 406, 435
  on Freud's identification with Emma Eckstein, 354
  Freud's Oedipal theory, 427, 430
  The spectral mother, , 2
Stahl, Reinhold, 176
Steiner, Maxim, 351–352
Strachey, James, 209, 423, 440
Strauss, Richard, 334
Studies on hysteria, 152
suggestibility, 145–146, 145–148
suicide
  Freud's assisted, 344
  misunderstanding over Freud's intentions, 355–356
Sulloway, Frank, 104, 226
superstition, 237
  religion as, 119, 124
symbolization, and loss, 374–376

Thomson, J.J., 103
thought, directive and non-directive, 294–295
thought reading, 231–232
"Theme of the Three Caskets, The", 303, 335, 365–368, 369, 376
"Thoughts for the times on war and death", 327, 328, 338–342
Three essays on sexuality, 260
Tiy, Queen, 451
Totem and taboo, 235, 301, 306, 343, 380, 382, 400, 404, 443, 444
Toulmin, Stephen, 59

transference, 146, 157–158, 195, 230, 308
    Anna O.'s to Freud, 139–140
    countertransference, 115, 230, 306
    Freud's and Jung's debates on, 272–273
    Freud's to Charcot, 113–114
    Freud's to Fliess, 179–183, 189–190,
        214–217, 230, 281
    Freud's to Paris, 111
    maternal, 423
    religious, 272
    resistance to, 453
    Schreber's to Flechsig, 281, 282
    template, 33–34
transience, 332–338, 341, 375. *See also* "On
    Transience"
trauma, early, consequences for Freud, 49–53
Trimethylamin (TMA), 210, 211–212
truth ethic, Freud's, 397
"Two Principles of Mental Functioning",
    235, 280, 296, 298
Tyndall, John, 103
Tysmenitz, 18, 20, 21, 25

unconscious, 83–84, 118, 128, 144, 145,
    220–225, 326, 331
    active side of the, 222–224
    and consicous, 170
    ego and, 162–163, 164
unconscious-instinctual life, 165–167, 173
Unwerth, Matthew von, 313, 333–335

Valéry, Paul, 255
Vandermeersch, Patrick, 296
Vergänglichkeit, 335
Vienna, 57–61
    effect of the First World War, 324–325
    rapid modernization of, 251
Vienna College of Medicine, 141
Vitalism, 107–108
Vitz, Paul C., 45
Voltaire, François-Marie Arouet, 383

Wagner, Richard, 250, 274
Wahle, Fritz, 126
waking dreams., 114
Weber, Max, 17, 178, 250–252, 314,
    320, 402
    *Protestant ethic and the spirit of capitalism,
        The*, 252
    on religion, 385–386
wedding, of Freud and Martha's, 130
Weininger, Otto, 232
Winnicott, D.W., 3, 23, 50, 240, 369, 429
    on Carl Jung, 245
    climactic vs. nonclimactic pleasure, 165
wish fulfillment, 198, 296
Wissenschaft (Science), 7, 23
    Freud's conception of, 237, 239, 311,
        398–401
    magical thought and, 309
    non-positivist form of, 294
    and religion, 24, 254
    universality, 265
Wissenschaft des Judentums (Science of
    Judaism) movement, 22, 24
Wittels, Fritz, 94–96, 95
Wittgenstein, Ludwig, 61, 94, 99
Wollheim, Richard, 16
womb fantasies, 299
women
    Freud's intellectual friendships
        with, 314
    and homosexuality, 425

Yerushalmi, Yoseph Hayim, 28,
    378–379, 444
Yiddish, 66–67
Young-Bruehl, Elisabeth, 3
Yovel, Yirmiyahu, 11, 398

Zuider Zee metaphor, 163, 166
Zweig, Arnold, 431
Zweig, Stefan, 58, 73